Architectural Drawing & Light Construction

Architectural Drawing & Light Construction

Special Edition — Volume II

Compiled by James T. Darling

Taken from

Architectural Drawing and Light Construction
Sixth Edition
by Edward J. Muller, James G. Fausett and Philip A. Grau III

Reading Architectural Working Drawings: Commercial Construction,
Volume Two
by Edward J. Muller and Robert L. Myatt, J.R., P.E.

Taken from:

Architectural Drawing and Light Construction, Sixth Edition
by Edward J. Muller, James G. Fausett and Philip A. Grau III
Copyright © 2002, 1999, 1993, 1985, 1976, 1967 by Pearson Education, Inc.
Published by Prentice-Hall, Inc.
Upper Saddle River, New Jersey 07458

Reading Architectural Working Drawings: Commercial Construction, Volume Two
by Edward J. Muller and Robert L. Myatt, J.R., P.E.
Copyright © 1988 by Prentice-Hall, Inc.
A Pearson Education Company

This special edition published in cooperation with Pearson Custom Publishing.

Printed in the United States of America

10 9 8 7 6

ISBN 0-536-83538-1

2004520011

EH

Please visit our web site at *www.pearsoncustom.com*

PEARSON CUSTOM PUBLISHING
75 Arlington Street, Suite 300, Boston, MA 02116
A Pearson Education Company

Table of Contents

Preface

This second part of the custom edition of *Architectural Drawing and Light Construction Vol. II* presents the application side of translating drawings into working construction documents. The first part, *Architectural Drawing and Light Construction Vol. I*, covers drafting conventions, color, shading, drawing, and organization of working drawings, while this text covers the elements of construction including: Building layout, structural design and implementation, construction material and techniques, building codes, architectural details, specification writing, and reading of commercial working drawings.

Volume II presents an overview of the use of Computer Assisted Drafting or CAD in order to provide the learner with a survey of how computer technology is being used to develop working drawings in the construction industry.

This text outlines a detailed survey of different building materials and their application on the construction site as well as their representation on paper. The appendix offer more detailed information including span tables, code requirements, metric conversions, architectural abbreviations, heat loss calculations, and structural data for wood products.

Chapter 8, 9, and 10 provide the student with three examples of commercial working drawings that can be used to interpret the building processes outlined throughout the text.

"Would you tell me, please, which way I ought to go from here?"
"That depends a good deal on where you want to get to," said the Cat. "I don't much care where—" said Alice. "Then it doesn't matter which way you go," said the Cat. Alice and the Cheshire Cat in Alice's Adventures in Wonderland
—LEWIS CARROLL

Computer-Aided Drafting and Design

Although somewhat lighthearted, Lewis Carroll's point is important: "If you don't know where you're going, then any road will get you there." This principle is important when you are learning about computers. Keep your needs and applications in mind so as not to be confused by the multitude of options available in hardware and software.

A basic understanding of graphic principles is also important before you learn how to operate computer-aided drafting and design (CADD) equipment and software. A beginner should already know the meaning and use of lines, the various types of drawings, and the graphic symbols used in technical drawing. It is also very useful to have an understanding of three-dimensional (3D) drawings such as axonometric and perspective drawings. CAD does not eliminate the need for knowledge of these principles. Sketching is still used by technicians and designers as a means of communicating preliminary ideas, basic design schemes, and rough drawings of details.

1.1

HISTORICAL OVERVIEW

Historians tend to divide history by materials (Stone Age, Bronze Age, Iron Age) and to mark progress by inventions. Starting with the development of language around 40,000 years ago, inventions that improved the collection and transmission of information—such as writing, printing, and the computer—have been the driving force behind society's evolution and have made progress in other areas possible.

The beginning of the Paper Age can be traced to the invention of the printing press 500 years ago. This invention marked the beginning of an information explosion that changed how society functioned. Over time, the main challenge to society became access to and transmission of this information. In the Information Age this challenge is being met by digital technology. Computers,

initially designed as fast calculating machines, are now accepted as the primary tool to access, understand, and communicate large quantities of information.

Computers were introduced to the architecture and building professions as automated drafting machines. Their purpose was to make the most tedious and expensive part of traditional practice more efficient. Architects and builders are reinterpreting the computer as a tool for developing, processing, and communicating information about buildings. Included in this process is the development of animation, virtual reality scenes, interactive facilities management models, sun studies, real-time cost analyses, and working drawings. The goal in this Information Age is to increase the amount and change the nature of information available about a proposed or an existing building.

In the past 15 years, the design and construction field has realized that CADD (computer-aided drafting and design) can work and can be cost-effective. CADD can make a real difference in the way architecture is created, and it can improve the overall quality and value of design. Clients no longer see CADD as a novelty, and they have come to expect CADD work as a matter of course. CADD helps architects perfect building concepts and produce cost-effective construction drawings. Hours that would be spent hand drawing can be eliminated. Potential design mistakes can be caught early, before construction begins and corrections become expensive.

Computer-aided, design-based software such as AccuRender, 3D Studio, Virtus WalkThrough, QuickTime VR, AutoCAD, and ArchiCAD make it possible to move from designing on paper to designing on the computer. Once all the details have been entered in the computer and the computer-generated models have been created during a 16- to 20-hour development process, clients can be guided on a "flyby" or "walkthrough" adventure. They can explore their house or building on a predetermined path or a path of their own choosing. They can move

ELEVATIONS

Computer-aided presentation elevations of a home for a young family. (Paul M. Black AIA, architect)

around the house exterior for a 3D view of the roof and landscaping. This technology forms the basis for highly interactive computer-based presentations in which the designer and the client explore variations together and experiment with all aspects of a project.

CADD further enhances design by providing better communication of information among design professionals. A CADD drawing becomes an information resource readily accessible to all professionals involved in the design and construction process. Architects, project managers, engineers, and builders can work with "intelligent" building objects—walls, doors, pipes, ducts—that will have the same properties as those of the actual components. These objects automatically adjust themselves in relation to other drawing objects and accurately maintain these relationships throughout design changes. Building owners see the value of this shared electronic drawing information and increasingly require it for their own future building management and maintenance. Once completed, a CADD drawing can be modified and reused for facilities management with little effort.

Making the process even more realistic is the introduction of virtual reality headgear. The software company Virtus WalkThrough Pro introduced the first stereoscopic headgear to the architecture industry. This headgear provides a more realistic viewing of computer-digitized models using standard virtual reality modeling language and fitting two sets of images to each eye,

thereby producing the actual feeling you have when walking around. This software can combine real photographs with computer-generated renderings. For example, photographs taken of a skyline and surrounding landscape can be scanned into the computer, and a computer-generated building model can then be superimposed on the scanned background.

1.2

SYSTEM COMPONENTS

CADD systems are composed of several components; some involve hardware (electronic gear), and others involve software (programs). All of the components are used together to make the whole system work, but each must be in its proper place and interconnected with the other parts to function correctly. Figure 1–1 is helpful in

Figure 1–1 Components of a computer/CADD system.

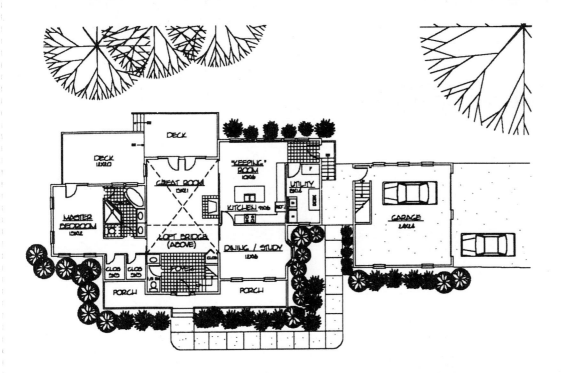

MAIN LEVEL

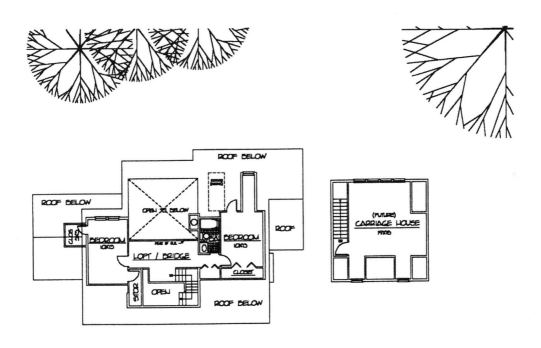

UPPER LEVEL

Computer-aided presentation floor plans of a home for a young family.

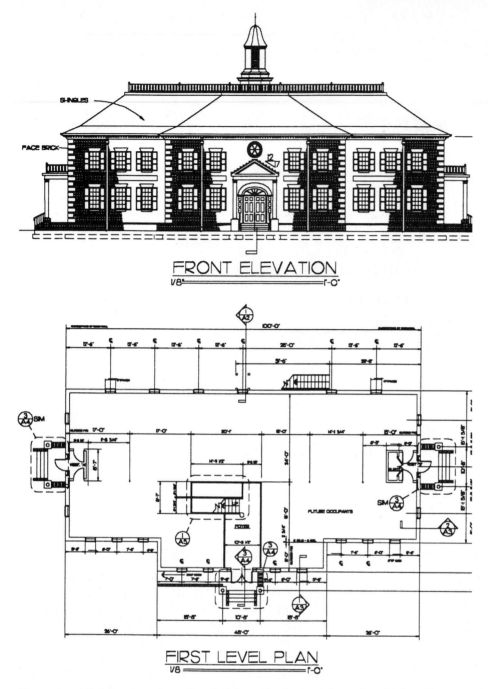

FRONT ELEVATION
1/8" = 1'-0"

FIRST LEVEL PLAN
1/8 = 1'-0"

Computer-aided drawing of an office building elevation and floor plan. (Robert Foreman Assoc., architect, Paul M. Black, AIA, project manager)

picturing how each system works with the others to produce electronic drawings. Each component will be discussed in detail in the following sections.

1.3
OPERATING SYSTEMS

An operating system (OS) is the software between the applications that a person uses and a computer's hardware (memory, disk drives, and input/output devices). It is the foundation upon which all other programs are built. The performance and usability of software applications are determined by the performance and usability of the operating system.

Architectural software programs run on a variety of operating systems including Windows 95/98/2000, Windows NT, and MacOS. Today most architects use Windows, Macintosh, or a combination of both computer systems.

Some important features of current operating systems include multitasking, 32-bit memory addressing, and integrated networking.

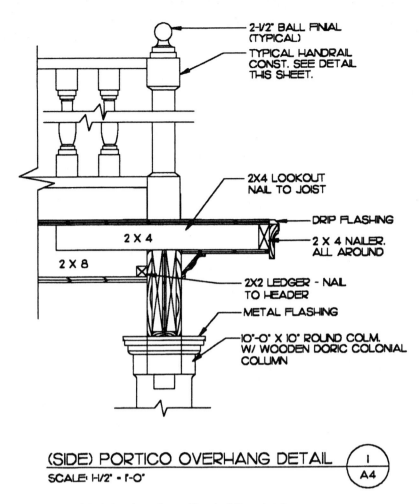

(SIDE) PORTICO OVERHANG DETAIL
SCALE: I-1/2" = I'-0"

2-1/2" BALL FINIAL (TYPICAL)

TYPICAL HANDRAIL CONST. SEE DETAIL THIS SHEET.

2X4 LOOKOUT NAIL TO JOIST

DRIP FLASHING

2 X 4 NAILER. ALL AROUND

2X2 LEDGER - NAIL TO HEADER

METAL FLASHING

IO"-O" X IO" ROUND COLM. W/ WOODEN DORIC COLONIAL COLUMN

2 X 4

2 X 8

Computer-aided drawing of an office building detail.

Multitasking refers to the ability of a computer to run more than one program at the same time; however, the term is misleading. A multitasking system switches back and forth quickly between different programs. This gives the illusion that two or more things are happening at the same time.

The *32-bit memory addressing* feature means that the operating system can access up to four gigabytes (4 billion bytes) of memory at any given time.

Integrated networking includes the capabilities for built-in networking, e-mail, and access to online services.

1.3.1 Windows 95

Windows 95 is a replacement for three operating systems: MS-DOS, Windows 3.1, and Windows for Workgroups 3.11. It supports plug-and-play hardware and includes an integrated information manager, built-in access to Microsoft Network (an online service), and universal e-mail. Windows 95 also supports 32-bit memory addressing as well as 16-bit memory addressing. Windows 95 still supports DOS applications, although DOS is no longer required to run it.

1.3.2 Windows 98SE/ME

Windows 98SE (Second Edition) is an upgrade to Windows 98, which was an upgrade to Windows 95. One of the major differences between Windows 95 and Windows 98 is the integration of Internet Explorer into Windows 98. Windows 98SE fine-tunes this integration with a number of enhancements, the most important of which is the upgrade to Internet Explorer 5.0. Windows ME (Millenium) is the upgrade to Windows 98SE.

1.3.3 Windows NT

Windows NT is Microsoft's alternative to the performance and sophistication of UNIX. NT provides true multitasking, security, multiprocessing, and 32-bit software development tools. Windows NT has no DOS component and runs on a number of different kinds of multiprocessors. This makes it better suited for use as a network file server or database server.

1.3.4 Windows 2000

Windows 2000 was originally developed as Windows NT 5.0. This version combines the extra security and reliability of NT with the familiar interface of Windows 98. This is an operating system intended for corporate users and medium to large businesses, but not single desktop PCs.

1.3.5 MacOS

The Macintosh represents only about 10 percent of all desktop computer sales, even though it is generally recognized as more thoughtfully designed than Windows. The Mac's strength is in the fields of desktop publishing, digital image editing, digital music editing, visualization, and multimedia authoring tools.

1.4

COMPUTER HARDWARE

Test driving different desktop computers using key software applications is always the best way to evaluate their price and performance. Over the past decade several key hardware technologies have become available and affordable to architects, including color scanners, digital cameras, color printers, and video capture hardware. Collectively they provide firms of all sizes—even the sole practitioner—access to publication and presentation techniques that only a few years ago were the exclusive domain of the largest architectural firms.

1.4.1 Desktop PC Components

Typical CADD hardware is shown in Fig. 1–2. The various components are described in the following paragraphs.

CPU The CPU (Central Processing Unit) is the microprocessor brain of the computer. Intel and AMD are the main CPU manufacturers for desktop computers. Other CPU manufacturers include Apple (PowerPC), Sun Microsystems (SPARC), Silicon Graphics (MIPS), and DEC (Alpha).

Some desktop computer buyers estimate the performance of a computer by the clock speed of the CPU, usually measured in megahertz (MHz). The clock speed of a CPU is roughly equivalent to the rpm (revolutions per minute) of a car engine. The faster the rpm of an engine in a given gear, the faster the speed of the car. Upshifting or downshifting the gears, however, also affects the speed, which is comparable to shifting between different brands of CPU. A computer clock speed is only one measure of performance and can be misleading.

Motherboard The motherboard of a desktop computer is the printed circuit board that contains the CPU, memory, input/output chips, slots for expansion cards, and other specialized circuitry for video sound or networking. Some components of a computer motherboard may operate at a slower clock speed than the CPU itself. This imbalance causes "wait states" in the CPU where the CPU pauses to allow the motherboard to catch up.

Memory RAM (Random Access Memory) is the fast, silicon memory accessed by the CPU and is used to store programs and data for fast access. In general the more memory the faster the performance of the computer, depending on the software applications. Most RAM is packaged in what is known as SIMMS (Standard In-line Memory Modules). These modules are small cards with

Figure 1–2 Typical CADD hardware. Shown are the "box" containing the motherboard, a 3.5-inch diskette hard drive, and a CD-ROM drive. Also shown are a standard keyboard, a 17-inch monitor, speakers, a digitizing tablet with a four-button puck, a mouse, and a laser printer.

memory chips that snap into memory slots on the motherboard. Memory capacity is measured in megabytes (MB—about one million bytes of data). A minimum of 128MB RAM is standard on CAD systems. RAM is a volatile storage medium, which means it will not retain information when the computer is turned off.

Cache memory is a special, very expensive, high-speed type of memory provided on desktop computers. A cache is a temporary holding area for data and programs used by the CPU. Cache memory provides access to information much faster than ordinary RAM. The cache memory is located on the chip itself and runs at the full processor speed. CAD systems today provide two levels of cache memory: L1 and L2. High-end systems provide 128KB of L1 cache and 256KB of L2 cache, both on the chip itself, for a total of 384KB full-speed system cache.

Magnetic Disk Drives Most desktop computers come with one 3.5-inch diskette drive, as well as an internal hard disk drive that can store up to 75GB (gigabyte, or 1,000 megabytes) of data. Software and data stored on magnetic disks are retained when the computer is turned off. One measure of how fast the disk drive can access a track is called seek time. Between 9 and 13 milliseconds seek time is average, with particularly fast drives having times around 5 milliseconds.

Optical Disks Optical disks are an excellent medium for information publishing and distribution, and for archiving large amounts of digital data. A 5.25-inch CD-ROM (read only) can store up to 650MB of data. This is enough storage capacity for tens of thousands of pages of text, thousands of graphics, or hundreds of photographs. CD-ROM drives are inexpensive and are standard equipment on computers. Read/write optical disk drives, CD-R and CD-RW, capable of storing 128–256KB of data (3.25) to 500MB–4GB (5.25) are also available. CD-R discs cannot be altered once they have been recorded; CD-RW discs can be erased and reused but can be read only by fairly recently manufactured CD-ROM and DVD-ROM drives. Relatively new DVD-ROM drives are becoming standard equipment on new desktop and notebook computers. These drives are much faster and versatile than other drives, although they are not rewritable. The fastest DVD-ROM drives are over three times faster than the fastest CD-ROM drives and are capable of reading multiple formats including CD-ROM, CD-R, and CD-RW discs. DVD-RAM drives, the rewritable version of the DVD-ROM drive, are very new. These first-generation drives read discs fairly slowly although the technology is developing quickly and second-generation drives are expected that will be significantly faster than the first-generation versions.

Display Monitor/Graphic Card The display monitor is where the user and the computer meet eye to eye. For CAD, rendering, image editing, desktop publishing, or word-processing applications that require high graphics resolution, a 19-inch monitor is necessary.

"Dot Pitch" refers to the resolution of the screen and is an important criteria for determining screen sharpness. A 0.25 mm dot pitch is a typical value for most desktop computer displays.

The quality of a digital image on your computer display depends on the dimensional size of the monitor, the resolution and color depth of the image, and the amount of display memory.

The display memory available and how many bits are used to store the color value of each pixel of the image determines the number of colors available and the maximum resolution of the screen. The CGA display standard of early IBM-compatible PCs was a 4-bit color display (16 colors) with a resolution of 320×200. Storing a CGA image in memory required $320 \times 200 \times 4$ bits (32,000 bytes). Computers equipped with standard VGA displays ($640 \times 480 \times 8$ bits) required 307,200 bytes of display memory. The requirements of present-day 24-bit high-resolution graphics displays are much higher. The standard CAD system includes a graphics card with 32MB of display memory and many high-end systems are equipped with graphics cards with 64MB of display memory. The graphics card should be able to provide 1024×768 resolution with 16.7 million colors and a $1280 \times 1024 \times 24$-bit double-buffered accelerator.

Keyboard Keyboards should be slightly below the work surface to minimize bending of the wrists. Ergonomic keyboards, which look like they've been sawn in half, are designed to minimize the amount of wrist rotation by users. They are available from Apple and Microsoft, among others (Fig. 1–3).

Pointing Device The mouse is the most common pointing device used with desktop computers (Fig. 1–4). A mouse is a "relative" pointing device because the cursor movement depends on the relative movement of the mouse.

Digitizing tablets are "absolute" pointing devices. They contain a grid of wires just below their surface that detect the location of a puck moved over it. An area of the tablet represents the screen drawing area (Fig. 1–5). Digitizing tablets are typically used in CAD applications.

Modems Modem is an acronym for *mo*dulator-*dem*odulator. It is the hardware component responsible for converting the digital signal of a computer into an analog signal that can be transmitted over telephone lines. A modem is required for your computer to access online services such as AIA-ONLine, CompuServe, or the Internet. Modems support different speeds. One capable of connecting to a v.90 server at 56Kbps is recommended.

Figure 1–3 Examples of keyboards. (A) Standard. (B) With a touchpad. (C) Ergonomic with a touchpad. (GLOBAL Computer Supplies catalog)

A

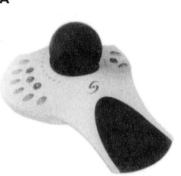

B

Figure 1–4 Mouse. (A) Microsoft IntelliMouse Optical with left and right buttons and a middle scroll wheel. (Reproduced with permission from *Cadalyst,* Vol. 17, Number 5, May 2000, pg. 28. Copyright by Advanstar Communications Inc. Advanstar Communications Inc. retains all rights to this photo.) (B) Labtec Spaceball 4000 FLX is a 3D motion control device that has 12 buttons and a smooth rubber ball that can be controlled in six axes. (Courtesy of Cadence)

Tape Drives   A tape drive may be necessary for backing up and storing large amounts of data for networked systems. Small, tape backup systems can store between 8GB and 20GB of data; large systems can store between 50GB and 100GB of data on one tape. The major limitation of backup tape drives is its sequential linear format. Accessing a file that is stored at the end of a tape takes time if the tape has to be forwarded and rewound.

Digital Cameras   Digital cameras can be used to capture images without needing to store the images on film (Fig. 1–6). Some cameras, such as Apple's QuickTake cameras and Kodak's digital camera, combine a scanner with the optics of a traditional camera.

A few years ago affordable digital cameras had resolutions of 640 × 480 pixels (picture elements). Today most digital cameras offer megapixel resolutions that capture images made up of more than 1 million pixels. More pixels mean higher resolution and sharper images. Many digital cameras offer more than one resolution setting, ranging from 640 × 480 up to 1280 × 960, with some newer cameras having resolutions as high as 2048 × 1536. These 3.2 megapixel resolution (2048 × 1536) cameras are approaching the quality of 35mm film photography.

Storage options include a variety of interchangeable memory sticks. The new Sony Digital Mavica also allows you to store images on standard high density 3.5″ computer disks. Costs for these higher resolution cameras range between $500–$1000, with the newer 3-megapixel cameras falling in the $800–$1000 range.

Figure 1–5 Digitizing tablet. Shown here is the Kurta XGT tablet with a four-button puck.

A

B

Figure 1–6 Digital cameras. (A) Sony Digital Mavica (Courtesy of Sony Electronics Inc.)
and (B) Toshiba PDR-M70. (Courtesy of Popular Science)

Photographic service bureaus provide Kodak PhotoCD scanning services for slides or film negatives at a cost of $1–$2 per image. Kodak PhotoCD provides a cost-effective way to convert existing slide libraries into digital images. Kodak's low-cost viewing software, PhotoEdge, can be used to browse CD-ROMs that contain PhotoCD images.

1.4.2 Peripheral Devices

Over the last fifteen years a variety of plotting technologies have been introduced. Pen, thermal, electrostatic, inkjet, and electrophotographic (LED) plotters have been introduced with great fanfare. Today only the LED and inkjet plotters continue to hold significant market share. The number of pen plotters and electrostatic plotters being sold to the AEC market are small. Many users are trading in their older plotters in favor of new inkjet and LED plotters. The resolution of most printers and plotters (except for pen/pencil plotters) is typically measured in dots per inch (dpi).

Inkjet Plotter Inkjet plotters range in price from $2000 to $7500 and are available from companies such as Hewlett-Packard, CalComp, Encad, Summagraphics, Mutoh, and Selex (Fig. 1–7).

Inkjet has become the choice for many firms. Inkjet plotters use standard ink cartridges, the same kind used in inexpensive desktop inkjet printers. They provide very good print quality with little or no operator intervention. All that is required is loading a new ink cartridge when the old one runs out. Most inkjet plotters are capable of creating a D-size draft quality plot in less than three minutes.

A

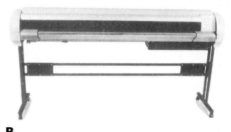

B

Figure 1–7 Inkjet plotters. (A) Hewlett-Packard DesignJet 1055 CM. (Courtesy of Cadence) (B) Mutoh America Inc. RJ-6100/62. (Reproduced with permission from *Cadalyst*, Vol. 17, Number 7, July 2000, pg. 16. Copyright by Advanstar Communications Inc. Advanstar Communications Inc. retains all rights to this photo.)

The standard language used by inkjet plotters is HP-GL/2—Hewlett-Packard's graphic language. Although most manufacturers offer specific driver software for their inkjet plotters, most plotters will run quite acceptably with the built-in software drivers that ship with the ink plotters.

Inkjet plotters are available both in monochrome and color models. Higher-end color models, like the Hewlett-Packard DesignJet 1055CM, are suitable for printing photorealistic images when loaded with specially coated media. Larger format color inkjet plotters are also available, such as the Mutoh RJ-6100/62 62" printer.

There are some limitations associated with inkjet plotting. For example, inkjet plotting involves spraying ink on paper and filling large black areas of paper, which is costly. Also the ink used in inkjet plotters is water based, which creates questions about the permanence of the image; however, some of the newer inkjet cartridges use inks containing a polymer-based pigment that are more resistant to fading and more archival than earlier inks. Media manufacturers also offer specially coated inkjet media that are designed to be stable for long-term storage.

Led Plotter The high end of the plotter market is dominated by electrophotographic (LED) plotters (Fig. 1–8). Prices for these units start at around $20,000 and range upwards to $110,000. They are available from Xerox, Cal-Comp, Oce, JDL, Shacoh, and Mutoh. LED plotters have a resolution of 400 dpi and are designed for unattended operation. They are configured for roll-feed media, automatic cutting, and automatic data format recognition.

Top-end LED plotters are generally available as part of hybrid digital copying systems that combine a plotter and a scanner. Xerox, Oce, and Shacoh offer units that copy and plot equally well. These units can scan a number of drawings and then create multiple collated sets without having to rescan the drawings. LED printed sets are fully collated, have no errors, and are of original quality. Large-format LED plotters are economical when used for high volume production. The fastest LED plotter, currently the Oce 9800, can create up to eight E-size copies per minute.

Desktop Printers The preferred resolution for desktop small-format printers is 600 dpi; the minimum is 300 dpi. One of the most important recent developments in printing technology for architects is the affordable 600 dpi 11 × 17-inch black-and-white laser printer. This Hewlett Packard 4MV printer is fast (16 pages per minute), and is an excellent printer for CAD checkplots. The 11 × 17-inch format, at 600 dpi, is suitable for a wide range of small projects, and excellent for reduced-size printing of large projects. Also, the new Hewlett-Packard DesignJet Color Pro CAD (Fig. 1–9) inkjet printer provides color and monochrome printing in a variety of paper sizes.

Scanners Document scanning is a technology in which an existing paper drawing is captured as electronic data. Once converted the "virtual" drawing is available for use in any number of CAD applications, and for transmittal and reprinting.

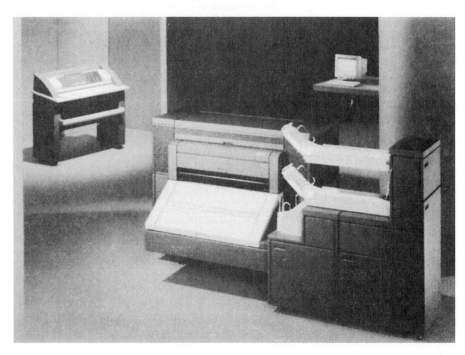

Figure 1–8 LED plotters. The Océ 9800 plotter/copier is designed to maximize productivity and ensure quality in digital, hard copy, or hybrid environments. (*A/E/C Systems,* Sept./Oct. 1995)

Figure 1–9 Desktop inkjet printer. Hewlett-Packard/Design Jet Color Pro CAD Printer. (Courtesy of Cadence)

Document scanners range from desktop A-sized units to large scanners capable of reproducing full E-sized and larger drawings. They can record a range of images from simple lines to full continuous color tones. They can clean up badly damaged documents so that subsequent prints are better than the original.

The scanning process consists of taking a snapshot of a drawing with a digital camera. This photographic process uses one or more cameras that record a narrow portion of a drawing as it is moved on rollers past the camera. The digitized data is then passed to a computer, which processes the information.

Scanner capability is based on image resolution and can range from 150 (dpi) up to 1000 (dpi). This resolution directly relates to what you intend to do with the data. The higher the resolution, the finer the detail. If the drawings are simple and relatively clean, then a lower resolution may be acceptable. Older drawings or drawings that are faded or damaged should be scanned at a higher resolution.

Several very high speed scanners are now available. At the very high end is the OCE 9800 system—a full function hybrid scanning/plotting/copying system featuring a 800 dpi scanner. The OCE 9800 is expensive—a complete system, including printer, starts at $162,000. At the economy end of the wide-format scanning market, there have been some interesting developments. Recently, VIDAR introduced its TruScan Atlas Plus (800 dpi) scanner at $26,000.

Color Scanners Color desktop scanners that support resolutions up to 600 dpi are available for under $600 (Fig. 1–10). These are excellent for scanning small-format sketches or photographic prints.

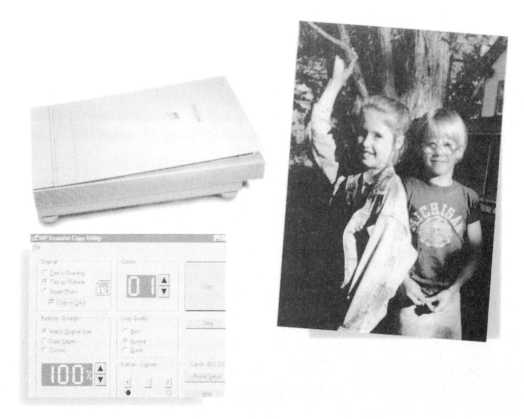

Figure 1–10 Color desktop scanner. Hewlett-Packard ScanJet 4c is a 30-bit, 600-dpi color scanner. It comes with Copy Utility, which lets you turn the scanner and the color printer into a color copier. (*PC* magazine, December 1996)

Figure 1–11 Notebook computer, Dell Inspiron 7500. (Courtesy of Dell Home Systems)

1.4.3 Notebook Computers

Most portable computers today are sold with optional docking stations that connect the monitor, keyboard, modem, mouse, and network through a single adapter (Fig. 1–11). Connecting a portable computer to any of these resources simply requires plugging the notebook into the port. Notebook displays are starting to rival those of desktop computers with 1400 × 1050 resolution and true 24-bit color at 640 × 480 resolution.

1.4.4 Hardware Recommendations

The best way to decide what kind of computer you should purchase is to talk to other people who have recently purchased hardware. Current high-end PC systems are running Intel Pentium or AMD Athlon 600MHz to 1GHz, or MAC PowerPC G4 450MHz chips. Systems should have a minimum of 128MB RAM; however, 256MB is better. Hard drives should be 20GB to 75GB with seek times no less than 9 ms. CD-ROM drives should be 40X speed. Most high-end systems today come with, in addition to or in place of, the standard CD-ROM drive, a 12X Max DVD-ROM drive, and/or an 8X/4X/32X Max CD-RW drive. Portable backup systems include the 250MB or 100MB Iomega Zip drives or the Imation 120MB SuperDisk. You will need a fax/modem that supports a 33.6Kbps transmission rate and that can connect to a v.90 server at 56Kbps. Finally, a 19-inch monitor with 0.25 mm dot pitch is a minimum for CAD work.

1.5

SOFTWARE

The types of software applications used by most architects have expanded dramatically. In addition to CADD, software programs used by architects include word processing, spreadsheets, databases, contract management, project scheduling, desktop publishing, multimedia presentation, digital image editing, e-mail, and online services. Three-dimensional model building, visualization, animation, and virtual reality tools are becoming part of the design and communication process for many firms.

1.5.1 Computer Drafting Software

Many graphics software packages are available in the marketplace. A full-featured architecture and engineering software package provides a vector format for the storage of data and the means to create, change (edit), combine, and print drawings. It contains features that allow for the drawing of three-dimensional objects (solids modeling), the addition of shade and color to the drawings, and the creation of moving pictures of the objects described in the database. AutoCAD is a widely used, general-purpose package that can be combined with many special-purpose programs to accomplish a variety of tasks. MicroStation is another general-purpose package that also can be combined with special-purpose programs. DataCAD, written primarily for architects, features commands and procedures commonly used by architects in manual drafting. A few programs, such as ArchiCAD and MiniCAD, are available in both Windows and Macintosh versions.

CADD software, especially 3D-model building and visualization, is one of the most complicated and difficult tools that architects learn to use. This complexity stems partly from the practice of software developers of continually adding features so that the scope of CADD programs expands to become an all-in-one modeling and documentation tool.

Object-Oriented Software Most software programs are organized into small modules that perform a specialized function on a set of data stored in files outside the program. This program structure is followed by most of the software currently used by architects. Each is a fairly large, complex program that provides hundreds of commands or operations that can be performed on a set of external data such as in a CADD drawing, a publication, an image, or a written document.

Unfortunately, most software programs arrange data in a very specialized way that makes it very difficult to share information between or among different programs. It is important, however, to architects, engineers, and clients for their electronic drawings to be compatible so that they can check and consult with one another. DXF and IGES standards have been developed to allow a drawing created in one package to be displayed in another, but they are not always accurate.

CADD is best understood as a design information management system, and it should be well integrated as a general-purpose tool with other software applications. In many architectural firms the documents that describe the total building process are being developed using not a single, monolithic, CADD program but rather a variety of smaller, general-purpose software applications that share information with each other.

The basic idea of object-oriented software is to combine software and data into the same object. Object-oriented concepts are applied today in software applications that support Microsoft's OLE (object linking and embedding). Using OLE, developers build applications that allow information from other applications to be combined into compound documents. Users can drag and drop objects from one document to another and create a link between the two. OLE is implemented on both Windows-based and Macintosh computers. Most major CAD software developers, including AutoDesk and Bentley Systems, are working on new object-oriented versions of their software.

Over time, traditional CADD software packages have become systems that supply all of the features needed within a self-contained environment. Object-oriented CADD software will provide the opportunity to use Windows systems resources more effectively. Whereas the traditional CADD file was an all-inclusive monster document, the new software will be a compact set of Windows-based files with intelligent links. The linked technologies will make it possible to experiment with changes wherever it is most convenient to do so. Making changes in the design module will also update the spreadsheet, database, and word-processing documents.

Making changes in the spreadsheet or database program will update the drawing and the word-processing document. The new software will make it easier for architects and builders to balance all considerations when planning and designing buildings.

1.5.2 Resources

In the very near future, architects will no longer maintain shelves of printed product catalogs. Instead, they will use the Internet and other private online resources to access more current information. For most product manufacturers and distributors, digital publishing will be less expensive than producing catalogs and distributing updates. However, external online resources do not yet provide high enough throughput. Downloading CAD drawings or high-resolution, full-color images can take minutes, and sometimes hours, even with fast modems.

CD-ROM resources, on the other hand, do provide fast access. CD-ROM drives, now standard equipment for most desktop computers, provide throughput and performance that are substantially faster than what can be achieved online at present. The January 1996 issue of *The Construction Specifier* has a listing of more than 250 construction industry companies that offer manuals, specifications, construction details, and other reference on computer disk and CD-ROM. The most recent edition of *Architectural Graphic Standards* is now available on CD-ROM as well (Fig. 1–12).

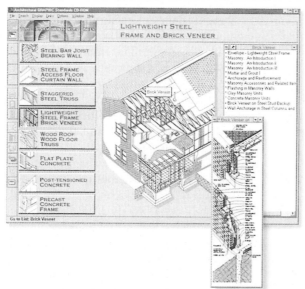

Figure 1–12 Graphics standards on CD-ROM. Shown is one option to locate data organized by systems and components for several common building technologies. (John Wiley & Sons, Inc., Product Information brochure)

Sweet's CD, developed by Sweet's Group, is an interactive product selection tool that operates within Microsoft Windows and over the Internet (Fig. 1–13). Sweet's CD allows you to quickly find information on a specific building product or manufacturer. Information on a specific product may contain text describing the technical features, CAD drawings, tables of product data, and photographs. You can copy or export these elements to other software products including word processors, graphics applications, and CAD programs.

A fairly recent development allows builders and buyers to peruse house plans and elevations in a 3D format. The presentation shows 20 to 30 photorealistic views of a simple floor plan from both inside and out. The viewer can tour the house from room to room, stopping or panning to see a closer view or a different angle of a room. This product was developed through a collaboration among architect Larry Garnett, Houston; software engineering firm Macromedia Technologies Inc., Minneapolis; Pella Corporation, Pella, Iowa; and *Professional Builder* magazine. Additional CD-ROM house plans are also available from HomeDesigns Multimedia Encyclopedia (HomeStyles Interactive), AbbiSoft's Home Plan Finder, Design Search, and Turning Point Publishing.

1.6
THE INTERNET

Imagine potential clients looking up your office listing in a directory and finding a history of your work, including drawings and photos. Also imagine these clients quickly looking up the testimonials of other clients and the credentials of your staff and consultants, finding a map to your office, or receiving an invitation to call or correspond by e-mail to review information and services that might be of value to them. A home page and a site on the World Wide Web can offer these services and can provide a chance for prospective clients to see what you have to offer, to see what sets you apart from others, and to see what you offer that most closely matches their needs.

The Internet, born in 1995, is a term used to describe an interconnection of worldwide computer networks. Operating on the Internet are a variety of computer services, such as e-mail, Use Net newsgroups, and the World Wide Web. The Internet is a massive global network of networks connecting literally millions of computers.

Virtually every possible potential design client will be reachable on the Internet. Some will be accessible directly through their own Web sites, whereas others will be available through their membership in professional and trade associations.

Designing and deploying a Web site requires a notable commitment of time and resources, but the benefits can be quite impressive. The Internet ends traditional limitations of state and international borders. It is especially exciting for those whose specialized services have had limited local markets or those with small practices who could not see themselves offering services in other locales. Clients, consultants, and employees are accessible from all over the world.

The Internet is becoming a growing source of information. Research data from many sources, satellite images, and reference information from standards organizations such as ASTM are all available. The Internet will be both a global library and a universal communications medium.

Progressive design firms are already using the Internet. E-mail is displacing the fax as the medium of preference in many firms, and the global e-mail capabilities of the Internet make it possible for project managers to operate "virtual offices" anywhere. Some firms are already upgrading their brochures using 3D, sound, ani-

A

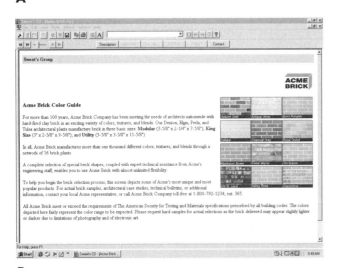

B

Figure 1–13 Sweet's CD. This set of CD-ROMs contains product information developed by Sweet's Group, a division of McGraw-Hill. (Compliments Acme Brick Co.)

mation, and walkthroughs in their Web pages. Firms search for new personnel by reviewing portfolios and resumés on the Internet. Many students have already created personal portfolio Web sites.

Architects and their consultants are working together on data maintained on Web servers. There are online "Project Management Information Groups" that not only house drawings and meeting minutes but also allow project managers to view project information wherever and whenever they wish. Drawing sketches and specifications are sent back and forth between architects, engineers, clients, associates, consultants, contractors, and job-site representatives.

There is a growing presence of design resources on the Internet as well. A number of vendors have current product information available at their Web sites.

Builder Online (http://www.builderonline.com), from *Builder* magazine, provides, among other things, a house plan section containing all the magazine's house plans, instant price quotes, and online ordering (Fig. 1–14). Products made for direct transfer to your computer are the wave of the future.

The Internet, using a technique called *virtual reality modeling language* (VRML), will provide a means of manipulating images in 3D space. This technique will apply to a variety of activities, including construction staging on difficult sites, interior design simulations, signage visibility studies, and space planning.

VRML is meant to be a way to interact with 3D models over the Internet. You see the 3D object and interact with it: move closer to it, walk around it, or jump to other

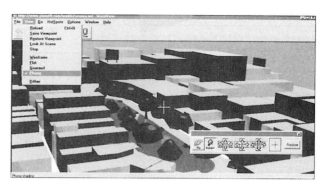

Figure 1–15 VRML SOMA. Shown is a south view of the Market Area in San Francisco. (Developed by WorldView, from InterVista, the first VRML browser for Windows-based computers; from *Cadence*, April 1996)

linked models. VRML lets project data and building design and construction personnel to be located anywhere in the world with an Internet connection.

TriSpectives (3D-Eye), WalkThrough VRML (Virtus), StudioPro (Strata), and Fountain (Caligari) are 3D drawing packages that output VRML directly. However, you do not have to create any VRML worlds because WRL files abound on the Internet. You can walk along a street in Poland as it appears in local time; witness the collision of two black holes; fly over downtown San Francisco's SOMA district; and design a custom kitchen—all over the Internet via VRML (Fig. 1–15).

Another option for Internet users is WebTV, often referred to as the "empty computer." The concept is that the Internet, and through it the World Wide Web, will contain much of the computing horsepower needed and that the desktop unit will simply provide access to the network. You will be connected to powerful servers all over the world through a low-cost modem in order to access data and execute programs. Low-cost systems are available now, although their long-term viability is still uncertain.

1.7

FUTURE DEVELOPMENTS

Converting from manual drafting to computer-aided design and drafting was a small step compared to the potential of today's technology. The next major advancement will be the linking of digital data and remote construction activities by affordable telecommunications. Tomorrow's industry will be an interactive environment of virtual buildings constructed from binary bits, design and construction teams connected by keyboards and video eyeballs, and a new set of uniform drawing standards to help organize the entire design-build process.

Figure 1–14 *Builder Online.* This Web site gathers in one place all of the information that home builders need. (Courtesy of Builder)

1.7.1 Building Design and the Construction Process

Some of the endless possibilities in store for the design professional of the twenty-first century include code research, virtual design, live construction documents, interactive plan checking, online bidding, and a construction process using 3D models.

In the area of code research, current updates could be downloaded soon after agency approval. Notification of changes could be made through code compliance forums whereby design professionals communicate with code enforcement officials and code development agencies to clarify unusual design situations.

Another aspect of this virtual model is that a project will be represented digitally by objects in space rather than by lines, arcs, and so forth. These objects will represent familiar construction components such as doors, windows, stairs, and structural items, and they will be able to respond to criteria established for a project. If the interior changes, the object will adjust to what is appropriate for the new conditions. For example, a roof structure designed for heavy snow loading in one part of the country will automatically recalculate component member sizes if the loading conditions change, such as in moving the building to a climate with no snow. Linked to these objects will be information that can be used in the generation of schedules and project specifications.

Interactive plan check will allow plan checkers access to the 3D model database. Comments will be added to a plan check database for review by the design professional as the project proceeds.

Bidders will have read-only remote access to the project's graphic and written databases. A bidders' forum will allow questions in the form of messages, and the responses will be available to all bidders electronically. During construction, the drawing data will remain accessible to users by remote access, and the contractor will update a copy of the drawing data to produce project record drawings. Progress photos can be taken with digital cameras and incorporated as graphic files.

1.7.2 Building Form and Design

Changes in technology will influence building form and design as well. For most of history, architects and builders have been concerned with the body's immediate sensory environment. Their goal has been to provide shelter, warmth, and safety. Buildings are distinguished from one another by their different uses, and their physical plan organization reflects these differences. The floor plan of a library, school, bank, office, or home clearly shows how it works. The various activities that are housed together are integrated with a circulation system of doors and passageways.

In the future, activities and the buildings that house them will be transformed in response to the emergence of digital technologies. Buildings will become computer interfaces, and computer interfaces will become buildings. The task of designing will be fundamentally redefined: It will no longer be one of laying out and constructing a building with storage and circulation areas. It will become one of designing and programming the computer tools.

Traditional home builders may well become extinct. Their role will most certainly be different. Existing technologies will give clients control over decisions on residential building projects. Clients will have the ability to design a new home from a computer, with every house becoming a customized, "one-of-a-kind" home.

Designers today have to consider the "cyber home." Computer-controlled displays of various sizes can be built into houses. Wires to connect components are installed during construction and thought has to be given to the placement of displays in relation to windows in order to minimize reflection and glare. When information appliances are connected there will be less need for many items such as reference books, stereo receivers, compact disks, fax machines, file drawers, and storage boxes for records and receipts.

The living room might contain an information appliance connected to a display device such as a large-screen television (Fig. 1–16). This display will become a powerful organizer of space and activities. Provisions will have to be made for groups of people to sit around them in living rooms, view them from a distance of eight to ten feet, and probably control them with hand-held remote devices. Appliances such as this are already available. The Destination Big Screen PC/TV developed by

Figure 1–16 The appliance of the future. Shown is the Gateway Destination D5-166 Big Screen PC/TV with 31-inch monitor, wireless keyboard, and Boston Acoustics MicroMedia 3-piece speaker system.

Gateway 2000, but no longer available, was described as a "group-computing, TV-viewing, multimedia-blasting, Internet-cruising mothership." It had a 31-inch monitor, wireless keyboard, remote control, an Intel 300 MHz Pentium II processor, 64MB RAM, an 8GB hard drive, and a DVD-ROM drive with a DVD decoder card.

1.8
KEY GRAPHIC PRINCIPLES FOR CAD

1.8.1 Increased Accuracy and Precision

Computers can store information about graphics in two ways. In the most precise, known as *vector format*, lines and curves are stored according to their mathematical coordinates. In the other, known as *rastor format*, graphic images are stored as a picture composed of a series of dots. Most full-featured CAD software packages use the vector format, but drawings are occasionally converted to rastor format during scanning, plotting, or printing.

As drawings are created in CAD, each item is given an exact mathematical description; therefore, it is more precise. In architectural drawing, the size of a component drawn can be approximated only to as close as the scale of the drawing will permit. For example, in a $\frac{1}{4}'' = 1'-0''$ scale drawing, using a drafting scale, nothing smaller than $1''$ can be accurately drawn. With CAD, since every item is entered by its exact size, it is drawn exactly to size.

1.8.2 Cartesian Coordinate System

In a full-featured microcad software package, all objects are stored by their mathematical coordinates in a coordinate system. Long the basis for analytic geometry, the Cartesian coordinate system is the basis for describing objects in CAD. In its two-dimensional form, it contains X and Y axes projecting vertically and horizontally from a point known as the *origin* (Fig. 1–17). Positive numbers are indicated on the top and right quadrants. Negative numbers are indicated in the left and bottom quadrants. Motion to the left or down is indicated by a negative number, and motion to the right or up is indicated by a positive number.

Each point in the description of an object is indicated by an X and Y value, usually displayed as (X, Y). Because a line is defined by two points, lines in microcad are defined by two points, each with an X an Y coordinate on the coordinate system. "Displacements," in CAD terminology, are the distance one wishes to move along an axis (X, Y, Z) described in terms of points on the coordinate system.

1.8.3 Linear Displacement

Linear displacement is motion along an axis from point to point (Fig. 1–18). It is the most fundamental method of drawing. At the keyboard you would draw from point (X, Y) to point (new X, new Y). There are two types of linear displacements. One is by absolute coordinates, which measure the location of all points from the origin. With other types, relative coordinates allow the user to reset the origin temporarily to the last point entered so that the new distances can be entered relative to the last point. Relative coordinates are frequently used because they are quicker.

1.8.4 Angular Displacement

Angular displacement (Fig. 1–19) is motion from a known (X, Y) point with a distance and an angle. This type of drawing is called *drawing with polar coordinates*. Angles in the electronic drawing area in CAD are generally measured from east. North, then, represents 90° west; 180°; and so on. Angles measured counterclockwise have a positive number; measured clockwise, they have a negative number.

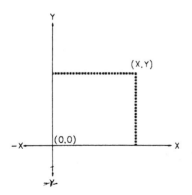

Figure 1–17 Cartesian coordinate system.

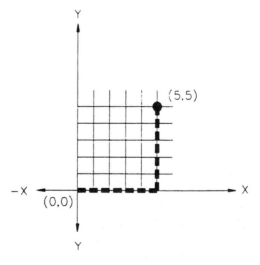

Figure 1–18 Linear point displacement.

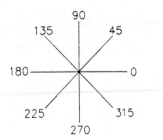

Figure 1–19 Angular displacement.

1.8.5 Database

All of the points and lines that define the objects in the drawings, taken together, represent the database of that drawing. Each time the drawing is added to or otherwise changed, the database is updated. As you might imagine, it takes many numbers to define the complex objects often depicted in CAD drawings; therefore, CAD requires special equipment and software and large amounts of computer memory.

1.8.6 Three-Dimensional Space (X, Y, Z Coordinates)

Even though we have discussed only the X and Y axes so far the third coordinate, Z, has been there all along (Fig. 1–20). The third axis helps to describe three-dimensional objects. In three-dimensional CAD, a 3D model is being created, not just a drawing. Therefore, the model can be rotated and viewed from any direction. Most CAD packages display 3D drawings as axonometric drawings, and most can create perspective views that make attractive presentations. For example, once the model is created, it can be shaded. Moving pictures or "animations" can be made to simulate a walk-through or fly-over, making truly dynamic presentations.

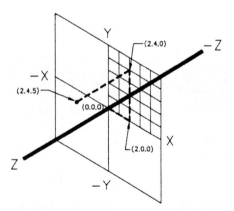

Figure 1–20 Three-dimensional coordinate system.

BASIC COMPUTER-AIDED DRAFTING

Once loaded onto a computer, most CAD packages can be started with a short keyword or by choosing an application icon from the screen menu. Once the program has begun, there are often several ways to drive it, including typing from the keyboard, pointing with a mouse or a digitizing tablet, or by interacting with items as they appear on the screen.

1.9.1 Menus

When the drawing editor is active, a *screen icon menu* can be displayed on the edge of the graphics screen (Fig. 1–21). This menu lets you enter a command by simply pointing to the icon on the screen with a pointing device.

- *Pull-down menus*, which you pull down from the menu bar at the top of the screen (Fig. 1–22).
- *Dialog boxes* (Fig. 1–23) are screens that appear when you need to make changes in values and it would be advantageous to review the current settings of those values. These boxes provide a quick visual means of viewing the current setup and for making changes.
- *Tablet menus* (Fig. 1–24) are stiff cards attached to the digitizing tablet. They contain a pointing area that equates to the screen on the monitor for drawing, and they have illustrations of the drawing commands that allow the user to select an operation quickly with the cursor while drawing.

1.9.2 Commands

The work in CAD is created primarily by a series of operations known as *commands*. Each allows for the creation or change of entities within the drawing. Once started, a command may have several steps to define what is to be done before it can be executed. Commands can be invoked from the keyboard, from screen menus, from pull-down menus, or from the digitizing tablet with a tablet menu.

Draw Commands These commands take the user's input and create the geometric entities intended to be shown in CAD. Most systems have commands that will create points, lines, circles, polygons, ellipses, and the basic geometric shapes. Each shape is constructed by establishing first its location and then its size in accordance with its geometric properties. For example, a point must be defined by two coordinates, a line by two points, a circle by its center point and radius, and a polygon by its number of sides. Beyond simple geometric entities, Draw commands allow for more complex operations. Sketching consists of creating freehand lines with the cursor or arrow keys. Hatch patterns can be added to enclosed geo-

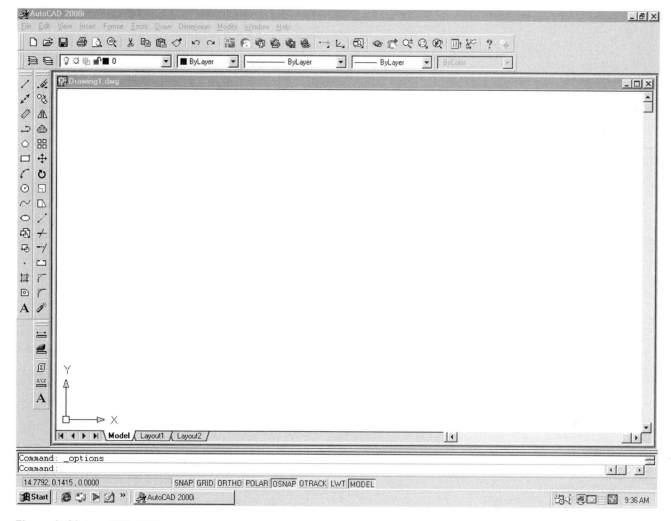

Figure 1–21 AutoCAD 2000 screen menu. (Courtesy of Autodesk Inc.)

metric shapes showing brick, concrete, steel, and much more. The annotating (lettering) of drawings is simplified with CAD. Select a typeface or font, and the size and location, and then type the text from the keyboard. Notes can be easily changed and moved.

Edit Commands   These commands are used to revise entities that have already been created within the program. The power of CAD becomes obvious with the Edit commands. Entities can be erased and then restored if necessary. Lines can be cut or trimmed to meet others. Items can be easily moved from place to place on the drawing. They can be enlarged and reduced in size and rotated a full (or any part of) 360°. Entities can be stretched or enlarged in any direction. Through a process known as *mirroring*, upside-down or reverse copies can be made, yet the writing on the drawing can stay "right reading." Probably the most powerful edit command, Array, allows for multiple copies of an entity in a circle or a rectangular matrix.

Inquiry Commands   These commands enable the user to obtain details from the database and to obtain the status of the drawing environment. They can provide a listing of the size and a geometric description of the entities in the drawing, and they can calculate the perimeter and area of shapes. You can use inquiry commands to identify the location in the Cartesian coordinate system of points, lines, and shapes.

1.9.3 The Drawing Environment

Recall the Cheshire Cat. Most CAD software packages offer so much flexibility that the user can easily become confused. Many CAD packages can be used for a wide variety of applications. The drawing environment is extremely flexible in CAD, and when this flexibility is understood, it becomes another of its many advantages.

As our prime concern here is architectural drawing, think of the decisions that must be made before starting

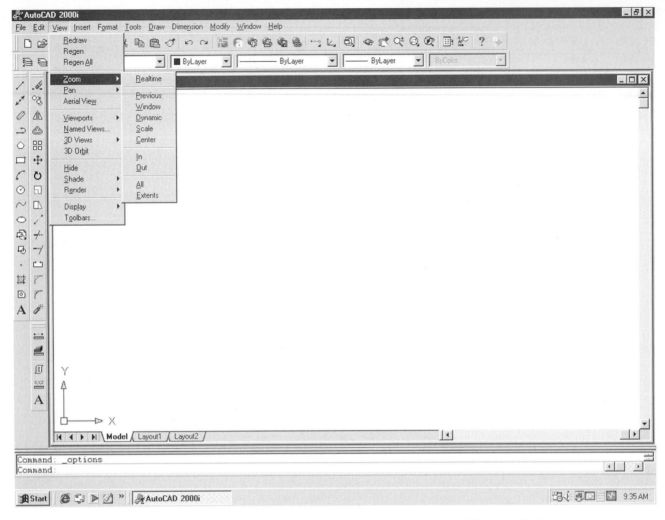

Figure 1–22 AutoCAD pull-down menu. Shown are the View, Zoom, Out menus. (Courtesy of Autodesk Inc.)

to draw with a pencil. How big a drawing table is necessary? What units will be used to draw? Architectural? Decimal-feet? Will a paper with a grid be used? Will the drawing be full size or scaled?

CAD programs have *settings* to control all of these factors and more. Settings control the size of the area in which the object will be drawn, the units in which it will be measured, and the relative size or scale at which it will be depicted. Furthermore, drawing aids are available that can set up a reference grid in the background to help keep your place. Other drafting aids, impossible in manual drafting, allow you to draw only straight lines, draw only from grid point to grid point, and draw from one particular part of an object to another.

Layers in CAD drawings help to sort and organize data. They are derived from a drafting technique known as *overlay drafting*. In overlay drafting, a series of translucent sheets were used to create a composite drawing. All of the drawings were held in registration with a pin bar attached to the drawing board. The walls and doors were drawn on one layer, and the electrical plan and HVAC

plans on others. A composite print could be made by placing the drawings together on a flat-bed diazo machine and making a blueline print.

CAD software packages offer the same capability and more. Using layers in a single "drawing," you can clearly organize the work and make it much easier to revise later. Each layer can have a separate name, color, and type of line (dashed, dotted, continuous, and so on). Each layer can be turned off, making it invisible on the screen, and then on again. Layers can also be temporarily excluded from the database (frozen) to save time. Items can be moved from layer to layer as desired. Only one layer can be edited at a time; therefore, only the active layer can be changed.

The Display command is used to enlarge a portion of a drawing. If you are creating an object as large as an Olympic-sized (50-meter) swimming pool in CAD and looking through a 19-inch monitor, it will probably appear too small to work on, especially when drawing the pattern of slots in the grid on the drain at the bottom. Although this example illustrates another advantage of

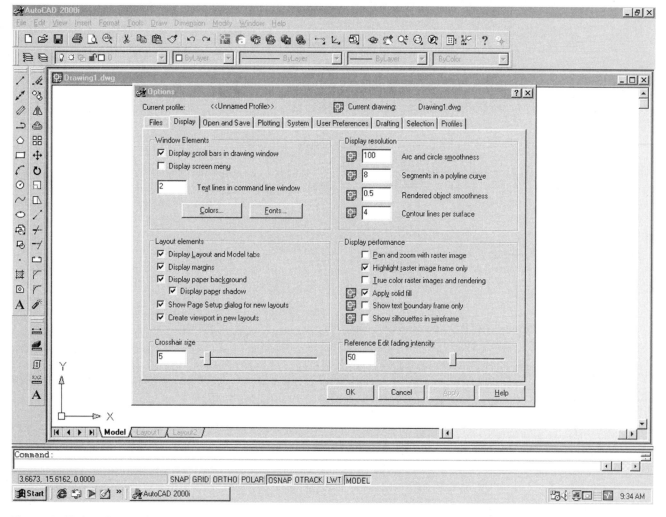

Figure 1–23 AutoCAD dialog boxes. (Courtesy of Autodesk Inc.)

CAD, the ability to draw infinite detail, there must be a way to move closer and farther away from your subject; and there is. A group of *Display commands* helps to control the point of view. The primary command for moving in or out on an object is Zoom. With this command, you can move in or out at specified increments. The primary way to move from side to side on an object is Pan. A linear displacement is required for Pan. It can be entered either from the keyboard or graphically on the screen. When zooming and panning, you should remember that the object always remains the same; only the viewpoint changes.

1.9.4 Polylines

A complex CAD drawing can have a large database. It is not uncommon for a single architectural drawing to require more than one diskette. It is important, then, that CAD drawings be kept to a manageable size. A series of detailed architectural elevations, for example, would best be stored as a series of separate drawings, known as *poly-*

lines. They can be combined just prior to plotting, or each can be plotted separately on the same sheet. CAD packages, however, are designed to minimize the database whenever possible. One way to accomplish this goal is to put related objects together as polyline groups.

1.9.5 Combining Drawings

Architectural drawings are often composed of symbols that are transferred from drawing to drawing. Sometimes they contain actual parts from other drawings. Drafters of the past laboriously copied drawings from one set to another or, more recently, copied, cut, and pasted them into new drawings. Just the ability to copy an entity in a single drawing would relieve this tedium, but there is even more.

The Block feature allows the reuse of drawings and symbols within a drawing or from drawing to drawing. In some CAD systems these blocks are called *parts*. Whatever the name, it is one of the most powerful features of CAD. When the Block command is invoked, the user is

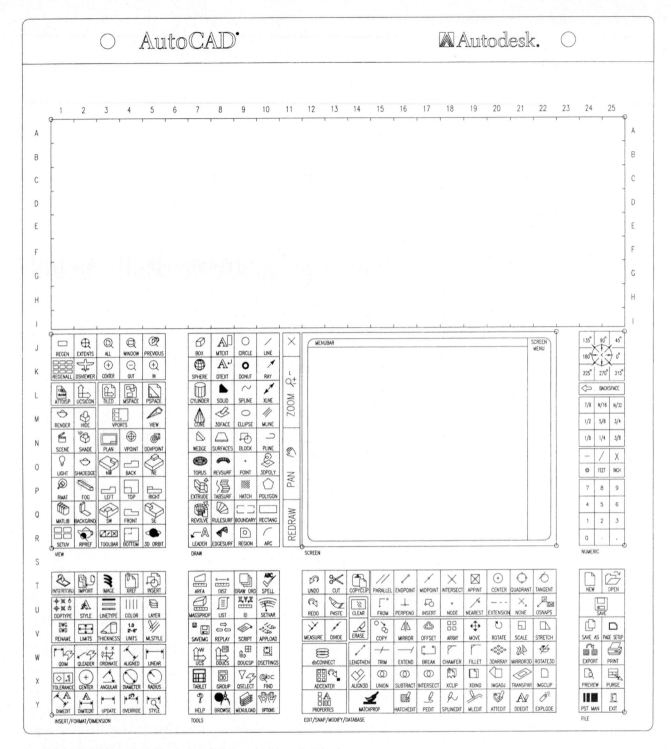

Figure 1–24 AutoCAD Tablet menus. (Courtesy of Autodesk Inc.)

prompted to select the items to be included. After selection, the items are saved as a part of the drawing file. They can be recalled into the drawing with the Insert command. If the user wishes to use those items in another drawing, then the block is converted into a drawing file with the WBlock (for Write Block) command. The items contained in the block are now contained in a drawing file. When the items are needed again *in any drawing*, they can be recalled with the Insert command. The beauty of these commands is that any drawing can be combined with any other drawing in CAD.

The power of blocks has two primary implications. First, drawing symbols that are frequently used, such as doors, windows, plumbing fixtures, and furniture, can be created just one time and reused. Symbol libraries are composed of these items. Second, parts of drawings can be combined with other drawings. For example, a title block can be created for a 24 × 36 sheet one time and then called into other drawings as required. With Attributes, another powerful CAD feature associated with Blocks, the user can be prompted to input the sheet number and date. Finally, details commonly used in an office can easily be reused on other projects.

1.9.6 Customization

The Prototype Drawing CAD packages are very flexible, but they can also be customized for a particular use or user. Blocks are the first step in customization. The next step is automating the procedure by which the drawing environment is created. Normally, while booting up, the CAD software looks for a seed drawing or a *prototype* or template. Much as a word-processing system starts with an 8.5 × 11 sheet, CAD packages must have something from which to start; therefore, the manufacturer usually provides one with the package. The exact information contained in the prototype drawing is normally duplicated in a new drawing. Therefore, you can duplicate the drawing environment of previous drawings with ease simply by changing the prototype drawing.

In some applications, *other prototype drawings* or templates are required, for example, title blocks for 18 × 24 sheets, 24 × 36 sheets, and 30 × 42 sheets. In this case, not only the previous settings but also the previous drawing (the title block) should be duplicated. It is possible to set any one of these drawings as the pattern (prototype) for a new drawing, thus saving the time required to create again.

Macro is short for "macro command," meaning a large or long command. A macro is a series of commands attached together so as to perform a task. Menus actually consist of prewritten macros. An advanced user can rewrite these menus or add new ones to string together series of frequently used commands. Keyboard characters have special meanings in the menu, almost like a primitive programming language. The result is a customized menu. In the case of the tablet menu, blank spaces or cells are available that can be assigned to custom macros so that they can be activated with the cursor.[1] Macros can be written for the buttons on a cursor and the screen menu. An example of a simple two-step macro would be created to enter the command Zoom Window in one step, thereby minimizing input from the user. Zoom Window could then be included on and activated from a screen menu.[2]

LISP is a programming language that was derived from XLISP. AutoLISP[3] is a dialect of LISP and coexists with AutoCAD itself within the AutoCAD program.[4] *LISP* is short for "list processing." It can be used to create programs within AutoCAD using more than just the resident commands. "An example of an AutoLISP program would be one that would expedite creation of a staircase in a building. If properly written, the program would prompt you for the distance between the upper and lower floors, ask you for the size and/or number of steps (risers and treads), and automatically draw the detailed staircase for you."[5]

1.9.7 Third-Party Development

Many software packages are general purpose, that is, intended for many different applications. Unfortunately, what is gained in flexibility is lost in utility. In other words, the basic package can be used for several different disciplines, but each discipline must adapt it for its particular way of drawing.

We have just had a brief overview of customization in which new menu features and LISP routines can be added to increase speed and efficiency. Many users not proficient in customization and programming prefer to use customized features developed by others and incorporate them into their system. These include special type fonts, hatch patterns, text editors, macros, and LISP routines. Users sometimes share these add-ons through user groups, bulletin boards, and personal contacts, taking care not to violate copyright law. Some items are available directly from the developer, such as text fonts. Macros and LISP routines are regularly published in customization books and in CAD industry journals.

Some construction product manufacturers prepare details of their products in CAD; write custom programs that enable the user to select one of their products, including model, size, and features; and combine the product with the working drawings. Such programs are now available from a number of manufacturers.

Furthermore, packages that contain entire detail files are available that work within a CAD software package. Within these packages, the designer can choose among thousands of predrawn details, verify that they apply to the current project, change them if necessary, and then incorporate them into the working drawings. Currently, third-party software developers and construction product manufacturers are working together to combine their details into massive databases.

---

[1] D. Raker and Harbort Rice, *Inside AutoCAD*, 5th ed. (Thousand Oaks, CA: New Riders Publishing, 1989) 18–1 through 18–8.

[2] Terry T. Wohlers, *Applying AutoCAD*, *Step by Step* (Mission Hills, CA: Glencoe Publishing, 1989), 350.

[3] AutoLISP™ is a registered trademark of Autodesk, Inc.

[4] Raker and Rice, *Inside AutoCAD*, 20–1.

[5] Wohlers, *Applying AutoCAD*, 380.

1.9.8 Applications Packages

A special type of software known as an *applications package* is available. Each is for use with specific CAD packages. In some cases they are developed by the primary CAD software company, but frequently they are produced by another company, a third party. They run within the primary CAD software and are a coordinated set of customized features, such as a drawing setup routine, layering schemes, drawing settings, menus, symbols, and macros.

Some CAD vendors provide versions of their programs incorporating features specifically geared for architectural applications. Autodesk, the parent company of AutoCAD, has AutoCAD Architectural Desktop, Bentley Systems has MicroStation TriForma, and Data-CAD has DataCAD Plus. These programs utilize computer-based objects that represent real-world objects such as furniture and building materials. These objects are "smart." They understand what they represent in the real world and respond accordingly in the 3D model. A window or door knows what wall it is attached to, and where in that wall it is supposed to be. If changes are made to the wall that affect the window or door they adapt accordingly. As the development of "smart" objects has advanced, the focus has shifted somewhat from simply drawing construction plans to creating 3D models from premade objects. The building plans, sections, elevations, and details are then derived from these 3D models.

Welcome to CADD

Home Design of the Future: Computer Integration

With available software, the following scenario is not only possible today but will be commonplace in the near future for home builders.

You have purchased a piece of land on which you want to build your "dream" house and have just sold your current house. You determine that you have a $160,000 budget for your new house and a deadline of September 1 to move out of your present house.

You have three factors to consider: design, cost, and time. Cost must be your primary consideration because it is inflexible. You do not qualify for more than a $160,000 mortgage. Timing is next. You have a deadline of when you have to be out of your current house. You could put your things in storage for a month, but this entails additional expenses. Design comes last. You have definite ideas of what you want in a house, but it is the one place where you have some flexibility.

Keeping these criteria in mind, you sit down at your computer and start designing. Once you have the basics down and are within budget and on time, you can start playing with options. You decide that you would like to put an arched window above the front door. You add it to your design and, thanks to a link to the spreadsheet, find that it keeps you within budget. Unfortunately, you also find out that it will take 8 weeks to order the model you have selected. Another arched window is available now, but it costs much more than your original choice and puts you over budget. Subsequently you find that all of the arched windows available are either too expensive or not available soon enough. You decide to choose a standard window instead. You have compromised on the design somewhat but have done so knowing all of your options. There has been no guesswork.

Text and figures are from the article "The 'New CADD' Trades Brawn for Smarts" by Barbara Goode, Softdesk, Inc., in the May 1996 issue of *Design/Build* magazine.

FIG. 1: *Highlighted text is hot-linked to your drafting and spreadsheet files.*

The "New CADD" software has intelligent links with other applications such as word processors and spreadsheets. This layout links with standard Microsoft Word and Excel programs, so that changes you make—in the letter (Fig. 1), invoice (Fig. 2), spreadsheet (Fig. 3) or layout (Fig. 4)—are updated in all four. This means you can accomplish work wherever it's easier for you.

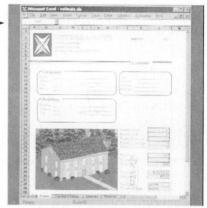

FIG. 2: *The view from the invoice.*

FIG. 3: *The spreadsheet changes as you change the design—or vice-versa!*

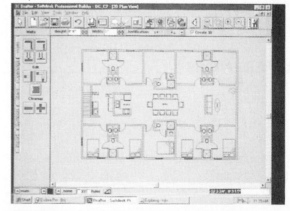

FIG. 4: *It may look like your typical CADD software, but it's more flexible.*

REVIEW QUESTIONS

1. Why doesn't learning to draw with a computer eliminate the need to learn to draw by hand?

2. What is meant by the term *model* in computer-aided design?

3. In what ways can computer-aided design aid creativity?

4. Which two major technological developments with computer hardware have fueled the rapid rise in popularity of microcomputers?

5. What is the proper name of the main printed circuit board that contains the microprocessor, the numeric coprocessor, and expansion slots?

6. How many pages of text can be stored on a typical CD-ROM disk?

7. Why is it important that CAD users develop good typing skills?

8. Discuss the advantages and disadvantages of pen and electrostatic plotters.

9. What device (other than a fax) is used to transmit files electronically over telephone lines?

10. What are the major purposes of an operating system?

11. Using CAD conventions, give an example of each of the following:

   a. linear displacement by absolute coordinates
   b. linear displacement by relative coordinates
   c. angular displacement by polar coordinates

12. What are four different techniques used to issue CAD commands?

13. In a typical CAD drawing session, which type of command is used more frequently, Draw or Edit?

14. Why does a square, 1 inch long on each side, require the same amount of computer memory as a square 1 mile long on each side?

15. Points, lines, and circles are examples of *entities*. What is the name of a compact group of entities in CAD?

16. Polylines can greatly increase the *speed* of CAD work, but they can hinder *detailed work*. Why?

17. What are the advantages of combining drawings?

18. Explain how symbol libraries are created in CAD.

19. Explain the difference between graphic images stored in *vector format* and *raster format*.

20. When objects are drawn at full scale in CAD, how are scale drawings generally produced?

BIBLIOGRAPHY

Autodesk, Inc., *AutoCAD User's Guide Release 14*, 1997.

Conner, Frank L., *The Student Edition of AutoSketch, User's Manual*. Reading, MA: Addison-Wesley Publishing and Benjamin/Cummings Publishing, 1991.

Hart, Roger. Plotters, Teaming Up Your Compaq with the Right One. *PAQ Review* (Summer 1988).

Hoskins, Jim. *IBM Personal System/2, A Business Perspective*. New York: John Wiley & Sons, 1987.

Jeffris, Alan, and David Madsen. *Architectural Drafting and Design*. 2d ed. Albany, NY: Delmar Publishers, 1991.

Lloyd, Bill. *Technical Notes, Note 102, Electrostatic Technology*. Versatec, 1989.

Popular Electronics. "World's First Minicomputer Kit to Rival Commercial Models . . . 'Altair 8800.' " January 1975.

Raker, Daniel, and Harbort Rice. *Inside AutoCAD*. 5th ed. Thousand Oaks, CA: New Riders Publishing Co., 1989.

Sheldon, Thomas. *Hard Disk Management in the PC & MS DOS Environment*. New York: McGraw-Hill Book Company, 1988.

Wohlers, Terry T. *Applying AutoCAD, Step by Step*. Mission Hills, CA: Glencoe Publishing, Division of Macmillan, Inc., 1989.

REFERENCES

Books

Gates, Bill. *The Road Ahead*. New York: Viking Penguin, 1995.

Guidelines Publishing. *The Internet for A/E's*. Orinda, CA, 1995.

Mitchell, William. *City of Bits*. Cambridge, MA: MIT Press, 1995.

Omura, George. *Mastering AutoCAD Release 12*. Alameda, CA: Sybex, Inc., 1992.

Sanders, Ken, AIA. *The Digital Architect*. New York: John Wiley & Sons, 1996.

Smith, Bud, Jake Richter, and Mark Middlebrook. *AutoCAD Power Tools*. New York: Random House, 1993.

Periodicals

A/E/C System. Sept./Oct. 1995; Nov./Dec. 1995; May/June, 1996.

Architecture. June 1995; August 1995; May 1996.

Builder. April 1994; July 1995; May 1996; June 1996.

Cadalyst. July 1993.

Cadence. April, 1996.

The Construction Specifier. January 1996.

Design/Build Business. May 1996.

PC Magazine. December 1995; February 1996; April 1996.

PC World. February 1995.

Professional Builder. December 1994; Mid-January 1995.

Progressive Architecture. September 1995.

Sun Coast. May 1995.

Windows Sources. May 1996.

PUBLISHERS' ADDRESSES

Books

Guidelines Publishing
P.O. Box 456
Orinda, CA 94563

MIT Press
5 Cambridge Center
Cambridge, MA 02142

Random House, Inc.
201 East 50th Street
New York, NY 10022

Sybex, Inc.
2021 Challenger Drive
Alameda, CA 94501

Viking
A Division of Penguin USA
375 Hudson Street
New York, NY 10014

John Wiley & Sons, Inc.
605 Third Avenue
New York, NY 10158

Periodicals

A/E/C Systems Computer Solutions
A/E/C Systems, Inc.
P.O. Box 310318
Newington, CT 06131

Architecture
BPI Communications
1515 Broadway
New York, NY 10036

Builder
Builder Magazine
655 15th Street N.W., Suite 475
Washington, DC 20005

Cadalyst
Advanstar Communications, Inc.
859 Williamette Street
Eugene, OR 97401

Cadence
Miller Freeman, Inc.
600 Harrison Street
San Francisco, CA 94107

The Construction Specifier
Construction Specifications Institute
601 Madison Street
Alexandria, VA 22314

Design/Build Business
McKellar Publications, Inc.
333 E. Glenoaks Boulevard, Suite 204
Glendale, CA 91207

PC Magazine
Ziff-Davis Publishing Company, L.P.
One Park Avenue
New York, NY 10016

PC World
PC World Communications, Inc.
501 Second Street #600
San Francisco, CA 94107

Professional Builder
Professional Builder
1350 E. Touhy Avenue
P.O. Box 5080
Des Plaines, IL 60017-5080

Progressive Architecture
Penton Publishing
1100 Superior Avenue
Cleveland, OH 44114

Sun Coast
McKellar Publications, Inc.
333 E. Glenoaks Boulevard, Suite 204
Glendale, CA 92107

Windows Sources
Ziff-Davis Publishing Company, L.P.
One Park Avenue
New York, NY 10016

"Ah, to build, to build. That is the noblest
art of all the arts."
—HENRY WADSWORTH LONGFELLOW

This chapter introduces and explains many of the accepted principles and methods of light construction found in residences and small commercial buildings. The written material is supplemented with typical sections taken through walls, floors, roofs, and structural members. Pictorial drawings are also used when necessary to present this information as simply as possible. Some of the methods shown are adaptable to one area of the country; others are common construction practice in other areas, depending on building codes and local conditions. Some methods are conventional practice, having been in use for years; others are comparatively new. Together, they form details widely used and generally found satisfactory. More exhaustive treatments of construction details can be found in specialized texts to supplement this material. The actual drawings of details is treated later, but you should not attempt design drawing until you have made a thorough study of construction methods. Tables and charts from the Uniform Building Code, referenced usually as, for example, "Table D–1," are found in Appendix D.

2.1
DEVELOPING A BACKGROUND IN LIGHT CONSTRUCTION METHODS

At this point in their training, students should acquire as much information and background relative to construction as they can find from various sources. Whether it is pursued by people who create and design the most elaborate structures or by others called on to draw the various working drawings of the simplest buildings, architecture requires a searching interest and enthusiasm about the methods of building. To be successful in this field not only requires skill in knowing *how to draw*, but, equally important, requires the acquisition of background information in knowing *what to draw*. Unless drafters continuously strive to increase their knowledge of construction details, they can expect to become no more than junior drafters or merely tracers.

Technical courses in architectural print reading, building materials, and construction methods, which in technical schools often precede or are prerequisites to architectural drawing, provide this needed background. Students and drafters should continually read monthly periodicals and trade magazines containing current information. Literature from the many building construction trade organizations will be found valuable. Various governmental agencies concerned with housing and standardized construction practice, including the U.S. Government Printing Office, offer inexpensive manuals that should not be overlooked. Drafters must become familiar with *Sweet's Architectural Catalog File* (F. W. Dodge Corp., New York) for convenient reference on many construction materials. Many good books on construction are available in libraries.

Part-time employment with builders or contractors, as an adjunct to drafting training, is desirable for learning construction methods. In fact, actual on-the-job observation of a building in the process of construction is time well spent by drafters. Not only is it a thrilling experience, but it offers the opportunity of seeing many of the building materials in use and the way that they are put together within the building—mainly the structural members that are often concealed once the building is completed. Students who have familiarized themselves with the methods and techniques of construction will certainly be better equipped to draw more intelligently, progress more rapidly, and grow in stature as architectural drafters.

This text makes no attempt to treat special situations requiring structural engineering design to solve the problems. Such information, which is beyond the scope of this book, is left to specialized texts.

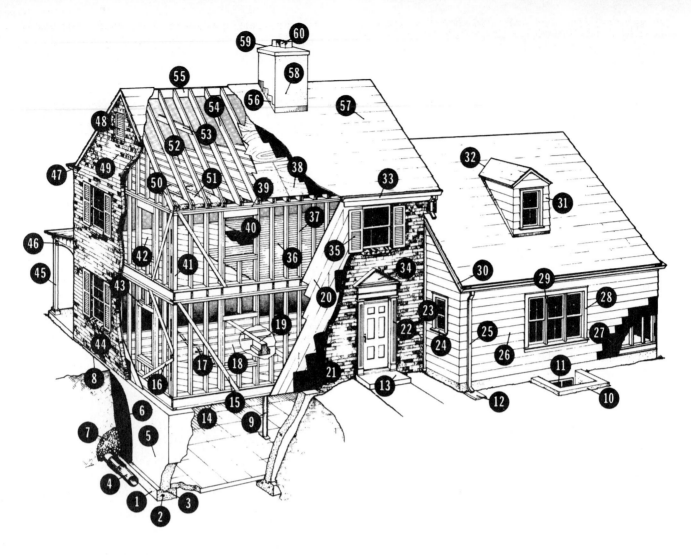

Figure 2–1 Typical residential terms.

1. Footing
2. Reinforcing rod
3. Keyway
4. Drain tile
5. Foundation wall
6. Waterproofing
7. Gravel fill
8. Grade line
9. Metal column
10. Areaway wall
11. Basement window
12. Splash block
13. Stoop
14. Sill plate
15. Corner brace
16. Knee brace
17. Bridging
18. Floor joist
19. Beam; girder
20. Sheathing

21. Building paper
22. Trim pilaster
23. Double-hung window
24. Window sill
25. Downspout; leader
26. Bevel siding
27. Fiberboard sheathing
28. Window trim
29. Mullion
30. Rake mold
31. Dormer
32. Valley
33. Gutter
34. Pediment door trim
35. Shutter
36. Finish flooring
37. Stud
38. Roof decking
39. Double top plate
40. Flooring paper

41. Corner post
42. Subfloor
43. Lintel; header
44. Brick sill
45. Porch post
46. Porch frieze board
47. Return cornice
48. Louver
49. Brick veneer; gable
50. End rafter
51. Insulation
52. Ceiling joist
53. Collar beam
54. Common rafter
55. Ridge board
56. Flashing
57. Shingles
58. Chimney
59. Cement wash; cap
60. Chimney flues; pots

CONSTRUCTION TERMINOLOGY

Figure 2–1 is a guide to the terms found in light construction. You should memorize these terms and know where they apply within a typical building. Definitions of other terms that may be unfamiliar can be found in the Glossary of Construction Terms following the Appendices. You will occasionally encounter several different designations for similar features in construction terminology because workers frequently use terms that are indigenous to their particular region; elsewhere the terms might have quite different applications. Despite widespread national distribution of building construction products, terminology has not been entirely standardized, but as you continue to improve your vocabulary and construction background, the ambiguities will become less confusing.

Some of the present terms used in residential construction, especially in wood framing, have been handed down from New England colonial history, for example, *collar beam*, *soleplate*, and *ridge pole*. Some terms have come from the ancient Greek civilization, especially terms relative to classic building exteriors, such as *frieze*, *plinth*, and *dentils*. Other parts derive their names from their physical shapes. For instance, the *box sill*, which has a boxed-in characteristic, the *K brace*, which has the shape of the letter *K*, and the *T post*, which resembles the letter *T* when shown in cross section, are just a few of the terms that are so labeled because of their shape. Most of the terms, however, have been derived from the logical use or placement of the part in relation to the building, for example, *footing*, *foundation*, *baseboard*, *shoemold*, and *doorstop*.

Girders, *beams*, and *joists* are terms given to horizontal structural members used in buildings. Often the heavy, structural support for the floor framing in light construction is referred to as either a *girder* or a *beam*. In more complex construction, however, the heaviest members are referred to as *girders*. They support the beams that are of intermediate weight and that support the joists, the lightest members of the floor or roof structure.

FOOTINGS AND FOUNDATIONS

Every properly constructed building must be supported by an appropriate foundation that will support the weight of the building and sustain the structure throughout all weather conditions to which it may be subjected. The *footing*, the enlarged base of the foundation wall, must be massive enough, depending on local soil conditions, to distribute the weight of the building to the ground below, and it must be deep enough to prevent frost action below. Poured concrete is usually the best and most widely used material. Footings can be formed and poured where soils are stable enough to hold their shape; trenches are dug the proper depth, and concrete is poured directly into the trenches to form adequate footings.

Figure 2–2 illustrates the method of laying out footings and foundation walls. Leveled batter boards are used to lay out the foundation of a building. Wooden stakes are driven into the soil several feet outside the corners of the proposed building. The top of the batter board is positioned at the finished floor elevation of the building. The batter board is then securely nailed to the wooden stakes. A taut string line that locates the exterior wall of the building and foundation is run between batter boards, as shown in Fig. 2–2.

Frost action below the footing would raise and lower the building during freezing and thawing and would soon fracture the foundation, as well as disrupt other parts of the building. Naturally, frost lines vary throughout the country; local building codes usually indicate the depth to which footings must be placed below grade. Figure 2–3 shows average frost depths throughout the

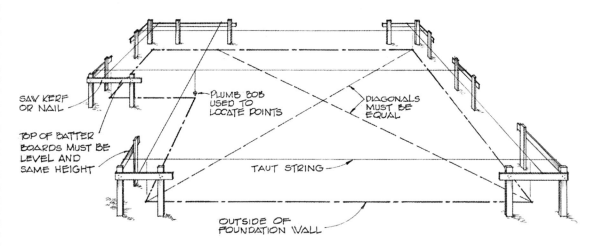

Figure 2–2 Leveled batter boards are used to lay out the foundation of a building.

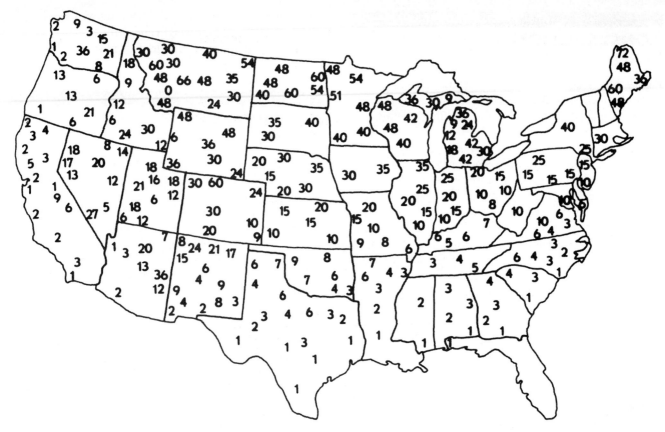

Figure 2–3 Average depth of frost penetration in inches for locations throughout the United States. (U.S. Department of Commerce Weather Bureau)

country, compiled by the U.S. Weather Service. The Uniform Building Code prescribes footings to be placed a minimum of 1′-0″ below the frost line. Footings of buildings with basements are deep enough so that frost lines usually need not be considered. In northern areas, the cost of excavating for deep footings often makes the basement more economical than in southern areas, where footings are often merely trench footings several feet below grade.

Footings should also be placed on undisturbed soil. Occasionally, if a building must be put over a fill, the soil should be well compacted, and sufficient steel reinforcing should be in the footing to prevent cracking (Fig. 2–5). Local codes in some areas require steel reinforcing in the footings to counteract specific conditions (for example, the Florida Hurricane Code, and the California Seismic Code). In cold weather, care must be taken to ensure that foundations are neither placed on frozen soil nor poured in freezing weather. Footings should project a maximum of 6″ beyond the face of the foundation wall. Table D–7 and Figure 2–4 contain guidelines for determining minimum footing depth and width based on building wall size and height.

The soil on which footings rest must be level and compact. In weak soils in which the load-bearing qualities are questionable, it is advisable to introduce steel reinforc-

ing rods at intersecting points between chimney or fireplace footings and wall footings. In soft soils, this is advisable also at corners, at offsets, and at breaks in the direction or size of the footings. When footings are subjected to heavier loads, calculations should be made to determine their correct size in order to balance the various footings in relation to their various loads. The first consideration is the load-bearing qualities of the soil on which the footings rest.

Table 2–1 indicates typical supporting capacities of different types of soil conditions in tons and pounds per square foot. The soil capacities are only general, and we cannot rely on them entirely for calculating critical footing sizes. Soils vary considerably even in local areas; also, the moisture content of some soils changes its supporting qualities. Only a soil expert or a local testing laboratory after numerous tests will be able to analyze load-bearing characteristics of a soil for critical footing design. Local practices that have been found successful should be relied on for this purpose. Careful builders generally have the soil tested before footings are poured. If local codes require steel reinforcing rods, they should be placed near the bottom in wall footings and in column or isolated footings. Engineers have found that the steel is usually effective in case of uneven settlement in resisting tensile stresses (Fig. 2–5).

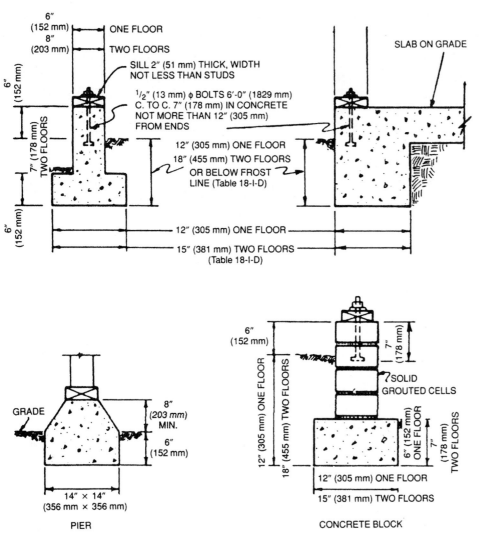

Figure 2–4 Footings: Recommended depths and sizes. (Dwelling Construction Under the Uniform Building Code, 1994. International Conference of Building Officials.)

Because residences and frame buildings are comparatively light, they seldom require accurate footing design. However, if the soil is not trustworthy or if the building gives indication of being heavier than usual, the following method can be used to calculate the necessary size of the footings (Tables 2–2, 2–3, and 2–4). Both dead load and live load must be considered in the calculations. *Dead load* refers to the weight of the structure as well as any stationary equipment fastened to it; *live load* refers to varying weights and forces to which parts of the building are subjected (people, furnishings, storage, wind, snow, and so on). Both weights are designated in pounds per square foot (lb/sq ft) (Fig. 2–6). Local codes generally require residential floors to be able to carry 40 lb/sq ft live load.

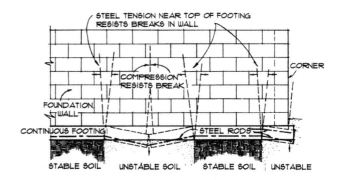

Figure 2–5 Reinforcing steel becomes most effective if placed in the lower part of a footing-supporting C.M.U.

Table 2-1 Presumptive values of allowable bearing pressures for spread foundations.

Type of Bearing Material	Consistency in Place	Allowable Bearing Pressure (Tons/Sq Ft)	
		Range	Recommended Value for Use
Massive, crystalline igneous and metamorphic rock: granite, diorite, basalt, gneiss, thoroughly cemented conglomerate (sound condition allows minor cracks).	Hard, sound rock	60 to 100	80.0
Foliated metamorphic rock: slate, schist (sound condition allows minor cracks).	Medium-hard, sound rock	30 to 40	35.0
Sedimentary rock: hard, cemented shales, siltstone, sandstone, limestone without cavities.	Medium-hard, sound rock	15 to 25	20.0
Weathered or broken bedrock of any kind except highly argillaceous rock (shale). RQD less than 25.	Soft rock	8 to 12	10.0
Compaction shale or other highly argillaceous rock in sound condition.	Soft rock	8 to 12	10.0
Well-graded mixture of fine- and coarse-grained soil: glacial till, hardpan, boulder clay (GW-GC, GC, SC).	Very compact	8 to 12	10.0
Gravel–gravel sand mixtures; boulder-gravel mixtures (SW, SP, SW, SP)	Very compact	6 to 10	7.0
	Medium to compact	4 to 7	5.0
	Loose	2 to 6	3.0
Coarse to medium sand; sand with little gravel (SW, SP)	Very compact	4 to 6	4.0
	Medium to compact	2 to 4	3.0
	Loose	1 to 3	1.5
Fine to medium sand; silty or clayey, medium to coarse sand (SW, SM, SC)	Very compact	3 to 5	3.0
	Medium to compact	2 to 4	2.5
	Loose	1 to 2	1.5
Homogeneous inorganic clay; sandy or silty clay (CL, CH)	Very stiff to hard	3 to 6	4.0
	Medium to stiff	1 to 3	2.0
	Soft	0.5 to 1	0.5
Inorganic silt; sandy or clayey silt; varved silt–clay–fine sand	Very stiff to hard	2 to 4	3.0
	Medium to stiff	1 to 3	1.5
	Soft	0.5 to 1	0.5

SOURCE: Foundations and Earth Structures, Design Manual 7.02, Naval Facilities Engineering Command.

NOTES:

1. Compacted fill, placed with control of moisture, density, and lift thickness, has allowable bearing pressure of equivalent natural soil.
2. Allowable bearing pressure on compressible, fine-grained soils is generally limited by consideration of overall settlement of the structure.
3. Allowable bearing pressure on organic soils or uncompacted fills is determined by investigation of the individual case.
4. If the tabulated recommended value for rock exceeds the unconfined compressive strength of the intact specimen, allowable pressure equals unconfined compressive strength.

Table 2–2 Typical weights of materials used in light construction.

Roof	lb/sq ft
Wood shingles	3
Asphalt shingles	3
Fiberglass shingles	2.5
Copper	2
Built-up roofing, 3-ply and gravel	5.5
Built-up roofing, 5-ply and gravel	6.5
Membrane roofing, without ballast	1
Slate, $1/4''$ thick	10
Mission tile	13
$1''$ wood decking, with felt	2.5
$2'' \times 4''$ rafters, $16''$ o.c.	2
$2'' \times 6''$ rafters, $16''$ o.c.	2.5
$2'' \times 8''$ rafters, $16''$ o.c.	3.5
$1/2''$ plywood	1.5

Walls	
$4''$ stud partition, plastered both sides	22
Window glass, DSB	2
$2'' \times 4''$ studs, $1''$ sheathing, paper	4.5
Brick veneer, $4''$	42
Stone veneer, $4''$	50
Wood siding, $1''$ thickness	3
$1/2''$ gypsum wallboard	2.5

Floors and Ceilings	
$2'' \times 10''$ wood joists, $16''$ o.c.	4.5
$2'' \times 12''$ wood joists, $16''$ o.c.	5
Oak flooring, $25/32''$ thick	4
Clay tile on $1''$ mortar base	23
$4''$ concrete slab	48
Gypsum plaster, metal lath	10

Foundation Walls	
$8''$ poured concrete, at 150 lb/cu ft	100
$8''$ concrete block	55
$12''$ concrete block	80
$8''$ brick, at 120 lb/cu ft	80

Table 2–3 Calculation for exterior wall footings (Fig. 2–6).

Given: 1-story brick veneer frame, wood shingle roof, plaster interior walls, poured concrete foundation. Load-bearing value of soils = 2000 lb/sq ft.

Roof

	1. Live load, snow, wind (varies locally)	30.0 lb/sq ft	
Dead load	2. Shingles, wood	3.0	
	3. Wood deck, 1″ thick, and felt	2.5	
	4. Rafters, 2″ × 6″, 16″ o.c.	<u>2.5</u>	
	(Length of rafters measures 13′-0″.)	38.0 lb/sq ft × 13′	= 494 lb

First-Floor Ceiling

	1. Live load (attic storage)	20.0	
Dead load	2. Wood floor, 1″ thick	2.5	
	3. Wood joists, 2″ × 8″, 16″ o.c.	3.5	
	4. Ceiling plaster, metal lath	<u>10.0</u>	
	(Half-span of ceiling is 5′-0″.)	36.0 lb/sq ft × 5′	= 180 lb

Exterior Wall

	1. Brick veneer	42.0	
Dead load	2. Sheathing, wood, 1″ thick, and felt	2.5	
	3. Studs, 2″ × 4″, 16″ o.c.	2.0	
	4. Plaster, metal lath, interior	<u>10.0</u>	
	(Height of wall measures 9′-0″.)	56.5 lb/sq ft × 9′	= 509 lb

Floor

	1. Live load (usual code requirements)	40.0	
Dead load	2. Finished oak floor	4.0	
	3. Subfloor, 1″ thick	2.5	
	4. 2″ × 10″ joists, 16″ o.c.	<u>4.5</u>	
	(Half-span of floor to center beam is 5′-0″.)	51.0 lb/sq ft × 5′	= 255 lb

Foundation

Dead load	1. Concrete wall, 8″ thick (Height of foundation wall is 9′-0″.)	100.0 lb/sq ft × 9′	= 900 lb
	2. Concrete footing, 16″ × 8″	100.0 lb/sq ft × 1.33′	= <u>133 lb</u>
	Total load on soil per lin ft of wall		**= 2471 lb**

$$\text{Required area of footing} = \frac{\text{load}}{\text{soil-bearing capacity}} = \frac{2471}{2000} = 1.23 \text{ sq ft}$$

Total area of footing required per linear foot of wall = 1.23 sq ft

For convenience, use 1.25: 12″ × 1.25 = **15″ wide footing required.** To be on the safe side, it would be practical to make the footing 16″ wide, which would be the width if calculated by rule of thumb.

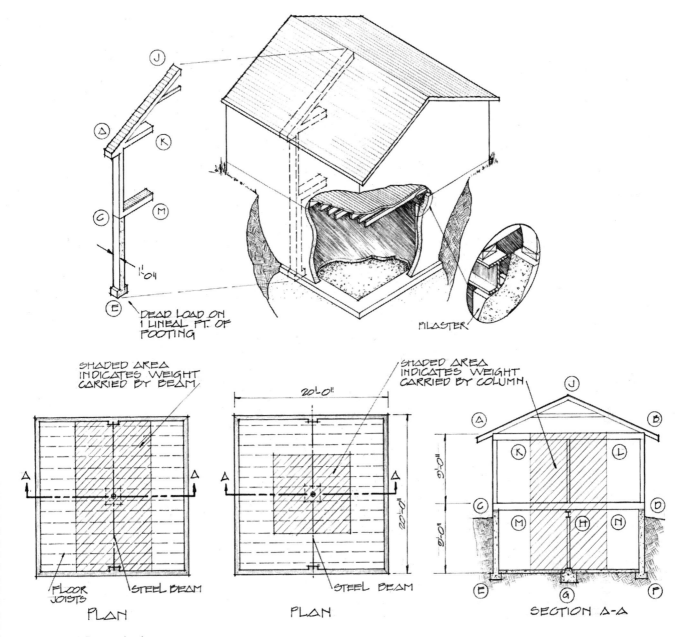

Figure 2–6 Footing loads.

Table 2–4 Calculation for column footing (Fig. 2–6).

1. Ceiling	180 lb/lin ft
2. Partitions	100
3. First floor	255
Total	535 lb/lin ft

The column supports 10 lin ft of beam

$$535 \times 10' = 5350$$

Dead load of beam: 250

Total 5600 lb carried by column

$$\frac{\text{Total load}}{\text{soil capacity}} = \frac{5600}{2000} = 2.8 \text{ sq ft footing required}$$

$$X = \sqrt{2.8} = 1.7 = 1'\text{-}8''$$

Required column footing size = $1'\text{-}8'' \times 1'\text{-}8''$

Make footing $2'\text{-}0'' \times 2'\text{-}0'' \times 12''$ deep.

2.3.1 Footing and Foundation Design

Good foundation design and construction depend on a number of strategies. For example, appropriate structural design should be combined with insulation, and with moisture-, termite-, and radon-control techniques where needed.

The choices involved reflect the decision-making process used by a designer, builder, or homeowner dealing with foundation design development (Fig. 2–7). You must decide which type of foundation and which construction system will be used. If the foundation is a basement, you must decide whether the below-grade space will be heated and/or cooled. Second, you must choose the construction system: concrete, masonry, or wood.

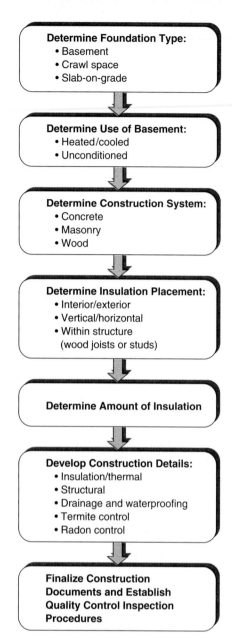

Determine Foundation Type:
- Basement
- Crawl space
- Slab-on-grade

Determine Use of Basement:
- Heated/cooled
- Unconditioned

Determine Construction System:
- Concrete
- Masonry
- Wood

Determine Insulation Placement:
- Interior/exterior
- Vertical/horizontal
- Within structure
  (wood joists or studs)

Determine Amount of Insulation

Develop Construction Details:
- Insulation/thermal
- Structural
- Drainage and waterproofing
- Termite control
- Radon control

Finalize Construction Documents and Establish Quality Control Inspection Procedures

Figure 2–7 The decision-making process for foundation design.

Third, the placement of insulation needs to be addressed. Be sure to check local codes to determine the minimum amount of insulation required for the type of foundation and construction system. Finally, once the amount and location of the insulation have been determined, the necessary construction details can be developed and construction documents can be finalized.

Radon Controlling radon is a relatively new concern in the design and construction of basements and foundations. Radon is a colorless, odorless, tasteless gas found in soils and underground water at varying levels throughout the United States. It is potentially harmful if it decays while in the lungs. Because radon is a gas, it can

travel through the soil and into a building through cracks, joints, and other openings in the foundation wall and floor (Fig. 2–8).

The initial step in addressing the radon problem is to determine to what degree it is present on the site. Various techniques to control radon levels can then be applied.

The Council of American Building Officials (CABO) has adopted the standards of the Environmental Protection Agency (EPA) for radon-resistant new residential construction. The methods for radon mitigation have been added as an appendix to the code. Many of the techniques that resist radon entry are already described in other sections of CABO's code because they effectively insulate buildings from temperature extremes and moisture. There are three basic approaches to dealing with radon:

1. the barrier approach,
2. soil gas interception, and
3. indoor air management.

The *barrier approach* is a set of techniques for constructing an airtight building foundation in order to prevent soil gas from entering. This approach is different for each foundation type.

Soil gas interception uses vent pipes and fans to draw soil gas from a gravel layer beneath the foundation floor slab (Fig. 2–9). This approach can be used for basements and slab-on-grade foundations.

Air management techniques reduce the suction that a building applies to the surrounding soil gas by reducing the pressure differential across the building envelope. It is necessary to make the entire building envelope airtight and to control the amount of the incoming fresh air, the exhausted inside air, and the air supplied for combustion devices.

Many of these principles are essentially the same as those recommended for moisture vapor control and energy-efficient design. Figure 2–10 illustrates the CABO recommendations, and Figures 2–11, 2–12, and 2–13 show radon-mitigation strategies for the three basic foundation types.

Termite Control Controlling the entry of termites through residential foundations is advisable in much of the United States. Be sure to consult with local building officials and codes for specific strategies that are acceptable.

The following general recommendations apply where termites are a potential problem:

1. Minimize soil moisture around the basement. Use gutters, downspouts, and runouts to remove roof water, or install a complete subdrainage system around the foundation.
2. Remove all roots, stumps, and scrap wood from the site.

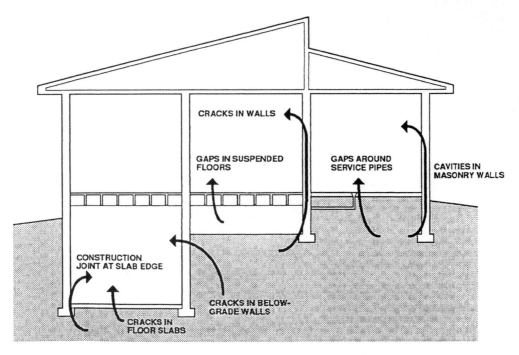

Figure 2–8 Points of radon entry into buildings.

3. Place a bond beam or a course of cap blocks at the top of all concrete masonry foundation walls; or fill all cores on the top course with mortar, and reinforce the mortar joint beneath the top course.

4. Be sure that the sill plate is at least 8″ above grade. It should be pressure-preservative treated to resist decay, and it should be visible from the inside for inspection. Termite shields are often damaged or installed incorrectly. They should be considered optional and should not be regarded as sufficient by themselves.

5. Be sure that the exterior wood siding and trim are at least 6″ above grade.

6. Construct porches and exterior slabs so that they slope away from the foundation wall and are at least 2″ below existing siding. They should also be separated from all wood members by a 2″ gap visible for inspection or by a continuous metal flashing soldered at all seams.

7. Form a termite barrier between the foundation wall and the slab floor by filling the joint with urethane caulk or coal-tar pitch.

8. Place wood posts on flashing or a concrete pedestal raised 1″ above the basement floor, or use pressure-preservative-treated wood posts on the basement floor slab.

9. Flash hollow steel columns at the top.

Plastic foam and mineral wood insulation materials have no food value to termites, but they can provide protective cover and easy tunneling. Exterior insulation system installations can be detailed to facilitate inspection, but they usually sacrifice thermal efficiency. Restrictions on widely used termiticides may make soil treatment unavailable or may cause the substitution of products that are more expensive and possibly less effective.

Figures 2–14, 2–15, and 2–16 show termite-control strategies for the three basic foundation types.

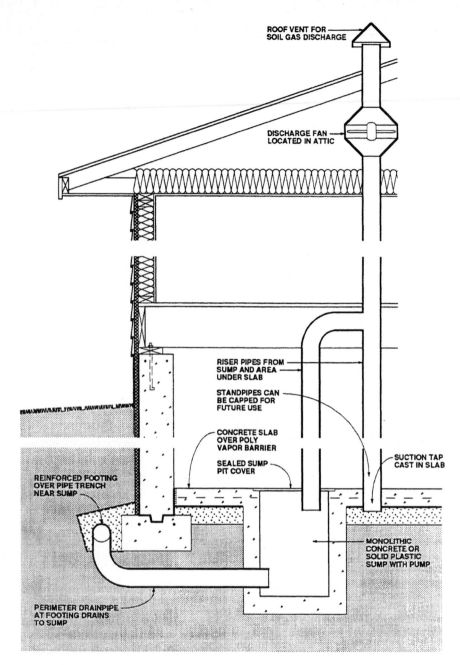

Figure 2–9 Soil gas collection and discharge techniques. (*AIA Architect*)

Labels within the figure:

ROOF VENT FOR SOIL GAS DISCHARGE

DISCHARGE FAN LOCATED IN ATTIC

RISER PIPES FROM SUMP AND AREA UNDER SLAB

STANDPIPES CAN BE CAPPED FOR FUTURE USE

CONCRETE SLAB OVER POLY VAPOR BARRIER

SEALED SUMP PIT COVER

SUCTION TAP CAST IN SLAB

REINFORCED FOOTING OVER PIPE TRENCH NEAR SUMP

MONOLITHIC CONCRETE OR SOLID PLASTIC SUMP WITH PUMP

PERIMETER DRAINPIPE AT FOOTING DRAINS TO SUMP

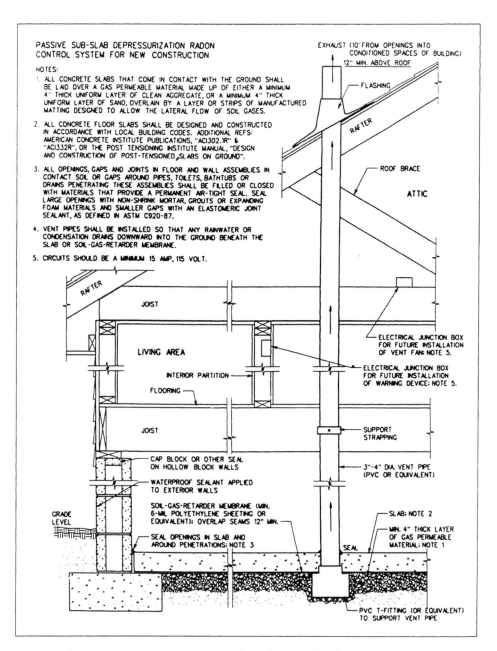

PASSIVE SUB-SLAB DEPRESSURIZATION RADON CONTROL SYSTEM FOR NEW CONSTRUCTION

NOTES:

1. ALL CONCRETE SLABS THAT COME IN CONTACT WITH THE GROUND SHALL BE LAID OVER A GAS PERMEABLE MATERIAL MADE UP OF EITHER A MINIMUM 4" THICK UNIFORM LAYER OF CLEAN AGGREGATE, OR A MINIMUM 4" THICK UNIFORM LAYER OF SAND, OVERLAIN BY A LAYER OR STRIPS OF MANUFACTURED MATTING DESIGNED TO ALLOW THE LATERAL FLOW OF SOIL GASES.

2. ALL CONCRETE FLOOR SLABS SHALL BE DESIGNED AND CONSTRUCTED IN ACCORDANCE WITH LOCAL BUILDING CODES. ADDITIONAL REFS: AMERICAN CONCRETE INSTITUTE PUBLICATIONS, "ACI302.1R" & "ACI332R", OR THE POST TENSIONING INSTITUTE MANUAL, "DESIGN AND CONSTRUCTION OF POST-TENSIONED SLABS ON GROUND".

3. ALL OPENINGS, GAPS AND JOINTS IN FLOOR AND WALL ASSEMBLIES IN CONTACT SOIL OR GAPS AROUND PIPES, TOILETS, BATHTUBS OR DRAINS PENETRATING THESE ASSEMBLIES SHALL BE FILLED OR CLOSED WITH MATERIALS THAT PROVIDE A PERMANENT AIR-TIGHT SEAL. SEAL LARGE OPENINGS WITH NON-SHRINK MORTAR, GROUTS OR EXPANDING FOAM MATERIALS AND SMALLER GAPS WITH AN ELASTOMERIC JOINT SEALANT, AS DEFINED IN ASTM C920-87.

4. VENT PIPES SHALL BE INSTALLED SO THAT ANY RAINWATER OR CONDENSATION DRAINS DOWNWARD INTO THE GROUND BENEATH THE SLAB OR SOIL-GAS-RETARDER MEMBRANE.

5. CIRCUITS SHOULD BE A MINIMUM 15 AMP, 115 VOLT.

EXHAUST (10' FROM OPENINGS INTO CONDITIONED SPACES OF BUILDING) 12" MIN. ABOVE ROOF

FLASHING

RAFTER

ROOF BRACE

ATTIC

RAFTER

JOIST

LIVING AREA

INTERIOR PARTITION

FLOORING

JOIST

ELECTRICAL JUNCTION BOX FOR FUTURE INSTALLATION OF VENT FAN: NOTE 5.

ELECTRICAL JUNCTION BOX FOR FUTURE INSTALLATION OF WARNING DEVICE: NOTE 5.

SUPPORT STRAPPING

CAP BLOCK OR OTHER SEAL ON HOLLOW BLOCK WALLS

WATERPROOF SEALANT APPLIED TO EXTERIOR WALLS

3"-4" DIA. VENT PIPE (PVC OR EQUIVALENT)

SOIL-GAS-RETARDER MEMBRANE (MIN. 6-MIL POLYETHYLENE SHEETING OR EQUIVALENT); OVERLAP SEAMS 12" MIN.

GRADE LEVEL

SEAL OPENINGS IN SLAB AND AROUND PENETRATIONS: NOTE 3

SLAB: NOTE 2

MIN. 4" THICK LAYER OF GAS PERMEABLE MATERIAL: NOTE 1

SEAL

PVC T-FITTING (OR EQUIVALENT) TO SUPPORT VENT PIPE

Figure 2–10 CABO recommendations for radon mitigation. (*AIA Architect*)

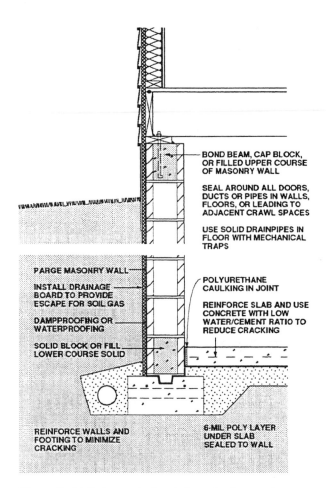

BOND BEAM, CAP BLOCK, OR FILLED UPPER COURSE OF MASONRY WALL

SEAL AROUND ALL DOORS, DUCTS OR PIPES IN WALLS, FLOORS, OR LEADING TO ADJACENT CRAWL SPACES

USE SOLID DRAINPIPES IN FLOOR WITH MECHANICAL TRAPS

PARGE MASONRY WALL

INSTALL DRAINAGE BOARD TO PROVIDE ESCAPE FOR SOIL GAS

DAMPPROOFING OR WATERPROOFING

SOLID BLOCK OR FILL LOWER COURSE SOLID

POLYURETHANE CAULKING IN JOINT

REINFORCE SLAB AND USE CONCRETE WITH LOW WATER/CEMENT RATIO TO REDUCE CRACKING

REINFORCE WALLS AND FOOTING TO MINIMIZE CRACKING

6-MIL POLY LAYER UNDER SLAB SEALED TO WALL

Figure 2–11 Radon-control techniques for basements.

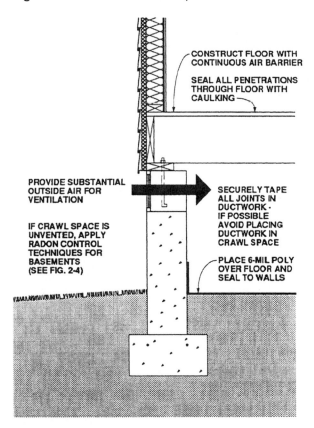

CONSTRUCT FLOOR WITH CONTINUOUS AIR BARRIER

SEAL ALL PENETRATIONS THROUGH FLOOR WITH CAULKING

PROVIDE SUBSTANTIAL OUTSIDE AIR FOR VENTILATION

IF CRAWL SPACE IS UNVENTED, APPLY RADON CONTROL TECHNIQUES FOR BASEMENTS (SEE FIG. 2-4)

SECURELY TAPE ALL JOINTS IN DUCTWORK - IF POSSIBLE AVOID PLACING DUCTWORK IN CRAWL SPACE

PLACE 6-MIL POLY OVER FLOOR AND SEAL TO WALLS

Figure 2–12 Radon-control techniques for crawl spaces.

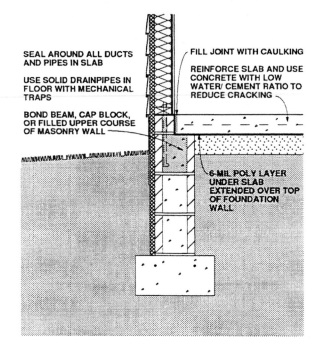

SEAL AROUND ALL DUCTS AND PIPES IN SLAB

USE SOLID DRAINPIPES IN FLOOR WITH MECHANICAL TRAPS

BOND BEAM, CAP BLOCK, OR FILLED UPPER COURSE OF MASONRY WALL

FILL JOINT WITH CAULKING

REINFORCE SLAB AND USE CONCRETE WITH LOW WATER/ CEMENT RATIO TO REDUCE CRACKING

6-MIL POLY LAYER UNDER SLAB EXTENDED OVER TOP OF FOUNDATION WALL

Figure 2–13 Radon-control techniques for slab-on-grade foundations.

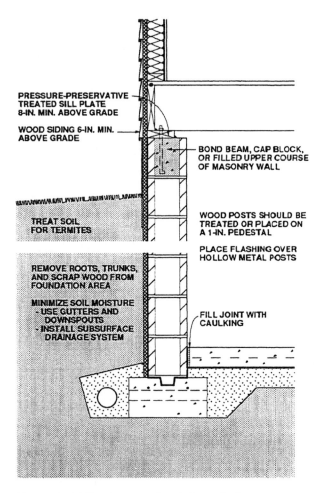

PRESSURE-PRESERVATIVE TREATED SILL PLATE 8-IN. MIN. ABOVE GRADE

WOOD SIDING 6-IN. MIN. ABOVE GRADE

BOND BEAM, CAP BLOCK, OR FILLED UPPER COURSE OF MASONRY WALL

TREAT SOIL FOR TERMITES

WOOD POSTS SHOULD BE TREATED OR PLACED ON A 1-IN. PEDESTAL

PLACE FLASHING OVER HOLLOW METAL POSTS

REMOVE ROOTS, TRUNKS, AND SCRAP WOOD FROM FOUNDATION AREA

MINIMIZE SOIL MOISTURE - USE GUTTERS AND DOWNSPOUTS - INSTALL SUBSURFACE DRAINAGE SYSTEM

FILL JOINT WITH CAULKING

Figure 2–14 Termite-control techniques for basements.

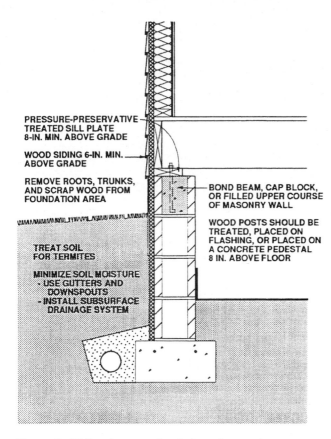

Figure 2–15 Termite-control techniques for crawl spaces.

PRESSURE-PRESERVATIVE
TREATED SILL PLATE
8-IN. MIN. ABOVE GRADE

WOOD SIDING 6-IN. MIN.
ABOVE GRADE

REMOVE ROOTS, TRUNKS,
AND SCRAP WOOD FROM
FOUNDATION AREA

TREAT SOIL
FOR TERMITES

MINIMIZE SOIL MOISTURE
- USE GUTTERS AND
  DOWNSPOUTS
- INSTALL SUBSURFACE
  DRAINAGE SYSTEM

BOND BEAM, CAP BLOCK,
OR FILLED UPPER COURSE
OF MASONRY WALL

WOOD POSTS SHOULD BE
TREATED, PLACED ON
FLASHING, OR PLACED ON
A CONCRETE PEDESTAL
8 IN. ABOVE FLOOR

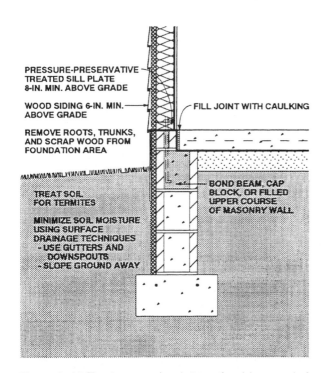

Figure 2–16 Termite-control techniques for slab-on-grade foundations.

PRESSURE-PRESERVATIVE
TREATED SILL PLATE
8-IN. MIN. ABOVE GRADE

WOOD SIDING 6-IN. MIN.
ABOVE GRADE

REMOVE ROOTS, TRUNKS,
AND SCRAP WOOD FROM
FOUNDATION AREA

TREAT SOIL
FOR TERMITES

MINIMIZE SOIL MOISTURE
USING SURFACE
DRAINAGE TECHNIQUES
- USE GUTTERS AND
  DOWNSPOUTS
- SLOPE GROUND AWAY

FILL JOINT WITH CAULKING

BOND BEAM, CAP
BLOCK, OR FILLED
UPPER COURSE
OF MASONRY WALL

2.3.2 Foundation Types

The three basic types of foundations are full basement, crawl space, and slab-on-grade (Fig. 2–17). Each foundation type can be built using several construction systems. The most common systems, cast-in-place concrete and concrete block foundation walls, can be used for all foundation types. Other systems that can be used include pressure-preservative-treated wood foundations, precast concrete foundation walls, masonry or concrete piers, cast-in-place concrete sandwich panels, and various insulated masonry systems.

Slab-on-grade construction with an integral concrete grade beam at the slab edge is common in climates with shallow frost depths. In colder climates, deeper, cast-in-place concrete walls and concrete block walls are more prevalent. Site conditions, overall building design, climate, and local market preferences and costs can all affect the choice of foundation type and construction system.

Basement Foundations Basement walls must be designed to resist lateral loads from the soil and vertical loads from the structure above (Fig. 2–18). These walls are usually constructed of cast-in-place concrete, concrete masonry units (C.M.U.s), or pressure-preservative-treated wood.

Concrete spread footings provide support beneath basement concrete and masonry walls and columns. The footings must be of an adequate size in order to distribute the building loads to the soil. A compacted gravel bed serves as the footing under a wood foundation wall. Concrete slab-on-grade floors are generally designed to have sufficient strength to support floor loads without requiring reinforcing if they are placed on undisturbed or compacted fill.

In areas of expansive soils or high seismic activity, special foundation construction techniques may be necessary. In these cases, consultation with local building officials and a structural engineer is recommended.

Keeping water out of basements is a major concern in many areas of the United States. Water sources may include rainfall, snow melt, and sometimes surface irrigation (Fig. 2–19). There are three basic approaches to preventing water problems in basements:

1. surface drainage,
2. subsurface drainage, and
3. dampproofing or waterproofing on the wall surface.

Surface drainage is designed to keep water from surface sources away from the foundation by sloping the ground surface and by using gutters and downspouts for roof drainage.

Subsurface drainage is designed to intercept, collect, and carry away any water in the ground surrounding the basement. A subsurface drainage system can include placement of porous backfill, drainage mat materials or insulated drainage boards, and perforated drainpipes that

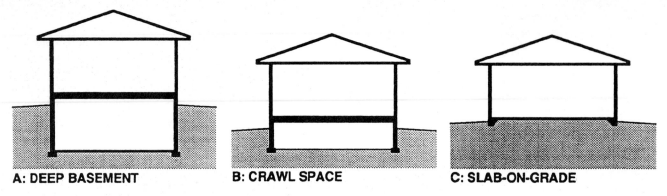

A: DEEP BASEMENT   **B: CRAWL SPACE**   **C: SLAB-ON-GRADE**

Figure 2–17 Basic foundation types.

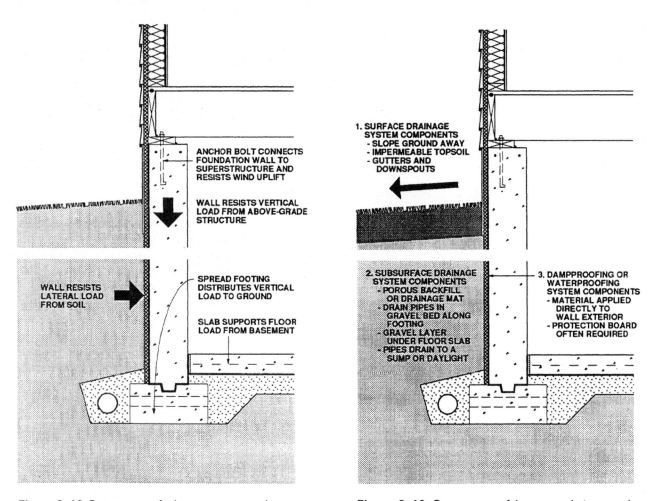

ANCHOR BOLT CONNECTS
FOUNDATION WALL TO
SUPERSTRUCTURE AND
RESISTS WIND UPLIFT

WALL RESISTS VERTICAL
LOAD FROM ABOVE-GRADE
STRUCTURE

WALL RESISTS
LATERAL LOAD
FROM SOIL

SPREAD FOOTING
DISTRIBUTES VERTICAL
LOAD TO GROUND

SLAB SUPPORTS FLOOR
LOAD FROM BASEMENT

1. SURFACE DRAINAGE
SYSTEM COMPONENTS
- SLOPE GROUND AWAY
- IMPERMEABLE TOPSOIL
- GUTTERS AND
  DOWNSPOUTS

2. SUBSURFACE DRAINAGE
SYSTEM COMPONENTS
- POROUS BACKFILL
  OR DRAINAGE MAT
- DRAIN PIPES IN
  GRAVEL BED ALONG
  FOOTING
- GRAVEL LAYER
  UNDER FLOOR SLAB
- PIPES DRAIN TO A
  SUMP OR DAYLIGHT

3. DAMPPROOFING OR
WATERPROOFING
SYSTEM COMPONENTS
- MATERIAL APPLIED
  DIRECTLY TO
  WALL EXTERIOR
- PROTECTION BOARD
  OFTEN REQUIRED

Figure 2–18 Components of a basement structural system.

Figure 2–19 Components of basement drainage and water-proofing systems.

lie in a gravel bed along the footing or beneath the slab and that drain to a sump or to daylight.

Waterproofing is intended to keep out water that finds its way to the wall of the structure. It is important to distinguish between the need for dampproofing versus waterproofing. A dampproofing coating covered by a 4-mil layer of polyethylene is recommended in most cases to reduce vapor and capillary draw transmission through the basement wall. However, a dampproofing coating is not

effective in preventing water from entering through the wall. Waterproofing is recommended (1) on sites with anticipated water problems or poor drainage, (2) in a building for which a finished basement space is planned, or (3) on any foundation where intermittent hydrostatic pressure occurs against the basement wall.

Whether to place insulation inside or outside the basement walls is a key question in foundation design (see Appendix F). Placement of a rigid insulation on the exterior surface of a concrete or masonry basement has some advantages over locating the insulation on the inside:

- It can provide continuous insulation with no thermal bridges.
- It protects and maintains the waterproofing and structural wall at moderate temperatures.
- It minimizes moisture condensation problems.
- It will not reduce usable basement floor area.

Exterior insulation at the rim joists also leaves joists and sill plates open to inspection from the interior for termites and decay. On the other hand, exterior insulation can provide a path for termites if it is not properly treated, and it can prevent inspection of the wall from the exterior.

Insulation placed on the inside is generally less expensive if the cost of interior finish materials is not included. It does not leave the wall with a finished, durable surface, however. Another concern is that energy savings may be reduced due to thermal bridges with some systems and details. Insulation can be placed on the inside of the rim joist, but it creates a greater risk of condensation problems on the rim joist. It also limits access to wood joists and sills for termite inspection from the interior.

Placing insulation in the ceiling of an unconditioned basement is another alternative. This approach should be used with caution in colder climates where pipes may freeze and structural damage may result from lowering the frost depth. With a wood foundation system, insulation is normally placed in the stud cavities.

In addition to more conventional interior or exterior placement, there are several systems that incorporate insulation into the construction of the concrete or masonry walls:

1. rigid foam plastic insulation cast within a concrete wall,
2. polystyrene beads or granular insulation materials poured into the cavities of conventional masonry walls,
3. systems of concrete blocks with insulating foam inserts,
4. framed interlocking rigid foam units that serve as permanent insulation forms for cast-in-place concrete, and
5. masonry blocks made with polystyrene beads instead of aggregate in the concrete mix.

Crawl Spaces

Crawl spaces vary in their height and in their relationship to exterior grade. A standard crawl space has walls that are 2′ high with only the upper 8″ exposed above grade on the exterior side (Fig. 2–20). Support can be either (1) structural foundation walls with continuous spread footings or (2) piers or piles with beams between. The beams between piers support the structure above and transfer the loads back to the piers. Because the interior temperature of a vented crawl space

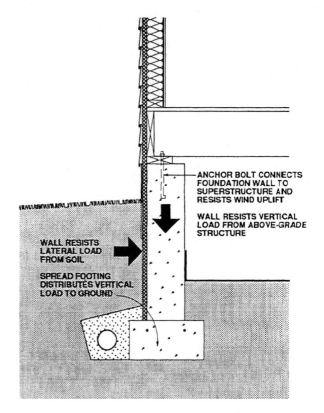

Figure 2–20 Components of a crawl space structural system.

may be below freezing in very cold climates, footings must be below the frost depth with respect to both interior and exterior grade.

Although a crawl space foundation is not as deep as a full basement, it is best to keep it dry. Good surface drainage is recommended, and subsurface drainage may be necessary (Figs. 2–21 and 2–22). Where the crawl

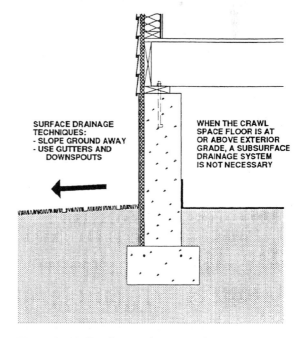

Figure 2–21 Crawl space drainage techniques.

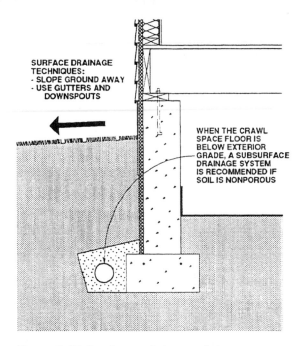

SURFACE DRAINAGE
TECHNIQUES:
- SLOPE GROUND AWAY
- USE GUTTERS AND
  DOWNSPOUTS

WHEN THE CRAWL
SPACE FLOOR IS
BELOW EXTERIOR
GRADE, A SUBSURFACE
DRAINAGE SYSTEM
IS RECOMMENDED IF
SOIL IS NONPOROUS

Figure 2–22 Crawl space drainage techniques.

space floor is at the same level or above the surrounding exterior grade, no subsurface drainage system is required. On sites with a high water table or poorly draining soils, keep the crawl space floor above or at the same level as the exterior grade. On sites with porous soil and no water table near the surface, place the crawl space floor below the surface. If it is necessary to place the crawl space floor beneath the existing grade, and if the soil is nonporous, a subsurface perimeter drainage system similar to that used for a basement should be used. Waterproofing or dampproofing on the exterior foundation walls of crawl spaces is not considered necessary if there is adequate drainage.

The insulation in a vented crawl space is always located in the ceiling. Batt insulation is typically placed between the floor joists, leaving sill plates open for inspection for termites or decay.

With an unvented crawl space, you must decide whether to place insulation inside or outside the walls, similar to the situation for a full basement. Vertical exterior insulation on a crawl space wall can extend as deep as the top of the footing. You can supplement it by extending the insulation horizontally from the face of the foundation wall. Placing crawl space wall insulation inside is more common than placing it on the exterior, primarily because it is less expensive.

Interior wall insulation may be less desirable than exterior insulation for the following reasons:

- It increases the exposure of the wall to thermal stress and freezing.
- It may increase the likelihood of condensation on sill plates, band joists, and joist ends.

- It often results in some thermal bridges through framing members.
- It may require installation of a flame-resistant cover.

Rigid insulation board is easier to apply to the interior wall than is batt insulation. It is continuous and may not need an additional vapor barrier.

Batt insulation is commonly placed inside the rim joist. This rim joist installation should be covered on the inside face with a polyethylene vapor retarder or a rigid foam insulation sealed around the edges to act as a vapor retarder.

With a pressure-preservative-treated wood foundation system, insulation is placed in the stud cavities, similarly to above-grade insulation in a wood frame wall.

Most major building codes require venting of crawl spaces in order to control moisture condensation within the crawl space. Generally, natural ventilation by reasonably distributed openings through foundation walls or exterior walls is required. A number of exceptions do allow for reducing or eliminating the openings. For example, when the ground surface within the crawl space is covered with an approved vapor barrier, the net vent area can be reduced to $1/10$ of that required. In this case, the ventilation openings can be equipped with operable louvers, allowing additional energy conservation benefits during the times of the year when moisture condensation is unlikely. Another exception allows the omission of ventilation openings on one side. This exception assumes that the remaining three sides will provide the necessary crossflow. The remaining three sides, however, must provide the total minimum net area as required. Under-floor spaces used as supply plenums for distribution of heated and cooled air do not have to be vented. Figure 2–23 shows the conditions used in calculating the required crawl space vent area for the following examples:

EXAMPLE 1: A house having a crawl space area of 1300 sq ft would require a total net clear area of openings not less than 8.7 sq ft (1300/150). With the 10 openings shown in Fig. 2–23, an opening size of 8″ × 16″ (0.87 sq ft) would be acceptable.

EXAMPLE 2: If an approved vapor barrier were placed over the ground surface of the crawl space, the total area of openings to the exterior in Example 1 could be reduced to 0.87 sq ft (8.7 sq ft/10).

There are several advantages to designing crawl spaces as semiheated zones. Duct and pipe insulation can be reduced, and the foundation can be insulated at the perimeter instead of at the ceiling. As a result, less insulation is usually required, installation difficulties are simplified in some cases, and the design can be detailed to minimize condensation hazards.

Concrete Slab-on-Grade Construction In recent years, basements have been eliminated in many 1-story houses. Formerly, a basement was definitely necessary,

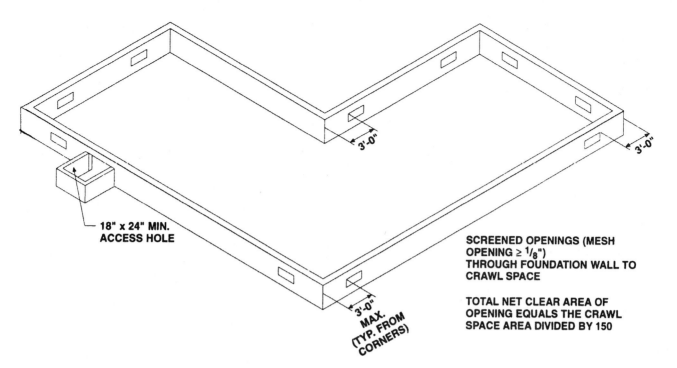

Figure 2–23 Crawl space ventilation.

for heating plants, fuel storage, and laundry or utility areas. With the advent of liquid and gas fuels, however, the need for bulky fuel and ash storage space has been eliminated. Both heating plants and laundry equipment have become more compact, thus requiring little space in the modern home. Basementless residences have become popular, especially in warmer climates where footings need not be placed so deep in the ground. With the elimination of the basement, one type of floor construction that has been found successful, if properly executed, is the concrete slab-on-ground construction (Fig. 2–24).

Precaution should be used in placing a slab on certain lots. Not only do sloping lots require considerable excavation, but they also present drainage problems. Low lots where moisture often accumulates would also be unfavorable. The ideal area would be a nearly level lot that requires a minimum of excavation and that is free of moisture problems. Finish floor should be at least 8″ above grade. Concrete floors have a tendency to feel cold and damp during winter and wet seasons; you can eliminate this coldness by introducing either radiant heating coils or perimeter heating ducts into the slab. Care must be taken to have an absolutely watertight membrane below the slab to prevent moisture from penetrating from the ground; and, particularly in northern climates, the periphery of the slab must be well insulated.

Concrete slabs can be finished with any of the many types of flooring materials: clay, ceramic, vinyl, or cork tile in mastic; carpeting over padding, or plywood block flooring in mastic; or hardwood strip flooring laid on sleepers over a concrete slab.

The following construction requirements should be met in using a concrete slab on ground:

1. Finish-floor level should be high enough above natural grade so that the finished grade will provide good drainage away from the building.
2. All debris, topsoil, and organic matter must be removed from below the slab. Loose soil must be compacted. Earth fill should be placed in 6″ layers.
3. All sewer, water, gas, and oil supply lines must be installed before the slab is poured. Gas lines must be placed in a pipe sleeve.
4. At least a 4″ layer of coarse gravel or crushed rock or coarse sand must be placed above the soil and must be well compacted.
5. A watertight vapor barrier must be placed over the crushed stone before the slab is poured to prevent moisture from seeping up into the slab from the soil.
6. A permanent, waterproof, nonabsorptive type of rigid insulation must be installed around the perimeter of the slab in accordance with the requirements of the climate. In very mild climates, insulation may not be required, but an expansion joint should be used.
7. The slab must be reinforced with wire mesh designated w 1.4 × w 1.4 fabricated in a 6″ × 6″ grid from No. 10 gauge steel wire. The slab must be at least 4″ thick and must be troweled to a smooth, hard finish.
8. When ductwork is placed in the slab, it should be of noncorrodible, nonabsorbent material with not

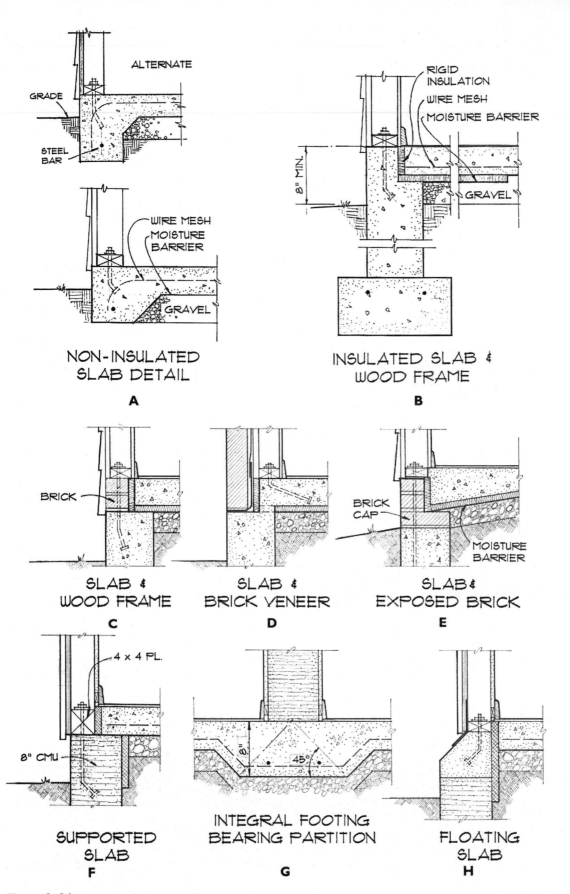

Figure 2–24 Sill details of slab-on-grade construction.

less than 2" of concrete completely surrounding the ductwork. Heating coils and reinforcement, if used, must be covered with at least 1" of concrete.

Slab-on-grade floors permit a lower silhouette in the overall appearance of the house. In areas where outdoor living spaces adjacent to the house are popular, the slab floor eliminates the need for four or five steps leading from interior floor levels the surface of the outdoor terrace areas. Consequently, the terrace becomes more usable and more easily accessible from the interior of the house.

Slabs can be supported by the foundation wall (Fig. 2–24F), or they can be independent of the foundation and supported entirely by the soil below the slab (Fig. 2–24H). Either method is satisfactory if the soil below is well compacted. If settlement should occur below the slab, the floating-slab construction would be less likely to eventually crack or fracture. If considerable fill is necessary under a slab, it should be placed under the supervision of a soil engineer in accordance with acceptable engineering practice. Such a slab should be supported by the foundation wall and should have reinforcing steel bars placed in the slab and in thickened portions of the slab throughout the slab area (Fig. 2–25). All load-bearing partitions and masonry nonbearing partitions should be supported on foundations bearing on natural ground independent of the slab, unless the slab is thickened and reinforced to distribute adequately the concentrated load (Fig. 2–24G).

In northern areas, where insulation from heat loss is of prime importance, several inches of Zonolite® or insulating concrete can be used below the regular concrete. Proper rigid insulation should also surround the entire slab (Fig. 2–24).

Structural Concrete Slabs

These slabs are designed on the basis of a structural analysis of their intended load. They contain steel reinforcing to make them strong enough to withstand the load that they will bear, independent of any central supports below. For example, garages with basements underneath may require structural slab floors.

Integral Slab and Footing

Where frost lines are very shallow, slabs and their footings can be poured at one time, thus providing an integral foundation and floor, economical for 1-story buildings (Fig. 2–24A). The footing is merely a flared thickening of the slab around its perimeter. For best results the bottom of the footing should be at least 1' below the natural grade line and must be supported on solid, unfilled, and well-drained soil. Several No. 4 bars are placed near the bottom of the footing, and the wire mesh of the slab is rolled into the shape of the footing to tie the entire concrete mass together. Gravel fill and a waterproof membrane must be placed below the slab, similar to the other types of slabs. This type of slab is difficult to insulate, but construction time is gained by its use.

Insulation for Floor Slabs

In most areas of the United States, perimeter insulation must be installed around residential concrete slabs if the construction is to be satisfactory. Because of the density of concrete, it can be classified as a conductor of heat rather than an insulator (the reverse is true of wood and other cellular types of building materials).

Heating engineers maintain that practically all of the exterior heat loss from a slab on grade takes place along and near the edges of the slab. Very little heat is dissipated into the ground below the slab (Fig. 2–26).

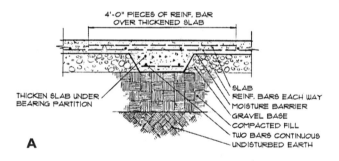

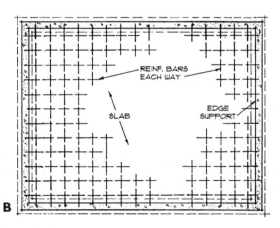

Figure 2–25 Use steel reinforcing in slabs placed on fill.

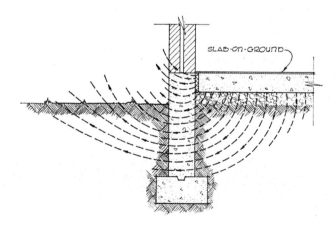

Figure 2–26 Heat loss of slab on ground.

Table 2–5 Resistance (R) values for determining slab-on-ground perimeter insulations.

Heating Design Temperature (°F)	Depth That Insulation Extends Below Grade	Resistance (R) Factor	
		No Floor Heating	Floor Heating
−20	2'-0"	2.00	3.00
−10	1'-6"	1.75	2.62
0	1'-0"	1.50	2.25
+10	1'-0"	1.25	1.87
+20	1'-0"	1.00	1.50

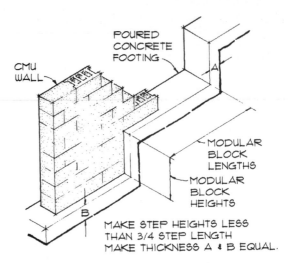

Figure 2–27 Stepped footings. Check local codes for various restrictions.

Therefore, careful consideration must be given to the insulation of the slab edges, especially in colder areas. Insulation should be rigid; resistive to dampness; immune to fungus and insect infestation; easy to cut and work; high in crushing strength; and, of course, resistive to transmission of heat.

Insulating qualities, referred to as *R* factors, are usually given for different insulation materials. The *R* factor for a material is the temperature difference in degrees Fahrenheit necessary to force 1 Btu/h through 1 sq ft of the material 1" thick. Table 2–5 lists the resistance values, or *R* factors, that should be used in determining the minimum amount of insulation recommended for various design temperatures, with and without floor radiant heating. The table also indicates the minimum depth that the insulation should extend below grade.

For example, if the table indicates that an *R* factor of 2.62 is needed, and if the insulation selected has an *R* factor of 1.50 per inch of thickness, then the total thickness needed would be calculated as follows:

$$\frac{2.62}{1.50} = 1.74'' \text{ of insulation}$$

For convenience and reliability, a 2" thickness should be used, making the *R* factor $2 \times 1.50 = 3.00$.

Cellular glass insulation board, asphalt-coated glass-fiber board, and synthetic plastic foam are favorable types of perimeter insulation for concrete slabs.

Stepped Footings

These footings are often required on sloping or steep lots where straight horizontal footings would be uneconomical (Fig. 2–27). The bottom of the footing is always placed on undisturbed soil and below the frost line, and horizontal runs should be level. The vertical rises of the footings are usually the same thickness as the horizontal portion and are poured at the same time. The vertical distance between steps should not exceed 2'; if concrete masonry units (C.M.U.s) are used for the foundation wall, the vertical height of each step should be compatible with the unit height of the C.M.U. Horizontal lengths for the steps are usually not less than 3'.

Column or Post Footings

These footings are required to carry concentrated loads within the building. Usually, they are square with a pedestal on which the column or post will bear. A steel pin is usually inserted into the pedestal if a wooden column is to be used. The footing will vary in size, depending on the load-bearing capacity of the soil and the load that it will have to carry. Ordinary column footings for small residences might be 24" square by 12" deep, which would support 16,000 lb if the soil-bearing capacity were 4000 lb/sq ft (Table 2–6).

Footings for chimneys, fireplaces, and the like, should be poured at the same time as other footings, and they should be large enough to support the weights that they will have to carry. You can calculate total weights of different types of masonry construction by using Table 2–6.

Freestanding Pier Foundations

In warmer areas where floors need not be insulated, it is more economical to put 1-story houses on freestanding piers of ma-

Table 2–6 Masonry weights.

Material	Weight (lb/cu ft)
Poured concrete	150
Concrete block (C.M.U.)	75
Solid brick	120
Stone	160

sonry rather than on continuous foundations around the entire exterior wall (Fig. 2–28). The piers must be of solid masonry: brick, poured concrete, or concrete masonry units. Customarily, piers 18″ or 24″ high above grade are used, and they are never more than three times their least horizontal dimension unless reinforced. Usually 8″ × 16″ or 12″ × 16″ piers spaced not more than 8′ apart are sufficient. Piers should be spanned with either wood or metal beams large enough to carry the weight of the exterior walls. The beams act as sills, and the floor is built above the beams, which are well anchored to the piers.

Brick veneer can be used with freestanding piers if the brick veneer is started on a poured footing below grade. The footings must be poured integrally with the pier footings, and each must be the proper size. Despite the use of masonry piers, this brick-veneer curtain wall gives the exterior the appearance of a continuous foundation. When a brick-veneer curtain wall is used, sufficient ventilation and an access door must be provided as in continuous foundations (Fig. 2–29).

Piers Piers are freestanding masonry posts. In basementless houses with wood floors, they are spaced 6′ to 8′ apart to support the girders. Usually, they need to be only several feet high and 16″ square in section and capped with a 4″ solid cap unit. The units should be laid in a lapped bond for strength, and if the piers support heavy loads, they should be made larger and filled with concrete.

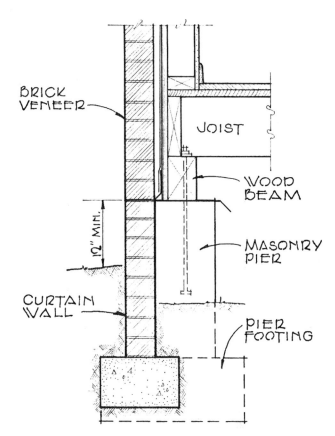

Figure 2–29 Economical pier construction with brick veneer and crawl space.

Grade Beam Foundations One-story frame buildings can be adequately supported on foundations made of a system of poured concrete piers with suitable footings, with the piers spanned by reinforced concrete beams that have been formed with trenches dug into the ground (Fig. 2–30). The concrete beams must be designed in accordance with good engineering practice to carry the weight of the building above. Unless the soil below the beam has been removed and replaced with coarse rock or gravel not susceptible to frost action, the bottom of the grade beam must be below the frost line. If structural analysis has not been made, the following minimum conditions (F.H.A.) or conditions according to local building codes should be met, based on a 1-story structure with average soil conditions:

1. *Piers:*
   (a) Maximum pier spacing, 8′-0″ o.c.
   (b) Minimum size of piers, 10′ diam. Pier should be reinforced with a No. 5 bar for the full length of the pier and extending into the beam.
   (c) Depth of pier should extend below the frost line and have a bearing area of at least 2 sq ft for average soils.
2. *Grade beam:*
   (a) Minimum width for frame buildings: 6″, an 8″ beam can be flared if covered by base trim.

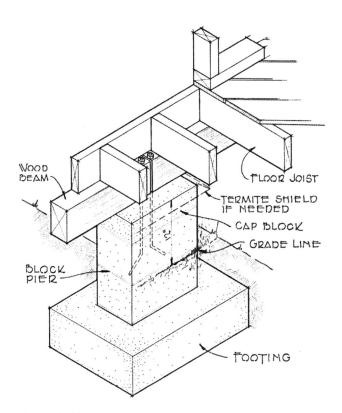

Figure 2–28 Freestanding masonry pier.

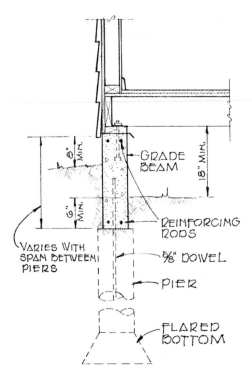

Figure 2–30 Detail showing the use of grade beam with frame construction.

Masonry or masonry veneer should be 8″ wide.

(b) Minimum effective depth, 14″. If grade beam supports a wood floor, the beam must be deep enough to provide a minimum of 18″ crawl space below the wood floor.

(c) Reinforce the beam with two top bars and two No. 4 bottom bars, if frame construction. If masonry or masonry veneer construction, reinforce with two top bars and two No. 5 bottom bars. If grade beam is flared at top, reinforce top with one No. 6 bar instead of two No. 4 bars.

Foundation Walls For light construction, foundation walls are generally built of poured concrete or C.M.U. Poured concrete requires time to set and harden. The integral, one-solid-piece concrete foundation will resist fracturing from settling and differential soil pressures. It lends itself to steel reinforcement at critical points, and dimensions are not restricted by unit sizes, as is the case with C.M.U., brick, or other materials. A good rule of thumb is to limit the height of unreinforced concrete foundation walls to *10 times their thickness;* otherwise, vertical reinforcing rods should be used.

Frequently, the thickness of the wall is determined by the thickness of the superstructure rather than the load that it is to carry. If masonry is used above, the foundation should be as thick as the masonry. If the brick or stone veneer frame construction is used, an 8″ thick foun-

dation will be sufficient for 1-story heights. The height of a 2-story building with a basement will require a 10″ thick foundation wall.

Brick cavity walls, which are usually 10″ thick, can be supported on an 8″ foundation, provided that the 8″ thickness is *corbeled* with solid masonry to the thickness of the cavity wall. Long foundation walls, over 25′, should be increased in thickness or designed with integral pilasters at points in the wall where girders or beams rest. The pilasters should be extended ½ the thickness of the foundation wall (Fig. 2–31).

When concrete walls are poured separately from the footings, a key is used at their intersection to resist lateral ground pressures (Fig. 2–32).

Concrete Masonry Unit (Concrete Block) Because of their economy and speed of erection, these foundations are used for residences as well as other types of buildings. Concrete masonry units are acceptable when correct design has been used and good construction methods have been followed. The majority of foundation walls are made with the nominal 8″ × 8″ × 16″ and/or 8″ × 12″ × 16″ sizes. Their actual sizes are 7⅝″ × 7⅝″ × 15⅝″ and 7⅝″ × 11⅝″ × 15⅝″ (standard sizes vary slightly in different areas). The smaller height and length allow for vertical and horizontal mortar joints to attain modular dimensions. This feature can be a convenience to the designer or drafter. Common brick can be incorporated into C.M.U. walls if necessary—three brick courses are equivalent to the 8″ C.M.U. thickness; three brick wythes are the same as the 12″ C.M.U. thickness; and so on.

Concrete masonry unit foundation walls should be capped with 4″ high solid cap units. This cap provides a smooth, continuous bearing surface for wood sills and makes the walls more resistive to termite infestation. Corner, joist, jamb, header, and other special units are also made in the standard sizes (Fig. 2–33). Basement interior partitions can be built with 4″ or 6″ thick partition units. Very often, C.M.U. walls are veneered with face brick to produce economical yet pleasing masonry walls of different thicknesses.

Points on foundation walls of C.M.U. on which beams or girders rest should have the cores filled with 1:2:4 concrete from the footing to the bearing surface. If heavy loads are anticipated, vertical steel rods should also be introduced to the cores. In long C.M.U. walls, 8″ × 16″ vertical pilasters should be incorporated in the inside of the wall at a maximum of 10′-0″ intervals (or as local building codes require) and filled with concrete for rigidity (Fig. 2–31).

The load put on C.M.U. walls should be limited to 70 or 80 lb/sq in., which usually makes the 8″ or 12″ thick blocks adequate for foundations in the majority of light construction buildings. In most situations, the mortar joints are the weakest part of the wall. Codes usually require units to be laid in full beds of portland cement

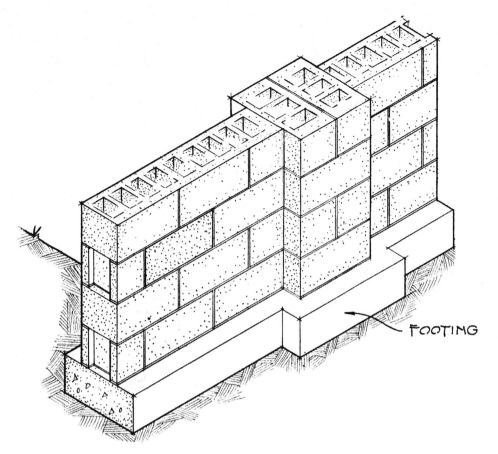

Figure 2–31 Block wall pilaster.

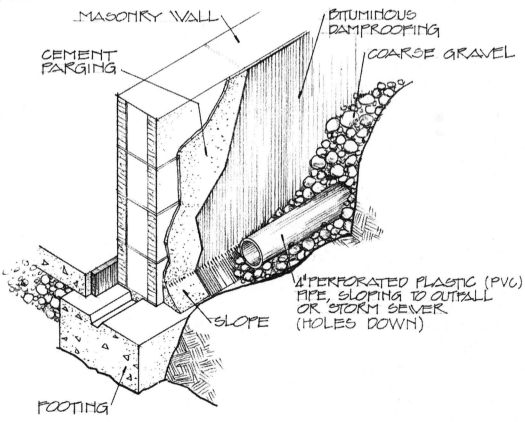

MASONRY WALL

BITUMINOUS DAMPROOFING

COARSE GRAVEL

CEMENT PARGING

4" PERFORATED PLASTIC (PVC) PIPE, SLOPING TO OUTFALL OR STORM SEWER (HOLES DOWN)

SLOPE

FOOTING

Figure 2–32 Dampproofing foundation walls.

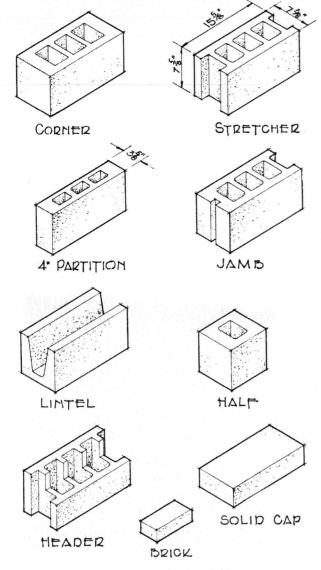

Figure 2–33 Typical concrete masonry units.

CORNER

STRETCHER

4" PARTITION

JAMB

LINTEL

HALF

HEADER

BRICK

SOLID CAP

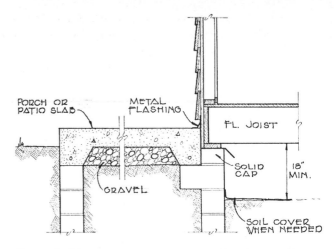

Figure 2–34 Anchoring exterior slabs to foundation walls.

PORCH OR
PATIO SLAB

METAL
FLASHING

FL. JOIST

SOLID
CAP

18"
MIN.

GRAVEL

SOIL COVER
WHEN NEEDED

mortar. Fully loaded walls would still have a safety factor of approximately 4 against failure. Walls supporting wood frame construction should extend at least 8″ above the grade line. Entrance platform slabs, porch slabs, and areaways should be supported or anchored to foundation walls (Fig. 2–34). In straight walls, units should be laid in lap bond (Fig. 2–31) so that vertical joints in every other course are directly above each other. Intersecting block walls should also be bonded for rigid construction by interlocking or lapping of alternate courses.

For economy and the sake of good construction, care should be taken to design C.M.U. walls so that units will not have to be cut by the mason. Wall lengths should be in modules of 8″ if the 16″ long unit is used. Openings for doors and windows should be placed, if possible, where vertical joints occur; both the width and the placement of the opening in the wall must be considered. Similarly, heights of C.M.U. walls should be determined by

the heights of the units used. If care is taken on the drawing board to provide wall lengths and openings compatible with the C.M.U. measurements used, sounder walls and neater construction will result.

Anchor bolts are required by codes in foundation walls. They are especially necessary to tie frame constructions such as open structures, carports, or garages to the foundations. Spaced 6′-0″ apart with at least two bolts in each sill member, anchors will resist winds if they are long enough to extend down into the second course of C.M.U. construction. You can bend or secure the lower ends of the bolts by embedding a 4″ square steel washer into the mortar joints and filling the cavities with concrete.

In areas subject to earthquakes, C.M.U. walls are not practical for foundations. To resist earthquakes, they must be reinforced with vertical rods in cores, and there must also be horizontal reinforcement in mortar beds.

Basement C.M.U. walls should be carefully laid with full, tight mortar joints. If the wall is to be waterproofed, the exterior surface below grade should be parged with a $1/2$″ layer of cement mortar and coated with hot tar or asphalt. In case of extreme moisture conditions, roofing felt is applied over the hot asphalt and is given another coat of hot asphalt. A foundation drainpipe set in gravel around the edge of the footings should also be used to carry off water that may build up around the wall (Fig. 2–32).

Lintels Lintels over wall openings should be reinforced concrete rather than wood. Wood incorporated into C.M.U. walls for support often shrinks and causes cracks in the masonry work. Some codes require a reinforced bond beam capping the entire block wall. Precast concrete lintels are available that can be set in mortar above openings by the mason. Because of their weight in handling, split precast lintels are often used over wider openings. Lintel units can also be made into satisfactory lintels. The units are set on forms over the opening and are

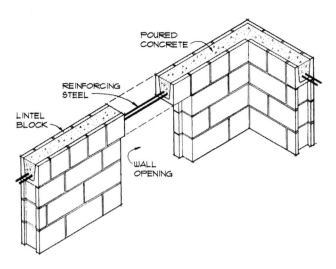

Figure 2–35 Lintel unit in masonry wall.

filled with concrete and several reinforcing rods (Fig. 2–35).

Areaways Basements in residences require some method of ventilation and natural lighting. If the basement wall extends only 1′ or 2′ above grade, an areaway is needed so that basement windows that are on or below grade do not allow moisture to get into the basement (Fig. 2–36). The areaway walls must be tied to the basement walls, and the same masonry materials are usually used for the areaway as for the foundation.

Small areaways can be made of semicircular, corrugated, galvanized steel. The bottom of the areaway can have a masonry floor with a drain leading to the storm sewer, or it can be filled with sufficient crushed gravel or stone with drainage tile below to carry the water away from the foundation wall. The areaway walls should extend several inches above grade and at least 4″ below the bottom of the basement window. If the areaway is over 24″ deep, it should be provided with a grill above to prevent children or animals from falling into it.

Steel Reinforcement Poured concrete used in foundations for lintels or structural beams must be reinforced with steel rods to carry the weight imposed on it. For structural use, concrete in itself possesses good compression resistance qualities but has relatively poor tensile strength. Mild steel and concrete have nearly the same coefficients of expansion and contraction; they are, therefore, compatible in that they will expand and contract practically the same amount during temperature changes and thus will not lose their bond when combined. When a force or weight is exerted downward on the top of a concrete beam, the tensile stresses will react outward on the lower part of the beam and cause it to break. For example, if a heavy weight were put on the center of a horizontal beam, supported on each end, the beam would crack open on its underside. To counteract this effect, steel, with its high tensile strength, should be placed in the lower part of the beam where the steel becomes the most effective. If the beam has a column or support below it at any point, the steel in the beam should continue over the column but be raised to the upper part of the beam directly over the column (Fig. 2–37A). The tensile stresses directly above the column are in the upper part of the beam.

Steel wire mesh, used in concrete slabs on grade, should be placed in the upper part of the slab for most effectiveness; in a 4″ slab the mesh should be placed 1″ from the top of the slab. Steel mesh, also known as *welded wire fabric*, is available in 5′ wide rolls, and the 6″ × 6″ mesh opening size is usually used in slab reinforcement unless structural slabs are required; W 1.4 × W 1.4 wire size is sufficient (Table 2–7A).

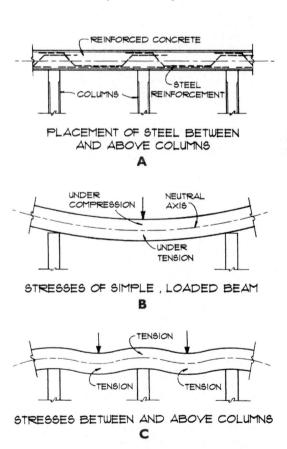

PLACEMENT OF STEEL BETWEEN AND ABOVE COLUMNS
A

STRESSES OF SIMPLE, LOADED BEAM
B

STRESSES BETWEEN AND ABOVE COLUMNS
C

Figure 2–37 Loading stresses of reinforced concrete beams. Similar stresses exist in wood beams.

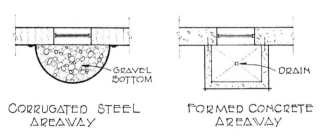

CORRUGATED STEEL AREAWAY

FORMED CONCRETE AREAWAY

Figure 2–36 Areaways for basement windows.

Table 2–7 (A) Common stock styles of welded wire fabric.

New Designation (W-Number)	Old Designation (Wire Gauge)	Steel Area (In./ft²) Long.	Trans.	Weight (lb/100 Sq ft)
Sheets + Rolls				
6 × 6 – W1.4 × W1.4	6 × 6 – 10 × 10	.028	.028	21
6 × 6 – W2.0 × W2.0	6 × 6 – 8 × 8	.040	.040	29
6 × 6 – W2.9 × W2.9	6 × 6 – 6 × 6	.058	.058	42
6 × 6 – W4.0 × W4.0	6 × 6 – 4 × 4	.080	.080	58
4 × 4 – W1.4 × W1.4	4 × 4 – 10 × 10	.042	.042	31
4 × 4 – W2.0 × W2.0	4 × 4 – 8 × 8	.060	.060	43
4 × 4 – W2.9 × W2.9	4 × 4 – 6 × 6	.087	.087	62
4 × 4 – W4.0 × W4.0	4 × 4 – 4 × 4	.120	.120	85

Spacing   Wire Size

6 × 12   –   W16 × W8

LONGITUDINAL   TRANSVERSE
WIRE   WIRE

METHOD OF DESIGNATION FOR WELDED WIRE FABRIC

(B) Standard sizes of reinforcing bars.

To determine the strength of a given size of rebar, multiply its yield stress (40,000 psi and 60,000 psi for grades 40 and 60) times its cross-sectional area.

Bar Size	Weight per ft lb.	kg.	Diameter in.	cm.	Cross-Sectional Area in.	cm.
#3	0.376	0.171	0.375	0.953	0.11	0.71
#4	0.668	0.303	0.500	1.270	0.20	1.29
#5	1.043	0.473	0.625	1.588	0.31	2.00
#6	1.502	0.681	0.750	1.905	0.44	2.84
#7	2.044	0.927	0.875	2.223	0.60	3.87
#8	2.670	1.211	1.000	2.540	0.79	5.10
#9	3.400	1.542	1.128	2.865	1.00	6.45
#10	4.303	1.952	1.270	3.226	1.27	8.19
#11	5.313	2.410	1.410	3.581	1.56	10.07
#14	7.650	3.470	1.693	4.300	2.25	14.52
#18	13.600	6.169	2.257	5.733	4.00	25.81

In brickwork, steel angles are usually used above openings, unless brick arches or other types of masonry lintels are used. Steel angle sizes, $3\frac{1}{2}'' \times 3\frac{1}{2}'' \times \frac{5}{16}''$ and $6'' \times 4'' \times \frac{3}{8}''$, are often used because they lend themselves to the width of the brick and the mortar joint thickness. However, the thickness and the size of the lintel depend on the load above and the span of the opening.

Steel reinforcement rods are available in sizes from No. 2 to No. 11, and they are labeled by their number or by their diameter (Fig. 2–38) and Table 2–7(B). The number labeling is preferable because it indicates how many eighths of an inch the rod is in diameter. A No. 5 rod, for example, would be $\frac{5}{8}''$ in diameter; a No. 7 rod; $\frac{7}{8}''$ in diameter; and so on. Deformed rods are rods that

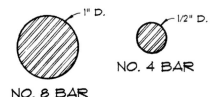

Figure 2–38 Reinforcing steel is sized according to its diameter.

have ridges on their surfaces that provide a more mechanical bond between the steel and concrete. When drawing section details, you should indicate steel reinforcement and place it correctly.

Wood Foundations   The All-Weather Wood Foundation System is fabricated of pressure-treated lumber and plywood approved for below-grade use by an approved inspection agency (Fig. 2–39). All parts of the supporting element for the house structure are included in the foundation system. Foundation sections of nominal 2″ lumber framing and plywood sheathing may be factory fabricated or constructed at the job site. A good drainage system is an integral part of the wood foundation to keep the basement dry. Gravel is a key element, providing an unobstructed path for water to flow away from the foundation to a sump.

The construction is essentially a below-grade, load-bearing, wood frame system that serves both as the en-

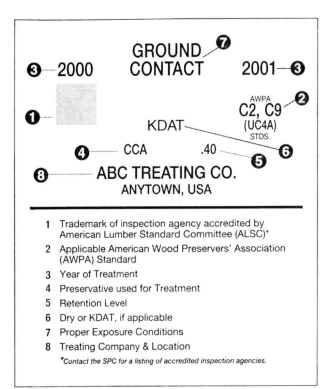

1 Trademark of inspection agency accredited by American Lumber Standard Committee (ALSC)*
2 Applicable American Wood Preservers' Association (AWPA) Standard
3 Year of Treatment
4 Preservative used for Treatment
5 Retention Level
6 Dry or KDAT, if applicable
7 Proper Exposure Conditions
8 Treating Company & Location

*Contact the SPC for a listing of accredited inspection agencies.

Figure 2–39 Typical label for pressure-treated wood.

closure for basements and crawl spaces and as the structural foundation for the support of light frame structures. Footings plates for the foundation are nominal 2″ pressure-treated wood planks resting on a 4″ or thicker leveled bed of gravel or crushed stone (Figs. 2–40 and 2–41).

For most house designs and loading conditions, nominal 2 × 6 or 2 × 8 footing will be adequate. Brick veneer exterior construction requires the use of 2 × 10 or 2 × 12 footing plates to provide added width for supporting the veneer. The height of brick should not exceed 16′-0″ unless the knee wall, footing plate, and gravel base are designed to support greater height (Tables 2–8 and 2–9).

The depth of the gravel bed under the footing plate for a continuous wall is ¾ of the required plate width. The bed extends from both edges of the plate a distance of ½ the plate width. For columns or posts, the depth and the width of the gravel bed should be greater to accommodate the concentrated load.

Lumber framing members in foundation walls enclosing a basement are designed to resist the lateral pressure of fill as well as vertical forces resulting from live and dead loads on the structure. The plywood sheathing is designed to resist maximum inward soil pressure occurring at the bottom of the wall. Foundation walls for crawl space construction can be designed to resist only vertical loads if the difference between the outside grade and the ground level in the crawl space is 12″ or less.

The exterior of basement foundation walls is covered with a 6-mil polyethylene film. The film is bonded to the plywood, and the joints must be sealed and lapped 6″ with a suitable construction adhesive. The top edge of the film is completely sealed to the plywood wall with adhesive. A polyethylene film 6 mils in thickness is applied over the gravel bed, and a concrete slab at least 3″ thick is poured over the film. The slab should be high enough to provide at least 2 sq in. of bearing against the bottom of each stud to resist the lateral thrust at the bottom of the wall. Backfill should not be placed against the foundation walls until after the concrete slab is in place and has set and the top of the wall is adequately braced. Where the height of backfill exceeds 4′, gravel should be used for the lower portion.

For habitable basement space, insulation can be installed between studs, and an interior vapor barrier and interior finish applied to wall framing. Permanent wood foundation basements are easy to finish: Nailable studs are already in place, no furring is needed to install paneling or insulation, and plumbing and wiring are simplified.

Cold weather precautions should be taken in the installation of the wood foundation system. The composite footing consisting of a wood plate supported on a bed of stone or sand fill should not be placed on frozen ground. Most important is the use of proper sealants during very cold weather. All manufacturers of sealants and bonding agents impose temperature restrictions on the use of their products. Only sealants and bonding agents

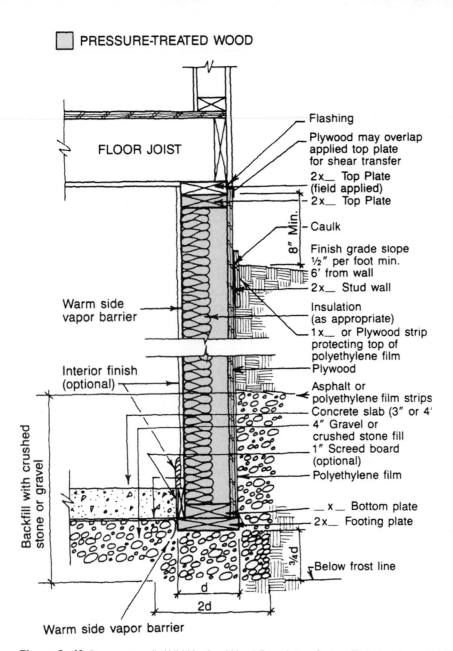

☐ PRESSURE-TREATED WOOD

FLOOR JOIST

Flashing

Plywood may overlap applied top plate for shear transfer

2x__ Top Plate (field applied)

2x__ Top Plate

Caulk

8" Min.

Finish grade slope ½" per foot min. 6' from wall

2x__ Stud wall

Warm side vapor barrier

Insulation (as appropriate)

1x__ or Plywood strip protecting top of polyethylene film

Plywood

Asphalt or polyethylene film strips

Interior finish (optional)

Concrete slab (3" or 4'

4" Gravel or crushed stone fill

1" Screed board (optional)

Polyethylene film

__ x __ Bottom plate

2x__ Footing plate

Backfill with crushed stone or gravel

¾d

Below frost line

d

2d

Warm side vapor barrier

Figure 2–40 Basement wall. (All-Weather Wood Foundation System Technical Report, 1972. American Forest and Paper Association.)

specifically produced for cold weather conditions should be used.

Maxito® Foundation   The Maxito® foundation was designed for use with modular prefab houses.[1] The building is leveled on jacks above the foundation trenches; then the Maxito formwork panels are attached around the perimeter, extending down into the trenches. Each panel has a solid plastic exterior face and a foam plastic interior face joined by plastic form ties. A woven fabric bag is attached to the bottom of the panel. When concrete is poured into the form, the bag fills with concrete and molds itself to the contours of the bottom of the excavation. Soil height variations up to 8" are accommodated automatically (Fig. 2–42).

[1] The Maxito foundation is manufactured by Maxito Industries, Ltd., Unit 224, 2570 King George Highway, South Surrey, British Columbia, V4P 1H5 Canada (1–604–535–7160).

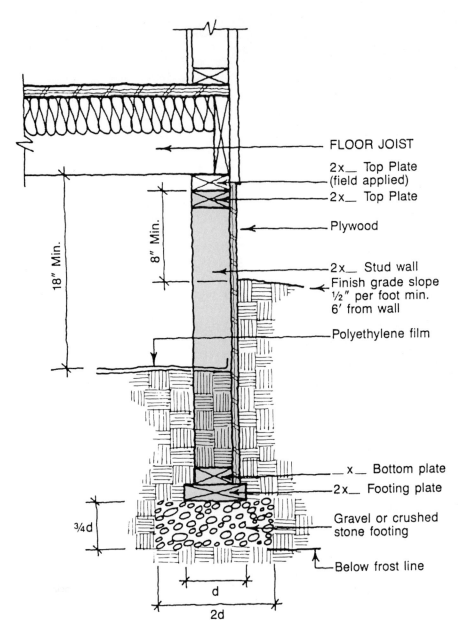

□ PRESSURE-TREATED WOOD

FLOOR JOIST

2x__ Top Plate
(field applied)

2x__ Top Plate

Plywood

2x__ Stud wall
Finish grade slope
½" per foot min.
6' from wall

Polyethylene film

x__ Bottom plate

2x__ Footing plate

Gravel or crushed
stone footing

Below frost line

18" Min.

8" Min.

¾d

d

2d

Figure 2–41 Crawl space wall. (All-Weather Wood Foundation System Technical Report, 1972. American Forest and Paper Association.)

Table 2–8 Pressure-treated wood foundation: Minimum structural requirements for lumber framing.

Construction	House Width (ft)	Number of Stories	Height of Fill (in.)	25 lb/cu ft of Soil Pressure				30 lb/cu ft of Soil Pressure			
				Species and Grade of Lumber[a] Required	Stud and Plate Size (Nominal)	Stud Spacing (in.)	Size of Footing (Nominal)	Species and Grade of Lumber[a] Required	Stud and Plate Size (Nominal)	Stud Spacing (in.)	Size of Footing (Nominal)
Basement		1	24	C	2 × 4	16	2 × 6	C	2 × 4	16	2 × 6
	24 to 28		48	B	2 × 4	12	2 × 6	B	2 × 4	12	2 × 6
				C	2 × 6	16	2 × 8	C	2 × 6	16	2 × 8
			72	B	2 × 6	16	2 × 8	A	2 × 6	16	2 × 8
				C	2 × 6	12	2 × 8	B	2 × 6	12	2 × 8
			86	A	2 × 6	12	2 × 8	A	2 × 6	12	2 × 8
	29 to 32	1	24	B	2 × 4	16	2 × 8	B	2 × 4	16	2 × 8
				C	2 × 4	12	2 × 8	C	2 × 4	12	2 × 8
			48	B	2 × 4	12	2 × 8	C	2 × 6	16	2 × 8
				C	2 × 6	16	2 × 8				
			72	B	2 × 6	16	2 × 8	A	2 × 6	16	2 × 8
				C	2 × 6	12	2 × 8	B	2 × 6	12	2 × 8
			86	A	2 × 6	12	2 × 8	A	2 × 6	12	2 × 8
	24 to 32	2	24	C	2 × 6	16	2 × 8	C	2 × 6	16	2 × 8
			48	C	2 × 6	16	2 × 8	C	2 × 6	16	2 × 8
			72	B	2 × 6	16	2 × 8	A	2 × 6	16	2 × 8
				C	2 × 6	12	2 × 8	B	2 × 6	12	2 × 8
			86	A	2 × 6	12	2 × 8	A	2 × 6	12	2 × 8
Crawl space	24 to 28	1		B	2 × 4	16	2 × 6				
				C	2 × 6	16	2 × 8				
	29 to 32	1		B	2 × 4	16	2 × 8				
	24	2		C	2 × 6	16	2 × 8				
	25 to 32	2		B	2 × 6	16	2 × 8				
				C	2 × 6	12	2 × 8				

[a]Species and species groups having the following minimum properties as provided in National Design Specification (surfaced dry or surfaced green):

		A	B	C
F_b (repetitive member) psi:	2 × 6	1750	1450	1150
	2 × 4		1650	1300
F_c psi:	2 × 6	1250	1050	850
	2 × 4		1000	800
F_{cl} psi:		385	385	245
F_v psi:		90*	90	75
E psi:		1,800,000	1,600,000	1,400,000

*Length of end splits or checks at lower end of studs not to exceed width of piece.

Table 2–9 Pressure-treated wood foundation: Structural plywood requirements.

Height of Fill (in.)	Stud Spacing (in.)	Minimum Plywood Grade and Thickness for Basement Construction[a]											
		Face Grain Parallel to Studs[b]						Face Grain Across Studs[b,c]					
		25 lb/cu ft Soil Pressure			30 lb/cu ft Soil Pressure			25 lb/cu ft Soil Pressure			30 lb/cu ft Soil Pressure		
		Grade[d,e]	Minimum Thickness	Identification Index	Grade[d,e]	Minimum Thickness	Identification Index	Grade[d]	Minimum Thickness	Identification Index	Grade[d]	Minimum Thickness	Identification Index
24	12	B	1/2	32/16	B	1/2	32/16	B	1/2	32/16	B	1/2	32/16
	16	B	1/2	32/16	B	1/2	32/16	B	1/2	32/16	B	1/2	32/16
48	12	B	1/2	32/16	B	1/2	32/16	B	1/2	32/16	B	1/2	32/16
	16	A / B	1/2 / 5/8	32/16 / 42/20	A / B	5/8 / 3/4	42/20 / 48/24	B	1/2	32/16	B	1/2	32/16
72	12	A / B	1/2 / 5/8	32/16 / 42/20	A / B	1/2 / 5/8	32/16 / 42/20	B	1/2	32/16	B	1/2	32/16
	16	A / B	5/8 / 3/4	42/20 / 48/24	B	3/4	48/24	B	1/2	32/16	A	1/2	32/16
86	12	A / B	1/2 / 5/8	32/16 / 42/20	A / B	5/8 / 3/4	42/20 / 48/24	B	1/2	32/16	B	1/2	32/16

[a]For crawl space construction, use grade and thickness required for 24" fill depth.

[b]Panels that are continuous over fewer than three spans (across fewer than three stud spacings) require blocking 2' above the bottom plate. Offset adjacent blocks and fasten through studs with two 16d, corrosion-resistant nails at each end.

[c]Blocking between studs is required at all horizontal panel joints fewer than 4' from the bottom plate.

[d]Minimum grade: A—STRUCTURAL I C–D; B—STANDARD C–D (exterior glue). If a major portion of the wall is exposed above ground, a better appearance may be desired. In this case, the following exterior grades would be suitable: A—STRUCTURAL I A–C, B–C, or C–C (plugged); B—Exterior Group I A–C, B–C, or C–C (plugged).

[e]All panels shall be 5-ply minimum.

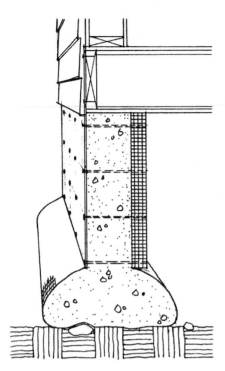

Figure 2–42 Maxito® foundation.

CONVENTIONAL WOOD FRAME CONSTRUCTION

The majority of houses built in North America employ wood frame construction. A frame structure will give many years of satisfactory service if careful planning has been done on the drawing board and if this careful planning is followed during construction. Correct details and good workmanship are two important factors in realizing durability from a frame building. However, the following methods will further ensure maximum service life from the use of wood:

1. Control the moisture content of the wood.
2. Provide effective termite and insect barriers throughout.
3. Use naturally durable or chemically treated wood in critical places in the structure.

To ensure that wood materials performing a load-carrying function conform to a minimum quality-control standard, all load-bearing lumber, plywood, and particleboard are required to be properly identified. In the case of load-bearing lumber, such information must be adequate to determine the bending strength and the modulus of elasticity for the purpose of using the allowable span tables found in the Uniform Building Code. For examples of grade marks, see Figs. 2–43 and 2–44.

To allow the widest range of lumber grades and species in floor construction, the code provides a series of tables permitting the selection of joists based on the clear span of the floor joist, the modulus of elasticity, and the bending strength properties of the wood members (see Appendix D). Tables are organized to allow a different member spacing and, in codes where the floor joists are spaced not more than 24″ o.c., a repetitive member use bending value may be used.

2.4.1 Platform Frame Construction

Platform frame construction (also referred to as *western frame*) is identified by its story-level construction erected by the workers on each subfloor or platform (Fig. 2–45). This method of construction has become popular throughout the country in recent years, mainly for the following reasons:

1. Long studding pieces required in balloon framing are not always available and are usually more costly.
2. The platform built at each level is convenient for carpenters to work on (the construction builds its own interior scaffolding).
3. The construction prevents flue action within the walls in case of fire, thus eliminating the need for firestop material in critical places.
4. It lends itself to modern prefabrication methods.
5. It is quicker to erect; wall sections can be assembled quickly on the horizontal platform and tilted into place.

Beams or Girders Under wood floor framing, unless the joists are long enough to span between exterior walls, some type of heavy beam must be used to support the inner ends of the joists (Fig. 2–46). If a building is wider than 15′ or 16′, which is generally the case, it is necessary to use additional support under the floor joists to avoid using excessively heavy floor joists. For this, wood or metal beams are used, and they are supported by the exterior foundation walls and piers or columns (Fig. 2–47).

The beams under floors carry concentrated loads, and their sizes should be carefully considered. If steel is selected, S beams are usually used; their sizes for general residential construction can be selected from Table 13–6 (in Chapter 3). Steel has the advantage of not being subject to shrinkage. Wood beams can be either solid or built-up of nominal 2″ lumber, usually of the same-size lumber used for the floor framing joists. Solid wood beams contain more cross-sectional lumber than built-up beams of similar nominal size. For example, a 6″ × 8″ solid wood beam would have an actual size of 5½″ × 7¼″, whereas a built-up beam of 6″ × 8″ nominal dimension would be actually 4½″ × 7¼″. However, from a practi-

Lumber grade. *Listed below are grades established under the National Grading Rules for Dimension Lumber and used by inspectors at mills throughout the country. Nationwide grading rules were first established in the 1920s through the cooperative efforts of mill operators, builders, architects and officials from the U. S. Department of Commerce.*

Abbreviation of grade name	Category	Dimension*	Use
CONST—construction STAND—standard UTIL—utility	Light framing	2 in. to 4 in. thick, 2 in. to 4 in. wide	This category is intended for use where especially high strength values are not required.
SEL STR—select structural #1 & BTR—#1 and better #1 #2 #3	Structural light framing	2 in. to 4 in. thick, 2 in. to 4 in. wide	These grades, typically used for trusses and tall concrete forms, are appropriate where higher strength is needed in light framing sizes.
SEL STR—select structural #1 #2 #3	Structural joists and planks	2 in. to 4 in. thick, 5 in. and wider	These grades commonly are used as joists and rafters.
STUD	Stud	2 in. to 4 in. thick, 2 in. and wider	A separate grade with lengths of 10 ft. or less. Relatively high strength and stiffness values make this grade suitable for use in load-bearing walls.

*Nominal

Reading a grade stamp

Lumber is graded to supply builders, architects, building officials and others with reliable information about its quality, characteristics and origin. Most grade stamps are composed of five elements: grade, species, moisture content, certifying agency and mill.

Mill. *The mill where lumber was sawn or manufactured, or the company that owns the mill, is identified by a name or a number. There are approximately 1,500 mills in the United States and about 500 in Canada. More than 95% of these mills belong to regional certifying agencies such as those listed in the box below.*

Species. *Species and species groups are identified by abbreviated symbols. Some of the more common symbols are shown below.*

DOUG. FIR-L	Douglas fir-larch
D FIR S	Douglas fir-south
HEM FIR	Hemlock-fir
SPFS	Spruce-pine-fir (south)

Certification. *Listed below are a few of the agencies that supervise lumber grading at individual mills. There are ten such agencies in the United States and 15 in Canada that are accredited by the American Lumber Standard Committee. ALSC writes standards under which lumber is milled and graded.*

Northeastern Lumber Manufacturers Association Inc.
272 Tuttle Road
P. O. Box 87A
Cumberland Center, Maine 04021
(207) 829-6901

Western Wood Products Association
Yeon Building
522 SW Fifth Ave.
Portland, Ore. 97204-2122
(503) 224-3930

SPIB®

Southern Pine Inspection Bureau
4709 Scenic Highway
Pensacola, Fla. 32504
(904) 434-2611

Moisture content. *Below are the abbreviations typically included in a grade stamp that provide information about the lumber's moisture content.*

Abbreviation	
S-GRN	Surfaced-green. This mark indicates that the moisture content of the lumber when it was planed was more than 19%.
S-DRY	Surfaced-dry. Indicates moisture content of the lumber when planed was 19% or less.
KD-19 or KD	Kiln-dried 19%. Indicates the lumber has been dried in a kiln to a moisture content of 19% or less.
MC-15 or KD-15	Moisture content 15%. Indicates the lumber has been dried to a moisture content of 15% or less.

Figure 2–43 Examples of grade stamps found on lumber.

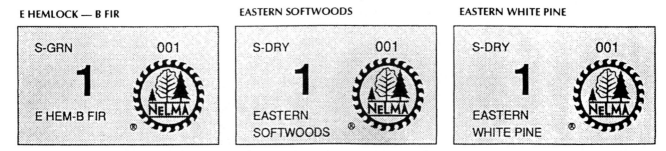

GRADE:
The grade of lumber is shown by number or an abbreviation of the grade name ...

SEL. STR.	= Select Structural
1	= No. 1
2	= No. 2
3	= No. 3
CONST.	= Construction
STAND.	= Standard
UTIL.	= Utility
STUD	= Stud

SPECIES:
Species is best indicated by name or an abbreviation of species or species group. Examples are listed below.

MOISTURE CONTENT:
This is the moisture content at the time of surfacing and is noted by the appropriate abbreviation.

S-GRN = (surfaced green) standard size unseasoned lumber with moisture content 20% or more.

S-DRY = (surfaced dried) standard size lumber dried to moisture content of 19% or less.

MILL IDENTIFICATION:
The original manufacturer is identified by a mill number or the name of the company.

CERTIFIED AGENCY:
Indicates lumber has been graded under the supervision of Northeastern Lumber Manufacturers Association.

Figure 2–44 Examples of grade stamps found on lumber.

cal standpoint the built-up wood beams have several advantages:

1. Stock-size framing lumber is more readily available.
2. Smaller pieces are easier to handle.
3. They reduce splitting and checking.
4. They can be nailed to the frame more easily.

It is desirable to locate beams, if possible, under major interior partitions in order to eliminate the need for double joists under the partitions. Bathrooms and kitchens have heavier dead loads, and their weights should be considered in placement of the beams. If living space in basements is important, beam sizes are generally made larger to avoid numerous columns throughout the basement. Columns are usually spaced 8' to 10' o.c. in basements, depending on the beam sizes. Under basementless houses, piers are spaced no more than 7' to 8' o.c. Wood beams should have at least a 3″ bearing on

masonry walls or pilasters, with a ½″ air space around the ends of the beams for adequate ventilation if they are surrounded with masonry (Fig. 2–48). If splices are necessary in wood built-up beams, they should be staggered and should be placed near the column for sound construction. The top edge of the beams must be the same height as the sill plates if joists are to rest on the beams (Fig. 2–49). If the joists are to butt into the beams, a ledger strip is nailed to the beam, and either notched or narrower joists are toe-nailed over the ledger strip to the beams (Fig. 2–45). Metal angle connectors or steel joist hangers can also be used for butt-fastening joists and beams.

Joists butting into beams allow more headroom in basements and facilitate the installation of ductwork and plumbing under the floor; basement ceilings can be finished without difficulty with unbroken surfaces; and plywood subfloors can be more easily put over in-line joists.

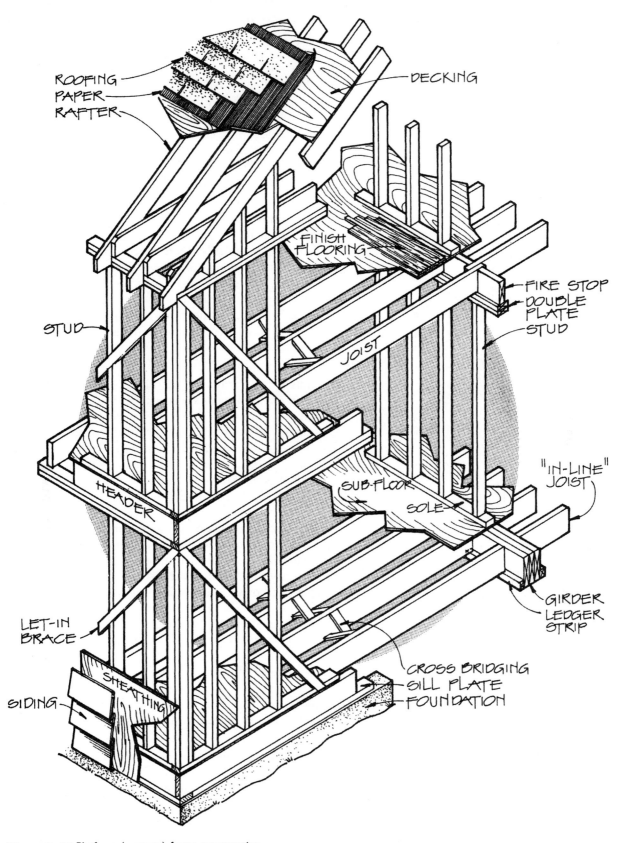

Figure 2–45 Platform (western) frame construction.

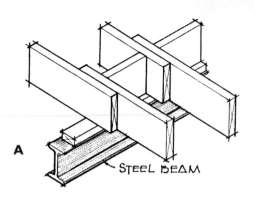

A

STEEL BEAM

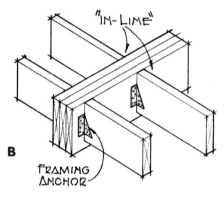

"IN-LINE"

B

FRAMING ANCHOR

C

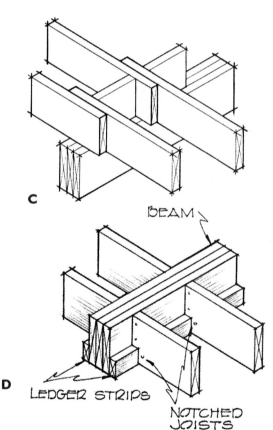

BEAM

D

LEDGER STRIPS

NOTCHED JOISTS

Figure 2–46 Joist and beam framing.

However, the simpler method of floor framing is to use joists resting on the beams.

Beams carry half the weight imposed on all of the joists that rest on or are attached to the beams (Fig. 2–6). In 2-story houses, considerable weight is transferred from the upper story to the beams. For convenient selection of beam or girder sizes under wood floor construction, see Table 3–5 (in Chapter 3), which designates maximum spans for the usual beam sizes used. Beams supporting unusually heavy loads would have to be designed according to established engineering practice.

Columns In residential basements, either wood or metal columns can be used under the beams. The columns are usually 6×6 wooden posts or, preferably, round steel columns of 3″ or 4″ diameter with cap plates welded to both ends (Fig. 2–50). Steel columns are available in stock lengths, or they can be fabricated in any lengths desired. Other types are adjustable. Select wood column sizes according to loads, unsupported heights, and lumber species (Table 3–3 in Chapter 3).

Sills The box type of sill (Fig. 2–49) is generally used with platform frame construction. The sill plate, generally measuring 2×6 or 2×8, is placed over the foundation wall and is anchored with 1/2″ diameter anchor bolts, spaced according to local codes (usually 6′ o.c.). All plates, sills, and sleepers must be treated wood or foundation-grade redwood or cedar. Use of these woods reduces the hazard of termites.

Anchor bolts must be 1/2″ diameter bolts set 7″ deep in concrete or masonry foundations at least every 6′. There must be at least two bolts in every piece of plate material, and neither may be more than 12″ from the end. Occasionally, builders use a 4×6 or 4×8 treated sill plate in box sill construction. The wood sill must be at least 6″ to 8″ above finished grade. If exterior wood siding is used on the building, the outside surface of the framing should be placed within the outer edge of the foundation so that the outside surface of the sheathing becomes flush with the outer surface of the foundation wall (Fig. 2–45). This allows the finish siding to come down over the joint between the sill plate and the masonry wall to make a weathertight joint.

Floor Joists Floor joists are the structural members of the wood floor. Joists rest on the sill plate, with a minimum of 1 1/2″ bearing surface (preferably 3″ on the plate); this should be worked out on the sill detail. Joists are selected for strength and rigidity. The strength is required to carry both dead and live floor loads; the rigidity is needed to prevent vibration and movement when live load concentrations are shifted over the floor. Joists are usually of 2″ (nominal) dimension thickness. The 6″, 8″, 10″, or 12″ (nominal) depths are used, depending on the load, span, spacing, and species and grade of lumber in-

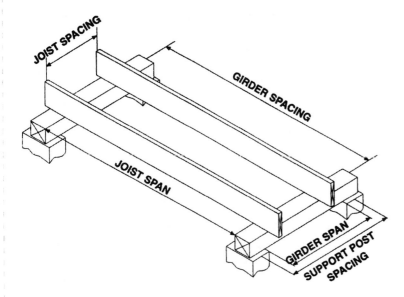

Figure 2–47 Girder span-spacing relationship.

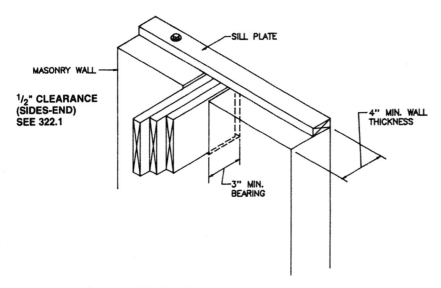

Figure 2–48 Beam or girder bearing on masonry.

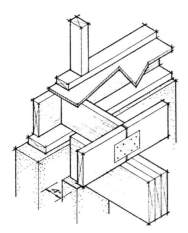

Figure 2–49 Box sill and girder support construction.

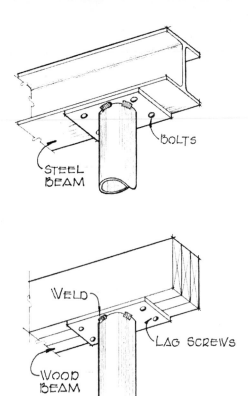

Figure 2–50 Steel columns supporting beams.

ing lumber finished on only two sides [the narrow edges (S2E)], although rough lumber will ignite more quickly in case of fire, and some codes prohibit its use. If joists lap over beams or supports, the lap should be no more than 6″ to 8″ and no less than 4″ for proper nailing of joists (Fig. 2–46A). If the lap is excessive, any sag or reflection at the center of the joists will cause the ends of the joists extending over the beams to raise the floor. If joists are supported by a steel beam, a 2″ × 4″ nailing strip should be bolted to the beam and the joists fastened to it.

For economy, the lengths of the joists should be limited to 2′ increments. The header joists are end-nailed to each joist with 16-penny nails, and both the headers and the joists are toenailed to the sill plate or are attached with metal joist anchors. If the bearing surface at the ends of the joists is critical, blocks between the joists can be used as a header; the blocks will function very much as block bridging (Fig. 2–51B).

Local codes usually indicate the minimum joist sizes for various conditions. A rule of thumb for joist sizes using Douglas fir, southern yellow pine, western larch, or hemlock (J & P Grade) would be to make their spans in feet 1½ times their depth in inches, if the joists are spaced 16″ o.c. Thus, a 2″ × 10″ joist of the species indicated will span 15′ if a 40-lb live load is required. Usually, lumber of a higher grade does not increase the allowable span, because rigidity is the controlling factor, which is not contingent on grades. For more accurate joist size selection according to spans required, refer to Chapter 3.

volved. Generally, joists are spaced 16″ o.c.; however, 12″ or 24″ spacing can be used when load concentrations vary.

Floor framing is simpler if the same-depth joists are used throughout the floor, and for greatest rigidity they should run in the direction of the shorter span. Builders can gain additional strength and stiffness in joists by us-

Bearing To ensure the adequate transfer of floor loads to supporting elements, minimum lengths of bearing for several alternative support systems are specified by code. For joists, a minimum bearing of 1½″ on metal or wood must be provided (Fig. 2–52). When joists bear on masonry, a minimum bearing of 3″ is required (Fig. 2–53). Joists may

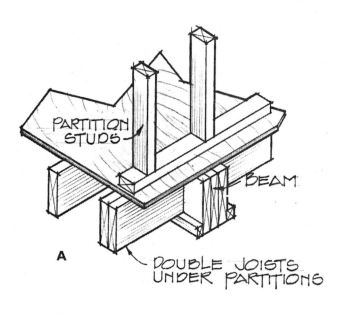

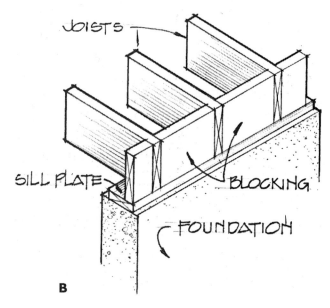

Figure 2–51 Double joist and header blocking.

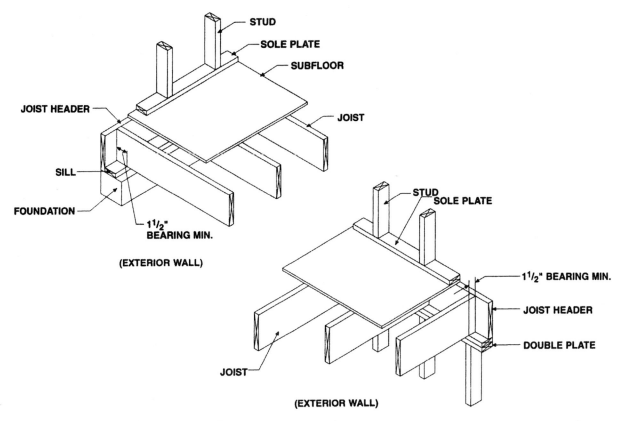

Figure 2–52 Floor joist bearing on wood.

be supported by a 1″ × 4″ ribbon strip when they are nailed to adjacent studs, or they may be secured by the use of approved joist hangers (Figs. 2–54 and 2–55).

To ensure a reasonably concentric application of load from the joist to supporting beams or girders, joists framing from opposite sides of a beam or girder are required to lap at least 3″ or the opposing joists must be tied to-gether in an approved manner (Fig. 2–56). Joists framed into the side of a wood beam or girder must be supported by approved framing anchors or by ledger strips having a minimum nominal dimension of 2″ (Fig. 2–57).

Lumber associations have a unified standard for siz-ing lumber. Examples for a few of the more commonly used lumber sizes are shown in the following list:

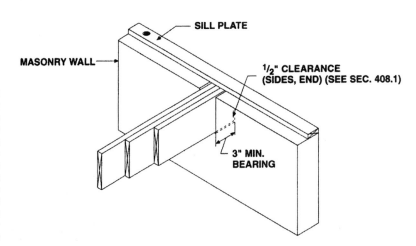

Figure 2–53 Floor joist bearing on masonry.

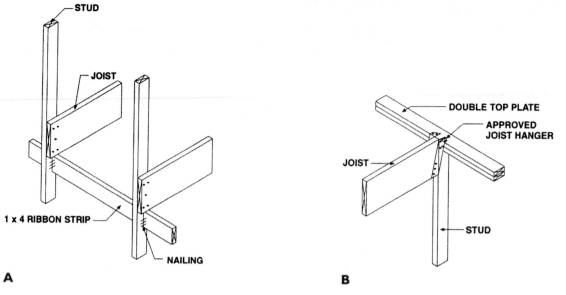

Figure 2–54 (A) Floor joist bearing on ribbon strip. (B) Joist hanger at double top plate.

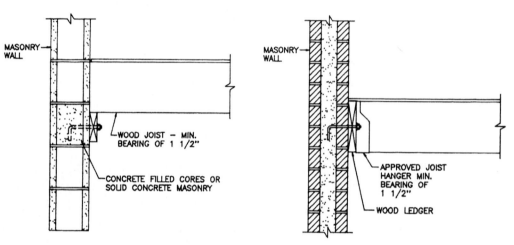

Figure 2–55 Joist-bearing minimums.

Dressed Size (S4S) in Inches

Nominal Size	Surfaced Dry	Surfaced Green
2 × 4	1½ × 3½	1⁹⁄₁₆ × 3⁹⁄₁₆
2 × 6	1½ × 5½	1⁹⁄₁₆ × 5⁵⁄₈
2 × 8	1½ × 7¼	1⁹⁄₁₆ × 7½
2 × 10	1½ × 9¼	1⁹⁄₁₆ × 9½
2 × 12	1½ × 11¼	1⁹⁄₁₆ × 11½

Double joists should be used under all partitions running parallel with the joists, or some method of blocking must be employed so that partitions bear on framing rather than on the subfloor between the joists (Fig. 2–51A).

Trimmers and Headers Openings in floor framing for chimneys, stairways, and the like, must be surrounded by additional framing members for support. The joists that run parallel to the two sides of the opening are doubled and are called *trimmers*. The members that surround the other two sides of the opening are also doubled and are called *headers;* into these headers are framed the shortened joists called *header joists* or *tail joists* (Fig. 2–58).

Header joists the same size as floor joists may be used for spans not exceeding 4′. Trimmers must be doubled to carry the additional load (Fig. 2–59). When the header joist span exceeds 4′, the header joist must be either doubled or of sufficient size to support the floor joist framing (Fig. 2–60). Sometimes nailing is insufficient to transfer vertical loads. In these cases, positive connections must be employed. These hangers are required when the

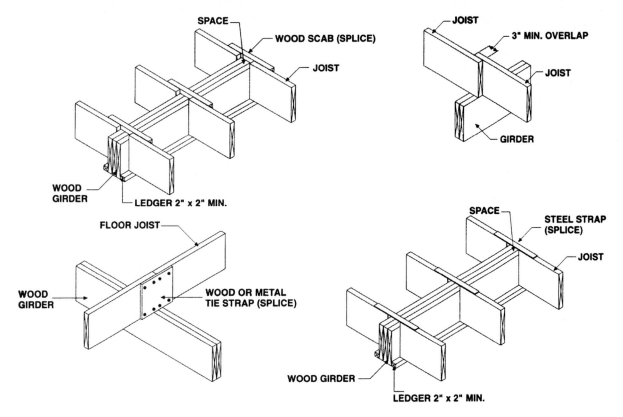

Figure 2-56 Joist at girder.

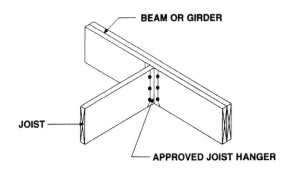

Figure 2-57 Joint hanger at girder.

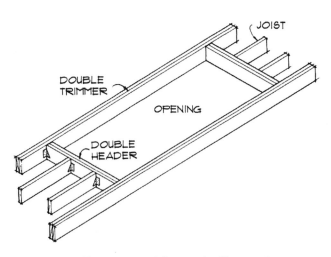

Figure 2-58 Framing around floor and ceiling openings.

header joist span exceeds 6' (Fig. 2–61). Headers should not be over 10'-0" long; if the spans are short and loads around the opening are not heavy, the assembly can be spiked together; otherwise, joist hangers or additional support must be used. Framing should not be fastened into chimneys; fire codes require a 2" space around chimneys between the framed opening, which should be filled with incombustible insulation. If the chimney flues are well surrounded with masonry, corbel masonry may be extended from the chimney on which framing may rest. Tail joists over 6'-0" long must be connected to beams or girders.

Cutting Openings in Joists The cutting or drilling through of joists that have been set in place should be avoided if possible. However, plumbing or wiring must occasionally pass through floor joists. Small holes, if placed properly, are not too objectionable, but larger cuts often result in weakened or dangerous conditions (Fig. 2–62). A horizontal structural member, such as a floor joist, with a load imposed on it can be considered to be under compression throughout the upper half of its depth; it is under tension throughout its lower half, with a neutral axis in the center of its depth. The farther away the wood fiber is from the center of the depth of the joist, the more important the fiber is to the strength of the

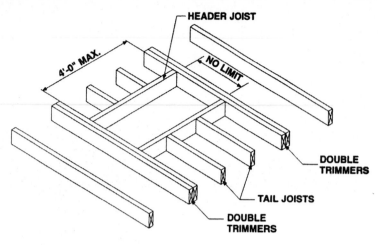

Figure 2–59 Floor framing for maximum 4' openings.

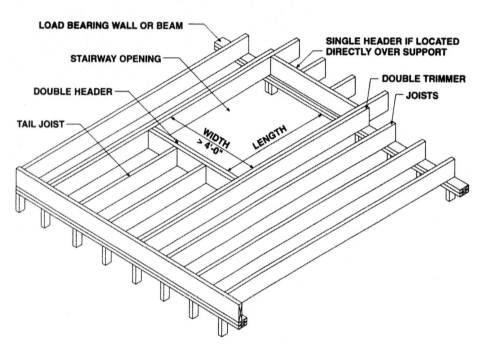

Figure 2–60 Floor framing for greater than 4' openings.

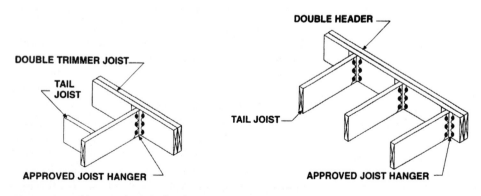

Figure 2–61 Hangers for joist-header connections.

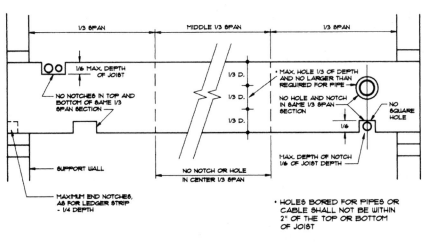

JOIST SIZE	MAX. HOLE	MAX. NOTCH DEPTH	MAX. END NOTCH
2 x 4	NONE	NONE	NONE
2 x 6	2"	1"	1 1/2"
2 x 8	2 1/2"	1 1/4"	2"
2 x 10	3"	1 1/2"	2 1/2"
2 x 12	4"	2"	3"

Figure 2–62 Cutting openings in wood floor joists.

member. Therefore, the closer to the center axis a hole is cut, the less destructive it will be.

Joists may be notched at top or bottom if the notch does not exceed one-sixth of the depth of the joist, as long as the notch does not occur within the center one-third of the span. Holes with a maximum of 2″ diameter can be bored within 2″ of the edges of the joist without causing excessive damage.

Bridging   Bridging consists of rows of short members between joists to produce a firm, rigid floor. Bridging not only prevents the deep, narrow shape of the floor joists from buckling sideways, but it also distributes concentrated live loads to adjoining joists. Rows of bridging should be uninterrupted throughout the floor. Three types of bridging are seen in floor framing:

1. 1 × 3 pieces of wood nailed diagonally between the joists.
2. Blocks the same depth as the joists nailed in staggered fashion perpendicular to the joists.
3. Light metal bridging pieces nailed diagonally between the joists.

Crossbridging allows wiring and piping to pass through without cutting (Fig. 2–63). Joists with more than 8′ of span should have one row of bridging, but rows of bridging should be no more than 7′ or 8′ apart in longer spans.

To ensure that joists are reasonably held in line and do not twist out of the plane of the applied load bridging, blocking or some other acceptable means of holding the joists in place is required. Lateral support at ends may be provided by full-depth solid blocking not less than 2″

in thickness; or the ends of the joists may be nailed or bolted to a header band, rim joist, or an adjoining stud (Fig. 2–64).

In addition to the lateral support at the ends, joists may also be required to have intermediate lateral support at intervals not exceeding 10′ when such members have a depth-to-thickness ratio exceeding 6:1 based on nominal dimensions. Intermediate blocking is not required for joists 2″ × 12″ or smaller.

Floor Trusses   An alternative to framing floors with conventional floor joists is to use floor trusses or truss joists (Fig. 2–65). These systems of floor framing are appropriate when long spans are required and the use of load-bearing walls or columns to support floor loads is undesirable. Floor trusses or truss joists are used for first-floor framing in residences where open space in basements is essential.

Floor trusses are usually factors-assembled units fabricated from 2 × 4 structural-grade lumber. Engineered as flat trusses with top chords, bottom chords, and web members connected by stamped metal plates, these structural members are capable of spanning greater distances than wood floor joists. Most floor trusses are spaced at 24″ o.c., thus requiring a ¾″ thick or thicker subfloor. Diagonal bridging and continuous lateral bracing are required between floor trusses. Wiring and ductwork can easily be routed through openings between web members of floor trusses.

Glued Engineered Wood Products   Glued engineered wood products make up an increasing percentage

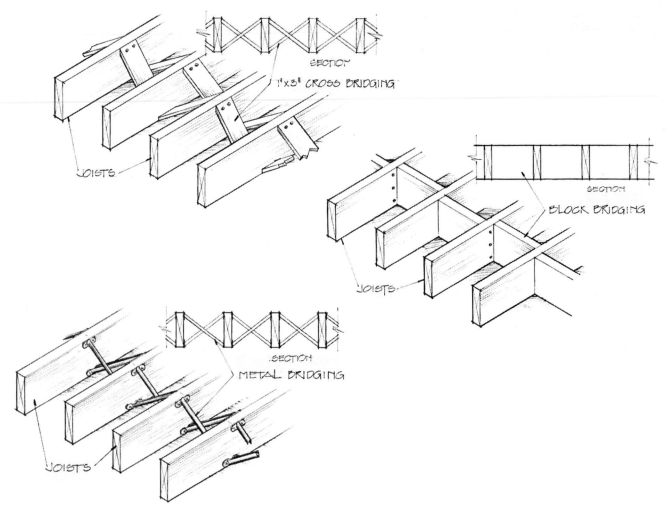

Figure 2–63 Types of bridging used in wood framing.

of the wood used in all forms of residential and nonresidential construction. Glued engineered wood is classified by the APA/Engineered Wood Association into four general groups:

1. Structural wood panels
2. Glued laminated timber (glulam)
3. Structural composite lumber (SCL)
4. Wood I joists

Structural adhesives are used to bond individual elements of wood in strands, veneers, or lumber to create structural shapes. Recent market studies project that the use of some of these products will more than double by the year 2000, partly because they use resources efficiently.

The most widely used of the glued engineered wood products are *structural wood panels*, which include plywood, oriented-strand board (OSB), and composite panels. *Plywood* is manufactured by bonding the veneers in a crossband orientation using structural adhesives. The crossbanding provides strength and dimensional stability. *OSB* is produced by bonding individual wood strands into

a mat-formed product. The mat consists of multiple crossbanded layers. *Composite panels* consist of wood-face veneers and a reconstituted wood core. The face veneers are positioned parallel to the long dimension of the panel, with the wood-based core oriented 90° to the face veneers.

Glulam, introduced in the United States in 1935 after almost 40 years of use in Europe, is an engineered, stress-rated product created by adhesively bonding individual pieces of lumber having a net thickness no greater than 2″. The individual pieces are end-joined to create long lengths referred to as *laminations*. These laminations are face-bonded to create the finished glulam product. The direction of the grain in all laminations is approximately parallel (Fig. 2–66).

Glulam, one of the most versatile engineered wood products, is used for a variety of structural applications, including floor and header beams in residential construction and beams in a variety of light commercial projects. Glulams come in several finish grades. Header grade is specified for concealed applications. Beam widths

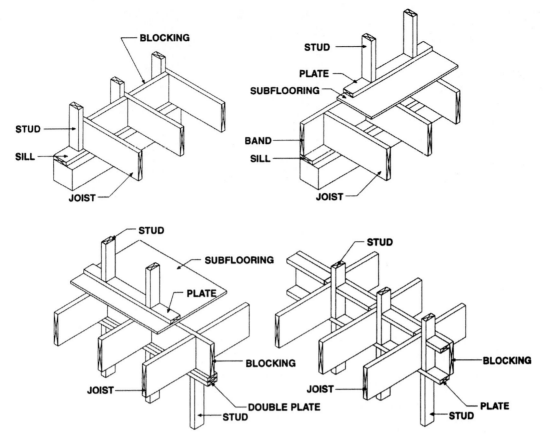

Figure 2–64 Blocking of joists.

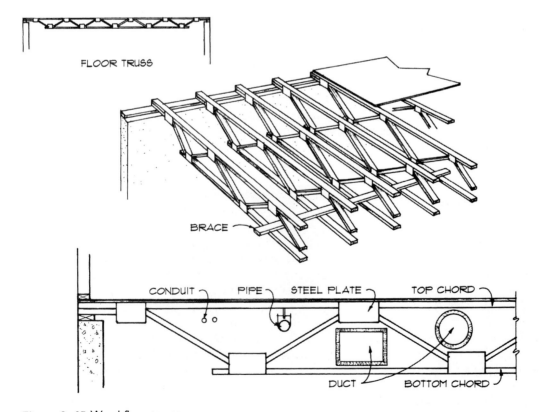

Figure 2–65 Wood floor trusses.

Figure 2–66 Glue-laminated timber. (APA/Engineered Wood Association)

Figure 2–68 Parallel-strand lumber. (Courtesy Arizona Public Service Co.)

are the same as those for standard framing and provide added load capacity compared to faced glulam sizes. Widths are 3½", 5½", and 7¼". Industrial-appearance-grade glulams are inexpensive timbers used in warehouses, garages, and other structures where appearance is not important. Architectural-appearance grade is for projects where appearance is important. Premium-appearance grade and clear-appearance grade are used where tight control of surface defects is of prime concern.

Structural composite lumber (SCL) refers to a family of products including laminated-veneer lumber (LVL), parallel-strand lumber (PSL), and other composite lumber products (Figs. 2–67 and 2–68).

LVL, the most widely used of the SCL products, is produced by adhesively bonding thin wood veneers, not greater than 0.25", such that the grain of all veneers is approximately parallel to the long direction of the member. LVL members are typically used for dimension lumber in beams and headers. They are also used as flanges for wood I joists.

PSL is created by adhesively bonding relatively long strands of wood fiber such that the strands are oriented

parallel to the long axis of the member. The most common sizes are comparable to those of dimension lumber, although members having cross sections up to 11" × 19" can be produced. PSL members are typically used in beams, headers, and columns.

Prefabricated wood I joists are probably the fastest-growing of the glued engineered wood products. Wood I joists are manufactured using either sawn lumber or LVL flanges and plywood or OSB webs (Fig. 2–69).

I joists are used extensively in residential floor construction. In general, nominal 10" and 12" deep I joists can be substituted on an equal-depth basis for most grades and species of 2 × 10 and 2 × 12 sawn lumbers. Special design verifications need to be made where I joists support concentrated loads or where they are cantilevered over supports. Because I joists can be supplied in long lengths, they are often used in multiple-span applications.

Diagonal bridging is essential between truss joists. Unlike with floor trusses, ductwork cannot be placed through the solid web; however, small openings can be cut through the webs to allow room for electrical wiring and plumbing pipes (Fig. 2–70). Such openings should

Figure 2–67 Laminated-veneer lumber. (Courtesy Arizona Public Service Co.)

Figure 2–69 Wood I joists. (Courtesy Arizona Public Service Co.)

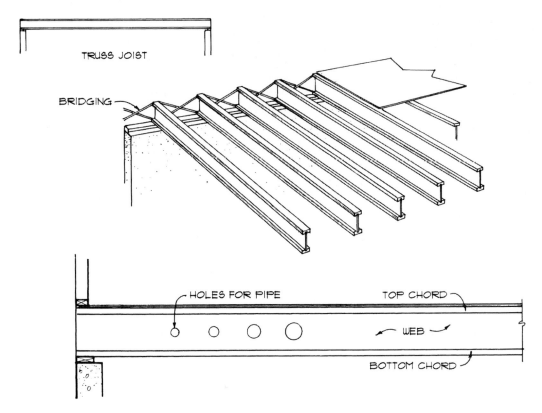

Figure 2–70 Truss joists.

be placed at strategic locations designated by the manufacturer of the truss joists.

Subfloor   Nominal 1″ boards 4″, 6″, or 8″ wide, securely nailed to the joists, were traditionally used for subfloors. The boards were square edged, tongue and groove, or shiplap, and it was preferable to lay them diagonally (45° to the joists). Finish strip flooring was then laid in either direction over the subfloor. Joists in the subflooring fall in the center of the joists and are staggered. Square-edge boards laid up too tight produce squeaky floors; rather they should be nailed about ⅛″ apart. When subflooring is laid perpendicularly to the joists, the finish floor must be laid perpendicularly to the subfloor.

Because of the speed of erection, plywood is the most popular material for subflooring today. Plywood that is used in floor construction and that performs a load-carrying function must conform to a known quality-control standard. Compliance is indicated by a grade mark issued by an approved agency (Fig. 2–71).

Allowable spans for plywood used as subflooring are shown in Table D–16. The span limitations are based on the grade of plywood used. In the case of rated sheathing used as structural subflooring, the maximum span is easily identified through the use of the panel span rating stamp, where the denominator represents the allowable span of the plywood floor sheathing.

Particleboard used in floor construction that performs a load-carrying function must conform to known quality-

control standards, as do plywood and lumber; see Fig. 2–72 for examples of approved marks. Plywood produces a smooth surface for block flooring, tile, carpeting, and other nonstructural flooring materials. Sheets of plywood, usually ½″, ⅝″, or ¾″ thick for subfloors, should be laid with their face grain across the joists; the end joints of the sheets should be staggered, and should fall midway between adjoining sheets (Fig. 2–73). If flooring other than strip wood is used, the joints around the plywood should have blocking below, or tongue-and-groove edge plywood can be used. Plywood must be securely nailed around its edges as well as throughout central areas where backing occurs.

A hardboard or particleboard overlayment ¼″, ⅜″, ½″, or ⅝″ thick should be placed over plywood subfloors ½″ or ⅝″ thick. Tongue-and-groove plywood ¾″ thick or thicker does not require an overlayment when installed with screws and construction adhesive on floor joists spaced 16″ o.c. or less. Structural-oriented strand board or wafer board ⁷⁄₁₆ and ¾″ thick is used as subflooring in locations where it is acceptable to building codes.

Subfloor Under Ceramic Tile   In bathrooms and other areas requiring ceramic tile floors, some method must be used to lower the subfloor so that a concrete base for the tile can be provided for. If the joists are adequate for the load, they can be dropped several inches, or the top of the joists can be chamfered and the subfloor dropped 3″ between the joists. If there is no objection to

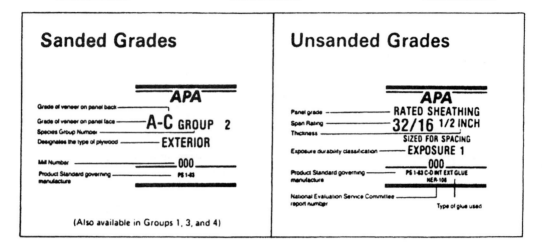

Figure 2–71 (A) Plywood-grade mark examples. (B) Identification of plywood subfloor span limitations. (APA/Engineered Wood Association)

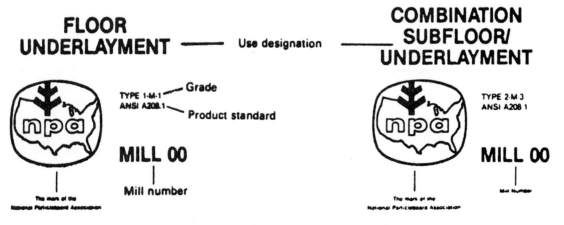

Figure 2–72 Particleboard-grade mark examples. (NPA)

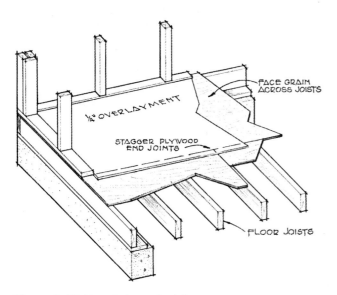

Figure 2–73 Use of plywood subflooring.

the finished tile floor being an inch or so above the other finished floor surface, the regular subfloor could be left as is. In economical construction, ceramic tile can be laid on mastic, on top of a substantial wood subfloor, which neither requires a concrete subfloor nor entails dropping of the wood floor.

Soleplates After the subfloor is in place, 2 × 4 plates, called *soles*, *shoe plates*, or *bottom plates*, are nailed directly over the subfloor to form the layout for all walls and partitions. Dimensions for this layout must be taken from the floor plan working drawing. Note that unless floor plans show dimensions from the outer edge of the exterior wall framing to the center line of partitions, accurate layout of soleplates by workers becomes rather difficult. The plates are generally run through door openings and are then cut out after the framing and rough openings have been established. Plumbing walls must be built of 2 × 6 or 2 × 8 studs to enclose soil stacks; partitions between closets can be built of 2 × 4 studs set sideways to increase usable space.

Studs Studs, usually 2 × 4 (16″ o.c.), are toenailed to the soleplate and are capped with a double 2 × 4 cap plate. Double studs, which support proper-size lintels or headers above the openings, should be used around all door and window openings. In 1-story buildings, studs can be spaced 24″ o.c., unless limited by the wall covering.

The size, height, and spacing of studs shall be in accordance with Table D–15. Studs shall be placed with their wide dimension perpendicular to the wall. To ensure minimum load-carrying capabilities for conventional wood frame walls, a minimum grade of No. 3 standard- or stud-grade lumber is specified.

To allow the more economical use of lumber for bearing studs not supporting floors and for nonbearing studs,

an exception is given permitting the use of utility-grade lumber. Utility-grade studs shall be spaced not more than 16″ o.c.; nor shall they support more than a roof and a ceiling or exceed 8′ in height for exterior walls and load-bearing walls or 10′ for interior, nonload-bearing walls.

Bearing and exterior wall studs shall be capped with double top plates installed to provide overlapping at corners and at intersections with other partitions. End joints in double top plates shall be offset at least 48″.

When stud spacing is 24″ o.c., the code allows for three options to account for the increased loading. The first option is an increase in the minimum top plate size (Fig. 2–74). The second option is a limitation on the location of the floor joists, floor trusses, or roof trusses being placed within 5″ of the supporting studs below (Fig. 2–75). The third option is solid blocking used as reinforcement for a double plate (Fig. 2–76).

With the advent of wider framing to accommodate increased thickness of insulation, a desire to save on material costs led to the allowance of a single top plate alternative. The use of a single top plate in bearing and exterior walls is permitted as long as adequate top plate ties are provided (Fig. 2–77).

If ceiling heights are to be 8′-0″ high, the studs are generally cut between 7′-8″ and 7′-9″ in length. Blocking, halfway up the height of the studs, stiffens the wall and prevents the studs from warping. If vertical paneling is to be used as interior wall covering, horizontal blocking must be inserted between the studs in rows every 2′-0″ of vertical height throughout the wall, or else 1 × 3 horizontal furring strips will have to be nailed to the studs to back up the vertical paneling.

With platform framing, it is convenient for workers to lay out each wall horizontally on the platform, nail the pieces together without the second cap plate, and then lift the wall into place where it can be temporarily braced. All of the walls and partitions are set in place and carefully trued. The top piece of the double cap plate is then attached so that all of the walls and partitions are well-lap-jointed (Fig. 2–78). Corner posts, T posts, and posts forming intersections of partitions are built up of 2 × 4s, well-spiked together in a manner to provide for both inside and outside nailing surfaces at the corners (Fig. 2–79).

Drilling and Notching Limitations on drilling and notching of studs used to frame partitions are based on ensuring the retention of structural or functional integrity (Figs. 2–80 and 2–81). In exterior walls and bearing partitions, any wood stud may be cut or notched to a depth not exceeding 25% of its width. Cutting or notching of studs to a depth not greater than 40% of the width of the stud is permitted in nonbearing partitions. A hole not greater in diameter than 40% of the stud width may be bored in any wood stud. Bored holes not greater than 60% of the width of the stud are permitted in nonbearing partitions or in any wall where each bored stud

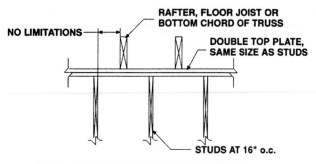

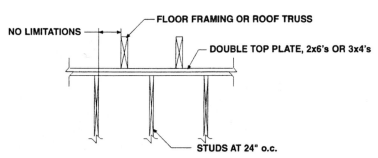

Figure 2–74 (A) Top plate with 16″ stud spacing. (B) Top plate with 24″ stud spacing.

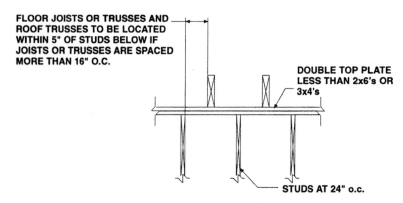

Figure 2–75 Top plate with 24″ stud spacing and bearing point limitations.

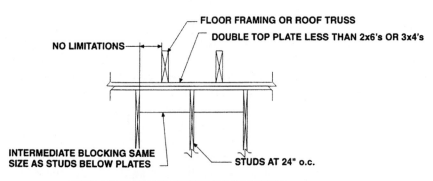

Figure 2–76 Blocked top plate with 24″ stud spacing.

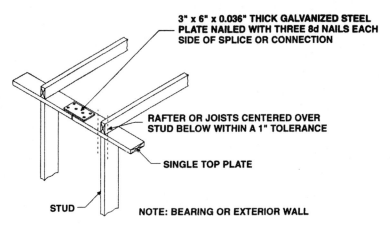

Figure 2–77 Single top plate splice.

is doubled, provided that no more than two successive double studs are bored. In no case shall the edge of the bored hole be nearer than ⅝″ to the edge of the stud. Bored holes shall not be located at the same section of studs as a cut or a notch.

Fire Blocking Fire blocking is required to restrict movement of flame and gases to other areas of the building through concealed combustible passages in building components such as floors, walls, and stairs. Such firestopping is required in order to cut off all vertical and horizontal concealed combustible spaces and to form a fire barrier between stories and between a top story and the roof space. The following locations shall be firestopped in wood frame construction:

1. In concealed spaces of stud walls and partitions, including furred spaces at the ceiling and floor levels and at 10′ intervals both vertically and horizontally (Fig. 2–82).
2. At all interconnections between concealed vertical and horizontal spaces, such as soffits, drop ceilings,

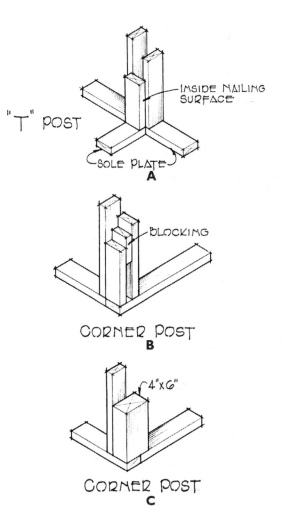

Figure 2–79 Stud framing at corners and intersections of walls.

Light Construction Principles

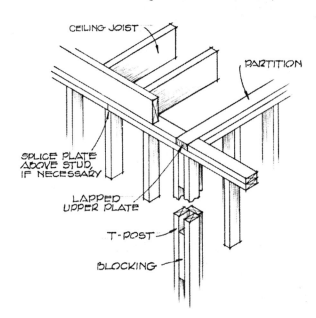

Figure 2–78 Framing at intersections of walls.

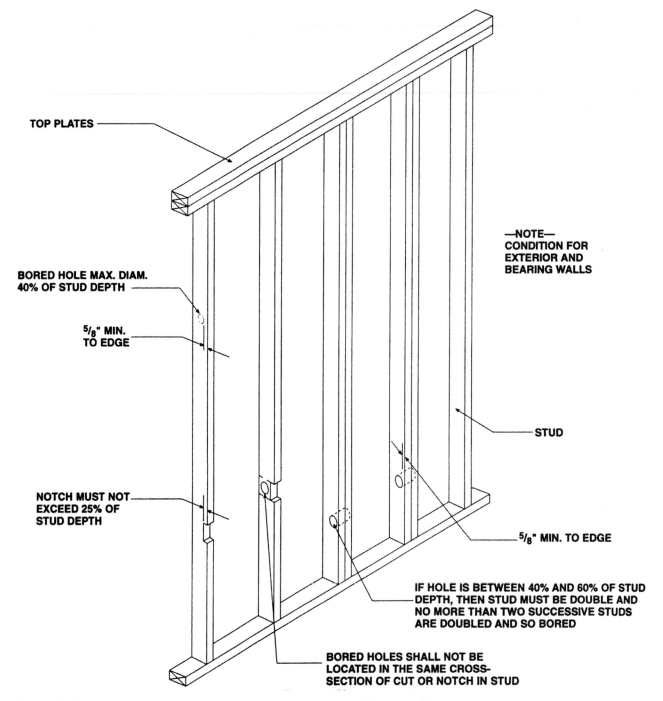

TOP PLATES

BORED HOLE MAX. DIAM.
40% OF STUD DEPTH

⁵/₈" MIN.
TO EDGE

NOTCH MUST NOT
EXCEED 25% OF
STUD DEPTH

—NOTE—
CONDITION FOR
EXTERIOR AND
BEARING WALLS

STUD

⁵/₈" MIN. TO EDGE

IF HOLE IS BETWEEN 40% AND 60% OF STUD
DEPTH, THEN STUD MUST BE DOUBLE AND
NO MORE THAN TWO SUCCESSIVE STUDS
ARE DOUBLED AND SO BORED

BORED HOLES SHALL NOT BE
LOCATED IN THE SAME CROSS-
SECTION OF CUT OR NOTCH IN STUD

Figure 2–80 Notching and bored-hole limitations for exterior walls and bearing walls.

cove ceilings, and bathtubs (Figs. 2–83, 2–84, 2–85, and 2–86).

3. In concealed spaces between stair stringers at the top and bottom of the run (Fig. 2–87).
4. At openings around vent pipes, ducts, chimneys, and fireplaces at ceilings and floor levels with non-combustible materials (Figs. 2–88 and 2–89).

Materials approved by code for use as firestopping include the following:

■ 2″ nominal lumber

■ Two thicknesses of 1″ nominal lumber with broken lap joints
■ One thickness of ²³/₃₂″ plywood with joints backed by ²³/₃₂″ plywood
■ One thickness of ¾″ Type 2-M particleboard with joints backed by ¾″ Type 2-M particleboard.

Other approved materials that may be used include gypsum board, glass fiber mesh–reinforced backer board, or mineral fiber, glass fiber securely fastened in place.

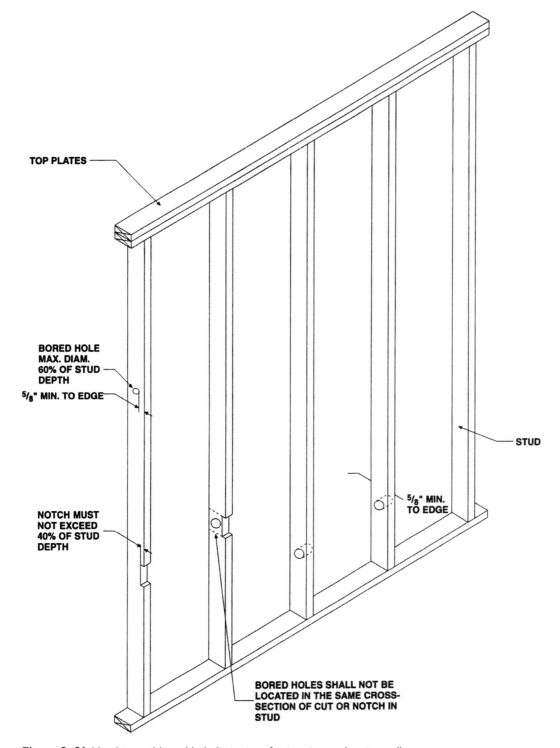

TOP PLATES

BORED HOLE MAX. DIAM. 60% OF STUD DEPTH

5/8" MIN. TO EDGE

NOTCH MUST NOT EXCEED 40% OF STUD DEPTH

STUD

5/8" MIN. TO EDGE

BORED HOLES SHALL NOT BE LOCATED IN THE SAME CROSS-SECTION OF CUT OR NOTCH IN STUD

Figure 2–81 Notching and bored-hole limitations for interior nonbearing walls.

Draftstopping Draftstopping is required to limit the spread of fire through combustible spaces in floor–ceiling assemblies when such spaces create a connected area beyond the normal joist cavity so that the area of the concealed space does not exceed 1000 sq ft. The concealed space must be divided into approximately equal areas. The material must be placed parallel to the main framing members (Fig. 2–90).

Materials used to meet draftstopping requirements are $1/2''$ gypsum board, $3/8''$ plywood, or $3/8''$ Type 2-M-W particleboard adequately attached to supporting members.

Bracing Wall bracing is usually one of two types: *let-in bracing* or *structural sheathing*. Both types serve to carry or transmit forces from the upper portion of the structure to the foundation. When subjected to wind loads or

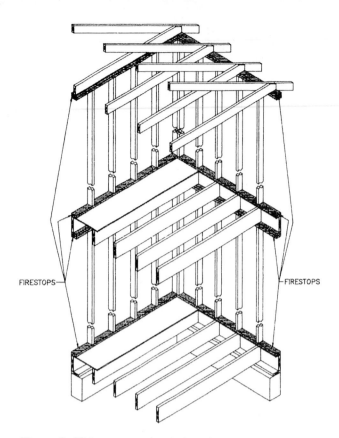

Figure 2–82 Firestopping by platform framing.

FIRESTOPS

FIRESTOPS

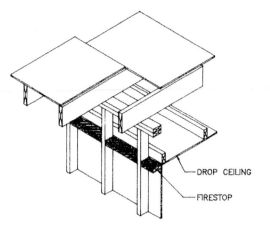

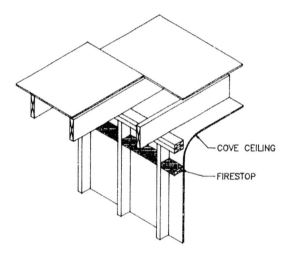

DROP CEILING

FIRESTOP

Figure 2–84 Firestopping by dropped ceiling.

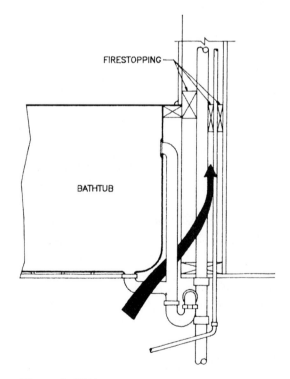

COVE CEILING

FIRESTOP

Figure 2–85 Firestopping by cove ceiling.

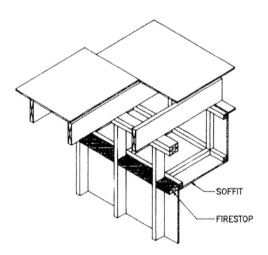

SOFFIT

FIRESTOP

Figure 2–83 Firestopping by furred soffit.

FIRESTOPPING

BATHTUB

Figure 2–86 Firestopping at tub.

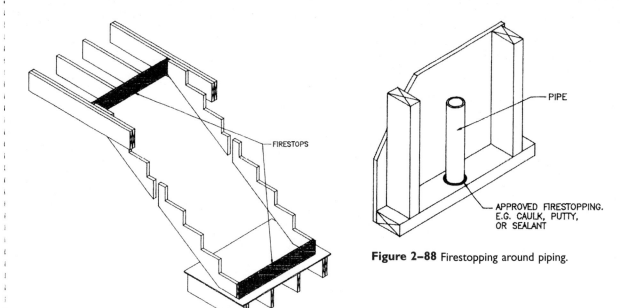

Figure 2–88 Firestopping around piping.

Figure 2–87 Firestopping at stairways.

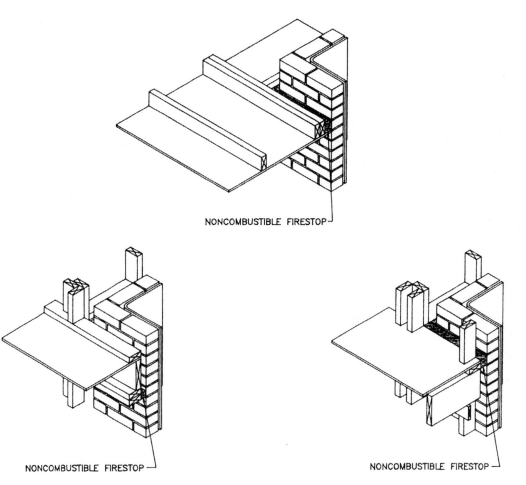

Figure 2–89 Firestopping around chimneys and fireplaces.

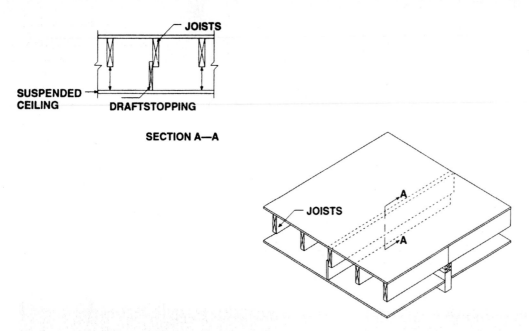

Figure 2–90 Draftstopping between floor joists and ceiling.

seismic activity, the upper portion of the structure moves horizontally while the lower portion is restrained at the ground level. Bracing resists this movement and thus prevents damage to the building.

Sufficient diagonal bracing must be used at the corners (Fig. 2–91) as well as in major partitions to counteract wind pressures and to prevent lateral movement of the framing.

Let-in, 1 × 4 braces, placed as close to 45° as possible and not over 60°, should be used and they should be tied into both the top and the bottom plates of the wall. If windows or openings are close to the corners, K braces can be used (Fig. 2–1). Diagonal bracing can be eliminated if structural sheathing is used and is nailed diagonally to the studs or if the frame is sheathed with plywood.

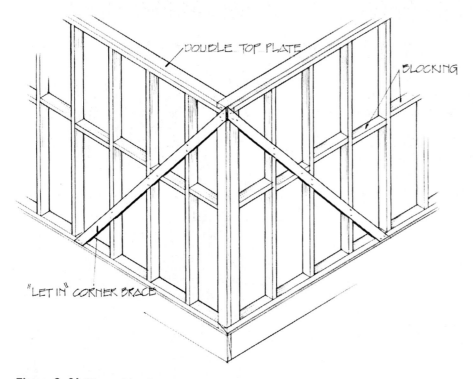

Figure 2–91 Diagonal bracing at corners.

Lintels The horizontal supports above openings are usually built up of two pieces of nominal 2 × 4, 2 × 6, 2 × 8, 2 × 10, or 2 × 12 lumber with the wide dimension vertical. Extra strength and the exact 3½″ stud width can be gained by sandwiching a ⅜″ plywood panel between the two vertical lintel pieces (Fig. 2–92).

Headers and lintels over openings 4′ wide or less can be made of double 2 × 4s on edge. For each 2′ of opening over 4′, increase the lumber size 2″. Use 2 × 4s on edge over a 4′ opening, 2 × 6s over a 6′ opening, 2 × 8s over 8′, and so on.

All headers and lintels must have at least 2″ solid bearing at each end to the floor or the bottom plate unless you use other approved framing methods or joist brackets. Many builders use double 2 × 12 lintels above all wall openings, thereby eliminating the need for cripples or vertical blocking between the lintel and the top plate (Fig. 2–92). For volume construction, some builders use a double 2 × 6 cap plate, set vertically, over all bearing walls, thus eliminating lintels. Such buildings generally have openings no wider than 4′-0″ (Fig. 2–93).

Second-Floor Framing Each story in platform framing is a separate unit; if two stories are planned, the second-floor joists and headers are attached to the top plate of the first floor. The second-story walls are built on the platform or subfloor of the second floor. Second-story floor joists then become the first-floor ceiling joists. If possible, second-story partitions should fall directly above partitions below; otherwise, additional floor joists or blocking is required. Occasionally, second stories are cantilevered out beyond exterior walls below. Joists below cantilevered walls should be perpendicular to the walls and well anchored (Fig. 2–94).

Ceiling Joists Ceiling joists generally rest on the top wall plate if the roof is put directly above. If an attic floor is required (Fig. 2–95), headers and joists can be built up to the outside surface of the walls, with the attic floor nailed to the joists and 2″ × 4″ soleplate nailed over the floor around its perimeter on which the rafters bear. In ceiling framing, if a gable-type is used, it is more desirable to put the ceiling joists parallel to the roof rafters, making the ceiling joists actually bottom chords for the truss shape of the roof rafters. Ceiling joists are nailed to both the top plate and the roof rafters (Fig. 2–96). A lateral brace or a catwalk brace for ceiling framing is shown in Fig. 2–97.

When ceiling joists must be placed at right angles to the rafters, short joists are run perpendicularly to the long joists over the plate and are nailed to both the plate and the rafters. The inner ends of the short joists are butted and anchored to a double-long joist. Metal straps are used to tie the tops of the short joists across at least three of the long joists if no wood flooring is used (Fig. 2–98).

Gable-Roof Rafters Wind pressures against gable roofs (and hip roofs as well) not only exert downward forces on the windward side, but also exert upward pressures on the leeward side, especially if the roof has a considerable overhang. Therefore, rafters must be well anchored at their lower ends or bearing cuts. The triangular notch cut into the rafters for horizontal bearing is called a *bird's-mouth* (see Fig. 2–99 for roof-framing terminology). It should be deep enough so that the rafter bears on the full width of the 2 × 4 plate. The bird's-mouth is toenailed to the plate, and the rafter is also nailed to the ceiling joist; metal anchors are sometimes employed for more positive anchorage. Rafters are placed directly opposite each other at the ridge so that they brace against each other. Rafter lengths and cuts are carefully laid out on a pattern piece to ensure uniformity of all common rafters and to simplify their cutting. The ridgeboard can be either 1″ or 2″ nominal lumber, but it should be 2″ wider than the rafters so that the entire beveled ridge cut will make contact with the ridgeboard.

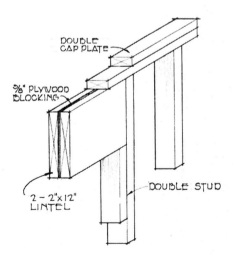

Figure 2–92 Lintels over typical wall openings.

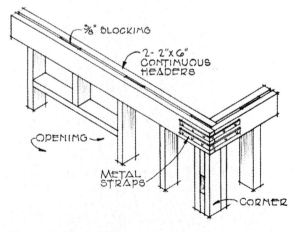

Figure 2–93 Wall framing with continuous headers instead of double cap plate.

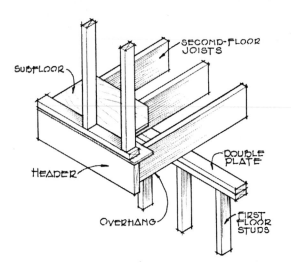

Figure 2–94 Framing a second-floor overhang.

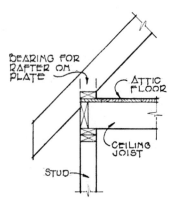

Figure 2–95 Fastening rafters to an attic floor.

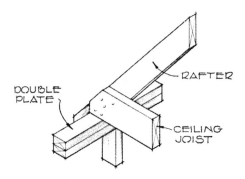

Figure 2–96 Fastening rafters and ceiling joists.

Valley Rafters   Valleys are formed by the intersection of two sloping roofs; the rafter directly below the valley is called the *valley rafter* (Fig. 2–100). Valley rafters carry additional loads and should be doubled as well as widened to allow full contact with the diagonal cuts of the jack rafters.

Jack Rafters   Jack rafters are shorter than common rafters and run from hip or valley rafters to the plates. If roofs with different ridge heights intersect, the higher roof is framed first, and the valley is formed by nailing a plate over the higher roof surface. The jack rafters of the lower roof are then nailed to the plate. Or the valley rafter can be incorporated into the larger roof framing if attic communication is needed between the gables or hips (Fig. 2–100).

Hip Rafters   Like ridgeboards, hip rafters do not carry any loads and are therefore the same size as the common rafters (Fig. 2–101).

Gambrel-Roof Framing   This roof framing requires two sets of generally different length rafters. The first set of longer rafters receives a bird's-mouth cut and is nailed to the top plate of the exterior bearing walls. A knee wall or a full stud wall is used to support these steeply pitched rafters at the opposite end of the span. The second set of rafters with less pitch is framed into the top end of the longer rafters and to a ridge beam at the center line of the structure. Collar beams or ceiling joists are placed at the junction between the two sets of rafters (Fig. 2–102).

Dormer Framing   This framing is similar to gable-roof framing. Double headers and double trimmers must be framed around the opening in the roof. Studs are nailed to the top of the double trimmers to form the vertical sides of the dormer. A ridge beam and rafters frame the gable roof structure of the dormers (Fig. 2–103).

Flat-Roof Framing   Flat-roof framing consists of roof joists bearing on the top plate of stud walls. The roof joists may cantilever over the bearing wall to create an eave or an overhang. When an overhang is desired around the perimeter of the structure, a double trimmer is placed to support cantilevered lookouts. These lookouts are perpendicular to the roof joists and form the overhang at the side of the structure (Fig. 2–104).

Collar Beams   Collar beams are short lengths of 2 × 4s or 1 × 6s nailed across opposite gable rafters about ⅓ the distance down from the ridge (Fig. 2–99). They stiffen the roof against wind pressures. If the attic is used for occupancy, the collar beams act as ceiling joists as well as rafter ties and must be placed at ceiling height. When the roof pitch is low and the rafter span is long, collar beams are nailed to each pair of rafters; otherwise, to every third pair.

Gable Studs   Gable studs must be framed with the same spacing as studs in the lower walls; they are diagonally cut and notched to fit the underside of the end rafters and butt to the double wall plate (Fig. 2–105). If a boxed overhang is required above the gable wall, a ladder-type framing can be cantilevered over the gable wall (Fig. 2–106). If wood siding is used on the gable

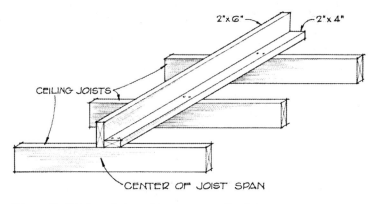

Figure 2–97 Catwalk lateral brace over ceiling joists.

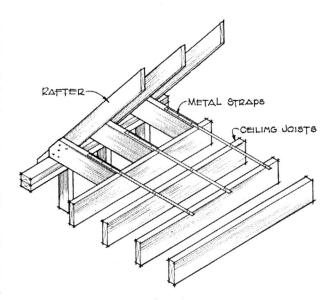

Figure 2–98 Framing with ceiling joists at right angles to rafters.

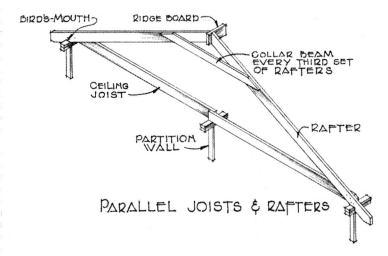

Figure 2–99 Arrangement of opposite rafters and ceiling joists.

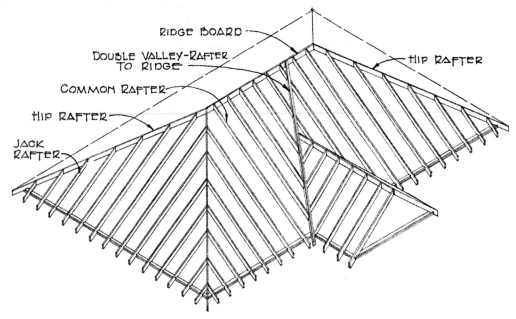

Figure 2–100 Hip-roof framing.

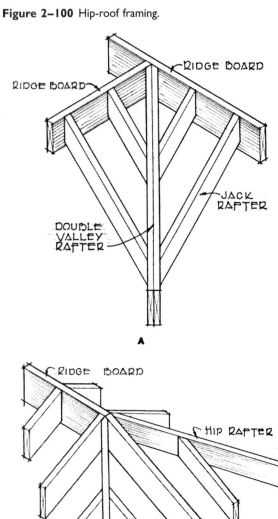

A

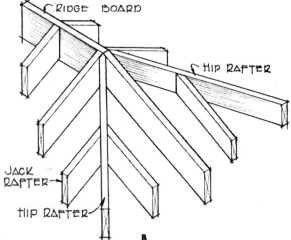

B

Figure 2–101 Roof framing. (A) Valley rafter. (B) Hip rafter.

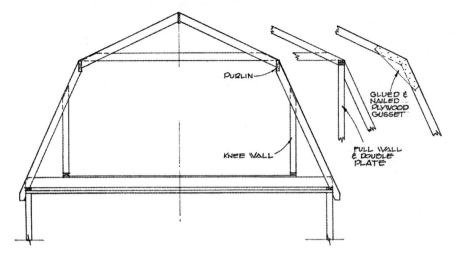

Figure 2–102 Gambrel-roof framing.

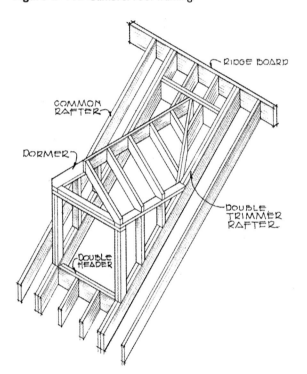

Figure 2–103 Dormer framing.

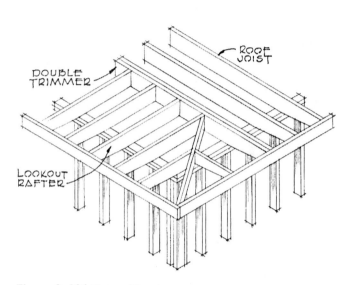

Figure 2–104 Flat-roof framing at corners.

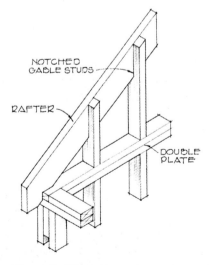

Figure 2–105 Gable studs.

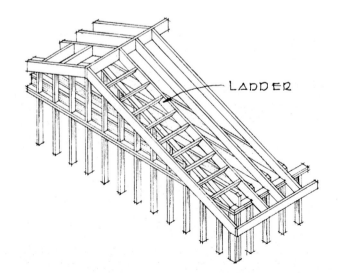

Figure 2–106 Gable-end roof framing.

wall, and if brick veneer is used below, 2 × 8 gable studs can be used to bring the gable siding out flush with the brick veneer.

Roof Venting

Building codes generally require that the vent area be 1/150 of the horizontal roof area. The area may be 1/300 of the horizontal roof area if 50% of the required ventilating area is located at least 3′ above the eave or the cornice vents, with the balance provided by eave or cornice vents. The vent area may be 1/300 if a vapor barrier with a transmission rate not exceeding 1 perm (see Section 2.16.2) is installed on the warm side of the attic insulation. Venting should be equal between eaves and ridges to provide active flow. Gable-end louvers and other mechanical systems interfere with the natural venting process and should not be combined with traditional eave/ridge venting. For proper venting, an open ridge should be used (Figs. 2–107, 2–108, and 2–109).

In the past several years, shingle problems have been attributed to the lack of venting often in "compact" roofs, that is, roofs with exposed deck ceilings and no attics. Compact roofs have the shingles applied directly onto insulation covered by plywood or onto foam insulation bonded to OSB. In some cases the shingles may be nailed directly to a roof deck that serves as an exposed cathedral ceiling. Some manufacturers have claimed that excessive heat loads on unvented roofs cause shingles to buckle and split; the Owens-Corning Company has made available a 10-year warranty on shingles installed over unvented attics or cathedral ceilings.

Roof Decking

There are several methods of covering roof framing, depending on the materials used and on the type of roof covering. Nominal 1″ matched boards, usually 6″ wide and nailed perpendicularly to the rafters, can be used. They are started at the edge of the roof overhang and are laid up tight to the ridge. Use of shiplap or tongue-and-groove lumber will result in a tighter deck and more solid surface for the roof covering. Splices should be well staggered and made over the center of the rafters. Long pieces of lumber are desirable for roof decking.

Softwood plywood makes a satisfactory roof deck; it goes on fast and makes a rigid roof when properly nailed down. Plywood joints should fall on the rafters, and vertical joints should be midway on succeeding rows. The face grain of the plywood should be laid perpendicularly to the rafters (Fig. 2–110). Plywood that is ½″ thick can be used as decking when light roof coverings are used; ⅝″ or ¾″ thickness is necessary for the heavier roof coverings. All plywood edges should be well covered with molding or trim at the edges of the roof. As soon as the roof deck is completed, it is covered with a good grade of roofing felt, preferably 2 layers of 15-lb felt. The felt is 2″ side lapped and is end lapped 4″ to 6″, depending on the roof covering. This covering is very important be-

cause it is rainproof and therefore protects the structure while the work is in progress.

Wall Sheathing

Wall sheathing is the outer subwall, which is nailed directly to the studs and the framework. Wall sheathing adds both strength and insulation to the building and forms a base for the exterior siding. The following types of materials are used for wall sheathing:

1. *Wood boards,* 1″ nominal thickness, usually 6″ or 8″ wide; wider lumber will shrink more and leave wider gaps. Wood sheathing can be applied either horizontally or at a 45° angle. The horizontal method is more economical but requires diagonal let-in bracing at the corners. Diagonal sheathing adds greatly to the rigidity of the wall and eliminates the need for corner bracing. It also provides an excellent tie between the framing and the sill plate. Wood sheathing can be either square edged, shiplap, or tongue-and-groove. End joints should be staggered and made over studs; two 8-penny nails are used at each stud bearing. Number 2 common lumber is usually specified.

2. *Fiberboard asphalt-coated sheathing* is available in 4′ widths and 8′, 10′, and 12′ lengths. It can be applied either horizontally or vertically. The latter method usually requires a 9′ long sheet to cover a wall that has 8′-0″ ceilings. Fiberboard sheathing ½″ thick is easy to handle by carpenters, and it goes on quickly compared to wood sheathing. Other types of fiberboard measure 2′ × 8′ and have shiplap or tongue-and-groove edges; they are applied horizontally. Fiberboard must be carefully nailed with galvanized roofing nails.

3. *Plywood* used for sheathing usually comes in 4′ × 8′ sheets and should be a minimum of 5⁄16″ thick over studs spaced 16″ o.c. and ⅜″ thick over studs spaced 24″ o.c. Six-penny nails should be used and should be spaced not more than 6″ apart for edge nailing and 12″ apart for intermediate nailing. Plywood is usually applied vertically to permit perimeter nailing without additional blocking. When the 8′ dimension is horizontal, blocking is desirable along the horizontal joints between the studs as a base for the finish-wall nailing. When the finish-wall material requires nailing between the studs (as with wood shingles), the plywood should be at least ⅜″ thick. Wood shingles must be nailed to stripping if 5⁄16″ plywood or other non-nail-holding sheathing is used. Plywood can be applied with power-driven staplers using galvanized wire staples. Asphalt building felt is placed over plywood sheathing in some locations.

4. *Gypsum sheathing,* composed of moisture-resistant gypsum filler faced on both sides with lightweight paper, can be used as a subwall. It is available in 2′ × 4′ and 2′ × 8′ sizes and ½″ thick.

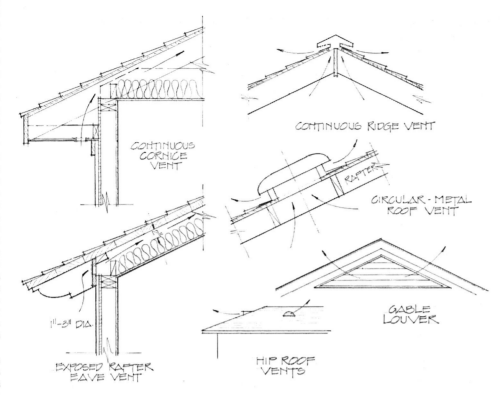

Figure 2–107 Methods of roof venting.

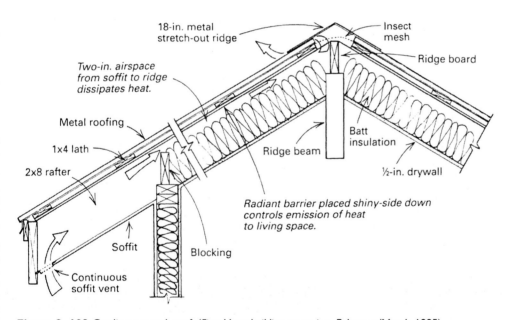

Figure 2–108 Cooling a metal roof. (*Fine Homebuilding* magazine, February/March 1995)

Some gypsum sheathing has V-joint edges for easier application and better edge ties; this type is applied horizontally and is nailed securely with galvanized roofing nails. Vertical joints are always staggered and made on the center of the studs. If finish siding is used that requires both nailing strips and a smooth base, the nailing strips are fastened directly to the studs, and the gypsum sheathing is nailed over the nailing strips.

5. ***Styrofoam® and urethane sheathings,*** usually ¾″ or 1″ thick, some foil-covered on one or both sides for added reflective insulation and resistance to

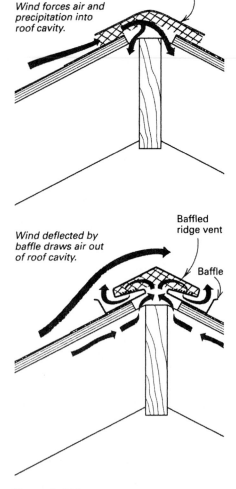

Wind forces air and precipitation into roof cavity.

Unbaffled ridge vent

Wind deflected by baffle draws air out of roof cavity.

Baffled ridge vent

Baffle

Figure 2–109 A baffled versus an unbaffled ridge vent. (*Fine Homebuilding* magazine, June/July 1996)

moisture features, are light but fragile. They are obtainable in sheet sizes similar to those of plywood, and they must be carefully fastened to framing with large-headed nails or staples. Either has excellent insulating but poor structural qualities.

6. *Particleboard,* available in ¼″ and ⁷⁄₁₆″ thicknesses and in 4′ × 8′ sheets, is used for sheathing. This material can be applied vertically or horizontally over studs. Particleboard is fastened in the same manner as plywood.

2.4.2 Balloon Frame Construction

The distinguishing feature of balloon construction (Fig. 2–111) is that the studs run from the sill to the top plate. These vertical lengths of wall framing minimize the amount of wood shrinkage in the total height of the building. Because the stud lengths are long, there is less

chance that the wood frame will reduce in height when used with brick or stone veneer or stucco in 2-story buildings. Houses built after 1930 are more likely to be platform framed due to the advent of plywood and an increasing scarcity of framing lumber. If a house is more than 60 years old and has a wood frame, it probably has a balloon frame.

Wood shrinks considerably more across grain than on end grain; therefore, the absence of horizontal members, with the exception of the sill and the plate, provides end-grain fiber almost throughout the entire height of the building. Even though balloon framing is not used as often as a platform frame, it has features that are noteworthy, and it is sometimes used in combination with platform construction.

Sill The sill plate, as in the platform frame, is well anchored to the foundation with ½″ diameter anchor bolts. If the top of the foundation wall needs trueing, a bed of grout or mortar is placed below the sill. The sill is usually a 2 × 6 or a 2 × 8; sometimes a double sill of well-spiked members is used. Both the studs and the first-floor joists rest on the sill plate, forming the solid sill. Usually, the sill plate is set the thickness of the sheathing inside the outer edge of the foundation wall (Fig. 2–51B).

Floor Joists As in the platform frame, the size and the spacing of the floor joists in the balloon frame depend on their loads and span. Generally, the joists are spaced 16″ o.c. and are toenailed to the sill plate and the beam within the building. Joists can be butted to the beam and anchored, or they can be lapped over the beam. A row of bridging should be used if the joists span more than 10′-0″. There are no headers at the ends of the joists.

Studs The studs are usually spaced 16″ o.c., as in other framing, and they run to the top plate. Each stud carries its own load from plate to sill without any lateral distribution by headers or beams. For this reason, studs must be carefully selected, especially in balloon frame, 2-story houses, where the studs must be considerably longer. The spacing of the studs must be compatible with the spacing of the floor joists and ceiling joists to allow the joists in all floors to be nailed directly to the studs. Openings for doors and windows must be surrounded with double studs, and headers or lintels must be carefully selected. Openings in first-story walls must have lintels or headers over them that are capable of carrying the entire weight of the studs above the openings.

One of the shortcomings of balloon framing is the ease with which a fire in the basement can burn through the sill and enter the cavities between the studs, causing flue action and rapid spread of the conflagration through the entire structure. To eliminate this hazard, codes require 2″ blocking between the joists and studs above the sill plate and often prescribe that the cavity at the sill

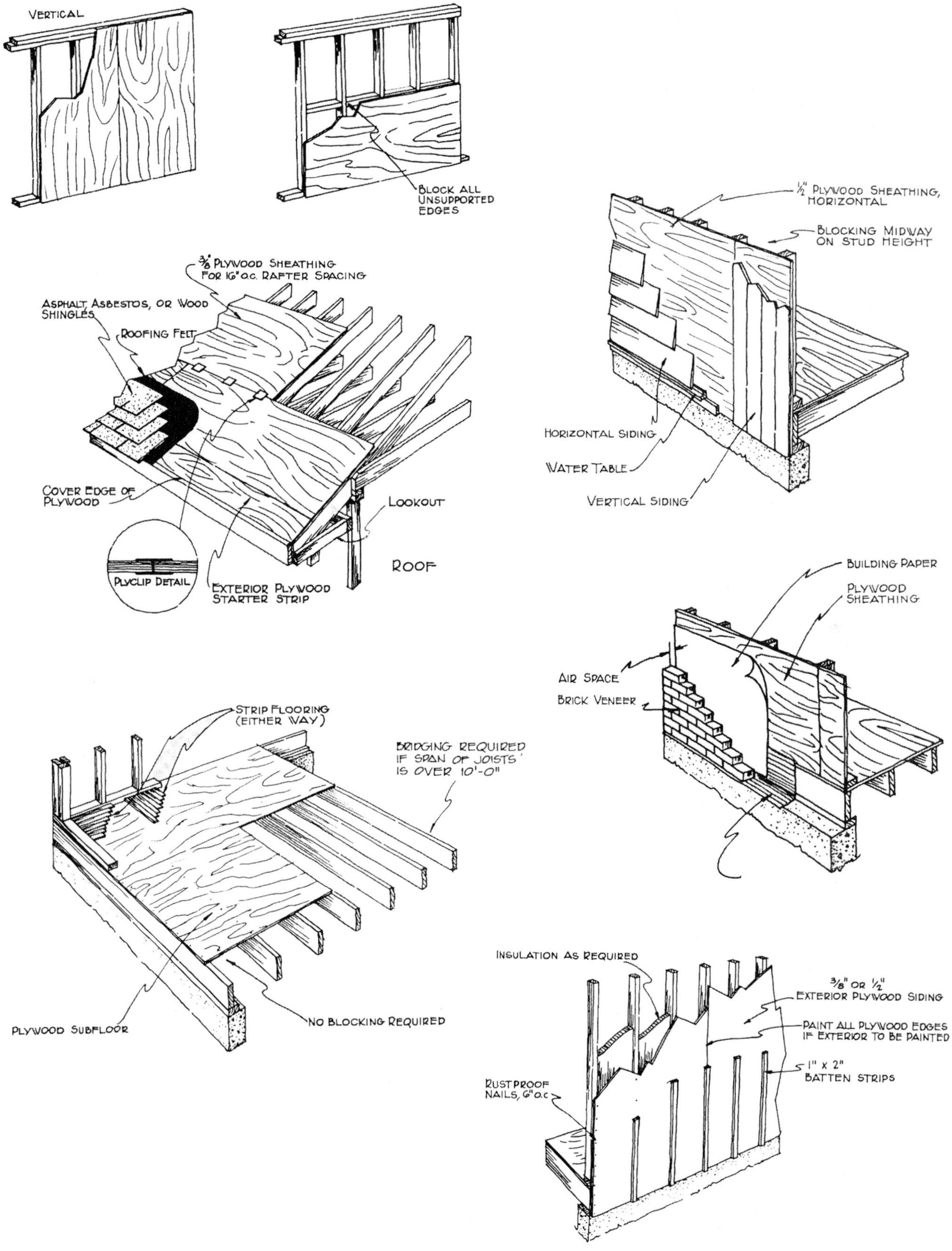
VERTICAL
BLOCK ALL UNSUPPORTED EDGES
½" PLYWOOD SHEATHING, HORIZONTAL
BLOCKING MIDWAY ON STUD HEIGHT
⅜" PLYWOOD SHEATHING FOR 16" o.c. RAFTER SPACING
ASPHALT, ASBESTOS, OR WOOD SHINGLES
ROOFING FELT
COVER EDGE OF PLYWOOD
LOOKOUT
PLYCLIP DETAIL
EXTERIOR PLYWOOD STARTER STRIP
ROOF
HORIZONTAL SIDING
WATER TABLE
VERTICAL SIDING
BUILDING PAPER
PLYWOOD SHEATHING
AIR SPACE
BRICK VENEER
STRIP FLOORING (EITHER WAY)
BRIDGING REQUIRED IF SPAN OF JOISTS IS OVER 10'-0"
PLYWOOD SUBFLOOR
NO BLOCKING REQUIRED
INSULATION AS REQUIRED
⅜" OR ½" EXTERIOR PLYWOOD SIDING
PAINT ALL PLYWOOD EDGES IF EXTERIOR TO BE PAINTED
1" x 2" BATTEN STRIPS
RUSTPROOF NAILS, 6" o.c.

Figure 2–110 The use of plywood for sheathing and decking.

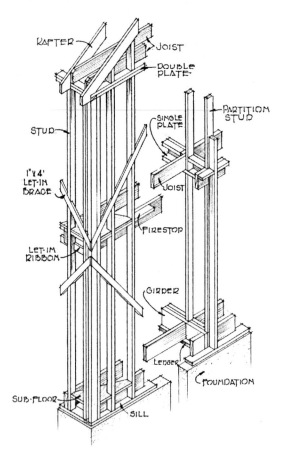

Figure 2–111 Balloon (eastern) frame construction.

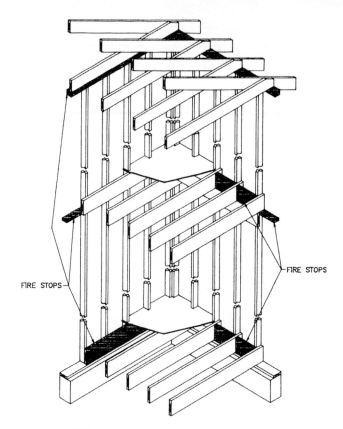

Figure 2–112 Firestopping in balloon framing.

be filled with masonry or a noncombustible material (Fig. 2–112).

Ribbon Another typical feature of the balloon frame is the method of supporting second-floor joists. Ceiling or second-floor joists rest on a 1 × 6 board, let into the studs, called a *ribbon*. The joists are also spiked to the studs. The ribbon is necessary only on those walls taking the ends of the joists. Firestopping and fireblocking are also needed at the intersection of second-floor joists and the walls. In addition, horizontal blocking between the studs is required midway between room heights.

Posts Corner studs and posts at intersections of partitions and walls are built up, similarly to the platform frame, so that nailing surfaces will be found on both inside and outside corners.

Braces If horizontal board sheathing is used for the subwall, 1 × 4 let-in bracing must be used throughout the framing to resist raking stresses. The use of diagonal wood sheathing or plywood eliminates the need for the bracing. Diagonal 2 × 4 blocking at the corners does not have the strength that the let-in braces have, especially if the blocking is not tightly fitted into the stud spacings.

Subfloor Boards, measuring 1 × 6 and laid diagonally, or plywood is generally used for the subfloor. The subfloor extends to the outer edge of the wall framing and is notched around the studs.

Top Plate and Roof Framing The top plate consists of a double 2 × 4, lapped at the corners and the intersections of partitions, and well-spiked together. If nailing surfaces are necessary for the application of gypsum board or other ceiling coverings, blocking must be inserted between the ceiling joists and spiked to the top plate. Rafters rest on the top plate and are nailed to both the plate and the ceiling joists, similar to platform framing. Metal framing anchors can be used to fasten rafters to the top plate if more rigidity is desired. The roof framing is done similarly to the method indicated in platform framing, and the treatment of the overhang varies with the type of architectural effect required. Some houses have very little overhang at the eaves; others may have as much as a 3′ overhang. Rafters can be left exposed at the eaves, or they can be boxed in with a horizontal soffit. The treatment of the detail at the junction of the wall and the roof plays an important part in the general character of the building (see Fig. 2–71).

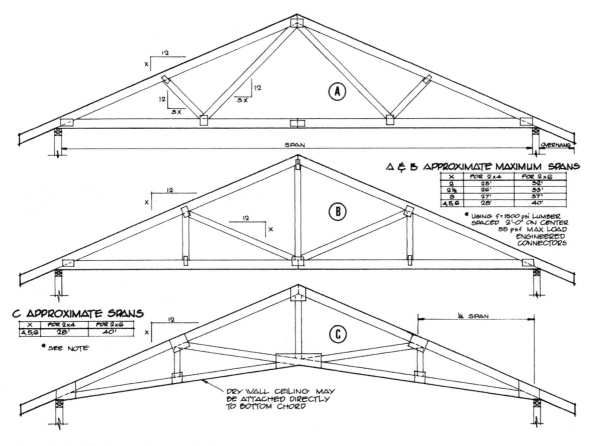

A & B APPROXIMATE MAXIMUM SPANS

X	FOR 2x4	FOR 2x6
2	25'	32'
2½	26'	35'
3	27'	37'
4,5,6	28'	40'

* USING f = 1500 psi LUMBER SPACED 2'-0" ON CENTER 55 psf MAX LOAD ENGINEERED CONNECTORS

C APPROXIMATE SPANS

X	FOR 2x4	FOR 2x6
4,5,6	28'	40'

* SEE NOTE

Figure 2–113 Prefabricated trusses for light construction.

2.4.3 Wood Roof Trusses

Lightweight, prefabricated wood trusses offer many advantages in roof framing of small- or average-size residences (Fig. 2–113). Wood trusses can be used with either platform or balloon framing; when spaced 24″ o.c., which is usually the case in small buildings, they become compatible with sheet sizes of plywood and other materials. Trusses can be lifted into place and quickly anchored on the job. Complete freedom can be exercised in the placement of partitions within the building. They can be made thinner and, when they are not load bearing, the foundation can be simplified, which constitutes a saving.

The basic shape of the truss is a rigid, structural triangle and, with the addition of strut members, the basic shape subdivides into smaller triangles, each reducing the span of the outer members or chords. This reduction of individual member spans allows narrower members and less material is required to carry similar loads as compared with conventional framing.

The fasteners used to join the members of the truss can be nails, bolts, split rings, barb-pointed plates, or plywood gusset plates fastened with nails and glue. Many lumber dealers stock engineered trusses of standard lengths and roof pitches. Volume builders prefabricate their own trusses with simple jigs and production-line efficiency. Fabrication of trusses requires careful workmanship and attention to detail; the joints between members are critical, especially the heel joint, which is subjected to more lateral stresses. The heel joint should bear on the wall plate below (Fig. 2–114). If an overhang is required, the top chords can be extended beyond the heel joint to support the overhang (Figs. 2–113 and 2–114).

Modified trusses are available for complete framing of hip-type roofs. Occasionally, conventional framing is combined with trussed-rafter framing; the trusses then replace the common rafters of the pitched roof, and conventional framing is used at the intersections of sloping roofs and around the hips of hip roofs. Trusses are as varied as the houses they go on and can be combined to create complex roof shapes (Fig. 2–115).

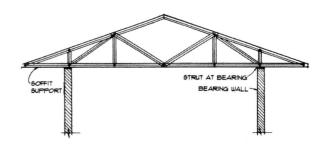

Figure 2–114 An alternate overhanging truss that provides for stable overhang.

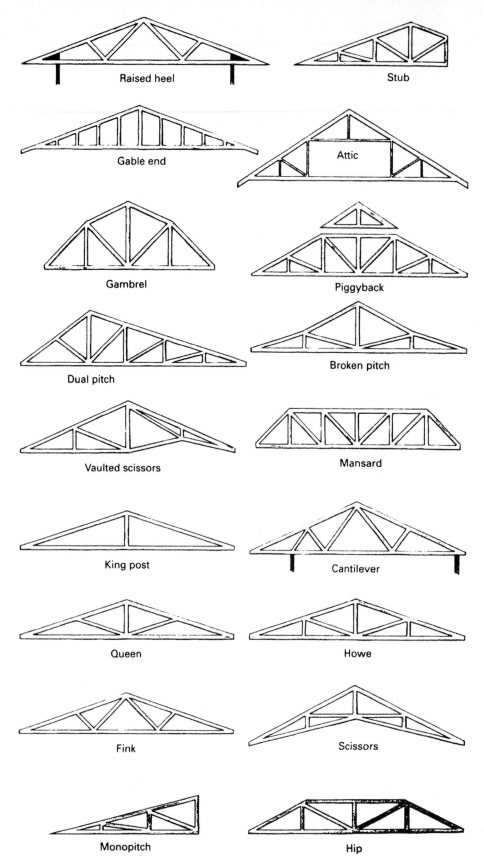

Figure 2–115 Roof choices. (*Fine Homebuilding* magazine, June/July 1994)

Residential roof trusses range from 15′ to 50′ long and from 5′ to 15′ high. Length and height are determined by roof pitch and roof span plus cantilever, if any. Special trusses can be made for virtually any situation. Attic trusses provide room-sized central openings, and vaulted scissor trusses provide a raised ceiling effect where wanted. Common trusses are fabricated with a variable top chord overhang, a variety of soffit returns, and details for box and closed cornicles. Unlike with conventional framing, trusses cannot be modified in the field without radically altering their strength. Truss manufacturers typically provide all engineering services required for fabrication, along with the placement diagrams for construction.

2.5

PLANK-AND-BEAM FRAME CONSTRUCTION

Plank-and-beam wood framing (Figs. 2–116 and 2–117), now an established method of residential construction, has been adapted from the older type of mill construction that utilized heavy framing members and thick wood floors and roofs. Plank-and-beam framing is similar to steel skeleton framing in concept: It develops structural stability by concentrating loads on a few large members, which in turn transfer their loads directly to the foundation by the use of posts or columns. In structures, these lines of load transfer from the beams should not be interrupted unless special provision has been made for their placement. Posts needed to support beams in light construction must be at least 4″ × 4″. Where heavy, concentrated loads occur in places other than over main beams or columns, supplementary beams are necessary to carry the loads.

One structural advantage of plank-and-beam framing is the simplicity in framing around door and window openings. Because the loads are carried by posts uniformly spaced throughout the walls, large openings can be easily framed without lintels. Large window walls, which are characteristic of contemporary construction, can be formed by merely inserting fixed glass between the posts. However, a window wall should have several solid panels in appropriate places to stabilize it against lateral movement. All walls must be braced with diagonal bracing or suitable sheathing.

Plank-and-beam framing requires disciplined planning; savings will be realized by employing modular dimensions to the framing members and to the wall and roof coverings. It lends itself to the use of plywood. Stock plywood sizes can be used with a minimum of cutting and waste. Massive, exposed structural members within a house are instrumental in giving it a feeling

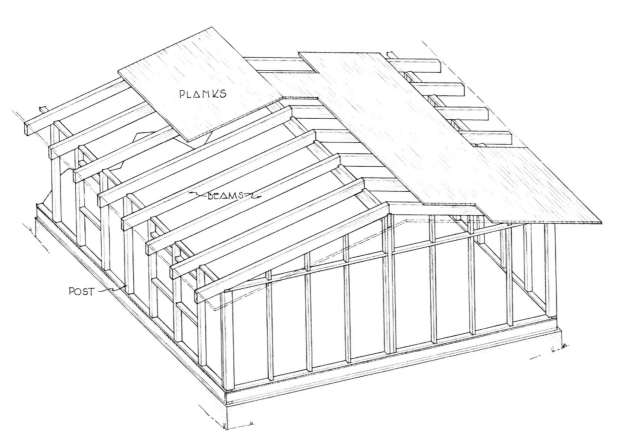

Figure 2–116 Plank-and-beam construction with transverse beams.

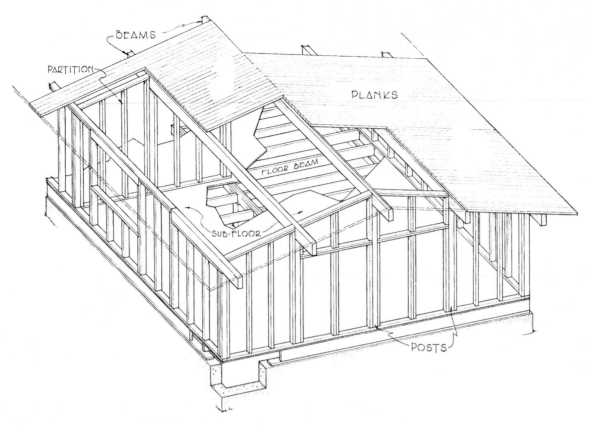

Figure 2–117 Plank-and-beam construction with longitudinal beams.

of stability and rhythmic beauty, attributes that testify to the architect's competence.

With rising relative costs of labor in home building, plank-and-beam framing, which requires the handling of fewer pieces than does conventional framing, offers structural economies to home builders. In a study made by the National Lumber Manufacturers Association, the plank-and-beam method saved 26% on labor and 15% on materials over conventional joist framing. Bridging is eliminated between joists, nails are fewer and larger, and inside room heights are increased with no increase in stud or building heights. Masonry piers can be used instead of continuous foundation walls for economy. (The piers must be located under the structural posts.) Eave details and roof overhangs are simpler; usually, the 2″ roof decking is cantilevered over the wall, and no material is needed for boxing in the cornice.

Conventional framing can be successfully combined with plank-and-beam framing within the same building. Sometimes a plank-and-beam roof is used in only one room of the house, often the living or family area (Fig. 2–118). If so, sufficient column bearing must be provided within the stud walls for the beams of the one roof. If plank-and-beam wall framing supports conventional roof framing, a continuous header should be used at the top of the walls carrying the roof loads to transfer

the load from the closely spaced rafters to the posts (Fig. 2–93).

There are limitations to plank-and-beam framing, and attention to special details is necessary at these points of construction: Partitions must be located over beams, otherwise supplemental framing must be installed; partitions perpendicular to the beams must rest on a 4 × 4 or 4 × 6 soleplate to distribute the load across the beam of the floor. Additional beams are needed under bathtubs and other concentrated loads. Because of the absence of concealed air spaces in floors and roofs, wiring and plumbing are more difficult to install. Often built-up cavity beams are used through which wiring or piping can pass. Flexible wiring cable can often be laid in the V joint on the top of 2″ roof decking. Surface-mounted electrical raceways may have to be used for electrical outlets. Plumbing, especially in 2-story houses, may have to be hidden within false beams or furred spaces. Moldings and raceways may have to be employed, and top surfaces of beams may have to be grooved to conceal wiring or piping.

Plank roofs with no dead air space below often require additional insulation and vapor barriers. Insulation is usually applied above the decking and must be rigid enough to support workers on the roof. The thickness of the insulation must conform to local climatic conditions. Vapor barriers should be installed between the decking and

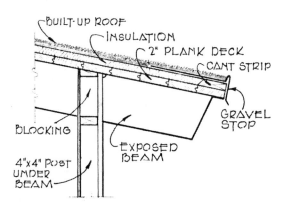

Figure 2–119 Typical plank-and-beam cornice detail.

Figure 2–118 Plank-and-beam interiors.

the insulation. Prefinished insulation board, 2″ to 4″ thick, is available in large sheets to replace decking and insulation combinations. It is light and can be installed rapidly by workers; no decorating of the underside ceiling is necessary. Prefinished insulation tile or panels can also be applied to the underside of regular wood decking. They can be attached directly to the decking, or furring strips can be used between the underside of the decking and the insulation. When rigid insulation is used above the decking, wood cant strips of the same thickness are fastened around the edges of the roof for application of flashing or gravel stops (Fig. 2–119). Light-colored cov-

erings for plank roofs also keep the house cooler in summer and warmer in winter.

Another consideration in plank-and-beam framing is the quality of the exposed structural lumber. Higher grades of framing lumber are required, because large knots, streaks, and resin blemishes are objectionable if painted and are even more unsightly if natural finishes are used. Workmanship in installing the structural pieces is especially important. Finishing nails must be used; metal anchors, if used, must be carefully fastened; and no hammer marks should be left on the exposed structural surfaces. Planking should be accurately nailed to the beams; joints should occur above the beams; and the tongue-and-groove planking should be nailed up tightly so that shrinkage between planks will not be objectionable. Kiln-dried lumber should be specified, especially for visible ceilings. Blocking, or filler wall, between beams on exterior walls must be carefully fitted and detailed, otherwise leaky joints and air infiltration will result when the blocking dries and shrinks. Particular care must be given to connections where beams abut each other and where beams join the posts. These connections must be strong and neatly done. Where gable roofs are used, provision must be made to absorb the horizontal thrust produced by the sloping roof beams (Fig. 2–120). Partitions and supported ridge beams help relieve this thrust. Metal straps fastened over the ridge beam or metal ridge fasteners are effective in resisting the lateral stresses.

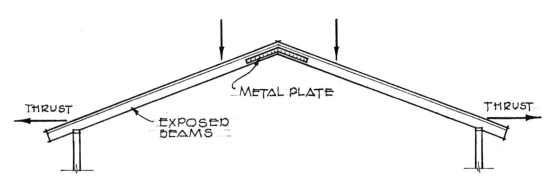

Figure 2–120 Horizontal thrust of a beam ceiling.

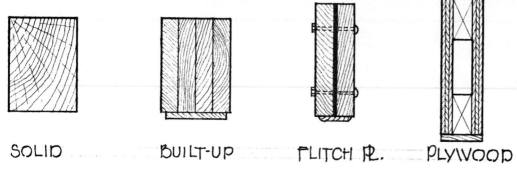

SOLID   BUILT-UP   FLITCH PL.   PLYWOOD

Figure 2–121 Types of beams used in plank-and-beam construction.

Plank-and-beam roofs can be supported with either transverse beams or longitudinal beams (Figs. 2–116 and 2–117).

2.5.1 Transverse Beams

Transverse beams are usually supported at the ridge by a heavy ridge beam and by the long, exterior walls of the building. The planks then span the beams perpendicularly to the slope of the roof, if it is a gable type. Beams may be solid, glue laminated, or built up (Fig. 2–121) of 2″ lumber, securely fastened together (fasteners are usually concealed). Strength and rigidity of the planks are improved if the planks are continuous over more than one span. Tests show that a plank that is continuous over two spans is nearly 2½ times as stiff as a plank extending over only one span under the same conditions. Planks, usually 6″ or 8″ wide, can be tongue-and-grooved or splined (Fig. 2–122) and are designed to support moderate loads. If beams are spaced more than 6′ or 7′ apart, noticeable deflection of common species of nominal 2″ planking will result; 3″ T & G planking will span up to 12′.

2.5.2 Longitudinal Beams

Longitudinal beams running the entire length of the building can be used instead of transverse beams. In that case, the planking is applied parallel to the slope of the roof—down the slope. For either method, tables are used for the proper selection of beam size, span, and spacing, after the other architectural considerations have been resolved. Exterior beams at corners of gable ends are usually false or short beams, which are cantilevered out from the corner of the long, exterior walls (Fig. 2–117). Beam

sizes can be reduced when interior partitions become supports for the beams.

When either method of plank-and-beam framing is employed, interior partitions are often more difficult to frame than when conventional framing is used. If ceilings are sloping, the top of the partition must meet the underside of the slope and must be made diagonal. Other partitions, running perpendicularly to the slope of the ceiling, will have horizontal cap plates but must be built to different heights. Interior partitions, using 2 × 4 studs, can be framed by several methods. First, they can be framed with the studs cut the same length as the exterior walls, and a double cap plate can be put over all of the exterior and interior walls, tying them securely together as in platform framing. Short studs are then attached above the plate to a single top plate that conforms to the slope of the ceiling and is attached to it. Or the partitions can be erected after the roof is completed. The various-length studs are cut to fit the slope of the ceiling, and each partition with a single 2 × 4 cap is fitted into its proper place.

Finish strip flooring should be nailed at right angles to the plank subfloor, similarly to conventional construction. Care must be taken to be sure that flooring or roofing nails do not penetrate through the planks when the planks serve as a ceiling. The inside appearance should be considered when the beams are spaced; moving a beam several inches one way or another near a partition will often be an improvement. Partitions, on the other hand, should be placed in relation to beams so that the beams seem to form a uniform pattern throughout the room. The appearance of exposed beams on the exterior of the building is also of importance. Plank-and-beam framing lends itself to open planning, a characteristic of contemporary houses.

TONGUE & GROOVE -"V" JT.   SPLINE & "V" JT.

Figure 2–122 Wood decking used on plank-and-beam ceilings.

Figure 2–123 A California redwood home with an interesting roof of planks over laminated beams. (Courtesy Dandelet)

In most areas, the structural design of plank-and-beam framing will be controlled by the local building code to the extent of specifying live load requirements. A live load of 40 lb/sq ft is usually specified for floors. For roofs, some codes specify 20 lb/sq ft; others, 30 lb. Beam sizes, beam spacing, and the wood species necessary for various spans of both roofs and floors can be taken from the plank-and-beam tables found in Chapter 13.

2.5.3 Glue Laminated Structural Members

Glue laminated structural members offer many design possibilities in plank-and-beam construction that other-

wise would be restricted by the structural limitations of sawed wood members (Fig. 2–123). Many stock beam shapes are available (Fig. 2–124), providing variations in conventional building silhouettes. Many church buildings successfully employ either laminated beams or arches for interesting ceilings and roof structures. Special waterproof glues are used for exterior exposures. Usually, comparative sectional sizes span one-third more than sawn timbers. Consult manufacturers' catalogs for specific shapes, loads, and spans.

In larger buildings, structural systems such as rigid frames, two-hinged barrel arches, and three-hinged arches, as well as bowstring arches and domes, use laminated members. Rigid frames are made of separate leg

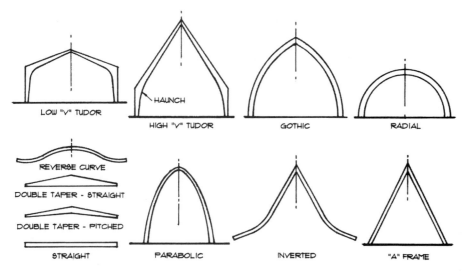

Figure 2–124 Glue laminated structural shapes available in wood.

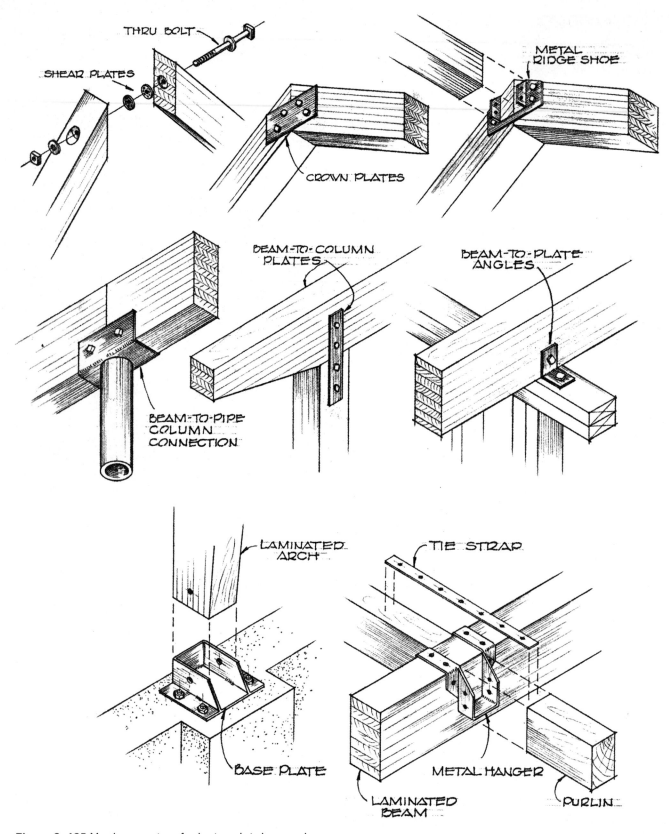

Figure 2–125 Metal connections for laminated timber members.

and arm members carefully joined at the haunch to maintain the desired roof slope. The two-hinged barrel arches must have provision for counteracting outward thrust at their bases with the use of foundation piers, tie rods, or concrete foundation buttresses. Each support must be engineered to resist the horizontal thrust of the arch. Three-hinged arches such as Tudor and Gothic are popular in contemporary church architecture because of their beauty. Their spans vary typically from 30′ to 100′. Their base construction is similar to that of the two-hinged arches. Because of the distance between arches, purlins are commonly placed perpendicularly between arches to carry the roof decking. Arch design data vary with the roof slope and span distance. Metal connectors at critical points ensure neat, engineered joining of the laminated members (Fig. 2–125).

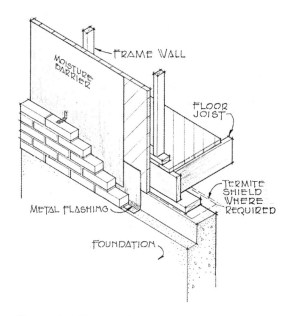

Figure 2–126 Wood frame construction with brick veneer.

BRICK AND STONE VENEER CONSTRUCTION

In areas of the country where brick or building stone is economical, veneered frame dwellings are popular. Masonry veneer over wood framing is more economical than solid masonry; the combination wall (masonry over wood) utilizes the good qualities of both materials. The exterior masonry is durable and requires no maintenance; the wood is economical, more flexible, and a good insulator. Any of the previously mentioned types of wood framing can be used with veneer; the wood frame supports the entire weight of the floors and the roof—no loads are put on the masonry veneer. The single wythe of brick or stone is merely an exterior wall covering for the structure (Fig. 2–126).

Bricks or 4″ or 5″ maximum cut stone can be used for veneering. Hard-burned, moisture-resistant brick should be used. Sandstones and limestones are commonly used for stone veneers. Standard-size brick as well as oversized brick (jumbo, utility, or Norwegian) is available (Fig. 2–137). Bricks are manufactured in a wide range of colors and finishes. A better-quality brick has the same clay throughout the brick, whereas a less expensive brick may have a color or sand finish applied only to the face of the brick. Wood-mold brick is available, which resembles the handmade brick of colonial times. Adobe brick is popular in the Southwest.

It is common practice to start the veneer at the grade line. Provision must be made on the foundation for the width of the veneer and a 1″ minimum air space between the veneer and the wall sheathing; at least 5″ bearing width on the foundation wall is allowed (Fig. 2–127). Good construction usually starts the veneer lower than the wood sill on the foundation wall. Brick may be corbeled ¾″ beyond the edge of the foundation wall. Condensation often develops within the air space, and provisions must be made to keep the moisture from penetrating the wood members. Veneer is tied to the wood frame wall with rustproof, corrugated metal ties (Fig. 2–128). The ties are nailed through the sheathing to every other stud and are laid into the mortar joints of every sixth course (about every 16″ to 20″ of vertical masonry).

Wall ties must be corrosion resistant and either sheet metal or wire. If sheet metal, they must be a minimum size of 0.030″, No. 28 galvanized sheet gauge by ¾″. If wire, they must have a minimum diameter of 0.148″. Wall ties must be spaced so they support no more than 2 sq ft of wall area but no more than 24″ o.c. horizontally. Areas of the country subject to special seismic considerations require additional reinforcement (Fig. 2–129).

The exterior wood sheathing must be covered with a moisture barrier, such as roofing felt. If asphalt-coated sheathing board is used, the asphalt coating acts as a moisture barrier. Styrofoam and urethane sheathing are water-resistant materials and do not require a moisture barrier.

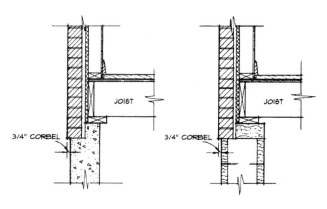

Figure 2–127 Brick veneer may be corbeled on foundation.

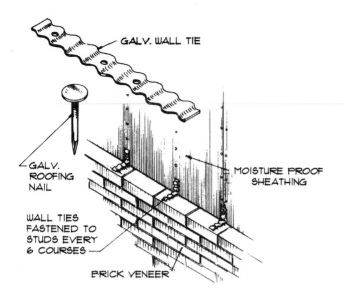

Figure 2–128 Brick wall ties.

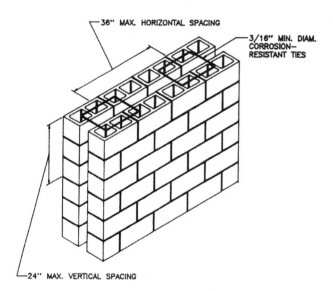

NOTE: TIES IN ALTERNATE COURSES TO BE STAGGERED
ONE METAL TIE FOR EACH 4½ SQ. FT. OF WALL AREA

Figure 2–129 Masonry bonding metal ties.

WEEP HOLE	RECOMMENDED MAXIMUM SPACING (Center to Center)
Wick Material	16 in.
Open Head Joints	24 in.
Other: Inserts Tubes Oiled Rods (removable)	24 in.

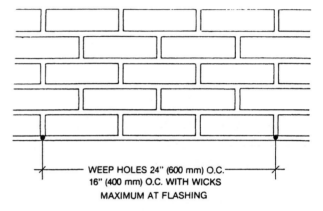

WEEP HOLES 24" (600 mm) O.C.
16" (400 mm) O.C. WITH WICKS
MAXIMUM AT FLASHING

Figure 2–130 Recommended spacing of weep holes.

At the bottom of the air space, a rustproof base flashing must be inserted under the felt and extended into the lower mortar joint of the veneer. This flashing prevents any moisture from penetrating the wood sill members after gathering at the bottom of the air space. Weep holes can be provided at the bottom course by leaving mortar out of vertical joints about 4′ apart (Fig. 2–130).

Brick or masonry sills under window and door openings must be flashed in the same manner. Water running off from windows and doors onto their sills must be kept from entering the air cavity. Masonry will absorb moisture unless it is waterproofed (Figs. 2–131 and 2–132).

Sloping sills of brick, set on edge, are usually used under all openings of brick veneer, and a similar sloping sill must cap brick veneer when it extends only partially up an exterior wall. Combination brick and wood siding exteriors require a bead of caulking where the two materials join together. Stone veneer usually has a cut stone sill under all openings. It also extends out from the face of the veneer, similarly to brick, and has a sloping top surface, called a *wash*, and a drip underneath to prevent water from running back to the wall. All mortar joints in veneers should be well tooled to prevent moisture penetration.

Steel angle iron, usually $3\frac{1}{2}'' \times 3\frac{1}{2}'' \times \frac{5}{16}''$ or $6'' \times 3\frac{1}{2}'' \times \frac{3}{8}''$ depending on loads and spans, is used for lintels above openings in brick veneer (Fig. 2–133 and Table 2–10). Often brick *soldier courses:* (Fig. 2–134) are put directly above openings. Some builders eliminate the use of steel lintels above veneer openings in 1-story houses by using a wide-trim frieze board and molding above all window and door openings. If a low, boxed-in cornice is used, no masonry is necessary above the openings. The wide frieze board continues around the entire house below the cornice, and blocking is used to fur out to the face of the veneer above the windows and doors.

Brick or stone is often used to veneer concrete masonry units (Fig. 2–135). In low walls, corrugated metal ties can be used to tie the two materials together; in larger walls, more positive bonds are attained with *header courses* called "bonding" of brick set into the masonry backing.

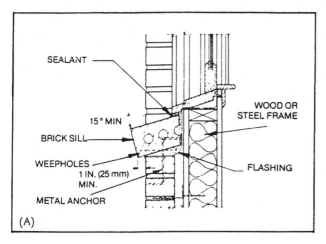

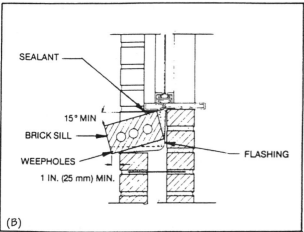

Figure 2–131 (A) Sill in frame/brick veneer construction. (B) Sill in cavity wall construction.

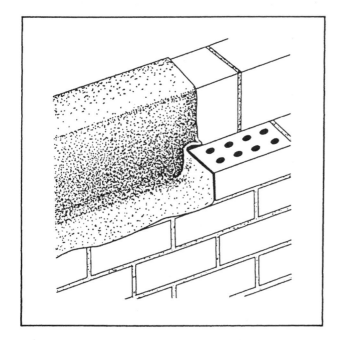

Figure 2–132 End dams.

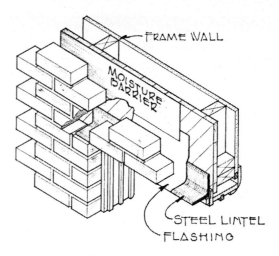

Figure 2–133 Steel lintel above brick veneer openings.

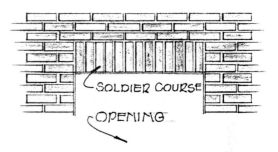

Figure 2–134 Brick soldier course above opening.

Table 2–10 Steel angle lintels for light frame, brick veneer construction.

Span	Size
0'–5'	$3\frac{1}{2}'' \times 3\frac{1}{2}'' \times \frac{5}{16}''$
5'–7'	$4'' \times 3\frac{1}{2}'' \times \frac{5}{16}''$
7'–9'	$5'' \times 3\frac{1}{2}'' \times \frac{3}{8}''$
9'–10'	$6'' \times 3\frac{1}{2}'' \times \frac{3}{8}''$

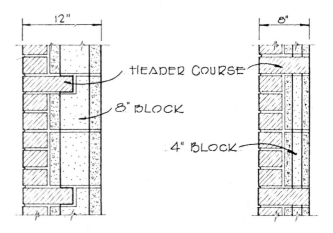

Figure 2–135 Concrete block and brick veneer wall details.

SOLID MASONRY AND CAVITY WALL CONSTRUCTION

Solid masonry, especially brick and stone, has served people well for centuries as a desirable construction material. Many structures still standing and still beautiful provide evidence of its pleasing as well as durable characteristics. Both brick and stone are available in many different colors, textures, and sizes to challenge the creativity and artistry of modern designers and builders. Although many solid masonry buildings have been built of these materials in the past, the present-day trend is to use these materials as exterior veneers only, with wood frame, metal studs, concrete block, or reinforced concrete as the structural, load-bearing material. Solid stone in residential work is limited to small walls; in contemporary residences it is often used to create contrasting walls where the texture and the color of the brick or stone are exposed both inside and outside. Many architects feel that the natural beauty of stone provides sufficient textural interest to make any further decoration of the walls unnecessary.

Local codes in some residential areas require solid masonry exterior walls in all structures. Usually 8″ thick brick walls are used in 1-story houses; local codes must be invoked if higher walls are involved. This type of construction, where solid masonry walls carry the weight of the floors and roof, is known as *bearing-wall construction*. The floors and the roof are constructed of wood framing members, similarly to conventional framing, except that the floor joists are set into the masonry walls and transfer their loads to them; the rafters rest on wood plates well anchored to the top of the walls. All of the wood structural members of the floors, partitions, and roof are surrounded by the shell-like exterior masonry wall. This shell of incombustible material has the advantage of restricting the spread of fire to surrounding buildings. Floor joists that are in the masonry wall must have a diagonal cut, called a *firecut*, on their ends to prevent the joists from rupturing the wall should a fire burn through the joists and cause them to drop to the bottom of the building (Fig. 2–136). The firecut allows full bearing at the bottom surface of the joist, yet it is self-releasing in case of fire.

Because of the porous and noninsulating nature of solid brick or masonry, some method must be used to prevent moisture penetration and to insulate the exterior walls. The conventional method is to waterproof the inside surface of the masonry with hot asphalt or tar and then fasten 1 × 2 furring strips to the inside masonry surface, to which the interior wall covering is applied. Rigid insulation can also be inserted between the furring strips. Another method of furring the masonry wall, to create an air space between the exterior and interior surfaces, is by using a self-furring metal lath over which ¾″ plaster is applied.

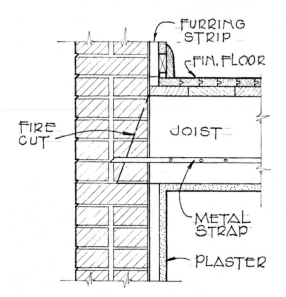

Figure 2–136 Wood joists in solid-brick wall detail.

In economical 1-story buildings with wall heights not exceeding 9′, 15′ at the gable peak, a single-wythe brick called *Norwegian brick* can be used for the masonry load-bearing walls (Fig. 2–137). Since Norwegian brick is larger than common brick, a wall can be laid up much faster. It is 5½″ wide, 2³⁄₁₆″ high, and 11½″ long and can be furred with 2″ × 2″ furring strips, fastened to metal clips that are set into the mortar joints throughout the wall. Interior finish materials can be fastened to the furring strips.

Many other hollow brick units are available up to 8″ thick that are suitable for single-unit masonry walls. Many small commercial buildings are built with this method. For residential construction, however, small brick units are preferable because their texture imparts more interest than that of the larger units.

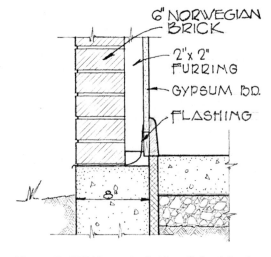

Figure 2–137 Norwegian brick wall detail for 1-story walls.

If a brick surface is required for both the outside and the inside walls, a *brick cavity* wall can be used (Fig. 2–138). This method of construction was introduced from Europe in the late 1930s and has been widely accepted in this country. A 2″ air cavity is used between the wythes of common brick, making the wall usually 10″ thick. Rigid metal ties are placed in the mortar joints spaced 16″ o.c. horizontally and vertically to tie the two wythes together. No furring is necessary, since the air cavity prevents moisture penetration and insulates the wall. In colder climates, air stops are used at corners to minimize air circulation throughout the cavity. Added insulation can be given by the application of rigid insulation to the inside wall of the air cavity; insulation should not touch the outside wythe of brick. Flashing must be used at floor levels, sills, heads of openings, and other critical places. Weep holes must be used in the outer base course to dissipate moisture accumulating in the lower part of the air cavity. Such weep holes can be accomplished by omission of the mortar from header joints at intervals of 3′ to 4′.

Wood floor joists can rest on the inside wythe of brick; additional metal ties must be used in the course below the joists, and the joists must not project into the cavity. Girders and beams must be supported by solid, 8″ wide pilasters that bond the inner and outer wythes together. Roof and ceiling construction must be supported by a 2″ thick wood plate that rests on both wythes and is anchored with ½″ anchor bolts 6′-0″ o.c. The anchor bolts must extend down into the air cavity about 15″, and a 3″ × 6″ × ¼″ plate is welded to the head of the bolt and is anchored in the mortar joints of the brick (Fig. 2–138). Mortar joints should be well tooled on both the outer and the inner finish surfaces.

2.7.1 Concrete Masonry Units (Concrete Block)

Concrete blocks have become the most economical building material for small buildings, even for above-ground construction. It is estimated that a C.M.U. wall costs about 10% less than conventional stud wall with insulation construction. It is a widely available material that combines structure, insulation, and exterior and interior finish surfaces. Many various shapes and sizes of blocks are manufactured; as previously mentioned, the most used sizes are nominal 8″ × 8″ × 16″ and 8″ × 12″ × 16″. (Refer to Fig. 2–33 for other sizes and shapes.) The units are made either of dense concrete mixes, which give them good structural qualities, or of lightweight aggregate mixes, which result in blocks that are weaker structurally, but that provide better insulation. Lightweight blocks of foamed concrete are available in some areas; they have the same insulating qualities as stud walls with wood sheathing, siding, and 2″ of insulation.

Improperly cured units often result in cracks in C.M.U. walls. The blocks should be air cured for at least 28 days, or they should be cured under high-pressure steam, which is the better method for reducing ultimate shrinkage. Steam-cured units will shrink from ¼″ to ⅜″ in a 100′ wall; air-cured units will shrink about twice that amount. Cracking can often be eliminated by the introduction of wire mesh or lightweight C.M.U. steel reinforcement into every second or third horizontal mortar joint (Fig. 2–139). Extra reinforcement is required above and below all wall openings. In long C.M.U. walls, control joints must be used to relieve contraction and other stresses; they are continuous, vertical joints through the wall and are spaced at 20′-0″ intervals.

Concrete masonry unit walls are not successful in areas subjected to earthquakes, unless heavy reinforcement is used extensively at each floor and ceiling level. Refer to local seismic codes if blocks must be used.

In warm areas such as Florida, Arizona, and parts of Texas, concrete masonry units are a very popular above-ground construction material, even in fine houses. Units can be waterproofed on the exterior with waterproof, cement-base paints, or they can be directly covered with stucco. The inside is usually furred and plastered. Florida hurricane codes require continuous, reinforced concrete bond beams above each story level of C.M.U. work, which must be tied to the foundation with vertical corner reinforcement (Fig. 2–35).

Different architectural effects can be achieved by the use of different-sized units in various combinations; however, the *half-lapped bond* is used in structural walls. A *stacked bond* is occasionally used for novelty effects, but horizontal reinforcement must then be used in the

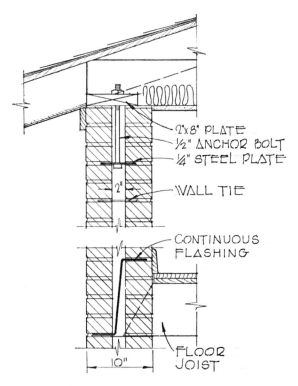

Figure 2–138 Brick cavity wall detail.

- 2″x8″ PLATE
- ½″ ANCHOR BOLT
- ¼″ STEEL PLATE
- WALL TIE
- 2″
- CONTINUOUS FLASHING
- FLOOR JOIST
- 10″

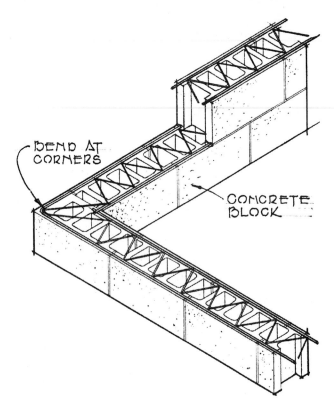

Figure 2–139 Horizontal reinforcement in C.M.U. courses.

horizontal joints. As mentioned in the material on foundations, use unit modules for lengths, heights, and opening sizes, as well as for placement of the openings (Fig. 2–27). Hollow units must be capped with solid cap blocks where framing joists or beams rest on them. Non-load-bearing partitions can be made with 4″ thick hollow units.

Ribbed or split-faced concrete masonry units in a wide variety of styles and colors are available from certain manufacturers. Although more expensive than standard units, the split-faced units eliminate the need for painting or furring the exterior or interior faces of the walls to apply other finishes.

2.7.2 Steel and Concrete Joists

Steel joists are often used in small commercial buildings for the structural support of roofs and light-occupancy floors. Several different types of open-web steel joists are manufactured; details and allowable spans can be obtained from manufacturers' catalogs.[2]

Total dead and live loads must be calculated, and preliminary considerations must be studied, before open-web steel joists are adopted. After they have been found

---

[2] Specifications and details can also be obtained from the Steel Joist Institute, 1346 Connecticut Avenue NW, Washington, DC 20036.

adaptable in the preliminary planning, a thorough engineering calculation is made of all aspects of their use before the steel joist construction is finally selected for the structure.

H-series steel joists are available in standard depths of 8″, 10″, 12″, 14″, 16″, 18″, 20″, 22″, 24″, 26″, 28″, and 30″, each in different weights that can span up to 60′ for roofs. Maximum permissible spacing of the joists for floors is 24″ o.c.; for roofs it is 30″ o.c. In flat roof construction with 2″ thick tongue-and-groove decking, a 2″ × 4″ nailing strip is fastened to the top of the joists with metal clips or bolts to receive the decking. Some joists are made with wood nailing strips already attached to both the top and the bottom chord. If a ceiling is required below the roof joists, ³⁄₈″ ribbed metal lath can be clipped to the bottom chord, and plaster applied over it (Fig. 2–140). This construction will give the roof a ³⁄₄-h fire rating according to the National Bureau of Standards Report TRBM-44.

Flat-type roof construction with steel joists also employs a 2″ concrete slab poured over paper-backed steel mesh or a 2″ gypsum slab as the deck. Usually, built-up roofing is applied directly over the slabs, unless rigid insulation is needed. Lightweight, insulating concrete makes a desirable roof. The steel joists rest on the load-bearing masonry walls or, in wider buildings requiring a steel girder through the center, they rest on the girder as well as on the walls. Metal bridging is attached to joists between spans. Suspended ceilings of acoustical tile can be supported with hangers and metal channels below the steel joists; the open-web character of the joists allows pipes, ducts, and wiring to be run through the dead air space above the ceiling.

In floor construction with steel joists, the joists are supported in the masonry wall similarly to wood framing, as well as on steel girders through the center if the building is wider than the span of one joist. A 2″ or 2½″ poured concrete slab is placed over one of several types of permanent forming material—paper-backed 6″ × 6″

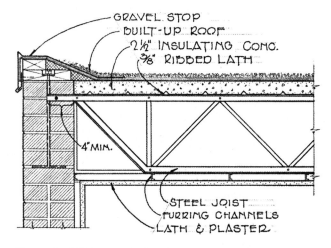

Figure 2–140 Bearing wall and steel joist detail.

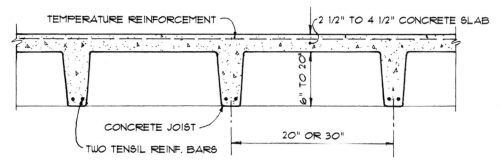

TEMPERATURE REINFORCEMENT · 2 1/2" TO 4 1/2" CONCRETE SLAB

6" TO 20"

CONCRETE JOIST · TWO TENSIL REINF. BARS · 20" OR 30"

Figure 2–141 Reinforced concrete joist detail.

No. 10 wire mesh, corrugated steel sheets, or $\frac{3}{8}''$ expanded metal rib lath. The forming material is left in place. Floor slabs are reinforced with $\frac{1}{4}''$ (N0. 2) bars, 12" o.c. both ways, or with the $6'' \times 6''$ welded wire mesh; generally, no other reinforcing is used.

Precast, reinforced concrete slabs of similar thickness can also be used on floors. Asphalt tile or other floor finishes can be put over the concrete slabs.

2.7.3 Reinforced Concrete Joists

Occasionally, reinforced concrete joists are used in light construction (Fig. 2–141). In the case of either a concrete floor with a basement below or a fireproof flat roof, the use of concrete joists is appropriate. These roofs are manufactured in many areas, so a source can usually be found near any given building site. Depth and reinforcing size are custom designed according to the loads and the spans required. Concrete joists are generally spaced 24" o.c. and bear on concrete block walls. The slab can be poured over wood forming placed between the joists, or the permanent forming materials, mentioned above, can be used.

Another method utilizes filler block laid tightly between the concrete joists and resting on the joists. A 2" slab is poured over the filler block to form the floor or the roof. Precast concrete joists are designed for each specific job and are delivered to the site, ready to be installed.

2.8
STEEL FRAME CONSTRUCTION

The American Iron and Steel Institute estimates that steel will capture 25% of the building market by the year 2000. Just as today's standard for design and construction of wood frame houses has evolved over time, the best techniques for engineering a steel frame house are still being developed.

A steel frame house is similar to a stick frame house but with some significant differences. Steel framing

members consist of two basic components that are C-shaped in section. Studs, joists, and rafters are made with members that have flanges folded inward about $\frac{1}{4}''$ at their open corners. Studs come with prepunched holes in their webs for electrical conduits. Joists and rafters can have solid webs, or they can be prepunched. The other basic components are tracks; they have solid webs and do not have the folded corners on the legs. Tracks are used both as sill plates and top plates and as part of posts or headers when combined with studs.

Steel studs, joists, rafters, and tracks come in various dimensions that differ in regular increments. Unlike wood dimensions, steel dimensions are a net figure; that is, 6" means 6". Studs are measured from their outside dimensions, and tracks are measured from the inside of their legs. A 6" stud fits snugly into the track. The assembly is held together by self-tapping screws driven through the legs of the track and the legs of the stud.

Steel components are surprisingly light for their strength. Studs are often shipped nested together in bundles of ten, and one person can pick up and carry a bundle of 10′ studs with relative ease. Another attractive aspect of steel framing is its strength. You can increase the strength and the load-bearing capabilities of the member simply by increasing the thickness or gauge of the material. You do not have to increase the dimensions of the member; 12 gauge is stronger and heavier than 20 gauge.

A steel house is put together in small pieces, just as the typical platform frame house of wood. The foundations are the same for wood or steel, but with steel it is important to trowel the top of the foundation smooth because the steel track is not as forgiving as a wood mudsill atop a layer of sill sealer. A flat, level foundation is essential.

Accurate layout of framing members is important in any system, but with steel, layout accuracy takes on greater importance. Rafters must be over either a post or a double stud. If the house is more than 1 story tall, posts and studs bear on a plate that is supported either by a joist or by a short piece of stud called a *web stiffener* placed in the joist track directly under the post or the stud (Figs. 2–142 through 2–145). Loads are transferred to the foundation by corresponding posts and studs in the

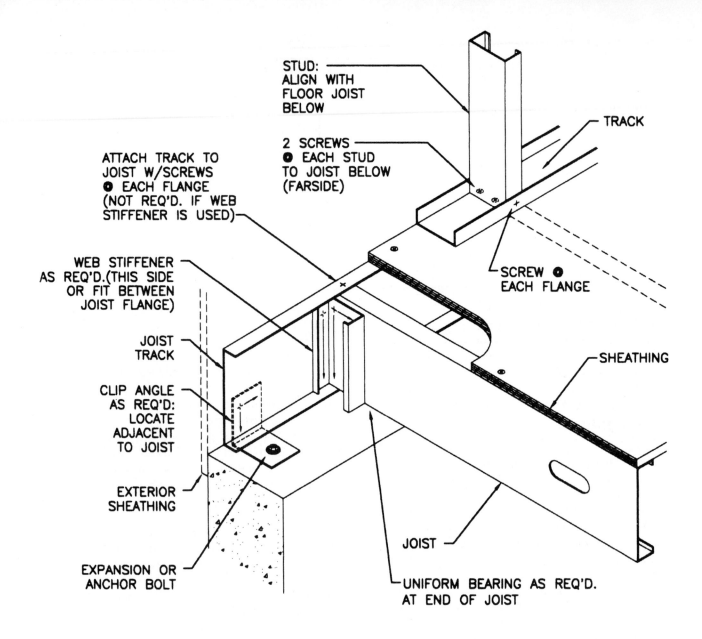

STUD:
ALIGN WITH
FLOOR JOIST
BELOW

TRACK

2 SCREWS
● EACH STUD
TO JOIST BELOW
(FARSIDE)

ATTACH TRACK TO
JOIST W/SCREWS
● EACH FLANGE
(NOT REQ'D. IF WEB
STIFFENER IS USED)

SCREW ●
EACH FLANGE

WEB STIFFENER
AS REQ'D.(THIS SIDE
OR FIT BETWEEN
JOIST FLANGE)

JOIST
TRACK

SHEATHING

CLIP ANGLE
AS REQ'D:
LOCATE
ADJACENT
TO JOIST

EXTERIOR
SHEATHING

JOIST

EXPANSION OR
ANCHOR BOLT

UNIFORM BEARING AS REQ'D.
AT END OF JOIST

NOTE: SEE B.21 FOR
ALTERNATE DETAILS

Figure 2–142 Floor joists bearing on the foundation.

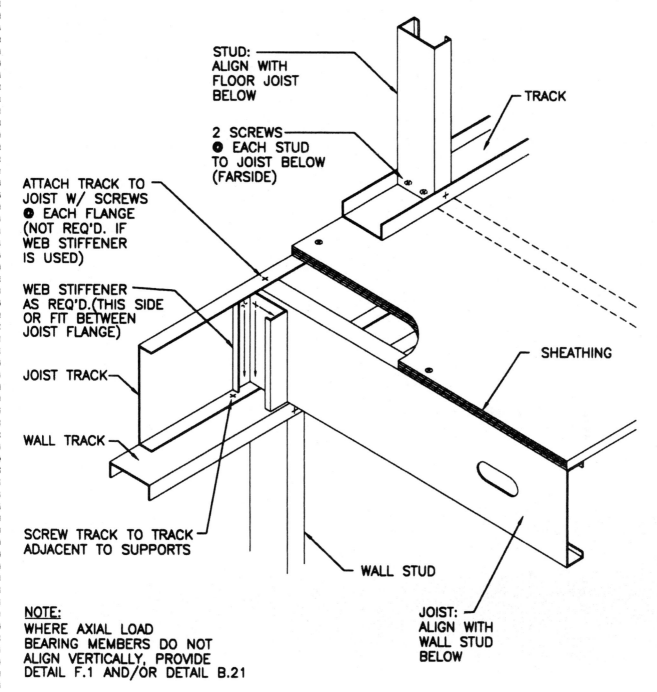

STUD:
ALIGN WITH
FLOOR JOIST
BELOW

TRACK

2 SCREWS
⊙ EACH STUD
TO JOIST BELOW
(FARSIDE)

ATTACH TRACK TO
JOIST W/ SCREWS
⊙ EACH FLANGE
(NOT REQ'D. IF
WEB STIFFENER
IS USED)

WEB STIFFENER
AS REQ'D.(THIS SIDE
OR FIT BETWEEN
JOIST FLANGE)

JOIST TRACK

WALL TRACK

SCREW TRACK TO TRACK
ADJACENT TO SUPPORTS

WALL STUD

SHEATHING

JOIST:
ALIGN WITH
WALL STUD
BELOW

NOTE:
WHERE AXIAL LOAD
BEARING MEMBERS DO NOT
ALIGN VERTICALLY, PROVIDE
DETAIL F.1 AND/OR DETAIL B.21

Figure 2–143 Floor framing at an exterior wall.

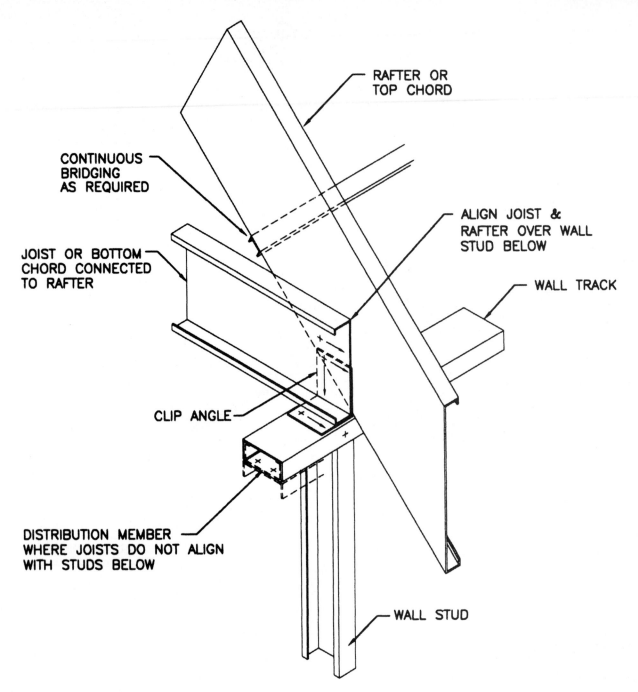

RAFTER OR
TOP CHORD

CONTINUOUS
BRIDGING
AS REQUIRED

ALIGN JOIST &
RAFTER OVER WALL
STUD BELOW

JOIST OR BOTTOM
CHORD CONNECTED
TO RAFTER

WALL TRACK

CLIP ANGLE

DISTRIBUTION MEMBER
WHERE JOISTS DO NOT ALIGN
WITH STUDS BELOW

WALL STUD

Figure 2–144 Roof eave.

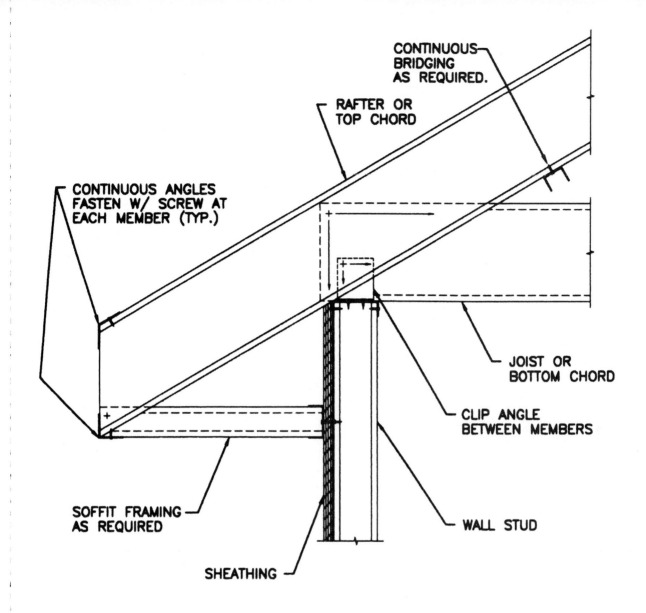

CONTINUOUS BRIDGING AS REQUIRED.

RAFTER OR TOP CHORD

CONTINUOUS ANGLES FASTEN W/ SCREW AT EACH MEMBER (TYP.)

JOIST OR BOTTOM CHORD

CLIP ANGLE BETWEEN MEMBERS

SOFFIT FRAMING AS REQUIRED

WALL STUD

SHEATHING

NOTE:
WHERE AXIAL LOAD BEARING MEMBERS DO NOT ALIGN VERTICALLY, PROVIDE DETAIL F.1

Figure 2–145 Roof eave and soffit.

lower floors. When you lay out first-floor walls, you are laying out the roof framing. Screws for steel frame walls must be driven from both sides of the track into the legs of the stud. Screwing steel framing components to one another is not difficult, but it is time-consuming.

Complicated roofs, low-pitch roofs, and most hip roofs can be built with wood for less cost than steel because wood truss assemblies are standardized and factory built. However, almost all roofs can be framed with steel if you have the time and the budget.

Potentially severe energy penalties can accompany steel framing. Steel has very high conductive capabilities, which provide a direct flow of heat out of a building in heating climates and into a building in cooling climates. Steel framing conducts 10 times more heat than wood framing. When a building envelope is insulated only in the cavities between framing members, the steel framing reduces the insulation's performance by more than 50%, versus 10% to 15% for wood framing (Table 2–11).

In an attempt to understand the energy loss problems associated with steel framing, the American Iron and Steel Institute, in conjunction with the NAHB Research Center, ran tests on a variety of wall systems. The results of these tests are published in the *Thermal Design Guide for Exterior Walls*, which includes tables of expected *R* values for several steel stud wall sections (Table 2–12 and Fig. 2–146). These tests looked at simple walls built with steel studs without openings, headers, corners, and partition leads, all of which increase heat loss. The tests also did not study the conductive heat loss from stud walls through their connections to concrete foundations and steel roof trusses.

While performing infrared thermography of a steel frame home, the Bonneville Power Administration (BPA) staff found interior wall surface temperatures of 45° over steel studs when the outside temperature was 40°. These temperatures occurred even though the exterior of the wall was sheathed with *R*-6 foam and the 6″ wall cavities were filled with insulation. This study discovered that heat traveled vertically down through the steel to the foundation. The engineers also found that where steel walls connected directly to steel roof trusses, exterior foam on the studs only redirected heat flow up through studs and through the uninsulated truss tails. Another finding of these studies was that *R*-6 foam located inside the studs worked more effectively than foam on the exterior.

Recommendations to address energy concerns include using foam sheathing (*R*-5 to *R*-10) over steel frame walls and filling wall cavities with *R*-11 batts that are a full 16″ or 24″ wide. Spacing studs 24″ o.c. rather than 16″ o.c. can reduce the amount of thermal loss by about 10%. The use of steel from the foundation wall up requires that exterior foam insulation extends below grade. The bottoms of cantilevers and steel floor joists must be covered when they are over unheated garages, attic spaces, and vented crawl spaces. If you use foam sheathing, you must install steel bracing in the frame; also, you should fill headers and corners with fiberglass before assembling them. Attaching siding can be a problem because it cannot be attached to the foam sheathing directly. You may use a layer of plywood or OSB underneath the foam and nail it through to the sheathing. Some steel framers reduce heat loss by using wood trusses and wood sills instead of steel.

Some companies are designing proprietary framing systems using steel in more efficient configurations. For example, Techbuilt Systems, Inc., of Cleveland, Ohio, has installed Thermotech 21® in over two hundred structures. Only four bolts penetrate the thermal break that separates 1″ × 2″ steel tubes at the exterior and interior of the wall (Fig. 2–147).

Table 2–11 Framing and wall R values.

Framing and Spacing	Nominal Cavity Insulation	Wood Frame[c]	Steel Frame[d]
2 × 4, 16″ o.c.[a]	R-11	R-9.0	R-5.5
	R-13	R-10.1	R-6.0
	R-15	R-11.2	R-6.4
2 × 4, 24″ o.c.[b]	R-11	R-9.4	R-6.6
	R-13	R-10.7	R-7.2
	R-15	R-11.9	R-7.8
2 × 6, 16″ o.c.[c]	R-19	R-15.1	R-7.1
	R-21	R-16.2	R-7.4
2 × 6, 24″ o.c.[d]	R-19	R-16.0	R-8.6
	R-21	R-17.2	R-9.0
2 × 8, 16″ o.c.[a]	R-25	R-20.1	R-7.8
2 × 8, 24″ o.c.[b]	R-25	R-21.2	R-9.6

SOURCE: *Environmental Building News*, Vol. 3, No. 4.
NOTES:
C-channel metal studs are 16 gauge or thinner.
Wall R-values are without sheathing or air films.
[a]Assumes that 11.9% of wall area is framing.
[b]Assumes that 8.9% of wall area is framing.
[c]Values for wood are calculated using the parallel path method.
[d]Values for steel are from ASHRAE Standard 90.1.

Table 2–12 Expected *R* values for steel stud wall sections.

(A) Suggested Insulation Levels for Steel Frame Construction (Refer to Thermal Zone Map of Fig. 2–146 for Steel Framing)				
Zone	Annual Degree-Day Demand	Cavity Insulation	Wall Construction	Exterior Insulated Sheathing	Effective Wall R Value
Blue	>7000	R-19	2 × 6	R-10	20
		R-11	2 × 4	R-13	21
Green	5000–7000	R-19	2 × 6	R-5	15
		R-11	2 × 4	R-7	15
Yellow	4000–5000	R-19	2 × 6	R-2.5	12.5
		R-11	2 × 4	R-5.0	13.5
Red	<4000	R-19	2 × 6	0	10
		R-11	2 × 4	0	8.5

(B) Equivalent Insulation Systems for Steel Frame Construction								
Wall R value	13		13.5		15		20	
Framing	Wood	Steel	Wood	Steel	Wood	Steel	Wood	Steel
ASHRAE ref.	RW55		RW45B		RW13A		RW58	
Cavity insulation R value	12	11	11	13	11	11	12	15
Exterior sheathing	½″ plywood + alum.siding	1″ XPS	⅝″ cedar + 4″ brick	1″ XPS	1″ polyiso. + stucco	1½″ XPS	1½″ polyiso. + alum. siding	2″ XPS

NOTES:
1. Steel studs are $3\frac{5}{8}″ \times 1\frac{5}{8}″$ @ 24″.
2. Wood studs are nominal 2″ × 4″ @ 16″.
3. Interior sheathing is ½″ gypsum wallboard for both.
4. Information on the wood system is from the *ASHRAE Handbook*.

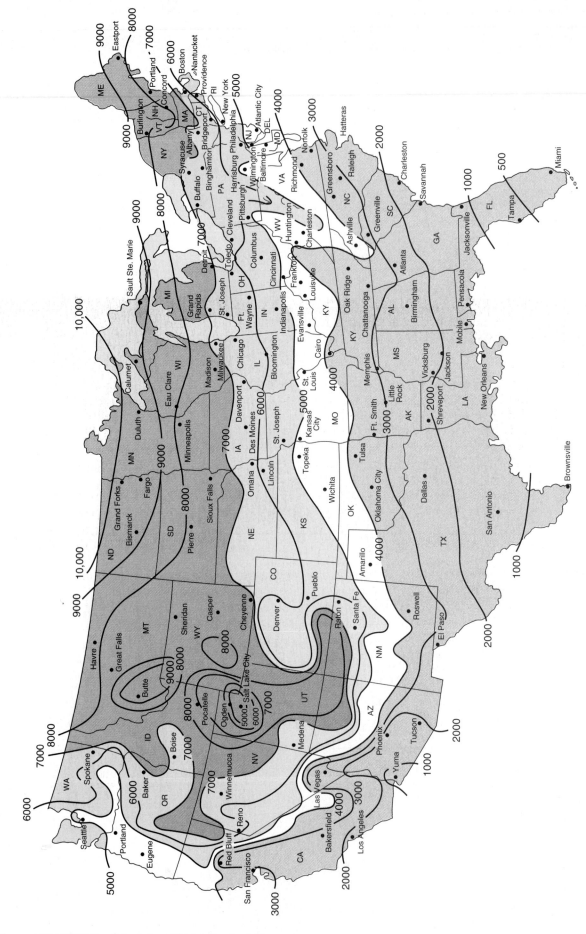

Figure 2–146 Thermal zone map for steel framing.

CHAPTER 2 Principles of Light Construction

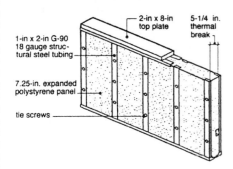

Figure 2–147 The Thermotech wall is one of a number of alternatives that use a thermal break to reduce energy loss. (*Architectural Record,* September 1995)

2.9

INSULATING CONCRETE FORM (ICF) SYSTEMS

Stay-in-place, insulating concrete forms (ICFs) made from expanded or extruded polystyrene foam have become a much-discussed alternative to wood framing. ICFs are hollow blocks, panels, or planks that are made of rigid foam and that are erected and filled with concrete to form the structure and insulation of exterior walls. ICFs are cost competitive with frame construction and deliver a product that is more energy efficient, comfortable, durable, and resistant to natural elements. Virtually any house design that can be built with wood or steel frame can be built with ICFs, although an ICF wall has greater thickness, greater weight, and a higher *R* value.

Table 2–13 lists the ICFs available in the United States as of the summer of 1995. They all work on the same principle—filling forms with concrete—but there are

three major differences:

1. the size of the form unit and the ways they connect to one another,
2. the shape of the cavities into which the concrete goes, and
3. whether the formwork has surfaces that materials can be fastened with a screw or nail.

This table classifies the systems according to size and connection method: panel, plank, and block (Fig. 2–148). It also classifies the systems by the type of concrete wall that is created: flat, grid, and post-and-beam (Fig. 2–149).

Panel systems are the largest units, as big as 4′ × 8′. Plank systems consist of long (usually 8′), narrow (8″–12″) planks of foam held a constant distance apart by steel or plastic ties. Block systems include units ranging from standard concrete block size, 8″ × 16″, to a much larger 16″ high by 4′ long.

Each system has one of three distinct cavity shapes: flat, grid, or post-and-beam (Figs. 2–150 through 2–153). These systems produce different shapes of concrete beneath the foam. Flat cavities produce a concrete wall of constant thickness. Grid cavities are "wavy," both horizontally and vertically. Post-and-beam cavities are filled with concrete only every few feet horizontally and vertically. Many of the systems have a fastening surface, which is of material other than the foam, embedded in the units that can be nailed into, similarly to a stud or a furring strip (Fig. 2–154).

Detailed information on ICF systems and construction procedures is contained in *Insulating Concrete Forms: A Construction Manual* by Pieter A. VanderWert and W. Keith Munsell. This manual, published by McGraw-Hill, was sponsored by the Portland Cement Association and is available through the association or the publisher.

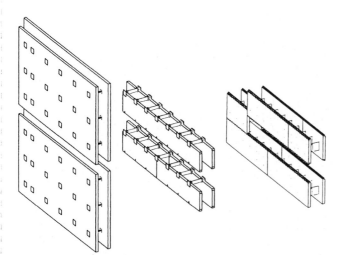

Figure 2–148 ICF formwork made with the three basic units: panel (left), plank (center), and block (right).

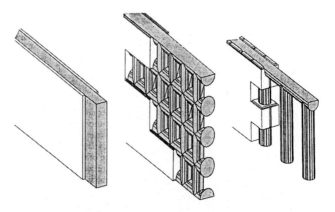

Figure 2–149 Cutaway diagrams of ICF walls with the three basic cavity shapes: flat (left), grid (center), and post-and-beam (right).

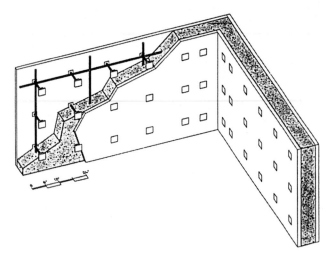

Figure 2–150 Cutaway diagram of a flat panel wall.

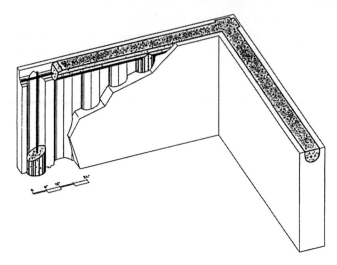

Figure 2–152 Cutaway diagram of a post-and-beam panel wall.

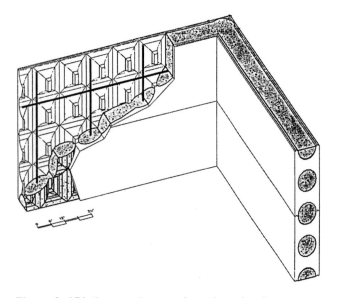

Figure 2–151 Cutaway diagram of a grid panel wall.

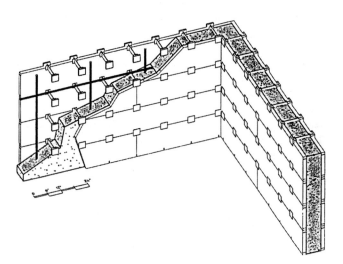

Figure 2–153 Cutaway diagram of a flat plank wall.

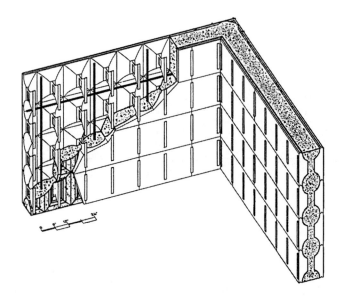

Figure 2–154 Cutaway diagram of a grid block wall with fastening surfaces.

Table 2–13 Available ICF systems.[a]

System	Dimensions[b] (Width × Height × Length)	Fastening Surface	Notes
1. Panel systems:			
Flat panel systems			
R-FORMS	8″ × 4′ × 8′	Ends of plastic ties	Assembled in the field; different lengths of ties available to form different panel widths.
Styrofoam	10″ × 2′ × 8′	Ends of plastic ties	Shipped flat and folded out in the field; can be purchased in larger/smaller heights and lengths.
Grid panel systems			
ENER-GRID	10″ × 1′3″ × 10′	None	Other dimensions also available; units made of foam/cement mixture.
RASTRA	10″ × 1′3″ × 10′	None	Other dimensions also available; units made of foam/cement mixture.
Post-and-beam panel systems			
Amhome	9⅜ × 4′ × 8′	Wooden strips	Assembled by the contractor from foam sheet. Includes provisions to mount wooden furring strips into the foam as a fastening surface.
2. Plank systems			
Flat plank systems			
Diamond Snap-Form	1′ × 1′ × 8′	Ends of plastic ties	
Lite-Form	1′ × 8″ × 8′	Ends of plastic ties	
Polycrete	11″ × 1′ × 8′	Plastic strips	
QUAD-LOCK	8″ × 1′ × 4′	Ends of plastic ties	
3. Block systems			
Flat block systems			
AAB	11.5″ × 16¾″ × 4′	Ends of plastic ties	
Fold-Form	1′ × 1′ × 4′	Ends of plastic ties	Shipped flat and folded out in the field.
GREENBLOCK	10″ × 10″ × 3′4″	Ends of plastic ties	
SmartBlock Variable Width Form	10″ × 10″ × 3′4″	Ends of plastic ties	Ties inserted by the contractor; different-length ties available to form different block widths.
Grid block systems with fastening surfaces			
I.C.E. Block	9¼″ × 1′4″ × 4′	Ends of steel ties	
Polysteel	9¼″ × 1′4″ × 4′	Ends of steel ties	
REWARD	9¼″ × 1′4″ × 4′	Ends of plastic ties	
Therm-O-Wall	9¼″ × 1′4″ × 4′	Ends of plastic ties	
Grid block systems without fastening surfaces			
Reddi-Form	9¼″ × 1′ × 4′	Optional	Plastic fastening surface strips available.
SmartBlock Standard Form	10″ × 10″ × 3′4″	None	
Post-and-beam block systems			
ENERGYLOCK	8″ × 8″ × 2′8″	None	
Featherlite	8″ × 8″ × 1′4″	None	
KEEVA	8″ × 1′ × 4′	None	

[a]All systems are listed by brand name.
[b]"Width" is the distance between the inside and outside surfaces of the foam of the unit. The thickness of the concrete inside will be less, and the thickness of the completed wall with finishes added will be greater.

AUTOCLAVED, AERATED CONCRETE BLOCK

A solid but lightweight concrete block that has an *R* value of about 30 is now being distributed in the United States by Hebel Southeast of Atlanta, Georgia.[3] The Hebel Group of Germany, the parent company, has been producing the system for sale outside the United States for more than fifty years (Fig. 2–155).

The block, called *precast, autoclaved, aerated concrete*, is 25″ long and 10″ tall, and it comes in three widths: 4″, 8″,

and 10″. The blocks, which can be cut with a bandsaw, are made of sand, lime, cement, and water. The wider blocks can be used for exterior load-bearing walls, and the narrower 4″ version is designed for partition walls.

The blocks have a high *R* value, exceeding 30 for the 8″ width, because they contain a lot of air. According to Michael Sweeney, Hebel's marketing manager, the blocks are about 80% air by volume. The air is contained in what Hebel calls *noncapillary pockets*, or *bubbles*. The air comes from an expanding agent added to the raw materials while they are in liquid form. The mix is then poured into a mold and allowed to rise. The blocks are cut to dimension and are then steam cured under pressure in a huge oven called an *autoclave*.

The company says that the 8″ blocks have a 4-h fire rating and the 4″ blocks have a 2-h rating. The blocks

_____

[3] The company distributing the material is Hebel Southeast, 3340 Peachtree Road NE, Suite 150, Atlanta, GA 30326 (1–404–812–7400).

Figure 2–155 Workman lifts a lightweight Hebel unit into place.

are available in three strength categories, and they have an average compressive strength ranging from 363 psi to 1090 psi. They are commonly covered with stucco but can be left unfinished. The Southern Building Code Congress has evaluated the material and has found it suitable for use in building load-bearing exterior walls.

STRAW BALE CONSTRUCTION

Baled straw is an inexpensive and environmentally sound material for the construction of low-scale buildings. Straw bale construction dates back 400 years in Germany, but it was first used for housing in the United States only a century ago in the Sand Hills of southwestern Nebraska.

The density of straw bales makes them a highly energy efficient building material. Straw buildings are less expensive to cool in the summer and heat in the winter, and their walls tend to absorb excess sound. Bale sizes range from 18″ deep by 35″–40″ long with an *R* value of 43, to 23″ deep by 43″–47″ long with an *R* value of 55.

Straw bale construction can be of two types: (1) load-bearing, in which the straw bales carry roof, wind, and other loads (Figs. 2–156 and 2–157); and (2) nonload-bearing, in which a post-and-beam structural system supports building loads with the straw bales acting as infill (Fig. 2–158).

A concrete foundation wall is poured, and reinforcing steel rods are embedded vertically around the perimeter. The first row of straw bales is impaled on the reinforcing steel. Subsequent rows are stacked like large bricks in a running bond pattern. Interior and exterior walls are typically finished with cement or adobe plaster.

The roof of a load-bearing straw bale building is connected to a wood roof plate or a concrete bond beam that rests on the stacked straw bales. The roof plate is also tied to the building foundation with threaded rods driven through the bales. The rods are connected at the bottom to anchors embedded in the foundation, and they are bolted at the top to the roof plate or the bond beam.

Foundations for post-and-beam straw bale systems are similar to those in load-bearing construction except that the structural frame and the roof are assembled before the straw bale walls are raised. The bales are attached to vertical posts at every course with strips of expanded metal lath, which are nailed to the post. Metal lath strips attach the bales to the horizontal roof plate or bond beam.

Building code officials generally prefer post-and-beam straw bale houses over load-bearing structures, although both types have been approved by Arizona and California building departments under the Uniform Building Code provisions for experimental structures.

The greatest danger to straw bale construction is moisture. If bales become wet and are not permitted to dry

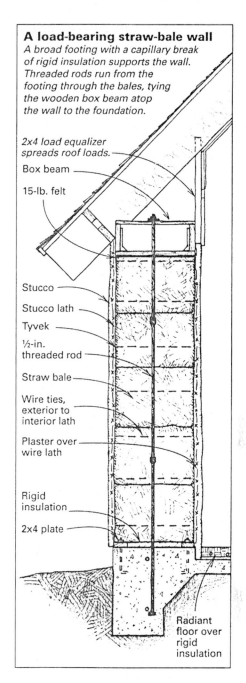

A load-bearing straw-bale wall
A broad footing with a capillary break of rigid insulation supports the wall. Threaded rods run from the footing through the bales, tying the wooden box beam atop the wall to the foundation.

2x4 load equalizer spreads roof loads.
Box beam
15-lb. felt

Stucco
Stucco lath
Tyvek
½-in. threaded rod
Straw bale
Wire ties, exterior to interior lath
Plaster over wire lath
Rigid insulation
2x4 plate
Radiant floor over rigid insulation

Figure 2–156 Example of load-bearing straw bale construction.

out, they will rot. It is important to start with dry bales and to keep them dry during construction. A vapor barrier is installed on the foundation below the first course of bales to keep water from wicking up into the straw. Vapor barriers are usually not applied to wall surfaces because they do not allow the straw to breathe.

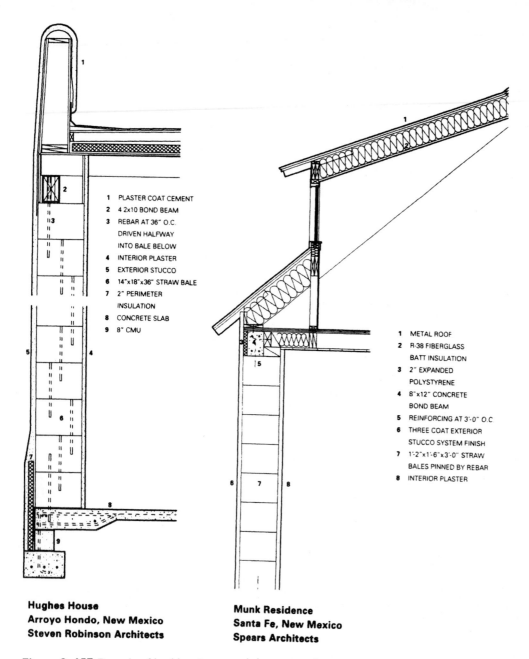

Hughes House
Arroyo Hondo, New Mexico
Steven Robinson Architects

1 PLASTER COAT CEMENT
2 4 2x10 BOND BEAM
3 REBAR AT 36" O.C.
  DRIVEN HALFWAY
  INTO BALE BELOW
4 INTERIOR PLASTER
5 EXTERIOR STUCCO
6 14"x18"x36" STRAW BALE
7 2" PERIMETER
  INSULATION
8 CONCRETE SLAB
9 8" CMU

Munk Residence
Santa Fe, New Mexico
Spears Architects

1 METAL ROOF
2 R-38 FIBERGLASS
  BATT INSULATION
3 2" EXPANDED
  POLYSTYRENE
4 8"x12" CONCRETE
  BOND BEAM
5 REINFORCING AT 3'-0" O.C.
6 THREE COAT EXTERIOR
  STUCCO SYSTEM FINISH
7 1'-2"x1'-6"x3'-0" STRAW
  BALES PINNED BY REBAR
8 INTERIOR PLASTER

Figure 2–157 Example of load-bearing, straw bale construction.

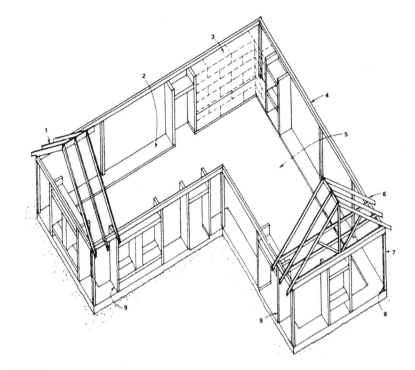

1. 2x10 ROOF JOISTS AT 24" O.C. WITH NONBEARING RIDGE BOARD AND COLLAR TIES AS REQUIRED
2. 4" CONCRETE LEDGE AT PERIMETER WITH WATERPROOFING AS REQUIRED
3. STRAW BALE INFILL BETWEEN DOOR AND WINDOW ASSEMBLIES
4. PERIMETER BEAM ABOVE TOP BALE COURSE, SIZE AS REQUIRED
5. POURED CONCRETE FOUNDATION AND FLOOR SLAB
6. PRE-ENGINEERED WOOD TRUSSES AT 24" O.C.
7. 4x4 WOOD POST
8. 1/8-INCH STEEL POST-BASE CONNECTOR
9. WINDOW AND DOOR ASSEMBLIES CONSTRUCTED OF 2x4s AND PLYWOOD OR PRESSED STRAWBOARD

Tillman House
Tucson, Arizona
Paul Weiner, Architect

Figure 2–158 Example of nonload-bearing, straw bale construction.

ROOF TYPES AND ROOF COVERINGS

The roof is a very important part of any building, large or small, and it should therefore receive careful consideration. We might say that a house is no better than the roof that covers it. Like an umbrella, it protects the structure from the elements; in some climates it is subjected to intense heat, almost everywhere to rain and dampness, and in many areas to driving winds. Not only is the roof extremely functional, but its shape and nature play a vital role in the architectural appearance and styling of a house, which is often designated by its roof type. In commercial buildings, however, the roof is often flat and obscured by parapet walls, and it is therefore less important as far as the building's appearance is concerned.

In years past, the snow load of buildings in northern areas required steep roofs. However, with the improvement of roofing materials and more engineering design in buildings, the design of modern roofs has become less restrictive. Because architects and builders now have available a generous selection of roof coverings for any desired architectural treatment, we find successful roofs of all types and slopes in almost every area of the country, regardless of climatic conditions.

All roofs should be built to provide positive drainage. Flat roofs should have a minimum pitch or have tapered rigid insulation to provide a minimum slope to roof drains.

2.12.1 Roof Types

The Flat Roof The flat roof is one of the simplest and most economical roofs as far as material is concerned (Fig. 2–159). The roof joists become the framing members of both the roof and the interior ceiling. Sizes and spans of joists must be adequate to support both the live load of the roof and the dead loads of the roofing and the finished ceiling. The spacing of wood roof joists is generally 16" o.c. Comparatively little air space is provided in a flat roof; therefore, batt-type or blanket insulation, with the vapor barrier near the interior side, is recommended between roof joists. All of the air cavities between the roof joists must be ventilated. Solid bridging should not be used in flat roofs; the blocking would prevent uniform air circulation.

Overhangs, for reason of weather protection or appearance, vary in width from 1' to 4'. The usual overhang is 2', so 4'-0" wide plywood panels can be conveniently ripped and used for soffits. Overhangs of the flat roof are simply cantilevered over the exterior wall plates; the joists are toenailed to the plates, or metal framing anchors can be used. If a boxed-in overhang is used, a header joist is recommended around the periphery of the roof (Fig. 2–160). The header joist becomes the backing for the finish fascia board, provides blocking for the soffit material, and tends to straighten the roof line. Overhangs from exterior walls that are parallel to the joists must be framed with *lookout joists* sometimes called *tail joists* (Figs. 2–104 and 2–160). Lookout joists are short and butt into a double long joist. Generally, the distance from

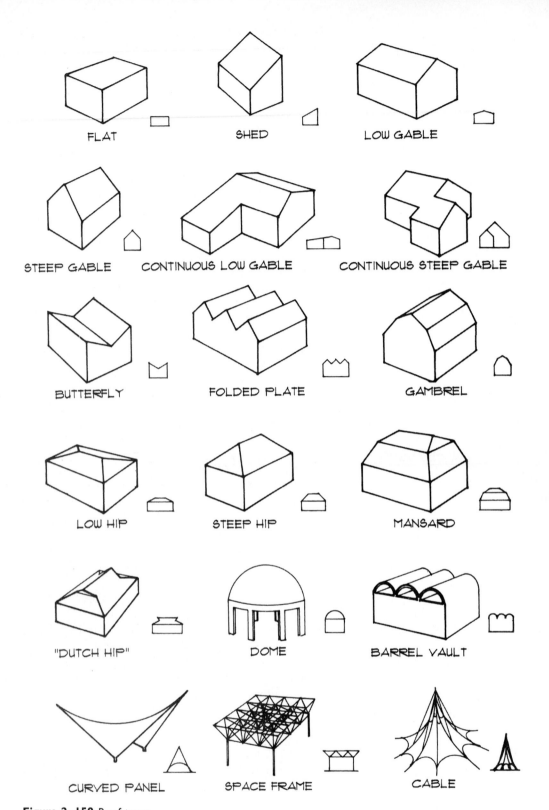

FLAT SHED LOW GABLE

STEEP GABLE CONTINUOUS LOW GABLE CONTINUOUS STEEP GABLE

BUTTERFLY FOLDED PLATE GAMBREL

LOW HIP STEEP HIP MANSARD

"DUTCH HIP" DOME BARREL VAULT

CURVED PANEL SPACE FRAME CABLE

Figure 2-159 Roof types.

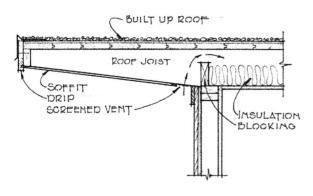

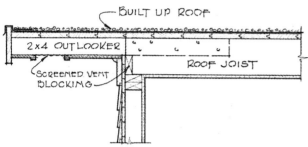

Figure 2–160 Flat roof with narrow fascia details.

the double-long joist to the wall line is the same as to the overhang. If wide joists are necessary, because of the span, the joist width is often tapered from the exterior wall to the outside end of the joist. This tapering of the joists prevents the fascia board from appearing too wide and heavy. Occasionally, to avoid wide fascias, narrow outlookers are lap nailed to the roof joists. Blocking is required on the top wall plate between each roof joist to provide nailing strips for the soffit and crown molding.

Flat roofs have the advantage of ease and flexibility of framing over odd building shapes and offset exterior walls. Other types of roofs often restrict the general shape of the building. Many architects resort to a flat roof when living spaces within the building do not conform to traditional shapes and relationships. Space planning can be almost unrestricted if a flat roof is used. However, the straight, horizontal roof line of a flat roof often appears hard and monotonous; variety and interest can be gained by combining other roof shapes with the flat roof, or by using several roof levels throughout the building. A watertight, built-up or single-ply membrane roof covering must be used on a flat roof, and metal gravel stops are put around the edges.

The Shed-Type Roof

The shed-type roof is framed very similarly to a flat roof, yet it has a definite slope (Fig. 2–159). As a rule, the slopes are made low, unless the shed is used in combination with gable-type roofs. Ceilings can be applied directly to the rafters to provide interest and variety to interior living spaces. The span of a sloping rafter is the horizontal distance between its supports. Shed rafters should be well anchored to the plates of the exterior wall.

The Gable Roof

Used for centuries, the gable roof is the traditional shape of most roofs. It consists of two inclined planes that meet at a ridge over the center of the house and slope down over the side walls. The inclined planes form a triangular shape at the ends of the house called a *gable* or *gable end* (Fig. 2–106). Framing of the gable roof is discussed in Section 2.4.1, "Platform Frame Construction." Many different slopes or pitches can be used with the gable roof, depending on the architectural treatment and roofing materials.

Roof pitches must be indicated on drawings, and there are several methods of expressing the slope (refer to Section 2.3).

Details of the framing and architectural treatments of the intersection of the roof and the walls (Fig. 2–161) are shown in *cornice details*. Steep gable roofs allow enough headroom for second-story living space, even though the floor area may not be as large as that of the first floor. Light and ventilation can be provided by dormers with windows that are framed out from the main roof (Fig. 2–103). In traditional, colonial-type houses, dormers must be symmetrically spaced on the roof; they should have good proportions so that they will appear light and neat. Massive dormers often ruin an otherwise attractively designed colonial-type house.

Low-slope gable roofs are characteristic of the newer, rambling ranch-type house; they usually have wide overhangs. The space below the roof can be used, if at all, for minor storage.

The Hip Roof

The hip roof is another conventional-type roof that is popular in many areas of the country (Fig. 2–159). The inclined roof planes slope to all outside walls, and the treatment of the cornice and roof overhang is identical around the entire house. It eliminates gable-end walls but requires more roofing material than a gable roof of comparative size. Usually, the plan is rectangular, in which case common rafters are used to frame the center portion of the roof. Hip rafters, which carry very little of the load, are used at the exterior corners of the sloping intersections. Valley rafters (Figs. 2–100 and 2–101), on the other hand, carry considerable loads and are used at the interior intersections of the roof planes. Short jack rafters join either the hip rafter and the wall plate or the valley rafter and the ridge.

More complex framing is required in hip roofs; hip, valley, and jack rafters require compound diagonal cuts at their intersections. For simple hip roofs, a roof layout is not necessary on the working drawings, but more complex roofs with ridges of different heights and other offsets would definitely require a roof layout drawing.

Trussed rafters are available in some areas for framing standard span and pitch hip roofs. Regular trusses are used in the center section along the ridge, and modified trusses are made to conform to the end slope of the hip.

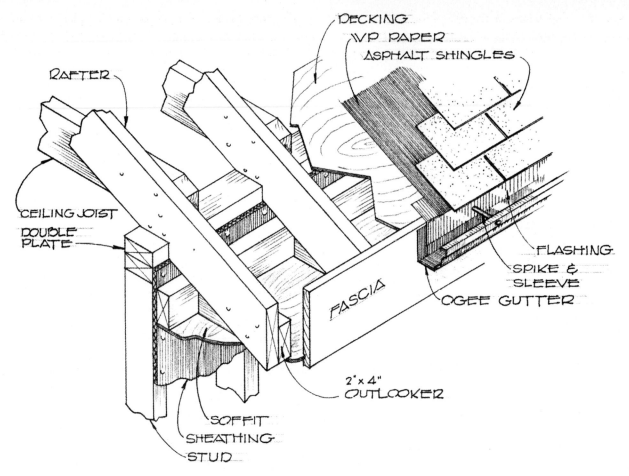

Figure 2–161 Roof construction at overhang with a boxed-in eave.

Like other roofs, hip roofs must be properly ventilated; because the roof covering is continuous over the higher areas of the roof, small metal vents or louvers are often employed on the rear side near the ridge to allow warm air to escape. Air inlets are provided by vents under the eaves.

Steep hip roofs often allow additional living space under the roof, similar to steep gable roofs. To be consistent, dormers on hip roofs usually have hip roofs as well.

The Dutch Hip Roof
A variation of the hip roof, the Dutch hip roof is framed similarly to the gable roof throughout the center section to the ends of the ridge, where double rafters are used (Fig. 2–159). The end hips are attached to the double rafters, are started below a louver, and extend over the corners of the building. The louvers at each end of the ridge allow more positive ventilation under the roof.

Because a hip roof can become more complex to frame than other roofs, the following method is offered *to lay out a working drawing for a hip roof:*

Using Fig. 2–162 as an example, draw the outline of the building, including all ells and offsets. Draw the main roof formed by the rectangle *ABCD*; the 45° hip

lines are drawn from the main corners and corners of the ells. The intersections of the 45° hip lines will locate the ridge lines.

Draw the 45° valley lines connecting all roof intersections. A Dutch hip is indicated at point *E*; the ridge end can be indicated at any location along the diago-

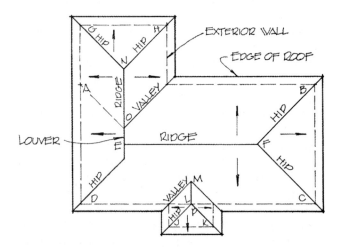

Figure 2–162 Layout of a hip roof.

nal hip lines, depending on the size of the louver used on the end elevation of the building.

Uniform overhangs can be drawn around the exterior wall lines, and hip lines can be extended to the corners of the overhangs.

This layout can be used regardless of the pitch that has been selected—low or steep slope. Hip roofs are more pleasing if the same pitch has been used on all planes of the roof. Rafters are drawn using either 16″ or 24″ o.c. spacing.

The Gambrel Roof The gambrel roof is typical of Dutch colonial houses, and it is also found on many farm buildings. Each slope has a break or change of pitch: the lower part is always steeper than the upper (Fig. 2–102). From a practical standpoint, this roof allows more headroom compared with a gable roof with the same ridge height. More labor is involved in framing a gambrel roof; as a result, it is seldom used in modern construction except on strictly colonial houses.

The Butterfly Roof The butterfly roof is similar to an inverted gable roof (Fig. 2–159). Caution should be exercised in the selection of a butterfly roof; roofers indicate that the intersection of the two inclined planes produces severe strain on the roof covering. Drainage of the valley is difficult, yet this drainage can be accomplished with the use of tapered cant strips under the roofing, which act very much as a saddle that is used to spread water away from a chimney on a sloping roof. A bearing partition should be used below the valley for a stable support for the rafters.

The Barrel-Vault Roof This roof employs precurved plywood panels or regular plywood attached to curved ribs (Fig. 2–159). The panels are custom designed and are made by authorized plywood manufacturers. With relatively thin cross sections, the curved, stressed-skin panels permit spanning long distances because of their arching action. Tie rods are usually required to counteract the thrust action when thinner panels are used. Insulation can be incorporated into the panels, and the underside of the panels can be used as the finished ceiling. Supported beams are uniformly spaced below the intersections of the vaults.

The Folded-Plate Roof This roof creates a roof line that is truly contemporary in profile (Fig. 2–159). Its form is the result of engineered functional design. Reinforced-concrete, folded-plate roofs have been in use for years. Corrugated metal, on a small scale, obtains its stiffness similarly because of its folded characteristic. However, it has been largely through the efforts of the American Plywood Association that the shape has been adapted to wood construction, mainly because of the high shear strength and rigidity of plywood.

The construction of a plywood folded-plate roof differs from conventional pitched roof construction in that the roof sheathing and framing are designed to act together as a large inverted V-shaped beam to span from end to end of the building. A multiple-bay roof is made of several such beams connected together side by side.

The inclined planes of the roof transfer their vertical loads to adjoining ridge and valley intersections, very much as crossbridging in conventional floor construction transfers a concentrated load to surrounding floor joists. Loads on the inclined planes are carried in shear by the plywood diaphragm action to the ends of the building and by horizontal thrust action to the sides of the building.

Vertical supports are necessary at the ends of the building under the valleys and along the sides of the building. Either a beam or a bearing wall can be used along the sides. Horizontal thrust that is transferred to the sides of the building must be counteracted by horizontal ties of steel or wood.

The analysis of a multiple-bay folded plate differs slightly in that at the interior valleys, additional support is gained by each plane supporting the other; for this reason, walls or vertical beams are not required, provided that the valley chords are adequately connected. Omission of supports below valleys, of course, increases the shear that must be resisted by the interior sloping planes. Horizontal chord stresses are greater then as well.

The following lists point out the advantages and disadvantages of the folded-plate roof as compared with other methods of roof construction:

Advantages

1. Trusses or other members that span from valley to valley are eliminated, thereby resulting in clear, uncluttered interiors.
2. Inasmuch as the plywood sheathing constitutes part of the structural unit, long spans are possible with small framing units.
3. A plywood ceiling can be used as a finish as well as for additional resistance to shear.
4. Assembly can be with nails only; no gluing is required, although it will improve rigidity.
5. Either conventional site construction or prefabrication can be employed. Components of the folded plate can be stressed-skin panels, or one or more full-length plates can be prefabricated.
6. Interesting form can be achieved economically for buildings of all sizes, from residences to large industrial structures.

Disadvantages

1. Drainage requires special attention on multiple-bay structures.
2. A well-designed folded-plate roof necessitates more roofing material. At least a 5:12 slope is recommended, since shear in the roof diaphragm diminishes with increase in slope.

3. Folded plates do not readily lend themselves to incorporation of a flat ceiling.

2.12.2 Roof Coverings

Many roofing materials are available for small buildings, and each has its advantages and limitations. Consequently, selection of the proper roofing material is of paramount importance. Thus, in selection of roofing materials, the following points should be considered:

- Slope of the roof, if any
- Quality or permanence required of the roof
- Inherent architectural features of the roofing in relation to the rest of the structure
- Cost of the roofing material

In areas subject to wind-driven snow or to the buildup of roof ice, which forms ice dams, the underlayment application in the eave area is modified to prevent ice dams from forcing water under the roofing, there by damaging ceilings, walls, and insulation (Fig. 2–163). Two layers of underlayment consisting of nonperforated Type 15 felt should be cemented together with asphalt cement from the edge of the roof up to a point that is at least 24′ inside the interior wall line of the building (Fig. 2–164). For wood shingle or wood shake roofs, this double underlayment should extend 36″ inside the interior wall line of the building.

The environment within the envelope of the building provides adequate warmth to prevent ice dams from forming above the heated space.

Built-Up Roofing A flat roof or a roof of very little slope must, of necessity, be covered with a completely watertight material. The majority of flat roofs are now covered with built-up roofing (see Fig. 2–165), which, if properly installed, is durable. On a wood deck, the first heavy layer of felt is nailed to the decking with galvanized roofing nails. Each succeeding layer of felt is mopped with either hot asphalt or hot coal-tar pitch. The top layer is then well mopped and covered with a thin layer of pea gravel, fine slag, or marble chips. This mineral surface protects the roof to some degree from the elements, and the lighter colors reflect the sun's rays from the building. For every 100 sq ft of roof, the use of 400 lb of gravel or 300 lb of slag is recommended.

Over smooth concrete decks, fewer piles are required, and the first layer of felt is mopped directly to the slab. Asphalt pitch can be used on steeper slopes than can coal-tar pitch, but the limiting slope for a built-up roof is 2:12, if gravel is expected to stay on the roof. Even on a 2:12 slope, gravel will lose its grip during heavy rains. Metal gravel stops, preferably copper, are fastened to the wood deck surrounding the entire roof. Proper use of base and cap flashing is shown in Figs. 2–166 and 2–167.

On flat roofs as well as pitched roofs, substantial and rigid roof decks play an important part in the success of the roof covering. Decks should be well nailed, clean, and dry before coverings are applied.

In roofing terminology, a *square* is an area of 100 sq ft; thus, a square of roofing material is the amount necessary to cover 100 sq ft. Requirements for built-up roof construction are summarized in Table D–6.

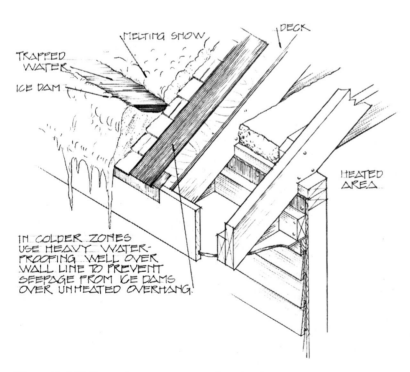

Figure 2–163 Preventing water seepage from ice dams.

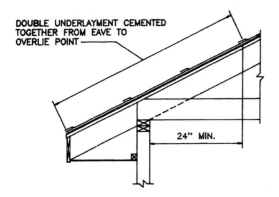

Figure 2–164 Eave flashing for asphalt shingles.

DOUBLE UNDERLAYMENT CEMENTED TOGETHER FROM EAVE TO OVERLIE POINT

24" MIN.

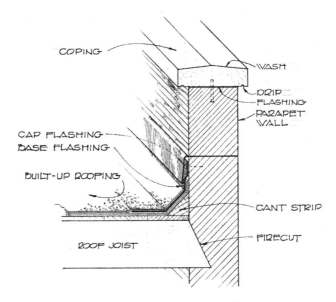

Figure 2–166 Roof flashing at a parapet wall.

COPING
WASH
DRIP FLASHING
PARAPET WALL
CAP FLASHING
BASE FLASHING
BUILT-UP ROOFING
CANT STRIP
FIRECUT
ROOF JOIST

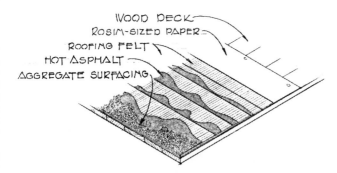

Figure 2–165 Built-up roof on wood deck (level to 2:12 pitch).

WOOD DECK
ROSIN-SIZED PAPER
ROOFING FELT
HOT ASPHALT
AGGREGATE SURFACING

Membrane Roofing In recent years, major advances have been made in the membrane roofing industry. High-strength, reinforced, synthetic sheets suitable for single-ply roofing systems have been developed. Although many membrane systems are installed over concrete roof decks or rigid insulation on metal decks, they can also be applied over wood decks. Most systems use mechanical fasteners to anchor the sheets to the roof deck. Special

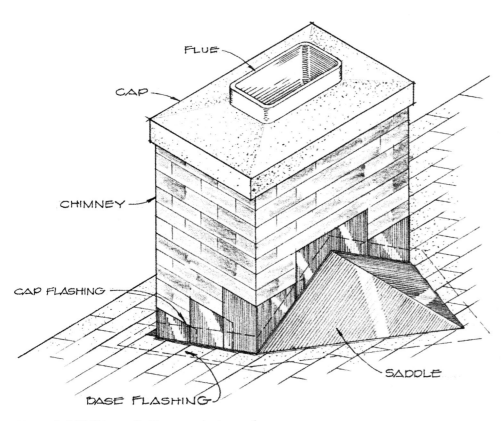

Figure 2–167 Chimney flashing on a sloping roof.

FLUE
CAP
CHIMNEY
CAP FLASHING
BASE FLASHING
SADDLE

flashings are installed at roof penetration. Seams are usually heat welded. Some systems require a stone ballast to stabilize the membrane during high winds. The majority of such systems are easily repaired, if damaged, and have a warranty.

Shingle Roofing

When a building has a sloping roof, more consideration must be given to the appearance of the roofing material. Shingles or multiple-unit type roofing materials are designed for sloping roofs; the incline allows water to drain off quickly without readily challenging the watertightness of the roof. The small, individual units of such roofing are also not subjected to stresses or shock from severe temperature changes; each piece can expand and contract individually without producing a noticeable effect, as in a built-up roof.

The degree of resistance to water penetration of shingle materials varies directly with the slope of the roof and indirectly with the amount of exposure of each unit to the weather. Usually, steeper slopes will allow more exposure of the units than flatter slopes because the water drains off more quickly. Strong winds tend to drive moisture under roof units unless some provision is made for sealing the edges or holding them down. This tendency is especially noticeable on lower slopes. Exposure to the weather is specified in inches. Some roofing materials are exposed 4″ between laps; other materials, for example, can be allowed 10″ exposure. However, manufacturers' recommendations should be followed in application of all roofing materials.

Currently, almost all shingles are based on either organic or glass fiber felt (Fig. 2–168). Each has its advantages. Glass fiber shingles are more fire resistant than organic shingles. They may lower insurance costs and may be required by code in certain locales. They are also more mildew resistant, are less affected by moisture absorption, and weigh less than organic shingles.

On the other hand, glass fiber shingles have poorer wind resistance and lower tear strength than organic shingles, and they are therefore more likely to crack in cold weather. They also show underlayment irregularities more than organic shingles. Requirements for asphalt shingle construction are summarized in Table D–1.

Sloping roofs in light construction are generally covered with one of the following roofing materials:

- Asphalt shingles
- Fiberglass shingles
- Wood shingles
- Wood shakes
- Slate shingles
- Clay tile units
- Cement tile units
- Metal shingles or panels

Asphalt Shingles

Asphalt-saturated felt, coated with various-colored mineral granules, is manufactured into strip shingles of different shapes and sizes. The most popular shape is the square-butt strip shingle, 12″ wide and 36″ long, with slotted butts to represent individual shin-

OWENS-CORNING'S FIBERGLAS® SHINGLE

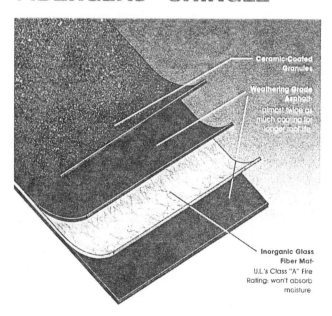

Ceramic-Coated Granules

Weathering Grade Asphalt
almost twice as much coating for longer roof life

Inorganic Glass Fiber Mat-
U.L.'s Class "A" Fire Rating; won't absorb moisture

THE ORGANIC SHINGLE

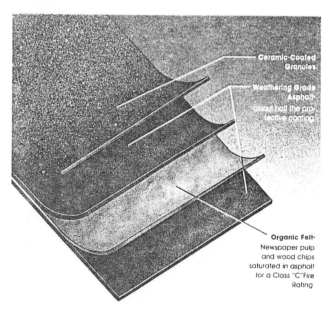

Ceramic-Coated Granules

Weathering Grade Asphalt
about half the protective coating

Organic Felt-
Newspaper pulp and wood chips saturated in asphalt for a Class "C" Fire Rating

Figure 2–168 Fiberglass and organic shingles. (Owens-Corning Product Information brochure)

gles at the exposure. Strips with hexagonal exposures are also made. The amount of 4″ or 5″ is the usual exposure to the weather, and weights per square vary according to the quality of the shingles. Quality shingles should weigh at least 235 lb/square.

The shingles are attached to the wood deck with 1¼″ galvanized roofing nails; four nails are needed for each strip. Each nail is driven about ½″ above each slot on the square-butt shingles. Two layers of shingles are then fastened with each nail, and the nailhead is just covered with the succeeding course. A double course is fastened at the eave. Occasionally, a starter strip of 53-lb roll roofing is used under the double layer of strip shingles at the eave. Along the gable edge of the roof, a strip of wood bevel siding is often nailed to the deck with the thin edge in, to guide water from the edge as it drains along the incline. Metal edge flashing can also be used at gable edges. Roof decks should be first covered with 15-lb asphalt felt, lapped 2″ horizontally and 4″ vertically, before asphalt shingles are applied.

Asphalt strip shingles can be used on low-slope roofs if self-sealing shingles are used. This type has asphalt adhesive under the exposed edges, which seals the edges against driving rains and capillary action. Often, starter strips near the eaves are full mopped with adhesive, rather than nailed, to prevent this moisture penetration.

To cover ridges and hips, strip shingles are cut into smaller pieces and are nailed over the ridges in a lapped fashion called a *Boston lap* (Fig. 2–169). Intersections of roofs and walls must be flashed with durable metal flashing. Valleys are flashed with either 28-gauge (minimum), galvanized, corrosion-resistant sheet metal or woven asphalt shingles. Both require an underlayment of Type 15 felt. Metal shall extend at least 8″ each way from the

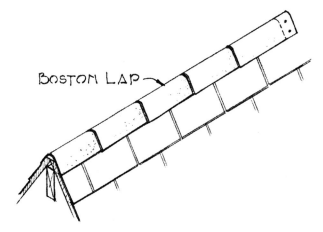

Figure 2–169 Covering a ridge with fiberglass shingles.

center line of the valley, with a minimum section overlap of 4″. The underlayment below a woven shingle valley must extend 18″ each way from the center line of the valley. A woven valley performs well when installed by a skilled worker. However, with some of the premium-grade laminated shingles, the adjacent shingles do not lie flat, so woven valleys should not be used. In an open valley, the shingles must be cemented, and exposed corners must be clipped to avoid lateral pick-up of water that runs down-slope (Figs. 2–170 and 2–171).

Although they burn readily when ignited, asphalt shingles are more resistant to combustion than wood shingles, and many local codes that prohibit wood shingle roofs will allow the use of asphalt shingle materials. Shingles are available in a variety of patterns (Fig. 2–172).

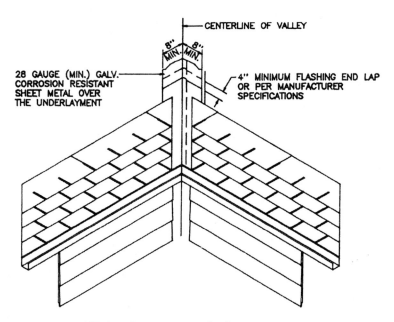

Figure 2–170 Flashing for an open roof valley.

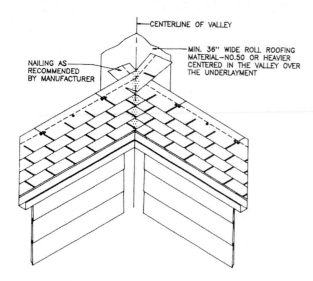

Figure 2–171 Flashing for a woven valley.

Fiberglass Shingles A variation of the asphalt shingle is known as the fiberglass roof shingle. It has better fire- and weathering-resistance qualities than the conventional asphalt shingle because of the inorganic fiberglass-mat base. With these additional properties, it is rapidly replacing the organic-based asphalt shingle in the marketplace. Those with self-sealing adhesive strips below each shingle can be used on low-slope (2:12 minimum) roofs if additional underlayment is provided. The self-sealing adhesive is activated by the heat of the sun to seal down the shingle tabs and help to prevent wind damage.

The worst problem with fiberglass shingles is thermal splitting. Fully adhered, self-sealing shingles with a low tear strength often split when cold shrinks them. Some splits are horizontal, between the line of shingle fasteners and the fully adhered bottom edge of the shingle, and some are vertical, usually directly over abutting shingles or slots. Organic-based shingles have about twice the tear strength of glass-fiber-based shingles and rarely, if ever, split.

Wood Shingles Wood shingles have been used for many years in residential construction. Because of their inherent combustibility, standard wood shingles or shakes are prohibited by many local fire codes. Recently, a chemical treatment process has been developed that makes it possible to obtain a wood shingle or shake with a Class B or Class C fire rating. In other than restricted areas, the standard wood shingle and shake is being used; they make handsome, durable roofs when properly installed. Wood weathers to a soft, mellow color after exposure to the elements and, if properly installed, can be expected to last 25 years.

Wood shingles are made chiefly of western red cedar, redwood, or cypress, all highly decay-resistant woods. Wood shingles are manufactured in 24″, 18″, and 16″ lengths and are graded into three categories. Table 2–14

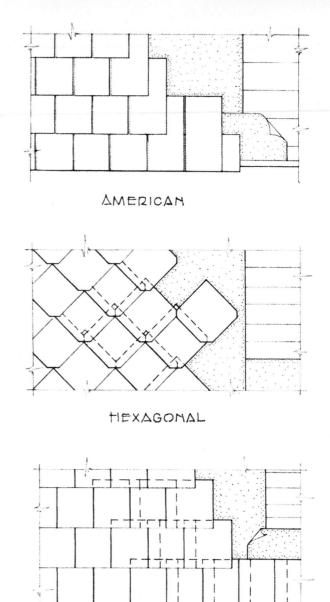

AMERICAN

HEXAGONAL

DUTCH LAP

Figure 2–172 Shingles are available in a variety of patterns.

describes each grade, and Figure 2–173 shows an example label. Each bundle of shingles should have a label specifying the grade in accordance with the rules of the Red Cedar Shingle and Handsplit Shake Bureau.

Shingles may be applied to roofs with solid or spaced sheathing. Shingles should be laid with a side lap of at least 1½″ in adjacent courses. Each shingle should be laid approximately ¼″ from an adjacent shingle and nailed with two corrosion-resistant nails only, placed not less than ¾″ from each edge and 1″ above the exposure line (Fig. 2–174). To prevent cupping after exposure, the better grades are cut from the logs so that the annular rings of the log are perpendicular to the flat surfaces of the shingles. Butt ends vary in thickness from ½″ to ¾″.

Table 2–14 Wood shingles grade description.

Grade	Length	Thickness (at Butt)	No. of Courses Per Bundle	Bdls. Cartons Per Square	Description
No. 1 BLUE LABEL	16″ (Fivex) 18″ (Perfections) 24″ (Royals)	0.40″ 0.45″ 0.50″	20/20 18/18 13/14	4 bdls. 4 bdls. 4 bdls.	The premium grade of shingles for roofs and sidewalls. These top-grade shingles are 100% heartwood, 100% clear, and 100% edge-grain.
No. 2 RED LABEL	16″ (Fivex) 18″ (Perfections) 24″ (Royals)	0.40″ 0.45″ 0.50″	20/20 18/18 13/14	4 bdls. 4 bdls. 4 bdls.	A good grade for many applications. Not less than 10″ clear on 16″ shingles, 11″ clear on 18″ shingles, and 16″ clear on 24″ shingles. Flat grain and limited sapwood are permitted in this grade.
No. 3 BLACK LABEL	16″ (Fivex) 18″ (Perfections) 24″ (Royals)	0.40″ 0.45″ 0.50″	20/20 18/18 13/14	4 bdls. 4 bdls. 4 bdls.	A utility grade for economy applications and secondary buildings. Not less than 6″ clear on 16″ and 18″ shingles, 10″ clear on 24″ shingles.
No. 4 UNDER-COURSING	16″ (Fivex) 18″ (Perfections)	0.40″ 0.45″	14/14 or 20/20 14/14 or 18/18	2 bdls. 4 bdls. 2 bdls. 4 bdls.	A utility grade for undercoursing on double-coursed sidewall applications or for interior accent walls.
No. 1 or No. 2 REBUTTED-REJOINTED	16″ (Fivex) 18″ (Perfections) 24″ (Royals)	0.40″ 0.45″ 0.50″	33/33 28/28 13/14	1 carton 1 carton 4 bdls.	Same specifications as above for No. 1 and No. 2 grades but machine trimmed for parallel edges with butts sawn at right angles. For sidewall application where tightly fitting joints are desired. Also available with smooth, sanded face.

Wood Shakes Wood shakes are manufactured in three different types: (1) handsplit and resawn, (2) taper split, and (3) straight split. The shakes are cut into 15″, 18″, and 24″ lengths. Each bundle should have a label specifying the grade in accordance with the requirements of the Red Cedar Shingle and Handsplit Shake Bureau.

Figure 2–173 Example label of wood shingle grade.

Table 2–15 describes each grade, and Figure 2–175 shows an example label.

Wood shakes are split from the log to reveal a natural, irregular, wood-grain surface. Their butts are thicker, ranging from ⅝″ to 1¼″, which produces strong horizontal course lines that give the roof a rustic quality. Thick, natural butt shingles are popular on ranch-type houses. In dry areas, wood shingles are usually put directly on plywood or tight wood decks. In damp areas, installation of nailing strips, spaced the same distance apart as the shingle exposure, provides ventilation directly below the shingles (Fig. 2–176). Air space below the shingles prolongs the life of the roof.

Shakes may be applied to roofs with solid or spaced sheathing. In areas with wind-driven snow, sheathing should be solid, and the shakes should be applied over an underlayment of not less than Type 15 felt applied single fashion. Shakes should be laid with a side lap of not less than 1½″ between joints in adjacent courses. Spacing between shakes should not be less than ⅜″ or more than ⅝″. Spacing of preservative-treated shakes can range

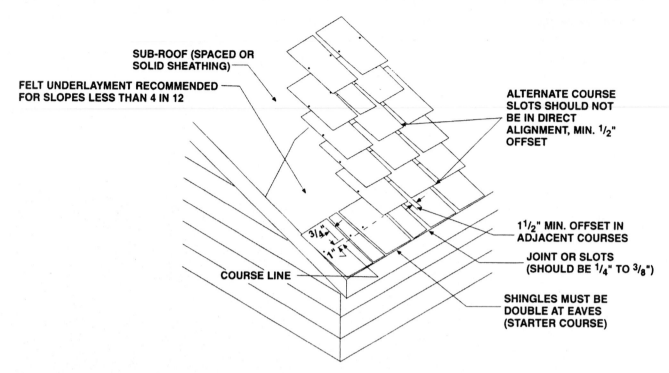

Figure 2–174 Wood shingle application.

Table 2–15 Wood shake grade description and example label.

| Grade | Length and Thickness | 18" Pack | | Description |
		Courses per Bdl.	Bdls. per Sq.	
No. 1 HANDSPLIT & RESAWN	15" Starter-Finish	9/9	5	These shakes have split faces and sawn backs. Cedar logs are first cut into desired lengths. Blanks or boards of proper thickness are split and then run diagonally through a bandsaw to produce two tapered shakes from each blank.
	18" × 1/2" Mediums	9/9	5	
	18" × 3/4" Heavies	9/9	5	
	24" × 3/8"	9/9	5	
	24" × 1/2" Mediums	9/9	5	
	24" × 3/4" Heavies	9/9	5	
No. 1 TAPERSAWN	24" × 3/8"	9/9	5	These shakes are sawn both sides.
	18" × 3/8"	9/9	5	
No. 1 TAPERSPLIT	24" × 1/2"	9/9	5	Produced largely by hand, using a sharp-bladed froe and a wood mallet. The natural shingle-like taper is achieved by reversing the block, end-for-end, with each split.
		20" Pack		
No. 1 STRAIGHTSPLIT	18" × 3/8" True-edge	14 Straight	4	Produced in the same manner as tapersplit shakes except that by splitting from the same end of the block, the shakes acquire the same thickness throughout.
	18" × 3/8"	19 Straight	5	
	24" × 3/8"	16 Straight	5	

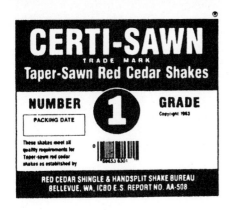

Figure 2–175 Example labels of wood shake grades.

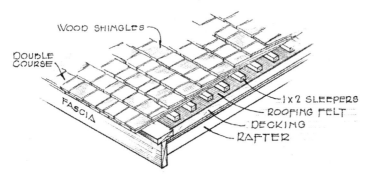

Figure 2–176 Installing wood shakes.

from ¼″ to ⅜″. Shakes are fastened to sheathing with two nails positioned approximately 1″ from each edge and 2″ above the exposure line. The starter course at the eave is doubled. Shakes should be laid with not less than 18″ interlayment of Type 30 felt shingled between each course so that no felt is exposed to the weather below the shake butts and between the shakes.

More course-line texture can be obtained by doubling each course, usually with No. 2 grade shingles below. Careful nailing technique must be used to ensure that joints in preceding and successive courses are staggered or are off-set at least 1½″ to allow good drainage and eliminate water penetration into the roof along the edges of the shingles. Shingles are loosely spaced to allow for swelling and shrinking, and zinc-coated or copper three-penny nails should be used; thicker shingles require larger nails.

Valley flashing for both wood shingles and wood shakes must be a minimum No. 28, galvanized, corrosion-resistant metal over an underlayment of at least Type 15 felt. Sections of flashing must overlap a minimum of 4″ and must extend 8″ from the center line each way for shingles and 11″ for shakes (Fig. 2–177). Maximum weather exposures are given in Table D–3, and requirements for wood shingle and shake construction are summarized in Table D–2. Hips and ridges can be covered by several methods, but the alternating Boston lap is the most popular as it retains the shingle texture to the edge of the ridge.

Many variations can be used in laying shingles. Sometimes every fifth or sixth course is doubled to vary the shadow line throughout the roof; sometimes the shingles are laid at random with no set course. Sometimes they are staggered so that alternate shingles project beyond adjoining ones; sometimes the course lines are made wavy to stimulate thatch roofs, with even the rakes and eaves turned over slightly to emphasize the effect of the thatch. Stained shingles are occasionally used to give definite color to the roof; staining also prolongs the life of the shingles. Regardless of the treatment and variations that are possible with wood shingles, the basic ware shedding principles of application must be followed.

Slate Roofing Natural slate taken from quarry beds and split into thin sheets has provided builders with one of our more aristocratic roofing materials. The marked cleavage of the slate rock imparts a natural, irregular, and pleasing surface to a roof, and the natural color variations of slate from different quarries produce subtle shades ranging from blacks and grays to blues and greens, and even browns and reds. Some slate changes in color after weathering. A well-laid slate roof is very durable and will outlast the life of the building. Slate is used only on the finest homes and more formal commercial buildings, yet its use has diminished in recent years.

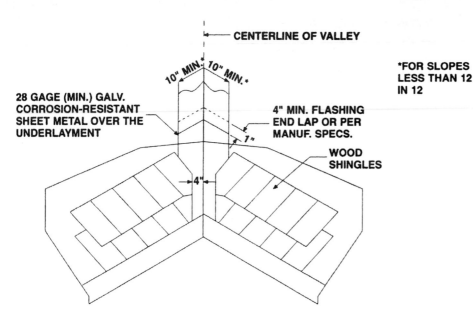

Figure 2–177 Wood shingle valley flashing.

Slate is split, cut into sheets, and punched for nails at the quarry. Common commercial sizes of the sheets are 12″ × 16″ and 14″ × 20″ and ³⁄₁₆″ or ¹⁄₄″ thick. Random sheets vary in size and thickness. Each sheet is attached with at least two copper nails; pieces near ridges and hips are often secured with copper wire and roofing cement. Slate roofs are heavy, and therefore the roof-framing members must be more substantial than those for wood or asphalt shingles or other light roofing materials. Because of the weight of the slate, the sheets hug the roof well against driving wind. Damaged slate sheets are difficult to replace after the roof has been completed; experienced slate roofers are required to install a slate roof properly.

Under most conditions, at least a 6:12 pitch is necessary for slate. Roof boards are nailed up tight over which a heavy roofing felt is applied and secured with roofing nails. A cant strip is used at the eaves to give the starter course the same slant as that of successive courses. Usually, the starter course is laid along the eave with the long dimension parallel to it, and the doubled course is started flush with the edge. Depending on the slope of the roof, slate should be laid with a 3″ or 4″ head lap. The head lap is the amount that a lower edge of a course laps or covers the top edge of the second course underneath it. To determine the amount of slate exposure, deduct the lap from the total length of the sheet, and divide the difference by 2. For example, the exposure of a 16″ long sheet with a 4″ head lap is $\frac{1}{2}(16 - 4) = 6$.

Slate can be laid with different exposures on the same roof, however. As with wood shingles, all joints must be staggered to shed water effectively. After random sizes are sorted, it is preferable for the slater to attach the large, thick slates near the eaves and the medium slates near the center, and to leave the smaller, thin pieces for the ridge area. This method produces rather interesting slate textures on a roof.

Hips and ridges are generally finished with the Boston-lap method. Both flashing and roofing cement are used to make the ridges and hips water resistant. Closed valleys, made with trapezoidal pieces of copper flashing placed under each course and lapped at least 3″, are the most popular on slate roofs.

Simulated slate shingles manufactured of fiber-reinforced cement resemble natural slate shingles in appearance. The simulated slate is lighter in weight and stronger than natural slate. The installation procedure for these shingles is similar to that for natural slate. Simulated slate carries a Class A fire rating and can be guaranteed up to 30 years.

Clay Tile Roofing Many variations of clay roofing tile are manufactured. They are generally very durable, made from different types of clay, and burned in kilns, as are many other types of terra-cotta building products. Roofs of clay tile are characteristic of Mediterranean and Spanish architecture. The early Jesuits of Mexico first brought tile roof construction to this country when they built the old Spanish missions of California and the Southwest.

Traditionally, clay tiles were available in natural, burnt-orange colors. Today a wide selection of natural colors, ranging from light tan to dark brown, is available. Some manufacturers produce a glazed ceramic roofing tile that comes in a spectrum of colors from white to dark blue.

Although there are various patterns or shapes, all clay tile can be divided into two general categories: flat and roll type (Fig. 2–178). The flat tiles vary from simple

Figure 2–178 Examples of roll and flat tiles.

pieces to pieces with interlocking edges and headers. Roll tiles are available in semicircular shapes, reverse-S shapes, and pan and cover types. Each type requires a tightly sheathed roof covered with heavy roofing felt. On low-pitched roofs and on all ridges and hips, the paper should be doubled; cant strips are needed at the eaves, as in slate roofs. Although some flat tile is fastened by hanging it on wooden cleat strips across the roof, the majority is secured with copper nails through prepunched holes. Semicircular roll tiles require wooden strips running from the eaves to the ridges between the pans.

Clay tile application requires careful planning inasmuch as tile pieces must fit together, and very little latitude is allowed in their placing. Allowance must be made for expansion and contraction of the roofing at intersections of walls and projections. Because clay tile is one of the heavier roofing materials, roof framing must be adequate to support it.

Open valleys are usually used with tile and copper flashing is placed below (Fig. 2–179). Manufacturers furnish special shapes and pieces for covering hips and ridges, as well as pieces for rake edges and starter strips at the eaves (Figs. 2–180, 2–181, and 2–182). Often, starter pieces at the eaves, as well as ridge and eave pieces, are set in mastic or cement, both of which are available in colors to match the tile. Ridge rolls often require wood strips along the ridge for fastening the tile. Some tile shapes tend to look bulky on residential roofs; however, if carefully chosen to complement the style of the house, tile will help in creating a picturesque effect.

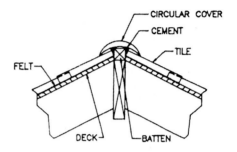

Figure 2–180 Tile roof ridge section.

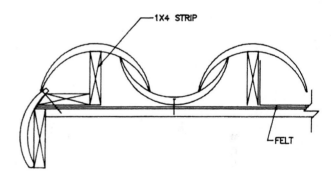

Figure 2–181 Tile roof gable rake section.

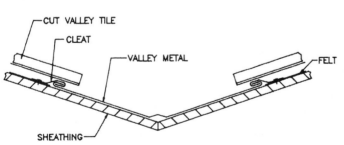

Figure 2–179 Tile roof flashing at a valley.

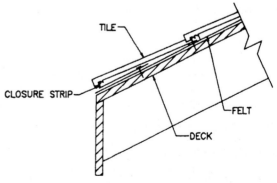

Figure 2–182 Tile roof eave section.

Cement Tile Roofs This type of roof has become popular in Florida for residential construction. Precast concrete tiles with wide exposures are attached to the roof and are neatly grouted with mortar. Heavy roofing felt is used below, and white waterproofing, cement-base paint is applied as a finish over gray cement tiles. Cement tile can be used on low pitches, and the roof becomes resistant to sun and heat.

Cement tiles are now available in a number of colors. Colored cement is used in the manufacture of the tiles, eliminating the need for painting the tiles after installation. Requirements for roofing tile construction are summarized in Tables D–4 and D–5.

Metal Roofing Occasionally, metal roofing is the most appropriate material to cover residences or light construction buildings. The principal metals used in roofing are copper, terneplate, aluminum, painted steel, and galvanized iron. Because of the cost of material and labor, metal is generally restricted to use in finer residences and more expensive structures. On moderately priced residences, we often see metal employed for small dormers, projections over front entrances, and minor roofs, in combination with other roofing material on the major roof. Metal must be applied by experienced roofers, who are aware of the individual properties of the different metals.

Copper is the most durable as well as one of the more expensive metals for roofing. It is malleable, tenacious, and easy to work, and it does not require maintenance after installation. It weathers to a gray-green color and blends well with other building materials.

Terneplate is made of sheet iron or steel coated with an alloy of 25% tin and 75% lead. Metal roofers purchase the metal in small sheets that have been shop-coated with an oil-base paint. After application, the top surface must be painted with two coats of paint long in oil. If properly maintained, terneplate will last from 30 to 50 years. One advantage of terneplate is its light weight; also, it expands less than copper.

Both copper and terneplate are applied on tight board roof decks covered with rosin-sized paper. On roof pitches from 3″ to 12″, either the standing-seam or the batten-seam method is used (Fig. 2–183). After the small sheets have been joined into long strips, the standing seam is formed by turning up one edge 1½″ and the adjoining edge 1¼″. The edges are bent and are locked together without soldering. Cleats are nailed to the roof deck and are incorporated into the seam to hold the metal to the deck, but no nails are driven through the sheets.

Batten seams are formed by nailing wood strips, ranging in size from 2″ × 2″ to 4″ × 4″, to the deck; the strips run from the eaves to the ridge and are parallel to each other. Metal lengths are put between the battens and are bent up along the edges of the battens to form pans down the slope of the roof. Cleats of the same metal are nailed to the edges of the battens and are incorporated into lock joints, which are formed by the edges of metal caps that rest on the battens, as well as the edges of the metal pans. Batten strips are used on the ridges and the hips where necessary. The ends of wood batten strips at the edges of the roof must be covered with metal.

Several types of aluminum and steel roofing are used on residences and small buildings. Both aluminum and steel sheets, flat or corrugated, with baked enamel and other patented finishes are popular metal roofing materials. Some are laid beginning at the ridge and continuing down to the eave; others are laid beginning at the eave and proceeding up to the ridge, similarly to the method of applying copper sheets. Snap-on battens usually seam the joints between sheets, which are commonly 12″, 16″, or 24″ wide. Special caps are designed to cover ridges and hips. Pressed aluminum or steel shingles and tiles are available that resemble wood shakes and roll tiles. Like metal sheets these roofing materials have baked enamel or special finishes. Available in strips, the roofing is nailed in place; concealed locking devices connect one strip to the other at each end. Metal sheets, shingles, and tiles can be installed on wood furring strips nailed perpendicularly to the roof framing members. These roofing materials can be installed over roofing felt on a plywood deck.

Corrugated aluminum sheets are employed mainly for temporary buildings. They are fastened directly to the deck with aluminum nails and neoprene washers; the fastening is done through the high portion of the lapped corrugations.

On economy roofs, corrugated galvanized iron sheets can be used. However, galvanized iron has a limited service life as well as an unpleasing appearance. This mate-

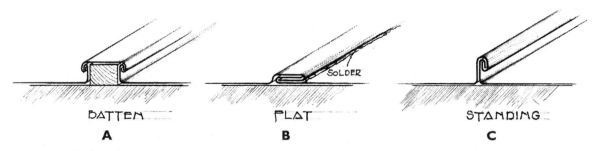

Figure 2–183 Metal roof seams.

rial should be reserved for temporary or less important structures.

2.13
EXTERIOR FINISH MATERIALS

The exterior finish material plays a very important part in the esthetics of a building, and if maintenance is a factor, the selection of the finish is especially important. Many finish materials are available; some of the more common materials for wood construction are wood siding, wood shingles, plywood, hardboard, aluminum, stucco, exterior insulation and finish systems (E.I.F.S.s), and masonry veneer (see Section 2.6 on masonry veneer).

Wood siding has been used successfully for years and is typical of American-built houses. Much of it requires periodic repainting; some of the durable wood species, such as redwood, western red cedar, and cypress, can be left natural with merely an application of several coats of water repellent. Kiln-dried lumber is preferred, and select grades with a minimum of know and defects should be used. Figures 2–184 and 2–185 illustrate some of the more common types of wood siding available.

2.13.1 Bevel Siding

Bevel siding is widely used in present-day construction. It is cut into widths varying from 4″ to 12″, and butt thicknesses range from 7/16″ to 3/4″. The usual amount of lap is

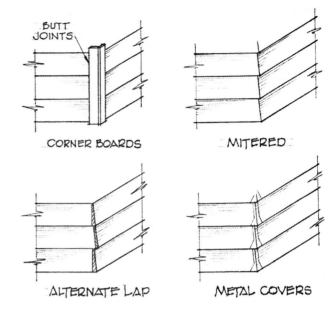

Figure 2–185 Treatments of outside corners on horizontal wood siding.

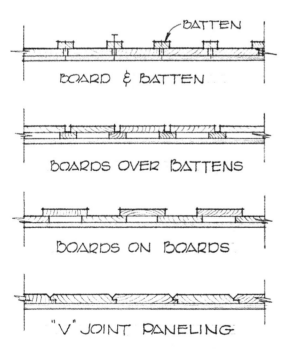

Figure 2–184 Various vertical wood siding as shown through horizontal sections.

from 1″ to 2″. For example, a bevel siding 6″ wide is usually applied with 4½″ to the weather, and a siding 10″ wide is usually applied with 8″ to the weather. Wider sizes have a tendency to cup and warp.

Much of the warping in siding can be prevented by the application of a prime coat of paint to all sides of the siding, including ends, before installation. Rustproof nails should be used, because rust stains bleed through the paint film. Figure 2–186 describes nailing recommendations for a number of types of siding. Notice in the figure that the nails do not pass through the underpiece of the lap. This method allows for expansion in the lap without the risk of splitting the thin portion of the underpiece, should the nails be put through both pieces of the lap.

Strong, horizontal shadow lines are characteristic of bevel siding. Various corner treatments are shown in Fig. 2–185. A starter strip must be nailed to the bottom of the sheathing so that the first course of siding will slope the same amount as succeeding courses. The bottom course is started about 1″ below the top of the foundation wall to weatherproof and hide the wood and masonry joint. Bevel siding exposures are worked out exactly by carpenters so that horizontal butt lines coincide with sill and head edges of windows and doors, and courses are similar throughout the wall height. Minor variations of exposure on a wall are permissible inasmuch as they are not readily noticeable. Water tables should be used above all windows and doors; a rabbeted trim member is generally used at the top of the wall to cover the thin edge of the top course. Rabbeted bevel siding is also available in various widths and thicknesses.

On economy walls, drop siding, also known as *novelty siding*, is acceptable without sheathing. Building felt is

Nailing recommendations

Nailing patterns vary depending on the profile of the siding. But no matter what the pattern, one thing remains the same: Don't nail through overlapping pieces. To do so will eventually split the siding as it seasonally expands and contracts. Nails should penetrate at least 1½ in. into studs or blocking (1¼ in. for ring-shank or spiral-shank nails). Spacing should be no more than 24 in. o. c. Use box or siding nails for face nailing and casing nails for blind nailing.

Estimating coverage

To calculate the amount of material required to side a house, first figure the square footage of the walls minus any openings. Add 10% for trim and waste. Now multiply your answer by the appropriate board-ft. factor or linear-ft. factor to tally the amount.

Bevel

6 in. and narrower: 1 in. overlap. One nail per bearing, just above the 1 in. overlap.

8 in. and wider: 1 in. overlap. One nail per bearing, just above the 1 in. overlap.

Nominal width	Dressed width	Exposed face	Factor for linear feet	Factor for board feet
4	3½	2½	4.8	1.6
6	5½	4½	2.67	1.33
8	7¼	6¼	1.92	1.28
10	9¼	8¼	1.45	1.21

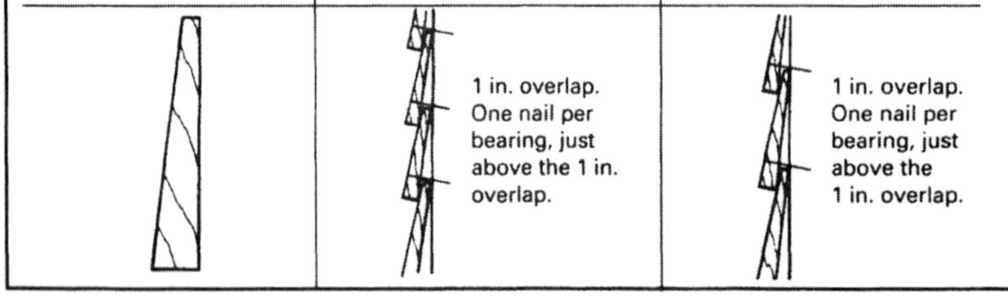

Shiplap (Dolly Varden)

6 in. and narrower: One nail per bearing, 1 in. up from bottom edge.

8 in. and wider: One nail per bearing, 1 in. up from bottom edge.

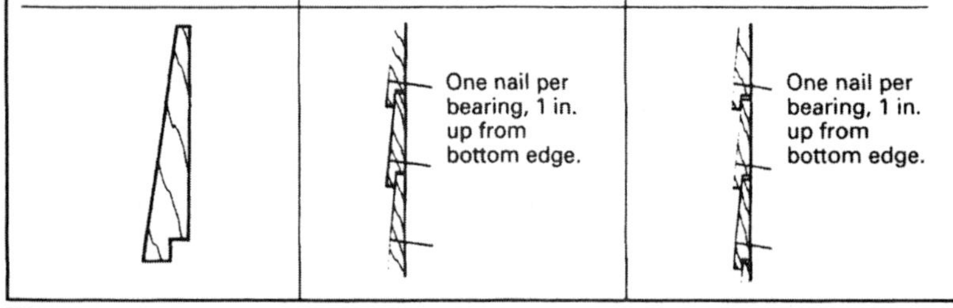

Nominal width	Dressed width	Exposed face	Factor for linear feet	Factor for board feet
4	3½	3	4	1.33
6	5½	5	2.4	1.2
8	7¼	6¾	1.78	1.19
10	9¼	8¾	1.37	1.14
12	11¼	10¾	1.12	1.12

Channel rustic

6 in. and narrower: One nail per bearing, 1 in. up from bottom edge.

8 in. and wider: Use two siding or box nails, 3 in. to 4 in. per bearing.

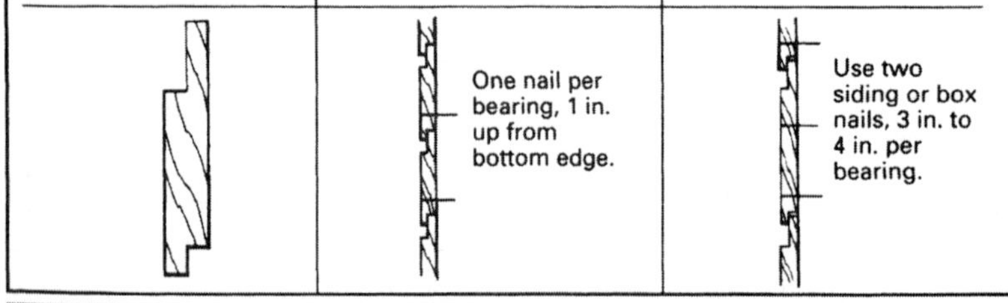

Nominal width	Dressed width	Exposed face	Factor for linear feet	Factor for board feet
4	3⅜	3⅛	3.84	1.28
6	5⅜	5⅛	2.34	1.17
8	7⅛	6⅞	1.75	1.16
10	9⅛	8⅞	1.35	1.13

Drop

6 in. and narrower: T&G pattern. Shiplap pattern. Blind nail T&G patterns; lace nail shiplap patterns, 1 in. up from bottom edge.

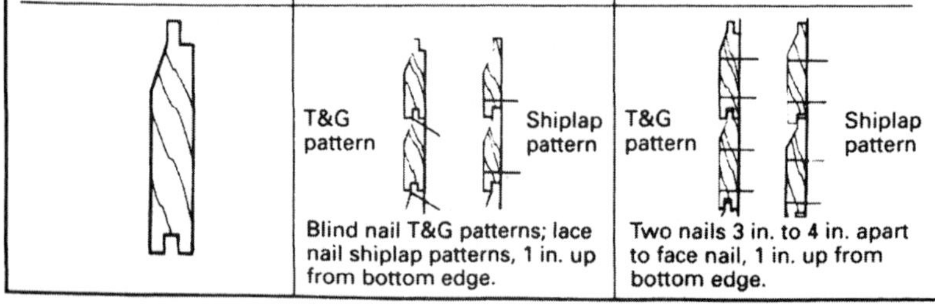

8 in. and wider: T&G pattern. Shiplap pattern. Two nails 3 in. to 4 in. apart to face nail, 1 in. up from bottom edge.

Nominal width	Dressed width	Exposed face	Factor for linear feet	Factor for board feet
4	3⅜	3⅛	3.84	1.28
6	5⅜	5⅛	2.34	1.17
8	7⅛	6⅞	1.75	1.16
10	9⅛	8⅞	1.35	1.13

Figure 2–186 Nailing recommendations for wood siding. (*Fine Homebuilding*, September 1995)

tacked directly to the studs, and the drop siding is nailed over the felt. Corners can be treated as mentioned previously, or square-edged corner boards can be nailed directly over the siding.

2.13.2 Board-and-Batten Siding

Board-and-batten siding can be used to obtain a rustic texture on exterior frame walls (Fig. 2–184). Either sur-faced or unsurfaced, square-edged boards can be used. The wide boards are nailed vertically with at least ⅛″ space between them for expansion. Battens of the same type of lumber, usually only 2″ wide, are nailed over the vertical joints of the wide boards. The 2″ batten strips are also used for trim around doors and windows, as well as along the top of the wall. Joints between the wide boards are often caulked before the batten strips are applied. Horizontal blocking must be installed in the stud wall if insulation board sheathing has been used so that the boards and the battens can be nailed at a minimum of four levels of vertical height throughout a 1-story wall. If nominal 1″ wood or plywood sheathing has been used, the boards and the battens can be secured by nailing into the sheathing. Care should be exercised in nailing the batten strips; the nails should pass between the wide boards in the joint, or the nails can pass through the batten and one of the wide boards *only*. This method allows expansion of the joint without splitting either the boards or the batten. Only rustproof nails should be specified.

Another interesting effect can be gained by applying the wide boards over the narrow batten strips. This application becomes a reverse board-and-batten method, which produces narrow grooves and a slightly different overall effect. Redwood lumber is frequently applied in this manner.

2.13.3 V-Joint, Tongue-and-Groove Paneling

V-joint, tongue-and-groove paneling can also be used for vertical siding. Adequate wood sheathing or horizontal blocking must also be installed to provide proper nail anchoring; blind nailing is generally used along the tongue to hide the nails within the joint. Kiln-dried lumber with minimum shrinkage characteristics should be selected, and joints should be nailed up tight so that moisture will not penetrate between the boards. Either random-width or uniform-width paneling can be used. Bottom cuts at the base of the wall should be beveled to provide a drip. Because of cupping, paneling over 8″ wide should be avoided.

In recent years, rough-sawn cedar paneling has been widely used in contemporary-style homes and small commercial buildings, in many applications with diagonal coursing. The paneling can be stained to gain various color treatments or left to weather with natural wood appearance. Both cedar and redwood are soft and require careful nailing with rustproof nails.

2.13.4 Wood Shingles

Wood shingles produce warm and charming exterior finishes that are popular in many areas of the country. The shingles are versatile in that many effects can be obtained by various applications. They can be painted, stained, or left to weather naturally. Unfinished shingles weather unevenly because of projections, overhangs, and the like. Handsplit shakes can be used for rustic effects; double courses of regular shingles can be used for strong horizontal shadow lines; or regular shingles can be applied in staggered course lines for unusual effects (Fig. 2–187). More exposure widths can be allowed on wood shingle walls than is necessary when applying similar shingles to a roof. Table D–8 lists wood shingle and shake side-wall exposure requirements.

Western red cedar is the most popular wood used for commercial shingles, and the method of application to walls is similar to the methods mentioned under Section 2.12.2, "Roof Coverings." For siding, No. 1 grade is usually specified; No. 2 or 3 grade can be used for underlays of double courses. Wood shingles must have substantial wood backing for nailing; if insulation board sheathing is used on the wall, horizontal nailing strips, usually 1 × 3, are nailed over the insulation board. The strips are spaced the same distance apart as the exposure width of the shingles.

2.13.5 Exterior Plywood

Exterior plywood is now used extensively for siding. Plywood must be of the exterior type and not less than ³/₈″ thick. Panel siding must be installed according to Table D–9. Plywood can be applied vertically with 1 × 2 batten strips placed vertically either 16″ or 24″ o.c. to hide the joints of the plywood (Fig. 2–188). Plywood must be well painted or stained. Also, texture one-eleven plywood, ⁵/₈″ thick, with rabbeted joining edges, can be nailed vertically on stud walls to resemble vertical paneling. Plywood is also available in strips to be applied horizontally, similar to shingles.

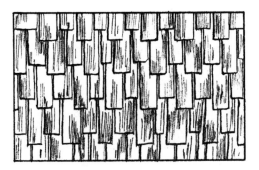

RANDOM COURSING

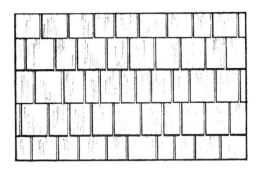

REGULAR COURSING

Figure 2–187 Wood shingle textures.

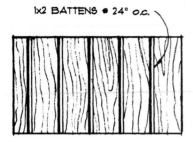
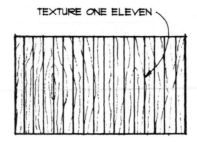

Figure 2–188 Plywood siding. Battens can be spaced either 24″ or 16″ o.c.

2.13.6 Sheet Hardboard

Sheet hardboard is a popular exterior siding material that, if properly applied and painted, will give years of satisfactory service. Hardboard is made from natural wood fibers that are subjected to heat and pressure to form sheets or strips of various sizes and thicknesses. It comes in various surface textures: smooth, grooved, and ribbed. Hardboard must have solid backing support and is durable if kept painted. Strips can be applied horizontally to resemble bevel siding, or larger panels can be applied vertically to resemble board-and-batten siding.

The horizontally applied panels are usually 8″ to 1′ wide by 16′ long by ³⁄₈″ to ⁷⁄₁₆″ thick, applied generally with 7″ or 11″ exposures. Starter strips at the base of the wall and corner treatments are handled similarly to wood bevel siding. Vertical joints should be made over studs, and nailing is done through the lap at each stud location.

For vertical application, 4′ wide panels are used. Lengths are obtainable up to 16′, and recommended thicknesses are ¼″ and ⁵⁄₁₆″. Vertical wood battens spaced 16″ o.c. can be used to hide vertical joints on smooth hardboard edges; a ⅛″ space must be left between panels, and joints are caulked before batten strips are applied. Grooved-and-ribbed panels have shiplap edges for concealing the joints. The builder should follow manufacturers' directions in applying either type of hardboard exterior panels. Hardboard siding must be installed according to Table D–11.

2.13.7 Aluminum Siding

Aluminum siding is a low-maintenance material used for both residential and commercial construction; it is also popular for remodeling exterior walls. Two types of aluminum panels are most popular: those applied horizontally to resemble either narrow- or wide-bevel siding, and those applied vertically to resemble board-and-batten siding. Both styles are available with baked-on enamel finishes of various colors, and both can be painted if necessary, similarly to wood siding. Aluminum siding is light in weight, easy to apply, and resistant to weathering.

The horizontal panels are started at the base of the sheathing with a wood cant strip nailed below the bottom edge of the first course, and each course is nailed to the sheathing along its top edge. Courses are held to the adjacent course with a lock joint. Matching corner pieces, backer strips for end joints, and trim pieces are furnished by the manufacturers for each type of panel. Horizontal panels are made 12½′ long, with either a bevel exposure 8″ wide or two 4″ bevel exposures. Some panels have foam insulation backing.

To apply vertical aluminum panels, first nail a starter corner strip vertically along one corner; then lock the first panel into the strip, and nail the panel along the edge opposite the lock joint. This procedure is continued across the wall. You can cut aluminum with a hacksaw or tinsnips when fitting it around openings and such; appropriate pieces are furnished by manufacturers to form water tables and trim members. Vertical panels are made in lengths to cover 1-story heights so that joints are eliminated.

2.13.8 Vinyl Siding

Vinyl siding is available in a wide range of colors and does not require painting. Manufactured from polyvinyl chloride sheets, the siding comes in 10′ and 12′ long panels. The panels are preformed to resemble either horizontal or vertical wood siding. The surface of the siding may be smooth or embossed to replicate wood graining. Both the vertical and the horizontal panels have perforated edge strips for nailing. Galvanized nails should be used to attach the siding to solid, nailable sheathing. A variety of vinyl trim pieces are available to complement the siding. These pieces are especially convenient for finishing corners, cornices, soffits, and fascias and around doors and windows (Fig. 2–189).

2.13.9 Stucco

Stucco has been used for years as a satisfactory exterior siding material, but present-day use is limited largely to direct application over concrete block and other masonry materials. Some application for stucco over wood frame walls in residential construction is still found, however.

On masonry walls of concrete block, tile, or brick, two coats of portland cement stucco are applied like plaster to form a coat ¾″ thick. This particular stucco should be made of 1 part portland cement, 3 parts sand, and 10% by volume hydrated lime. It must have a minimum compressive strength of 1000 lb/sq in. Or a prepared port-

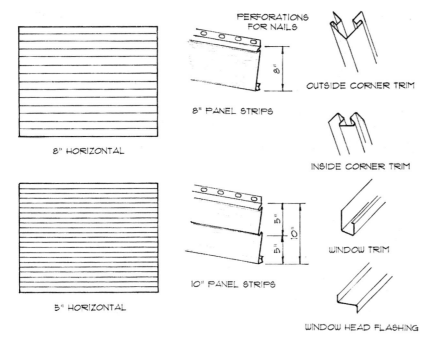

Figure 2–189 Vinyl siding.

land cement stucco may be used and applied according to the manufacturer's directions. The masonry wall is first cleaned with a wire brush, and a scratch coat is applied. After the scratch coat is thoroughly dry, the finish coat is applied and is given whatever surface texture is desired. A finish may be smoothed with a metal trowel finish, sand-finished with a wood float, or stippled by application of various tooling or stroking effects. To render the finish waterproof, cement-base paints are usually applied after the finish coat is completely dry. Colored stucco can be obtained by mixing mineral pigments into the finish coat, or colored cement-base paints may be applied to the final stucco surface.

On wood frame walls, stucco is applied over ribbed metal lath that is backed up with heavy asphalt-treated paper (Fig. 2–191). Wood or metal furring strips 15″ o.c. can also be used under galvanized wire fabric, or galvanized furring nails can be used to keep the fabric at least ¼″ away from the paper and sheathing. Foundations must be adequate to prevent settling and subsequent cracking of the stucco. Stucco-covered, 2-story buildings should be constructed with balloon framing to minimize vertical shrinkage. Usually, a rustproof metal ground strip is placed at the base of the wood wall to close the opening between the stucco and the sheathing. Flashing must be used above all doors and windows, and the tops of stucco walls must be protected by overhangs and trim members. When applied over wood frame walls, a three-coat stucco job is standard (consisting of scratch coat, brown coat, and finish coat) to make the stucco ⅞″ thick.

Stucco is used to produce imitation, half-timber-type exterior walls used mainly in Normandy-style houses.

Treated boards representing the timbers are fastened directly to the sheathing, and stucco is applied to the furring lath in the areas between the timbers. In this construction, attention must be given to the prevention of moisture penetration between the timbers and the stucco. Flashing must be used liberally over horizontal timber pieces as well as joints in the timber pieces, which are especially susceptible to the accumulation of moisture.

All of the aforementioned exterior siding materials must be applied over a suitable moisture-resistant building paper that has been fastened to the wall sheathing. This paper is important in preventing moisture penetration under and between siding pieces and in preventing air infiltration through the exterior walls from wind pressures.

2.13.10 Exterior Insulation and Finish Systems (E.I.F.S.s)

Exterior insulation finish systems were introduced into the United States in 1969. The system originated in post–World War II Europe as a finish system applied over masonry and concrete in building renovations. American manufacturers have adapted the European system for use on metal and wood frame walls (Fig. 2–190). E.I.F.S.s were initially used in commercial applications but have been used more extensively in the residential market in the last 10 years. There are now an estimated 250,000 houses clad in E.I.F.S.

E.I.F.S. can be applied to smooth masonry walls or to stud walls that have exterior-grade gypsum sheathing. The application is generally a four-step process. First, an

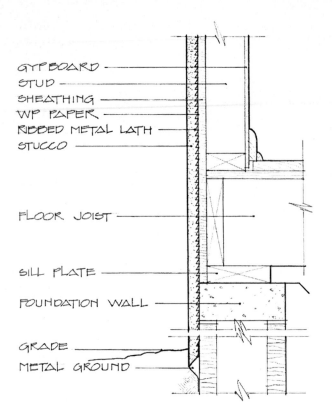

GYPBOARD
STUD
SHEATHING
WP PAPER
RIBBED METAL LATH
STUCCO

FLOOR JOIST

SILL PLATE

FOUNDATION WALL

GRADE
METAL GROUND

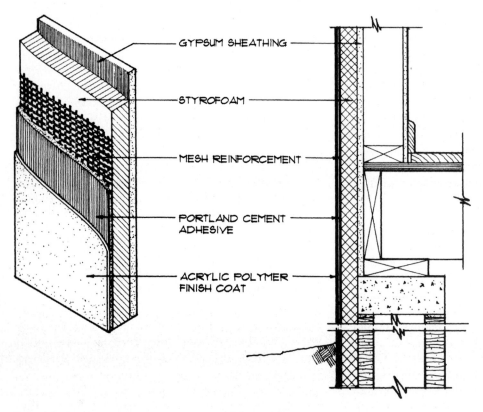

GYPSUM SHEATHING

STYROFOAM

MESH REINFORCEMENT

PORTLAND CEMENT
ADHESIVE

ACRYLIC POLYMER
FINISH COAT

Figure 2–190 Stucco and exterior insulation finish system.

adhesive is applied to one side of an insulating panel such as Styrofoam, which is then attached to the masonry wall or gypsum sheathing. Next, an adhesive with an admixture of portland cement is troweled over the insulating panel. Third, a fiberglass mesh reinforcement is embedded into the wet adhesive, which is allowed to cure. Last, an acrylic polymer finish coat is troweled over the exterior wall surface. Color tints can be added to the finish coat. The tints are usually blended into the acrylic polymer at the factory.

The E.I.F.S. treatment adds insulating value to the wall system, will not crack as will stucco, and is a low-maintenance material. Sharp objects or strong impacts can damage the soft surface; however, a heavy-duty reinforcing mesh with substantial impact resistance can be used. Creative designs and trims are easily achieved by varying the thickness or cutting sculptural shapes into the Styrofoam.

Recently, North Carolina's New Hanover County Inspection Department has observed significant problems with E.I.F.S.-clad houses. An investigation of 72 randomly selected E.I.F.S.-clad houses less than three years old revealed that 70 of them suffered from water infiltration. A subsequent study of 209 E.I.F.S.-clad houses, conducted by the Wilmington section of AIA North Carolina, drew similar conclusions: 90% registered high moisture levels.

In most cases, water had managed to get into the walls and through joints between the cladding and the windows, doors, and other penetrations such as roof flashings. Improperly caulked windows, poor sealants, and inadequate flashing will ruin an E.I.F.S. wall by allowing moisture to penetrate. Once moisture enters, it is not able to escape. A traditional E.I.F.S. has no internal drainage provision if moisture gets past the system membrane.

Another recently discovered problem concerns termite infestation of the expanded polystyrene foam in E.I.F.S. The termite problem and the wood rot problem are both exacerbated by the same cause—moisture. In typical E.I.F.S. installations, the exterior foam insulation extends from the above-grade walls down into the ground, providing a convenient path for termites to get almost anywhere in the above-grade structure. If water gets trapped in the E.I.F.S., termites do not have to return to the ground, because they have ready access to food, moisture, and warmth.

In response to these problems, the E.I.F.S. Industry Members Association (EIMA) has implemented a third-party builder certification program. The National Association of Home Builders Research Center has agreed to certify qualified participants based on EIMA-specified installation techniques. EIMA is also revising 10 basic construction details that were published in 1994. These details cover generic installation conditions at foundations, windows, parapet caps, dissimilar substrates, and expansion points. A supplementary set, published in 1996, addresses more complex circumstances such as a balcony wall intersection and penetrations.

2.14
INTERIOR FINISHES AND TRIM

2.14.1 Gypsum Wallboard

Gypsum wallboard (commonly called gypsum drywall) construction is now used as the interior finish in the majority of American homes under construction. The paper-covered gypsum sheets are made in $4' \times 8'$, $4' \times 10'$, and $4' \times 12'$ sizes. Standard thicknesses are $3/8''$, $1/2''$, and $5/8''$. Gypsum has good thermal and fire-resistance qualities. The sheets can be easily cut and nailed to framing; joints and nailheads can be smoothly finished with joint compound and perforated tape; and very little moisture is introduced into the structure from the material, which is the case when plaster is used (Figs. 2–191 and 2–192).

Building codes require inspection of gypsum wallboard installation before board joints and fasteners are taped and finished. Also, gypsum wallboard may not be installed until weather protection is provided.

Water-resistant gypsum board is used as a base for tile or wall panels for tub, shower, or water closet compartment walls. Water-resistant gypsum board cannot be used over a vapor barrier, in areas subject to continuous high humidity such as saunas, or on ceilings where frame spacing exceeds 12″ o.c.

Wallboard can be fastened with nails, screws, or adhesive. Supports and nailings for wallboard are indicated in Table D–20 for single-ply applications, and in Table D–21 for two-ply applications.

Two-ply installation is usually used where extra thickness is required for fire resistance because it is much easier to lay up two pieces of $3/8''$ wallboard than one piece that is $3/4''$ thick. One advantage of two-ply installation is that you can get a smoother wall. You can secure it with adhesive rather than nailing it, thereby reducing the amount of taping required.

2.14.2 Plaster

Two types of plaster are used in construction today: (1) portland cement plaster for both indoor and outdoor work and (2) gypsum plaster only on interior work. Both require three coats when applied over metal lath or wire fabric lath. You must apply at last two coats over any other material allowed by code, but you can never apply plaster directly to fiber insulation board.

2.14.3 Prefinished Plywood Sheets

Prefinished plywood sheets in various natural wood finishes are becoming popular in many room interiors. They

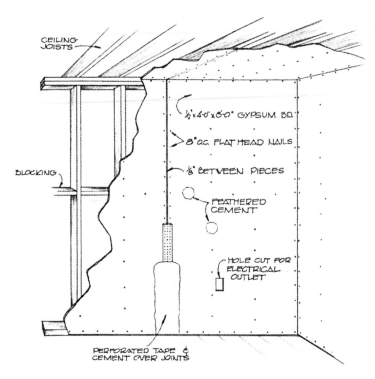

Figure 2–191 Application of gypsum board applied vertically for interior walls.

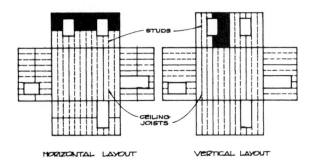

Figure 2–192 Two methods of gypsum board layout.

are blind nailed directly to studs and never require painting or finishing. Other manufactured sheet materials as well as solid wood paneling are also available for various wall coverings. To straighten nailing surfaces when using sheet materials or ceiling acoustical tile, you can apply furring strips perpendicularly to studs or ceiling joists.

2.14.4 Trim

Trim is the general term given to molding, base, casing, and various other finish members that must be carefully fitted by finish carpenters to complete the appearance of a structure (Fig. 2–193). Many stock pieces and patterns are available at lumber dealers. In higher-class construction, custom-made moldings and trim pieces are often shown in detail on the working drawings and therefore must be specially milled. Care must be taken to select consistent patterns to be used throughout a building so that harmony in the trim results. Colonial interiors traditionally require ogee profiles, whereas contemporary styles usually appear best with simpler tapered or teardrop profiles. Casing and finishing nails are used to apply trim members; the nails are driven below the surface of the wood with a nail set so that the holes can be filled, and care must be exercised to prevent hammer marks from injuring the surface of the wood.

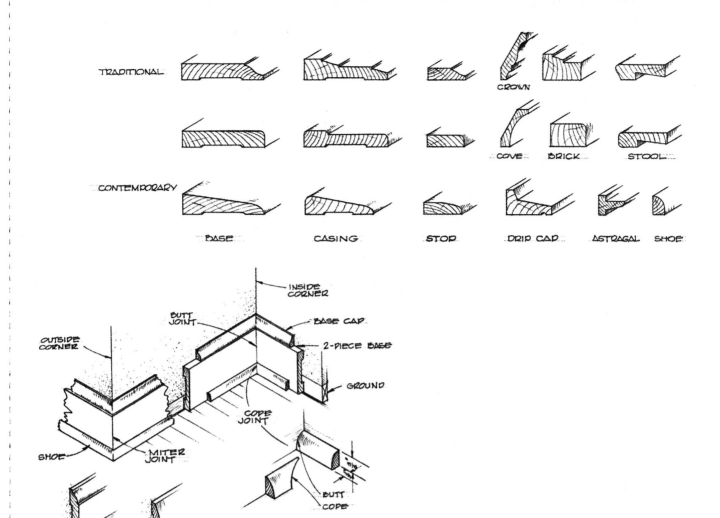

Figure 2–193 Stock trim and base applications.

INSULATION AND MOISTURE CONSIDERATIONS IN FRAME STRUCTURES

Builders are fully aware that indoor comfort is of primary importance to the individual. Consequently, proper insulation becomes a major consideration in warm climates as well as in cold. Many types of insulation are available. The most suitable usually depends on the details of the construction; the amount depends on the extent of comfort desired. When care in selection and installation is taken, optimum benefit will be realized.

Heat-loss calculations and the design of heating and cooling systems are not discussed in this material; however, the general aspects of insulation, such problems as water vapor within buildings, and the ventilation of unheated air spaces are of concern to the drafter if details of construction are to be correctly conceived and drawn.

All construction materials can be classified more or less as either insulators or conductors, depending on their porosity or density. Still air is an excellent insulator if confined into small spaces such as the matrix of insulation materials or small cavities within walls. On the other hand, dense materials, such as glass or masonry, are relatively poor insulators. All materials, however, resist the flow of heat to a certain extent, the resistance of the given material being directly proportional to its thickness (Fig. 2–194).

Heat may be transmitted by three different methods: conduction, convection, and radiation.

- **Conduction** is the transfer of heat by direct molecular contact. Metals, for instance, conduct heat

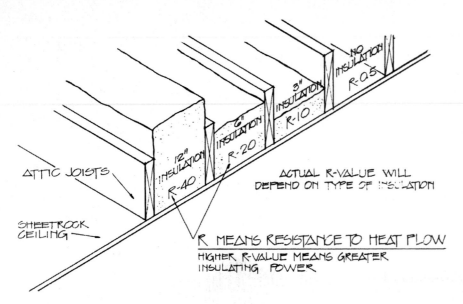

Figure 2–194 Insulation *R* values.

more readily than wood, yet all materials conduct heat if a temperature difference exists between their surfaces. Remember that *heat flows from warm to cold surfaces.*

- **Convection** is the transfer of heat by air or another agent in motion. Although air is a good insulator, when it circulates, it loses part of its value as an insulator. Air spaces about ¾″ wide within walls or ceilings are the most restrictive to circulation. In larger spaces, air acts as a conveyor belt, taking heat from warm surfaces and depositing it on cold surfaces.

- **Radiation** is the transfer of heat through space from a warm surface to a cold surface, very much as light travels through space. Effective resistance to radiation can be provided by shiny surfaces, such as aluminum foil; the more actual surfaces a heat ray has to penetrate, the more effective the reflective insulation becomes.

Actual heat transfer through walls and ceilings usually employs all three of the above-mentioned methods of transfer, to various degrees. Of course, some heat is also dissipated from buildings through openings around doors and windows.

To compare the suitability or insulating qualities of different building materials and insulations, a standard of reference must be used. By accurate experimentation, the thermal qualities of individual building materials have been determined. When these materials are incorporated into typical combinations found in walls, floors, roofs, and so on, including occasional air spaces, the rate of heat flow or the coefficient of transmission, known as the *U factor*, can be calculated. This factor can be defined as the number of Btu's (British thermal units—heat units) that will flow through 1 sq ft of the structure from one air re-

gion to another due to a temperature difference of 1°F in 1 h.

Easy reference can be made from tables giving the *U* factors with and without insulation; these tables are published by the American Society of Heating, Refrigeration, and Air Conditioning Engineers (A.S.H.R.A.E.). Tables for *U* factors of typical constructions and various insulation combinations can also be found in the *Forest Products Laboratory Report R1740*. Comparisons of these *U* factors make it possible to evaluate different combinations of materials and insulations on the basis of overall heat loss, potential fuel savings, influence on comfort, and cost of installation.

Other than the reflective insulators, commercial insulations are usually made of glass fibers, glass foam, mineral fibers, organic fibers, polystyrene, and polyurethane. The best materials should be fireproof and vermin-proof, as well as resistant to heat flow. The cellular materials utilize tiny, isolated air cells to reduce conduction and convection; the fibrous materials utilize tiny films of air surrounding each fiber. These efficient insulating materials are manufactured into blankets, batts, and sheets in sizes and shapes that fit conveniently into conventional structural spaces. Some have tabs or edges for stapling to wood frame members; others are sized so that they can be tightly wedged into conventional structural cavities. Proper selection depends on initial cost, effectiveness, and the adaptation of the insulation to the construction features. Figure 2–195 illustrates the proper placement of insulation within typical frame buildings.

2.15.1 Insulation

Heat transfer through the building envelope is probably most affected by the way that the insulation is used and installed. Insulated spaces must be completely filled with material. There should be no gaps or voids, and the ma-

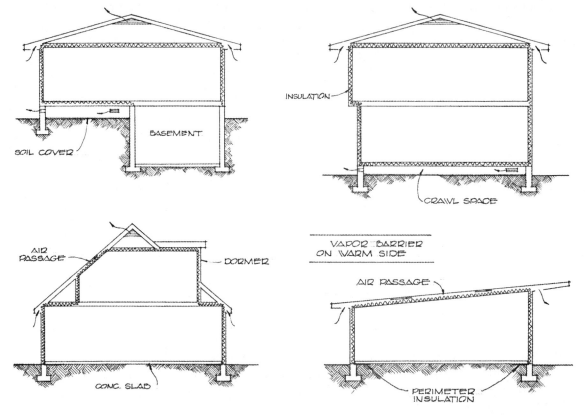

Figure 2–195 Placement of insulation in wood frame buildings. Ventilation of attic and crawl spaces is necessary.

terial must be kept dry. Insulation materials available include batt-type, loose fill, boardstock, spray-type, and radiant barriers.

Batt Type Batt-type insulation is made from glass or mineral fibers. These materials are acceptable for interior use such as on inside exterior walls and on foundation walls. Insulation values of the various products depend on the density of the material. Increased density generally increases the resistance of the material and reduces convective air movements within a building cavity. Performance of batt-type insulation products is directly related to installation practices. Gaps around wiring and plumbing must be prevented, and batt materials must fill cavities completely and evenly.

Loose Fill Glass fiber and mineral wool insulations are also available as loose fill. Loose fill insulation is blown into place using special equipment. It can be used in attics and inside above-grade exterior walls. It is important that it be installed at the correct density in order to provide acceptable performance. Cellulose fiber insulation is made from shredded, recycled newsprint that has been treated with chemicals to prevent the growth of molds, to keep rodents out, and to control flammability.

Boardstock Boardstock insulations can be rigid or semirigid and are available in five types:

1. **Expanded polystyrene** is made by expanding polystyrene beads in a mold. Large blocks are then cut into sheets of various thicknesses. Low-density polystyrene can be used as a sheathing material for above-grade exterior walls and can be used to insulate interior basement walls, flat roofs, and cathedral ceilings. High-density polystyrene can be used to insulate below-grade exterior walls because it will withstand high pressures. Both materials can be used to insulate interior walls above and below grade, but, due to their combustibility, they must be covered with a fire-protective covering such as ½″ drywall if used to insulate living spaces.

2. **Extruded polystyrene** is manufactured by extruding a hot mass of polystyrene through a slit. It expands upon exposure to atmospheric pressure and creates a closed-cell foam material. It is acceptable for use in all situations described for high-density expanded polystyrene. A higher-density extruded polystyrene can be used in built-up roofing applications. These materials must be covered with a fire-protective material if used in living spaces.

3. **Rigid glass fiber insulation** can be used in built-up roofing applications, as exterior wall sheathing, and as below-grade exterior wall insulation. The fibers in this product are aligned vertically so that water runs down the fibers. Product densities are

three to five times higher than those of standard batt-type products.

4. **Polyurethane** and **polyisocyanurate** are insulations made in continuous slabs that are cut with hot wires. They can be used in all of the applications noted earlier for expanded polystyrene. They are also combustible and must be covered with fire-protective materials when used in living spaces.

5. **Phenolic insulation** is manufactured in much the same way as polyurethane and polyisocyanurate insulations. However, it is much less combustible and is suitable for use as wall sheathing and for use inside, both above and below grade.

Spray Type Spray-type insulations are recent innovations in the residential construction industry. Three different types are presently available:

1. **Spray cellulose insulation** is available in a variety of types. The material is applied using special applicators that mix the insulation with materials. They allow it to hold together and adhere to the surface to which it is applied. Wet spray materials offer thorough cavity coverage and reduce envelope air leakage characteristics.

2. **Two-component isocyanurate foam** is best suited for use in exterior stud wall cavities, in perimeter joist spaces, and in the shim spaces around windows and doors. Special applicators are used to mix the chemicals in the correct proportions.

3. **Polyurethane formulations** are available in a variety of spray applications. The material is mixed on site using special foaming equipment for large projects. Single-component polyurethane foam is available in cans with "gun-type dispenser" canisters for sealing shim spaces around windows and doors.

Radiant Barriers A radiant barrier is a sheet of reflective material that is installed between a heat-radiating surface and a heat-absorbing surface. The reflective material stops the radiant transfer of heat between the two surfaces. Radiant barriers reduce cooling loads in summer by reducing the radiation of heat from the attic through the ceiling. The *R* value of a radiant barrier depends on the direction of heat flow.

If the restriction of heat flow were the only consideration in the application of insulation within buildings, it would be a simple matter to provide enough insulation around heated spaces to theoretically reduce fuel bills sufficiently and thereby offset the initial cost of the insulation. However, air contains water vapor, and because water vapor acts as a gas to penetrate porous materials and always flows from areas of high temperature to areas of lower temperatures, many types of insulation soon lose their effectiveness if they become saturated with water vapor.

Air is saturated or has a relative humidity of 100% when it contains as much moisture as it will hold. Warm air has the ability to retain more moisture than cold air. If saturated air is lowered in temperature, some of its moisture will be given off as condensation. This point in temperature change at which a specimen of air gives off moisture in the form of condensation is known as its *dew point*. When high temperature differences exist between insulated wall surfaces (between inside and outside air), the dew point often occurs in the insulation itself, where the resistance to heat flow is greater than in the structural members. The condensation that can gather in the insulation from the cooling of the vapor as it passes through a wall not only may reduce the value of the insulation but may also eventually cause permanent damage to the structural members. This problem generally arises in winter, during the heating season, especially when the humidity within the building is high.

2.15.2 Moisture Considerations

Water moves from place to place in one or all of four ways: (1) gravity, (2) capillary action, (3) air flow, and (4) diffusion.

Gravity Gravity causes water to seek its lowest point by traveling the path of least resistance. If improper drainage directs surface runoff toward a basement wall, water will enter the building through cracks in the wall. Measures to prevent such leaks include proper grading to direct water away from the wall and appropriate dampproofing and footing drains to direct the flow.

Capillary Action Capillary action causes water to move upward, downward, or sideways through thin tubes in materials. It affects foundations made of concrete or other porous materials. The pores in the concrete are like long, thin tubes. Water will rise up the foundation wall until it is released into an area with a low water-vapor pressure. This action usually occurs inside the basement or the crawl space.

If the water is not allowed to diffuse into the basement or crawl space, it will rise to the top of the foundation wall where it may rot the sill plate, the headers, and the floor joists if they are not treated lumber. Capillary action can be minimized by sealing the pores in the foundation materials with coatings or membranes. The use of coarse materials, rather than sand or pit-run gravel, below floor slabs can also help.

Dampproofing foundation walls does not prevent water from rising through the footing. A water-impermeable membrane or foundation coating should be installed over footings. A through-the-footing drain tile will help to reduce water pressure under the slab (Fig. 2–196).

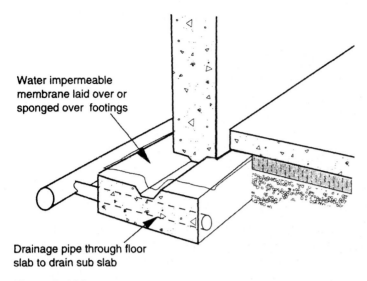

Water impermeable
membrane laid over or
sponged over footings

Drainage pipe through floor
slab to drain sub slab

Figure 2–196 Footing detail to prevent capillary action.

Air Flow Moisture enters attics and wall cavities through air flow. Figure 2–197 shows potential air leakage sites where warm, indoor air can carry water vapor into the shell of the building. All of these sites must be sealed to prevent warm, moist air from exfiltrating into the building envelope, where condensation can occur.

Diffusion Diffusion is a process in which water vapor passes through a seemingly solid material. Water vapor will flow from an area of high vapor pressure to an area of low vapor pressure.

Some materials slow the diffusion of moisture better than others. Since vapor diffusion is never stopped, but

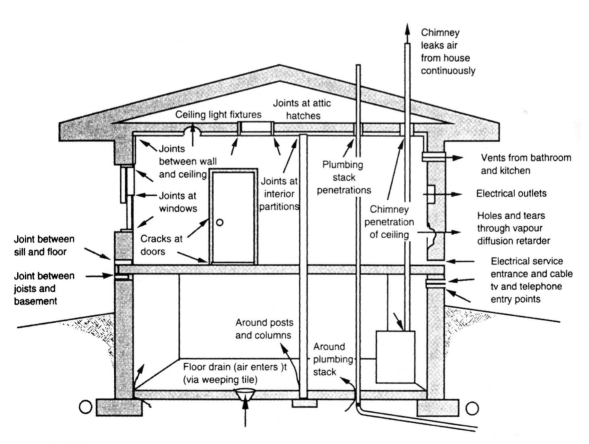

Figure 2–197 Air leakage sites.

Table 2-16 Typical moisture sources per day in houses.

Occupant-Related Sources		Building-Related Sources	
Four occupants	5 liters (1.3 gal)	Seasonal building storage (i.e., framing, drywall, concrete)	8 liters (2.1 gal)
Clothes drying indoors	1.2 liters (0.32 gal)		
Floor washing 10 m³ (107 sq ft)	1 liter (0.26 gal)	Exposed, uncovered earth crawl space	40–50 liters (10.5–13.2 gal)
Cooking (three meals/day)	1 liter (0.26 gal)	Drying and burning of firewood	5 liters (1.3 gal)
Dishwashing (three meals/ day)	½ liter (0.13 gal)	New construction–drying of framing and concrete over first 18 months	4–5 liters (1–1.3 gal)

merely retarded, the term *vapor diffusion retarder* (VDR) should be used instead of the term *vapor barrier*. A VDR must be placed on the warm side of a wall in order to ensure that water vapor does not reach a temperature at which it can condense.

Moisture levels are considerably higher inside a heated house than outside under normal winter conditions because warm air can hold more water vapor than cold air. Moisture is generated by normal daily activities such as cooking, bathing, washing and drying clothes, and breathing. Furniture, drywall, and the framing materials inside the house absorb moisture from humid air in the summer and release it to the interior during the winter. This process is termed *seasonal storage*. Moisture also enters a house from concrete in the basement and from crawl space foundations and floor slabs. An earthen floor in a crawl space or a basement of an older house can be a significant source of moisture.

Table 2–16 shows the amount of moisture that various activities contribute in a home. In a well-built home, indoor humidity levels are controlled by a combination of better building practice and the use of a properly designed and operated mechanical ventilation system.

2.16
CONSTRUCTION STRATEGIES

Houses are subjected to a range of weather conditions. Building assemblies must include elements to protect the structural members from exposure to excessive humidity levels and to ensure that wind does not adversely affect the performance of thermal insulation materials. The four most common approaches include the use of (1) air barriers, (2) vapor diffusion retarders, (3) weather barriers, and (4) moisture barriers/dampproofing.

2.16.1 Air Barriers

In cold climates, air barriers are designed to reduce the outward migration of moisture-filled air (Fig. 2–198). The air barrier is one of the most critical elements of all building envelope components because almost all water vapor is carried by air movement, with only a small amount diffusing through materials. An air barrier must be continuous at all corners, all partition walls, all floors, and all ceiling-wall junctions.

An effective air barrier is impermeable to air flow, continuous over the entire envelope, and durable over the expected lifetime of the building. The smallest cracks, holes, or tears can greatly reduce the effectiveness of an air barrier. All joints and seams must be carefully sealed.

Several different building systems are commonly used to achieve a continuous air barrier. Polyethylene is used as the primary interior air barrier in combination with sealants and header wraps. A second approach, known as the *airtight drywall air barrier (ADA)*, uses drywall in combination with sealants, gaskets, framing members, and

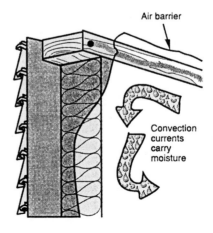

Figure 2–198 Air barrier.

other rigid materials. Exterior air barrier systems are a third option.

Membrane Air Barrier
Polyethylene is one of the most common air barrier systems. Its primary advantage is its dual function in providing the air barrier and the vapor diffuser retarder (VDR). Seams in the polyethylene should occur over solid backing and should be overlapped, caulked with an acoustical caulking, and sandwiched between rigid materials. Detailing at penetrations through the envelope, such as electrical boxes, pipes, and ducts, require special attention. In many instances, an exterior air barrier housewrap is used to provide continuity of the air barrier between floors.

The membrane air barrier cannot be accessed after construction, and certain steps should be taken to ensure its longevity (Fig. 2–199). These steps include the following:

- Locate the membrane on the warm side of the wall.
- Use UV-stabilized, 6-mil polyethylene.
- Overlap seams by a minimum of 6".
- Locate seams over rigid backing such as framing members.
- Caulk seems with a flexible, nondrying sealant.
- Staple seams through the sealant into the solid backing.
- Sandwich polyethylene seams between two solid materials such as the stud and the drywall.

Rigid Air Barrier
The rigid air barrier approach was developed as an alternative to the use of polyethylene. It stresses the use of rigid materials such as drywall as components of the air barrier system. An effective air barrier can be achieved by sealing the drywall at all junctions.

The rigid air barrier offers several advantages. It is not easily damaged in construction. If damaged, it can easily be repaired. It will stand up to high wind pressures on the walls and ceilings. The vapor diffusion retarder can be a number of materials such as polyethylene, foil-backed drywall, or low-permeance interior paints.

Seams between all components of the air barrier must be adequately sealed. Drywall is usually sealed to the framing using adhesive-backed foam tape. Most commonly used is a $1/2'' \times 3/16''$, low-density, closed-cell PVC foam tape. This tape is stapled to wood framing to ensure that it will stay in place during drywalling. It is important that the drywall be screwed or nailed at an 8" spacing over the tape to provide an airtight seal (Fig. 2–200). A rigid air barrier does not act as a vapor diffusion retarder. Most rigid air barriers are installed with a vapor barrier primer or paint used as a VDR.

Exterior Air Barrier
An exterior air barrier can consist of certain rigid insulation materials or more often a housewrap such as spun-bonded polyolefin or spun-bonded polypropylene sheeting. These materials must have the ability to allow adequate vapor transmission while stopping air movement, or they must be located so they prevent condensation of moisture in the wall. Exterior air barriers have the advantage of eliminating the labor required in sealing interior air barrier penetrations on walls and ceilings.

Seams in sheets should be taped with a compatible material as specified by the manufacturer. The membrane

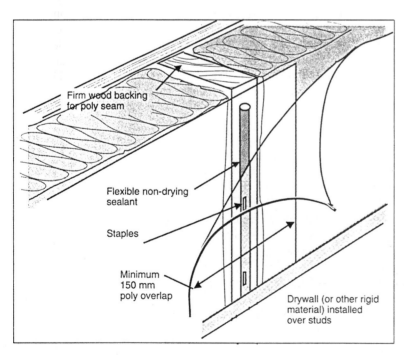

Firm wood backing for poly seam

Flexible non-drying sealant

Staples

Minimum 150 mm poly overlap

Drywall (or other rigid material) installed over studs

Figure 2–199 Sealing polyethylene.

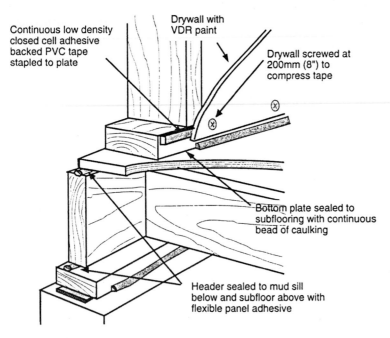

Continuous low density
closed cell adhesive
backed PVC tape
stapled to plate

Drywall with
VDR paint

Drywall screwed at
200mm (8") to
compress tape

Bottom plate sealed to
subflooring with continuous
bead of caulking

Header sealed to mud sill
below and subfloor above with
flexible panel adhesive

Figure 2–200 Rigid air barrier.

air barrier can be sandwiched between rigid materials to provide protection against wind pressure. Typically, fiberboard is used for this purpose. The air barrier must be made continuous and must be properly sealed to both the sill plate and the roofing members (Fig. 2–201).

2.16.2 Vapor Diffusion Retarders

A vapor diffusion retarder (VDR) is a membrane, material, or coating that slows the diffusion of water vapor. VDRs are classified according to their permeability and are measured in *perms*. The lower the perm rating, the more effectively the material will retard diffusion. One perm represents a transfer of one grain (0.002285 oz) of water per square foot of material per hour under a pressure difference of 1″ of mercury (1.134 ft of water). Polyethylene, aluminum foil, and certain kinds of paint can be used as VDRs.

Polyethylene film is very resistant to the flow of water vapor. If the film is made from virgin polyethylene resins, it will be clear. If it is cloudy, it probably contains reused resins. Choose crosslaminated film for best performance.

Paint can also be used as a vapor diffusion retarder. Varying numbers of coats of different types of paints will provide the required resistance to the flow of water vapor. Using paint as the VDR can have advantages because it is applied at the end of the construction process and serves as the finish as well. Care is required to ensure adequate coverage to attain a suitable perm rating.

2.16.3 Weather Barriers

Weather barriers are materials placed on the exterior of the wall or ceiling assembly to protect the interior components of the wall from the effects of wind, rain, snow, and sun. They resist the harmful effects of rain and snow, keeping the insulation and structural members dry. They also improve the thermal performance of the system by keeping wind out. If wind penetrates the insulation cavity, it may reduce the effectiveness of fiber insulations such as glass fiber batts (Fig. 2–202). If rain or snow penetrates the weather barrier, the insulation may become wet, and structural members may rot.

Housewrap materials have gained considerable market share over the last several years, both as sheet-applied materials and as a product laminated to rigid fiberglass sheathing. Spun-bonded polyolefin and woven polypropylene shed liquid water and resist air flow, but they are permeable to the diffusion of water vapor. They are tough enough to withstand severe wind and the rough handling that they might receive during the construction process. They should be covered within 60 days to prevent potential deterioration caused by ultraviolet radiation. Special sheathing tape is used to seal seams, holes, and openings around windows, doors, and service penetrations. Housewrap applications may not provide the desired airtightness unless considerable attention is paid to air sealing the house interior. For most purposes housewrap materials should be considered as a weather barrier, not an air barrier.

Asphalt-impregnated building papers have been used for decades. They must be lapped and secured to per-

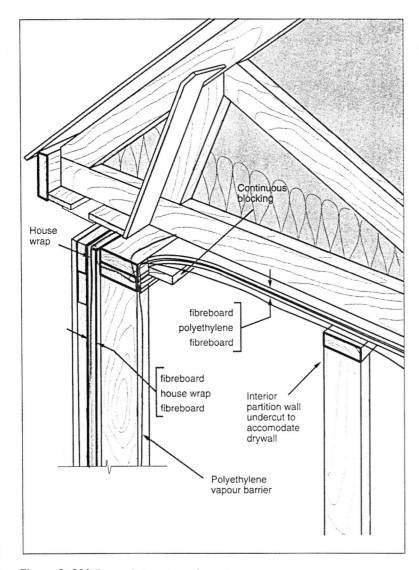

Continuous
blocking

House
wrap

fibreboard
polyethylene
fibreboard

fibreboard
house wrap
fibreboard

Interior
partition wall
undercut to
accomodate
drywall

Polyethylene
vapour barrier

Figure 2–201 External air system elements.

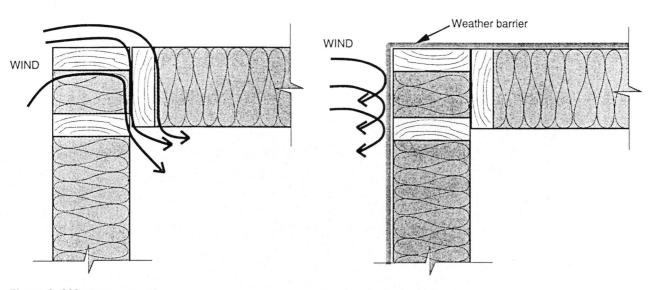

Weather barrier

WIND

WIND

Figure 2–202 Weather barrier.

form adequately. Both solid and perforated building papers are available.

A weather barrier should be resistant to the flow of air, be able to shed rain or snow, be able to withstand forces that may act on it, and last the lifetime of the building.

2.16.4 Moisture Barriers/Dampproofing

Soil vapor pressure can cause moisture to move from the ground through the foundation wall by diffusion, where it is released into the air in the basement or crawl space. To avoid this, dampproofing is required on the exterior of foundation walls located below grade. The material most commonly used for dampproofing is a spray- or mop-applied bituminous substance. It fills the pores in concrete, reducing the penetration of liquid water due to pressure against the wall and capillary action.

A moisture barrier is a material, membrane, or coating used to keep moisture that might come through the foundation wall from penetrating the interior foundation insulation or the wood members supporting the insulation and interior finishes. It is installed only on the below-grade portion of the foundation walls or under floor slabs. Asphalt emulsions applied to the interior surface of a wall provide a continuous membrane. Sheet materials, such as 2-mil polyethylene or building papers, can be fastened to the wall using adhesives or a cold asphalt mastic such as plastic roof cement. All seams must be overlapped and sealed. Newer, specially designed foundation membranes provide protection from moisture and also promote free-flow drainage.

Even good vapor barriers do not prevent some moisture from penetrating through minor breaks in the barrier around pipes, electric outlets, joints, and the like; some moisture will even permeate the barrier itself, not necessarily through minor breaks. Water vapor that has possibly found its way into walls can be released to the outside by *cold side venting*. This condition requires sheathing paper to be weather-resistant but not vapor-proof. Lightweight roofing felt is satisfactory—it can breathe. Siding materials must not be airtight, yet they must have the ability to shed water and resist driving rains. Many of the newer, water-based exterior paints possess this feature of allowing water vapor from the inside to escape through the paint film.

Another suggestion that will help minimize the vapor problem in homes is the installation of forced-air fans in rooms of excess humidity, such as bathrooms, kitchens, and utility areas. The use of exhaust fans directly to the outside relieves the home of much of the otherwise destructive concentrations of humidity.

The following exercises should be done on 8¹/₂″ × 11″ drawing paper with a ¹/₂″ border. Some of the drawings require the use of instruments; others may be done freehand.

1. Using guidelines ¹/₄″ high and ⁵/₁₆″ between each set, divide the sheet into three equally spaced columns. Using architectural style lettering, number 1 through 39 vertically (each vertical row will contain thirteen ¹/₄″ high guidelines and thirteen numbers). Using Fig. 12–1, cover the written terms with opaque paper, read the numbers on the drawing of the house, and letter on the numbered lines the proper term for the items identified by numbers 1 through 39.

2. Using the scale ¹/₄″ = 1′-0″, draw dashed lines to represent the outside wall of a 24′-0″ long by 12′-0″ wide building. Illustrate in plan view the placement of batter boards, string lines, and diagonal measurements that are required to locate the foundation wall and footings for this small structure.

3. Lay out a floor framing plan at a scale of ¹/₄″ = 1′-0″ with 2 × 8 floor joists at 16″ o.c. for the 24′-0″ × 12′-0″ building. Show headers and two rows of bridging. Label materials and sizes on the drawing.

4. Using the scale ¹/₄″ = 1′-0″, lay out a hip-roof framing plan with 2 × 6 rafters at 16″ o.c. for the 24′-0″ × 12′-0″ building using 2′-0″ projection beyond the exterior wall to form an overhang eave. Label materials and sizes on the drawing.

5. Draw the elevation view of a standard W-pattern truss with an 8:12 pitch and a clear span of 28′-0″ at a scale of ¹/₄″ = 1′-0″. Top and bottom chords are 2 × 6s, web members are 2 × 4s, and gussets are ¹/₂″

plywood. Eaves extend 1′-6″ beyond the face of the exterior wall. Label materials and sizes on the drawing.

6. Draw freehand sketches of the front elevation and one side elevation of small buildings with these roof types: gable, hip, shed, mansard, folded-plate, and gambrel. Scale the sketches to fit neatly on the sheet.

7. Draw a freehand section sketch through a 1-story wood frame structure with crawl space below the floor framing and a pitched gable roof with an attic. Using arrows, graphically show where the crawl space and attic should be ventilated. Label vents, and show the ratio of vent area to surface areas.

8. Draw nine 2″ wide by 1¹/₂″ high rectangles equally spaced on the sheet; sketch within each rectangle an elevation view of the following types of exterior siding: horizontal bevel, board-and-batten, novelty, boards-on-boards, V-joint, boards-over-boards, wood shingles with random coursing, wood shingles with regular coursing, and stucco.

9. Sketch a front elevation view of a 1-story gable-roof residence with a brick chimney penetrating the roof surface. Draw one side elevation of the same house, and show a saddle on the roof at the chimney.

10. Sketch four elevations of the end portion of a building with a hip roof. Show a different roofing material on each of the four sketches. Include the following roofing materials: fiberglass shingles, standing seam copper, Spanish clay tile, and wood shakes.

1. Why must you consider local frost depths when drawing footings?

2. What is a good rule of thumb for sizing footings in light construction?

3. Describe a stepped footing, and indicate its application.

4. What condition may require accurate calculation of footing sizes?

5. List three materials that are commonly used for foundation walls.

6. What is a *pier?*

7. Indicate the logical application of grade beam foundation construction.

8. What are the advantages of a slab-on-ground-floor construction in comparison with crawl space construction?

9. What are the identifying characteristics of platform (western) frame construction?

10. Why are trussed rafters widely used in small-home construction?

11. In plank-and-beam framing, how is the load on roof beams transmitted to the foundation?

12. Why should the location of beams in plank-and-beam framing be shown on the working drawings?

13. What part of construction limits the spacing of beams in plank-and-beam framing?

14. What is a *transverse beam?*

15. List the good points of brick veneer construction.

16. Explain modular sizing of concrete block walls.

17. What are the important factors in the selection of a roofing material?

18. What is the purpose of a vapor barrier in a wood wall, and why would it be placed facing the interior side?

19. What are *metal framing anchors,* and where are they used in construction?

20. What is *flashing?* Identify two places where flashing is used.

Product Research Using Computers

As we described in Chapter 2, "Computer-Aided Drafting and Design," CD-ROM resources provide relatively fast access to a wealth of information about construction-related products. The figures on pages 384–387 show screens generated for two different building products from the *SweetSource* CD. With *SweetSource,* you can collect and organize the products that you select. Information on a specific product may contain text describing the technical features, CAD drawings, tables of product data, and photographs. You can copy or export these elements to other software products, including word processors, graphics applications, and CAD programs.

The first three figures contain information about Hebel's aerated concrete products. Figure 1 shows an introductory page that contains a digitally reproduced photograph of a residence built using the Hebel products and a written description of the product. Either window can be enlarged to nearly full screen. Figure 2 shows three more windows containing construction details, product specifications, and a product spreadsheet table. Each window can be enlarged and printed independently, as shown in Figure 3.

Figure 4 describes a rigid Styrofoam exterior foundation drainage insulation manufactured by Dow Chemical Company. The initial screen contains three windows: a product photo, a product description and specifications, and a product properties table. The bottom of the figure shows enlarged portions of the product description window and the entire product properties table.

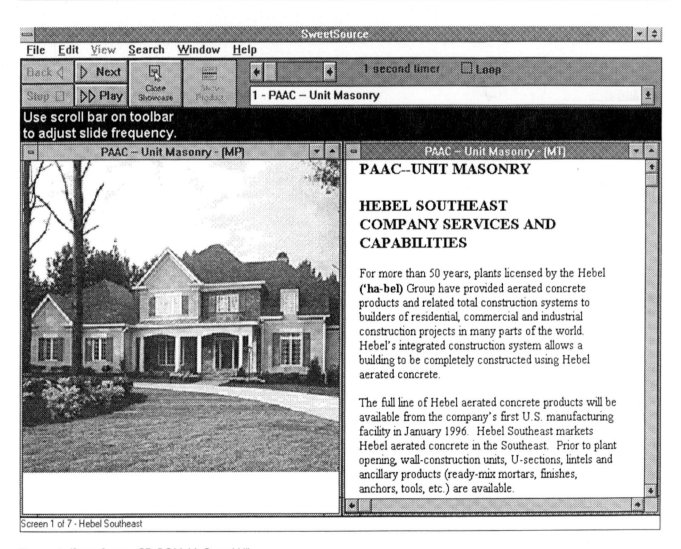

Figure 1 (SweetSource CD-ROM, McGraw-Hill)

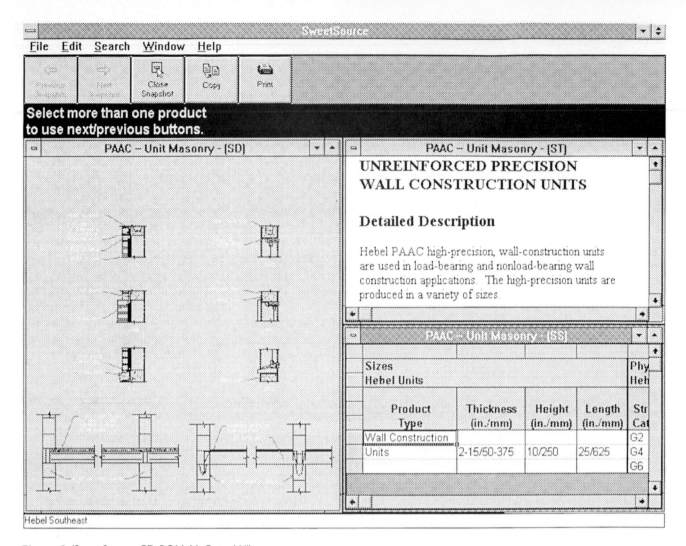

Figure 2 (SweetSource CD-ROM, McGraw-Hill)

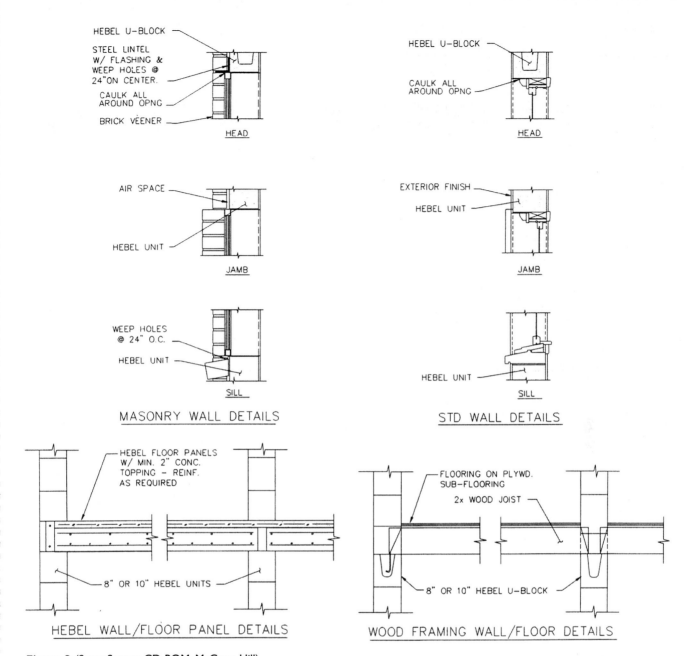

HEBEL U-BLOCK

STEEL LINTEL W/ FLASHING & WEEP HOLES @ 24"ON CENTER.

CAULK ALL AROUND OPNG

BRICK VEENER

HEAD

AIR SPACE

HEBEL UNIT

JAMB

WEEP HOLES @ 24" O.C.

HEBEL UNIT

SILL

MASONRY WALL DETAILS

HEBEL U-BLOCK

CAULK ALL AROUND OPNG

HEAD

EXTERIOR FINISH

HEBEL UNIT

JAMB

HEBEL UNIT

SILL

STD WALL DETAILS

HEBEL FLOOR PANELS W/ MIN. 2" CONC. TOPPING - REINF. AS REQUIRED

8" OR 10" HEBEL UNITS

HEBEL WALL/FLOOR PANEL DETAILS

FLOORING ON PLYWD. SUB-FLOORING

2x WOOD JOIST

8" OR 10" HEBEL U-BLOCK

WOOD FRAMING WALL/FLOOR DETAILS

Figure 3 (SweetSource CD-ROM, McGraw-Hill)

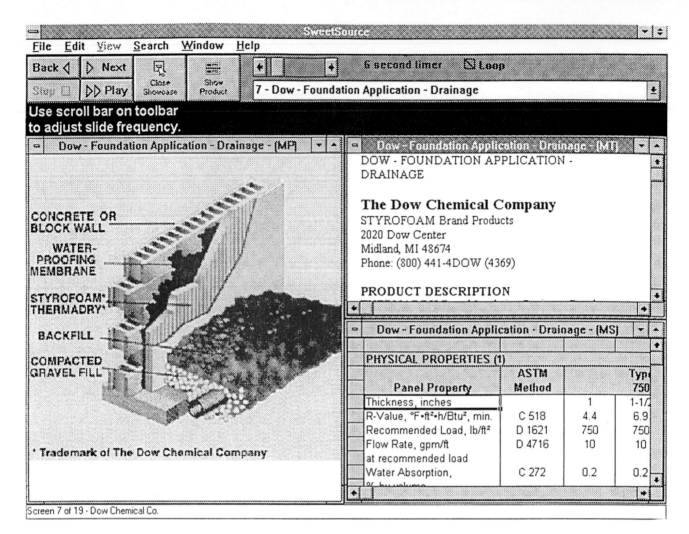

Figure 4 (SweetSource CD-ROM, McGraw-Hill)

"There is always a best way of doing everything, if it be to boil an egg."
—RALPH WALDO EMERSON

Structural Member Selection 3

It is common practice to indicate the sizes of structural members on working drawings. This chapter is concerned with this information and the span and loading tables that must be used to obtain the sizes. The tables are readily available to drafters and designers. On residential drawings this information is placed on the details, floor plans, or other views that seem the most appropriate. In a set of working drawings for a commercial building, structural information is found on separate structural drawings included with the architectural set—usually completed by a structural engineer or other specialist in the area involved.

The tables are compiled and published by various lumber manufacturing associations (for example, the National Forest Products Association) as well as by federal government departments involved with housing and construction. Some are included as part of local code manuals, that often include a nationally recognized building code, and are available at local building inspection offices. Drafters should consult these local code restrictions before making any decisions on structural members.

Notice that each species of framing lumber has its own loading table; a number of the tables are included in this chapter. The tables give minimum sizes, and sometimes good judgment may require that sizes taken from the tables be modified for structural soundness. Only experience in wood framing can provide this valuable background. Occasionally, it becomes feasible to use steel members in critical situations in wood framing; several steel tables are included here for that purpose. Many steel shapes and sizes are available to builders; consult the latest *Manual of Steel Construction* by the American Institute of Steel Construction for detailed information on steel shapes. Often a structural problem can be solved by the introduction of a steel member where wood may not be entirely adequate. For unusual framing problems, it is safest to employ the services of a competent structural engineer experienced in wood structures.

However, the drafter or designer should be familiar with the span tables and other structural information available for specifying and selecting the correct sizes of structural members needed in residential working drawings—mainly so that the builder will not be confronted with a hit-or-miss situation and so that the building will satisfactorily serve its intended purpose.

3.1
STRESSES IN MEMBERS

Let us begin by discussing lumber and its ability to support loads. Wood is a natural material as opposed to human-made, quality-controlled materials such as steel or aluminum; thus, it has inherent structural variations and limits. These variations are caused by species characteristics, natural defects, manufacture, moisture content, and so on. Some species, for example, oak and maple, have excellent resistance to the wear qualities needed on finish floors; other species resist weathering, insect and fungi attack, and decay, such as redwood, cedar, and cypress; yet they possess less desirable structural qualities. The widely cut Douglas fir and southern pine are especially suited for structural use. The majority of structural lumber manufactured today is made from these two species, although considerable amounts of lumber are made from several other minor species. Notice from the tables in this chapter that even those species that have less favorable load-bearing qualities are readily used if need be; yet their sizes must be increased or spans reduced to carry comparable loads.

Normal safety factors are reflected in some tables. Final selection of lumber, however, is usually based on economy and availability of the lumber locally. Higher grades of similar species of lumber can be expected to carry greater loads, as indicated by the tables. Although the innate character of the wood does not change with lower grades, the fewer defects in the better grades will no doubt result in more reliability (Table 3–1) and, as a result, longer spans are given on the tables.

For economy reasons, residential framing lumber is usually visually graded rather than machine graded as is needed for select structural lumber where critical strength and loading properties are needed.

The several structural species of lumber mentioned previously are usually stiffer than other types, especially under loads. The tendency for a member to bend when loaded is known as *deflection* (Fig. 3–1). In some situations within the structure, excessive deflection can cause serious damage, for example, in a plastered ceiling sup-ported by undersized ceiling joists. The deflection under load could cause plaster cracking. Therefore, many tables show several spans, each limited by a different deflection factor. The standard for maximum allowable deflection where very little deflection can be tolerated is $^1/_{360}$ of the span; for less critical situations, $^1/_{240}$ of the span is used. Deflection on long beams can be significant. For example, a horizontal beam or joist limited to, say, an $^1/_{240}$ deflection and selected to span 20'-0" would possibly deflect 1" near its center and still support its designed load. The less restrictive deflection factor is usually specified for rafters or other members where the actual deflection is not as visible as in floor or ceiling framing. Deflection

Table 3–1 Basic grade classifications for yard lumber.

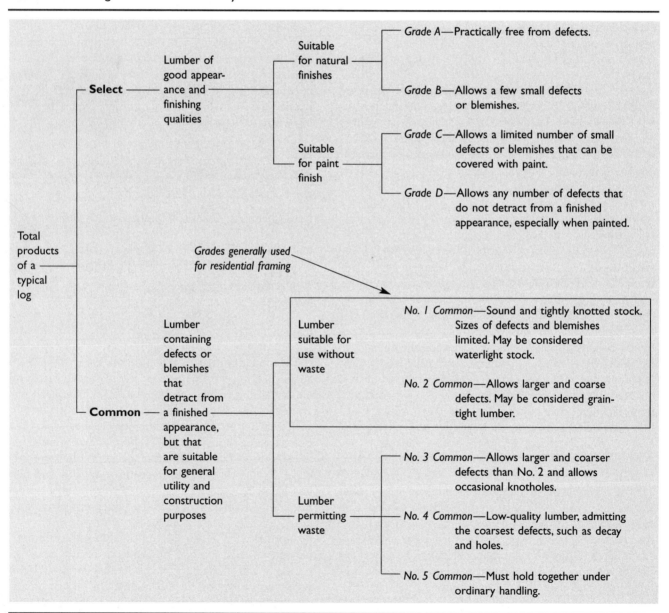

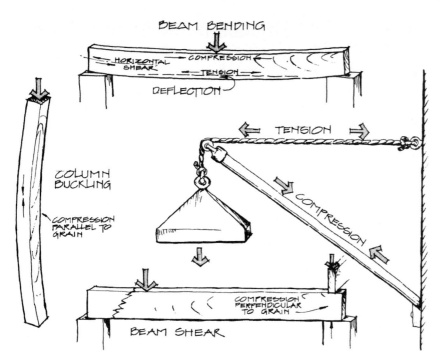

Figure 3–1 Stresses in structural members.

varies inversely with the depth of the beam; so, if suitable, you should select sizes with maximum depth. Members loaded with continuous heavy loads are affected by long-term deflection, often referred to as *live-load creep*. Over a period of years the deformation may be substantial. We see evidence of this creep in older buildings where floors are under continual heavy load; the loaded wood beams often sag considerably. To overcome creep, stiffer and larger members, or steel, can be used.

Elasticity is another important characteristic in selecting framing lumber; the greater the modulus of elasticity (*E*), the stiffer the lumber. Notice in the tables that both southern pine and Douglas fir rate high in this quality.

The stress to be considered in column selection is *buckling* (Fig. 3–1). The fiber in wood columns is under *compression* (parallel to grain) when loaded; some species can resist this squeezing-type stress better than others. *Tension* is a pulling-type stress, not of major concern in most light frame members, except those in triangular-shaped trusses. Whereas columns resist mainly compressive forces parallel to the grain, flexural members, such as beams and joists, are subject to a combination of stresses as shown by Fig. 3–1. This bending (flexure) produces longitudinal stress. For simply supported members, this stress results in compression at the top fiber and tension at the bottom fiber. Vertical applied loads are also resisted by internal shear stresses, which produce a sliding or cutting action. Where joists or beams are supported, compression stresses perpendicular to the grain are

developed; if the bearing length is too short, the bearing area is reduced, thus increasing the unit stresses to the extent that the wood fiber collapses.

3.2

MOISTURE CONTENT

Moisture content also affects the strength of lumber. It is the weight of the water in the wood, expressed as a percentage of the completely dry weight of the wood. Green lumber is not as strong as dried lumber, and we must remember that wood, especially dry wood, is a very good insulator from heat transfer. Lumber, however, tends to take on or give off moisture according to its environment. When it gives off moisture, it shrinks; when it takes it on, it swells. Lumber will shrink more in the dry, southwestern United States than it will in, for example, the coastal and southeastern states. The swelling and shrinking in various amounts is inevitable in wood structures, and the designer should be aware of it. Wood fiber, however, tends to shrink and swell less on end grain than across grain. Therefore, critical supports would be best placed with stresses against end grain (such as with studs and posts) wherever possible. Temperature changes, on the other hand, affect the structural properties of wood very little.

For economy and availability, residential framing lumber is universally specified at 19% moisture content; structural lumber used for more critical design loads is often specified at 15% moisture content. Check these criteria on tables, because values on identical members will vary. Finish lumber is usually specified at 12%; lumber with moisture content above 19% is considered unseasoned.

3.3
LOCAL CODES

Since every building must conform to building codes and restrictions, drafters must be familiar with these documents when doing residential drawings. The purpose of the codes is to provide for safety and to protect the health and welfare of the occupants. Live loads on floors and roofs are especially important in wood framing (Fig. 3–2). Local conditions throughout the United States vary considerably, and therefore local restrictions must be used to reflect these conditions. However, most local codes also include one of the national codes—the Uniform Building Code, the Standard Building Code, and the most recent International Residential Code 2000—as part of the document. Some areas use the F.H.A. Minimum Property Standards as a supplement to their codes. Remember that codes indicate minimum values, and any departures should be on the restrictive side.

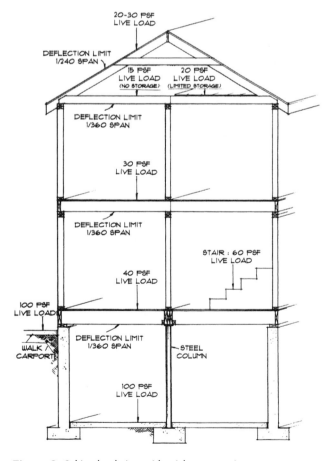

Figure 3–2 Live loads in residential construction.

3.4
FIRST DETERMINE THE LOADS

Before using the tables in this chapter to size framing members, calculate the total load that will be imposed on each supporting member. The weights of materials can be found in Table 2–2. More complete building material weights can be obtained from Architectural Graphic Standards. Include all materials that will form the tributary load (see Fig. 2–6). Roof loads are usually transmitted directly to exterior walls, especially roofs that are supported with prefabricated trusses, and they therefore do not need to be considered in column and girder loading. The total applied load supported by a structural member includes both the *dead load* and the *live load*. Refer to Table 3–2 for typical minimum live loads in residential framing.

Figure 3–3 presents an example of residential dead and live loads. The total design load at the base of the foundation wall or the footing of a typical single-family, wood frame house does not generally exceed 2500 lb per square foot (psf) for 1-story structures or 3000 psf for 2-story structures. The total design loads on center girder support columns generally do not exceed 7000 lb for 1-story structures or 10,000 lb for 2-story structures. Usually the local building code establishes the design snow load due to the regional variations in seasonal snowfall.

3.4.1 Columns

Indicate the size and the type of basement columns on the *basement plan*. Because steel columns are readily available and their smaller size allows more usable floor space, they have become more popular than wood columns, especially in 1-story heights (Fig. 3–2). Welded ¼″ steel plates are attached to each end for securing (see Fig. 2–50). The hollow center may be filled with concrete to increase their strength.

Table 3–2 Minimum residential live loads.

Location	Live load (psf)
Dwelling rooms (other than sleeping)	40
Dwelling rooms (sleeping only)	30
Attics (served by any type of stairs)	30
Attics (limited storage)	20
Attics (no storage)	15
Stairs	60
Public stairs, corridors (2-family duplex)	60
Garage or carport (passenger cars)	100
Walks	100

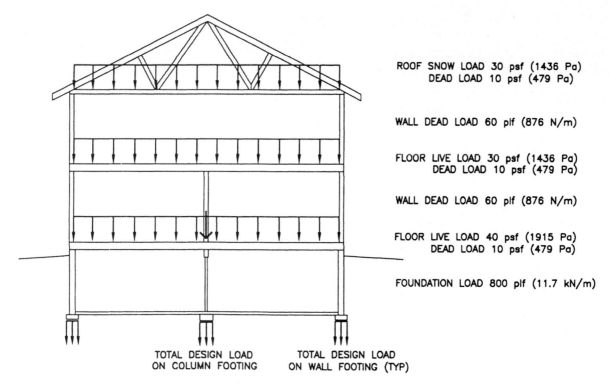

ROOF SNOW LOAD 30 psf (1436 Pa)
DEAD LOAD 10 psf (479 Pa)

WALL DEAD LOAD 60 plf (876 N/m)

FLOOR LIVE LOAD 30 psf (1436 Pa)
DEAD LOAD 10 psf (479 Pa)

WALL DEAD LOAD 60 plf (876 N/m)

FLOOR LIVE LOAD 40 psf (1915 Pa)
DEAD LOAD 10 psf (479 Pa)

FOUNDATION LOAD 800 plf (11.7 kN/m)

TOTAL DESIGN LOAD
ON COLUMN FOOTING

TOTAL DESIGN LOAD
ON WALL FOOTING (TYP)

Figure 3–3 Example of residential live and dead loads.

Try to locate columns at load points if possible. When the floor area to be framed is established, make several sketches on overlap paper above the plan to determine the best framing and support method possible. Columns used to support wood or steel girders are typically 3″ steel pipe or 4 × 4 or 6 × 6 timber. Table 3–3 shows the maximum column spacing for typical wood and steel columns that have a maximum unsupported length of 8′.

The American Iron and Steel Institute, in their publication RG-936, *Residential Steel Beam and Column Load/Span Tables* (1993), has developed load and span tables for column and beam sections commonly used in residential construction. The tables identify recommended spacing for columns of various sizes depending on the width of the house and the tributary area supported by the column. Roof loads are not included. It is assumed that the roof system spans between exterior bearing walls. Table 3–4 contains an example for supporting one floor only.

3.4.2 Beams

Indicate the size and the type of beams that support first-floor joists on the basement or foundation plan. Usually, a heavy broken line is a sufficient symbol. Again, if living space is important in the basement area, it may be advantageous to use a steel beam rather than wood to allow columns to be spaced farther apart. In crawl spaces use of steel beams is not critical; C.M.U. piers are uni-

versally used at ground level since they can be located at critical points under the framing and they can be somewhat closer together to minimize beam sizes.

Wood beams can be either solid or built up from 2″ framing lumber well spiked together. Notice that built-up beams span slightly shorter spans than similar-size solid members. This fact is reflected in the tables because more sides have been planed during finishing, which results in a smaller cross section. In small homes it is usually more practical to build up the wood beam using the same-size framing material as that used for joists, shown in Fig. 2–46D. If headroom or an uninterrupted ceiling is important below, or if a beam must be introduced into the joist framing and must be at the same level, ledger strips or hangers can be used (Fig. 2–46D) to support the joists against the beam rather than rest on the beam Table 3–5 indicates allowable spans for built-up wood girders for 1-, 2-, and 3-story structures of varying widths.

Steel beams are usually W sections; allow for a wood plate to be fastened above the beam for securing the wood joists (Fig. 2–46A). The wood joists can also be framed to the side of the steel beam. Steel column cap plates are welded or fastened to the beam with bolts (see Fig. 2–50). As mentioned previously, steel beams usually allow more headroom below.

Steel angle lintels, usually needed over brick veneer openings, are listed in Table 2–10. Table 3–6 shows allowable spans for steel girders for 1-, 2-, and 3-story structures of varying widths.

Table 3–3 Maximum spacing for typical wood and steel columns for support of center beams.

| Width of Structure in Feet (Meters) | Column Size | Maximum Spacing | | | | | |
| | | 1 Story | | 2 Story | | 3 Story | |
		ft-in.	m	ft-in.	m	ft-in.	m
24	4 × 4 wood	8-4	2.53	4-7	1.40		
(7.32)	6 × 6 wood	20-2	6.16	11-2	3.41	7-10	2.38
	3″ diameter STD	25-2	7.68	13-7	4.15	9-4	2.83
	TS 3 × 3 × 0.1875	27-4	8.32	14-10	4.51	10-1	3.08
	3.5″ diameter STD	34-7	10.55	18-8	5.70	12-10	3.90
28	4 × 4 wood	7-1	2.16	4-0	1.22		
(8.53)	6 × 6 wood	17-4	5.27	9-7	2.93	6-7	2.01
	3″ diameter STD	21-8	6.61	11-10	3.60	8-1	2.47
	TS 3 × 3 × 0.1875	23-6	7.16	12-10	3.90	8-10	2.68
	3.5″ diameter STD	29-10	9.08	16-2	4.94	11-1	3.38
32	4 × 4 wood	6-4	1.92				
(9.75)	6 × 6 wood	15-1	4.60	8-5	2.56	5-10	1.77
	3″ diameter STD	19-1	5.82	10-5	3.17	7-1	2.16
	TS 3 × 3 × 0.1875	20-8	6.31	11-4	3.44	7-8	2.35
	3.5″ diameter STD	26-2	7.99	14-4	4.36	9-10	2.99
36	4 × 4 wood	5-7	1.71				
(10.97)	6 × 6	13-5	4.08	7-6	2.29	5-2	1.58
	3″ diameter STD	17-0	5.18	9-4	2.83	6-5	1.95
	TS 3 × 3 × 0.1875	18-5	5.61	10-1	3.08	6-11	2.10
	3.5″ diameter STD	23-5	7.13	12-10	3.90	8-10	2.68

SOURCE: For pipe and tube columns: *Residential Steel Beam and Column Load/Span Tables—Pipe and Tube Columns,* American Iron and Steel Institute, Washington, DC, 1993. Used by permission of AISI.

NOTES:
1. Live load for the first floor is 40 psf (1915 Pa); for the second and third floors, 30 psf (1436 Pa).
2. Dead load is 10 psf (479 Pa) per floor. A clear-span, trussed roof is assumed; no attic or roof loads are included.
3. The unbraced length of a column is 8 ft (2.44 m).
4. Wood columns are limited by column compression buckling. Values are not applicable to adjustable-height columns.

Table 3–4 Steel column spacing in residential construction.

Steel Beam and Column Tables

Copyright 1993 by American Iron and Steel Institute

Residential Steel Column Load/Spacing Tables - Pipe and Tube Columns
MAXIMUM COLUMN SPACING, when C = D or MAXIMUM TRIBUTARY LENGTH, (C+D)/2, when C ≠ D; ft.
ONE FLOOR ONLY (no roof or attic loads) - Unbraced Length of Column = 8 feet

DL (psf) + 10   LL (psf)* 40

| COLUMN | Column Properties | | | | | TRIBUTARY WIDTH SUPPORTED BY THE CENTER BEAM - (A+B)/2 | | | | | | | | |
SIZE	Weight/Ft.	Fy	A	Pe	Pa	8'-0	10'-0	12'-0	14'-0	16'-0	18'-0	20'-0	22'-0	24'-0
3″dia. STD.	7.58	36	2.23	16	34	35.0	30.0	25.2	21.7	19.1	17.0	15.3	14.0	12.8
TS 3x3x0.1875	6.87	46	2.02	17	35	35.0	32.5	27.3	23.5	20.7	18.4	16.6	15.2	13.9
3.5″dia. STD.	9.11	36	2.68	22	44	35.0	35.0	34.6	29.8	26.2	23.4	21.1	19.2	17.7
TS 3x3x0.2500	8.81	46	2.59	21	44	35.0	35.0	33.7	29.1	25.5	22.8	20.6	18.7	17.2

DL (psf)+ 15   LL (psf)* 40

| COLUMN | Column Properties | | | | | TRIBUTARY WIDTH SUPPORTED BY THE CENTER BEAM - (A+B)/2 | | | | | | | | |
SIZE	Weight/Ft.	Fy	A	Pe	Pa	8'-0	10'-0	12'-0	14'-0	16'-0	18'-0	20'-0	22'-0	24'-0
3″dia. STD.	7.58	36	2.23	16	34	33.8	27.3	23.0	19.8	17.4	15.5	14.0	12.7	11.7
TS 3x3x0.1875	6.87	46	2.02	17	35	35.0	29.6	24.9	21.4	18.8	16.8	15.2	13.8	12.7
3.5″dia. STD.	9.11	36	2.68	22	44	35.0	35.0	31.6	27.2	23.9	21.3	19.2	17.5	16.1
TS 3x3x0.2500	8.81	46	2.59	21	44	35.0	35.0	30.8	26.5	23.3	20.8	18.7	17.1	15.7

DL (psf)+ 20   LL (psf)* 40

| COLUMN | Column Properties | | | | | TRIBUTARY WIDTH SUPPORTED BY THE CENTER BEAM - (A+B)/2 | | | | | | | | |
SIZE	Weight/Ft.	Fy	A	Pe	Pa	8'-0	10'-0	12'-0	14'-0	16'-0	18'-0	20'-0	22'-0	24'-0
3″dia. STD.	7.58	36	2.23	16	34	31.1	25.2	21.1	18.2	16.0	14.2	12.8	11.7	10.7
TS 3x3x0.1875	6.87	46	2.02	17	35	33.8	27.3	22.9	19.7	17.3	15.4	13.9	12.7	11.6
3.5″dia. STD.	9.11	36	2.68	22	44	35.0	34.6	29.0	25.0	22.0	19.6	17.7	16.1	14.8
TS 3x3x0.2500	8.81	46	2.59	21	44	35.0	33.7	28.3	24.4	21.4	19.1	17.2	15.7	14.4

Column loads are based on a maximum eccentricity of 1″ between the resultant (total) load and the centerline of the column.
Supported beams may be single span or continuous with a maximum eccentricity of 1″ for the resultant load.
Fy = Minimum design yield stress per the AISC Specification, ksi.   K = 1.0
A = Gross cross-sectional area of column per the AISC Manual, in.
Pe = Maximum axial load with an eccentricity of 1″, per the AISC Manual, kips.
Pa = Allowable axial load values from the 1989 AISC - ASD Manual, Allowable Concentric Load Tables, kips.
* No live load reductions have been included.   + DL is in addition to beam weight.
(C+D)/2 has been limited to 35 feet to correspond with the beam tables.
Column bearing design must be per the AISC Specification. Guidance on base plate design can be found on pages 3-106 through 3-111 of the 1989 AISC ASD Manual.

RESIDENTIAL STEEL FRAMING   June 1993

SOURCE: Copyright 1993 by the American Iron and Steel Institute.

Table 3–5 Allowable spans for built-up wood center girders.

| Width of Structure in Feet (Meters) | Girder Size | Maximum Clear Span | | | | | |
| | | 1 Story | | 2 Story | | 3 Story | |
		ft-in.	m	ft-in.	m	ft-in.	m
24	3-2 × 8	6-7	2.02	4-11	1.50	4-1	1.25
(7.32)	4-2 × 8	7-8	2.33	5-8	1.74	4-9	1.44
	3-2 × 10	8-5	2.57	6-3	1.92	5-3	1.60
	4-2 × 10	9-9	2.97	7-3	2.22	6-1	1.84
	3-2 × 12	10-3	3.13	7-8	2.33	6-4	1.94
	4-2 × 12	11-10	3.61	8-10	2.69	7-4	2.24
26	3-2 × 8	6-4	1.94	4-9	1.44	3-11	1.20
(7.92)	4-2 × 8	7-4	2.24	5-6	1.67	4-7	1.39
	3-2 × 10	8-1	2.47	6-1	1.84	5-0	1.53
	4-2 × 10	9-4	2.86	7-0	2.13	5-10	1.77
	3-2 × 12	9-10	3.01	7-4	2.24	6-1	1.87
	4-2 × 12	11-5	3.47	8-6	2.59	7-1	2.15
28	3-2 × 8	6-2	1.88	4-7	1.39	3-10	1.16
(8.53)	4-2 × 8	7-1	2.16	5-3	1.61	4-5	1.34
	3-2 × 10	7-10	2.38	5-10	1.78	4-10	1.48
	4-2 × 10	9-0	2.75	6-9	2.05	5-7	1.71
	3-2 × 12	9-6	2.90	7-1	2.16	5-11	1.80
	4-2 × 12	11-0	3.35	8-2	2.49	6-10	2.08
32	3-2 × 8	5-9	1.75	4-3	1.30	3-7	1.08
(9.75)	4-2 × 8	6-7	2.02	4-11	1.50	4-1	1.25
	3-2 × 10	7-4	2.23	5-5	1.66	4-6	1.38
	4-2 × 10	8-5	2.57	6-3	1.92	5-3	1.60
	3-2 × 12	8-11	2.71	6-8	2.02	5-6	1.68
	4-2 × 12	10-3	3.13	7-8	2.33	6-4	1.94

NOTES:
1. Values are for a clear-span, trussed roof, a load-bearing center wall on the first floor in 2-story construction, and a load-bearing center wall on the first and second floors in 3-story construction.
2. Spans are based on a species and grade of lumber having an allowable bending stress $F_b = 1000$ psi (6895 kPa) for repetitive members.

Table 3–6 Allowable spans for typical steel center girders.

| Width of Structure in Feet (Meters) | Beam Size | Maximum Center-to-Center Span | | | | | |
| | | 1 Story | | 2 Story | | 3 Story | |
		ft-in.	m	ft-in.	m	ft-in.	m
24	W 6 × 9	11-4	3.44	8-10	2.68	7-4	2.23
(7.32)	W 8 × 10	14-0	4.27	10-5	3.17	8-7	2.62
	W 10 × 12	16-10	5.12	12-4	3.75	10-2	3.11
	W 12 × 14	19-7	5.97	14-5	4.39	11-11	3.63
	W 14 × 22	26-0	7.92	20-0	6.07	16-6	5.03
28	W 6 × 9	10-10	3.29	8-2	2.50	6-10	2.07
(8.53)	W 8 × 10	13-2	4.02	9-8	2.96	8-0	2.44
	W 10 × 12	15-7	4.75	11-5	3.47	9-6	2.90
	W 12 × 14	18-2	5.55	13-5	4.08	11-0	3.35
	W 14 × 22	24-8	7.53	18-7	5.67	15-4	4.66
32	W 6 × 9	10-4	3.14	7-8	2.35	6-4	1.92
(9.75)	W 8 × 10	12-5	3.78	9-1	2.77	7-6	2.29
	W 10 × 12	14-7	4.45	10-8	3.26	8-11	2.71
	W 12 × 14	17-0	5.18	12-6	3.81	10-5	3.17
	W 14 × 22	23-7	7.19	17-5	5.30	13-6	4.11
36	W 6 × 9	9-10	2.99	7-2	2.19	6-0	1.83
(10.97)	W 8 × 10	11-8	3.57	8-7	3.11	7-1	2.16
	W 10 × 12	13-10	4.21	10-1	3.08	8-5	2.56
	W 12 × 14	16-1	4.91	11-10	3.60	9-8	2.96
	W 14 × 22	22-4	6.80	16-6	5.03	12-0	3.66

SOURCE: *Residential Steel Beam and Column Load/Span Tables——Wide Flange Beams*, American Iron and Steel Institute, Washington, DC, 1993. Used by permission of AISI.
NOTES:
1. Live load for the first floor is 40 psf (1915 Pa); for the second and third floors, 30 psf (1436 Pa).
2. The spans assume clear-span, trussed roof construction (no attic or roof loads are included).
3. Dead load is 10 psf (479 Pa) per floor.

Table 3–7 Relative strengths of engineered wood products.

Engineered Wood Product	Fiber Stress in Bending, F_b		Tension Parallel to Grain F_t		Shear Parallel to Grain, F_v		Compression Perpendicular to Grain, $F_{o\perp}$		Compression Parallel to Grain $F_{o\parallel}$		Modulus of Elasticity, E	
	psi	kPa	psi	kPa	psi	kPa	psi	kPa	psi	kPa	psi	kPA
Parallel-strand lumber[a]	2950	20,340	2400	16,547	290	1999	600	4137	2900	19,995	2,000,000	13,789,520
Laminated veneer lumber[b]	2875	19,822	1850	12,755	285	1965	500	3447	2700	18,616	2,000,000	13,789,520
Glue laminated lumber[c]	1600–2400	11,032–16,547	650–1300	4482–8963	90–200	621–1379	300–600	2068–4137	900–1750	6205–12,066	1,100,000–1,800,000	7,584,236–12,410,568

SOURCE: *Alternatives to Lumber and Plywood in Home Construction*, NAHB Research Center. Prepared for the U.S. Department of Housing and Urban Development, Washington, DC, 1993.
[a]Parallam PSL, 2 × 10.
[b]MicroLam, 2 × 10.
[c]Consult National Design Specification by American Forest and Paper Association (AFPA) for design values and adjustment factors for specific grades of glue laminated lumber.

3.4.3 Engineered Wood Girders

Engineered wood products such as glue laminated lumber (glulam), laminated veneer lumber (LVL), and parallel-strand lumber (PSL) are also available. These products generally have more uniform structural properties and a lower moisture content. Table 13–7 provides a comparison of the relative strengths of some of these products. Table 13–8, developed by the American Institute of Timber Construction (AITC), compares equivalent glulam sections for solid beams, steel beams, and LVL beams. It

Table 3–8 Equivalent glulam sections.

Equivalent Glulam Sections for Solid Sawn Beams

Sawn Section Nominal Size	Roof Beams Select Structural Douglas Fir	Roof Beams Select Structural Southern Pine	Roof Beams No. 1 Douglas Fir	Roof Beams No. 1 Southern Pine	Floor Beams Select Structural Douglas Fir	Floor Beams Select Structural Southern Pine	Floor Beams No. 1 Douglas Fir	Floor Beams No. 1 Southern Pine
3 × 8	$3\frac{1}{8} \times 6$	$3\frac{1}{8} \times 6\frac{7}{8}$	$3\frac{1}{8} \times 6$	$3\frac{1}{8} \times 5\frac{1}{2}$	$3\frac{1}{8} \times 7\frac{1}{2}$	$3\frac{1}{8} \times 6\frac{7}{8}$	$3\frac{1}{8} \times 7\frac{1}{2}$	$3\frac{1}{8} \times 6\frac{7}{8}$
3 × 10	$3\frac{1}{8} \times 7\frac{1}{2}$	$3\frac{1}{8} \times 8\frac{1}{4}$	$3\frac{1}{8} \times 6$	$3\frac{1}{8} \times 6\frac{7}{8}$	$3\frac{1}{8} \times 9$	$3\frac{1}{8} \times 9\frac{5}{8}$	$3\frac{1}{8} \times 9$	$3\frac{1}{8} \times 9\frac{5}{8}$
3 × 12	$3\frac{1}{8} \times 9$	$3\frac{1}{8} \times 9\frac{5}{8}$	$3\frac{1}{8} \times 7\frac{1}{2}$	$3\frac{1}{8} \times 8\frac{1}{4}$	$3\frac{1}{8} \times 12$	$3\frac{1}{8} \times 11$	$3\frac{1}{8} \times 10\frac{1}{2}$	$3\frac{1}{8} \times 11$
3 × 14	$3\frac{1}{8} \times 9$	$3\frac{1}{8} \times 11$	$3\frac{1}{8} \times 7\frac{1}{2}$	$3\frac{1}{8} \times 8\frac{1}{4}$	$3\frac{1}{8} \times 13\frac{1}{2}$	$3\frac{1}{8} \times 13\frac{3}{4}$	$3\frac{1}{8} \times 13\frac{1}{2}$	$3\frac{1}{8} \times 12\frac{3}{8}$
4 × 6	$3\frac{1}{8} \times 6$	$3\frac{1}{8} \times 6\frac{7}{8}$	$3\frac{1}{8} \times 6$	$3\frac{1}{8} \times 5\frac{1}{2}$	$3\frac{1}{8} \times 6$	$3\frac{1}{8} \times 6\frac{7}{8}$	$3\frac{1}{8} \times 6$	$3\frac{1}{8} \times 6\frac{7}{8}$
4 × 8	$3\frac{1}{8} \times 7\frac{1}{2}$	$3\frac{1}{8} \times 8\frac{1}{4}$	$3\frac{1}{8} \times 6$	$3\frac{1}{8} \times 6\frac{7}{8}$	$3\frac{1}{8} \times 9$	$3\frac{1}{8} \times 8\frac{1}{4}$	$3\frac{1}{8} \times 7\frac{1}{2}$	$3\frac{1}{8} \times 8\frac{1}{4}$
4 × 10	$3\frac{1}{8} \times 9$	$3\frac{1}{8} \times 9\frac{5}{8}$	$3\frac{1}{8} \times 7\frac{1}{2}$	$3\frac{1}{8} \times 8\frac{1}{4}$	$3\frac{1}{8} \times 10\frac{1}{2}$	$3\frac{1}{8} \times 11$	$3\frac{1}{8} \times 10\frac{1}{2}$	$3\frac{1}{8} \times 9\frac{5}{8}$
4 × 12	$3\frac{1}{8} \times 10\frac{1}{2}$	$3\frac{1}{8} \times 12\frac{3}{8}$	$3\frac{1}{8} \times 9$	$3\frac{1}{8} \times 9\frac{5}{8}$	$3\frac{1}{8} \times 12$	$3\frac{1}{8} \times 12\frac{3}{8}$	$3\frac{1}{8} \times 12$	$3\frac{1}{8} \times 12\frac{3}{8}$
4 × 14	$3\frac{1}{8} \times 10\frac{1}{2}$	$3\frac{1}{8} \times 12\frac{3}{8}$	$3\frac{1}{8} \times 9$	$3\frac{1}{8} \times 9\frac{5}{8}$	$3\frac{1}{8} \times 15$	$3\frac{1}{8} \times 15\frac{1}{8}$	$3\frac{1}{8} \times 13\frac{1}{2}$	$3\frac{1}{8} \times 13\frac{3}{4}$
4 × 16	$3\frac{1}{8} \times 12$	$3\frac{1}{8} \times 13\frac{3}{4}$	$3\frac{1}{8} \times 10\frac{1}{2}$	$3\frac{1}{8} \times 9\frac{5}{8}$	$3\frac{1}{8} \times 16\frac{1}{2}$	$3\frac{1}{8} \times 16\frac{1}{2}$	$3\frac{1}{8} \times 16\frac{1}{2}$	$3\frac{1}{8} \times 16\frac{1}{2}$
6 × 8	$5\frac{1}{8} \times 7\frac{1}{2}$	$5\frac{1}{8} \times 6\frac{7}{8}$	$5\frac{1}{8} \times 7\frac{1}{2}$	$5\frac{1}{8} \times 6\frac{7}{8}$	$5\frac{1}{8} \times 7\frac{1}{2}$	$5\frac{1}{8} \times 8\frac{1}{4}$	$5\frac{1}{8} \times 7\frac{1}{2}$	$5\frac{1}{8} \times 8\frac{1}{4}$
6 × 10	$5\frac{1}{8} \times 9$	$5\frac{1}{8} \times 8\frac{1}{4}$	$5\frac{1}{8} \times 9$	$5\frac{1}{8} \times 8\frac{1}{4}$	$5\frac{1}{8} \times 10\frac{1}{2}$	$5\frac{1}{8} \times 9\frac{5}{8}$	$5\frac{1}{8} \times 10\frac{1}{2}$	$5\frac{1}{8} \times 9\frac{5}{8}$
6 × 12	$5\frac{1}{8} \times 10\frac{1}{2}$	$5\frac{1}{8} \times 9\frac{5}{8}$	$5\frac{1}{8} \times 9$	$5\frac{1}{8} \times 9\frac{5}{8}$	$5\frac{1}{8} \times 12$	$5\frac{1}{8} \times 12\frac{3}{8}$	$5\frac{1}{8} \times 12$	$5\frac{1}{8} \times 12\frac{3}{8}$
6 × 14	$5\frac{1}{8} \times 12$	$5\frac{1}{8} \times 11$	$5\frac{1}{8} \times 10\frac{1}{2}$	$5\frac{1}{8} \times 11$	$5\frac{1}{8} \times 13\frac{1}{2}$	$5\frac{1}{8} \times 13\frac{3}{4}$	$5\frac{1}{8} \times 13\frac{1}{2}$	$5\frac{1}{8} \times 13\frac{3}{4}$
6 × 16	$5\frac{1}{8} \times 13\frac{1}{2}$	$5\frac{1}{8} \times 13\frac{3}{4}$	$5\frac{1}{8} \times 12$	$5\frac{1}{8} \times 12\frac{3}{8}$	$5\frac{1}{8} \times 16\frac{1}{2}$	$5\frac{1}{8} \times 16\frac{1}{2}$	$5\frac{1}{8} \times 16\frac{1}{2}$	$5\frac{1}{8} \times 16\frac{1}{2}$
6 × 18	$5\frac{1}{8} \times 15$	$5\frac{1}{8} \times 15\frac{1}{8}$	$5\frac{1}{8} \times 13\frac{1}{2}$	$5\frac{1}{8} \times 13\frac{3}{4}$	$5\frac{1}{8} \times 18$	$5\frac{1}{8} \times 17\frac{1}{8}$	$5\frac{1}{8} \times 18$	$5\frac{1}{8} \times 17\frac{1}{8}$
6 × 20	$5\frac{1}{8} \times 18$	$5\frac{1}{8} \times 16\frac{1}{2}$	$5\frac{1}{8} \times 16\frac{1}{2}$	$5\frac{1}{8} \times 15\frac{1}{8}$	$5\frac{1}{8} \times 19\frac{1}{2}$	$5\frac{1}{8} \times 19\frac{1}{4}$	$5\frac{1}{8} \times 19\frac{1}{2}$	$5\frac{1}{8} \times 19\frac{1}{4}$
8 × 10	$6\frac{3}{4} \times 9$	$6\frac{3}{4} \times 8\frac{1}{4}$	$6\frac{3}{4} \times 9$	$6\frac{3}{4} \times 8\frac{1}{4}$	$6\frac{3}{4} \times 10\frac{1}{2}$	$6\frac{3}{4} \times 9\frac{5}{8}$	$6\frac{3}{4} \times 10\frac{1}{2}$	$6\frac{3}{4} \times 9\frac{5}{8}$
8 × 12	$6\frac{3}{4} \times 10\frac{1}{2}$	$6\frac{3}{4} \times 9\frac{5}{8}$	$6\frac{3}{4} \times 10\frac{1}{2}$	$6\frac{3}{4} \times 9\frac{5}{8}$	$6\frac{3}{4} \times 12$	$6\frac{3}{4} \times 12\frac{3}{8}$	$6\frac{3}{4} \times 12$	$6\frac{3}{4} \times 12\frac{3}{8}$
8 × 14	$6\frac{3}{4} \times 12$	$6\frac{3}{4} \times 12\frac{1}{8}$	$6\frac{3}{4} \times 12$	$6\frac{3}{4} \times 11$	$6\frac{3}{4} \times 13\frac{1}{2}$	$6\frac{3}{4} \times 13\frac{3}{4}$	$6\frac{3}{4} \times 13\frac{1}{2}$	$6\frac{3}{4} \times 13\frac{1}{4}$
8 × 16	$6\frac{3}{4} \times 13\frac{1}{2}$	$6\frac{3}{4} \times 13\frac{3}{4}$	$6\frac{3}{4} \times 13\frac{1}{2}$	$6\frac{3}{4} \times 12\frac{3}{8}$	$6\frac{3}{4} \times 16\frac{1}{2}$	$6\frac{3}{4} \times 17\frac{7}{8}$	$6\frac{3}{4} \times 16\frac{1}{2}$	$6\frac{3}{4} \times 17\frac{7}{8}$
8 × 18	$6\frac{3}{4} \times 16\frac{1}{2}$	$6\frac{3}{4} \times 15\frac{1}{8}$	$6\frac{3}{4} \times 15$	$6\frac{3}{4} \times 13\frac{3}{4}$	$6\frac{3}{4} \times 18$	$6\frac{3}{4} \times 17\frac{7}{8}$	$6\frac{3}{4} \times 18$	$6\frac{3}{4} \times 17\frac{7}{8}$
8 × 20	$6\frac{3}{4} \times 18$	$6\frac{3}{4} \times 17\frac{7}{8}$	$6\frac{3}{4} \times 16\frac{1}{2}$	$6\frac{3}{4} \times 15\frac{1}{4}$	$6\frac{3}{4} \times 19\frac{1}{2}$	$6\frac{3}{4} \times 20\frac{5}{8}$	$6\frac{3}{4} \times 19\frac{1}{2}$	$6\frac{3}{4} \times 20\frac{5}{8}$
8 × 22	$6\frac{3}{4} \times 19\frac{1}{2}$	$6\frac{3}{4} \times 17\frac{7}{8}$	$6\frac{3}{4} \times 18$	$6\frac{3}{4} \times 17\frac{7}{8}$	$6\frac{3}{4} \times 22\frac{1}{2}$	$6\frac{3}{4} \times 22$	$6\frac{3}{4} \times 22\frac{1}{2}$	$6\frac{3}{4} \times 22$

(continued)

Table 3–8 *(continued).*

Equivalent Glulam Sections for Steel Beams

Steel Section	Roof Beams — Douglas Fir		Roof Beams — Southern Pine		Floor Beams — Douglas Fir		Floor Beams — Southern Pine	
W 6 × 9	3⅛ × 10½ or 5⅛ × 7½		3⅛ × 9⅝	or 5⅛ × 8¼	3⅛ × 10½ or 5⅛ × 9		3⅛ × 11	or 5⅛ × 9⅝
W 8 × 10	3⅛ × 12	5⅛ × 9	3⅛ × 12⅜	5⅛ × 9⅝	3⅛ × 13½	5⅛ × 10½	3⅛ × 12⅜	5⅛ × 11
W 12 × 14	3⅛ × 16½	5⅛ × 13½	3⅛ × 16½	5⅛ × 12⅜	3⅛ × 18	5⅛ × 15	3⅛ × 17⅞	5⅛ × 15⅛
W 12 × 16	3⅛ × 18	5⅛ × 13½	3⅛ × 17⅞	5⅛ × 13¾	3⅛ × 19½	5⅛ × 16½	3⅛ × 19¼	5⅛ × 16½
W 12 × 19	3⅛ × 19½	5⅛ × 15	3⅛ × 19¼	5⅛ × 15⅛	3⅛ × 21	5⅛ × 18	3⅛ × 20⅝	5⅛ × 17⅞
W 10 × 22	3⅛ × 21	5⅛ × 16½	3⅛ × 20⅝	5⅛ × 16½	3⅛ × 19½	5⅛ × 16½	3⅛ × 20⅝	5⅛ × 16½
W 12 × 22	5⅛ × 16½	6¾ × 15	5⅛ × 16½	6¾ × 15⅛	5⅛ × 18	6¾ × 16½	3⅛ × 22	5⅛ × 19¼
W 14 × 22	5⅛ × 18	6¾ × 16½	5⅛ × 17⅞	6¾ × 15⅛	5⅛ × 21	6¾ × 18	5⅛ × 20⅝	6¾ × 17⅞
W 14 × 26	5⅛ × 21	6¾ × 18	5⅛ × 19¼	6¾ × 17⅞	5⅛ × 21	6¾ × 19½	5⅛ × 22	6¾ × 19¼
W 12 × 26	5⅛ × 19½	6¾ × 18	5⅛ × 19¼	6¾ × 16½	5⅛ × 21	6¾ × 18	5⅛ × 20⅝	6¾ × 19¼
W 16 × 26	5⅛ × 21	6¾ × 19½	5⅛ × 20⅝	6¾ × 17⅞	5⅛ × 22½	6¾ × 21	5⅛ × 23⅜	6¾ × 20⅝
W 12 × 30	5⅛ × 21	6¾ × 19½	5⅛ × 20⅝	6¾ × 17⅞	5⅛ × 21	6¾ × 19½	5⅛ × 22	6¾ × 19¼
W 14 × 30	5⅛ × 22½	6¾ × 19½	5⅛ × 22	6¾ × 19¼	5⅛ × 22½	6¾ × 21	5⅛ × 23⅜	6¾ × 20⅝
W 16 × 31	5⅛ × 24	6¾ × 21	5⅛ × 23⅜	6¾ × 20⅝	5⅛ × 25½	6¾ × 22½	5⅛ × 24¾	6¾ × 22
W 14 × 34	5⅛ × 24	6¾ × 21	5⅛ × 23⅜	6¾ × 20⅝	5⅛ × 24	6¾ × 22½	5⅛ × 22	6¾ × 22
W 18 × 35	5⅛ × 27	6¾ × 24	5⅛ × 26⅛	6¾ × 22	5⅛ × 27	6¾ × 25½	5⅛ × 27½	6¾ × 24¾
W 16 × 40	5⅛ × 28½	6¾ × 25½	5⅛ × 27½	6¾ × 23⅜	5⅛ × 27	6¾ × 25½	5⅛ × 27½	6¾ × 24¾
W 18 × 40	5⅛ × 30	6¾ × 25½	5⅛ × 27½	6¾ × 24¾	5⅛ × 28½	6¾ × 27	5⅛ × 28⅞	6¾ × 26⅛
W 21 × 44	5⅛ × 33	6¾ × 28	5⅛ × 30¼	6¾ × 27½	5⅛ × 33	6¾ × 30	5⅛ × 31⅝	6¾ × 28⅞
W 18 × 50	5⅛ × 34½	6¾ × 30	5⅛ × 31⅝	6¾ × 27½	5⅛ × 31½	6¾ × 28½	5⅛ × 31⅝	6¾ × 28⅞
W 21 × 50	5⅛ × 34½	6¾ × 30	5⅛ × 33		5⅛ × 34½	6¾ × 31½		6¾ × 31⅝
W 18 × 55		6¾ × 31½		6¾ × 30¼	5⅛ × 33	6¾ × 30		6¾ × 30¼
W 24 × 55		6¾ × 34½		6¾ × 31⅝		6¾ × 34½		6¾ × 34⅜
W 21 × 62		6¾ × 36		6¾ × 34⅜		6¾ × 34½		6¾ × 34⅜

Equivalent Glulam Sections for LVL Beams

LVL Section	Roof Beams — Douglas Fir		Roof Beams — Southern Pine		Floor Beams — Douglas Fir		Floor Beams — Southern Pine	
2pcs. 1¾ × 9½	3⅛ × 12	or 5⅛ × 9	3⅛ × 11	or 5⅛ × 9⅝	3⅛ × 10½ or 5⅛ × 9		3⅛ × 11	or 5⅛ × 9⅝
2pcs. 1¾ × 11⅞	3⅛ × 13½	5⅛ × 12	3⅛ × 13¾	5⅛ × 11	3⅛ × 13½	5⅛ × 12	3⅛ × 13¾	5⅛ × 11
2pcs. 1¾ × 14	3⅛ × 16½	5⅛ × 13½	3⅛ × 16½	5⅛ × 12⅜	3⅛ × 16½	5⅛ × 13½	3⅛ × 15⅛	5⅛ × 13¾
2pcs. 1¾ × 16	3⅛ × 18	5⅛ × 15	3⅛ × 17⅞	5⅛ × 15⅛	3⅛ × 18	5⅛ × 15	3⅛ × 17⅞	5⅛ × 15⅛
2pcs. 1¾ × 18	3⅛ × 21	5⅛ × 16½	3⅛ × 20⅝	5⅛ × 16½	3⅛ × 19½	5⅛ × 16½	3⅛ × 20⅝	5⅛ × 16½
3pcs. 1¾ × 9½	3⅛ × 13½	5⅛ × 10½	3⅛ × 13¾	5⅛ × 11	3⅛ × 12	5⅛ × 10½	3⅛ × 12⅜	5⅛ × 11
3pcs. 1¾ × 11⅞	3⅛ × 18	5⅛ × 13½	3⅛ × 17⅞	5⅛ × 13¾	3⅛ × 15	5⅛ × 13½	3⅛ × 15⅛	5⅛ × 12⅜
3pcs. 1¾ × 14	3⅛ × 21	5⅛ × 16½	3⅛ × 20⅝	5⅛ × 15⅛	3⅛ × 18	5⅛ × 15	3⅛ × 17⅞	5⅛ × 15⅛
3pcs. 1¾ × 16	5⅛ × 18	6¾ × 16½	5⅛ × 17⅞	6¾ × 15⅛	3⅛ × 21	5⅛ × 18	5⅛ × 17⅞	6¾ × 16½
3pcs. 1¾ × 18	5⅛ × 21	6¾ × 18	5⅛ × 20⅝	6¾ × 17⅞	5⅛ × 19½	6¾ × 18	5⅛ × 19¼	6¾ × 17⅞

SOURCE: American Institute of Timber Construction.

is important to consult the manufacturer of any of these products for design analysis for any particular situation.

3.4.4 Machine Stress-Rated (MSR) Lumber

Machine stress-rated (MSR) lumber is dimension lumber that has been evaluated by mechanical stress-rating equipment. Each piece of MSR lumber is nondestructively evaluated for bending stiffness (F_b) and is then sorted into modulus of elasticity (E) classes. One of the prime uses for MSR lumber is trusses. However, this product can also be used as floor and ceiling joists, as rafters, and for other structural purposes where assured strength is a primary concern. MSR lumber produced under an approved grading agency's certification and quality-control procedures is accepted by regulatory agencies and all major building codes.

Specifying MSR lumber is simple: Specify machine-rated, grade-stamped lumber, and list the strenght value (F_b) and the corresponding modulus of elasticity (E) values. Also indicate nominal sizes and lengths required. Refer to Fig. 3–4 and Table 3–9 for examples and interpretations of a grade stamp and design values, respectively.

Machine-rated lumber

Lumber that bears the stamp "machine rated" or "MSR" (machine stress rated) has been tested by a machine that measures the wood's stiffness. The designation "E" stands for modulus of elasticity and is listed in millions of pounds per square inch (psi). "Fb" stands for extreme fiber stress in bending and is measured in psi. Machine-rated lumber is also inspected visually.

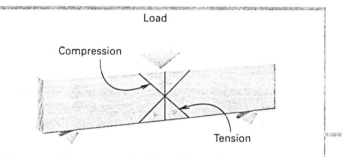

Extreme fiber stress in bending—Fb. *When a heavy load is applied to a structural member such as a joist, tension is produced in the surface of the opposite side of the board. At the same time, compression is produced in the fibers along the load-bearing surface. Extreme fiber stress in bending (Fb) is a measure of these forces, tension and compression.*

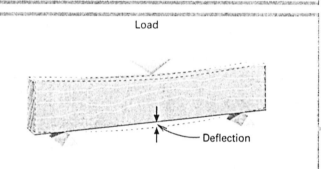

Modulus of elasticity—E. *Modulus of elasticity is a measure of stiffness. It is a ratio of how much a piece of lumber will deflect, or bend, in proportion to an applied load. E-values provide a conservative prediction of how much deflection might occur in a wall, floor or roof.*

How MSR lumber compares with visually graded lumber. *The table below shows four grades of visually graded lumber and their corresponding design values. The figures shown are base values that must be adjusted according to the width of the lumber. The figures represent the average that can be expected of a piece of lumber in a given grade. Each piece of MSR lumber is measured separately and marked with its particular strength and stiffness values.*

Species group	Grade	Extreme fiber stress in bending (Fb) (psi)	Modulus of elasticity (E) (psi)
Douglas fir-larch	Construction	1,000	1,500,000
	Standard	550	1,400,000
	Utility	275	1,300,000
	Stud	675	1,400,000

Figure 3–4 Interpretation of MSR lumber grade stamp. (Western Wood Products Association)

Table 3–9 MSR lumber design values for lumber 2″ and less in thickness and 2″ in width and wider.

Grade Designation[a]	Extreme Fiber Stress[b] in Bending, F_b Single	Modulus of Elasticity, E	Tension Parallel to Grain, F_t	Compression Parallel to Grain, $F_{c\|\|}$
2850 F_b–2.3E	2850	2,300,000	2300	2150
2700 F_b–2.2E	2700	2,200,000	2150	2100
2550 F_b–2.1E	2550	2,100,000	2050	2025
2400 F_b–2.0E	2400	2,000,000	1925	1975
2250 F_b–1.9E	2250	1,900,000	1750	1925
2100 F_b–1.8E	2100	1,800,000	1575	1875
1950 F_b–1.7E	1950	1,700,000	1375	1800
1800 F_b–1.6E	1800	1,600,000	1175	1750
1650 F_b–1.5E	1650	1,500,000	1020	1700
1500 F_b–1.4E	1500	1,400,000	900	1650
1450 F_b–1.3E	1450	1,300,000	800	1625
1350 F_b–1.3E	1350	1,300,000	750	1600
1200 F_b–1.2E	1200	1,200,000	600	1400
900 F_b–1.0E	900	1,000,000	350	1050

SOURCE: Grades are described in Section 52.00 of *Western Lumber Grading Rules*.

NOTE: Design values are in psi. Design values for compression perpendicular to grain ($F_{c\perp}$) and horizontal shear (F_v) are the same as those assigned to visually graded lumber of the appropriate species, unless indicated on grade stamp.

[a]For any given value of F_b, the average modulus of elasticity (E) and the tension value (F_t) may vary depending upon the species, the timber source, and other variables. The E and F_t values included in the Fb–E grade designations in the table are those usually associated with each F_b level. Grade stamps may show higher or lower values if the machine rating indicates that the assignment is appropriate. If the F_t value for the MSR grade is different from that shown in the table for the same F_b level, the assigned F_t value shall be included on the grade stamp. When an E or F_t varies from the designated F_b level in the table, the tabulated $F_{c\|\|}$, $F_{c\perp}$, and F_v values associated with the designated F_b value are applicable.

[b]The tabulated F_b values are applicable only to lumber loaded on edge.

3.4.5 Floor Joists

Floor framing requires careful consideration in residential construction. Often the type of subfloor (plywood or 1″ lumber), the span required, and the species of lumber available play a part in the selection of a satisfactory solution. Codes require 40 psf in living areas, but it is common practice to maintain the same live load throughout the building. Indicate joist size, spacing, and direction with a note and a short line with arrows at each end. Plan the joist layout so that the joists span the shorter dimension, which should be reflected in the overlap sketch.

Normally, joists are spaced 16″ apart, yet situations may arise where 12″ or 24″ spacing may be more suitable. Also, plan the joist layout so that a minimum of cutting is necessary; that is, plan joist lengths in 2′ increments if possible. Table 3–10 indicates allowable spans for floor joists, and selected floor joist span tables for southern pine and western wood species are given in

Appendix E. Table 3–11, published by the Southern Pine Council (SPC), provides maximum span comparisons for joists made from a number of different lumber species.

As an example of using the tables, a living room floor with a 40-lb live load and a span of 15′-0″ requires 2 × 10 joists spaced 16″ o.c. if No. 2 southern pine is used. Notice that the joists are capable of spanning 16′-1″ if necessary. Should a span of 17′-0″ be needed in another area of the house, for instance, it may be best to space this set of joists 12″ o.c. rather than go to larger 2 × 12 joists spaced at the same 16″ o.c. spacing. This solution results in neater and less complex framing unless a higher grade of lumber is used. Other situations occur where some latitude in joist selection must be available to arrive at the most economical yet sound arrangement. It is usually most practical to stay with one grade and one cross-sectional size throughout the entire floor framing. Ceiling joists that support another floor above must be considered as floor joists as well.

Table 3–10 Allowable spans for floor joists.

Joist Size	Spacing in.	Spacing mm	1.0 psi ft-in.	6.9 kPa m	1.2 psi ft-in.	8.3 kPd m	1.4 psi ft-in.	9.6 kPa m	1.6 psi ft-in.	11.0 kPa m	1.8 psi ft-in.	12.4 kPa m	2.0 psi ft-in.	13.8 kPa m
							Modulus of Elasticity, E, in 1,000,000 psi or kPa							
							30 psf (1436 Pa) Live Load							
2 × 6	16	406	9-2	2.79	9-9	2.97	10-3	3.12	10-9	3.28	11-2	3.40	11-7	3.53
	24	610	8-0	2.44	8-6	2.59	8-11	2.72	9-4	2.84	9-9	2.97	10-1	3.07
2 × 8	16	406	12-1	3.68	12-10	3.91	13-6	4.11	14-2	4.32	14-8	4.47	15-3	4.65
	24	610	10-7	3.23	11-3	3.43	11-10	3.61	12-4	3.76	12-10	3.91	13-4	4.06
2 × 10	16	406	15-5	4.70	16-5	5.00	17-3	5.26	18-0	5.49	18.9	5.72	19-5	5.92
	24	610	13-6	4.11	14-4	4.37	15-1	4.60	15-9	4.80	16-5	5.00	17-0	5.18
2 × 12	16	406	18-9	5.72	19-11	6.07	21-0	6.40	21-11	6.68	22-16	6.96	23-7	7.19
	24	610	16-5	5.00	17-5	5.31	18-4	5.59	19-2	5.84	19-11	6.07	20-8	6.30
F_b psi	16	406	889	6129	1004	6922	1112	7667	1216	8384	1315	9067	1411	9729
(kPa)	24	610	1018	7019	1149	7922	1273	8777	1392	9598	1506	10,384	1615	11,135
							40 psf (1915 Pa) LiΩ							
2 × 6	16	406	8-4	2.54	8-10	2.69	9-4	2.84	9-9	2.97	10-2	3.10	10-6	3.20
	24	610	7-3	2.21	7-9	2.36	8-2	2.49	8-6	2.59	8-10	2.69	9-2	2.79
2 × 8	16	406	11-0	3.35	11-8	3.56	12-3	3.73	12-10	3.91	13-4	4.06	13-10	4.22
	24	610	9-7	2.92	10-2	3.10	10-9	3.28	11-3	3.43	11-8	3.56	12-1	3.68
2 × 10	16	406	14-0	4.27	14-11	4.55	15-8	4.78	16-5	5.00	17-0	5.18	17-8	5.38
	24	610	12-3	3.73	13-0	3.96	13-8	4.17	14-4	4.37	14-11	4.55	15.5	4.70
2 × 12	16	406	17-0	5.18	18-1	5.51	19-1	5.82	19-11	6.07	20-9	6.32	21-6	6.55
	24	610	14-11	4.55	15-10	4.83	16-8	5.08	17-5	5.31	18-1	5.51	18.9	5.72
F_b psi	16	406	917	6322	1036	7143	1148	7915	1255	8653	1357	9356	1456	10,039
(kPa)	24	610	1050	7239	1186	8177	1314	9060	1436	9901	1554	10,714	1667	11,494

SOURCE: *Span Tables for Joists and Rafters,* American Forest and Paper Association, Washington, DC, 1993. Used by permission of AFPA.

NOTES:

1. The required bending design value F_b in Psi (kPa) is shown at the bottom of each section of the table and is applicable to all lumber sizes shown.
2. Allowable spans are based on a deflection of $1/360$ at design load.

Table 3–11 Maximum span comparisons for Joists.

Species and Grade	40 psf Live Load, 10 psf Dead Load, $1/360$ 2 × 10 16" o.c.	24" o.c.	2 × 12 16" o.c.	24" o.c.	360 psf Live Load, 10 psf Dead Load, $1/360$ 2 × 10 16" o.c.	24" o.c.	2 × 12 16" o.c.	24" o.c.
SP No. 1	16'-9"	14'-7"	20'-4"	17'-5"	18'-5"	16'-1"	22'-5"	19'-6"
DFL No. 1	16'-5"	13'-5"	19'-1"	15'-7"	18'-5"	15'-0"	21'-4"	17'-5"
SP No. 2	16'-1"	13'-2"	18'-10"	15'-4"	18'-0"	14'-8"	21'-1"	17'-2"
HF No. 1	16'-0"	13'-1"	18'-7"	15'-2"	17'-8"	14'-8"	20'-10"	17'-0"
SPF Nos. 1 and 2	15'-4"	12'-7"	17'-10"	14'-7"	17'-2"	14'-0"	19'-11"	16'-3"
DFL No. 2	15'-4"	12'-7"	17'-10"	14'-7"	17'-2"	14'-0"	19'-11"	16'-3"
HF No. 2	15'-2"	12'-5"	17'-7"	14'-5"	16'-10"	13'-10"	19'-8"	16'-1"
SP No. 3	12'-2"	9'-11"	14'-5"	11'-10"	13'-7"	11'-1"	16'-2"	13'-2"
DFL No. 3	11'-8"	9'-6"	13'-6"	11'-0"	13'-0"	10'-8"	15'-1"	12'-4"
HF No. 3	11'-8"	9'-6"	13'-6"	11'-0"	13'-0"	10'-8"	15'-1"	12'-4"
SPF No. 3	11'-8"	9'-6"	13'-6"	11'-0"	13'-0"	10'-8"	15'-1"	12'-4"

SOURCE: Southern Pine Council.

NOTES:

1. These spans were calculated using published design values and are for comparison purposes only. They include the repetitive member factor, $Cr = 1.15$, but do not include the composite action of adhesive and sheathing. Spans may be slightly different from other published spans due to rounding.
2. SP = southern pine; DFL = douglas fir–larch; HF = hem–fir; SPF = spruce–pine–fir.

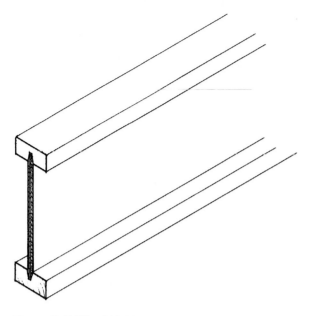

Figure 3–5 Wood I-joist.

In addition to sawn lumber floor joists, manufactured-type members are available. One is a wood I-shaped member, as shown in Fig. 3–5. It is made in depths of 9½″ to 24″ and in lengths to 40′. The flanges are made of microlaminated wood or solid wood, and the webs are made of plywood or oriented strand board. These members are lightweight, easy to handle, and dimensionally stable, and they have the capacity to support large loads. Members such as the residential TJI® joists are fabricated by Trus Joist MacMillian. Figure 3–6 shows examples of plywood I-beam uses in residential floor construction.

Another member is the fabricated wood flat truss. It is built up of 2 × 4 material and is assembled with metal truss plate connectors. It is usually available from roof trussed rafter suppliers. Large load capacity on longer spans means that load-bearing partitions and interior beams, posts, and footings can frequently be eliminated (Fig. 3–7). Table 3-12 lists floor truss spans for fabricated wood flat trusses. Table 3–13 contains span comparisons for wood trusses, I-joists, and dimension lumber.

3.4.6 Ceiling Joists

Indicate the ceiling joist size and direction with a symbol and a note on the floor plan that requires the ceiling above; always indicate framing information that is overhead or over the plane of the floor plan. Notice that ceiling joists may be subjected to various types of loads. Ceilings where storage above is necessary must be adequately framed to prevent objectional deflection. If ceiling joists are to tie with the rafters to counteract lateral thrust, consideration must be given to their direction; otherwise, joists are placed to result in the shortest span for economy. Table 3–14 indicates allowable spans for ceiling joists. Selected ceiling joist span tables for southern pine and western wood species are given in Appendix E.

3.4.7. Rafters

As we mentioned previously, roof loads are usually transmitted directly to exterior walls; occasionally, partial loads are transmitted to interior partitions. Rafter size can be affected by roof slope, with lower slopes generally requiring larger rafters. The span of a rafter is the horizontal distance from the wall plate to the ridgeboard (see Figs. 3–9 and 4–8). Collar beams, usually 1 × 4 or 1 × 6 ties, fastened midway between the ridge and the plate to opposing rafters, are meant to stiffen the roof. They are conventionally applied to every second or third set of rafters.

Design loads are figured from span to collar beam only, but in actual practice the full horizontal span of the rafter is used. The weight of roofing material is also important. Fiberglass or wood shingles are considered light roofing, whereas slate or mission tile is considered heavy roofing. Select rafter size from the table after roofing materials have been determined. Table 3–15 indicates allowable spans for roof rafters. Selected rafter span tables for southern pine and western wood species are given in Appendix E. Table 3–16, published by the Southern Pine Council (SPC), provides maximum rafter span comparisons for a number of different lumber species.

3.4.8 Headers

Structural headers are required to carry roof or floor loads over openings in load-bearing walls. Usually double 2 × lumber headers are installed above a wall opening with short "cripple" studs set between the header and the top plate. Table 3–17 and Figure 3–8 present allowable spans for conventional lumber headers with different roof and floor load conditions. Specific manufacturers will provide header span tables for other types of material such as parallel-strand lumber (PSL) and glue-laminated lumber.

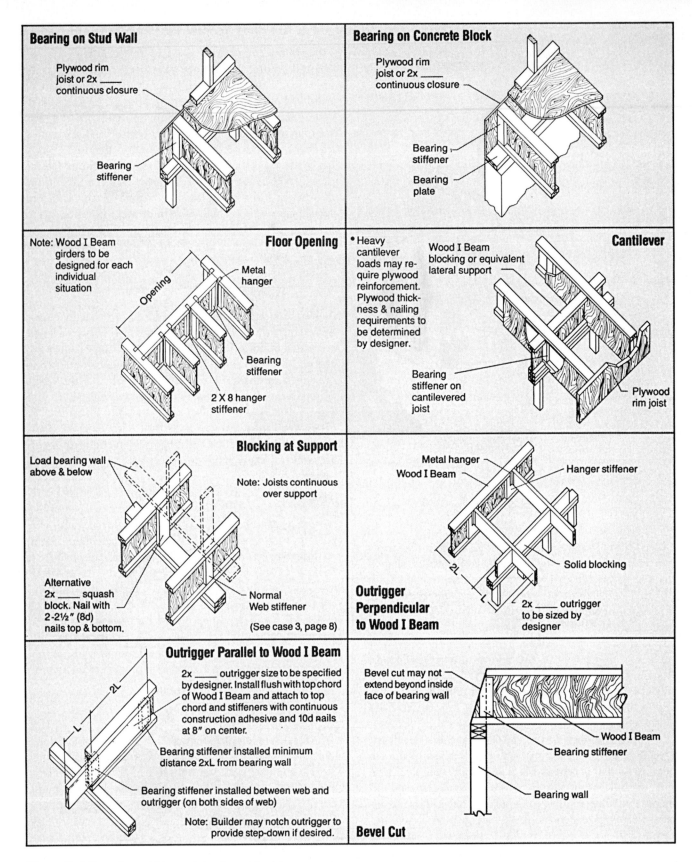

Figure 3–6 Use of wood I-beams/joists in residential construction.

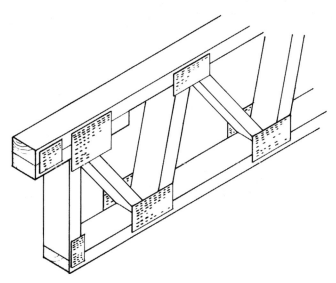

Figure 3–7 Factory-fabricated wood trusses.

Table 3–12 System 42 floor truss span tables.

TDO	Spacing	Allowable Total Loads (psf) Clear Span (ft)														
		17'	18'	19'	20'	21'	22'	23'	24'	25'	26'	27'	28'	29'	30'	31'
12"	16.0"	97	87	78	71	64										
	19.2"	80	72	65	59	53										
	24.0"	64	58	52	47	42										
14"	16.0"	101	97	94	85	77	70	64								
	19.2"	96	87	78	71	64	58	53								
	24.0"	77	69	62	56	51	46	42								
16"	16.0"	120	115	110	99	89	82	75	69	63	58	54				
	19.2"	112	101	91	82	74	68	62	57	53	49	45				
	24.0"	90	81	73	66	59	54	49	45	42						
18"	16.0"	120	120	120	111	102	93	85	78	72	67	62	58	54	50	47
	19.2"	120	112	104	94	85	78	71	65	60	55	51	48	45		
	24.0"	102	92	83	75	67	61	56	52	48	44	41				
20"	16.0"	120	120	120	117	114	105	96	89	82	75	69	64	60	56	53
	19.2"	120	118	117	106	95	87	80	74	68	63	58	54	50	47	44
	24.0"	115	104	93	84	76	69	63	58	54	50	46	43	40		
22"	16.0"	120	120	120	120	120	113	106	98	91	84	77	72	67	63	59
	19.2"	120	120	120	112	105	96	88	82	76	70	64	60	56	52	49
	24.0"	120	112	104	94	84	77	70	65	60	55	51	48	45		

NOTES:

1. These overall spans are based on NDS 91. Allowable design load is limited by deflection to $\frac{1}{360}$ under live load. Subtract the total dead load from the loads shown to determine the allowable live load.

2. TDO is overall truss depth in inches. Spacing of trusses is center to center (in inches). Other depths are available.

3. Allowable total loads are in psf. Top chord dead load = 10 psf; bottom chord dead load = 5 psf. Center line chase = 24" max.

4. Lumber basic design values are as follows: F_b = 2000 psi; F_t = 1100 psi; F_c = 2000 psi; E = 1,800,000 psi; duration of load = 1.00.

Table 3–13 Span comparisons.

	Truss	I Joist	Dimensional Lumber Joists				
				10" Nominal Depth			
	SP No. I Dense	I Joist	SP No. I	DF No. I	SP No. 2	DF No. 2	SPF No. I and No. 2
16" o.c.	19'-3"	17'-7"	16'-9"	16'-5"	16'-1"	15'-5"	15'-5"
24" o.c.	16'-10"	15'-5"	14'-7"	13'-5"	13'-2"	12'-7"	12'-7"
				12" Nominal Depth			
	SP No. I Dense	I Joist	SP No I	DF No. I	SP No. 2	DF No. 2	SPF No. I and No. 2
16" o.c.	22'-2"	21'-0"	20'-4"	19'-1"	18'-10"	17'-10"	17'-10"
24" o.c.	19'-3"	17'-11"	17'-5"	15'-7"	15'-4"	14'-7"	14'-7"
				14" Nominal Depth			
	SP No. I Dense	I Joist					
16" o.c.	24'-11"	23'-10"					
24" o.c.	21'-1"	17'-11"					

NOTES:
1. SP = southern pine; SPF = spruce–pine–fir; DF = Douglas fir.
2. Values are based on a 40-psf live load, a 10-psf dead load, and on $\frac{1}{360}$ deflection limitation.
3. This table is for comparison purposes only. All engineered products must be designed specifically for field conditions.
4. These spans do not include composite action of adhesive and sheathing.

Table 3–14 Allowable spans for ceiling joists.

Size	Joist Spacing in.	mm	Modulus of Elasticity, E, in 1,000,000 psi of kPa							
			1.0 psi ft-in.	6.89 kPa m	1.2 psi ft-in.	8.27 kPa m	1.40 psi ft-in.	9.65 kPa m	1.60 psi ft-in.	11.03 kPa m
					10 psf (479 Pa) Live Load (No Attic Storage)					
2 × 4	16	406	9-8	2.95	10-3	3.12	10-9	3.28	11-3	3.43
	24	610	8-5	2.57	8-11	2.72	9-5	2.87	9-10	3.00
2 × 6	16	406	15-2	4.62	16-1	4.90	16-11	5.16	17-8	5.38
	24	610	13-3	4.04	14-1	4.29	14-9	4.50	15-6	4.72
2 × 8	16	406	19-11	6.07	21-2	6.45	22-4	6.81	23-4	7.11
	24	610	17-5	5.31	18-6	5.64	19-6	5.94	20-5	6.22
2 × 10	16	406	25-5	7.75						
	24	610	22-3	6.78	23-8	7.21	24-10	7.57	26-0	7.92
F_b psi	16	406	909	6267	1026	7074	1137	7839	1243	8570
(kPa)	24	610	1040	7171	1174	8094	1302	8977	1423	9811
					20 psf (958 Pa) Live Load (Limited Attic Storage)					
2 × 4	16	406	7-8	2.34	8-1	2.46	8-7	2.62	8-11	2.72
	24	610	6-8	2.03	7-1	2.16	7-6	2.29	7-10	2.39
2 × 6	16	406	12-0	3.66	12-9	3.89	13-5	4.09	14-1	4.29
	24	610	10-6	3.20	11-2	3.40	11-9	3.58	12-3	3.73
2 × 8	16	406	15-10	4.83	16-10	5.13	17-9	5.41	18-6	5.64
	24	610	13-10	4.22	14-8	4.47	15-6	4.72	16-2	4.93
2 × 10	16	406	20-2	6.15	21-6	6.55	22-7	6.88	23-8	7.21
	24	610	17-8	5.38	18-9	5.72	19-9	6.02	20-8	6.30
F_b psi	16	406	1145	7895	1293	8915	1433	9880	1566	10,797
(kPa)	24	610	1310	9032	1480	10,204	1640	11,307	1793	12,362

SOURCE: *Span Tables for Joists and Rafters*, American Forest and Paper Association, Washington, DC, 1993. Used by permission of AFPA.
NOTES:
1. Allowable spans are based on a deflection of $\frac{1}{240}$ at design load.
2. Dead load is 10 psf (479 Pa). The required bending design value, F_b, in psi or kPa is shown at the bottom of each section of the table.

Table 3–15 Allowable spans for roof rafters.

Rafter Size	Spacing in.	Spacing mm	800 psi ft-in.	5516 kPa m	1000 psi ft-in.	6895 kPa m	1200 psi ft-in.	8274 kPa m	1400 psi ft-in.	9653 kPa m
20 psf (9-58 Pa) Live Load										
2 × 6	16	406	10-0	3.05	11-3	3.43	12-4	3.76	13-3	4.04
	24	610	8-2	2.49	9-2	2.79	10-0	3.05	10-10	3.30
2 × 8	16	406	13-3	4.04	14-10	4.52	16-3	4.95	17-6	5.33
	24	610	10-10	3.30	12-1	3.68	13-3	4.04	14-4	4.37
2 × 10	16	406	16-11	5.16	18-11	5.77	20-8	6.30	22-4	6.81
	24	610	13-9	4.19	15-5	4.70	16-11	5.16	18-3	5.56
E in 10^{6}psi	16	406	0.58	4.00	0.82	5.65	1.07	7.38	1.35	9.31
(kPa)	24	610	0.48	3.31	0.67	4.62	0.88	6.07	1.10	7.58
30 psf (1435 Pa) Live Load										
2 × 6	16	406	8-8	2.64	9-9	2.97	10-8	3.25	11-6	3.51
	24	610	7-1	2.16	7-11	2.41	8-8	2.64	9-5	2.87
2 × 8	16	406	11-6	3.51	12-10	3.91	14-0	4.27	15-2	4.62
	24	610	9-4	2.84	10-6	320	11-6	3.51	12-5	3.78
2 × 10	16	406	14-8	4.47	16-4	4.98	17-11	5.46	19-4	5.89
	24	610	11-11	3.63	13-4	4.06	14-8	4.47	15-10	4.83
E in 10^{6}psi	16	406	0.57	3.93	0.80	5.52	1.05	7.24	1.32	9.10
(kPa)	24	610	0.46	3.17	0.65	4.48	0.85	5.86	1.08	7.45
40 psf (1915 Pa) Live Load										
2 × 6	16	406	7-9	2.36	8-8	2.64	9-6	2.90	10-3	3.12
	24	610	6-4	1.93	7-1	7.08	7-9	2.36	8-5	2.57
2 × 8	16	406	10-3	3.12	11-6	3.51	12-7	3.84	13-7	4.14
	24	610	8-4	2.54	9-4	2.84	10-3	3.12	11-1	3.38
2 × 10	16	406	13-1	3.99	14-8	4.47	16-0	4.88	17-4	5.28
	24	610	10-8	3.25	11-11	3.63	13-1	3.99	14-2	4.32
E in 10^{6}psi	16	406	0.54	3.72	0.76	5.24	1.00	6.89	1.26	8.69
(kPa)	24	610	0.44	3.03	0.62	4.27	0.81	5.58	1.03	7.10
50 psf (2394 Pa) Live Load										
2 × 6	16	406	7-1	2.16	7-11	2.41	8-8	2.64	9-5	2.87
	24	610	5-10	1.78	6-6	1.98	7-1	2.16	7-8	2.34
2 × 8	16	406	9-4	2.84	10-6	3.20	11-6	3.51	12-5	3.78
	24	610	7-8	2.34	8-7	2.62	9-4	2.84	10-1	3.07
2 × 10	16	406	11-11	3.63	13-4	4.06	14-8	4.47	15-10	4.83
	24	610	9-9	2.97	10-11	3.33	11-11	3.63	12-11	3.94
E in 10^{6}psi	16	406	0.52	3.59	0.72	4.96	0.95	6.55	1.20	8.27
(kPa)	24	610	0.42	2.90	0.59	4.07	0.77	5.31	0.98	6.76

SOURCE: *Span Tables for Joists and Rafters*, American Forest and Paper Association, Washington, DC, 1993.
Used by permission of AFPA.
NOTES:
1. The live load plus the dead load of 10 psf (479 Pa) determines the required bending design value.
2. The modulus of elasticity, *E*, in 1,000,000 psi (kPa) is shown at the bottom of each section of the table.
3. Allowable spans are based on a deflection of $1/240$ at design load.

Table 3–16 Maximum span comparisons for rafters.

| Species and Grade | 30 psf Live Load, 15 psf Dead Load, $L/180$, $C_d = 1.15$, 6:12 Slope | | | | | | 20 psf Live Load, 10 psf Dead Load, $L/240$, $C_d = 1.25$, 3:12 Slope | | | | | |
| | 2 × 6 | | 2 × 8 | | 2 × 10 | | 2 × 6 | | 2 × 8 | | 2 × 10 | |
	16″ o.c.	24″ o.c.	16″ o.c.	24″ o.c.	16″ o.c.	24″ o.c.	16″ o.c.	24″ o.c.	16″ o.c.	24″ o.c.	16″ o.c.	24″ o.c.
SP No. 1	13′-6″	11′-1″	17′-0″	13′-11″	20′-3″	16′-6″	14′-4″	12′-6″	18′-11″	16′-6″	24′-1″	21′-1″
DFL No. 1	12′-0″	9′-10″	15′-3″	12′-5″	18′-7″	15′-2″	14′-4″	12′-6″	18′-11″	15′-10″	23′-9″	19′-5″
SP No. 2	11′-9″	9′-7″	15′-3″	12′-5″	18′-2″	14′-10″	14′-1″	12′-3″	18′-6″	15′-10″	23′-2″	18′-11″
HF No. 1	11′-9″	9′-7″	14′-10″	12′-1″	18′-1″	14′-9″	13′-9″	12′-0″	18′-1″	15′-6″	23′-1″	18′-11″
DFL No. 2	11′-3″	9′-2″	14′-3″	11′-8″	17′-5″	14′-3″	14′-1″	11′-9″	18′-2″	14′-10″	22′-3″	18′-2″
SPF Nos. 1 and 2	11′-3″	9′-2″	14′-3″	11′-8″	17′-5″	14′-3″	13′-5″	11′-9″	17′-9″	14′-10″	22′-3″	18′-2″
HF No. 2	11′-1″	9′-1″	14′-0″	11′-6″	17′-2″	14′-0″	13′-1″	11′-5″	17′-3″	14′-8″	21′-11″	17′-11″
SP No. 3	9′-1″	7′-5″	11′-7″	9′-6″	13′-9″	11′-3″	11′-8″	9′-6″	14′-10″	12′-2″	17′-7″	14′-4″
DFL No. 3	8′-6″	6′-11″	10′-9″	8′-10″	13′-2″	10′-9″	10′-10″	8′-10″	13′-9″	11′-3″	16′-9″	13′-8″
HF No. 3	8′-6″	6′-11″	10′-9″	8′-10″	13′-2″	10′-9″	10′-10″	8′-10″	13′-9″	11′-3″	16′-9″	13′-8″
SPF No. 3	8′-6″	6′-11″	10′-9″	8′-10″	13′-2″	10′-9″	10′-10″	8′-10″	13′-9″	11′-3″	16′-9″	13′-8″

Notes:

1. These spans were calculated using published design values and are for comparison purposes only. They include the repetitive member factor, $Cr = 1.15$, but do not include the composite action of adhesive and sheathing. Spans may be slightly different from other published spans due to rounding.

2. SP = southern pine; DFL = Douglas fir–larch; HF = hem–fir; SPF = spruce–pine–fir.

3. C_d = load duration factor.

Table 3–17 Maximum header spans based on house width and load condition (see Fig. 3–8).

| Load Condition | Header Size | House Width | | | | | | | | | |
		24 ft ft-in.	7.32 m m	26 ft ft-in.	7.92 m m	28 ft ft-in.	8.53 m m	30 ft ft-in.	9.14 m m	32 ft ft-in.	9.75m m
1. Roof only	2-2 × 3	2-1	0.63	2-0	0.61						
	2-2 × 4	2-11	0.89	2-10	0.85	2-8	0.82	2-7	0.79	2-6	0.77
	1-2 × 6	3-3	0.99	3-1	0.95	3-0	0.91	2-11	0.88	2-10	0.86
	1-2 × 8	4-3	1.30	4-1	1.25	4-0	1.21	3-10	1.16	3-8	1.13
	2-2 × 6	4-7	1.40	4-5	1.34	4-3	1.29	4-1	1.25	4-0	1.21
	1-2 × 10	5-5	1.66	5-3	1.60	5-1	1.54	4-11	1.49	4-9	1.44
	2-2 × 8	6-0	1.84	5-10	1.77	5-7	1.70	5-5	1.65	5-3	1.59
	1-2 × 12	6-8	2.02	6-4	1.94	6-2	1.87	5-11	1.81	5-9	1.75
	2-2 × 10	7-9	2.35	7-5	2.26	7-2	2.18	6-11	2.10	6-8	2.03
	2-2 × 12	9-4	2.86	9-0	2.75	8-8	2.65	8-5	2.56	8-1	2.47
2. Roof, second-story floor and wall	2-2 × 4	2-2	0.67	2-1	0.65	2-1	0.63				
	1-2 × 6	2-5	0.75	2-4	0.72	2-3	0.69	2-3	0.67	2-2	0.65
	1-2 × 8	3-3	0.98	3-1	0.95	3-0	0.92	2-11	0.89	2-10	0.86
	2-2 × 6	3-6	1.06	3-4	1.02	3-3	0.98	3-1	0.95	3-0	0.92
	1-2 × 10	4-1	1.26	4-0	1.21	3-10	1.17	3-9	1.13	3-7	1.10
	2-2 × 8	4-7	1.39	4-5	1.34	4-3	1.30	4-1	1.25	4-0	1.22
	1-2 × 12	5-0	1.53	4-10	1.47	4-8	1.42	4-6	1.38	4-5	1.33
	2-2 × 10	5-10	1.78	5-7	1.71	5-5	1.65	5-3	1.60	5-1	1.55
	2-2 × 12	7-1	2.16	6-10	2.08	6-7	2.01	6-5	1.95	6-2	1.89
3. Roof, second- and third-story floors and walls	1-2 × 6	2-1	0.64	2-0	0.62						
	1-2 × 8	2-9	0.84	2-8	0.82	2-7	0.79	2-6	0.76	2-5	0.74
	2-2 × 6	3-0	0.91	2-10	0.87	2-9	0.85	2-8	0.82	2-7	0.80
	1-2 × 10	3-6	1.08	3-5	1.04	3-4	1.01	3-2	0.97	3-1	0.95
	2-2 × 8	3-11	1.19	3-9	1.15	3-8	1.11	3-6	1.08	3-5	1.05
	1-2 × 12	4-4	1.31	4-2	1.26	4-0	1.22	3-11	1.19	3-9	1.15
	2-2 × 10	5-0	1.52	4-10	1.47	4-8	1.42	4-6	1.38	4-5	1.34
	2-2 × 12	6-1	1.85	5-10	1.79	5-8	1.73	5-6	1.68	5-4	1.63
4. Second-story floor only	2-2 × 3	2-8	0.80	2-6	0.77	2-5	0.74	2-4	0.72	2-3	0.70
	2-2 × 4	3-8	1.12	3-6	1.08	3-5	1.04	3-4	1.01	3-2	0.97
	1-2 × 6	4-1	1.25	3-11	1.20	3-9	1.16	3-8	1.12	3-7	1.08
	1-2 × 8	5-5	1.65	5-2	1.58	5-0	1.52	4-10	1.47	4-8	1.43
	2-2 × 6	5-10	1.77	5-7	1.70	5-4	1.64	5-2	1.58	5-0	1.53
	1-2 × 10	6-11	2.10	6-7	2.02	6-5	1.95	6-2	1.88	6-0	1.82
	2-2 × 8	7-8	2.33	7-4	2.24	7-1	2.16	6-10	2.08	6-7	2.02
	1-2 × 12	8-5	2.56	8-1	2.46	7-9	2.37	7-6	2.29	7-3	2.21
	2-2 × 10	9-9	2.97	9-4	2.86	9-0	2.75	8-9	2.66	8-5	2.57
	2-2 × 12	11-10	3.61	11-5	3.47	11-0	3.35	10-7	3.23	10-3	3.13

NOTES:

1. End splits may not exceed one times the header depth.

2. For design load conditions, see Fig. 3–8.

3. Minimum allowable bending stress F_b = 1000 psi (6895 kPa).

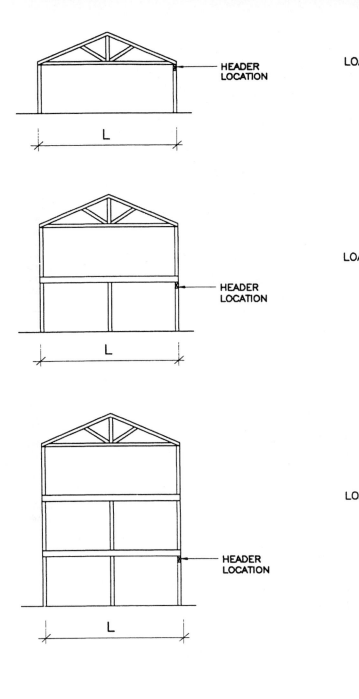

LOAD CONDITION #1:

    ONE STORY:
    ROOF LOADS ONLY

LOAD CONDITION #2:

    TWO STORY:
    UPPER FLOOR PLUS ROOF LOADS

LOAD CONDITION #3:

    THREE STORY:
    TWO FLOORS PLUS ROOF LOADS

LOAD CONDITION #4:

    TWO STORY:
    FLOOR LOADS ONLY

Figure 3–8 Load conditions for Table 13–17.

3.4.9 Roof Trusses

Wood trusses are easy to install, and they provide a means of rapidly enclosing a building shell. Trusses easily adapt to most roof designs and are normally designed for 24″ o.c. spacing. Truss fabricators normally have the capability of supplying the necessary engineering for each unique design condition. Maximum spans for selected Fink, Howe, scissors, and king post truss types at 24″ spacing are provided in Appendix E.

3.5

PLANK-AND-BEAM FRAMING[1]

Section 2.5 has additional information on plank-and-beam frame construction.

3.5.1 Design Data for Planks

Design data for plank floors and roofs are included in Table 3–18. Computations for bending are based on the live load indicated, plus 10 psf of dead load. Computations for deflection are based on the live load only. The table shows four general arrangements of planks as follows:

    Type A—Extending over a single span

    Type B—Continuous over two equal spans

    Type C—Continuous over three equal spans

    Type D—A combination of types A and B

On the basis of a section of planking 12″ wide, the following formulas were used in making the computations:

For type A:

$$M = \frac{wL^2}{8} \quad \text{and} \quad D = \frac{5wL^4(12)^3}{384EI}$$

---

[1] From *Plank-and-Beam Framing for Residential Buildings* (Manual No. 4). By and with permission from the National Forest Products Association.

For type B:

$$M = \frac{wL^2}{8} \quad \text{and} \quad D = \frac{wL^4(12)^3}{185EI}$$

For type C:

$$M = \frac{wL^2}{10} \quad \text{and} \quad D = \frac{4wL^4(12)^3}{581EI}$$

For type D:

$$M = \frac{wL^2}{8} \quad \text{and} \quad D = \frac{1}{2}\left(\frac{5wL^4(12)^3}{384EI} + \frac{wL^4(12)^3}{185EI}\right)$$

Notations In the preceding formulas and in the tables of Appendix E, the symbols have the following meanings:

    w = load in lb/lin ft

    L = span in ft

    M = induced bending moment in lb-ft

    f = fiber stress in bending in psi

    E = modulus of elasticity in psi

    I = moment of inertia in inches to the fourth power

    D = deflection in inches.

To use Table 3–18, first determine the plank arrangement (type A, B, C, or D), the span, the live load to be supported, and the deflection limitation. Then select from the table the corresponding required values for the fiber stress in bending (f) and the modulus of elasticity (E). The plank to be used should be of a grade and species that meets these minimum values. You can determine the maximum span for a specific grade and species of plank by reversing these steps.

For those who prefer to use random-length planks (instead of arrangements type A, B, C, or D), similar technical information is included in *Random Length Wood Decking*, a publication of the National Forest Products Association.

In addition to the nominal 2″ plank described above, decking is available in nominal 3″ thickness and in various laminated deck systems.

Table 3–18 Nominal 2″ plank: Required values for fiber stress in bending (f) and modulus of elasticity (E) to support safely a live load of 20, 30, or 40 psf within a deflection limitation of $1/240$, $1/300$, or $1/360$, respectively.

Plank Span in Feet	Live Load (psf)	Deflection Limitation	Type A f (psi)	Type A E (psi)	Type B f (psi)	Type B E (psi)	Type C f (psi)	Type C E (psi)	Type D f (psi)	Type D E (psi)
6′	20	$1/240$	360	576,000	360	239,000	288	305,000	360	408,000
		$1/300$	360	720,000	360	299,000	288	381,000	360	509,000
		$1/360$	360	864,000	360	359,000	288	457,000	360	611,000
	30	$1/240$	480	864,000	480	359,000	384	457,000	480	611,000
		$1/300$	480	1,080,000	480	448,000	384	571,000	480	764,000
		$1/360$	480	1,296,000	480	538,000	384	685,000	480	917,000
	40	$1/240$	600	1,152,000	600	478,000	480	609,000	600	815,000
		$1/300$	600	1,440,000	600	598,000	480	762,000	600	1,019,000
		$1/360$	600	1,728,000	600	717,000	480	914,000	600	1,223,000
7′	20	$1/240$	490	915,000	490	380,000	392	484,000	490	647,000
		$1/300$	490	1,143,000	490	475,000	392	605,000	490	809,000
		$1/360$	490	1,372,000	490	570,000	392	726,000	490	971,000
	30	$1/240$	653	1,372,000	653	570,000	522	726,000	653	971,000
		$1/300$	653	1,715,000	653	712,000	522	907,000	653	1,213,000
		$1/360$	653	2,058,000	653	854,000	522	1,088,000	653	1,456,000
	40	$1/240$	817	1,829,000	817	759,000	653	968,000	817	1,294,000
		$1/300$	817	2,287,000	817	949,000	653	1,209,000	817	1,618,000
		$1/360$	817	2,744,000	817	1,139,000	653	1,451,000	817	1,941,000
8′	20	$1/240$	640	1,365,000	640	567,000	512	722,000	640	966,000
		$1/300$	640	1,707,000	640	708,000	512	903,000	640	1,208,000
		$1/360$	640	2,048,000	640	850,000	512	1,083,000	640	1,449,000
	30	$1/240$	853	2,048,000	853	850,000	682	1,083,000	853	1,449,000
		$1/300$	853	2,560,000	853	1,063,000	682	1,354,000	853	1,811,000
		$1/360$	853	3,072,000	853	1,275,000	682	1,625,000	853	2,174,000
	40	$1/240$	1067	2,731,000	1067	1,134,000	853	1,444,000	1067	1,932,000
		$1/300$	1067	3,413,000	1067	1,417,000	853	1,805,000	1067	2,415,000
		$1/360$	1067	4,096,000	1067	1,700,000	853	2,166,000	1067	2,898,000

3.5.2 Design Data for Beams

Design data for beams along with tables for computations are included in Appendix E. Table 3-19 provides section properties of standard dressed (S4S) sawn lumber based on the American Forest and Paper Association's National Design Specifications Supplement, 1997. Tables 3–20 and 3–21 list base design values for visually graded dimension lumber for southern pine and other selected species. The National Design Specification for Wood Construction Supplement provides various tables of adjustment factors that are to be used in conjunction with the design values in the previous tables. Consult the National Design Specifications for the proper use of the adjustment factors. Expanded tables of design values for a wide range of lumber species are given in Appendix E.

Table 3–19 Properties of sections.

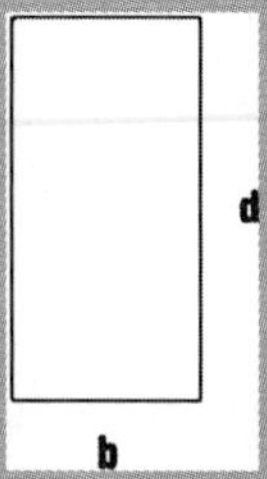

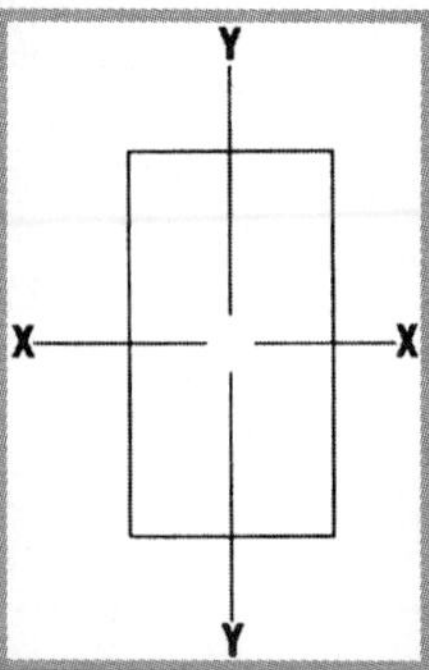

Nominal Size (in.) b d	Actual Size (in.) b × d	Area (in.²)	Axis XX S (in.³)	Axis XX I (in.⁴)	Axis YY S (in.³)	Axis YY I (in.⁴)	Board Measure per Lineal Foot	Weight per Lineal Foot (lb)
2 × 2	1½ × 1½	2.250	0.563	0.422	0.563	0.422	0.33	0.73
3	2½	3.750	1.563	1.953	0.938	0.703	0.50	1.10
4	3½	5.250	3.063	5.359	1.313	0.984	0.67	1.47
5	4½	6.750	5.063	11.391	1.688	1.266	0.83	1.83
6	5½	8.250	7.563	20.797	2.063	1.547	1.00	2.20
8	7¼	10.875	13.141	47.635	2.719	2.039	1.33	2.93
10	9¼	13.875	21.391	98.932	3.469	2.602	1.67	3.84
12	11¼	16.875	31.641	177.979	4.219	3.164	2.00	4.60
14	13¼	19.875	43.891	290.775	4.969	3.727	2.33	5.59
3 × 3	2½ × 2½	6.250	2.604	3.255	2.604	3.255	0.75	1.80
4	3½	8.750	5.104	8.932	3.646	4.557	1.00	2.30
6	5½	13.750	12.604	34.661	5.729	7.161	1.50	3.45
8	7¼	18.125	21.901	79.391	7.552	9.440	2.00	4.60
10	9¼	23.125	35.651	164.886	9.635	12.044	2.50	6.00
12	11¼	28.125	52.734	296.631	11.719	14.648	3.00	7.20
14	13¼	33.125	73.151	484.626	13.802	17.253	3.50	8.40
4 × 4	3½ × 3½	12.250	7.146	12.505	7.146	12.505	1.33	3.19
6	5½	19.250	17.646	48.526	11.229	19.651	2.00	5.00
8	7¼	25.375	30.661	111.148	14.802	25.904	2.67	6.68
10	9¼	32.375	49.911	230.840	18.885	33.049	3.33	8.33
12	11¼	39.375	73.828	415.283	22.969	40.195	4.00	10.00
14	13¼	46.375	102.411	678.476	27.052	47.341	4.67	11.68
*6 × 6	5½ × 5½	30.250	27.729	76.255	27.729	76.255	3.00	11.40
8	7½	41.250	51.563	193.359	37.813	103.984	4.00	15.20
10	9½	52.250	82.729	392.964	47.896	131.714	5.00	19.00
12	11½	63.250	121.229	697.068	57.979	159.443	6.00	22.80
14	13½	74.250	167.063	1127.672	68.063	187.172	7.00	26.60
*8 × 8	7½ × 7½	56.250	70.313	263.672	70.313	263.672	5.33	20.25
10	9½	71.250	112.813	535.859	89.063	333.984	6.67	25.35
12	11½	86.250	165.313	950.547	107.813	404.297	8.00	30.40
14	13½	101.250	227.813	1537.734	126.563	474.609	9.33	35.45
*10 × 10	9½ × 9½	90.250	142.896	678.755	142.896	678.755	8.33	31.65
12	11½	109.250	209.396	1204.026	172.979	821.651	10.00	38.00
14	13½	128.250	288.563	1947.797	203.063	964.547	11.67	44.35
*12 × 12	11½ × 11½	132.250	253.479	1457.505	253.479	1457.505	12.00	45.60
14	13½	155.250	349.313	2357.859	297.563	1710.984	14.00	53.20
*14 × 14	13½ × 13½	182.250	410.063	2767.922	410.063	2767.922	16.33	62.05

SOURCE: *National Design Specification Supplement*, 1991 Edition. American Forest and Paper Association, Washington, DC, 1991. Used by permission of AFPA.

*Properties are based on minimum dressed green size, which is ½″ off nominal in both b and d dimensions.

Table 3–20 Base design values for visually graded dimension lumber, selected species.

| Species and commercial grade | Size classification | Design values in pounds per square inch (psi) | | | | | | Grading Rules Agency |
		Bending F_b	Tension parallel to grain F_t	Shear parallel to grain F_v	Compression perpendicular to grain $F_{c\perp}$	Compression parallel to grain F_c	Modulus of Elasticity E	
DOUGLAS FIR-LARCH								
Select Structural		1500	1000	95	625	1700	1,900,000	
No.1 & Btr	2"-4" thick	1200	800	95	625	1550	1,800,000	
No.1		1000	675	95	625	1500	1,700,000	
No.2	2"& wider	900	575	95	625	1350	1,600,000	WCLIB
No.3		525	325	95	625	775	1,400,000	WWPA
Stud		700	450	95	625	850	1,400,000	
Construction	2"-4" thick	1000	650	95	625	1650	1,500,000	
Standard		575	375	95	625	1400	1,400,000	
Utility	2"-4" wide	275	175	95	625	900	1,300,000	
DOUGLAS FIR-LARCH (NORTH)								
Select Structural	2"-4" thick	1350	825	95	625	1900	1,900,000	
No.1/No.2		850	500	95	625	1400	1,600,000	
No.3	2"& wider	475	300	95	625	825	1,400,000	NLGA
Stud		650	400	95	625	900	1,400,000	
Construction	2"-4" thick	950	575	95	625	1800	1,500,000	
Standard		525	325	95	625	1450	1,400,000	
Utility	2"-4" wide	250	150	95	625	950	1,300,000	
HEM-FIR								
Select Structural		1400	925	75	405	1500	1,600,000	
No.1 & Btr	2"-4" thick	1100	725	75	405	1350	1,500,000	
No.1		975	625	75	405	1350	1,500,000	
No.2	2"& wider	850	525	75	405	1300	1,300,000	WCLIB
No.3		500	300	75	405	725	1,200,000	WWPA
Stud		675	400	75	405	800	1,200,000	
Construction	2"-4" thick	975	600	75	405	1550	1,300,000	
Standard		550	325	75	405	1300	1,200,000	
Utility	2"-4" wide	250	150	75	405	850	1,100,000	
HEM-FIR (NORTH)								
Select Structural	2"-4" thick	1300	775	75	370	1700	1,700,000	
No.1/No.2		1000	575	75	370	1450	1,600,000	
No.3	2"& wider	575	325	75	370	850	1,400,000	NLGA
Stud		775	450	75	370	925	1,400,000	
Construction	2"-4" thick	1150	650	75	370	1750	1,500,000	
Standard		650	350	75	370	1500	1,400,000	
Utility	2"-4" wide	300	175	75	370	975	1,300,000	
SPRUCE-PINE-FIR								
Select Structural	2"-4" thick	1250	700	70	425	1400	1,500,000	
No.1/No.2		875	450	70	425	1150	1,400,000	
No.3	2"& wider	500	250	70	425	650	1,200,000	NLGA
Stud		675	350	70	425	725	1,200,000	
Construction	2"-4" thick	1000	500	70	425	1400	1,300,000	
Standard		550	275	70	425	1150	1,200,000	
Utility	2"-4" wide	275	125	70	425	750	1,100,000	

SOURCE: *National Design Specification Supplement,* 1997 Edition. American Forest and Paper Association, Washington, DC, 1991. Used by permission of AFPA.

NOTES:

1. Tabulated design values are for normal load duration and dry service conditions. See National Design Specification 2.3 for a comprehensive description of design value adjustment factors.
2. *Lumber dimensions:* Tabulated design values are applicable to lumber that will be used under dry conditions such as in most covered structures. For 2" to 4" thick lumber, the DRY dressed sizes shall be used (see NDS® Table 1A) regardless of the moisture content at the time of manufacture or use. In calculation of design values, the natural gain in strength and stiffness that occurs as lumber dries has been taken into consideration, as well as the reduction in size that occurs when unseasoned lumber shrinks. The gain in load-carrying capacity due to increased strength and stiffness resulting from drying more than offsets the design effect of size reductions due to shrinkage.
3. *Stress-rated boards:* Stress-rated boards of nominal 1", 1¼", and 1½" thickness, 2" and wider, of most species, are permitted the design values shown for select structural, No. 1 and better, No. 1, No. 2, No. 3, stud, construction, standard, utility, clear heart structural, and clear structural grades as shown in the 2" to 4" thick categories herein, when graded in accordance with the stress-rated board provisions in the applicable grading rules. Information on stress-rated board grades applicable to the various species is available from the respective grading rules agencies. Information on additional design values may also be available from the respective grading agencies.

Table 3–21 Base design values for visually graded southern pine dimension lumber.

Species and commercial grade	Size classification	Design values in pounds per square inch (psi)						Grading Rules Agency
		Bending F_b	Tension parallel to grain F_t	Shear parallel to grain F_v	Compression perpendicular to grain $F_{c\perp}$	Compression parallel to grain F_c	Modulus of Elasticity E	
SOUTHERN PINE								
Dense Select Structural		3050	1650	100	660	2250	1,900,000	
Select Structural		2850	1600	100	565	2100	1,800,000	
Non-Dense Select Structural		2650	1350	100	480	1950	1,700,000	
No.1 Dense		2000	1100	100	660	2000	1,800,000	
No.1	2"-4" thick	1850	1050	100	565	1850	1,700,000	
No.1 Non-Dense		1700	900	100	480	1700	1,600,000	
No.2 Dense	2"-4" wide	1700	875	90	660	1850	1,700,000	
No.2		1500	825	90	565	1650	1,600,000	
No.2 Non-Dense		1350	775	90	480	1600	1,400,000	
No.3 and Stud		850	475	90	565	975	1,400,000	
Construction	2"-4" thick	1100	625	100	565	1800	1,500,000	
Standard		625	350	90	565	1500	1,300,000	
Utility	4" wide	300	175	90	565	975	1,300,000	
Dense Select Structural		2700	1500	90	660	2150	1,900,000	
Select Structural		2550	1400	90	565	2000	1,800,000	
Non-Dense Select Structural		2350	1200	90	480	1850	1,700,000	
No.1 Dense		1750	950	90	660	1900	1,800,000	
No.1	2"-4" thick	1650	900	90	565	1750	1,700,000	
No.1 Non-Dense		1500	800	90	480	1600	1,600,000	
No.2 Dense	5"-6" wide	1450	775	90	660	1750	1,700,000	
No.2		1250	725	90	565	1600	1,600,000	
No.2 Non-Dense		1150	675	90	480	1500	1,400,000	
No.3 and Stud		750	425	90	565	925	1,400,000	
Dense Select Structural		2450	1350	90	660	2050	1,900,000	SPIB
Select Structural		2300	1300	90	565	1900	1,800,000	
Non-Dense Select Structural		2100	1100	90	480	1750	1,700,000	
No.1 Dense	2"-4" thick	1650	875	90	660	1800	1,800,000	
No.1		1500	825	90	565	1650	1,700,000	
No.1 Non-Dense	8" wide	1350	725	90	480	1550	1,600,000	
No.2 Dense		1400	675	90	660	1700	1,700,000	
No.2		1200	650	90	565	1550	1,600,000	
No.2 Non-Dense		1100	600	90	480	1450	1,400,000	
No.3 and Stud		700	400	90	565	875	1,400,000	
Dense Select Structural		2150	1200	90	660	2000	1,900,000	
Select Structural		2050	1100	90	565	1850	1,800,000	
Non-Dense Select Structural		1850	950	90	480	1750	1,700,000	
No.1 Dense	2"-4" thick	1450	775	90	660	1750	1,800,000	
No.1		1300	725	90	565	1600	1,700,000	
No.1 Non-Dense	10" wide	1200	650	90	480	1500	1,600,000	
No.2 Dense		1200	625	90	660	1650	1,700,000	
No.2		1050	575	90	565	1500	1,600,000	
No.2 Non-Dense		950	550	90	480	1400	1,400,000	
No.3 and Stud		600	325	90	565	850	1,400,000	
Dense Select Structural		2050	1100	90	660	1950	1,900,000	
Select Structural		1900	1050	90	565	1800	1,800,000	
Non-Dense Select Structural		1750	900	90	480	1700	1,700,000	
No.1 Dense	2"-4" thick	1350	725	90	660	1700	1,800,000	
No.1		1250	675	90	565	1600	1,700,000	
No.1 Non-Dense	12" wide[4]	1150	600	90	480	1500	1,600,000	
No.2 Dense		1150	575	90	660	1600	1,700,000	
No.2		975	550	90	565	1450	1,600,000	
No.2 Non-Dense		900	525	90	480	1350	1,400,000	
No.3 and Stud		575	325	90	565	825	1,400,000	

NOTES:

1. Tabulated design values are for normal load duration and dry service conditions. See NDS® 2.3 for a comprehensive description of design value adjustment factors.

2. *Lumber dimensions:* Tabulated design values are applicable to lumber that will be used under dry conditions such as in most covered structures. For 2" to 4" thick lumber, the DRY dressed sizes shall be used (see Table 1A in NDS®) regardless of the moisture content at the time of manufacture or use. In calculation of design values, the natural gain in strength and stiffness that occurs as lumber dries has been taken into consideration, as well as the reduction in size that occurs when unseasoned lumber shrinks. The gain in load-carrying capacity due to increased strength and stiffness resulting from drying more than offsets the design effect of size reductions due to shrinkage.

3. *Stress-rated boards:* Information for various grades of southern pine stress-rated boards of nominal 1", 1¼", and 1½" thickness, 2" and wider, is available from the Southern Pine Inspection Bureau (SPIB) in the "Standard Grading Rules for Southern Pine Lumber."

4. *Spruce pine:* To obtain recommended values for spruce pine graded to SPIB rules, multiply the appropriate design values for mixed southern pine by the corresponding conversion factor shown in Table 3–22, and round to the nearest 100,000 psi for E; to the next lower multiple of 5 psi for F_v and $F_{c\perp}$; to the next lower multiple of 50 psi for F_b, F_t, and F_c if 1000 psi or greater, 25 psi otherwise.

5. For mixed southern pine, and wet and dry service condition design values, see the manufacturer's tables or the National Design Specification.

Table 3–22 Conversion factors for determining design values for spruce pine.

	Bending, F_b	Tension Parallel to Grain, F_t	Shear Parallel to Grain, F_v	Compression Perpendicular to Grain, $F_{c\perp}$	Compression Parallel to Grain, F_c	Modulus of Elasticity, E
Conversion Factor	0.78	0.78	0.98	0.73	0.78	0.82

Source: Derived from the *National Design Specification Supplement, 1997 Edition.* American Forest and Paper Association, Washington, DC, 1997. Used by permission of AFPA.

EXERCISES

The following exercise should be done on 8¹/₂" × 11" drawing paper with a ¹/₂" border, using drawing instruments; drawings do not have to be drawn to a particular scale.

1. Draw an elevation view and a section of a wood beam. Graphically illustrate which fibers are in tension and which fibers are in compression. Show where the neutral axis is located to illustrate that the stress changes from tension to compression.

2. Draw the elevation view of a beam that is supported by two columns and cantilevers beyond the end of one of the columns. Graphically illustrate which fibers are in tension and which fibers are in compression.

3. Draw the elevation view of a W-pattern truss. Identify the members of the truss that are in tension and the ones that are in compression. Use arrows to indicate tension and compression.

4. Draw a section of each of the following structural members: a wide flange beam (W section), a glue laminated beam, a flitch beam, and an I-shaped floor joist. Poché and label the materials.

5. Draw an elevation view of a flat floor truss with metal truss plate connectors. Show a bearing wall at one end of the trusses and a steel beam at the other end.

REVIEW QUESTIONS

1. What lumber grades are generally used for the major amount of residential framing throughout the country?

2. What physical characteristics must structural lumber possess?

3. List the two major species of wood that are now used for framing houses.

4. What is the main use in home construction for oak lumber?

5. Explain the word *deflection* as used in structural terminology.

6. To what type of stresses will wood columns used to support a girder in a structure be subjected?

7. What is the maximum amount of moisture allowed in seasoned framing lumber?

8. What minimum live load do local building codes require on living room floors?

9. Why must you consider both the live load and the dead load when determining the size of a structural framing member?

10. If you are using No. 2 Douglas fir for framing a kitchen floor, what size joists will be necessary if they are spaced 16" o.c. and span 11'-6"?

11. Specify the ceiling joist size for the following situation: no attic storage, No. 2 southern yellow pine, 16" o.c. spacing, and 13'-0" span.

12. Define the term *safety factor*.

13. Differentiate between light roofing and heavy roofing when sizing rafters.

14. Why is it important in conventional roof framing to have ceiling joists parallel to the rafters?

15. In planning a plank-and-beam roof with wide spacing of the beams, why is the stiffness of the planking an important consideration?

16. Is the rafter length or the rafter span used in selecting a proper size for a rafter from Table 13–16?

17. What is the maximum allowable span for 2×10 Douglas fir floor joists spaced at 16″ o.c. if the live load is 30 lb/sq ft?

18. What will be the length of a rafter if the roof slope is 9 : 12 and the horizontal span is 16′-0″? (See Fig. 13–9.)

19. What advantage is gained by the use of a flitch beam?

20. What size of standard steel pipe column is required to support 50 kips if the unsupported length is 10′-0″?

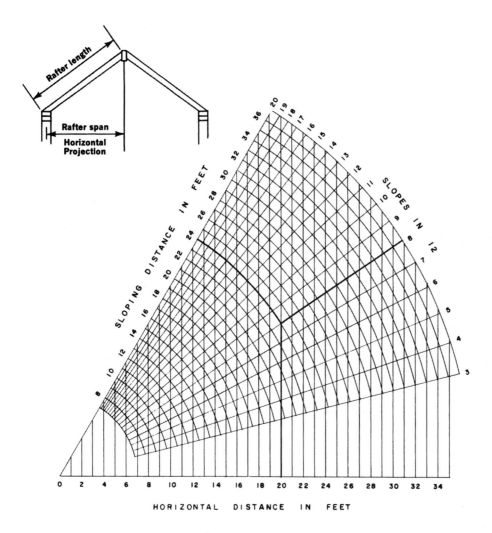

To use the diagram select the known horizontal distance and follow the vertical line to its intersection with the radial line of the specified slope, then proceed along the arc to read the sloping distance. In some cases it may be desirable to interpolate between the one foot separations. The diagram also may be used to find the horizontal distance corresponding to a given sloping distance or to find the slope when the horizontal and sloping distances are known.

Example: With a roof slope of 8 in 12 and a horizontal distance of 20 feet the sloping distance may be read as 24 feet.

Figure 3–9 Conversion diagram for rafters.

Computer-Based Building Structural Design Resources

Two examples of computer applications related to building structural design or components are included. The first example, Fig. 1, from Alpine Engineered Products, Inc., shows a sample output sheet for the design of a wood truss roof system. The second example, Fig. 2, from ParaVision Technologies, Inc., was downloaded from an Internet site.

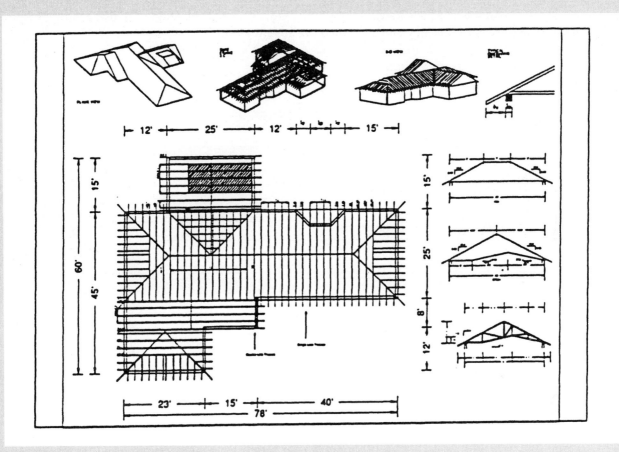

Figure 1

Truss Design and Manufacturing

Truss Design

The design and drafting of trusses can be a time-consuming and costly task. For manufacturers of trusses used in residential and commercial construction, the ability to quickly design, draft and estimate the cost of a project provides an important competitive advantage. With ParaGrafixtm the logic for design and drafting standards can be incorporated in the system so that fabrication information is available in minutes rather than hours.

ParaGrafix's ease of use and parametric capabilities allows easy optimization of design solutions. Better solutions means greater efficiency and a competitive advantage.

Here's a look at the application running under Windows 95:

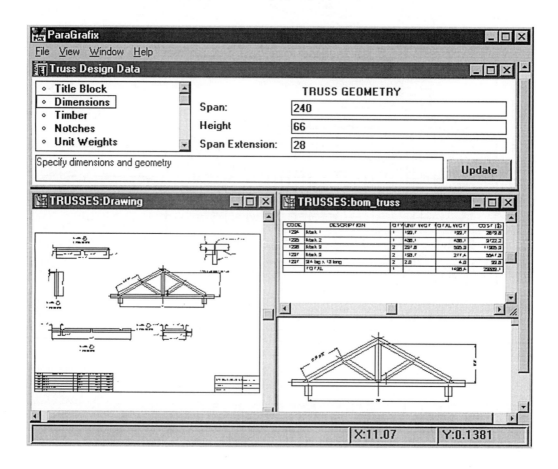

Return to previous page.

For more information, phone (604)733-8600, fax (604)733-8622 or E-mail info@paravision.ca
Copyright © 1995 ParaVision Technologies Inc

Figure 2

"*Genius is the ability to reduce the complicated to the simple.*"
—*C. W. CERAN*

The word *details* covers the broad category of the isolated and enlarged drawings that, together with the plans and the elevations, form a complete set of working drawings. Each detail furnishes specific information at key points throughout the construction. Almost every set of drawings requires a different set of details, the choice of which is determined by the architect or the drafter. Only a few standard details may be necessary, however, on drawings of modest structures incorporating conventional construction. In fact, some sets of drawings contain very few details, allowing the builders considerable latitude in the choice of construction, whereas other sets contain details for almost every construction arrangement in the building.

This chapter is limited to the basic general details found in sets of drawings for average residential and light construction.

4.1

SELECTING THE CORRECT SCALE FOR DETAILS

Before starting a detail drawing, take a minute or two to decide on the most appropriate scale. Suitable scale depends on the size of members in the detail, the amount of detail that must be shown, and the space available in the layout of the sheet; all of these factors must be considered. Plan the sheets so that details are placed for their most logical association with other drawings and so that all sheets of a set are utilized for economy as well as appearance. Scales for details range from $1/2'' = 1'\text{-}0''$ to full size. Small pieces, such as moldings, are usually drawn full size to show profiles and small detail clearly. Larger members or assemblies can be drawn at smaller scales. Note that the preferable larger scales can be used in minimum spaces if *break symbols* are employed to remove unimportant areas of long members. This method of con-

densing details to show only the significant points is common practice in architectural drawings since many members are necessarily large, and reducing the scale would only make smaller pieces difficult to show. However, if space permits, the true heights and lengths of important members of a detail are definitely more informative to workers. You should resort to break symbols only when limited space prevents drawing the entire detail.

The choice of scale may also be affected by the units in the detail. For example, if concrete block coursing is used, by selecting the $3/4'' = 1'\text{-}0''$ scale, you can easily lay out the $8''$ coursing with the $1/2'' = 1'\text{-}0''$ architect's scale. See Table 4–1 for a list of typical drawing scales.

Table 4–1 Drawing scale table.

Drawing	Range	Description
Site plan	1:30–1:20	Site plan and survey should be drawn at the same scale.
Detail of site plans	$1/8''$–$1/2''$ $11/2''$–$3''$	Large areas Small areas
Floor plans, exterior building sections	$1/16''$–$1/4''$	Very large to small
Detail plans	$1/4''$–$1/2''$ $11/2''$–$3''$	Large areas Small areas
Wall sections	$3/8''$–$3/4''$	Small-scale drawing should be sketchy.
Interior elevations	$1/4''$, $3/8''$, $3/4''$	$1/4''$–$3/8''$ are most common.
Details	$11/2''$–$3''$	Use the same scale for details in a family.
Schedules: door, window, and cabinet	$1/4''$, $3/8''$, $3/4''$	$1/4''$–$3/8''$ are most common.

DRAWING TYPICAL WALL DETAILS

If the construction of a house is identical throughout all exterior walls, only one wall section may be necessary; if the construction varies, several sections should be drawn. A typical wall section conveniently incorporates the *footing detail*, *sill detail*, and *cornice detail*—all properly in line for relative reference (Figs. 4–1, 4–2, and 4–3).

To draw a wall section, start with the poured footing (usually twice as wide and the same height as the thickness of the foundation wall), and center the foundation wall directly above. If footing depths vary below grades, and if a basement is required, the foundation wall can be drawn with a break symbol, and only a convenient amount of the wall need be shown.

The construction at the top of the foundation, known as the *sill detail*, is important, and various arrangements of the framing members at this point determine the height of the finished floor from grade. If the foundation is concrete masonry units, show the courses, and insert an anchor bolt through the sill plate into the C.M.U. Wood members should be kept at least 8″ from grade. If a wood floor over a crawl space has been decided on, allow at least 18″ clearance between floor joists and the grade line. This condition usually places the finished floor at least 28″ or 30″ above grade (unless excavation is done within the foundation). Exterior steps to the floor surface will then be necessary. If a basement is planned, the foundation must extend far enough above grade to meet local codes and to allow installation of basement windows. If slab-on-ground construction is required, the finish floor level will usually fall about 8″ above the grade level, requiring one step height for entry. Other variations of the sill detail may result in still other floor heights; usually, it is advantageous to keep the house as low as possible. Draw the grade line after the sill is completed. Be sure that the wood joists have at least 3″ bearing surface on the sill plate. In western frame construction, the box sill requires the soleplate and the studs to be placed over the subfloor.

In brick veneer construction, a better sill detail results if the brick starts at, or just below, grade and if the wood plate is raised above the bottom of the veneer and frame air space (Fig. 4–2B). This prevents moisture, which usually forms at the bottom of the air space during cold weather, from penetrating the wood framing. Otherwise, the wood members are identical to that used in frame construction. Brick rowlock sills (Figs. 4–4F and 4–5) must have flashing below.

In solid masonry construction, several methods can be used to support wood floor joists. A diagonal firecut can be used at the ends of the floor joists resting within the solid masonry walls (Fig. 4–4D), or the masonry wall can be widened to provide bearing for the floor joists.

The cornice detail shows all of the construction at the intersection of the walls and the roof, including the roof overhang. In conventional frame construction, both the notched bird's-mouth of the rafters and the ceiling joists bear on the double wall plate, and the joists are usually shown parallel to the rafters. A bird's-mouth cut provides horizontal bearing surface for the rafters, and because it supports the main weight of the roof, the surface should be a minimum of 3″ wide. Remember that members in details should be drawn *actual size rather than nominal size*.

Extend the rafters to form the overhang (often as much as 2′ on some homes). The overhang can be given various treatments, depending on the decisions made on the design sketches. If a wide, boxed-in cornice seems advisable, draw 2 × 4 horizontal outlookers from the studs to the rafter ends (Fig. 4–2A). Attach soffit material to the underside of the outlookers, and show a screened vent under the eave when applicable. At the ends of the rafters, draw either a vertical or inclined fascia board, making it wide enough to allow about a ¾″ drip below the surface of the soffit material. If a sloping soffit is desirable, the soffit material is attached directly to the underside of the rafter overhang; on other treatments, the rafters can be left exposed on the exterior. Cornice details showing exposed rafters, in either conventional or post-and-beam construction, must have blocking and exterior wall covering shown between the rafters. This detail must be carefully conceived to produce an airtight joint between the wall and the underside of the roof decking; exterior trim at this point also requires consideration.

Complete the decking, roofing material, gravel stops, gutter, and the like, and include all hatching, notes, and applicable dimensions. Avoid scattering descriptive notes on section views in a disorderly fashion. Plan the notes in a logical sequence, with noncrossing leaders touching the identifying part. Line up the notes on a vertical guide line insofar as possible, and make the spacing between notes uniform when they occur in groups. Keep the notes as close to their counterparts as practical to minimize misinterpretation. Outline the section with *bold lines*. (See Fig. 4–6 for cutting plane indications.) Roof slopes, as discussed below, should be indicated with a roof slope diagram.

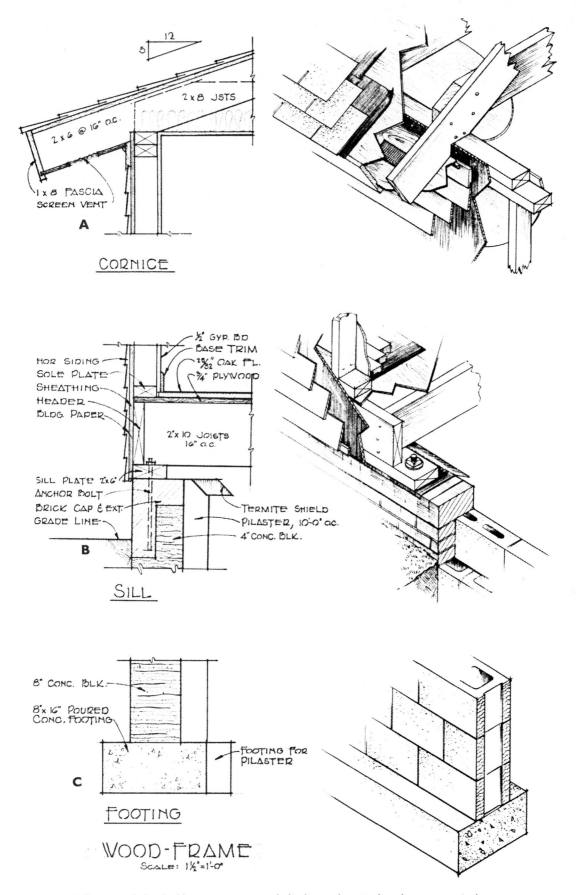

A

12
5

2 x 6 @ 16" O.C.

2 x 8 JSTS

1 x 8 FASCIA
SCREEN VENT

CORNICE

B

½" GYP. BD
BASE TRIM
²⁵⁄₃₂" OAK FL.
¾" PLYWOOD

HOR SIDING
SOLE PLATE
SHEATHING
HEADER
BLDG. PAPER

2' x 10 JOISTS
16" O.C.

SILL PLATE 2x6"
ANCHOR BOLT
BRICK CAP & EXT.
GRADE LINE

TERMITE SHIELD
PILASTER, 10'-0" O.C.
4" CONC. BLK.

SILL

C

8" CONC. BLK.

8"x 16" POURED
CONC. FOOTING

FOOTING FOR
PILASTER

FOOTING

WOOD-FRAME
SCALE: 1½"=1'-0"

Figure 4–1 Typical wall details (the isometric views help the reader visualize the construction).

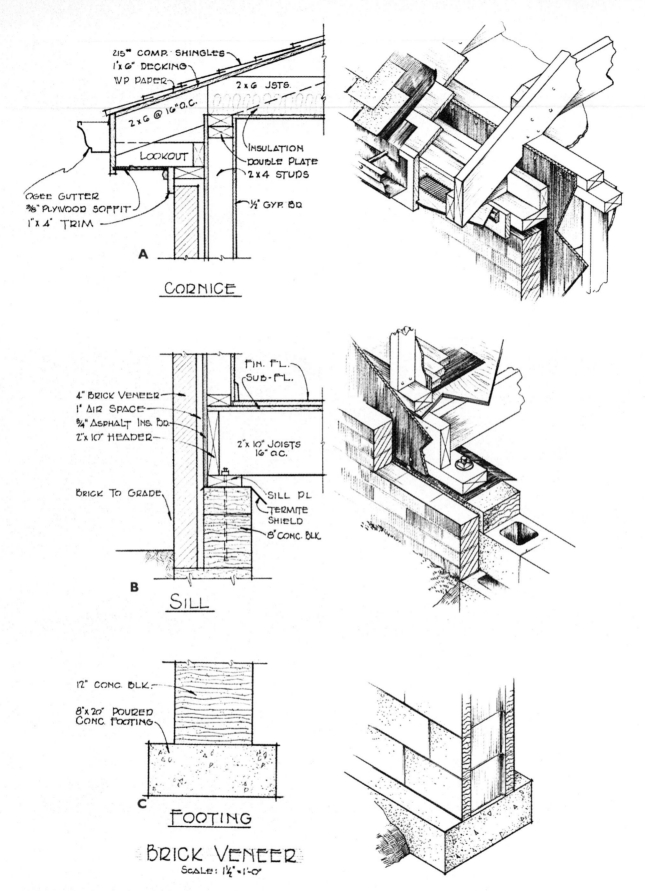

Figure 4–2 Typical wall details (the isometric views help the reader visualize the construction).

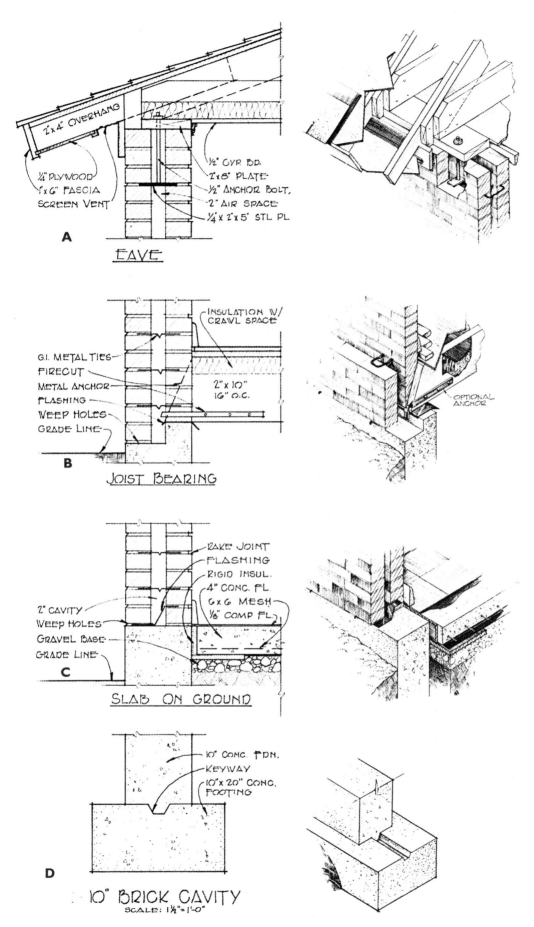

A EAVE

B JOIST BEARING

C SLAB ON GROUND

D 10" BRICK CAVITY
SCALE: 1½"=1'-0"

Detail A — EAVE:
2"x 4" OVERHANG
¼" PLYWOOD
1"x 6" FASCIA
SCREEN VENT
½" GYP. BD.
2"x 8" PLATE
½" ANCHOR BOLT
2" AIR SPACE
¼"x 2"x 5" STL. PL.

Detail B — JOIST BEARING:
INSULATION W/ CRAWL SPACE
G.I. METAL TIES
FIRECUT
METAL ANCHOR
FLASHING
WEEP HOLES
GRADE LINE
2"x 10" 16" O.C.
OPTIONAL ANCHOR

Detail C — SLAB ON GROUND:
RAKE JOINT
FLASHING
RIGID INSUL.
4" CONC. FL.
6x6 MESH
⅛" COMP. FL.
2" CAVITY
WEEP HOLES
GRAVEL BASE
GRADE LINE

Detail D — 10" BRICK CAVITY:
10" CONC. FDN.
KEYWAY
10"x 20" CONC. FOOTING

Figure 4–3 Typical wall details (the isometric views help the reader visualize the construction).

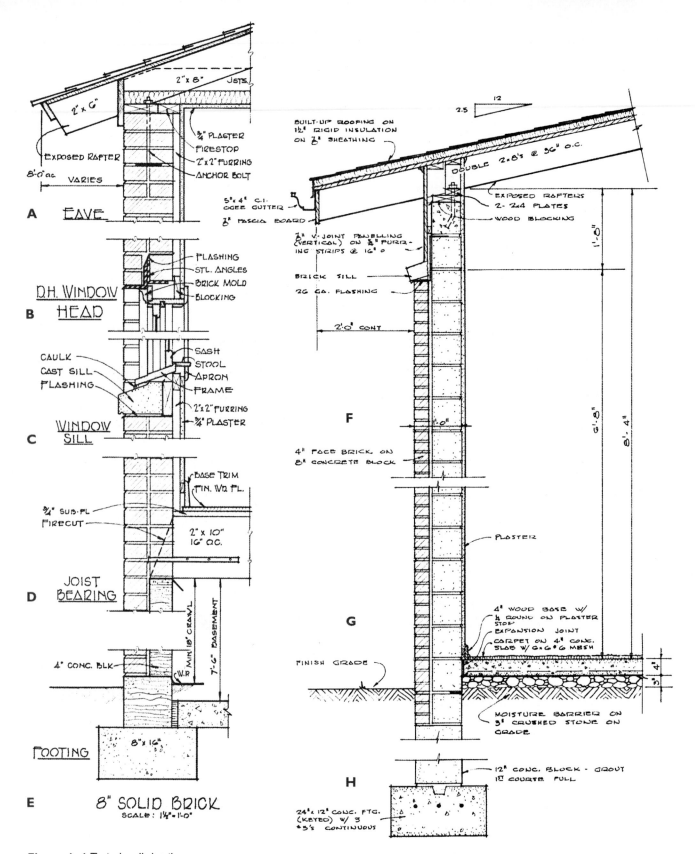

Figure 4–4 Typical wall details.

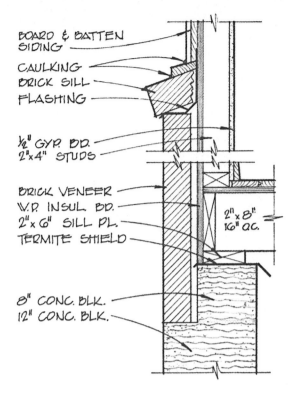

BOARD & BATTEN
SIDING
CAULKING
BRICK SILL
FLASHING

½" GYP. BD.
2"x 4" STUDS

BRICK VENEER
V.P. INSUL. BD.
2" x 6" SILL PL.
TERMITE SHIELD

8" CONC. BLK.
12" CONC. BLK.

2" x 8"
16" O.C.

Figure 4–5 Wood and brick half-wall detail.

4.3

INDICATING ROOF PITCHES ON DRAWINGS

The slope of a roof largely determines the kind of roofing; this in turn influences preliminary planning when pleasing roof lines have been established. Although any slope can be made workable, it is advisable to modify the roof lines of the sketch slightly if necessary so that the working drawings will have roof slopes that are not too difficult to measure. This modification affects the appearance very little and makes the construction of the roof somewhat simpler (see Fig. 4–7 for typical roof slopes).

Roof slopes or pitches can be shown by any of three methods on drawings:

1. slope-ratio diagram,
2. fractional pitch indication, and
3. angular dimension.

The *slope-ratio triangle* is drawn with its hypotenuse parallel to the roof profile. Its opposite sides, representing the rise-and-run slope ratio, are drawn vertically and horizontally. The horizontal leg of the triangle is usually measured 1″ long for convenience and is given a numerical value of 12. The rise value shown on the vertical leg of the triangle can then be easily measured off on the 1″ = 1′-0″ scale. This ratio of the rise of the roof to its run is stated, for example, as $3:12$, $7:12$, or $1\frac{1}{2}:12$, making it consistent with conventional references associated with roofing materials and other construction applications. In Fig. 4–8, the $4:12$ right-triangle symbol means, briefly, that for every 12″ of horizontal run, the roof rises 4″. Most architects use this method for slope indications.

The *fractional pitch* of a roof is derived from a standard formula:

$$\text{Pitch} = \frac{\text{rise}}{\text{span}}$$

The span is the total distance between top plate supports (twice the run). Fractional pitches are infrequently found on working drawings; yet carpenters have traditionally used fractional pitches for many of their rafter layouts.

Angular slopes are shown with an arc dimension line, revealing the angular dimension in degrees from the horizontal (Fig. 4–7). Use of an arc dimension line is limited mainly to minor construction features.

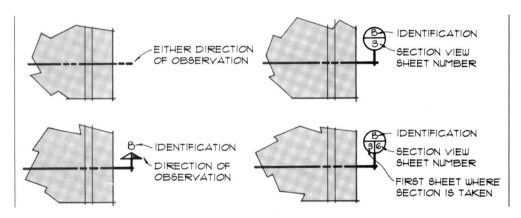

EITHER DIRECTION
OF OBSERVATION

B — IDENTIFICATION

3 — SECTION VIEW
SHEET NUMBER

B — IDENTIFICATION

DIRECTION OF
OBSERVATION

B — IDENTIFICATION

3 6 — SECTION VIEW
SHEET NUMBER

FIRST SHEET WHERE
SECTION IS TAKEN

Figure 4–6 Methods of indicating cutting planes for sections.

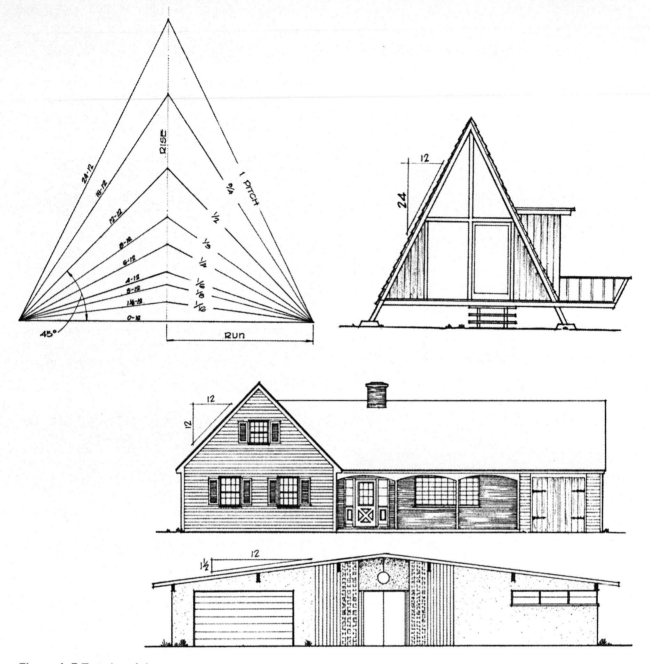

Figure 4–7 Typical roof slopes.

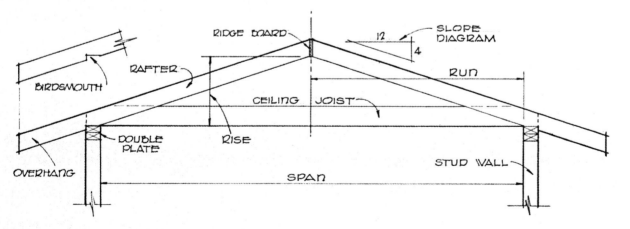

Figure 4–8 Roof slope and framing terms.

WINDOWS AND THEIR REPRESENTATION

Windows provide, first of all, the light and ventilation necessary in dwellings; they are the eyes through which the surrounding landscape can be enjoyed, bringing in the outdoors to make the interior more spacious and less confined. Windows must be carefully selected as to size, type, and placement if they are to provide the desired architectural character to the structure. Thus, both practical and esthetic considerations are important in their selection. As a rule, the total window area should be at least 10% of the floor space. Choosing windows can be a difficult task unless you pay close attention to three characteristics: (1) energy performance, (2) operation, and (3) service.

4.4.1 Energy Performance

Heat loss (the *U* value), solar heat gain, air infiltration, and condensation resistance are important areas to investigate. Whole-unit *U* values rather than middle-of-glass values should be studied. This information, found on the labels of the National Fenestration Rating Council (NFRC), provides a good comparison of the combined effectiveness of all of a window's components, including glazing, frame construction, and weatherstripping. Glazings that maximize solar gain in cold climates and minimize solar gain in warm climates should be chosen in order to reduce heating and cooling loads. Review the manufacturer's air infiltration ratings. Be sure that weatherstripping seals the entire perimeter and compresses or interlocks when the sash is closed and locked. Weatherstripping material should resist damage caused by ultraviolet radiation. Features that minimize potential condensation include thermal breaks in metal frames, warm-edge seals between multiple glazings, and glass coatings and air-space gases that improve performance.

The NFRC has developed a fenestration energy rating system based on whole product performance. This system accurately accounts for the energy-related effects of all of a product's component parts, and it prevents information about a single component from being compared in a misleading way to other whole product properties. At this time, NFRC labels on window units give ratings for the *U* value, the solar heat gain coefficient, and visible light transmittance. Soon labels will include air infiltration rates (FHR) and an annual fenestration cooling rating (FCR). Figure 4–9 is a sample NFRC label. Table 4–2 notes characteristics of typical windows and annual energy performance ratings.

4.4.2 Operation

Windows should operate smoothly and should be easy to clean; they should also have good-quality screens and storm sashes. Crank mechanisms should operate

National Fenestration Rating Council INCORPORATED		
AAA Window Company		
Energy Rating Factors	**Ratings** Residential / Nonresidential	**Product Description**
U-factor Determined in accordance with NFRC 100	0.40 | 0.38	Model 1000 Casement Low-e Argon Filled
Solar Heat Gain Coefficient Determined in accordance with NFRC 200	0.65 | 0.66	
Visible Transmittance Determined in accordance with NFRC 200	0.71 | 0.71	

NFRC ratings are determined for a fixed set of environmental conditions and specific product sizes and may not be appropriate for directly determining seasonal energy performance. For additional information contact:

Sample NFRC Label

Figure 4–9 Sample NFRC label.

smoothly: Latches should pull the sash closed without being forced. Weatherstripping should seal tightly but not bind or catch. Windows should also have a sash that you can tilt in order to clean the windows; easy-to-use sash removal mechanisms; a sliding sash that glides with little effort; and hardware, glass, and a sash that can be easily replaced if necessary.

4.4.3 Service

Purchase units from suppliers and manufacturers who support their products and who have representatives available to come to your site to address problems. Check out the warranties. Parts are usually covered for 1 year; glass and seals, from 1 to 20 years, with 5 years the most common. Factory-applied exterior finishes may be covered by a separate warranty. Be sure to follow the manufacturer's finishing instructions. Check on the company's replacement parts policy. Some manufacturers provide parts only as long as existing inventories last, whereas others try to provide lifetime service for any window that they have ever made.

Glassed areas can be either preassembled window units or *fixed glass*, which is directly affixed to the framing. Fixed glass allows large window areas to be installed with a minimum of expense, inasmuch as no operating sash, hardware, or screens are necessary. If ventilation is needed, occasional-opening sash or panels can be incorporated into window walls. Today's market offers a wide assortment of preassembled window units; most of them

Table 4–2 Characteristics of typical window types and annual energy performance ratings.

Window Description	Overall Window Characteristics					
	U-Factor (Btu/h-ft²-°F)	Solar Heat Gain Coefficient	Visible Transmittance	Air Leakage (cfm/ft²)	FHR	FCR
1. Single-glass, aluminum-frame no thermal break	1.30	0.79	0.69	0.98	0	0
2. Single-glass, bronze; aluminum-frame; no thermal break	1.30	0.69	0.52	0.98	−2	8
3. Double-glass, aluminum-frame, thermal break	0.64	0.65	0.62	0.56	19	12
4. Double-glass, bronze; aluminum-frame; thermal break	0.64	0.55	0.47	0.56	17	20
5. Double-glass, wood- or vinyl-frame	0.49	0.58	0.57	0.56	24	18
6. Double-glass, bronze; wood- or vinyl-frame	0.49	0.48	0.43	0.56	22	25
7. Double-glass; low-E, argon; wood- or vinyl-frame	0.33	0.55	0.52	0.15	32	19
8. Double-glass; low-E, argon; wood- or vinyl-frame	0.30	0.44	0.56	0.15	32	27
9. Double-glass; selective low-E, argon; wood- or vinyl-frame	0.29	0.32	0.51	0.15	30	36
10. Double-glass; selective low-E, argon; wood- or vinyl-frame	0.31	0.26	0.31	0.15	27	40
11. Triple-glass; low-E (2), krypton; insulated-vinyl-frame	0.15	0.37	0.48	0.08	38	33
12. Triple-glass, wood- or vinyl-frame	0.34	0.52	0.53	0.08	32	22

are made of wood, aluminum, or vinyl cladding, which eliminates the need for painting.

Wood windows make up about 50% of the residential market. Although all of the parts of a wood window are treated with a preservative prior to assembly, wood windows do require maintenance. Some manufacturers paint the exterior of their wood windows in the factory.

Many manufacturers make clad windows, which can have a relatively maintenance-free exterior with a wood interior. There are a number of different ways to clad a window. Some manufacturers attach the cladding by gluing it onto a wood frame. Others have designed their cladding so that it snaps onto a wood frame. Other companies make a vinyl or an aluminum frame to which a wood interior is attached.

All-vinyl windows are typically much less expensive than wood windows, and they never need painting. All-

vinyl windows should not be confused with vinyl-clad windows. In the past, some all-vinyl windows experienced problems. Vinyl expands and contracts at a different rate than glass, and on some windows, thermal cycling caused the vinyl to distort and to pull away from the seals around the glazing. Faulty seals affect a window's ability to withstand air and water infiltration. Vinyl is a brittle material that is 80% salt. In order to make vinyl pliable, a plasticizer is added so that the vinyl can be molded. With time, as the plasticizer evaporates, the vinyl becomes brittle. New vinyl formulas, called uPVCs (unplasticized polyvinyl chlorides), are supposed to be more stable and more resistant to distortion and movement. An important feature to look for in vinyl windows is welded corners rather than mitered and screwed corners.

In recent years some people have steered away from aluminum windows because they are not energy efficient.

Aluminum is a good conductor and thus a poor insulator. Aluminum windows are typically less expensive than wood windows or vinyl windows, and they should not require much maintenance. Aluminum can be painted, and manufacturers offer their products with a factory-applied colored coating. Another advantage of aluminum is that, because of its inherent strength, aluminum windows have a much larger glass area per window size. Aluminum-clad windows do not suffer from the energy disadvantages of all-aluminum windows because the heat-conducting properties of the aluminum are broken by the wood interior.

Fiberglass has advantages as a material for both window frames and sashes. Fiberglass expands and contracts at almost the same rate as window glass, so there should not be the kinds of problems associated with older all-vinyl windows. Other benefits include corrosion resistance and dimensional stability.

When choosing windows for a house, you will want to decide three things: (1) the type of windows—casement, double-hung, fixed, awning, or slider; (2) the kind of glass to use; and (3) the material used for the frames.

Insulating glass—two panes of hermetically sealed glass separated by a spacer—came into widespread use in the 1970s. Dead air space between two pieces of glass improves the energy efficiency of a window. The wider the air space between panes, the higher the insulating value of the window. Filling the space between the pieces of glass with gases that are less conductive than air, such as krypton or argon, improves a window's insulating ability.

Low-E glass is covered with a heat-reflective, low-emissivity coating. The direction in which low-E glass reflects heat is determined by the glass surface to which the coating is applied. In a cooling environment, low-E glass reflects the sun's heat away from the house. In a heating environment, low-E glass reflects heat back into the house instead of letting it pass through the window.

Heat mirror is a low-E film suspended in the space between the panes in a piece of insulating glass. Different types of heat mirror films perform different functions. Some are better at reflecting exterior heat away from a house; others are better at keeping heat inside the house. All heat mirror films are superb at keeping ultraviolet (UV) light out of a house. Window systems developed using the heat mirror system can cost up to twice as much as other systems using regular insulating glass.

4.4.4 Types of Windows

The two basic components of all windows are a sash and a frame. The sash is the part of the window that holds the glass, and the frame is the part that holds the sash. Windows are categorized by the method and direction in which the sash moves, or does not move, in the frame. Fig 4–10 shows the major types of window units currently used in residential construction.

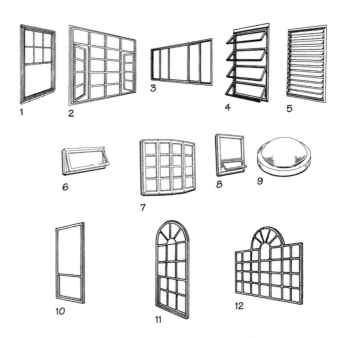

Figure 4–10 Major residential window types: (1) double-hung; (2) casement; (3) horizonal sliding; (4) awning; (5) jalousie; (6) basement; (7) bow or bay; (8) hopper and fixed; (9) skylight; (10) single hung; (11) arch top; (12) Palladian.

Double-Hung Windows These windows, also called *vertical-slide windows*, are the most familiar, having two sashes that operate vertically. A double-hung window allows a maximum of 50% ventilation and is typically American. The unit, including the two sashes, the frame, weatherstripping, and hardware, is set into the rough opening; then it is plumbed and is nailed to the double studs and header. Inside trim is applied after the interior walls are complete. If units are combined into groups, a structural mullion is shown between the units. The slopping sill member rests on the lower member of the rough opening (Fig 4–11).

Casement Windows Casement windows have their sash hinged on the side. Most of them open out, but some that open in are available. Casement sash windows have the advantage of directing breezes into the room when open, and 100% ventilation is possible. Operating cranks open and close the sash.

Horizontal Sliding Windows Horizontal sliding windows operate horizontally, like sliding doors. Like double-hung windows, horizontal sliding windows allow only 50% ventilation when open. Units are often combined with fixed picture-window sash.

Awning Windows These windows open out horizontally, with the hinges of each sash at the top and the cranking hardware operating all of the sash in each unit simultaneously. Their major advantage is that they can be

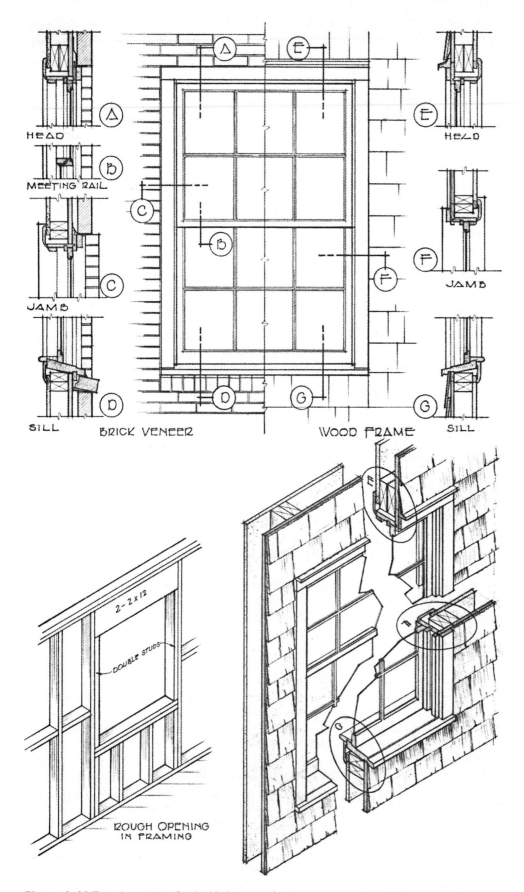

HEAD

MEETING RAIL

JAMB

SILL

BRICK VENEER

HEAD

JAMB

SILL

WOOD FRAME

2 - 2 x 12

DOUBLE STUDS

ROUGH OPENING
IN FRAMING

Figure 4–11 Typical sections of a double-hung window.

left open during rain without adverse effects. Dust collects on the opened windows readily, however.

Jalousie Windows Jalousie window units have small, horizontal glass panels that operate horizontally, much as an awning sash window does. The individual glass panels do not have frames. The advantages are similar to those of awning windows, except that jalousie windows are seldom as weathertight when closed. Therefore, they should be reserved mainly for glass-enclosed porches or for residences in warmer climates.

Hopper Windows Hopper windows have small sashes, opening either in or out, which are combined with larger fixed windows. The complete unit is set into the rough opening like other window units.

Palladian Windows Palladian windows are a comparitively recent adaptation from the sixteenth century Italian architect Andrea Pallidio. They are tall, semicircular center windows combined with straight-headed side windows; they have become popular in many American homes within the last 20 years. Often classical pilasters and heads are trimmed out in the interior to form very elegant windows, especially in rooms with high ceilings.

The Palladian window should be carefully proportioned to complement other windows and features. They must be properly placed without crowding other elements and spaces, and they should be used sparingly to avoid dominating the main architectural features. Usually small lights within the combined units are most pleasing.

These windows are generally used to provide added light to large rooms with high ceilings, as we mentioned, and often to illuminate stairways where a focal point might contribute style to the exterior. Manufacturers frequently refer to these arched windows as "cathedral windows." Stock windows properly sized can be combined using a larger central unit and semicircular head and two smaller side windows to form very satisfactory combinations.

Skylights Skylights are actually roof windows that can be placed over openings in roofs of little or no slope and sealed into the roofing material. Residential skylights are usually bubble-shaped, plastic units with flanges or sealing rims around the base. Small skylights are convenient for giving natural light to interior hallways or windowless bathrooms. However, in warm climates, the direct glare of the sun through a skylight can be troublesome unless some manner of light control is provided. Caution should be exercised in the use of skylights on roofs.

Clerestory Windows Clerestory windows are so named because of their placement—usually high in a wall above a lower roof level. They are often a series of small windows; their height affords privacy and permits them to cast dramatic light effects within the room.

Picture Windows So called because usually no muntins interfere with the framed view, picture windows are fixed-glass units (as a rule, rather large), which often become the center unit of several regular windows.

Study the many manufacturers' catalogs for more detailed information of various windows, and observe the recommended method of attaching each window in different wall openings (Fig 4–12).

4.4.5 Window Unit Measurements

There are four basic measurements associated with any one window unit: (1) unit size, (2) rough opening size, (3) sash size, and (4) glass size (Table 4–3 and Fig. 4–13). It is important to identify which one of the four measurements is being used when window dimensions are given. Window sizes are usually noted with the width first and the height second.

The *unit dimension* represents the overall outside dimensions of the window. This size can be taken from different places, depending on the type of window being described. A wood double-hung unit normally has preattached brick mold trim, so the unit size is the out-to-out size of the brick mold. Clad casement windows often come with plastic nailing flanges, and the unit size will be the same as the out-to-out dimensions of the jambs.

The *rough opening size* is the dimension required in the rough frame wall in order to receive the window. This size is most important for the builder. It determines the framing size for the exterior wall opening. It is usually ¼″ larger per side than the outside-of-jamb-to-outside-of-jamb measurement. It provides extra space needed for leveling and plumbing the window in the rough framing of the wall.

The *sash size* is the overall measurement of the window sash. The window sash fits between the two jambs and is the same as the distance between the jambs for the width size. The height dimension will vary, depending on the type of window. A casement window sash extends from the head to the sill, whereas a double-hung window has two or more sashes between the head and the sill.

The *glass size* is the measurement of the glass area as viewed in the sash. It is the sash minus the stile size (for the width) or minus the rails (for the height).

Figure 4–13 and Table 4–3 illustrate the sizes and their relationship to each other for a 24″ × 24″, double-hung window unit.

In Fig. 4–11, note the method of framing window openings in wood frame construction. As mentioned previously, the units are supported by the wood framing, and the section views reveal the relationship of the unit to the

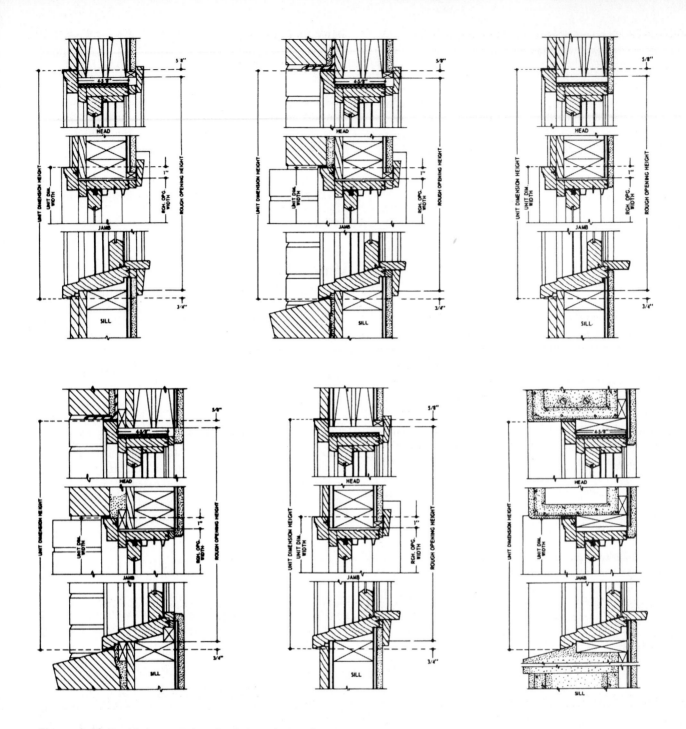

Figure 4–12 Double-hung window details in various walls.

framing: how they are attached and what trim is necessary for completion. These details should be shown on working drawings for proper installation of the windows.

To understand better the details of a double-hung window, observe the cutting planes shown on the elevation view of Fig. 4–11. The head, jamb, and sill sections to the left of the elevation clearly explain these important points in the construction. A meeting rail section is also shown merely to familiarize you with the relationship of the two sashes. Note that, for more information, the right side of the elevation appears to be in a brick veneer wall, and the same sections to the right show typical construction around the double-hung window in brick veneer construction. The isometric view in Fig. 4–11 describes the pictorial representations of the same head, jamb, and sill sections in wood frame. Study these details carefully. Details of windows vary with different manufacturers; therefore, after window selections have been made, details of the windows must be taken from the manufacturers' catalogs.

Table 4–3 Opening sizes of windows in inches.

Glass width (glass size)	24
Sash stiles (2″ each)	4
Side jambs (¾″ each)	28
Plumbing or fitting allowance (¼″ per side)	1½
	½
Rough opening width	30
Glass height (glass size)	48
Window rails	6
Head jamb	¾
Window sill	2
Plumbing or fitting allowance (¼″ top and bottom)	½
Rough opening height	57¼

To draw a window detail, first establish the wood frame members, or the rough openings of masonry if the window is to go into solid masonry. Use large scales such as 3″ = 1′-0″ or 1½″ = 1′-0″ if small members are present in the section. Then draw the sheathing and inside wall covering. Next locate the window frame in relation to the rough opening surface, and complete the sash, trim, and exterior wall covering. Use the conventional break symbol so that only the necessary amount of detail needs to be drawn. Be sure that the structural members line up vertically and that the head section is drawn at the top, the jamb in the center, and the sill section at the bottom.

DOORS AND THEIR REPRESENTATION

Because of their economy and the wide assortment of available sizes, stock doors are universally used in residential and light construction. Two major types are manufactured: flush and panel (Fig. 4–14).

4.5.1 Flush Doors

Flush doors are built of solid wood stiles and rails with various wood veneering glued to both sides, producing smooth, easy-to-paint surfaces. This type is popular in contemporary architecture because of its clean-cut appearance and easy-to-maintain features. Various-shaped lights can be introduced to flush doors for lighting dark entrances, and decorative moldings can be applied directly to the veneered surfaces for style treatments. Flush doors can be subdivided into two types: *hollow-core* and *solid-core*. The hollow-core have grillage-filled cavities, making them lighter and ideal for interior use. The solid-core have their cavities filled with wood blocking or other dense materials, making them heavier and more appropriate for exterior entrances. The heavier construction reduces warping during extreme temperature differences between inside and outside. Many decorative wood grain veneers are available on flush doors to match natural wood interior wall coverings. See Fig. 4–15 for typical sizes.

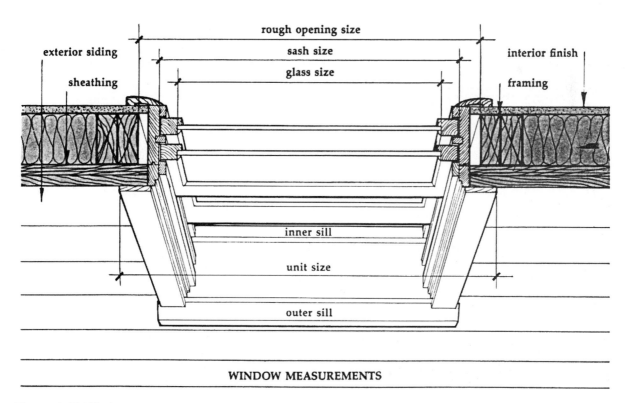

WINDOW MEASUREMENTS

Figure 4–13 Window unit measurements.

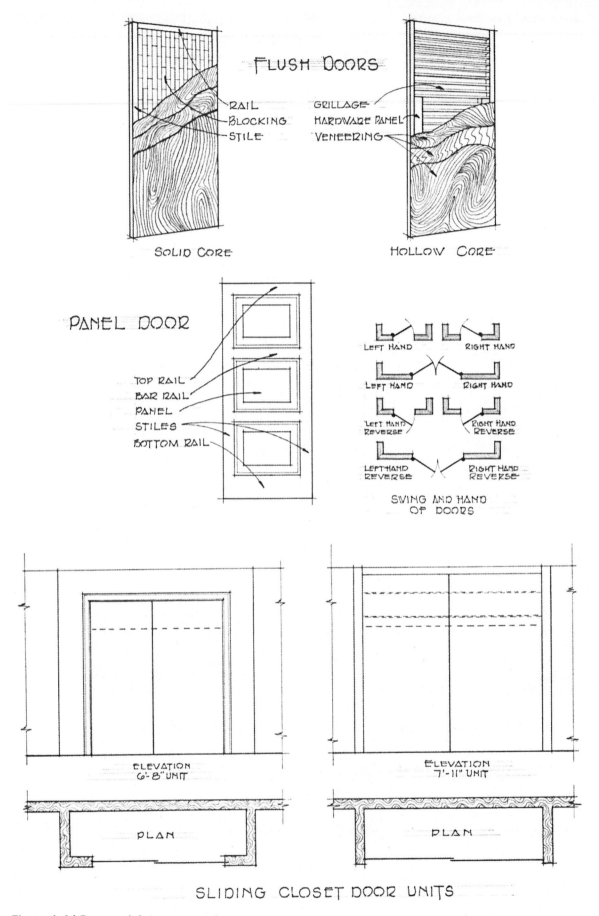

Figure 4–14 Doors and their representation.

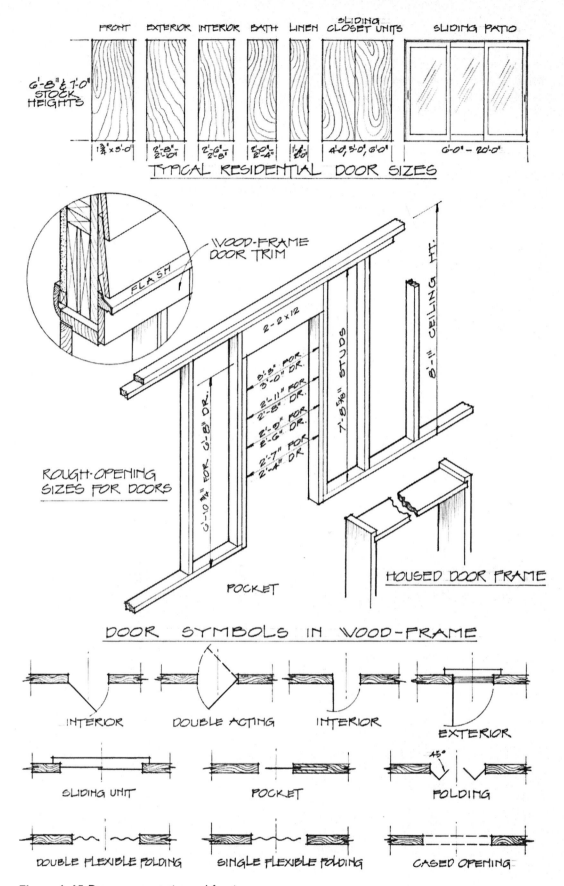

TYPICAL RESIDENTIAL DOOR SIZES

FRONT EXTERIOR INTERIOR BATH LINEN SLIDING CLOSET UNITS SLIDING PATIO

6'-8" & 7'-0" STOCK HEIGHTS

WOOD-FRAME DOOR TRIM

FLASH

ROUGH-OPENING SIZES FOR DOORS

POCKET

HOUSED DOOR FRAME

DOOR SYMBOLS IN WOOD-FRAME

INTERIOR DOUBLE ACTING INTERIOR EXTERIOR

SLIDING UNIT POCKET FOLDING

DOUBLE FLEXIBLE FOLDING SINGLE FLEXIBLE FOLDING CASED OPENING

Figure 4–15 Door representation and framing.

4.5.2 Panel Doors

Manufactured in a wide variety of styles, panel doors are generally made of ponderosa pine or Douglas fir. Various arrangements of the panels and lights are surrounded with stiles and rails, usually of solid wood, to produce handsome and sturdy doors. Panel doors have been used for many years in American homes. Some panel doors are manufactured with glue and veneer stiles and rails. They are sometimes preferred for exterior installation. For colonial and traditional homes, panel doors are the most authentic in character. Elaborate panel door and frame units are available for classic entrances (Fig. 4–16). Variations of the panel door include the following styles:

- **French doors** have glazed lights separated with muntins throughout, rather than panels. When additional light is needed, or when a view is desired between rooms, these doors find application, especially in traditional homes. Often they are used in pairs with an astragal molding between.
- **Dutch doors,** also typical of some colonial styles, are cut in half horizontally, and each half operates

on its own set of hinges. The bottom half can act as a gate while the top remains open.

- **Louver doors,** which have horizontal strips placed on the diagonal for vents instead of panels, are attractive in both traditional and contemporary settings. They are excellent for closet doors because of their venting characteristics, but they are time-consuming to paint.
- **Jalousie doors,** usually suitable for enclosed porches or exterior doors in warmer climates, have operating glass panel units inserted within the stiles and the rails.

4.5.3 Wood Stock Door Sizes

Both flush and panel doors are available in $1\frac{3}{8}''$, $1\frac{3}{4}''$, and $2\frac{1}{4}''$ stock thicknesses. Stock heights are 6'-8" and 7'-0"; narrow doors can be obtained in 6'-6" heights. Widths are available in 2" increments, from 1'-6" to 3'-0"; a few styles are made in 4'-0" widths. See Fig. 4–15 for the conventional door widths applicable to residential construction.

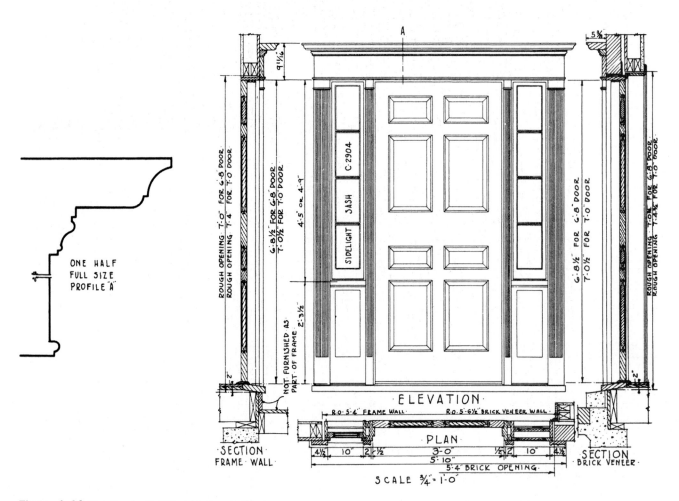

Figure 4–16 Details of a traditional entrance door.

4.5.4 Folding- or Sliding-Door Units

With the increase in private outdoor living areas, large sliding glass doors have found widespread acceptance. Sliding units are manufactured of aluminum, steel, or wood (Fig. 4–17). Stock heights are usually 6'-10", and unit widths, ranging from 6'-0" to 20'-0", utilize various sliding- and fixed-glass panel arrangements. Like other component sizing indications, door unit widths are given first, such as 8'-0" × 6'-10" or 12'-0" × 6'-10". Exact sizes and specifications should be taken from manufacturers' literature. Because of serious accidents involving large glass doors, many local codes require either tempered glass or protection bars across the doors.

For interior use, many types of folding- and sliding-door units are appropriate for closet doors and room dividers. Stock sizes conform to the 6'-8", 7'-0", and 8'-0"

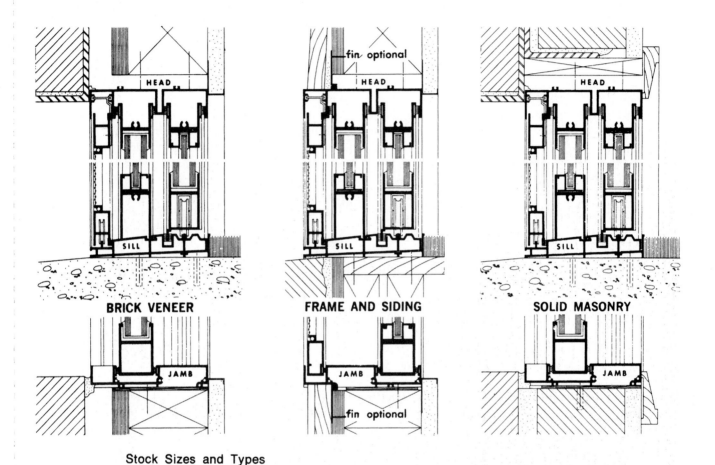

Stock Sizes and Types

Door Types Viewed from exterior	Door Sizes Width	Door Sizes Height	Stock Numbers	Glass Sizes Width only All heights 76¾"	Rough Openings All heights 6'–10½"
XO	5'–11"	6'–10"	G2- 6	33"	5'–11½"
	7'–11"	6'–10"	G2- 8	45"	7'–11½"
	9'–11"	6'–10"	G2-10	57"	9'–11½"
OX	5'–11"	6'–10"	G2- 6	33"	5'–11½"
	7'–11"	6'–10"	G2- 8	45"	7'–11½"
	9'–11"	6'–10"	G2-10	57"	9'–11½"
OXO	8'–10¼"	6'–10"	G3- 9	33"	8'–10¾"
	11'–10¼"	6'–10"	G3-12	45"	11'–10¾"
	14'–10¼"	6'–10"	G3-15	57"	14'–10¾"
OXXO	11'– 8⅞"	6'–10"	G4-12	33"	11'– 9⅜"
	15'– 8⅞"	6'–10"	G4-16	45"	15'– 9⅜"
	19'– 8⅞"	6'–10"	G4-20	57"	19'– 9⅜"

Figure 4–17 Details of an aluminum sliding glass door.

heights, and custom-built units are available from some manufacturers for special situations. The 8'-0" high closet door units (Fig. 4–14) allow an additional amount of accessible storage space in a closet in comparison to lower heights, and these units are highly recommended. Their use reduces the amount of framing around the door as well.

Accordion doors, available in 6'-8" and 8'-0" stock heights and in widths ranging from 2'-4" to 8'-2", are made of flexible plastic material and require little space at the jambs when open. Distinctive wood folding doors are also made of various wood panels. Sliding closet units come in 3', 4', 5', and 6' widths.

4.5.5 Fireproof Doors

Flush wood doors filled with heat-resisting materials and treated with fire-resisting chemicals (1-hour fire rating) are available for light construction. Some codes require fireproof doors between the house and its attached garage. Many types of metal doors having hollow, grillage-filled, or wood cores are manufactured mainly for commercial and industrial application and are labeled according to the amount of time of fire resistance: C = ³⁄₄, B = 1¹⁄₂, A = 2 hours.

4.5.6 Doorframes

Exterior wood doorframes are usually made and assembled at the mill and then delivered to the site, ready for installation into the rough openings. In wood frame floor construction, the header joist and the subflooring below an entrance must be cut out slightly to receive the sloping sill member of a doorframe (Fig. 4–16). Frames must be heavy enough to carry the weight of the doors and to take the strain of door closures. Generally, exterior frames are 1¹⁄₁₆" thick, and the sill member is made of hardwood to resist wear. Heavy doors may require thicker jamb members. A planted threshold of either hardwood or metal is necessary to hide the joint between the sill and the finished floor below entrance doors.

Interior doorframes are purchased in sets and are usually assembled on the job. Usually 1" or 1¹⁄₈" thick lumber is satisfactory for interior use. Other dimensions depend on the size of the door and the thickness of the walls in which they are installed. To provide simple door installation, planted doorstops are preferred on interior frames.

Metal doorframes, called *door bucks*, are being used by some housing developers. They are prefitted and predrilled, ready for the installation of the door hardware. Both wood and metal frames are available with prehung doors.

4.5.7 Overhead Garage Doors

Because of their size and weight, garage doors must be operated with counterbalances or springs on overhead tracks. Stock sizes range from 8'-0" × 7'-0" to 9'-0" × 7'-0" for single garage widths; double-garage openings require a 16'-0" × 7'-0" door size. Their symbol on plans is merely a line through the opening, accompanied by a dimensional note and the manufacturer's number.

4.5.8 Drawing Door Details

Although accurate details of door sections are seldom shown on working drawings involving conventional construction, the drafter must choose the size, type, and style to best fit the situation. If doors are incorporated into special framing, or if they are placed in walls of different construction, section views of the jambs and the surrounding construction, as well as the trim, must be drawn. To show the proper installation methods in various types of walls, several door details are included in this material.

In Fig. 4–16, note that the cutting planes on the door elevation indicate sections similar to window details, described previously. Profile A reveals the construction through the head jamb and sill, and the plan section reveals the construction through the side jambs. The sections are placed in a position for convenient projection of, as well as for analysis of the relationships among, the members. In drawing the sections, start by laying out the frame walls, then the wall coverings, and finally the doorjambs and surrounding trim. In solid masonry construction, the masonry outlines are drawn first; then the jambs and trim are added. Steel angles or reinforced concrete lintels must be used to support the weight of the masonry above the door opening and must be shown on the head section.

4.6

FIREPLACE DESIGN AND DETAILS

For centuries, fireplaces were the only method of heating homes, and even with our modern fuels and central heating systems, the fireplace is still as popular as ever because we have not found a substitute for the sheer fascination of an open fire, which provides warmth and a peaceful gathering place in the home.

Because the old-time fireplace mason, who knew by experience the necessary dimensional requirements of successful fireplaces, is slowly disappearing, complete working drawings of fireplaces must be included in plans to ensure their correct construction. If an honest house is to be built, the fireplace must be honest as well and must be designed to be workable.

Residential fireplaces of various forms and styles are being constructed (Fig. 4–18). Some are merely openings in massive interior masonry walls, with no mantel or decor other than the texture of the masonry. Some have provision for log storage near the opening; others may

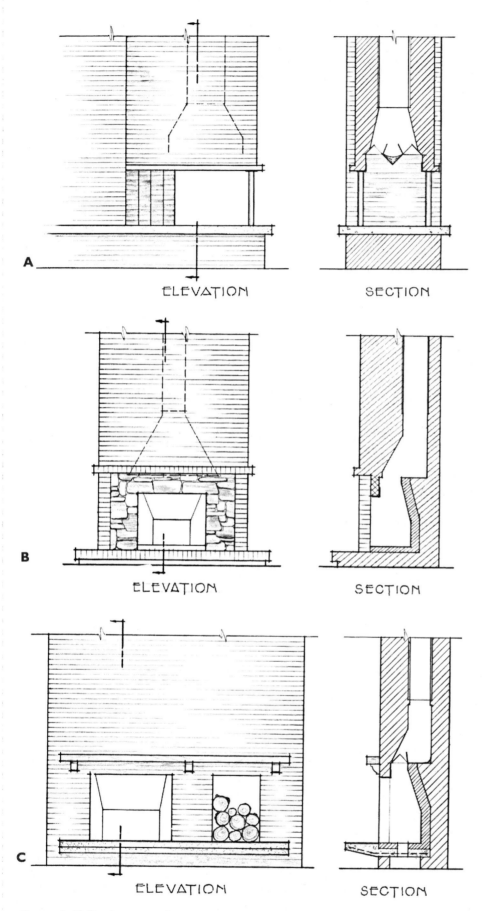

ELEVATION   SECTION

ELEVATION   SECTION

ELEVATION   SECTION

Figure 4–18 Fireplace suggestions.

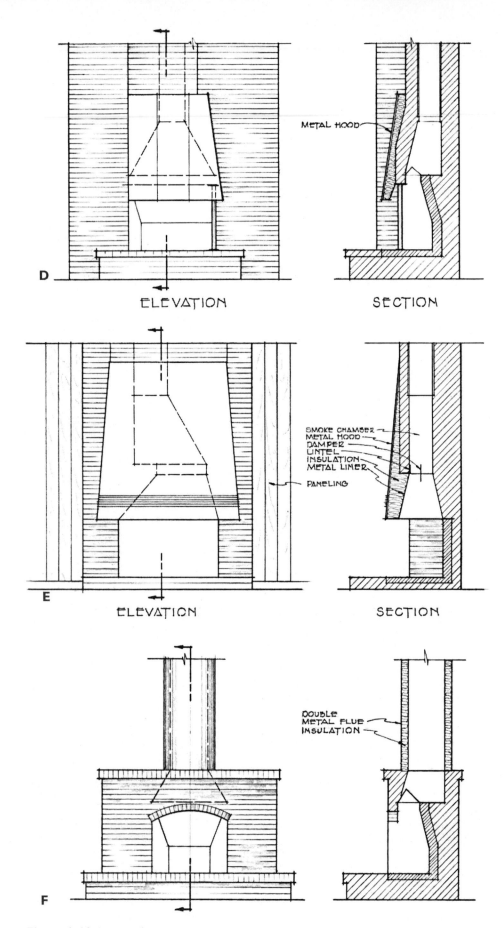

ELEVATION   SECTION

METAL HOOD

D

ELEVATION   SECTION

SMOKE CHAMBER
METAL HOOD
DAMPER
LINTEL
INSULATION
METAL LINER

PANELING

E

DOUBLE
METAL FLUE
INSULATION

F

Figure 4–18 *(continued)*

have outdoor barbecue grills incorporated into the chimneys. Many are masonry walls with metal hoods above to concentrate the draft and carry off hot gases and smoke. For general purposes, fireplaces can be divided into the following groups:

1. Single-face fireplaces (conventional)
   (a) Wall
   (b) Corner
   (c) Back-to-Back
2. Multiple-face fireplaces (contemporary)
   (a) Two adjacent faces (corner)
   (b) Two opposite faces (through opening)
   (c) Three faces: two long, one short
   (d) Three faces: one long, two short
   (e) Hooded
   (f) Freestanding

The successful operation of a fireplace depends on its construction. Even special fireplaces, which incorporate various shapes and materials, can be made workable if the designer follows the basic principles of fireplace design instead of resorting to chance or mere luck. The critical points in single-face fireplace design and construction are discussed in the following sections and illustrated in Fig. 4–19.

4.6.1 Size of Fireplace Opening

Not only should the fireplace be given a prominent position in a room, away from major travel routes, but the fireplace opening should also be in keeping with the room size. Small rooms should have small fireplace openings; large rooms, large ones. The opening should have pleasing proportions: A rectangle is more desirable than a square, and the width should exceed the height. A fireplace width of, for instance, 28″ to 36″ would be adequate for a room of 250-sq ft floor space. In Fig. 4–20, notice some of the more common opening sizes. A raised hearth, usually 16″ above the floor, brings the opening nearer to eye level and often makes the fireplace appear larger. Keep wood trim at least 8″ from the opening, and use a steel angle-iron lintel to support the masonry above the opening.

Figure 4–20 shows that fireplace openings have relative proportions of height, width, and depth; however, you can make minor variations to meet the various masonry courses and other restrictions of layout. The size of the opening becomes the starting feature in the design of a fireplace.

4.6.2 Flue Size and Chimney Height

Each fireplace in a building should have an independent flue, unconnected to other vents or flues, and it must start on the center line of the fireplace opening. A chimney can take care of a number of fireplaces, and each flue must continue to the top with as little offset as necessary. Each

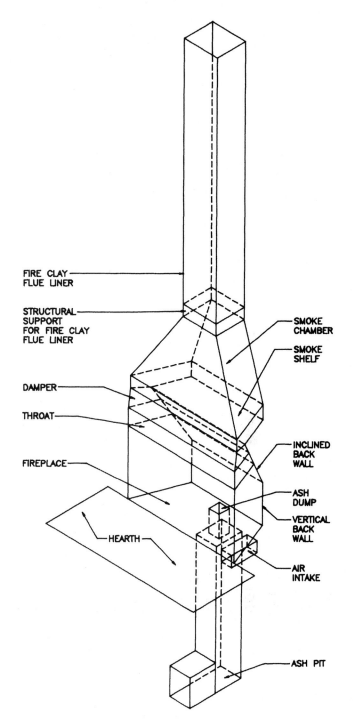

Figure 4–19 Masonry fireplace.

flue must be large enough in cross-sectional area to create the proper draft through the fireplace opening. Unless the sectional flue area is at least $^1/_{10}$ of the fireplace opening area (a rule of thumb), a troublesome condition may result (see the table that accompanies Fig. 4–22 for exact sizes). Chimney heights under 14′ may require even larger flue sizes, as the height of the chimney, surrounding buildings, and prevailing winds affect flue velocities. The higher the chimney, the more draft velocity. For fire protection of the roofing materials, the height of the

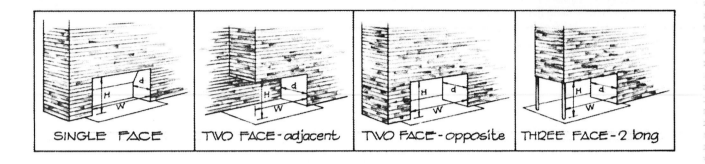

SINGLE FACE | TWO FACE - adjacent | TWO FACE - opposite | THREE FACE - 2 long

Fireplace Dimensions

Fireplace Type	Opening Height h, in.	Hearth Size w by d, in.	Modular Flue Size, in.
Single Face	29	30 × 16	12 × 12
	29	36 × 16	12 × 12
	29	40 × 16	12 × 16
	32	48 × 18	16 × 16
Two Face— adjacent	26	32 × 16	12 × 16
	29	40 × 16	16 × 16
	29	48 × 20	16 × 16
Two Face— opposite	29	32 × 28	16 × 16
	29	36 × 28	16 × 20
	29	40 × 28	16 × 20
Three Face— 2 long, 1 short	27	36 × 32	20 × 20
	27	36 × 36	20 × 20
	27	44 × 40	20 × 20

Figure 4–20 Typical fireplace openings and workable dimensions.

chimney should be as noted in Fig. 4–21. Flue sizes are important and therefore should be clearly indicated on the drawings; a flue that is too large is better than one that is too small. Vitrified clay flue linings are used to resist high chimney temperatures and to provide smooth flue interiors. Without the lining, cracks tend to develop in the chimney walls. Round linings operate more efficiently, but rectangular types can be more easily fitted into chimney spaces.

4.6.3 Shape of Combustion Chamber

The combustion chamber (Fig. 4–22) is lined with 4″ thick firebrick set in fireclay. It is shaped not only to reflect heat into the room, but also to lead hot gases into the throat with increased velocity. If the fireplace is too deep, less heat will be radiated into the room. The sections in Fig. 4–22 indicate the conventional shape of combustion chamber walls. The back and end walls should be at least 8″ thick. Slight variations are permissible in the layout of the chamber, but long experience has shown that the conventional shapes and proportions are the most satisfactory as far as operation is concerned.

4.6.4 Design of the Throat

The throat offsets the draft above the chamber, and if a metal damper is used, the door of the damper acts as a valve for checking downdrafts while the fireplace is in operation. The inclusion of a damper is a convenient method of preventing heat loss and outside drafts when the fireplace is not in use. Notice that the door of the damper hinges so that it opens toward the back of the fireplace. The opening of either the damper or the throat should be larger than the area of the flue lining. Also, the damper should be the same length as the width of the fireplace and should be placed at least 6″ (preferably 8″) above the top of the fireplace opening. Both steel and cast-iron dampers are available; check manufacturers' catalogs for types and sizes.

4.6.5 Shape of the Smoke Shelf and Smoke Dome

The location of the damper establishes the height of the smoke shelf, which is directly under the flue and which stops downdrafts with its horizontal surface. The smoke dome is the area just above the shelf. Notice that the back wall is built vertically; the only offset on the back is a cor-

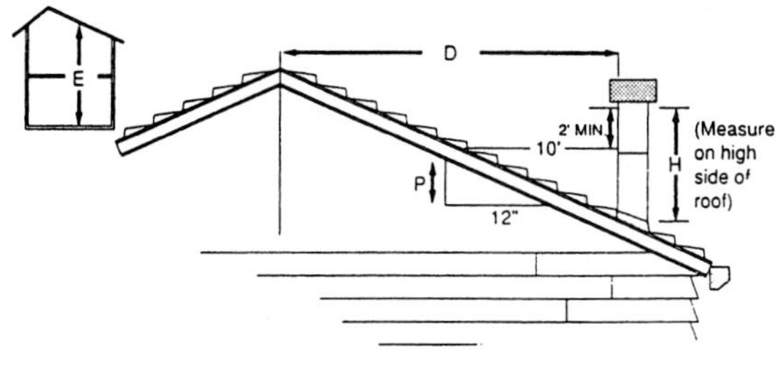

"P" Dim. Roof Pitch Inches	Minimum Required Chimney Height (H Dimension) (Do not include terminal cap in Dimension H) "D" Dimension (Feet) 1'	2'	3'	4'	5'	6'	7'	8'	9'	10' +
1"	3'	3'	3'	3'	3'	3'	3'	3'	3'	3'
2"	3'	3'	3'	3'	3'	3'	3'2"	3'4"	3'6"	3'8"
3"	3'	3'	3'	3'	3'3"	3'6"	3'9"	4'	4'3"	4'6"
4"	3'	3'	3'	3'4"	3'8"	4'	4'4"	4'8"	5'	5'4"
5"	3'	3'	3'3"	3'8"	4'1"	4'6"	4'11"	5'4"	5'9"	6'2"
6"	3'	3'	3'6"	4'	4'6"	5'	5'6"	6'	6'6"	7'
7"	3'	3'2"	3'9"	4'4"	4'11"	5'6"	6'1"	6'8"	7'3"	7'10"
8"	3'	3'4"	4'	4'8"	5'4"	6'	6'8"	7'4"	8'	8'8"
9"	3'	3'6"	4'3"	5'	5'9"	6'6"	7'3"	8'	8'9"	9'6"
10"	3'	3'8"	4'6"	5'4"	6'2"	7'	7'10"	8'8"	9'6"	10'4"
11"	3'	3'10"	4'9"	5'8"	6'7"	7'6"	8'5"	9'4"	10'3"	11'4"
12"	3'	4'	5'	6'	7'	8'	9'	10'	11'	12'
13"	3'1"	4'2"	5'3"	6'4"	7'5"	8'6"	9'7"	10'8"	11'9"	12'10"
14"	3'2"	4'4"	5'6"	6'8"	7'10"	9'	10'2"	11'4"	12'6"	13'8"
15"	3'3"	4'6"	5'9"	7'	8'3"	9'6"	10'9"	12'	13'3"	14'6"
16"	3'4"	4'8"	6'	7'4"	8'8"	10'	11'4"	12'8"	14'	15'4"
17"	3'5"	4'10"	6'3"	7'8"	9'1"	10'6"	11'11"	13'4"	14'9"	16'2"
18"	3'6"	5'	6'6"	8'	9'6"	11'	12'6"	14'	15'6"	17'
19"	3'7"	5'2"	6'9"	8'4"	9'11"	11'6"	13'1"	14'8"	16'3"	17'10"
20"	3'8"	5'4"	7'	8'8"	10'4	12'	13'8"	15'4"	17'	18'8"
21"	3'9"	5'6"	7'3"	3'9	10'9"	12'6"	14'3"	16'	17'9"	19'6"
22"	3'10"	5'8"	7'6"	9'4"	11'2"	13'	14'10"	16'8"	18'6"	20'4"
23"	3'11"	5'10"	7'9"	9'8"	11'7"	13'6"	15'5"	17'4"	19'3"	21'2"

Figure 4–21 Relationship between roof pitch and required chimney height.

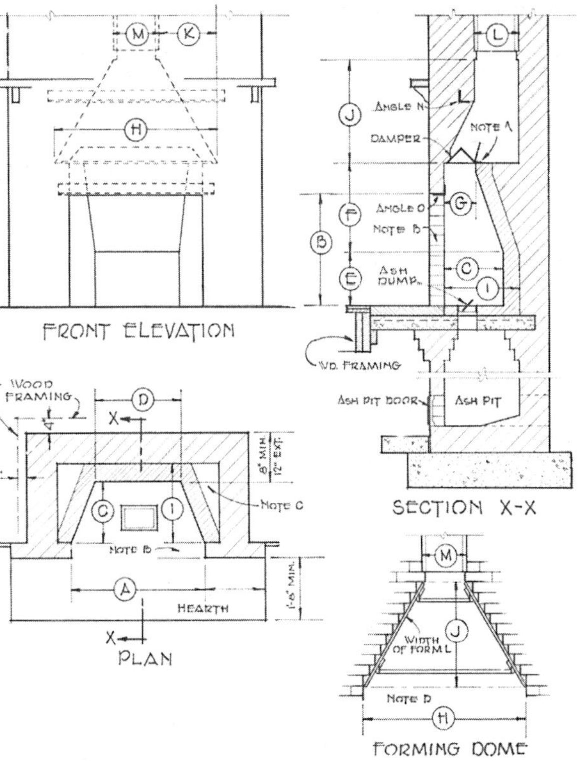

A

Fireplace Dimensions, Inches [1]

Rough Brick Work and Flue Sizes																		
Finished Fireplace Opening							New sizes[2]						Old sizes			Steel angles[2]	
A	B	C	D	E	F	G	H	I	J	K	L M	R[3]	K	L	M	N	O
24	24	16	11	14	18	8¾	32	20	19	10	8×12	8	11¾	8½	× 8½	A-36	A-36
26	24	16	13	14	18	8¾	34	20	21	11	8×12	8	12¾	8½	× 8½	A-36	A-36
28	24	16	15	14	18	8¾	36	20	21	12	8×12	10	11½	8½	×13	A-36	A-36
30	29	16	17	14	23	8¾	38	20	24	13	12×12	10	12½	8½	×13	A-42	A-36
32	29	16	19	14	23	8¾	40	20	24	14	12×12	10	13½	8½	×13	A-42	A-42
36	29	16	23	14	23	8¾	44	20	27	16	12×12	12	15½	13	×13	A-48	A-42
40	29	16	27	14	23	8¾	48	20	29	16	12×16	12	17½	13	×13	A-48	A-48
42	32	16	29	14	26	8¾	50	20	32	17	16×16	12	18½	13	×13	B-54	A-48
48	32	18	33	14	26	8¾	56	22	37	20	16×16	15	21½	13	×13	B-60	B-54
54	37	20	37	16	29	13	68	24	45	26	16×16	15	25	13	×18	B-72	B-60
60	37	22	42	16	29	13	72	27	45	26	16×20	15	27	13	×18	B-72	B-66
60	40	22	42	16	31	13	72	27	45	26	16×20	18	27	18	×18	B-72	B-66
72	40	22	54	16	31	13	84	27	56	32	20×20	18	33	18	×18	C-84	C-84
84	40	24	64	20	28	13	96	29	61	36	20×24	20	36	20	×20	C-96	C-96
96	40	24	76	20	28	13	108	29	75	42	20×24	22	42	24	×24	C-108	C-108

[1] Angle sizes: A. 3″ x 3″ x 3⁄16″; B. 3½″ x 3″ x ¼″; C. 5″ x 3½″ x 5⅙″.

[2] New flue sizes: Conform to modular dimensional system. Sizes shown are nominal. Actual size is ½″ less each dimension.

[3] Round flues.

Note A. The back flange of the damper must be protected from intense heat by being fully supported by the masonry. At the same time, the damper should not be built in solidly at the ends, but given freedom to expand with heat.

Note B. The thickness of the fireplace front will vary with the material used: brick, marble, stone, tile, etc.

Note C. The hollow, triangular spaces behind the splayed sides of the inner brickwork should be filled to afford solid backing. If desired to locate a flue in either space, the outside dimensions of the rough brickwork should be increased.

Note D. A good way to build a smoke chamber is to erect a wooden form consisting of two sloping boards at the sides, held apart by spreaders at the top and bottom. Spreaders are nailed upward into cleats. The form boards should have the same width as the flue lining.

B

Figure 4–22 Successful fireplace construction. (Courtesy Donley Bros. Co.)

beled brick course that supports the flue lining, where a corbeled brick course is also shown for flue support. Usually, the sloping walls are represented with lines drawn 60° from the horizontal.

4.6.6 Support for the Hearth

The hearth is best supported with a reinforced concrete slab resting on the walls of the fireplace foundation and extending in front at least 18″. (Previously, a brick trimmer arch was used to support the forward hearth against the chimney foundation in conventional construction.) Number 3 reinforcing rods are placed near the upper part of the slab, and brick, stone, or other masonry material is applied directly on the slab for a textured hearth covering. If an ash dump is feasible and is accessible to a basement ash pit or an outdoor cleanout door, the reinforced slab may simply be formed with ribbed metal lath having a hole cut for the ash dump and any upcoming flues; the concrete is poured over the lath.

In homes with slab floors, the fireplace and the hearth are built up from an isolated footing to the floor level. For easy cleaning, the fireplace floor can be made 1″ higher than the outer hearth.

4.6.7 Wood Framing Precautions Around the Fireplace and Chimney

Precautions must be taken when fireplaces or their chimneys pass through wood frame floors, roofs, and the like. Fire codes prohibit direct contact between framing members and chimney surfaces (Fig. 4–22). Usually a 2″ air space is provided between the masonry and wood; this space is filled with incombustible insulating material. Trimmers and headers around wood openings are doubled to give support to the cut joists or rafters, and the subflooring or decking is applied closer to the masonry.

The hearth slab, which is independent of the wood framing, usually has its outer edge resting on a ledger strip fastened to the headers or the floor joists.

4.6.8 Steel Fireplace Boxes

Prefabricated, one-piece, factory-built fireboxes are available (see Figs. 4–23, 4–24, and 4–25 and *Sweet's Architectural Catalog File*) that combine the combustion chamber, the smoke dome, and even a steel lintel for the masonry opening. The firebox is merely set on a masonry hearth, and the brick or stone enclosure is built up around it, thus eliminating any necessity for fireplace design other than the correct flue size. Because they are hollow, the fireboxes can utilize warm- and cold-air ducts and vents to improve heating efficiency. After the desired openings have been determined, correct catalog numbers can be established.

4.6.9 Special Fireplaces

Special fireplaces include variations of the multifaced and hooded types, often referred to as "contemporary." Because of their unusually large openings and their complexity of shapes, special fireplaces occasionally cause smoking in the room and have poor draw through their throats. Generally, if these fireplaces operate poorly, the flue is too small, the damper throat is too narrow, the chimney height is too low, or possibly nearby buildings or trees prevent proper draft through the flues. Also, fireplaces with the sides of the combustion chamber exposed to allow room drafts to pass directly through, such as freestanding or open-back fireplaces, will tend to allow smoke into the room unless room drafts are prevented or glass sides are installed. Special metal smoke dome and damper boxes are available to improve multiface fireplace operation (see *Sweet's File*). Hooded fireplaces require heat-resisting insulation below the metal hoods.

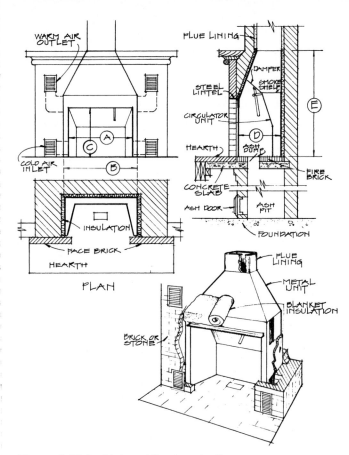

Figure 4–23 Prefabricated fireplace detail.

Freestanding, complete fireplace units are sold that require neither masonry enclosures nor a masonry chimney. The units, complete with chimney and hearth, can be installed in existing structures.

In drawing special fireplace details, you can take design data from the fireplace dimensions table and the accompanying drawings (Fig. 4–22); further information can be found in Ramsey and Sleeper's *Architectural Graphic Standards*. However, the best source for information about special fireplaces, as well as the equipment needed for regular fireplaces, is from manufacturers' catalogs and literature.

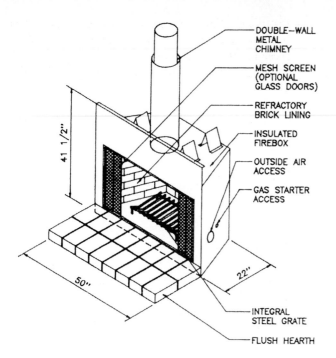

DOUBLE-WALL
METAL
CHIMNEY

MESH SCREEN
(OPTIONAL
GLASS DOORS)

REFRACTORY
BRICK LINING

INSULATED
FIREBOX

OUTSIDE AIR
ACCESS

GAS STARTER
ACCESS

41 1/2"

50"

22"

INTEGRAL
STEEL GRATE

FLUSH HEARTH

Figure 4–24 Traditional factory-built fireplace.

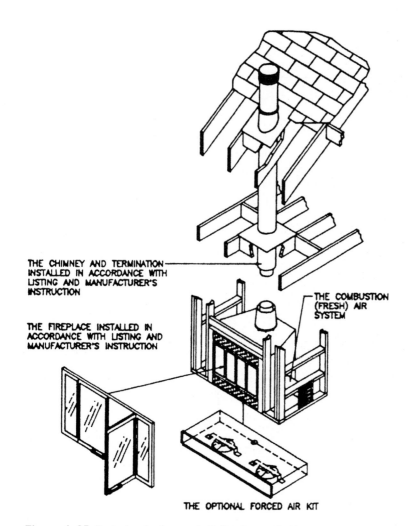

THE CHIMNEY AND TERMINATION
INSTALLED IN ACCORDANCE WITH
LISTING AND MANUFACTURER'S
INSTRUCTION

THE FIREPLACE INSTALLED IN
ACCORDANCE WITH LISTING AND
MANUFACTURER'S INSTRUCTION

THE COMBUSTION
(FRESH) AIR
SYSTEM

THE OPTIONAL FORCED AIR KIT

Figure 4–25 Example of a factory-built fireplace and chimney.

226   CHAPTER 4   Typical Architectural Details

STAIR DESIGN AND LAYOUT

Let us now consider the problems encountered in stair construction. A flight of stairs is part of the system of hallways communicating between the occupied floor levels of a building. In multistory buildings, the stairs, both interior and exterior, must be given careful consideration in the total design. Main stairways in homes, as well as in public buildings, have long been objects of special ornament by architects. Many beautiful staircases are evident in scores of buildings throughout the country. The present trend, however, is toward simplicity and comfort in residential stairs, although dramatic stairways are occasionally found in contemporary public buildings.

4.7.1 Stair Terminology

Stairs have their own terminology in construction work; the following terms are commonly encountered:

- **Balusters** The thin vertical supports for the handrail of open stairs.

- **Bullnose** The first step on an open stair; it has been extended out, forming a semicircle and often receiving the newel post.
- **Carriage** The rough structural support (usually $2'' \times 12''$) for treads and for risers of wood stairs, sometimes called *string* or *stringer*.
- **Closed stringer** The visible member of a stairs that abuts the risers and treads and that is not cut to show the profile of stairs.
- **Handrail** The round or decorative member of a railing that is grasped with the hand during ascent or descent.
- **Headroom** The narrowest distance between the surface of a tread and any ceiling or header above.
- **Housed stringer** The stringer that has been grooved to receive the risers and the treads.
- **Landing** The floor between flights of stairs or at the termination of stairs.
- **Newel** The main post of the railing at the bottom of a stair or at changes in direction of the railing.
- **Nosing** The round projection of the tread beyond the face of the riser.

- **Open stringer** The stringer that has been cut to fit the profile of the stairs; the riser cut is mitered, and the tread cut is square.
- **Platform** The intermediate landing between various parts of the stair flight.
- **Railing** The handrail and the baluster forming the protection on open stairs.
- **Rise** The total floor-to-floor vertical height of a stairs.
- **Riser** The vertical face of the step.
- **Run** The total horizontal length of a stairs, including the platform.
- **Stairwell** The enclosed chamber into which the stairs are built.
- **Step** The combination of one riser and one tread.
- **Stringer** The inclined member supporting the risers and treads; sometimes a visible trim member next to the profile of the stairs.
- **Tread** The horizontal surface member of each step, usually hardwood.
- **Winder** The radiating or wedge-shaped treads at turns of stairs.

4.7.2 Types of Stair Construction

Previously, stair building was a highly specialized craft, especially in home construction; many stairs required considerable hand labor. Today, stairways are often ordered directly from a mill or shops, fabricated according to details furnished by the designer. Usually, first-quality construction accepts only shop-made stair units (Fig. 4–26) that have expert crafting and that are delivered to the site and quickly installed by carpenters. Figure 4–27 shows a more economical stair that is built on the job. Usually, 2 × 12 carriages are cut to the profile of the stairs, and the treads are attached. Three carriages are preferred construction if the stair width is 3'-0" or over. Double trimmers and headers must surround the stairwell framing, and the carriages must have sufficient bearing at both ends.

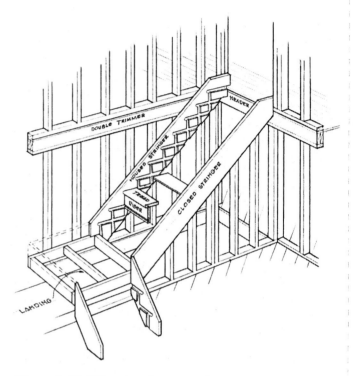

Figure 4–26 Mill-made stair construction.

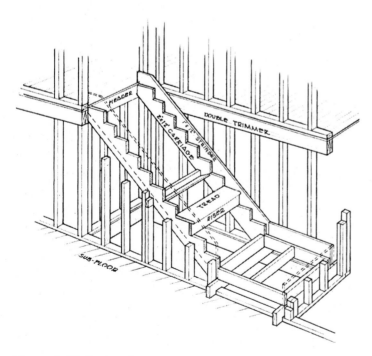

Figure 4–27 On-the-job stair construction.

Other structural methods of stair support have been devised by architects to produce both novel and sturdy stair flights.

Figure 4–28 and 4–29 illustrate familiar details for framing around stair openings but with wood I-beam joists and light-gauge steel. In these cases, special atten-tion must be paid to doubling up trimmers and headers. Wood filler pieces are used between webs to reinforce doubled wood I-beam joists near headers (Fig. 4–28), and steel joists are doubled by "tubing" them into pieces of joist track (Fig. 4–29). Be sure to use the recommended fasteners and fastening schedules.

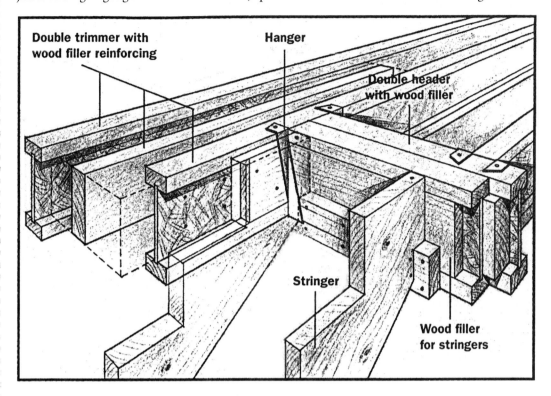

Figure 4–28 Stair framing with wood I-beam joists.

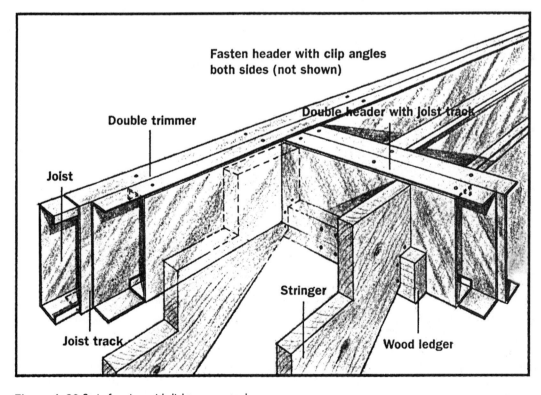

Figure 4–29 Stair framing with light-gauge steel.

4.7.3 Riser and Tread Proportions

Because considerable effort is expended in ascending and descending stairs, regardless of type, comfort and safety should be the first considerations in their design. In designing a comfortable stair, you must establish a definite relationship between the height of the risers and the width of the treads; all stairs should be designed to conform to established proportions. If the combination of riser and tread is too great, the steps become tiring, and a strain develops on the leg muscles and the heart. If the combination is too short, the foot has a tendency to kick the riser at each step in an attempt to shorten the stride, also producing fatigue. Experience has shown that risers 7″ high with an 11″ tread result in the most satisfactory combination for principal residential stairs.

4.7.4 Stair Formulas

The following three formulas have been devised for checking riser and tread proportions, exclusive of molding. Each will be satisfactory:

Two risers + 1 tread = between 24″ and 25″

Riser × tread = between 72″ and 77″

Riser + tread = between 17″ and 18″

As an example of formula application, suppose that an 11″ tread is found suitable on a preliminary stair layout. After examining each of the stair formulas, you will see that a riser height of 7″ satisfies any formula. If a 12″ tread is selected, the riser will have to be 6″; and so on. Minor variations would still make the stairs workable, but treads are seldom made less than 11″ or more than 12″ wide.

4.7.5 Angle of Stairs

Stair flights should be neither too steep nor too flat in incline. An angle from 30° to 33° from the horizontal is the most comfortable. Long flights are also tiring; usually a platform about midway in a long flight helps relieve fatigue. There will always be one fewer tread than there are risers in all stairs.

4.7.6 Plan Layout Variations

Various stair plan layouts are shown in Fig. 4–30. If space on the plan prohibits the use of a straight run, other layouts are shown to increase flexibility in fitting stairs in restricted spaces and to lend stairs various character treatments. In limited space, a winder stair (Fig. 4–30) can be used if necessary, yet it is more hazardous than a plat-

form arrangement. The winder-stair profile should be considered at a line 1′-4″ from the winder corner. Remember that a landing counts as a tread and should conform to the width of the rest of the stairs.

4.7.7 Headroom

Headroom should be between 6′-8″ and 7′-4″ over major stairs; 6′-6″ is usually sufficient over minor flights to the basement or attic. Individual conditions may necessitate slight variations of headroom. Disappearing stairs to attic storage spaces are usually prefabricated units, which can be shown on the plan with a dashed rectangle and a note.

4.7.8 Railings

Whether a stair is open or is enclosed between walls, a railing must be installed to be within easy reach in case of stumbling or loss of balance. It is general practice to use a continuous handrail from floor to floor. It can be plain or ornamental—in keeping with the design features of the building—but it should be smooth and sturdy. The most comfortable handrail height is 32″ above the tread surface measured from the edge of the tread to the top of the handrail. Landings in residences should have 36″ high railings, landings in commercial building, 42″ high.

4.7.9 Exterior Stairs

Exterior stairs are usually designed with smaller riser heights and therefore with wider treads than interior stairs. A popular proportion is a 6″ riser and a 12″ tread for maximum safety on long flights. Landings should be provided every 16 risers on continuous stairs. If slopes are gradual, ramps (up to 12°) are often preferable to steps for outside use. Usually, masonry with reinforcing and well-anchored footings is the most practical exterior material.

Requirements of all classes of stairs are given in the publication *NFPA 101, Life Safety Code*, published by the National Fire Protection Association. The design of all stairs should meet their specifications.

4.7.10 Drawing Stair Details (Figs. 4–31 and 4–32)

Step 1: *To draw a stair detail,* first you must know the finished-floor-to-finished-floor height, although carriages rest on rough framing. You can arithmetically determine the number of risers necessary to ascend the height by dividing the heights by 7″ (typical risers). If the floor-to-floor dimension is conveniently divisible by either typical riser height, calculation is simplified. However, seldom will it come out even, unless ceiling heights have

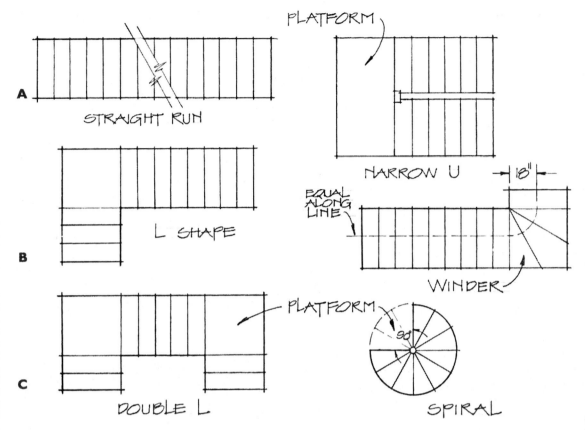

Figure 4–30 Various stair layouts.

been purposely figured. In Fig. 4–32, the total height or rise needed for the stairs is 108″ (8′-1⅛″ stud and plate height, plus 9¼″ joist height, plus 1⅝″ floor thickness). When we divide 108 by 7, the quotient is 15.42. Since all risers must be the same height, 16 risers can be adopted. Using 16 risers with 11¼″ tread width seems to satisfy the stair formulas:

$$\frac{108''}{16} = 6.75'' \text{ riser}$$

Formula 1: $2(6.75) + 11.25 = 24.75$

Formula 2: $\quad 6.75 \times 11.25 = 75.93$

Formula 3: $\quad 6.75 + 11.25 = 18$

Therefore, the stair data for Fig. 4–33 would be as follows:

Total number of risers	16
Total number of treads	15
Riser height	6.75″
Tread width	11.25″
Total rise	108″
Total run	168.75″

Step 2: Because odd fractions are difficult to measure on a drawing, the graphic method of stair profile layout is recommended. Scale the floor-to-floor height, and draw the floor lines between which the stair is to be drawn. Divide the between-floor space into 16 divisions graph-ically. You can use divisions on the scale by adopting 16 convenient divisions, adjusting them diagonally across the space, and marking them to form the tread surfaces (see the left side of Fig. 4–31). Draw the 15 vertical riser surfaces similarly, or measure them if feasible. The top riser meets the second-floor surface. The result is the correct stair profile from floor to floor. Strengthen the profile and erase the construction lines.

Step 3: Locate the ceiling or soffit surface above the stairs, keeping in mind that the headroom for important stairs should be 6′-8″ to 7′-4″ high, if possible; slightly less is permissible if the stairwell above must be made smaller. This headroom line locates the header framing and the sloping ceiling above. In basement stairs, less headroom is satisfactory. To conserve stairwell space, usu-ally two or more flights of stairs are superimposed di-rectly above one another in multistory buildings. Open-ings for the stairwell can now be dimensioned for the framing, and final adjustments on second-floor walls near the stairs can be made.

Step 4: If the carriage outline is to be drawn, the thick-ness of the treads (usually 1¹⁄₁₆″) is shown below the pro-file surface, and the thickness of the risers (usually ¾″) is shown within the vertical lines. The original profile will remain the surface of the risers and the treads. Usually, the carriage is cut from 2 × 10 or 2 × 12 lumber, and at least 3″ of solid material must remain below the depth of

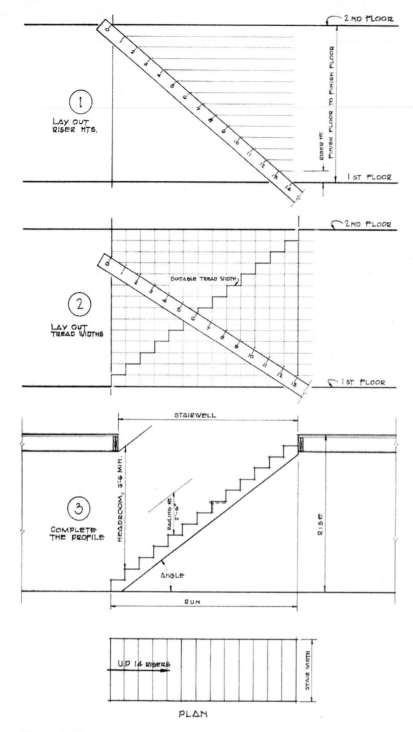

Figure 4–31 Drawing a stair detail.

the cuts for stability. Nosings commonly extend $1\frac{1}{8}''$ beyond the surface of the risers. Basement stairs seldom require covered risers.

Step 5: For safety, railings are a necessary part of the stairs and should be drawn next. If necessary, details of railings, ornamental newel posts, balusters, and trim can be taken from manufacturers' catalogs. Draw the railings 2'-6" above the surface of the treads. Major stairs should be

made from 3'-0" to 3'-6" wide in residences and 3'-8" wide or wider in commercial buildings.

Complete the stair plan layout by projecting the risers from the elevation detail. Show the riser surfaces, and indicate the number of risers; include either an UP or a DOWN note and an arrow (Fig. 4–32). About half of the complete stair symbol is shown on each floor plan, and a conventional diagonal break line is drawn near the symbol center. A concrete stair detail is shown in Fig. 4–33.

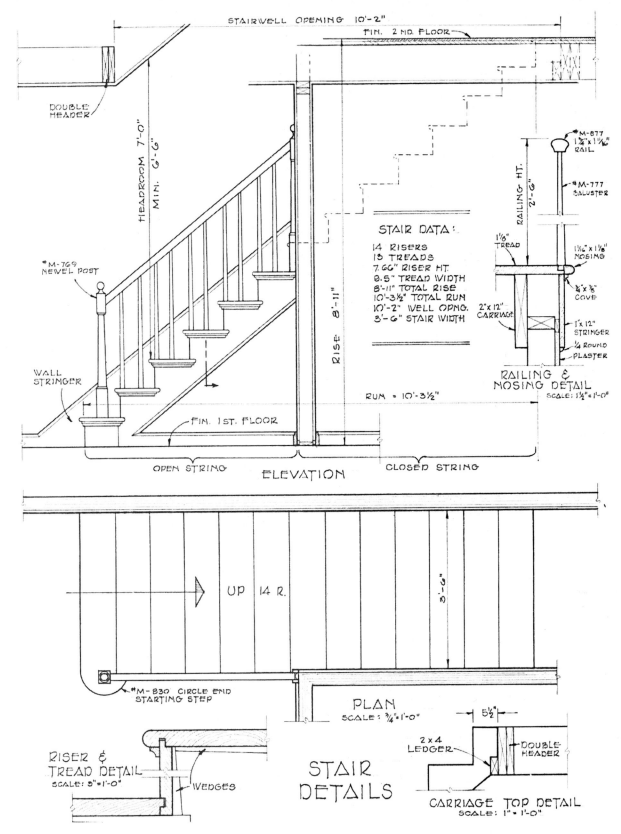

STAIRWELL OPENING 10'-2"

FIN. 2 ND. FLOOR

DOUBLE HEADER

HEADROOM 7'-0"

MIN. 6'-6"

#M-769 NEWEL POST

WALL STRINGER

RISE 8'-11"

STAIR DATA:
14 RISERS
15 TREADS
7.66" RISER HT.
9.5" TREAD WIDTH
8'-11" TOTAL RISE
10'-3½" TOTAL RUN
10'-2" WELL OPNG.
3'-6" STAIR WIDTH

RUN = 10'-3½"

FIN. 1ST. FLOOR

OPEN STRING   CLOSED STRING

ELEVATION

#M-877 1¾" x 1⅝" RAIL

RAILING HT. 2'-6"

#M-777 BALUSTER

1⅛" TREAD

1¾" x 1⅛" NOSING

⅜" x ⅝" COVE

2"x 12" CARRIAGE

1"x 12" STRINGER

¼ ROUND

PLASTER

RAILING & NOSING DETAIL
SCALE: 1½"=1'-0"

UP 14 R.

3'-6"

#M-830 CIRCLE END STARTING STEP

PLAN
SCALE: ¾"=1'-0"

RISER & TREAD DETAIL
SCALE: 3"=1'-0"

WEDGES

STAIR DETAILS

5½"

2 x 4 LEDGER

DOUBLE HEADER

CARRIAGE TOP DETAIL
SCALE: 1"=1'-0"

Figure 4–32 Details of a traditional stairs.

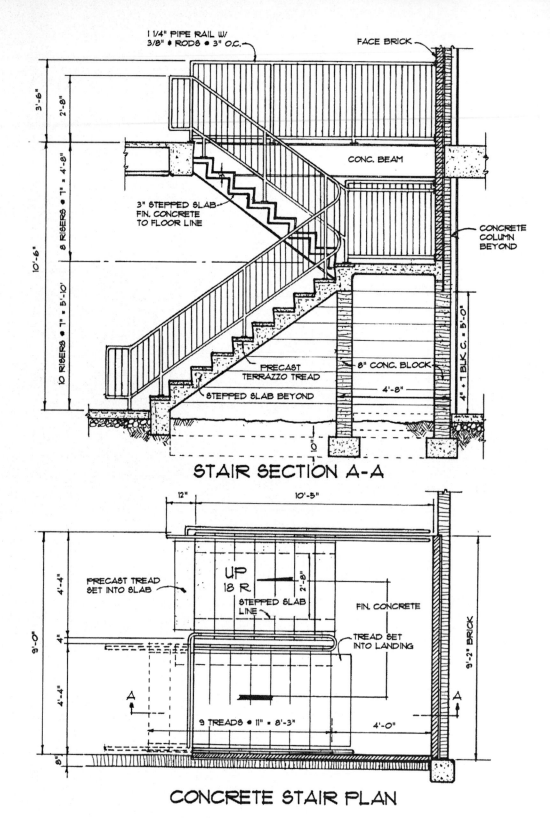

STAIR SECTION A-A

Labels in section:
- 1 1/4" PIPE RAIL W/ 3/8" ⌀ RODS ⌀ 3" O.C.
- FACE BRICK
- CONC. BEAM
- 3" STEPPED SLAB FIN. CONCRETE TO FLOOR LINE
- CONCRETE COLUMN BEYOND
- PRECAST TERRAZZO TREAD
- 8" CONC. BLOCK
- STEPPED SLAB BEYOND
- 4' + 1 BLK C. = 5'-0"
- 4'-8"
- 10"
- 3'-6"
- 2'-8"
- 8 RISERS ⌀ 7" = 4'-8"
- 10'-6"
- 10 RISERS ⌀ 7" = 5'-10"

CONCRETE STAIR PLAN

Labels in plan:
- 12"
- 10'-5"
- PRECAST TREAD SET INTO SLAB
- UP 18 R
- 2'-8"
- STEPPED SLAB LINE
- FIN. CONCRETE
- TREAD SET INTO LANDING
- 9'-2" BRICK
- 9'-0"
- 4'-4"
- 4"
- 4'-4"
- 8"
- A
- A
- 9 TREADS ⌀ 11" = 8'-3"
- 4'-0"

Figure 4–33 Details of a commercial (concrete) stairs.

NEW CONSTRUCTION SYSTEMS AND MATERIALS

In the period after World War II, America built 73.8 million homes that set world standards for comfort, quality, and design. The approach of the twenty-first century brings new issues and opportunities, especially in the areas of innovative structural systems that can be used as alternatives to wood framing and that provide increased energy efficiency.

The new structural systems reflect innovations in the material sciences in the areas of engineered wood products, concrete, and steel. All of the systems have implications for energy efficiency. Other technologies with a relationship to energy efficiency include innovative heating and air-conditioning equipment and photovoltaics.

It is important for students to be aware of the changes in building materials and systems that are appearing in the construction industry and to be able to detail the construction situations associated with these new materials and systems. One of the best, current examples of the use of innovative construction materials and systems is the 21st Century Townhouses built by the National Association of Home Builders. The products and systems described in the accompanying boxed material, "The 21st Century Townhouses: The NAHB Research Home Program", show significant promise for U.S. home building and are likely to enter the mainstream of housing construction during the balance of this decade or shortly thereafter.

The 21st Century Townhouses were built by the Research Center in the NAHB Research Home Park as part of the Research Center's research home program (Fig. 1). The purposes of the program are as follows:

- to test, demonstrate, and gain experience with innovative home products, systems, and technologies, for the purpose of assisting U.S. home building to maintain its position of world leadership;
- to disseminate information on the features of innovative systems and methods, and to assist promising new products, systems, and technologies to move into the mainstream of home construction; and
- to ensure that American home buyers get the highest quality and the greatest possible value when they purchase homes.

During construction as well as after completion, each research house is opened for a period of one to two years, for inspection, for tours, and for conducting research. The house is then placed on the market and sold. The location of the Research Home Park in a standard, attractive development, and the requirement that the research houses be sold on the commercial market, both assure that the new and innovative features are united in a home design that can meet the test of broad consumer acceptance.

ARCHITECT, PROJECT DIRECTOR, DEVELOPMENT MANAGER, AND PROJECT SUPERVISOR

Architect for the townhouses was John T. Stovall, President of John Stovall and Associates, Gaithersburg, Maryland. Daniel J. Ball, AIA, of Daniel Ball &

Figure 1 NAHB 21st Century Townhouses.

Associates, served as Project Director. Miles Haber of Monument Construction, Inc., served as Development Manager. J. Albert van Overeem of the NAHB Research Center staff served as Project Supervisor.

The 21st Century Townhouses were built with products that feature two themes:

1. innovative structural systems in home building and
2. approaches to achieving advanced residential energy efficiency.

LOT 7   LOT 8   LOT 9   LOT 10

FRONT ELEVATION
1/8" = 1'- 0"

INNOVATIVE STRUCTURAL SYSTEMS

Interest in alternative systems for home construction grew rapidly in the early 1990s, stimulated by sharp fluctuations in the price of dimensional lumber. Interest was also created by the performance characteristics of many innovative technologies that had not yet entered the mainstream of the marketplace. Many of these technologies show the promise of significant structural merits and excellent energy performance.

ADVANCED ENERGY EFFICIENCY

Increased energy efficiency of homes can make an important contribution to national energy conservation. The average U.S. home is a well-built structure that lasts for at least 75 years. Savings in energy consumption can add up to substantial amounts over the life span of even a single home. Energy-saving features that are not built into a home during construction can be difficult or impossible to introduce later.

In the 21st Century Townhouses, contributions to energy conservation are made by the structural systems, heating and air-conditioning equipment, wastewater heat reclamation, and the use of photovoltaics

to generate electricity. The performance of the structural systems will be compared to the minimum requirements of the Model Energy Code.

STRUCTURAL WALL AND FLOOR SYSTEMS

Each townhouse features a different structural system. The four systems are (1) structural insulated panels; (2) I.C.E. Block™ concrete forming system; (3) steel; and (4) Hebel precast, autoclaved, aerated concrete units.

House 1: Structural Ins\ulated Panels

Structural insulated panels (SIPs), used for the exterior structural system of House 1, consist of a form-core center that contains no environmentally harmful CFCs or HCFCs and is clad on both sides with oriented strand board (Fig. 2). The panels were precut, including some openings, before delivery to the site. SIPs were used for all walls above grade and for roof panels. Panels as large as 8′ × 24′ were incorporated into the exterior walls and roof structure (Figs. 3 and 4).

Benefits of structural insulated panels include the following:

Figure 2 SIP roof panel being lifted into place by a crane.

- SIPs contain relatively low levels of embedded energy. Manufacture involves moderate technological requirements and utilizes moderate amounts of energy.
- The joining systems that are used with SIPs reduce the use of dimensional lumber. The panels contain almost no conventional studs.
- SIP-clad houses present broad, seamless areas to the external environment, offering potential reduced air infiltration and energy savings.
- Construction with precut, structural insulated panels involves low waste generation at the site.

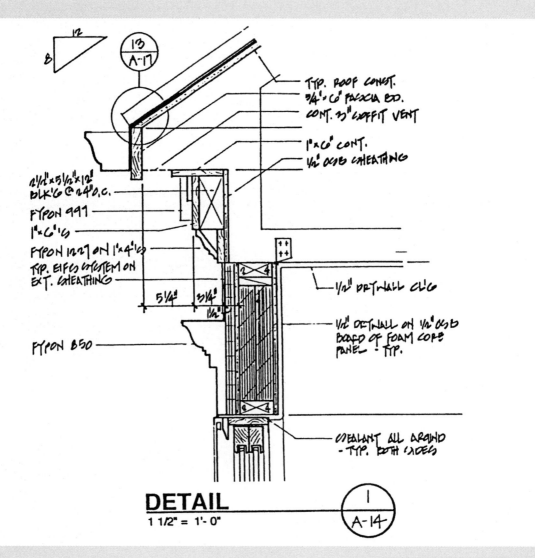

Figure 3 Head detail.

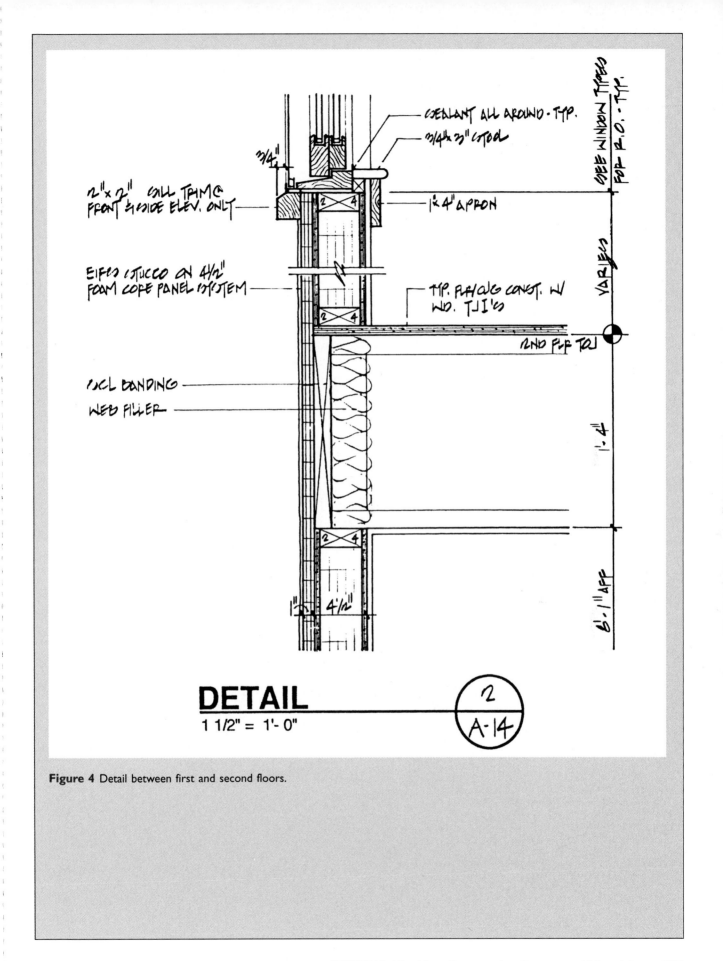

DETAIL
1 1/2" = 1'- 0"

2
A·14

Figure 4 Detail between first and second floors.

Concrete forming systems employing polystyrene forms originated 30 years ago in Europe and were introduced in the United States in modified and improved form in the 1990s. The concrete forming system used for the structural system of House 2, provided by I.C.E. Block™ Building Systems, Inc., utilizes forms that are made of expanded polystyrene (EPS) and that are stacked, reinforced with metal rebars, and filled with concrete. I.C.E. is an acronym for Insulate Concrete Efficiently. The system was used to create above- and below-grade exterior walls (Fig. 5).

The tongue-and-groove EPS forms used in the I.C.E. Block™ system are 48″ × 16″ and are either 9¼″ or 11″ thick. The concrete core thicknesses are 6″ or 8″, respectively.

When the concrete is poured, it produces a post-and-beam, grid-pattern concrete wall with 6″ or 8″ vertical columns, 12″ o.c., and horizontal concrete beams, 16″ o.c., with the horizontal links 2″ thick (Figs. 6, 7, and 8).

The blocks contain light-gauge steel sections, 1½″ wide and 13″ high, vertically embedded 12″ o.c. These sections provide attachment surfaces for interior and exterior finishing material. The sections are embedded ½″ inside the interior and exterior faces of the blocks, providing a thermal break. Marks on the inner and outer surfaces indicate the location of the sections, for attachment of drywall or siding.

In building with I.C.E. Block™, steel reinforcement bars are set, and the corners and window and door frames are braced. When stacking of the blocks reaches each floor level, concrete is poured. When the concrete sets, the bracing is removed. The forms remain in place and serve as exterior and interior insulation.

Concrete forming systems can be used both below and above grade. Standard designs can withstand sustained winds of hurricane force. The walls do not support combustion, soundproofing levels are high, and the manufacturer's product literature states that insulation value is also high. The system can be constructed at temperatures down to 0°F without special freeze protection in the concrete formulation.

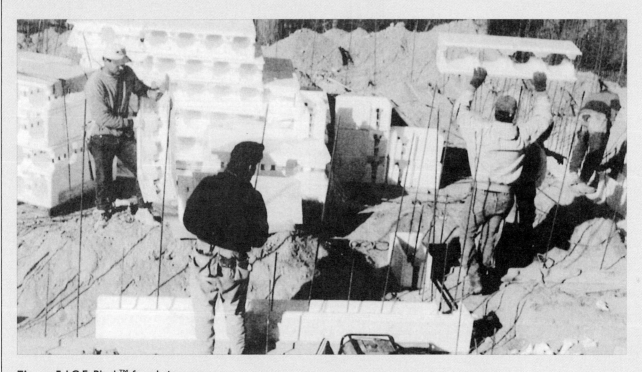

Figure 5 I.C.E. Block™ foundation system.

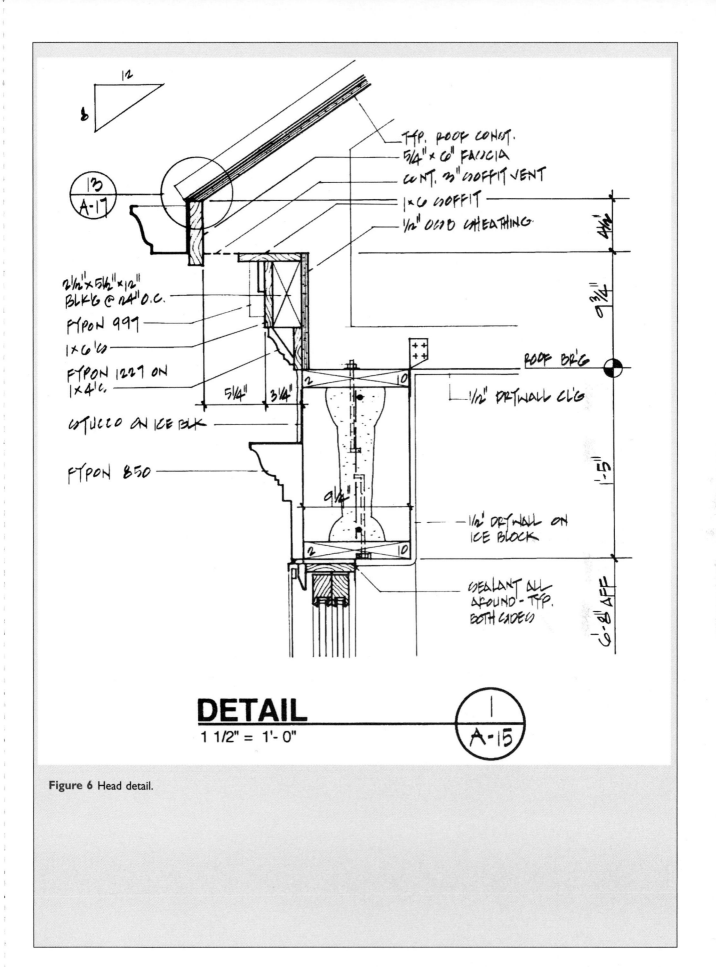

DETAIL
1 1/2" = 1'- 0"

Figure 6 Head detail.

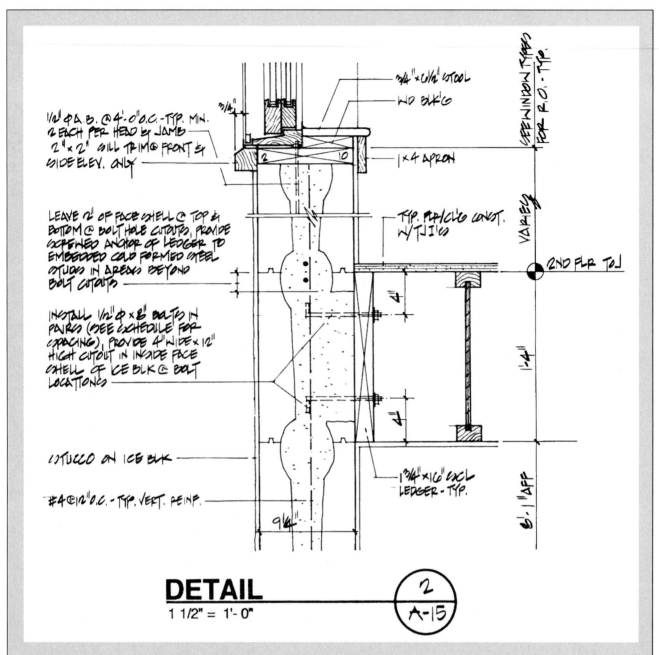

DETAIL
1 1/2" = 1'- 0"

2 / A-15

Figure 7 Detail between first and second floors.

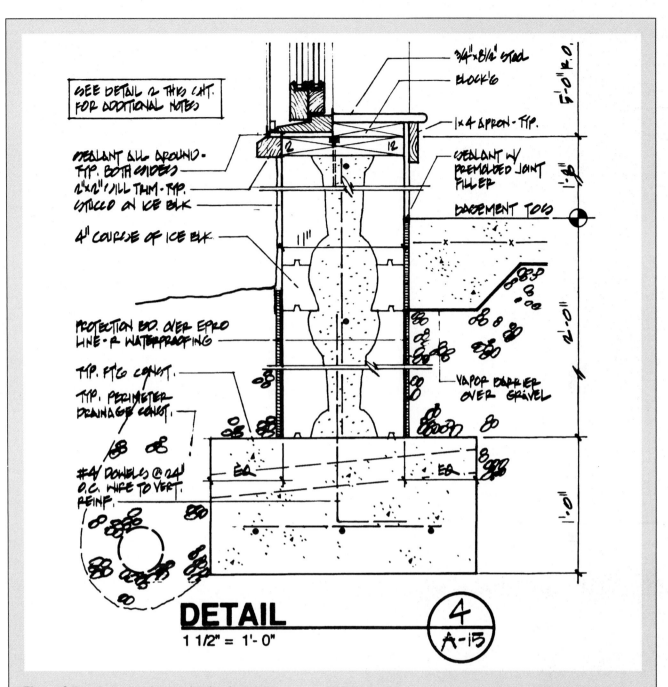

DETAIL
1 1/2" = 1'- 0"

④
A-15

Figure 8 Foundation and footing detail at basement.

Cold-formed steel provided by the American Iron and Steel Institute was used for the framing, the floor joists, and the roof trusses of House 3. Steel was also used for the interior partition walls and the roofs of all four townhouses. Steel used in the house's structural system was galvanized to provide corrosion protection (Fig. 9).

The framing consisted of 18-gauge (0.0043″) 2 × 6 studs, 24″ o.c. The same gauge was used for top and bottom wall tracks (the equivalent of plates in wood construction). Twenty-five-gauge (0.0018″) 2 × 4 studs were used in the interior nonload-bearing walls.

Studs were fastened to the tracks by No. 8 × ½″ drill-point, flat-head screws, to provide a smooth surface for drywall. A hex-drive system with No. 10 × ¾″ drill-point screws was used for structural connections such as clip angles, header connections, and truss connections (Figs. 10, 11, and 12).

Advantages of steel include the following:

- **Fire performance**   Steel is noncombustible.
- **Durability**   Steel is invulnerable to rot or termites and does not shrink, warp, or swell. Galvanized steel resists corrosion.

- **Quality control**   Steel is manufactured to exacting specifications, providing uniform dimensions and highly consistent quality. It is free of twisting, warping, or similar defects.
- **Light weight and strength**   The light weight of steel components makes them easy to handle and assemble. Steel has a high strength-to-weight ratio and utilizes framing screws that resist uplifting loads. It may perform better in earthquakes and hurricanes, although currently few field data are available.
- **Supply and pricing stability**   Steel has a relatively stable price history.
- **Environmental considerations**   A substantial proportion of steel is recycled, with old cars being a major source. Construction with steel produces small amounts of scrap, easily gathered and recycled.

An important consideration in the use of steel is its thermal conductivity. Cold-formed steel studs are much more conductive of heat and cold than wood studs. This problem is usually countered by the use of insulating sheathing, which provides a thermal break. In House 3, ⅝″ Durock™ cement board was placed over the exterior of the steel frame. A layer of 1″ thick

Figure 9 Cold-formed steel frame construction.

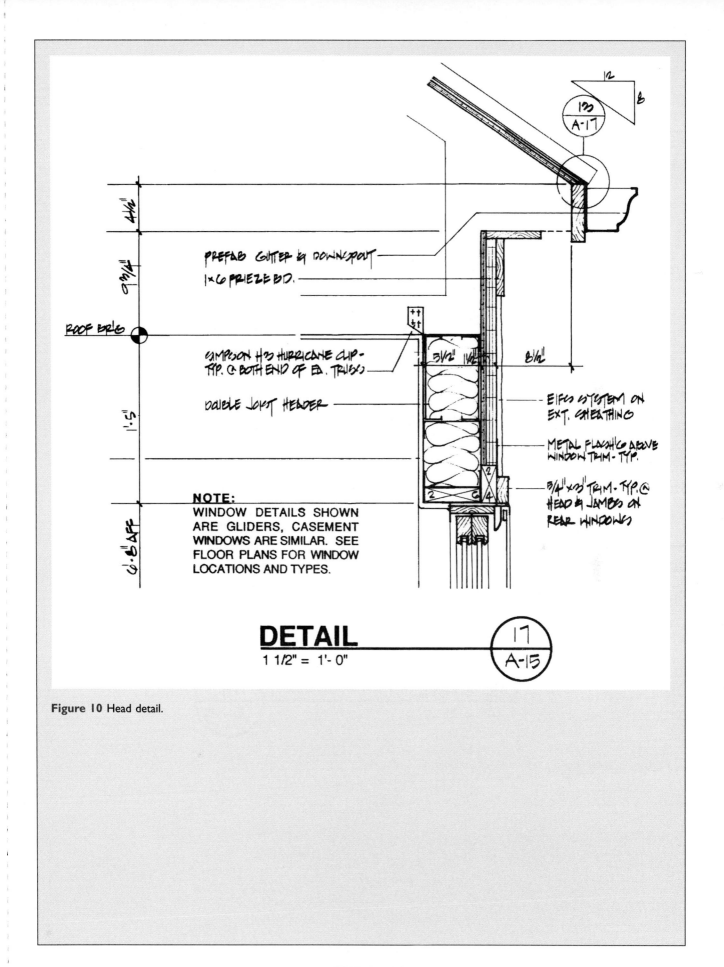

NOTE:
WINDOW DETAILS SHOWN
ARE GLIDERS, CASEMENT
WINDOWS ARE SIMILAR. SEE
FLOOR PLANS FOR WINDOW
LOCATIONS AND TYPES.

PREFAB GUTTER & DOWNSPOUT
1×6 FRIEZE BD.

SIMPSON H3 HURRICANE CLIP -
TYP. @ BOTH END OF EA. TRUSS

DOUBLE JOIST HEADER

EIFS SYSTEM ON
EXT. SHEATHING

METAL FLASH'G ABOVE
WINDOW TRIM - TYP.

3/4" ×3" TRIM - TYP. @
HEAD & JAMBS ON
REAR WINDOWS

ROOF BRG

DETAIL
1 1/2" = 1'- 0"

17
A-15

Figure 10 Head detail.

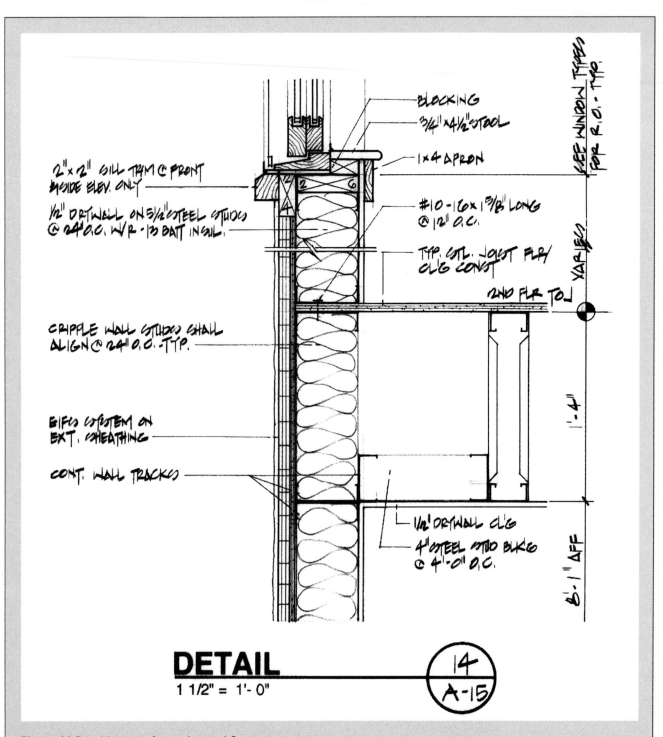

DETAIL
1 1/2" = 1'- 0"

14 / A-15

BLOCKING
3/4" x 4 1/2" STOOL
1 x 4 APRON

2" x 2" SILL TRIM @ FRONT
& SIDE ELEV. ONLY

1/2" DRYWALL ON 5 1/2" STEEL STUDS
@ 24" O.C. W/R-13 BATT INSUL.

#10-16 x 1 3/8" LONG
@ 12" O.C.

TYP. STL. JOIST FLR/
CLG CONST

2ND FLR T.O.

CRIPPLE WALL STUDS SHALL
ALIGN @ 24" O.C. TYP.

EIFS SYSTEM ON
EXT. SHEATHING

CONT. WALL TRACKS

1/2" DRYWALL CLG
4" STEEL STUD BLKG
@ 4'-0" O.C.

SEE WINDOW TYPES
FOR R.O. TYP.

VARIES

1'-4"

8'-1" AFF

Figure 11 Detail between first and second floors.

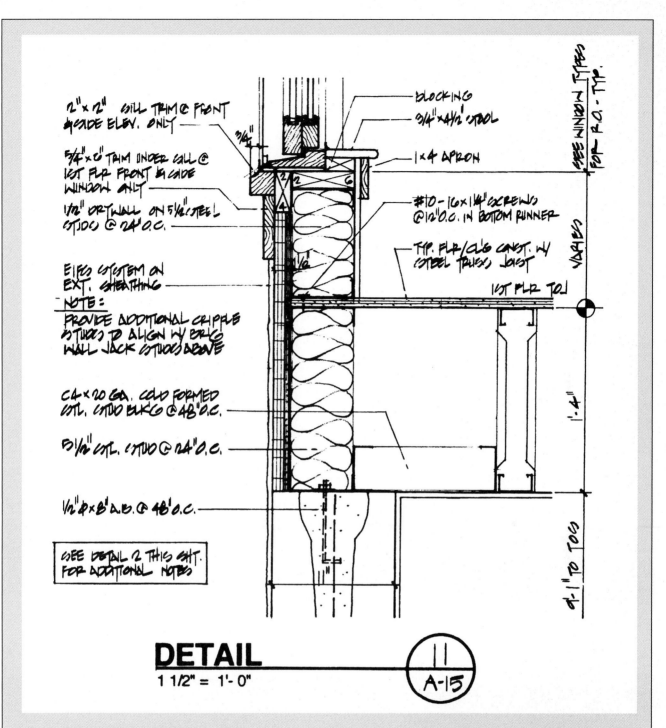

2" x 2" SILL TRIM @ FRONT & SIDE ELEV. ONLY

5/4" x 6" TRIM UNDER SILL @ 1ST FLR FRONT & SIDE WINDOW ONLY

1/2" DRYWALL ON 5 1/2" STEEL STUDS @ 24" O.C.

EIFS SYSTEM ON EXT. SHEATHING

NOTE:
PROVIDE ADDITIONAL CRIPPLE STUDS TO ALIGN W/ BRICK WALL JACK STUDS ABOVE

C4 x 20 GA. COLD FORMED STL. STUD BLKG @ 48" O.C.

5 1/2" STL. STUD @ 24" O.C.

1/2" Ø x 8" A.B. @ 48" O.C.

SEE DETAIL 2 THIS SHT. FOR ADDITIONAL NOTES

BLOCKING

3/4" x 4 1/2" STOOL

1 x 4 APRON

#10 - 16 x 1 1/4" SCREWS @ 12" O.C. IN BOTTOM RUNNER

TYP. FLR/CLG CONST. W/ STEEL TRUSS, JOIST

1ST FLR TOJ

SEE WINDOW TYPES FOR R.O. TYP.

VARIES

1'-4"

9'-1" TO TOS

DETAIL
1 1/2" = 1'- 0"

11
A-15

Figure 12 Detail between first floor and basement.

sheets of expanded polystyrene (EPS) was adhesively applied to the Durock™ cement board. These EPS sheets are part of an exterior insulation and finishing system.

House 4: Precast, Autoclaved, Aerated Concrete Units

Precast, autoclaved, aerated concrete (PAAC) units provided by Hebel USA were used for the structure of House 4. Hebel is a German firm that has been producing and selling the product for about 50 years. Hebel USA was established in 1988, and the first U.S. manufacturing facility was recently established in Adel, Georgia.

Standard Hebel units measure 8″ × 24″ on their interior and exterior surfaces; they are 8″ thick. The units are made with sand, cement, lime, water, and an expanding agent that, when combined, form a uniform cellular structure. Hebel units are about ½ the weight of concrete blocks of the same size, and they provide built-in insulation (Fig. 13).

Hebel base course wall units are laid on a Type M mortar bed. A thin-bed mortar, similar to tile-set-

Figure 13 Hebel USA precast, autoclaved, aerated concrete units being lifted into place.

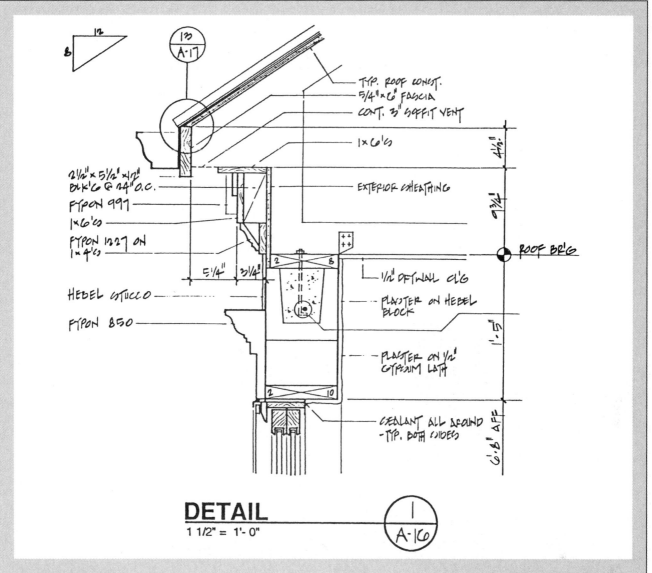

DETAIL
1 1/2" = 1'- 0"

1 / A-16

Figure 14 Head detail.

ting mortar, is used for subsequent horizontal and vertical joints. The units can be trimmed accurately with normal woodworking tools at the site. They can be drilled, nailed, or screwed for attachment of finishes. Raceways or channels for wiring and plumbing can be made by routing the interior face of the wall.

Hebel U-units can be field cut or factory supplied. They are laid at each floor level to create a bond beam that is filled with standard concrete and reinforcing (Figs. 14 and 15).

Hebel units contain no combustible materials and exceed building code requirements for fire resistance. They are also pest resistant and sound resistant, possess dimensional stability, and require little maintenance over the life of the house. In House 4, a plaster interior finish and a cement stucco exterior finish system were applied directly to the units.

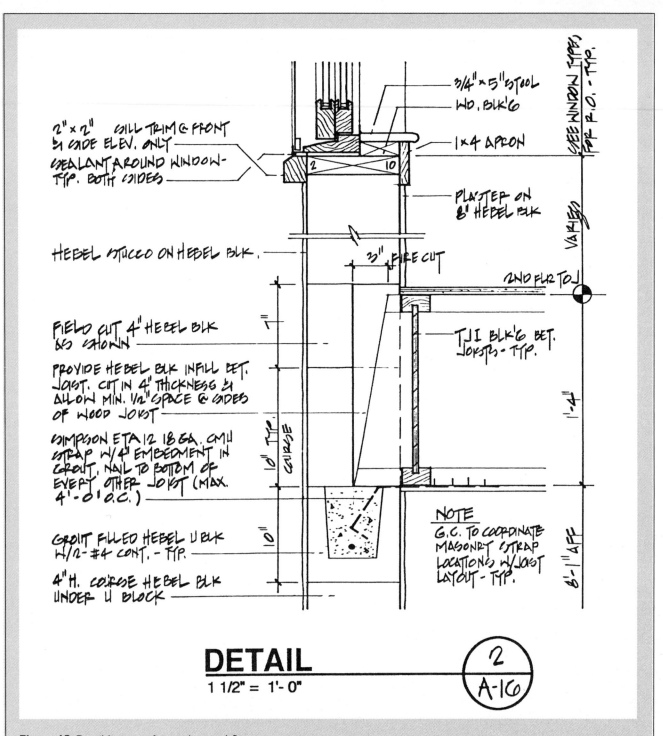

2" x 2" SILL TRIM @ FRONT & SIDE ELEV. ONLY
SEALANT AROUND WINDOW - TYP. BOTH SIDES

3/4" x 5" STOOL
WD. BLK'G

1 x 4 APRON

PLASTER ON 8" HEBEL BLK

SEE WINDOW TYPES FOR R.O. - TYP.

HEBEL STUCCO ON HEBEL BLK.

3" FIRE CUT

2ND FLR TOJ

VARIES

FIELD CUT 4" HEBEL BLK AS SHOWN

PROVIDE HEBEL BLK INFILL BET. JOIST. CUT IN 4" THICKNESS & ALLOW MIN. 1/2" SPACE @ SIDES OF WOOD JOIST

TJI BLK'G BET. JOISTS - TYP.

SIMPSON ETA12 18 GA. CMU STRAP W/ 4" EMBEDMENT IN GROUT. NAIL TO BOTTOM OF EVERY OTHER JOIST (MAX. 4'-0" O.C.)

GROUT FILLED HEBEL U BLK W/2 - #4 CONT. - TYP.

4" H. COURSE HEBEL BLK UNDER U BLOCK

10" TYP. COURSE

1"

1"

10"

1'-4"

8'-1" AFF

NOTE
G.C. TO COORDINATE MASONRY STRAP LOCATIONS W/ JOIST LAYOUT - TYP.

DETAIL
1 1/2" = 1'- 0"

2
A-16

Figure 15 Detail between first and second floors.

FOUNDATIONS

Houses 1, 2, and 3: I.C.E. Block™ System

The foundations of Houses 1, 2, and 3 utilize the I.C.E. Block™ system, which was also used for the exterior walls of House 2 (Figs. 8, 16, and 17).

House 4: Precast, Preinsulated System

House 4 utilizes a precast, preinsulated foundation system. The system, supplied by Superior Walls, Inc., utilizes a 1¾″ outer skin of high-strength, reinforced concrete, with a continuous sheathing layer of 1″ foam insulation on its inner surface and with steel-reinforced concrete studs to which wood nailing strips are affixed (Fig. 18).

Panels are made at the factory to fit the perimeter of the house. The panels are formed with door and window openings. Normally, 16′ is the maximum length. There are three standard wall heights: 4′, 8′-2″, and 10′.

Concrete footings are not required for installation of the Superior Walls system. The panels are placed directly over a gravel bed (Fig. 19). As they are installed, a sealant is applied between the panels to provide watertightness. The foam insulation panels have an *R* value of 5. Additional insulation can be added between the studs to provide a total of *R*-24.

The panels are made with 5000-psi concrete. According to the American Concrete Institute, a 4000-psi mix design is adequate to provide watertightness. It is therefore not necessary to parge or tar the exterior of the wall after installation.

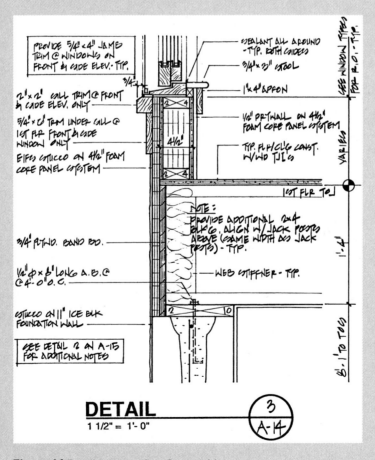

Figure 16 Detail between first floor and basement.

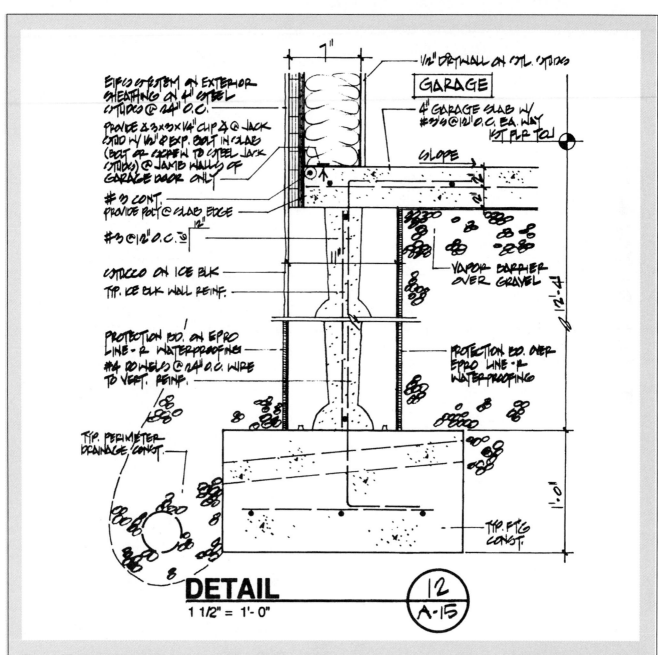

Figure 17 Foundation and footing at slab on grade.

Figure 18 Superior Walls, Inc., precast, preinsulated foundation system.

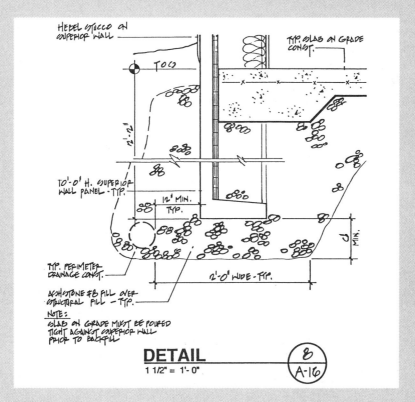

Figure 19 Superior Walls, Inc., foundation detail (no insulation required).

ROOFS

The townhouses have standing-seam steel roofs. The roofs are of various colors, which are applied as weather-resistant coatings during manufacture. The steel roof of House 1 is supported by structural insulated panels; of Houses 2 and 4, by wood trusses; and of House 3, by steel trusses.

The steel used to make the roofs is partially recycled. Steel roofs typically have a useful life of over fifty years, during which they require little or no maintenance.

EXTERIOR FINISHING SYSTEMS

Exterior Insulation and Finish System (E.I.F.S.)

Exterior Insulation and Finish Systems (E.I.F.S.s) are methods for covering and insulating the exterior of homes; these systems combine high insulating value with attractive external appearance. United States Gypsum Company (USG) provided two types of E.I.F.S.s for Houses 1, 2, and 3.

A USG Durock™ E.I.F. water-managed system was installed on House 3 (Fig. 12). The steps were as follows:

1. A water-resistive barrier was installed over the steel frame. For fire-rated party walls using gypsum wallboard, a vapor-permeable, water-resistive barrier is installed over the gypsum.
2. Durock™ cement board panels of ⅝″ thickness were installed.

3. A layer of 1″ thick sheets of expanded polystyrene (EPS) was adhesively applied to the Durock™ cement board.
4. The exterior surface of the EPS was rasped, and a ³⁄₃₂″ thick base coat of portland cement containing dry latex polymers was applied.
5. A glass fiber mesh was embedded in the base coat. The mesh was of 4.5-, 12.5-, or 24-oz/yd weight, depending on the location where it was installed.
6. A finish coat of USG Exterior Textured Finish was applied. Various tints and textures are available with the finish. For the townhouses, a coarse texture was utilized.

A standard E.I.F.S. application was provided over the structural insulated panels of House 1 (Fig. 20).

The walls of House 2, which was built with I.C.E. Block™ polystyrene forms, possess integral interior and exterior insulation (Fig. 21). The exterior surface of the forms was rasped, and a base coat, 12.5-oz/yd^2 glass fiber mesh, and finish were applied. The 12.5-oz. mesh was specified by USG for use with I.C.E. Block™.

Exterior Finish System for Hebel Units

House 4, built with Hebel PAAC units, received a ⅜″ base coat of a cement stucco, which was spray applied and smoothed (Fig. 22). This application was followed by a trowel-applied finish coat of the same material. The material chosen for the finish possesses the same coefficient of expansion as that of the Hebel units.

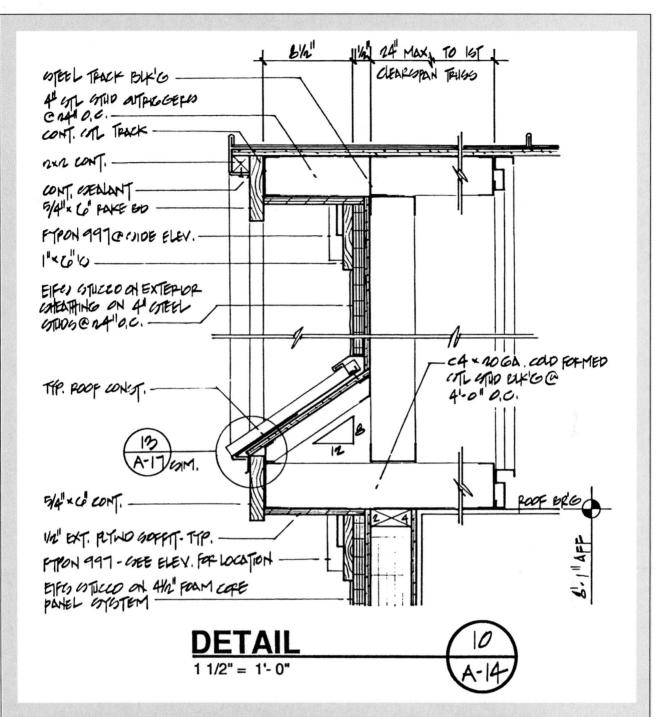

STEEL TRACK BLK'G
4" STL STUD STAGGERED @ 24" O.C.
CONT. STL TRACK
2x2 CONT.
CONT. SEALANT
5/4" x 6" RAKE BD
FYPON 997 @ SIDE ELEV.
1" x 6" 'S
EIFS STUCCO ON EXTERIOR SHEATHING ON 4" STEEL STUDS @ 24" O.C.

TYP. ROOF CONST.

13
A-17 SIM.

5/4" x 6" CONT.
1/2" EXT. PLYWD SOFFIT - TYP.
FYPON 997 - SEE ELEV. FOR LOCATION
EIFS STUCCO ON 4½" FOAM CORE PANEL SYSTEM

6½"   1½"   24" MAX. TO 1ST CLEARSPAN TRUSS

C4 x 20 GA. COLD FORMED STL STUD BLK'G @ 4'-0" O.C.

12   8
12

ROOF BR'G

6'-1" AFF

DETAIL
1 1/2" = 1'- 0"

10
A-14

Figure 20 E.I.F.S. on exterior sheathing.

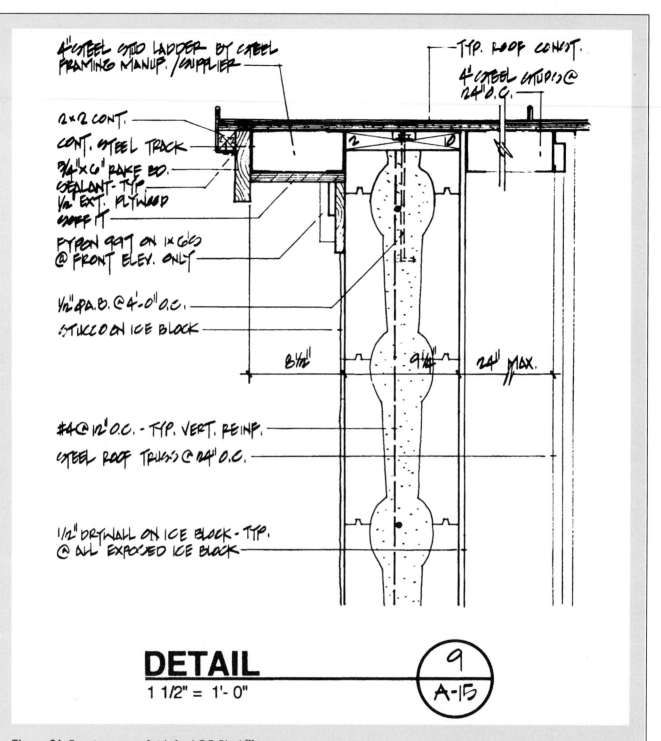

4" STEEL STUD LADDER BY STEEL FRAMING MANUF. / SUPPLIER

TYP. ROOF CONST.

4" STEEL STUDS @ 24" O.C.

2×2 CONT.

CONT. STEEL TRACK

3/4" × 6" RAKE BD.

SEALANT - TYP.

1/2" EXT. PLYWOOD

SOFFIT

FYPON 997 ON 1×6's @ FRONT ELEV. ONLY

1/2" A.B. @ 4'-0" O.C.

STUCCO ON ICE BLOCK

8 1/2"

9 1/4"

24" MAX.

#4 @ 12" O.C. - TYP. VERT. REINF.

STEEL ROOF TRUSS @ 24" O.C.

1/2" DRYWALL ON ICE BLOCK - TYP. @ ALL EXPOSED ICE BLOCK

DETAIL
1 1/2" = 1'- 0"

9

A-15

Figure 21 Exterior stucco finish for I.C.E. Block™ system.

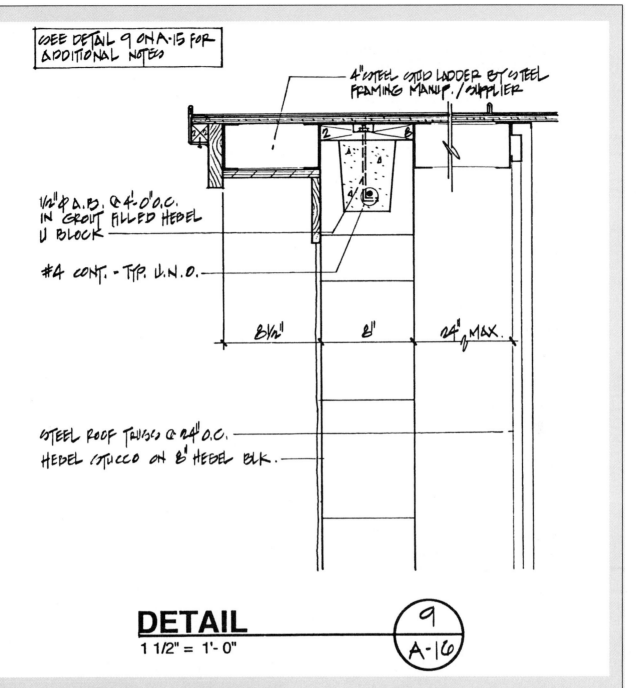

SEE DETAIL 9 ON A-15 FOR ADDITIONAL NOTES

4" STEEL STUD LADDER BY STEEL FRAMING MANUF./SUPPLIER

1/2" Ø A.B. @ 4'-0" O.C. IN GROUT FILLED HEBEL U BLOCK

#4 CONT. - TYP. U.N.O.

8½"

8"

24" MAX.

STEEL ROOF TRUSSES @ 24" O.C.
HEBEL STUCCO ON 8" HEBEL BLK.

DETAIL
1 1/2" = 1'- 0"

9
A-16

Figure 22 Exterior stucco finish for Hebel system.

WINDOWS AND DOORS

Energy-efficient glider and casement windows installed in the townhouses have high-performance, argon-filled glazing panels. When the windows are closed, cam action pulls the sashes together to inhibit air infiltration. Finger-jointed wood is used for the frames, to make use of short pieces of wood that would normally be discarded. The windows have a U-value rating of 0.33.

Energy-efficient entry doors were installed in all of the units. The fiberglass doors are insulated and can be finished with stain to look like traditional six-panel wood doors.

SPRAY-IN FOAM INSULATION

House 3, which was framed with steel, was insulated with the Icynene Insealation System™ (Fig. 23). The system was also used in Houses 1 and 4 to insulate the exposed floor above the garage, and in all of the town-houses to insulate joist ends and to seal attics, cantilevered fireplaces, cantilevered floors, and gable ends.

In this system, the foam insulating material is sprayed as a liquid at a temperature of about 150°F, and it expands at a ratio of 100:1. The material cures dry within seconds, adheres to the surface onto which it is sprayed, and does not undergo loss of pliancy or subsequent shrinkage. After spraying, excess insulation is easily removed with a standard handsaw.

Water in the formulation reacts with other components to produce carbon dioxide, which serves as the blowing agent. The product contains no ozone-destroying CFCs or HCFCs, and no formaldehyde. After 30 days, it produces no detectable emissions.

The material fills cavities completely, providing a nearly perfect fit and drastically reducing air leakage, convection, and airborne moisture. The material has an R value of 3.6 per inch of thickness. It virtually eliminates the need for detailed special air seals, vapor barriers, or air barrier treatment such as building wraps, taping, and caulking.

PHOTOVOLTAICS

Photovoltaics (PV) is the generation of electricity from sunlight. The technology involves the installation of both PV modules where they are accessible to the sun and equipment for storing the electricity that is generated by the shining of the sun on the modules. Residential applications of photovoltaics represent an important frontier of energy efficiency and home building technology.

Figure 23 Icynen Insealation System™ being sprayed into steel stud wall cavities.

Figure 24 Flexible photovoltaic modules installed on the roof of House 4.

An innovative approach to residential photovoltaics, involving flexible modules that have the appearance of standard roofing products and that can serve both as roofing and as solar collectors, will be tested and demonstrated in House 4. The steel roofing was removed from more than 400 sq ft of the south-facing roof of this house, and the PV modules were mounted directly on the roof sheathing. Installation methods and products common to the installation of standard metal roofing were used to mount the modules (Fig. 24).

The power output from the modules, which is expected to exceed 2 kilowatts in the full sun, will be stored in batteries. The system is expected to contribute between 50% and 75% of the home's 120-volt requirements, exclusive of space conditioning, cooking, and water heating. The electricity can be used during on-peak periods, to reduce both energy demands of the home and energy cost to the homeowner. It can also be used as a source of backup power if there is a power outage.

The system operation is programmable and will involve an interactive relationship among the utility grid, the PV output, and the battery storage, which will enable the utility to use the system for demand-side management. The system will be able to feed excess electricity generated by the modules into the utility grid. Functioning of the system will be automatic, with minimum user involvement.

HOME AUTOMATION

SMART HOUSE, LP, provided home automation systems for the townhouses. SMART HOUSE coordinated contributions from SMART HOUSE; AMP, Inc.; and Molex, Inc., to provide a different system package for each house. Services provided by the systems include advanced energy management.

PROBLEMS AND SPECIAL CONSIDERATIONS ENCOUNTERED IN CONSTRUCTION

Working with Steel Framing

Interior steel framing was used in all of the houses. In order to avoid electrolysis, no copper piping and no electrical wiring can touch the steel. Piping and wiring must pass through openings in the steel studs that are insulated with plastic grommets. In addition, care must be taken regarding the condition of electrical tools and cords that are used in the vicinity of the steel frame. Electrical contact could result in shock to anyone who was touching the frame at any point. These requirements for working with steel generally translate to increased labor time.

Evaluation Criteria

As the townhouses were constructed, evaluation of the materials and systems was carried out in three areas:

1. **Technical performance** This included comparisons of features and characteristics of the innovative materials with those of standard materials currently in use.
2. **Buildability** This comprised evaluation of the capability of the average subcontractor work force to work with and install the innovative products and systems. What tools were needed? What training was required? How long did it take workers to master new methods and techniques?
3. **Infrastructure** This included easy availability of technical information from local building supply outlets, on-shelf availability of such items as fasteners, and availability of information in building codes.

Delays in Securing Buildings Permits

Substantial delays were encountered in securing permits for construction. Certain supporting data and fitness-for-use justifications that the county required did not exist for the innovative products that were to be used, or they were not in a form that was acceptable to the county officials, particularly with regard to fire performance.

The Prince George's County Fire Department conducted an extensive review of the project's design. In response to the department's requirements, the Research Center put available data into a form acceptable to the county, or it retained experts to help develop technical information and to obtain approvals. A cooperative effort between manufacturers and Research Center staff was involved. The compliance documents that were generated through this effort will be useful in securing approvals for the products in other jurisdictions.

Lack of Informational Infrastructure

For all of the basic structural products used to build the townhouses, far less informational infrastructure exists than is available for conventional construction. Technical information, recommendations, and advice for wood and masonry construction have evolved through nearly universal use over a long period of time, and all are available to builders at places that range from their local lumber supply outlet to the national building codes. A major challenge facing the manufacturers and suppliers of the innovative products is to develop an adequate informational infrastructure to support widespread use and adoption of the materials.

Integration of Products and Systems

Integrating nonconventional and dissimilar materials posed significant challenges. For example, special attention and engineering were required to develop anchorage details for attaching the steel framing of House 3 to the I.C.E. Block™ forms of House 2.

House-by-House Summaries

Other problems and special considerations involved in working with the innovative materials used to build the townhouses are described in the following house-by-house summaries:

- **House 1.** No structural insulated panel (SIP) system that was available for the project possessed a 1-h fire rating on both sides of the panels. This rating was required by county officials for use in the common wall between Houses 1 and 2. The Research Center retained a leading fire engineer to study the problem and devise a method for meeting the county's requirements. The method recommended by the engineer, which met with the county's approval, was installation of two layers of 5/8″ drywall on each side of the wall.
- **House 2.** The initial design for House 2 involved the use of more reinforcing steel in the walls above

the basement than was indicated in manufacturer's recommendations. The Research Center respecified the system to the manufacturer's recommendations, making it fully safe at less cost.

- **House 3.** The steel studs were light and were easy to handle and put into place. They were also easy to alter in the field. They had been made too long, and shortening them posed no difficulty. However, there were no commercially available hangers, and these had to be made at the site. In addition, it was necessary to train the workers in the use of the screw gun, and the training requirement for this skill had been underestimated. The screws themselves could not be purchased at the local home building supply outlet.

The steel roof trusses that were installed on House 3 were light and easy to handle, but they were not as rigid as wood trusses. To set and brace the trusses required procedures different from those that are customarily used for wood trusses. It was not possible to stand either on the trusses or on the top of the interior steel frame. Auxiliary lifting equipment for the workers was therefore required.

- **House 4.** The learning curve of the workers was exhibited in their building of the structural system of House 4. It took experienced masons 2½ weeks, including minor weather delays, to lay the first-floor walls. It took 2½ days, including training of a new crew, to lay the second-floor walls.

Carpenters built one Hebel wall section. Contrary to what might be expected, carpenters worked more quickly and more accurately than masons in erecting the Hebel units. A carpenter, rather than a mason, constructed the gable wall on the house. Working with Hebel units resembles carpentry in many respects. Carpenters are accustomed to precise measurements and cuts. The Hebel units can be measured to exact dimensions, cut with a saw, and fitted together snugly. Masons are accustomed to ⅜″ to ½″ mortar joints, which reduces the degree of accuracy required for fitting. Due to the dimensional accuracy of the Hebel PAAC units, the mortar joint is only 2 to 3 mm (¹⁄₁₆″ to ¹⁄₁₂″).

The manufacturer notes that, whereas carpenters work well with Hebel PAAC units, construction has also been carried out successfully with masons or with crews made up of a lead mason or carpenter with three or four laborers.

RESEARCH ACTIVITIES

Research activities and programs that will be carried out in the townhouses include the following.

Energy and Thermal Performance

Analysis of the energy performance of the townhouses was initiated during construction and will continue after completion. Preliminary analysis included a review of the compliance of each of the townhouses with the Model Energy Code (MEC) minimum standards, using the *MECcheck* software package. Data on each house—such as structural dimensions, types of materials and their *R* values, fenestration, and HVAC equipment—will be integrated into the analysis.

An empirical analysis of the energy performance of each unit will be performed. This analysis will include compilation of data on outdoor air temperature, exterior wall surface temperature, indoor wall surface temperature, and HVAC gas and electric energy usage. A data acquisitions system has been installed that includes thermocouples in the outside south and north faces of the units to record surface temperatures. The thermocouples will be used to monitor diurnal temperature swings. The full set of data will be used to create a predictive model of the anticipated energy consumption of each house.

Focus Groups and Surveys

Focus groups in the townhouses will be conducted for the project's private-sector sponsors, the American Iron and Steel Institute, Hebel USA, the National Ready Mixed Concrete Association/Portland Cement Association, and United States Gypsum Company. These focus groups will provide a qualitative assessment of features and technologies used in the townhouses.

Two panel sessions will be held. One will include builders and members of trades directly associated with home building. The other will include real estate salespersons and potential home buyers. Participants will be briefed on the features of the houses, and their reactions and opinions will be elicited, recorded, and analyzed.

Two separate survey instruments will also be developed: one for home builders and associated tradespersons and one for real estate professionals and potential home buyers. All persons visiting and touring the houses will be asked to fill out a survey form. Results will be tabulated, and the results will be used to supplement the findings of the focus groups.

Study of Energy-Efficient Duct System

Under a contract with the Gas Research Institute, the Research Center is studying ways to improve duct energy efficiency in new residential construction. As part of the program. Research Center engineers will test the thermal efficiency of duct systems that are installed in the townhouses.

All of the units will be evaluated for distribution efficiency, with special studies being conducted in House 2. Redundant duct systems servicing the second floor were installed in this house. These systems consist of ceiling registers with ducting in the floor. The duct leakage and sealing techniques and the thermal distribution efficiency of ducts inside and outside the conditioned space will be evaluated. When the tests are completed, the information will be made available to builders, to enable them to make a cost-versus-benefits analysis of various alternatives for the benefit of their customers.

Photovoltaic System

Baltimore Gas & Electric will oversee the operation of the photovoltaic system and will monitor the output of the PV array as well as the operation of the battery storage. BG&E will also oversee the monitoring of the home loads and the interaction of the system with the utility grid.

The installation features of the photovoltaic roofing material will be evaluated, and input on its esthetic qualities will be secured from builders, code officials, and consumers.

ADDITIONAL PRODUCTS AND MATERIALS

Key Participants and Contributors

The following products and materials were provided by key participants and contributors:

- **Armstrong World Industries** Resilient flooring.
- **Benjamin Moore and Company** Interior coatings that are low in volatile organic compounds (VOCs). In these coatings, VOCs, which have an adverse environmental impact, have been virtually eliminated from the formulation.
- **Hearth Products Association** State-of-the-art technologies for fireplaces and free-standing stoves, including pellet stoves and gas-fired hearth products. Pellet stoves burn small, concentrated pellets, which are made from recycled waste products such as sawdust or cardboard. Gas-fired hearth products provide an esthetic simulation of a wood fire without the inconvenience, the environmental impact, and the sometimes high cost of burning wood.
- **International Paper Company, Masonite Division** Interior doors and garage doors, with facings simulating the appearance of dimension lumber, that are made from sawmill residue and wood scrap.

- **National Ready Mixed Concrete Association (NRMCA)** Driveways for Houses 2 and 3 that are certified in the Association's "Blue Ribbon" quality program. The driveways are designed to provide high durability. They are covered under a five-year limited warranty against major cracking and scaling.
- **Therma-Stor Products** Ventilation and dehumidification equipment, designated to prevent mold, mildew, dust mite infestations, and airborne allergens; dispel gaseous contaminates; and provide maximum indoor air quality through fresh air ventilation, humidity control, and air filtration.
- **Trus Joist MacMillan** The floor system for House 1, consisting of structural engineered lumber products that are designed to make efficient use of wood fibers.
- **Water Film Energy, Inc.** The drain-water, heat-recovery system, in which the heat from hot drain water is used to warm cold water circulating in a pipe wrapped around the hot-water drain pipe. According to the manufacturer, the system can typically recycle about half of the heat carried by a hot shower stream.
- **Wilsonart International** Solid sheet and molded sinks made of a structural material that can be carved and routed like wood, is renewable, and is produced by manufacturing processes designed to require minimal energy and produce minimal waste.
- **York International Environmental Systems** A natural gas heating and cooling system. Using a non-CFC refrigerant cycle, the system removes heat from the home in the summer and delivers heat in the winter. The system runs automatically at variable speeds in accordance with need, providing uniform temperature and humidity levels.

Other Products

Products donated for the project include the following:
- **Geothermal ground-source heat pump** This heat pump takes advantage of the stability of earth temperatures, as opposed to outdoor air temperatures, to operate at lower energy cost. Because the earth is a stable source of heat, the warmth delivered by ground-source heat pumps is not reduced when outdoor temperatures drop, as is the case with air-source heat pumps.
- **Pallet flooring** This flooring is made from old wooden pallets. The boards from the pallets are cut and shaped as tongue-and-groove flooring. After the flooring is laid, it is coated with a thin layer of filler, which fills the numerous nail holes in the boards. The floors are then sanded and finished.

1. Draw a typical wall detail of a brick veneer, 1-story residence, using the scale $1'' = 1'-0''$. Use a crawl space with concrete block foundation wall. Floor joists are $2'' \times 10''$; ceiling joists, $2'' \times 8''$; and roof slope, 4:12.

2. Draw a typical wall detail of a concrete block wall with a slab-on-ground floor, using the scale $3/4'' = 1'-0''$. Show a flat roof with $2'' \times 8''$ roof joists, and box in the $2'$ overhang (see roof overhang details in Section 12.12 in Chapter 12).

3. Draw a typical wall detail of a frame wall for a house with a basement of $8''$ poured concrete walls, using the scale $1/2'' = 1'-0''$. Use a plank-and-beam roof with $3'' \times 8''$ beams. The roof slope is 3:12; board-and-batten siding is used.

4. Draw a section detail of an aluminum awning window, using the scale $1'' = 1'-0''$. Select an actual window from *Sweet's File*.

5. Draw a section and an elevation of a wood hopper window, using the scale $1\frac{1}{2}'' = 1'-0''$. Use information from a manufacturer's catalog.

6. Draw the head, jamb, and sill section of a door detail in a solid-brick ($8''$) wall, using the scale $3/4'' = 1'-0''$. Use $1\frac{1}{4}''$ wood jambs, suitable trim, and a $1\frac{3}{4}''$ flush door.

7. Draw the elevation, plan, and vertical section details for a contemporary fireplace, using the scale $3/4'' = 1'-0''$. Use stone masonry with a flagstone hearth. The size of the fireplace opening is $42'' \times 28''$.

8. Design and draw the details for a single flight of colonial stairs, using the scale $3/4'' = 1'-0''$. The finish-floor-to-finish-floor height is $9'-8''$. Select a suitable scale, trim, and railing.

9. Draw a wall detail of a 2-story, contemporary, wood frame house with slab on ground, aluminum and glass sliding doors, 2×10 second-floor joists, $4'-6''$ high aluminum casement windows on the second floor, $18''$ deep flat roof trusses, membrane roofing with stone ballast, and a $2'-0''$ high parapet. The exterior walls and parapet have $1\frac{1}{2}''$ thick E.I.F.S.; the scale is $3/4'' = 1'-0''$.

10. Draw a section through a covered patio, slab on ground with $2''$ stone flooring, $8''$ square by $10'$ high wood posts, a 6×12 wood beam between the posts, 4×8 wood rafters, $3''$ laminated T&G decking, a Spanish tile roof with 5:12 slope, a $36''$ high railing with 2×4 top and bottom rails, and 2×2 vertical balusters between the posts. Use a scale of $1'' = 1'-0''$.

REVIEW QUESTIONS

1. What factors are used to determine the choice of scale when drawing details?

2. What information does a typical wall detail usually show?

3. Why are structural members in detail drawings drawn actual size rather than nominal size?

4. In gable-roof terminology, what is the difference between *span* and *run?*

5. Why must you consult manufacturers' catalogs when determining rough opening sizes for windows?

6. Differentiate between a *window sash* and a *window frame.*

7. Why are doorjambs usually the only sections needed when you are drawing door details?

8. What dimensions are first selected in fireplace design, and what should be the basis for their selection?

9. For a workable fireplace, what should be the proportion of the cross-sectional flue area to the fireplace opening area?

10. What two dimensions are the most critical in satisfactory stair design?

11. Describe how an architect's scale can be used to lay out the riser height and the tread width of stairs in elevation or section without measuring each riser and tread from floor to floor.

12. Write the three formulas for checking riser and tread proportions.

13. What is a fire door, and what do the labels A, B, and C designate?

14. What are anchor bolts, and where are they used in wood frame construction?

15. What is used to support brick masonry above a door or window opening?

16. What type of cut is usually placed on a rafter where it rests on a bearing wall?

17. What is the minimum headroom above stairs?

18. Where is a brick rowlock used in window detaining?

19. What is a clerestory window?

"Nothing is achieved before it is thoroughly attempted."
—SIR PHILIP SIDNEY

In light of what has been said about graphic description, it will seem obvious that working drawings, however well drawn, cannot be entirely adequate in completely revealing all aspects of a construction project. Many things cannot be shown graphically. For example, how would you show on a drawing the quality of workmanship required on a kitchen cabinet, except by an extensive hand-lettered note?

The information that is necessary for the construction of any structure is usually developed by means of two basic documents: drawings and specifications. These two documents represent distinct methods of transmitting information. They should complement one another and should not overlap or duplicate one another (Fig. 5–1). *Drawings* are a graphical portrayal, and *specifications* are a written description of the legal and technical requirements forming the contract documents. Working drawings describe the construction quantitatively, that is *how much*, whereas specifications describe the project qualitatively, or *how good/well*. Together, the working drawings and specifications communicate a complete picture of the construction.

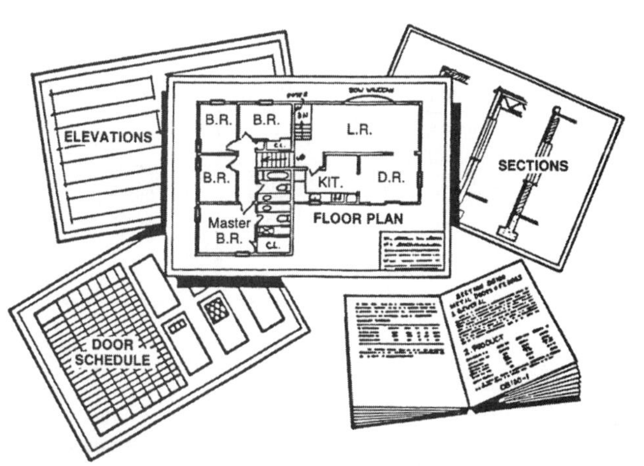

Good communication of any design depends on having complete and fully coordinated construction documents. Properly prepared drawings and specifications dovetail like a snugly fitted jigsaw puzzle with no overlaps or gaps. The project drawings show the form, quantity, and relationship of the construction materials and should identify but not describe a material or component. This should be done with a minimum of information. The specifications establish the quality of materials and workmanship and in comparison to the data shown on the drawings should contain detailed information needed to define the required quality of materials, equipment, and methods of installation. An important principle in specification writing is that each requirement should be stated only one time and in the most logical location in order to reduce the possibility of conflicts and discrepancies. Also, information in one document should not be repeated in any other document (Fig. 5–2).

This chapter examines the detailed instructions, often called *specs*, together with other written documents, and shows their relationship to working drawings.

Figure 5–1 Drawings and specifications complement each other.

5.1

RELATIONSHIP OF DRAWINGS TO THE SPECIFICATIONS AND OTHER WRITTEN DOCUMENTS

We have seen the importance of architectural drawings in conveying the architect's intent. However, in the world of construction, several other written documents are just as important as the drawings in establishing the contract between the owner and the contractor. We must remember that the purpose of these documents is to

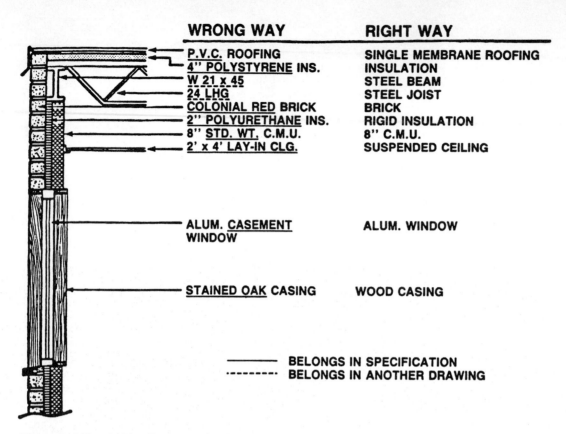

WRONG WAY	RIGHT WAY
P.V.C. ROOFING	SINGLE MEMBRANE ROOFING
4" POLYSTYRENE INS.	INSULATION
W 21 x 45	STEEL BEAM
24 LHG	STEEL JOIST
COLONIAL RED BRICK	BRICK
2" POLYURETHANE INS.	RIGID INSULATION
8" STD. WT. C.M.U.	8" C.M.U.
2' x 4' LAY-IN CLG.	SUSPENDED CEILING
ALUM. CASEMENT WINDOW	ALUM. WINDOW
STAINED OAK CASING	WOOD CASING

——————— BELONGS IN SPECIFICATION
- - - - - - - BELONGS IN ANOTHER DRAWING

Figure 5–2 Material identification on drawings.

provide communication that will allow the project (1) to be constructed by the general contractor and the sub-contractors in a fashion and to the quality intended by the architect and perceived by the owner, as indicated in the contract documents, and (2) to meet building codes and other applicable laws.

The term *contract documents* is accepted as meaning those documents that taken together make up the contract between the owner and the contractor for building construction. These documents are as follows (Fig. 5–3):

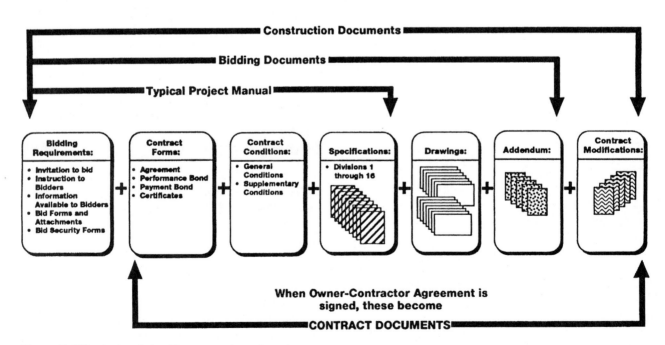

Figure 5–3 The basic relationships among the various documents.

1. Working drawings
2. Specifications
3. Contract conditions (general and supplementary)
4. Addenda (changes made before contract signing)
5. Change orders (changes made after contract signing)
6. Agreement (or the contract between the owner and the contractor)

In projects for which contracts are awarded through the bidding process, additional documents called *bidding requirements* must be added to the contract documents. These include the following:

1. Invitation to bid
2. Instructions to bidders
3. Bid form
4. Information available to bidders

Notice that bidding requirements are not contract documents, and, since they are not, they do not actually make up a part of the documents upon which a contract or an agreement is signed between the owner and the contractor.

In the past, there was a tendency to develop *precedence* of one document over another in case of dispute. Under that scenario, specifications usually had precedence over drawings, assuming that the written word was more correct than graphics. This assumption proved not to be true, and it is recommended that precedence not be incorporated into documents. Discrepancies should be referred to the architect for clarification.

5.2
TYPES OF PROJECTS

There are a number of types of project delivery, depending on the conditions surrounding the project and, to a lesser extent, on the project size. The most common form is the *bid* project, in which the bidding documents are distributed by the architect to several general contractors, called *bidders*. These contractors, along with their subcontractors, estimate the construction cost and bid for a project, with the contract award going to the bidder submitting the lowest-cost bid. This type of contract is used for most government and public projects where bidding is required by law. Many owners prefer this method, as it assures them of the lowest initial construction cost.

Also in widespread use is the *negotiated* type of contract. A negotiated contract eliminates bidding and has the owner select a contractor with whom he or she negotiates the cost and time for construction. When using this type of contract, the contractor uses every effort to control costs and stay within the owner's budget and construction time frame as established before construction begins. Many owners protect themselves from cost over-

runs in negotiated projects by establishing a *guaranteed maximum cost* ceiling. This ceiling assures the owner that the contract amount cannot exceed the given amount unless the nature of the work is changed. A private owner might select a negotiated contract to get a contractor on line who has experience with a particular type of construction or who has expertise in delivery of a project within a short period of time. Naturally, the architect and the contractor work more closely together as a team during pricing and construction.

A variation of the negotiated type contract is the *fast-track* type of delivery process. The procedure is much the same as in a negotiated-type contract, except that the contractor is involved much sooner in the process, advising the owner and the architect of systems, products, costs, and methods during the development of the contract documents. Construction may actually start prior to completion of the working drawings and specifications to shorten the construction time. This factor may be important when an owner has a commitment to a tenant for an early move-in date or when construction financing costs make it advantageous to the owner to gamble in order to reduce this "soft cost." As with negotiated contracts, fast-track contracts usually have guaranteed maximum cost caps. The architect, the contractor, and the owner must work very closely in fast-track construction, as decisions must be made quickly and can require input from all. Since construction may already be underway as documents are developed, it is incumbent on all that the proper decisions be made in a timely manner.

The *design–build* type of project delivery stipulates that one entity, the contractor, has a contract with the owner to perform design as well as construction. This process is opposite to the normal process in which the architect has a separate design contract with the owner. In this case, the contractor has control of the design process and integrates it within his or her estimation, schedule, and construction processes to take total responsibility for design and construction.

5.3
THE PROJECT MANUAL CONCEPT

The term *specifications*, used to describe the book often accompanying the working drawings, is actually a misnomer, as the book called *Specifications* in most cases includes documents, such as bidding requirements and contract conditions, that are not specifications. The American Institute of Architects (A.I.A.) developed the idea of the *Project Manual* in 1964, as the volume that would contain the specifications and any other data conveniently bound into one volume (Fig. 5–3). Although slow to gain acceptance, the term *Project Manual* has now come into wide usage. This definition is even more important with the increased inclusion of such items as door and finish schedules, traditionally designated as drawing items, in the Project Manual.

5.4

WHO WRITES SPECIFICATIONS

Regardless of which form a firm uses to define its specification-writing operation, the functions are essentially the same. The specifier has primary responsibility for producing the Project Manual, including performing the product research and the evaluation necessary to specify the right material to perform the right purpose. The specifier will prepare this text from a master specification that he or she maintains. The specifier must write specification sections from scratch when no master section exists. He or she sees product manufacturers' representatives who visit the office and discuss their products and the specifier's needs as they relate to the projects in the office. The specifier is generally the source for product and industry information for others in the office, and in many cases, he or she handles the field problems. The specifier is responsible for seeing that information gained is incorporated back into the system. The specifications may be written by one of several people.

In small architectural offices, *firm principals*, who have great experience with and appreciation for the liabilities of poorly written specifications, may do the specifying. In others, *project architects* and *construction administration personnel* who have had experience with materials and construction frequently compile the specifications.

In larger architectural offices, designated *specification writers* or *specifiers* often prepare specifications and related documents. They are registered architects or architectural personnel who have extensive experience both in material evaluation and selection and in-field applications and problems. In addition, specifiers usually have acquired an ability to write using correct English grammar and agreement and to use accepted words, spellings, and abbreviations consistently within established office policy.

Many multioffice firms maintain a *central specification department* in the home office, where specifications for projects the world over are prepared from the office's master specification system. Other firms prefer to keep specification personnel in various offices where they can be more conversant with local conditions, materials, and installations. At this time, there seems to be no clear-cut advantage to either system. Increasingly, specifiers are being assisted by office librarians, whose job it is to keep up with the building product catalogs and industry standards that are delivered to the office by mail and by manufacturers' representatives. It is virtually impossible for one person with several duties to be successful in maintaining a reference library used by an entire office.

In many firms, both large and small, the task of preparing project specifications from the firm's master system is the responsibility of the project architect. The master system is maintained by an in-house specification coordinator, who in a larger office performs the duties of the specifier but who leaves the preparation of the actual specification to the person who knows the most about the project—the project architect. This approach has grown greatly with the proliferation of commercially available master specification text and the personal computer.

A *specification consultant* specializes in the preparation of specifications and related documents for a number of architectural firms, while maintaining his or her independence as an outside consultant. The consultant's service makes expertly prepared specifications and related documents available to small- and medium-size firms so that these firms do not incur the cost of maintaining a full-time specification department. The specifier's expertise in material evaluation and selection, as well as knowledge of contract forms, makes him or her a valuable asset to firms that do not have or want in-house experience. Many specification consultants are members of the organization Specification Consultants in Independent Practice (S.C.I.P.), which deals with the particular problems and concerns of the consultant.

The correct preparation of construction documents is necessary in order to run economical and trouble-free projects. The construction industry today prefers that the person preparing the project specifications have demonstrated a minimum level of competency in the area of specification writing. The primary vehicles for demonstrating this competency are the certification exams sponsored by the Construction Specifications Institute (C.S.I.). The entry-level exam is the CDT (Certified Document Technician), and a person must pass this test before taking the advanced-level exam, the CCS (Certified Construction Specifier). C.S.I. also sponsors two additional certification programs: CCPR (Certified Construction Product Representative) and CCCA (Certified Construction Contract Administrator).

5.5

SPECIFICATION MATERIAL SOURCES

To write a completely new set of specifications for each job would be unnecessarily time-consuming. Instead, specifiers rely on various sources for reference material and standard specifications from which they can compile a set for each new job. They rely heavily on specifications that have repeatedly proved satisfactory in the past. Some specs may have to be modified to fit the conditions of a given job; many can be used word for word. Master specifications text, such as A.I.A.'s *Masterspec®*, A.I.A.'s *SPECSystem™*, and C.S.I.'s *Spec-Text®*, are often used to write new sections. These master systems contain guide specifications for many materials, allowing the specifier the luxury of editing out unnecessary text rather than generating new information each time. Master specifications also incorporate correct specification language and format for ease of specification preparation.

Most new specification sections are generated from master systems. Listed below are the major sources from which specification material is available:

- City and national codes and ordinances
- Manufacturers' catalogs (*Sweet's Catalog File, Man-U-Spec, Spec-data*)
- Manufacturers' industry associations (Architectural Woodworking Institute, American Plywood Association, Door and Hardware Institute, Tile Council of America)
- National standards organizations (American National Standards Institute, National Institute of Building Sciences)
- Testing societies (American Society for Testing and Materials, Underwriters Laboratories)
- Master specifications (*Masterspec®, SPECSystem™, Spec-Text®*)
- Individual files of previously written specifications
- Books on specifications
- Federal specifications (*Specs-In-Tact*, G.S.A., N.A.S.A., N.A.F.V.A.C.)
- Magazines and publications (*Construction Specifier, Architecture, Architectural Record*)

Not only must the specifier be familiar with construction methods, new materials, and building techniques, but he or she must also be able to accumulate reference material and organize it for easy access when it is needed.

5.6
SPECIFICATION ARRANGEMENT

The Construction Specifications Institute (C.S.I.) has for a number of years engaged in a program of standardizing specification format. After questioning its members, the institute concluded that a universal need existed for more uniformity in format arrangement and that a consistent national format would prove beneficial not only to the writers of specifications, but also to the contractors and material suppliers as well. After evaluating the various comments, the institute has compiled a format that provides the advantages of standardization yet has sufficient flexibility to allow writers throughout the country enough latitude in expression to accommodate local codes and trade practice variations. Only the arrangement in the format is restrictive, so that a set of specifications, like the alphabet or a numbering system, will be universally useful because of its consistency. The benefits of the format will be realized mainly from its

widespread usage. Although nearly every set of specifications varies in content because of variations in circumstance, it has been found that arrangement of content can be identical.

The C.S.I. format consists of the following:

- A universal numbering system applicable to all possible items of work
- Breakdowns for each technical item and group of related items
- A three-part designation for each technical item
- A suggested page layout

C.S.I. breaks down construction into a group of *sections*, where each section is an item of work represented by a five-digit number. This breakdown does not presume that the contractor will subcontract with regard to the section since the contractor has control over and charge of the construction, although the breakdown is so reasonable that in many cases this is possible. Each section can be *broadscope*, *mediumscope*, or *narrowscope* in nature, depending on how complex the project is and what the specifier chooses to include (Fig. 5–4). An example is a section for acoustical ceilings. As a broadscope section, the section entitled "Acoustical Ceilings" might include several types of lay-in ceiling panels, a concealed-grid acoustical ceiling system, and metal suspension systems for all. In a mediumscope section, the specifier might specify only the lay-in ceiling panels and the related metal

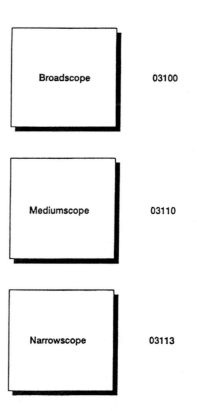

Figure 5–4 Levels of specifications detail.

suspension system in a section entitled "Lay-in Acoustical Ceiling Systems." Another mediumscope section would specify the concealed-grid system. Finally, a narrowscope section might be limited to only the metal suspension systems, entitled "Ceiling Suspension Systems," assuming that related narrowscope sections would be written for the acoustical panels themselves.

The C.S.I. format groups sections of like construction into *divisions*. This format is often referred to as the *16-division format* since there are 16 static divisions. Since these divisions are always the same, any person familiar with this format can easily find his or her way through the Project Manual. In the table of contents, divisions that are not applicable to the project in question are simply designated as "Not Used."

The specification user is further aided by the breakdown of each section into three *parts*. The three-part format locates data within each section with regard to its basic relationships:

- **Part 1: General** Those items relating in general to an item, such as shop drawing requirements and delivery procedures.
- **Part 2: Products** Relates to the material itself, including mixing and fabrication.
- **Part 3: Execution** Relates to the installation of the material.

Breakdown of the section into these parts provides a skeleton for the specifier, thus making it simpler to prepare the specification in a consistent manner. It also makes it easy for the user to find exactly what he or she is looking for without laboriously reading the entire section. See Fig. 5–5 for suggestions of article titles within the parts.

C.S.I. further simplifies the use of the section by using the *page format*. This suggested layout provides article, paragraph, and subparagraph numbering; spacing, tabs and margins; and other similar data necessary to create the most readable text.

The five-digit numbering system unifies the 16-division, three-part format. Under this system, broadscope and many mediumscope section titles are given static numbers. The first two digits represent the division, 1 through 16. The other three digits represent a somewhat arbitrary sequence of sections; by being organized into standard order, the sequencing promotes standardization. Creation of numbers for narrowscope sections rests with the specifier. The master list of titles and numbers is published by C.S.I. in conjunction with Construction Specifications Canada (C.S.C.) in *Masterformat*. See Fig. 5–6 for a list of divisions and broadscope section titles with appropriate five-digit numbers. *Masterformat* is available individually or as a part of the C.S.I. *Manual of Practice*, which contains a great deal more information regarding specification preparation and use than can be included in this text. It is recommended that the C.S.I. *Manual of Practice* be used by those having a need for greater detail.

ARTICLE TITLES BY PART

Part 1 GENERAL

1.01 SUMMARY
  A. Section includes.
  B. Products furnished but not installed under this section.
  C. Products installed but not furnished under this section.
  D. Related sections.
  E. Allowances.
  F. Unit prices.
  G. Alternates.
1.02 REFERENCES
1.03 DEFINITIONS
1.04 SYSTEM DESCRIPTION
  A. Design requirements.
  B. Performance requirements.
1.05 SUBMITTALS
  A. Product data, shop drawings, and samples.
  B. Quality control submittals.
  C. Design data, test reports, certificates, manufacturer's instructions, field reports.
  D. Contract closeout submittals.
  E. Project record documents, operation and maintenance data, warranty.
1.06 QUALITY ASSURANCE
  A. Qualifications.
  B. Regulatory requirements.
  C. Certifications.
  D. Field samples.
  E. Mock-ups.
  F. Preinstallation conference.
1.07 DELIVERY, STORAGE, AND HANDLING
  A. Packing and shipping.
  B. Acceptance at site.
  C. Storage and protection.
1.08 PROJECT/SITE CONDITIONS
  A. Environmental requirements.
  B. Existing conditions.
  C. Field measurements.
1.09 SCHEDULING AND SEQUENCING
1.10 WARRANTY
  A. Special warranty.
1.11 MAINTENANCE
  A. Maintenance service.
  B. Extra materials.

PART 2 PRODUCTS

2.01 MANUFACTURERS
2.02 MATERIALS
2.03 MANUFACTURED UNITS
2.04 EQUIPMENT
2.05 COMPONENT
2.06 ACCESSORIES
2.07 MIXES
2.08 FABRICATION
  A. Shop assembly.
  B. Shop/factory finishing.
  C. Tolerances.
2.09 SOURCE QUALITY CONTROL
  A. Tests, inspections.
  B. Verification of performance.

PART 3 EXECUTION

3.01 EXAMINATION
  A. Verification of conditions.
3.02 PREPARATION
  A. Protection.
  B. Surface protection.
3.03 ERECTION/INSTALLATION/APPLICATION
  A. Special techniques.
  B. Interface with other products.
  C. Tolerances.
3.04 FIELD QUALITY CONTROL
  A. Manufacturer's field service.
3.05 ADJUSTING/CLEANING
3.06 DEMONSTRATING
3.07 PROTECTION
3.08 SCHEDULES

Figure 5–5 Three-part format.

THE C.S.I. FIVE-DIGIT BROADSCOPE FORMAT

BIDDING REQUIREMENTS, CONTRACT FORMS, AND CONDITIONS OF THE CONTRACT

00010	PREBID INFORMATION
00100	INSTRUCTIONS TO BIDDERS
00200	INFORMATION AVAILABLE TO BIDDERS
00300	BID FORMS
00400	SUPPLEMENTS TO BID FORMS
00500	AGREEMENT FORMS
00600	BONDS AND CERTIFICATES
00700	GENERAL CONDITIONS
00800	SUPPLEMENTARY CONDITIONS
00900	ADDENDA

Note: The items listed above are not specification sections and are referred to as "Documents" rather than "Sections" in the Master List of Section Titles, Numbers, and Broadscope Section Explanations.

SPECIFICATIONS

DIVISION 1—GENERAL REQUIREMENTS

01010	SUMMARY OF WORK
01020	ALLOWANCES
01025	MEASUREMENT AND PAYMENT
01030	ALTERNATES/ALTERNATIVES
01035	MODIFICATION PROCEDURES
01040	COORDINATION
01050	FIELD ENGINEERING
01060	REGULATORY REQUIREMENTS
01070	IDENTIFICATION SYSTEMS
01090	REFERENCES
01100	SPECIAL PROJECT PROCEDURES
01200	PROJECT MEETINGS
01300	SUBMITTALS
01400	QUALITY CONTROL
01500	CONSTRUCTION FACILITIES AND TEMPORARY CONTROLS
01600	MATERIAL AND EQUIPMENT
01650	FACILITY STARTUP/COMMISSIONING
01700	CONTRACT CLOSEOUT
01800	MAINTENANCE

DIVISION 2—SITEWORK

02010	SUBSURFACE INVESTIGATION
02050	DEMOLITION
02100	SITE PREPARATION
02140	DEWATERING
02150	SHORING AND UNDERPINNING
02160	EXCAVATION SUPPORT SYSTEMS
02170	COFFERDAMS
02200	EARTHWORK
02300	TUNNELING
02350	PILES AND CAISSONS
02450	RAILROAD WORK
02480	MARINE WORK
02500	PAVING AND SURFACING
02600	UTILITY PIPING MATERIALS
02660	WATER DISTRIBUTION
02680	FUEL AND STEAM DISTRIBUTION
02700	SEWERAGE AND DRAINAGE
02760	RESTORATION OF UNDERGROUND PIPE
02770	PONDS AND RESERVOIRS
02780	POWER AND COMMUNICATIONS
02800	SITE IMPROVEMENTS
02900	LANDSCAPING

DIVISION 3—CONCRETE

03100	CONCRETE FORMWORK
03200	CONCRETE REINFORCEMENT
03250	CONCRETE ACCESSORIES
03300	CAST-IN-PLACE CONCRETE
03370	CONCRETE CURING
03400	PRECAST CONCRETE
03500	CEMENTITIOUS DECKS AND TOPPINS
03600	GROUT
03700	CONCRETE RESTORATION AND CLEANING
03800	MASS CONCRETE

DIVISION 4—MASONRY

04100	MORTAR AND MASONRY GROUT
04150	MASONRY ACCESSORIES
04200	UNIT MASONRY
04400	STONE
04500	MASONRY RESTORATION AND CLEANING
04550	REFRACTORIES
04600	CORROSION RESISTANT MASONRY
04700	SIMULATED MASONRY

DIVISION 5—METALS

05010	METAL MATERIALS
05030	METAL COATINGS
05050	METAL FASTENING
05100	STRUCTURAL METAL FRAMING
05200	METAL JOISTS
05300	METAL DECKING
05400	COLD FORMED METAL FRAMING
05500	METAL FABRICATIONS
05580	SHEET METAL FABRICATIONS
05700	ORNAMENT METAL
05800	EXPANSION CONTROL
05900	HYDRAULIC STRUCTURES

DIVISION 6—WOOD AND PLASTICS

06050	FASTENERS AND ADHESIVES
06100	ROUGH CARPENTRY
06130	HEAVY TIMBER CONSTRUCTION
06150	WOOD AND METAL SYSTEMS
06170	PREFABRICATED STRUCTURAL WOOD
06200	FINISH CARPENTRY
06300	WOOD TREATMENT
06400	ARCHITECTURAL WOODWORK
06500	STRUCTURAL PLASTICS
06600	PLASTIC FABRICATIONS
06650	SOLID POLYMER FABRICATIONS

DIVISION 7—THERMAL AND MOISTURE PROTECTION

07100	WATERPROOFING
07150	DAMPPROOFING
07180	WATER REPELLENTS
07190	VAPOR RETARDERS
07195	AIR BARRIERS
07200	INSULATION
07240	EXTERIOR INSULATION AND FINISH SYSTEMS
07250	FIREPROOFING
07270	FIRESTOPPING
07300	SHINGLES AND ROOFING TILES
07400	MANUFACTURED ROOFING AND SIDING
07480	EXTERIOR WALL ASSEMBLIES
07500	MEMBRANE ROOFING
07570	TRAFFIC COATINGS
07600	FLASHING AND SHEET METAL
07700	ROOF SPECIALTIES AND ACCESSORIES
07800	SKYLIGHTS
07900	JOINT SEALERS

DIVISION 8—DOORS AND WINDOWS

08100	METAL DOORS AND FRAMES
08200	WOOD AND PLASTIC DOORS
08250	DOOR OPENING ASSEMBLIES
08300	SPECIAL DOORS
08400	ENTRANCES AND STOREFRONTS
08500	METAL WINDOWS
08600	WOOD AND PLASTIC WINDOWS
08650	SPECIAL WINDOWS
08700	HARDWARE
08800	GLAZING
08900	GLAZED CURTAIN WALLS

DIVISION 9—FINISHES

09100	METAL SUPPORT SYSTEMS
09200	LATH AND PLASTER
09250	GYPSUM BOARD
09300	TILE
09400	TERRAZZO
09450	STONE FACING
09500	ACOUSTICAL TREATMENT
09540	SPECIAL WALL SURFACES
09545	SPECIAL CEILING SURFACES
09550	WOOD FLOORING
09600	STONE FLOORING
09630	UNIT MASONRY FLOORING
09650	RESILENT FLOORING
09680	CARPETING
09700	SPECIAL FLOORING
09780	FLOOR TREATMENT
09800	SPECIAL COATINGS
09900	PAINTING
09950	WALL COVERINGS

DIVISION 10—SPECIALTIES

10100	VISUAL DISPLAY BOARDS
10150	COMPARTMENTS AND CUBICLES
10200	LOUVERS AND VENTS
10240	GRILLES AND SCREENS
10250	SERVICE WALL SYSTEMS
10260	WALL AND CORNER GUARDS
10270	ACCESS FLOORING
10290	PEST CONTROL
10300	FIREPLACES AND STOVES
10340	MANUFACTURED EXTERIOR SPECIALITIES
10350	FLAGPOLES
10400	IDENTIFYING DEVICES
10450	PEDESTRIAN CONTROL DEVICES
10500	LOCKERS
10520	FIRE PROTECTION SPECIALTIES
10530	PROTECTIVE COVERS
10550	POSTAL SPECIALTIES
10600	PARTITIONS
10650	OPERABLE PARTITIONS
10670	STORAGE SHELVING
10700	EXTERIOR PROTECTION DEVICES FOR OPENINGS
10750	TELEPHONE SPECIALTIES
10800	TOILET AND BATH ACCESSORIES
10880	SCALES
10900	WARDROBE AND CLOSET SPECIALTIES

DIVISION 11—EQUIPMENT

11010	MAINTENANCE EQUIPMENT
11020	SECURITY AND VAULT EQUIPMENT
11030	TELLER AND SERVICE EQUIPMENT
11040	ECCLESIASTICAL EQUIPMENT
11050	LIBRARY EQUIPMENT
11060	THEATER AND STAGE EQUIPMENT
11070	INSTRUMENTAL EQUIPMENT
11080	REGISTRATION EQUIPMENT
11090	CHECKROOM EQUIPMENT
11100	MERCANTILE EQUIPMENT
11110	COMMERCIAL LAUNDRY AND DRY CLEANING EQUIPMENT
11120	VENDING EQUIPMENT
11130	AUDIO-VISUAL EQUIPMENT
11140	VEHICLE SERVICE EQUIPMENT
11150	PARKING CONTROL EQUIPMENT
11160	LOADING DOCK EQUIPMENT
11170	SOLID WASTE HANDLING EQUIPMENT
11190	DETENTION EQUIPMENT
11200	WATER SUPPLY AND TREATMENT EQUIPMENT
11280	HYDRAULIC GATES AND VALVES
11300	FLUID WASTE TREATMENT AND DISPOSAL EQUIPMENT
11400	FOOD SERVICE EQUIPMENT
11450	RESIDENTIAL EQUIPMENT
11460	UNIT KITCHENS
11470	DARKROOM EQUIPMENT
11480	ATHLETIC, RECREATIONAL, AND THERAPEUTIC EQUIPMENT
11500	INDUSTRIAL AND PROCESS EQUIPMENT
11600	LABORATORY EQUIPMENT
11650	PLANETARIUM EQUIPMENT
11660	OBSERVATORY EQUIPMENT
11680	OFFICE EQUIPMENT
11700	MEDICAL EQUIPMENT
11780	MORTUARY EQUIPMENT
11850	NAVIGATION EQUIPMENT
11870	AGRICULTURAL EQUIPMENT

DIVISION 12—FURNISHINGS

12050	FABRICS
12100	ARTWORK
12300	MANUFACTURED CASEWORKS
12500	WINDOW TREATMENT
12600	FURNITURE AND ACESSORIES
12670	RUGS AND MATS
12700	MULTIPLE SEATING
12800	INTERIOR PLANTS AND PLANTERS

DIVISION 13—SPECIAL CONSTRUCTION

13010	AIR SUPPORTED STRUCTURES
13020	INTEGRATED ASSEMBLIES
13030	SPECIAL PURPOSE ROOMS
13080	SOUND, VIBRATION, AND SEISMIC CONTROL

Figure 5–6 The C.S.I. five-digit broadscope format.

13090	RADIATION PROTECTION		13900	FIRE SUPPRESSION AND SUPERVISORY SYSTEMS		15500	HEATING, VENTILATING, AND AIR CONDITIONING
13100	NUCLEAR REACTORS		13950	SPECIAL SECURITY CONSTRUCTION		15550	HEAT GENERATION
13120	PRE-ENGINEERED STRUCTURES					15650	REFRIGERATION
13150	AQUATIC FACILITIES					15750	HEAT TRANSFER
13175	ICE RINKS		**DIVISION 14—CONVEYING SYSTEMS**			15850	AIR HANDLING
13180	SITE CONSTRUCTED INCINERATORS		14100	DUMBWAITERS		15880	AIR DISTRIBUTION
13185	KENNELS AND ANIMAL SHELTERS		14200	ELEVATORS		15950	CONTROLS
13200	LIQUID AND GAS STORAGE TANKS		14300	ESCALATORS AND MOVING WALKS		15990	TESTING, ADJUSTING, AND BALANCING
13220	FILTER UNDERDRAINS AND MEDIA		14400	LIFTS			
13230	DIGESTER COVERS AND APPURTENANCES		14500	MATERIAL HANDLING SYSTEMS		**DIVISION 16—ELECTRICAL**	
13240	OXYGENATION SYSTEMS		14600	HOIST AND CRANES		16050	BASIC ELECTRICAL MATERIALS AND METHODS
13260	SLUDGE CONDITIONING SYSTEMS		14700	TURNTABLES		16200	POWER GENERATION-BUILT-UP SYSTEMS
13300	UTILITY CONTROL SYSTEMS		14800	SCAFFOLDING		16300	MEDIUM VOLTAGE DISTRIBUTION
13400	INDUSTRIAL AND PROCESS CONTROL SYSTEMS		14900	TRANSPORTATION SYSTEMS		16400	SERVICE AND DISTRIBUTION
13500	RECORDING INSTRUMENTATION					16500	LIGHTING
13550	TRANSPORTATION CONTROL INSTRUMENTATION		**DIVISION 15—MECHANICAL**			16600	SPECIAL SYSTEMS
13600	SOLAR ENERGY SYSTEMS		15050	BASIC MECHANICAL MATERIALS AND METHODS		16700	COMMUNICATIONS
13700	WIND ENERGY SYSTEMS		15250	MECHANICAL INSULATION		16850	ELECTRICAL RESISTANCE HEATING
13750	COGENERATION SYSTEMS		15300	FIRE PROTECTION		16900	CONTROLS
13800	BUILDING AUTOMATION SYSTEMS		15400	PLUMBING		16950	TESTING

Figure 5–6 (continued)

A sample specification section incorporating the C.S.I. division, section, and page format is shown in Fig. 5–7.

In addition to the format described above, specifiers realize the need for other, shorter formats to accommodate smaller commercial projects and residential projects. Outline specifications are often useful as communication tools for commercial projects and may be all that is necessary to construct simpler projects. A sample outline specification section is shown in Fig. 5–8.

SECTION 07310

SHINGLE ROOFING

PART 1 GENERAL

1.01 SUBMITTALS
   A. Product data: Indicate material specifications and installation instructions.
   B. Samples: Submit full-size samples of shingles in selected color for architect's approval.
1.02 DELIVERY, STORAGE, AND HANDLING
   A. Stack bundles of shingles not more than 3'-0" high. Store roll goods on end.
1.03 QUALITY ASSURANCE
   A. Application standards: Standards of the following as referenced herein:
   1. American Society for Testing and Materials (ASTM).
   2. Underwriters Laboratories, Inc. (UL)

PART 2 PRODUCTS

2.01 SHINGLES
   A. Acceptable product: Celotex Corp. Presidential Shake.
   B. Characteristics:
      1. Type: Heavy-weight asphalt-saturated fiberglass laminate shingles meeting ASTM D3018-82 Type I and UL Class A rating for fire and wind resistance.
      2. Shingles shall be curved, double-laminated tabs, self-sealing, random tab style.
      3. Minimum weight: 365 lb./sq.
      4. Color: As selected by Architect from manufacturer's standard colors.
2.02 ACCESSORY PRODUCTS
   A. Roofing felts: Meeting ASTM D226-87, Type I, #15 felt, asphalt-saturated organic felt, 3'-0" width, unperforated.
   B. Nails: Hot-dipped galvanized, 10 ga. screw threaded shank, 3/8" head, length as required to penetrate roof deck 1" minimum.
   C. Underlayment, starter and ridge shingles: Types furnished by shingle manufacturer for use with specified shingles. Match color of selected shingle.

PART 3 EXECUTION

3.01 APPLICATION
   A. Install felt layer over roof sheathing, lapping each course over lower course 2" minimum horizontally and 4" minimum side laps at end joints. Lap 6" from both sides at ridge.
   B. Secure felt layer to deck with sufficient fasteners to hold in place until shingles are secured.
   C. Apply shingles in straight, even courses, parallel to eave and ridge line, with four nails per shingle; nail heads concealed. Drive nails tight without cutting into shingles.
   D. Apply a starter course using starter shingles in accordance with manufacturer's product data.
   E. Install shingles with exposure recommended by manufacturer, in regular pattern, in accordance with shingle manufacturer's product data.
   F. Construct ridges using two layers of ridge shingles.
   G. Furnish two extra squares of roofing shingles for Owner's maintenance use. Store where directed.

END OF SECTION

Smith Residence   07310-1
Atlanta, GA
October 1, 1992

Figure 5–7 Typical specification section.

DIVISION 7-THERMAL AND MOISTURE PROTECTION

Section 07310—Shingle Roofing

1. General requirements: Submit product data and samples for shingles. Provide 30-year warranty.
2. Materials: Fiberglass shingles shall be Certainteed Hallmark Shangle or similar by Celotex, Elk, or Tamco. Shingles shall be minimum 300 lb./sq weight in color selected by Architect from manufacturer's standard colors. Provide roofing felt and roofing nails.
3. Execution: Install shingle roofing in accorance with manufacturer's product data, in straight, even courses, parallel to eaves. Install one layer of 15# felt, shingle fashion over sheathing prior to shingle application. Attach each shingle with three roofing nails.

Smith Residence   07310-1
Atlanta, GA
January 15, 1991

Figure 5–8 Typical outline specification.

DIVISION I: GENERAL REQUIREMENTS

In examining the breakdown of the 16 divisions, note that all divisions except division 1 relate to the construction itself. Division 1, General Requirements, applies to all other divisions and acts as a bridge between the technical sections and other bidding and contract documents. Division 1 sections relate to administrative and procedural requirements and temporary facilities. Actual contract requirements might be specified by the agreement or contract conditions, but the rules for implementing would be specified in division 1 (Fig. 5–9).

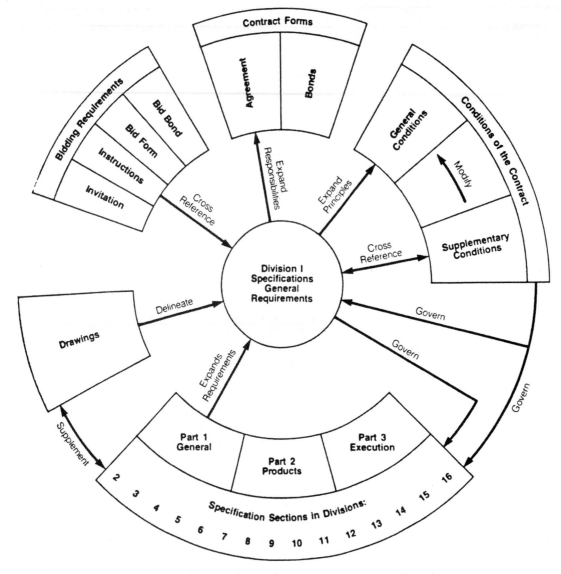

Figure 5–9 Division 1 relationship to other documents.

5.8

GENERAL POINTS FOR PREPARING SPECIFICATIONS

Keep the following points in mind when writing specifications:

1. Use simple, direct language and accepted terminology, rather than abstract legal terminology.
2. Use brief sentences requiring only simple punctuation.
3. Specify standard items and alternates where possible, in the interest of economy, without sacrificing quality.
4. Avoid repetition; use cross-references if they apply and seem logical.

5. Avoid specifications that are impossible for the contractor to carry out; be fair in designating responsibility.
6. Avoid including specifications that are not to be part of the construction.
7. Clarify all terms that may be subject to more than one interpretation.
8. Be consistent in the use of terms, abbreviations, and format and in the arrangement of material.
9. Specify numbers, names, and descriptions of materials from the *latest editions* of manufacturers' catalogs.
10. Capitalize the following: major parties to the contract, such as Contractor, Owner, Designer, Architect; the contract documents, such as Specifications, Working Drawings, Contract, Supplementary Conditions; specific rooms within

the building, such as Kitchen, Living Room, Office; grade of materials, such as No. 1 Douglas Fir, Clear Heart Redwood, FAS White Oak; and, of course, all proper names.

11. Differentiate between "shall" and "will"—"The Contractor shall. . ."; "The Owner or Architect will. . . ."

12. Avoid the term *a workmanlike job* or similarly vague phrases; rather, describe the quality of workmanship or the exact requirements expected.

13. Use accepted standards when specifying quality of materials or workmanship required, such as "Lightweight concrete masonry units: ASTM C-90-85; Grade N, Type 1."

14. Number all pages within a section consecutively, and include a table of contents for each section.

15. Keep in mind that bidders and subcontractors of different trades will have to use the specifications to look up information in their respective areas; remember that the information dealing with their work should be stated in the logical section and not hidden throughout the various sections.

5.9

METHODS OF SPECIFYING

One of the first things a specifier must do when writing a master specification section or an individual project section from scratch is to decide what method he or she will use to communicate with the contractor. Four basic types of specifications can be prepared, and most items can be specified by one or more methods.

The first and easiest method of specifying is the *proprietary specification*, which basically names the manufacturers or products acceptable to the architect. A proprietary specification may be written as a *closed* proprietary specification, in which only one product is acceptable and the contractor is so advised by the nature of the specification. The specification may also be written as an *open* proprietary section, in which multiple manufacturers or products are named or alternatives solicited. Naturally, an open proprietary specification results in more competition among vendors and may result in a lower installed price. However, an open proprietary specification may not be applicable if one specific product is desired.

An example of a closed proprietary specification is one for brick for an addition to an existing building, where the brick must match existing brick. Only one product is desired. By comparison, an open proprietary specification might be applicable for building sealants when multiple products with the same characteristics can be specified. However, the specifier should be sure that the product specified is equivalent to avoid an "apples and oranges" specification.

A word of caution about proprietary specifications is due with regard to use of the phrase "or equal." Frequently used in the past to convey the concept that the architect would consider products other than those specified, which he or she considered "equal" in quality, the term is unclear and leads to disagreement as to what is equal and in whose eyes. Thankfully, the use of the "or equal" clause has almost disappeared from specification writing and is most often used by persons unwilling to do the research and product evaluation necessary to specify the desired products.

The second method of specifying is the *descriptive specification*, which describes the product in detail without providing the product name. Descriptive specifications can be used when it is not desirable to specify a particular product. Some government agencies require that specifications be written in descriptive form to allow the greatest competition among product manufacturers. Descriptive specifications are more difficult to write than proprietary ones since the specifier must indicate all product characteristics for which he or she has concern in the specification.

A third type of specification in prevalent use is the *reference standard*. This standard simply references an accepted industry standard as the basis for the specification and is often used to specify generic materials such as portland cement and clear glass. In using a reference standard, the specifier should have a copy of that standard; should know what is required by the standard, including choices that may be contained therein; and should enforce those requirements for all suppliers.

A fourth type of specification is the *performance specification*. The performance specification gives the greatest leeway to the contractor because it allows him or her to furnish any product that meets the performance criteria specified. It is the most difficult for the specifier to prepare since he or she must anticipate all products and systems that could be used and must specify only those characteristics he or she desires—specifically those related to test results. A performance specification must provide sufficient data to ensure that product characteristics can be demonstrated. Performance specifications have their greatest use in specifying complex systems, such as a curtain wall, which can be easily custom designed for a certain application and engineered to perform to required levels, say, for wind loading and air infiltration. Testing for compliance is often required in performance specifications.

Most product specifications actually end up using a combination of methods to convey the architect's intent. A specification for brick masonry would use a proprietary specification to name the product or products selected by the architect; a descriptive specification to specify size and color; and a reference standard to specify the ASTM standard, grade, and type required.

ALLOWANCES, ALTERNATES, AND UNIT PRICES

No discussion of specification types is complete without mentioning three methods that the architect may need to use to delay making a product selection during bidding or early construction: (1) allowances, (2) unit prices, and (3) alternates.

An *allowance* is defined as follows:

1. an amount of money (a *cash allowance*) or a quantity of material (a *quantity allowance*) for which the quantity can be determined from the actual drawings but for which a decision as to what material to use has not been reached; or
2. a *lump sum* for a system that will be required but that has not been designed at the time bids are solicited.

An example of a cash allowance is one for a building's carpet, where an allowance of *X* dollars per square yard is specified. The quantity required can be determined from the working drawings. Or there might be a lump-sum cash allowance established for landscaping not yet designed. A quantity allowance could be used for tenant work, where historically a certain number of doors or linear footage of wall might be anticipated, but the space has not yet been designed.

Unlike allowances, *unit prices* are prices solicited from the contractor per unit of material when the system is defined but quantity is not. Requests for unit prices are often included in the bid form for such items as rock removal, where the soils report indicates the presence of rock to be removed, but the quantity is unknown until the rock is exposed.

Alternates are often included in the architect's bidding documents in order to obtain a price for an alternative system or material from the contractor. They stem from the fact that the architect does not do detailed estimates and depends on the contractor's estimating ability to determine the affordability of some items. The architect is in effect asking, "How much more (or how much less) does *X* cost than *Y*?" The inclusion of alternatives in bids demonstrates that the architect may be willing to compromise if the budget is exceeded. Alternates may also be suggested by the contractor, especially in negotiated contracts, as a means of cost reduction. Such suggestions should usually be *value engineering* items, meaning that systems or products of equivalent or better value can be substituted for less or the same cost. Value engineering is an important concept best practiced by someone experienced in that discipline.

PRODUCT EVALUATION

Perhaps the most important part of specification writing is proper product evaluation, or determining the applicability of a particular system or product. Product evaluation takes into consideration items such as esthetics, acoustics, fire safety, personal safety, stain resistance, interface, and replaceability. Other considerations include the desires of the owner, the manufacturer's reputation, initial and maintenance cost, and long-term maintenance and service requirements.

MASTER SPECIFICATIONS

As already discussed, master specification systems are one source of information for specifiers. Specification writing is not about creating original text; it is about using standardized text, combined with product and project knowledge, to communicate clearly, completely, concisely, and correctly with others who use the information created by the specifier. The use of master specification systems is not new. What is relatively new is the ability, through the personal computer, to utilize and manipulate master systems to a greater extent than ever before.

Many architectural firms maintain master systems of their own. These systems represent the attitudes of the firm principals, define the level of quality normally desired by that firm, and contain master specifications for systems and products normally specified by that firm. For example, a firm that does low-rise hospital work would need a highly refined specification for hydraulic, hospital elevators, but it probably would not spend the time to develop a master section for gearless elevators.

Many other firms, particularly smaller firms and firms doing a wide variety of work, normally rely on one of the several commercial master specification systems available. The A.I.A.'s *Masterspec*® and SPECSystem™ and C.S.I.'s *Spec-Text*® are some of the most successful. All are available in hard-copy form as well as on disks. These systems contain master sections for a myriad of products and are available for those who perform only interior design or for those who practice mechanical and electrical engineering. Master systems usually come complete with drawing coordination checklists and explanation sheets for those uninitiated in a particular type of construction. The biggest disadvantage of these systems is that by their nature their scope is at least national. Some even try to anticipate construction in other parts of North America and other continents. Their biggest advantage is the uniformity that they bring to construction. In an effort to eliminate the disadvantage, some firms buy these master systems and custom tailor the sections to their own practice.

5.13

TODAY AND TOMORROW

Specification production and reproduction have come a long way in just a few years, due to advances in technology. In the area of production, the norm today is for the specifier to edit his or her master system directly from the computer screen. The commercially available master systems are available in disk form using a number of word processors. The specifier simply loads the master system onto his or her personal computer, and he or she has instant access to the master system, complete with drawing checklist and explanation sheets. The master text itself will contain notes that explain certain articles and paragraphs. Once the specifier has edited the section, he or she can print out a draft copy complete with an audit trail. The audit trail tells what has been deleted or what decisions must be made. After reviewing sections for the entire project, making changes and spelling corrections, and perhaps inserting the current date on every page, the specifier can send the entire Project Manual to print at eight pages per minute on a laser jet printer. The printing can be done in a relatively short time period, eliminating the need to print until very late in document development. Thus, changes can be made until the last minute. The entire Project Manual is printed, complete with the name of the project on every page, and the table of contents is self-generated. The quality of the copy is far better than that previously available by typing.

Now the Project Manual is ready for copying and binding. Most copying is done today using high-speed copiers. The cost for reproduction in this manner has been reduced to the point that only the needed number of copies must be made, as opposed to previous methods in which economy was achieved only through making many copies at the same time. Now, other copies can be economically made later, if needed.

Most offices use an $8\frac{1}{2}'' \times 11''$ page size, with printing on one or two sides as preferred. The C.S.I. page for-mat accommodates either one- or two-sided printing. After copying, the Project Manual copies are bound usually with a heavy stock cover bearing the firm's name or logo. The manner of binding is an individual preference, with several options that a printer can explain. The basic idea in binding text is to use a system that will hold up as the Project Manual is used in the field.

The state of the art in specification preparation technique is the CD-ROM. *SPEC-SEARCH*, developed for C.S.I. by the Data Matic Systems Co., is designed to provide computer-based search and retrieval capabilities for SPEC-DATA® and MANU-SPEC® documents. The program is capable of displaying up to four product specifications simultaneously, enabling users to analyze up to four products at the same time. The program also allows users to copy specifications into a word processor and print or fax them. *SPEC-SEARCH* will work under Windows 95 and Windows 98, although at this time it is not an officially compatible product.

Sweet's CD is an interactive product selection tool available on CD-ROM. Developed by Sweet's Group/McGraw-Hill, Inc., it provides access to over 5500 manufacturers by C.S.I. classification. It is a complete reference to *Sweet's General Building & Renovation Catalog* file.

The National Institute of Building Sciences (N.I.B.S.), a government agency, has a CD-ROM that contains the *Masterspec* and *Spec-In-Tact* master specification systems; many Navy, NASA, and Army Corps of Engineers design and maintenance manuals; and ASTM standards and standards from many other industry associations. This process is continuing, as other manufacturers are providing master specification text as well as drawing details on disks to the design community.

As for future developments in the area of specification writing, as in the area of changes in the way we now design and draw, we cannot imagine the changes that will take place in just a few years. With CADD already in place in many architectural offices, the next step is to integrate specification production so that the first draft of the Project Manual is produced along with the drawings. Toward this end, we will see more sophisticated development of master specification systems.

REVIEW QUESTIONS

1. What qualifications are required of a construction specification writer?

2. Drawings depict the quantity of a certain material. What do specifications depict?

3. List five sources for specification reference material.

4. Why are construction material manufacturers' associations interested in furnishing material to specification writers?

5. Who requires a copy of the specifications? How are these copies usually made?

6. How is the information in the general conditions related to the other technical sections?

7. How do dimensions given in the specifications differ from the dimensions required on the working drawings?

8. Why must requirements in specifications be made fair and just to all parties of the contract?

9. List the three recommended parts of a typical technical section.

10. What are the major advantages in using the five-digit numbering system in spec writing?

11. Name several architectural or construction books that follow the five-digit numbering format.

12. What organization originated the 16-division *uniform* construction specification system?

13. Describe the differences between *broadscope*, *mediumscope*, and *narrowscope*.

14. List and describe the *three-part section* in specification writing.

Computerized Specification Writing

BSD SpecLink®

BSD SpecLink® is an interactive specification system that is meant to be used directly by the design professional. As you choose sections to include in your project and make product selections, SpecLink® includes related text and excludes incompatible options. BSD SpecLink® helps produce project specifications that are better coordinated and more up to date because of its unique relational database with built-in intelligence.

Over 125,000 links in the database make the master "intelligent." As you select paragraphs for your project, links add related text, exclude incompatible options, and highlight choices you may wish to make. All of these links are visible in the Links dialog box, so you can tell exactly why a particular paragraph has been included or excluded. You can add your own links, making your office master as intelligent as you wish.

BSD SpecLink® comes with a Master project configuration. When you create a new project, the first time you use the software the Master project configuration is the foundation upon which you generate the new project. You can subsequently use any project as the foundation for new projects. Editing a project in SpecLink® does not affect the master database. Each project is like an overlay that contains all the changes you make.

In BSD SpecLink® all information about a project, including all the sections in the project, is contained in a single file. Because everything about the project is contained in a single file, global decisions such as page format and choice of units of measure can be made in one place.

The master specification database is divided into folders that correspond to CSI's 16 Divisions (Fig. 1). These main folders are divided into Broadscope Heading folders (Fig. 2), which include sections arrayed in numerical order, using a 5-digit section number and a title based on the 1995 MasterFormat published by

The Construction Specifications Institute (CSI). You access a folder at the Tree Panel of the Project Window by picking it (Fig. 3). Each section is organized consistently using CSI's Three-Part Section Format: PART 1 General; PART 2 Products; and PART 3 Execution (Fig. 4).

The working environment for SpecLink® is more like an electronic spreadsheet than a word processor. Each paragraph is contained within a separate cell and adjacent cells contain additional information about the paragraph. The links connecting paragraphs are analogous to the formulae in a spreadsheet. You select the text you want instead of deleting text you don't want and the selected text is assembled into the final documents and printed. All the master text is available for use on future projects.

To prepare a project specification, you work in one of two areas of the Project Window—the Tree Panel or the Document Panel (Fig. 5). You can create a new project or open an existing one and make modifications to

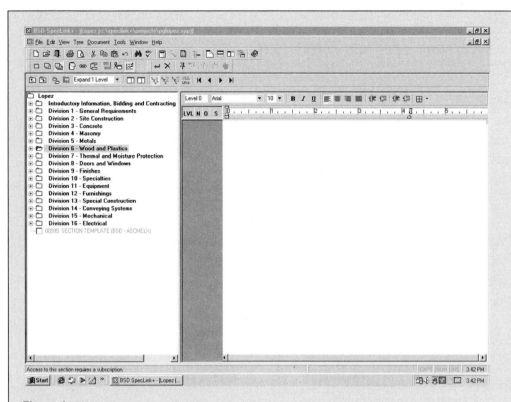

Figure 1 CSI 16 Divisions.

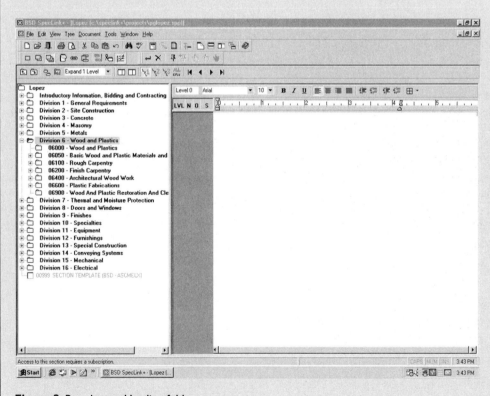

Figure 2 Broadscope Heading folders.

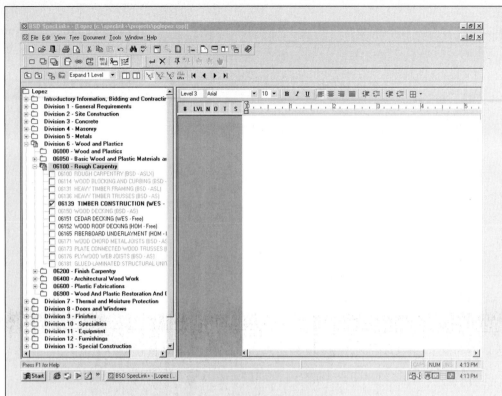

Figure 3 CSI Master Format 5-digit section numbers.

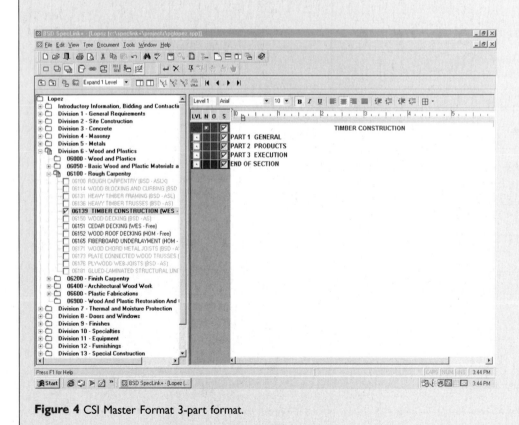

Figure 4 CSI Master Format 3-part format.

it. When you create a new project the Project Window and the Project Summary Information dialog boxes appear (Fig. 6). The Project Summary Information dialog box allows you to establish global settings for your project. Once you complete the Project Summary Information dialog box and choose OK, the dialog box disappears and the Project Window remains with both the Tree Panel and the Document Panel visible (Fig. 1). Here you select the sections to include in your project.

Use the Notes toolbar button to open a small "floating" Notes window that can display a brief description of the section contents and other information about the selected section to determine if you want to use this section in your project (Fig. 7). To open a section, click on its title in the Tree Panel. The section appears in the ad-

jacent Document Panel where you edit the section content. There are various levels of detail available from outline to detailed (Figs. 8A, B, C).

When all the necessary text has been selected or added and all modifications have been made, a section is ready to print. BSD SpecLink® provides the three most commonly used specification formats for use (Figs. 9A, B, C):

CSI style — Format recommended by the CSI Manual of Practice.

Military style — Conforms closely to the format used for U.S. Army Corps of Engineers and NAVFAC specifications in the SPECSINTACT program.

Block style — Basic block format.

Once you have decided on the format for your report, you can print the Specification Sections, a Table of Contents, and Requirement Reports, if you want, which summarize some provisions found in sections.

"BSD SpecLink" means the specification production system that comprises Windows, master specifications database sections that are copyrighted and owned by Building Systems Design, Inc. (BSD) and other entities, documentation and periodic newsletters copyrighted by BSD, and the electronic CD-ROM media through which the database and software are delivered. BSD can be contacted at 1175 Peachtree Street, 100 Colony Square, Suite 1900, Atlanta, GA 30361, or through their Web site—www.bsdsoftlink.com.

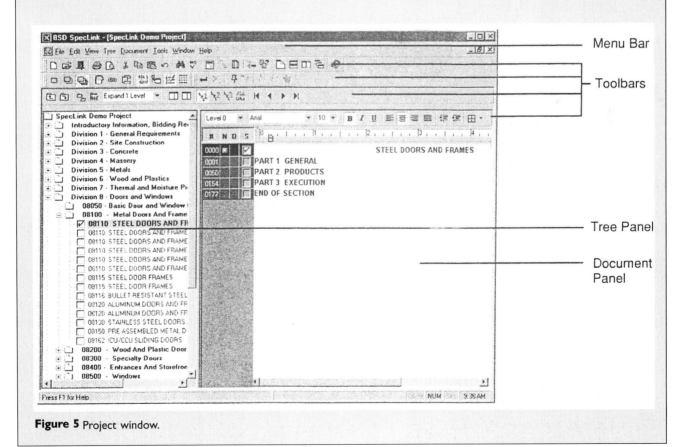

Figure 5 Project window.

Figure 6 Project Summary Information dialog box.

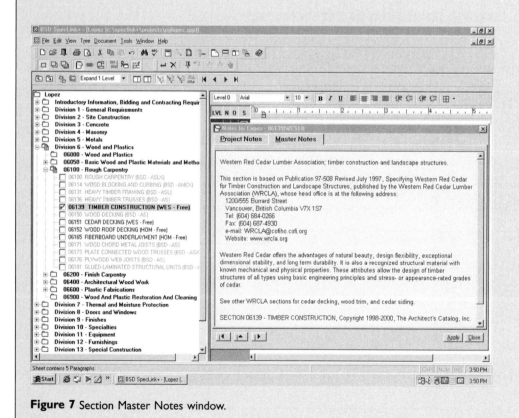

Figure 7 Section Master Notes window.

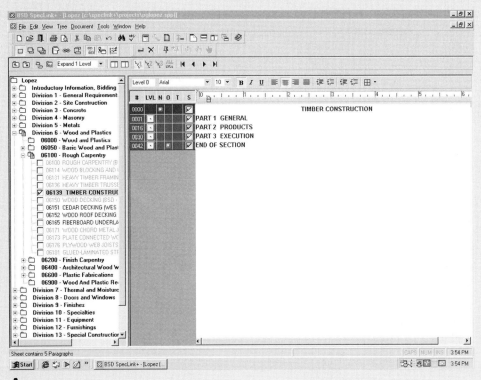

A

Figure 8 A, B, C Detail levels.

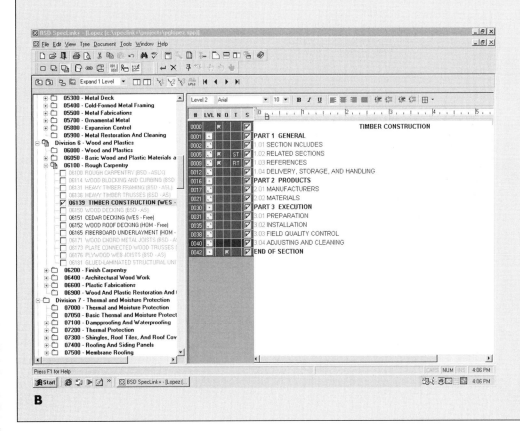

B

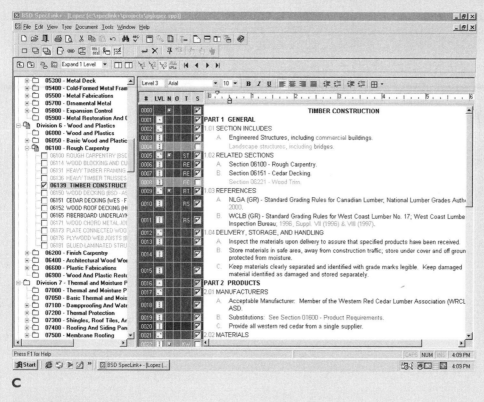

C

Figure 8 A, B, C *(continued)*

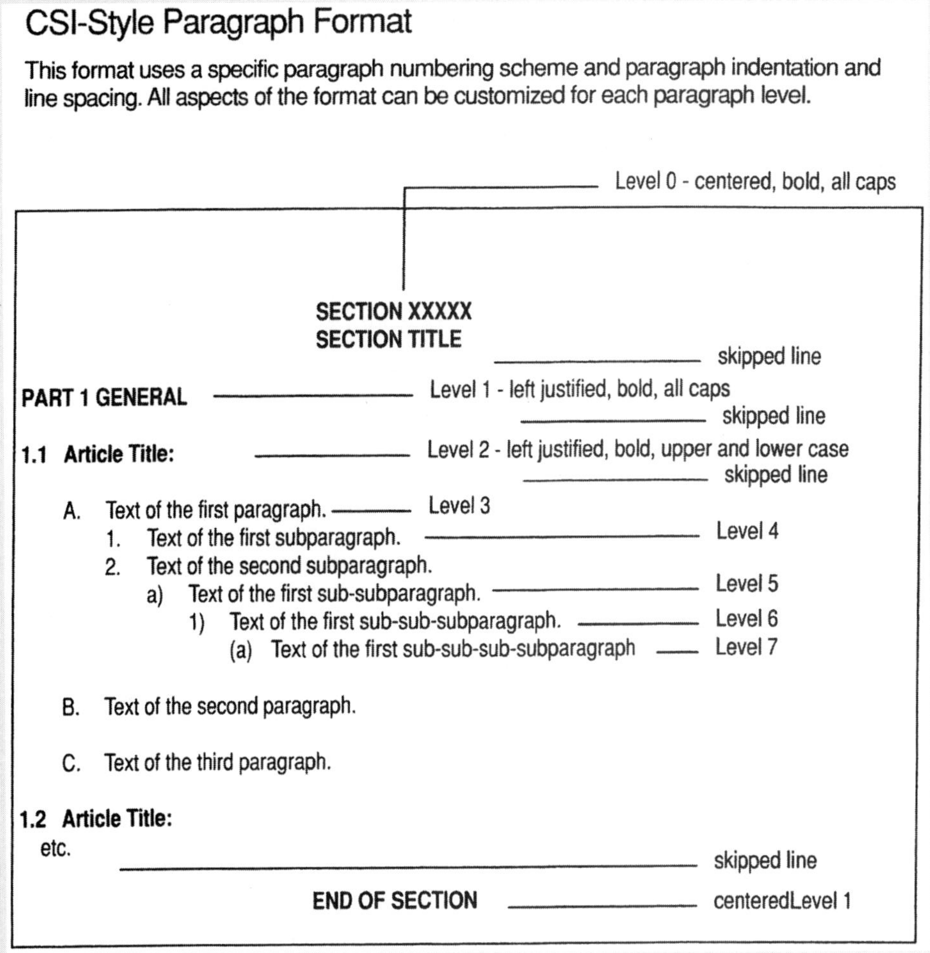

CSI-Style Paragraph Format

This format uses a specific paragraph numbering scheme and paragraph indentation and line spacing. All aspects of the format can be customized for each paragraph level.

Level 0 - centered, bold, all caps

SECTION XXXXX
SECTION TITLE
—————————————— skipped line

PART 1 GENERAL ————— Level 1 - left justified, bold, all caps
—————————————— skipped line

1.1 Article Title: ————— Level 2 - left justified, bold, upper and lower case
—————————————— skipped line

A. Text of the first paragraph. ——— Level 3
1. Text of the first subparagraph. ———————————— Level 4
2. Text of the second subparagraph.
a) Text of the first sub-subparagraph. ——————— Level 5
1) Text of the first sub-sub-subparagraph. ——— Level 6
(a) Text of the first sub-sub-sub-subparagraph —— Level 7

B. Text of the second paragraph.

C. Text of the third paragraph.

1.2 Article Title:
etc. —————————————— skipped line

END OF SECTION ————— centeredLevel 1

A

Figure 9A, B, C Optional specification formats.

Military-Style Paragraph Format

This format uses a specific paragraph numbering scheme and paragraph indentation and line spacing. All aspects of the format can be customized for each paragraph level.

Level 0 - centered, bold, all caps

SECTION TITLE

———————— skipped line

PART 1 GENERAL ———————— Level 1 - left justified, bold, all caps

———————— skipped line

1.1   Article Title: ———————— Level 2 - left justified, upper and lower case

1.1.1   Text of the first paragraph. ——— Level 3 - left justified

     a.   Text of the first subparagraph. ———————— Level 4

     b.   Text of the second subparagraph.

       (1)   Text of the first sub-subparagraph. ———————— Level 5

          (a)   Text of the first sub-sub-subparagraph.———————— Level 6

             (1)   Text of the first sub-sub-sub-subparagraph ——— Level 7

1.1.2   Text of the second paragraph.

1.1.3   Text of the third paragraph.

———————————————————— skipped line

1.2   Article Title:

  etc.

END OF SECTION ——— Level 0 - centered, bold, all caps

Level 2 and 3 numbers always start with the PART number; that is, 1, 2, or 3.

B

Figure 9A, B, C *(continued)*

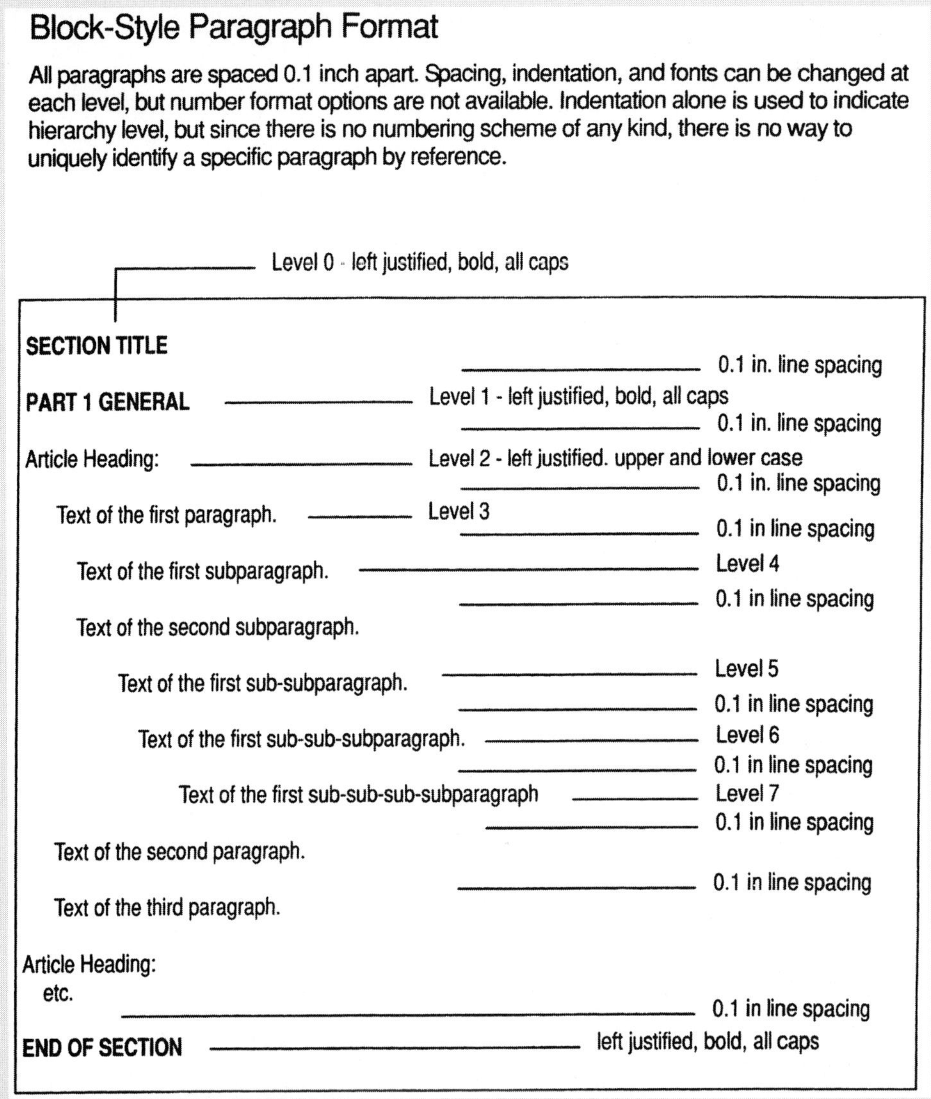

Block-Style Paragraph Format

All paragraphs are spaced 0.1 inch apart. Spacing, indentation, and fonts can be changed at each level, but number format options are not available. Indentation alone is used to indicate hierarchy level, but since there is no numbering scheme of any kind, there is no way to uniquely identify a specific paragraph by reference.

Level 0 - left justified, bold, all caps

SECTION TITLE

0.1 in. line spacing

PART 1 GENERAL ———————— Level 1 - left justified, bold, all caps

0.1 in. line spacing

Article Heading: ———————— Level 2 - left justified. upper and lower case

0.1 in. line spacing

   Text of the first paragraph. ———— Level 3

0.1 in line spacing

    Text of the first subparagraph. ———————— Level 4

0.1 in line spacing

   Text of the second subparagraph.

     Text of the first sub-subparagraph. ———————— Level 5

0.1 in line spacing

      Text of the first sub-sub-subparagraph. ———— Level 6

0.1 in line spacing

       Text of the first sub-sub-sub-subparagraph ———— Level 7

0.1 in line spacing

 Text of the second paragraph.

0.1 in line spacing

 Text of the third paragraph.

Article Heading:
  etc.

0.1 in line spacing

END OF SECTION ———————————— left justified, bold, all caps

C

Figure 9A, B, C *(continued)*

"Our eyes are made to see forms in light;
light and shade reveal these forms . . . "
—*LeCORBUSIER*

Commercial Construction

6

COMMERCIAL BUILDINGS

Commercial buildings, commonly classified as "heavy construction," encompass many types of construction projects. The term is commonly used by those in the construction industry to define not only *commercial* structures but many types of buildings that are not strictly "business ventures" and serve mainly public functions. Schools, churches, monuments, and government buildings fall into this category. As used in this text the term *heavy construction* is intended to include all types of commercial buildings, although others may use the term heavy construction to classify dams, water and sewage works, airports, docks, tunnels, power plants, and large industrial plants.

Because of the necessity to protect concentrations of people within these larger buildings, life-safety, building, and zoning codes are understandably more restrictive and thus require the use of fire-resistive materials such as steel, concrete, and masonry. Architects, engineers, and contractors must also conform to laws pertaining to access of spaces within these structures by the handicapped and to ensure safe construction practices during the building process.

Many commercial buildings are at least several stories high (see Fig. 6-1). This means that environmental factors, earthquake zones, and wind loads cause the components in these buildings to be more complex, as well as larger. To build these structures requires special construction equipment and workers that are highly trained, especially in their ability to read working drawings (see Fig. 6-2). More detailed planning in all phases of construction is necessary to make the finished building functional as well as economical.

Innovative construction products and structural systems such as precast wall components, high-strength steel bolts, prestressed concrete members, tilt-up construction, and composite beams of concrete and steel, to name a few,

have contributed to hold down the escalating cost of construction. Those people associated with commercial construction must have an understanding of these and other similar terms to be able to "read" working drawings.

The complete instructions for the construction of a commercial building consist of two major parts: a set of **working drawings** and a set of written **specifications** to accompany the drawings. Both are important in conveying the complete information. Together, with Bid Forms and Legal Contracts, they constitute what are known as the *Contract Documents*.

ARCHITECTURAL SERVICES

Whereas an owner usually deals primarily with the builder in residential construction, the *architect* or architectural firm is usually the principal contact of the owner in commercial construction and represents the owner's interest during the building process. Although an architect is sometimes involved in residential construction, typical architectural practice is concerned, almost exclusively, with commercial construction.

The architect usually provides *five* basic services for a client (owner). These are defined in AIA (American Institute of Architects) document B 141, the Standard Form of Agreement between Owner and Architect. They are:

1. Schematic Design Phase (Preliminary)
2. Design Development Phase
3. Construction Document Phase
4. Bidding and Negotiation Phase
5. Administration of the Construction Contract

During the discussion of the construction procedure later in this chapter, we will see how these services completely encompass the building process.

Figure 6–1 Downtown Atlanta, Georgia. Commercial buildings are a physical expression of an expanding economy. (Courtesy John Portman and Associates)

Figure 6–2 Construction is one of our major industries requiring accurate communication between designers and builders.

Drawings are the tools the architect uses to convey his or her ideas and, through which, the architect ensures that the finished building is properly constructed and will serve the requirements of the owner. Almost all architects are skilled drafters and must be able to communicate the building instructions to the people involved in a construction project through the various drawings he or she produces.

CONSTRUCTION DRAWINGS

Drawings associated with commercial construction projects may be divided into five categories that are closely associated with their purposes: (1) Sketches, (2) Presentation Drawings, (3) Preliminary Drawings, (4) Working Drawings, and (5) Shop Drawings.

6.3.1 Sketches

When an architect is retained to design a building, he or she must first determine from the owner those items that are important for the function of the building. The architect usually sets these down in the form of a *program*. Sketches are then made to fit ideas to the requirements of the program. Plans, elevations, and some typical details are sketched and submitted to the owner to determine if the architect's solution is compatible with the owner's requirements. Many changes can occur during this schematic design phase until an agreement is reached.

6.3.2 Presentation Drawings

Presentation drawings usually consist of perspective views of a tentative building along with sections and schematic floor plans. The perspective view (see Fig. 6-3), and sometimes even elevation views, are drawn to present, as nearly as possible, the actual appearance of the building, making it possible to view the design as a finished product before committing it to construction. The purpose of these *renderings*, carefully landscaped with shadows and color, is to "promote" the design (see Fig. 6-4). A building must be *sold* before it reaches the working drawing stage; therefore, architectural artists are often employed to prepare colorful and artistic renderings for this purpose. These are drawn with the esthetic characteristics of the building as the predominant consideration. (See Fig. 6-5). If the architect thinks that the project justifies it, a three-dimensional architectural model may be made for presentation to laypeople, who often have difficulty in interpreting architectural plans.

Figure 6–3 Presentation drawing of a multistory building.

LAKESIDE CENTRE BUILDING

Figure 6–4 Perspective drawing of Lakeside Centre Building discussed in Chapter 5. (Courtesy Stevens & Wilkinson, Inc.)

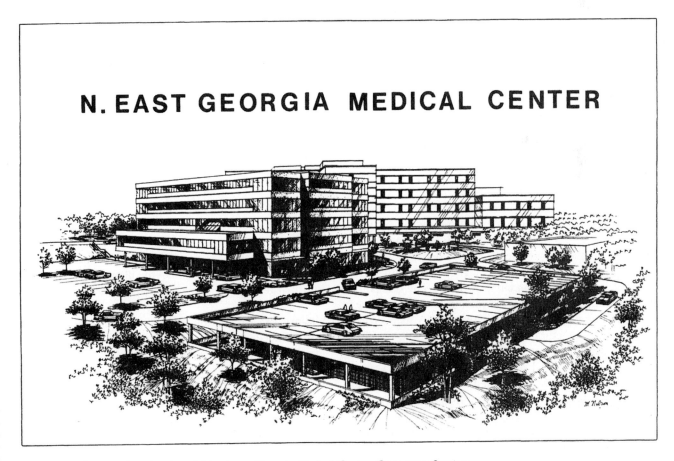

N. EAST GEORGIA MEDICAL CENTER

Figure 6–5 Presentation drawing of Northeast Georgia Medical Center, Outpatient Services Building discussed in Chapter 6. (Courtesy Chegwidden, Dorsey, and Holmes)

6.3.3 Preliminary Drawings

As the name implies, preliminary drawings are the beginning drawings prepared during the early part of the design development phase as a first step toward the preparation of the working drawings. Preliminary drawings are not meant to be used for construction and are usually stamped to indicate this. They are meant merely for exploration of original concepts, functional studies, material selection, preliminary cost estimates, preliminary approval by civil authorities, and as a basis for preparation of the final working drawings.

A large portion of the design work is reflected in the preliminary drawings. Although usually drawn at smaller scales ($\frac{1}{16}'' = 1'-0''$) than working drawings, they include much of the structural, mechanical, and electrical concepts, coordinated with the architectural features, to form a skeleton outline in graphic form. The preliminary architectural plans usually include only a Site Plan, Floor Plans, one or two Elevations, and Typical Wall Sections. The structural plans usually include a Foundation Plan (to show the type of footings), Typical Floor Framing Plans (with estimated member sizes), and a full Cross Section (to show floor heights and wall thicknesses). The architectural and structural preliminaries are used by the mechanical and electrical engineers to determine the best locations for the mechanical and electrical equipment.

Only a few sets of prints are made of the preliminary drawings, and corrections and revisions are commonly recorded only on the prints. *They are of no further use after the working drawings have been prepared.*

6.3.4 Working Drawings

The finished product of the research, thought, and design that an architect puts into a building project is reflected in the set of working drawings. These drawings are the technical directions to the general contractor, in graphic form, showing the size, quantity, location, and relationships of the building's components that make it possible to build the project and make it a functionally successful structure. The drawings are prepared on translucent paper or film (called *tracings*) so that a sufficient number of prints can be made from them. Usually between 10 and 30 sets of prints are necessary for an average job, with even more sets required on larger projects. The time and effort expended during the construction document phase to produce the working drawings constitutes a major part of the total architectural service.

Sheets within the set of working drawings for commercial buildings usually are numbered in a logical sequence. The Site Plans are labeled SP-1, SP-2, etc.; the Architectural Drawings are labeled A-1, A-2, A-3, etc.; the Structural Drawings are labeled S-1, S-2, etc.; the Mechanical Drawings are labeled M-1, M-2, etc.; and the Electrical Drawings are labeled E-1, E-2, etc. An index is usually shown on the title sheet or first sheet to facilitate finding a needed drawing.

A typical set of drawings for a medium-sized building would consist of from 20 to 60 tracings on $24'' \times 36''$, $22'' \times 34''$, or $36'' \times 42''$ sheets and would contain the following types of drawings:

Site Plan: This drawing(s) shows the location of the structure on the property. The location of utilities, bench marks, drainage facilities, driveways, parking lots, and the existing and final contour lines, etc., are shown on one or more drawings.

Floor Plans: A plan view of the foundation, each floor, and the roof is drawn to show the footing locations, location of walls and partitions and sizes and locations of all doors, windows, and other openings (see Fig. 6-6, 6-7, 6-8).

The first step in drawing a plan of this type is to lay out the exterior walls of the building. After the exact widths of the walls are determined, the outline of the plan is blocked in, and all partition walls are lightly drawn without regard for window and door openings. Then the door and window openings are located according to the scheme of the exterior and the traffic flow of the interior. Only construction lines are used up to this point.

The walls are then darkened and refined, window and door symbols are drawn, and minor wall outlines are completed. Manufacturers' literature is consulted before the doors and windows are drawn. Plumbing fixtures are drawn with the use of a template. Minor details are added throughout the plan. Exterior platform ramps and steps are drawn with the help of information from the site plan contour levels. Stair layouts are developed with the proper number of risers and treads between floors. (Codes are consulted for acceptable riser heights and tread widths.) Then door identification is shown, room titles are lettered, and all general callouts are added.

Next, dimensions are inserted in positions where they do not interfere with linework. Notice that, along with important exterior dimensions placed around the periphery of the plan, a continuous line of dimensions is shown through the interior in each direction to locate all partitions accurately.

In some cases, it is advisable to begin a project with a typical wall section rather than the plan. Much of the wall information must be known before the plan can be drawn.

Elevations: Elevation views of each side of the building are needed to indicate the materials required, finish grades, floor and ceiling heights, and general exterior architectural features (see Fig. 6-9, 6-10).

In starting the elevations, the designer first draws the finish floor levels. Then, after establishing the desired ceiling heights, he or she draws the major horizontal lines from information taken from the preliminary section view. Lengths of the elevation view features, however, are projected directly from the plan, as in residential drawings. Windows, offsets, doors, and other features are drawn from preliminary sketches with the help of manufacturers' literature. Where indicated, the trim members are completed, and the finish floor and the roof level are added. To complete the drawing, the grade line, footings, stairs, ramps, railings, material symbols, notes, and titles are added as shown. For convenience in construction, the footing surfaces are labeled for their correct elevation below grade.

Sections: Longitudinal or transverse vertical sections through the building show material placement and construction details. Many sections are drawn to larger scales than plan views to show specific information (see Fig. 6-11, 6-12, 6-13).

The longitudinal and transverse sections are drawn after all detail information has been completed on both the plan and the elevations. These section views reveal all visible interior information on the cutting planes completely through the building. To conserve time, the longitudinal section is blocked in on the sheet placed directly over the left-side elevation drawing and the transverse section over the front elevation drawing. In both cases, the floor plan is oriented and attached to the board above the section view so that interior features can be easily projected. In completing the sections, the designer must occasionally duplicate information found on elevation views.

Schedules: Wall and floor finishes, window and door information, and bath and plumbing materials are indicated on "chartlike" schedules. Many times these schedules are placed on the floor plans or sectional drawings (see Fig. 6-14).

Structural: These drawings include foundation plans, floor framing plans, roof framing plans, and sections showing the sizes and types of structural components of the building (see Fig. 6-15, 6-16, 6-17, 6-18, 6-19, 6-20).

The foundation, floor, and roof framing plans are developed by the structural engineer. Data concerning the soil conditions are important to the structural engineer to size the footings correctly and to determine the proper foundation system for the building. The structural engineer gives valuable guidance to the designer regarding the location of columns, beams, bearing walls, and roof framing systems. The civil engineer, the designer, and the structural engineer must meet frequently to exchange information concerning the structural integrity of the building.

Mechanical: Plumbing, heating, and air-conditioning features are shown in detail on these drawings. Isometric or other pictorial views are often used to show complicated piping or ductwork (see Fig. 6-21, 6-22, 6-23, 6-24, 6-25, 6-26, 6-27, 6-28, 6-29, 6-30, 6-31, 6-32).

Plumbing and HVAC drawings are prepared by the mechanical engineer. Plumbing plans show plumbing fixtures, hot- and cold-water supply pipes, and sanitary drainage pipe. Existing utility information gathered by the civil engineer, and the type, number, and location of plumbing fixtures determined by the designer, are important to the mechanical engineer.

The mechanical engineer is frequently asked to prepare an analysis of the space-conditioning needs for the building. Numerous types of heating and cooling systems are available. It is imperative that the proper type of system be selected. The designer, the structural engineer, and the mechanical engineer must carefully integrate the HVAC system into the design of the building. Adequate space for the mechanical equipment and sufficient structural supports for the system are essential.

Some buildings are required to have fire protection systems. The mechanical engineer usually develops a sprinkler system plan for fire protection for such buildings.

Electrical: Wiring, electrical switches, and electrical fixtures are shown on floor plans and in schedules. (see Fig. 6-33, 6-34, 6-35, 6-36, 6-37, 6-38, 6-39, 6-40, 6-41)

The electrical engineer prepares the lighting plan and the power wiring plan for commercial buildings. In addition to the basic electrical plans, the electrical engineer is usually responsible for developing communications plans, which consist of telephone, intercom, fire detection, and alarm systems. Even some small buildings have massive amounts of electronic equipment. The designer and the electrical engineer must stay abreast of the users' needs and must carefully coordinate the location of all of the electrical features of the building.

6.3.5 Shop Drawings

These are technical drawings prepared by the various trades participating in the construction and used mainly by their own mechanics. On many jobs, the architects and engineers must rely on specialists or material suppliers to furnish precise information. Details concerning reinforcing steel, elevators, conveyors, complex cabinetwork, etc., are commonly furnished by the suppliers. For example, even though the structural drawings show the size, location, and typical splicing laps for reinforcing bars, the steel fabrication firm in its own drafting department prepares drawings that show each type of bar required, the number needed, placing information, and the number and type of bar supports required to hold the bars in place during the concrete pouring operation. These shop drawings are submitted to the structural engineer, who checks for design only, and to the general contractor, who checks only for quantity. The drawings are then stamped with such phrases as "furnish as submitted," "furnish as corrected," or "revise and resubmit." When the review of the drawings indicates compliance with the contract documents, the reinforcing steel fabrication firm can then begin cutting and bending the steel for delivery to the job. Shop drawings also allow the architects and engineers to review the quality of the components that subcontractors propose to furnish.

CONSTRUCTION PROCEDURE

To understand the importance of drawings as the basis of dialogue throughout the developmental procedure of these complex projects, it is necessary to be familiar with the three major phases of development. These are (1) promotion, (2) design, and (3) construction (see Fig. 6-42).

6.4.1 Promotion

This phase is concerned with the preliminaries. In general, surveys must be made in the area for land cost,

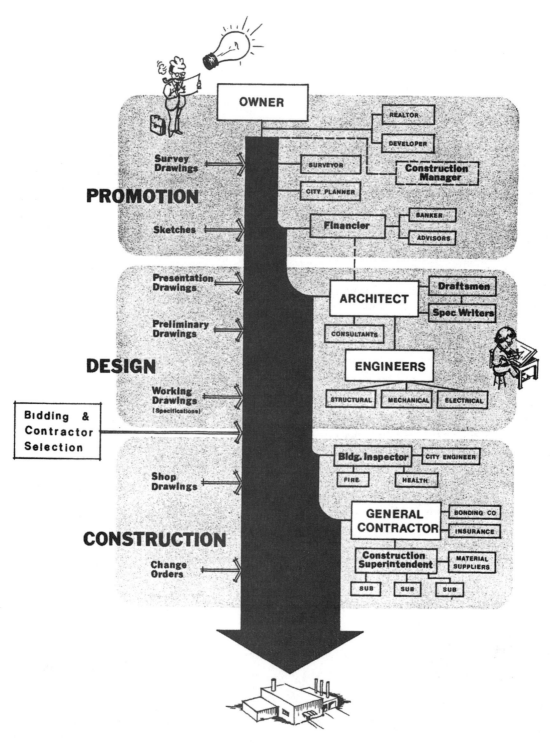

Figure 6–42 Phases in the development of a typical commercial building.

marketing, transportation facilities, water sources, and other economic factors to determine the feasibility of the proposed building. Surveys are done by personnel experienced in this work or by realtors who are retained to negotiate property purchases. If the surveys are positive, financing is arranged next. This is an important step, for no building can proceed without sound financial backing. Lenders must be satisfied that the building will pay a reasonable return on the investment before they will provide the financing. It is in the owner's interest to acquire the highest loan committal and in the lender's interest to secure a stable and sound investment.

The next step is to retain a competent architect. Many of the larger business organizations have their own planning and architectural personnel for the purpose of maintaining a continual building program. Individual developers seek the most competent architect on the basis of experience, reliability, interest, tastes, and other environmental aptitudes. The architect is often the catalytic agent who is able to produce a close harmony among the owner, contractors, financiers, material suppliers, and the public as well. The architect must expend considerable effort in examining the site, consulting, doing research, making *sketches*, and planning the construction. It is part of the architect's responsibility to see that the building will be economically and financially workable and that it will become an asset to the community.

Other specialists may also be consulted as to the feasibility of the project before final decisions are made. It is worth mentioning that a comparatively small percentage of the vast amount of proposed construction gets beyond the promotional phase. Stopping at this point is better than constructing buildings that lack integrity and genuine usefulness.

Some types of large or complex projects utilize an architect-engineer-management firm to provide all services, including the preliminary planning. In this arrangement, which was widely used during World War II, an A&E firm is given responsibility for the planning, design, and awarding of all the construction contracts for a given installation. The form of contract between the owner and the A&E firm is usually of the cost-plus-fixed-fee type, with the owner taking little part in the determination of the contract for the physical construction.

Another type of arrangement is the *turnkey* contract by which one company is given the responsibility for designing and building the project, with both the design and the construction personnel being employed by the same company. This design-and-build approach to building is an outgrowth of modern management methods. It applies the efficiency and control of good business organization to building construction. This process encourages the designer/builder to seek the best and most economical way to build, consistent with the owner's objectives. Many times it permits faster occupancy of a building and provides alternate ways to meet the building budget.

6.4.2 Design

The design of a building is the direct responsibility of the architect once the preliminary sketches have been approved and other decisions resolved. The architect's first step in developing the project, within a justified budget, is to produce a set of *preliminary drawings*. During this phase, the architect is assisted by consulting engineers who specialize in structural, mechanical, electrical, and other design categories. Interior decorators, landscape architects, kitchen consultants, and sanitation consultants, to name a few, are often called on to help during the design stage. Even trade representatives, skilled in their fields, are consulted to help solve critical problems that might arise. The design of highly specialized buildings, such as hospitals or industrial processing plants, definitely requires the aid of consultants. Civil authorities are also helpful in working with the architect to ensure that the design meets prevailing ordinances and local building codes.

Experienced drafters, under the supervision of a designated *project architect* (or "job captain"), prepare the *working drawings* in the architect's office, while specification writers compose the complete set of *specifications*. The completed working drawings and specifications then form the basis for accurately determining the type and extent of labor required, the material and equipment needed, and the estimated total cost of the project.

6.4.2A contractor selection

Competitive bidding on the estimated cost of a proposed structure is the usual method of selecting a construction contractor, known as the *general contractor*, with the idea of awarding the contract to the low bidder. However, the selection may be tempered by the reputation and general competence of the bidder. Competitive bidding consists of inviting more than one contractor (usually three to ten) to submit an estimate of the cost of building a project from a set of working drawings and specifications. These individual proposals are then submitted to the owner in scaled envelopes at an appointed time and place where they are opened and read publicly.

Estimating a job and submitting an accurate bid are therefore very important to the general contractor. The contractor's estimators must be able to correctly "read" or interpret the plans and specifications and must be familiar with the most economical construction practices. It is also important that the plans be correctly drawn and contain enough information from which to make a true estimate. The working drawings, then, are most important to both the contractor and the owner.

The competitive contract is used on almost all public works, and authorities are almost always obligated to select the lowest bidder. Private owners, however, may select the *lowest responsive bidding contractor* rather than the lowest bidder, although the lowest bidder is usually chosen. They sometimes negotiate directly with one or more favored contractors on the total cost of construction. The *negotiated contract* usually takes the form of a "cost-plus" basis, with the "cost" being the expense that will be required to complete the building and the "plus" being either a fixed fee or a percentage of the construction cost. A contract of this type permits construction to start before the working drawings are complete (which may be important when time of completion is a factor) and may result in less cost to the owner, since it eliminates the amount for contingencies that a contractor must include in a bid to cover the uncertainties and hazards of construction.

6.4.2B subcontractors

Before submitting a bid to the owner, the general contractor utilizes a similar bid procedure for the selection of the subcontractors, or "subs," who will be employed for various tradework. A reputation for quality work is often the basis for the selection of subcontractors by the general contractor, since the contractor is responsible to the owner for the acceptance of their finished work.

All bidding subcontractors, as well as the bidding general contractors, must have access to a set of working drawings and specifications of the proposed project. Some projects may have as many as 200 subcontractors interested in various parts of the job. Since the sub is providing a "free bid" to the general contractor, the sub may feel that this service does not justify the purchase of a set of prints and specifications. To help the subcontractors, many metropolitan areas provide a *Plan Room Service* that is available by subscription to the subs. Here they will find an array of prints and specifications for most of the current building projects. The service is a kind of clearinghouse for information on the major projects being readied for bid. Some of the plan rooms have equipment for showing microfilmed information. The drawings and specifications are projected on small table screens for easy interpretation, thus eliminating the necessity of handling large, bulky prints.

When the selection procedure is complete, a contract agreement is entered into between the owner and the general contractor. The information in both the working drawings and the specifications is part of the legal documents that are binding to both parties. The selected contractor then has the authority to secure the services of all subcontractors, tradespeople, and material suppliers unless other provisions have been expressly stated in the contract.

6.4.3 Construction

Once costs have been agreed on and contracts have been signed, the construction operation commences. The responsibility for this phase of the project is assumed by the general contractor, often called the *prime contractor*. Since most contracts call for a completion date, it is immediately necessary for the general contractor to submit a building construction production schedule in order that all the subcontractors will know when the various parts of their work must be started and completed. Both the owner and the architect deal directly with the general contractor, but not with the subcontractors. The subs are responsible to the general contractor. If a subcontractor's work is rejected by the owner because of noncompliance with the drawings or specifications, the owner would inform the general contractor (not the sub) concerning the work to be corrected.

The general contractor's key person at the construction site—and perhaps one of the most respected individuals in the construction industry—is the *construction superintendent*, conveniently called the "super" on the job. The super assumes most of the technical responsibility and must have a general knowledge of all the building trades and methods of construction. Among other things, the super's duties include supervising the building layout, coordinating the work, and seeing that materials and subcontractors arrive on the job on time. Expertise in these many duties comes only with experience, and the quality of the completed building often depends directly on the ability of the construction superintendent. Obviously one of the super's major duties is to read and interpret the working drawings and specifications. Although many of the tradespeople are concerned only with specific information on a drawing, the super must be concerned with all the drawings and the entire concept.

Traditionally, the building industry has always had a particular interpretation of the two words "superintend" and "supervise," and a distinction should be made at this point. To *superintend* has been understood to have direct control of the work in progress and to instruct personnel in the correct methods of construction. To *supervise*, on the other hand, was understood to mean to interpret the intent of the drawings and specifications when any misconceptions arose and to *inspect* the progress of the job. The words "supervise" or "inspect" have recently become questionable, legally, in relation to the architect's or engineer's duties during the construction phase. The words "review" or "observe" are usually preferred today. Part of the architectural service involves continual observation of the construction by the architect, the structural engineer, the mechanical engineer, and the electrical engineer, or one of their representatives. They are "observers" and have no superintending authority or responsibility.

The owner frequently employs a *resident engineer*, sometimes known as the *clerk of the works*, to continually observe the work in progress and make regular reports to the owner concerning the project. Job meetings are periodically called during which the architect's representative, the resident engineer, and the construction superintendent iron out any problems and discuss the progress of the job.

Local government agencies also concerned with the project have *building inspectors* who make periodic inspections during the progress of the construction to make sure that the work complies with local building codes and ordinances. A local *fire marshal* may also make similar inspections.

When the construction phase nears completion, the architect and the resident engineer make up lists of necessary work still to be completed, known as *punch lists*. This is an example of items on a punch list:

Office 109: Light fixture not installed, window glass broken, and switch plate missing.

Office 110: Door striker plate missing and ceiling tile damaged.

After all the items on the punch list are completed by the contractor, there is a final accounting of all changes in the work ordered by the owner before final payment is made. These changes consist of additions, deletions, or other revisions that affect the contract sum or the required time of completion. They are usually authorized by *change orders* to the contractor signed by the owner and the architect or engineer.

The contractor is usually required to furnish to the owner complete maintenance and operating instructions for mechanical, electrical, and specialty equipment and systems provided in the building. Most construction contracts require the contractor to furnish *as-built* records as well. These are called *record drawings* and are marked-up prints or drawings that show significant changes made during the construction process, such as the actual location of underground sewers, pipes, conduits, etc.

At completion, a *Certificate of Occupancy* must be obtained from the local building department before the building may be occupied by the owner. This certificate is issued when the building is found to comply with the provisions and regulations of the local building code and permits occupancy for its designated use.

Practically all construction contracts require the contractor to furnish a one-year warranty on all work in the project. The contractor is therefore responsible for correcting any failure or malfunction, and guarantees that repair or replacement of defective parts will be done, without charge, for a period of one year.

6.5

FAST TRACK CONSTRUCTION

A number of factors have led to the development of several innovations in the traditional construction procedure in recent years. The high cost of land, high interest rates, the expectation of a high return on investment once construction is finished, and other financial considerations have all put pressure on those involved in construction to reduce, to a minimum, the total time required to complete a building project. *Fast track* is a name given to a system of construction management that involves a continuous design-construct operation. The object is to get the construction underway at the earliest possible time and to complete the project at the earliest possible date. To accomplish this, the architectural services and the construction are telescoped into a coordinated schedule. For example, excavation may start before the floor plans and details are finished.

A number of different forms of this system have been tried. One recently successful fast track project involved an invitation to a number of selected contractors to submit a bid on the final cost of completing a building from a rather detailed set of preliminary drawings. The successful bidder became a member of the construction management team, with the architect, and assumed all cost-control functions. As such, he gave advice on design considerations and construction procedures that affected costs.

The scheduling of the completion time of the various drawings necessary for different phases of construction was another area in which the contractor had input. Bidding on this project required the contractors to present a proposed schedule (see Fig. 6-43) for the construction of the building and also to include a firm completion date. Thus, not only was the owner assured of a total cost, but was also advised of the least possible time for construction.

The *construction management* (CM) approach is another procedure that has been used successfully. This system involves the employment of an independent professional construction manager. Theoretically, the architect, the construction manager, and the owner work as a team for the success of the project. As team coordinator, the construction manager administers the designs, schedules, and budgets that express quality, time, and cost in a format that all team members can understand. Throughout the early design process, the construction manager may request the architect to try alternative schemes for different systems and materials, which could then be tested against the requirements and the budget of the project. By this method, trade-offs and alterations can be made before materials and systems have become fixed. For example, the construction manager might evaluate the probable costs and the construction time required by each of several schemes to aid in the best selection for the benefit of the owner. Because responsible estimating is one of the construction manager's most impressive tools, his or her ability to establish a probable cost in the early periods of design can avoid many potential problems.

Network planning through the *critical path method* (CPM) of scheduling can be an important tool in monitoring the construction program. This is a planning, scheduling, and control technique whereby a project is completely planned and scheduled and an arrow

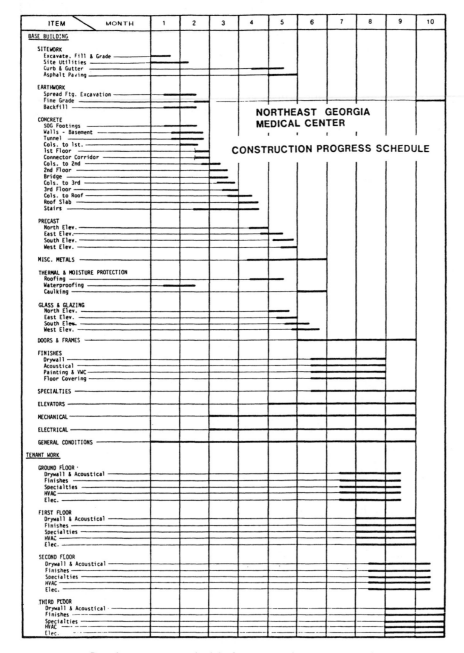

Figure 6–43 Bar chart progress schedule for proposed construction of Northeast Georgia Medical Center discussed in Chapter 6. (Courtesy Chegwidden, Dorsey, and Holmes)

diagram drawn (see Fig. 6-44) that shows the interconnected individual tasks involved within the total project. It permits the determination of the relative significance of each event and establishes the optimum sequence and duration of operations. Although well known in the construction industry, it is also applicable to the planning of drawings and related activities throughout large and complex projects. In fast track and CM systems, a periodically updated CPM chart will graphically illustrate the phasing and time-control essentials of the project.

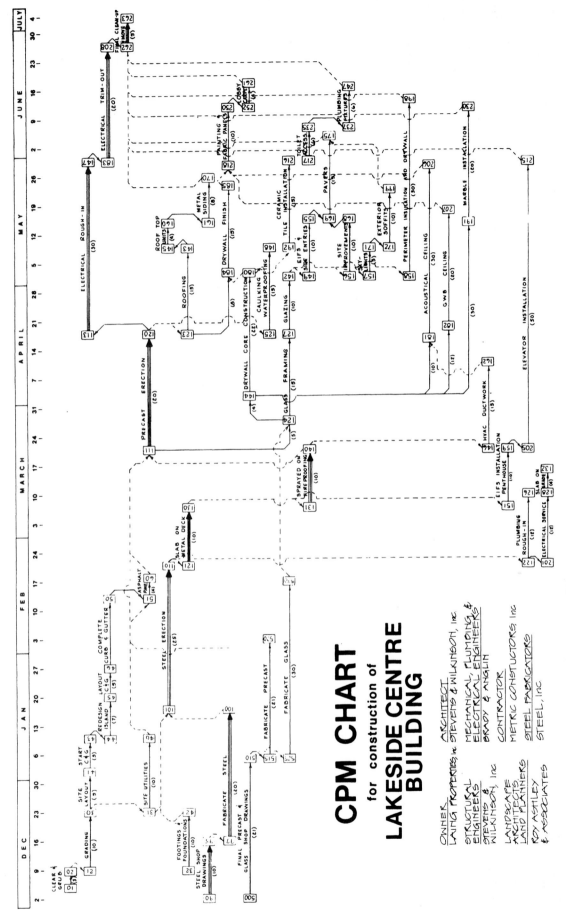

Figure 6–44 CPM chart for construction of Lakeside Centre Building discussed in Chapter 5. (Courtesy Metric Constructors, Inc.)

REVIEW QUESTIONS

1. Why must codes dealing with public buildings be carefully regulated?

2. List three general structural systems commonly used in commercial buildings.

3. Why are enclosed vestibules often used in public entrances?

4. When laying out plan views of buildings with multiple floor levels, why should the drafter reserve suitable space for vertical plumbing and mechanical chases?

5. What detail is commonly drawn before the plans and the elevations are started?

6. What factors must the designer consider in deciding on the spacing of modular columns in planning a commercial building?

7. In dimensioning, how does the designer make the features in detail views relate to major features on plan and elevation views?

8. Why must masonry coursing sizes be accurately drawn on details?

9. What types of professional services are usually engaged by architectural firms to complete their sets of working drawings for commercial buildings?

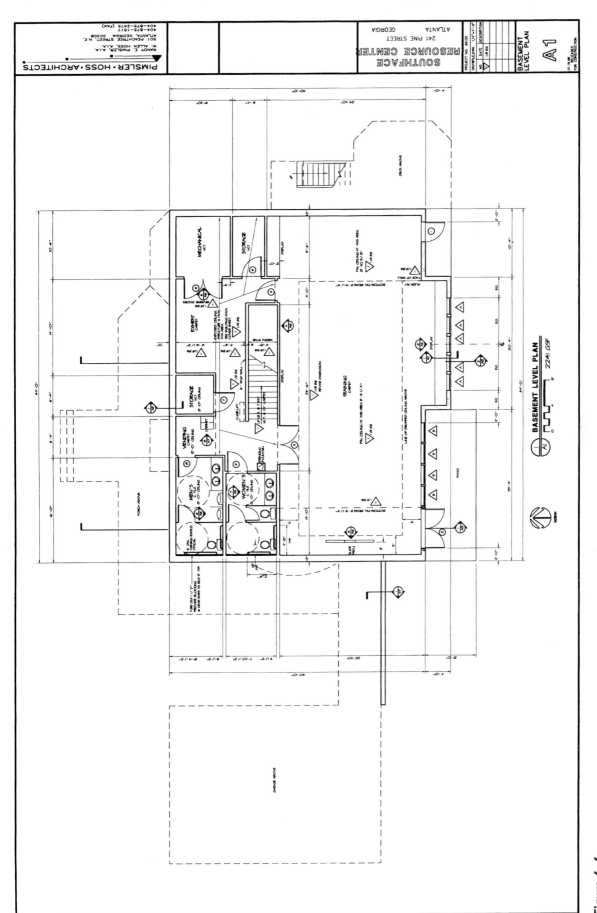

Figure 6-6

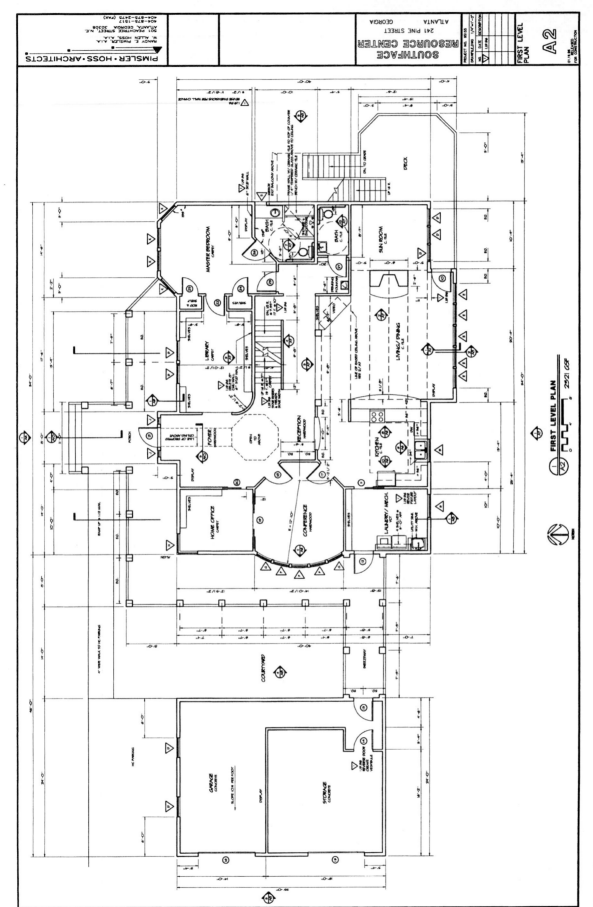

Figure 6-7

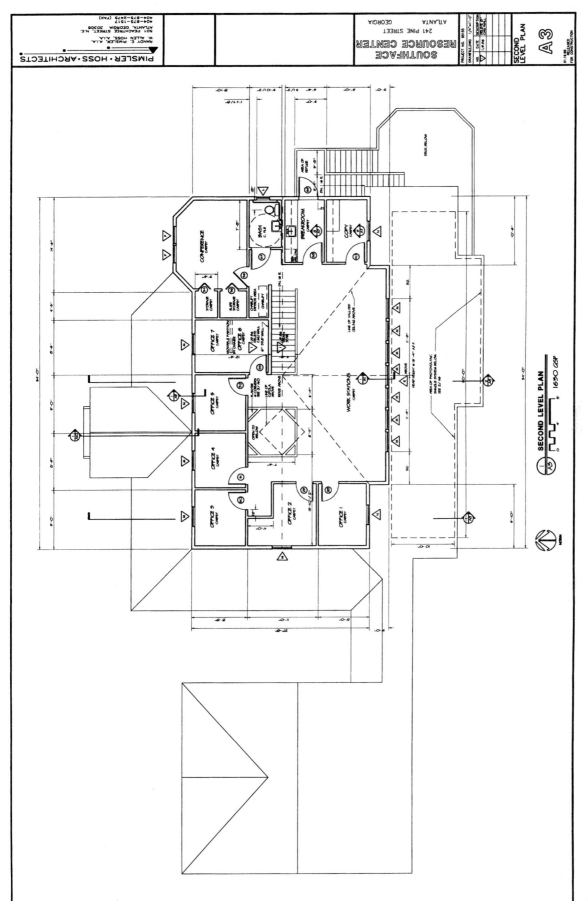

Figure 6-8

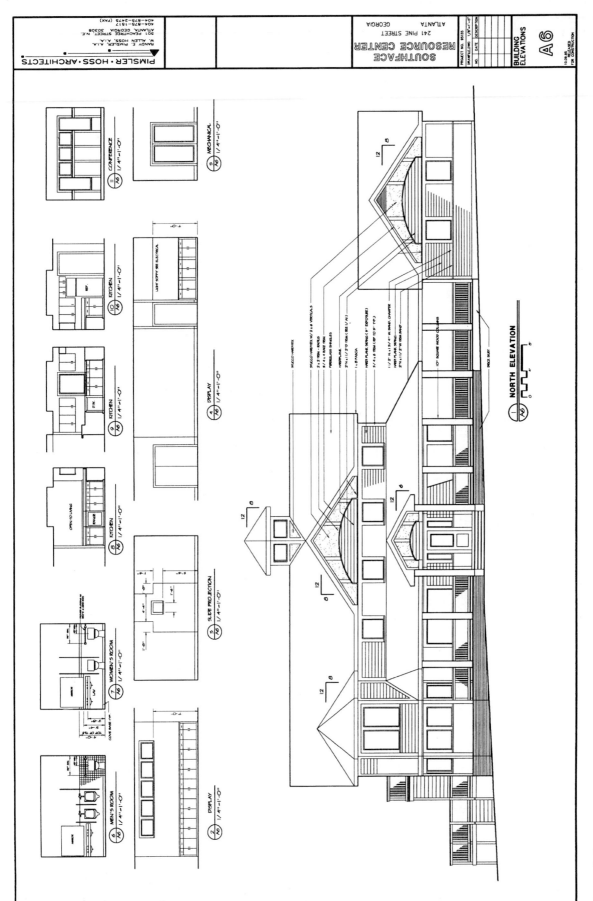

Figure 6-9

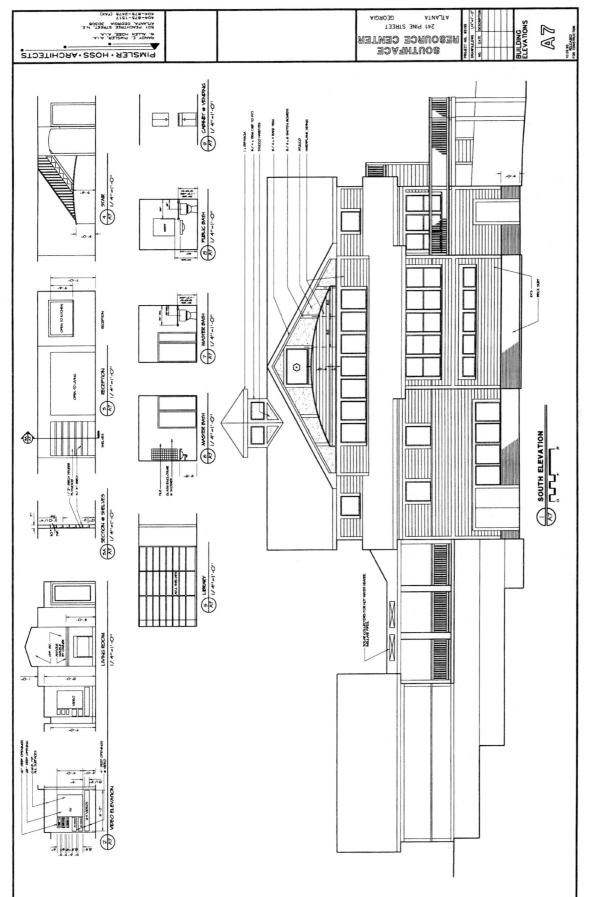

Figure 6-10

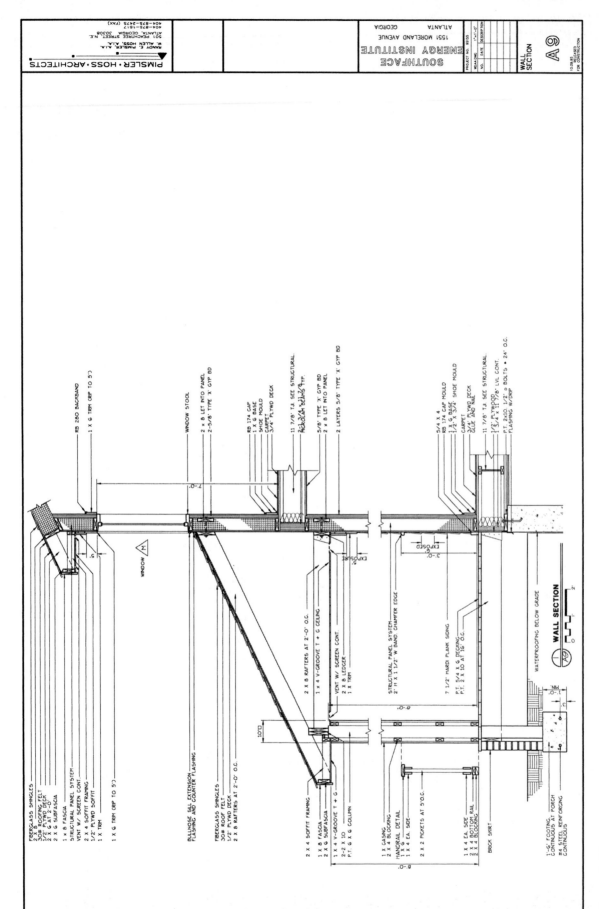

Figure 6-11

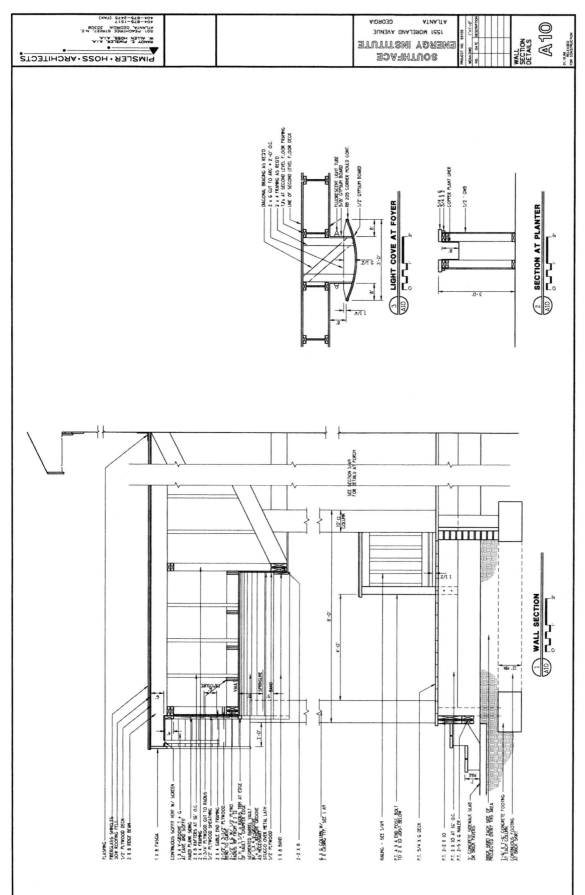

Figure 6-12

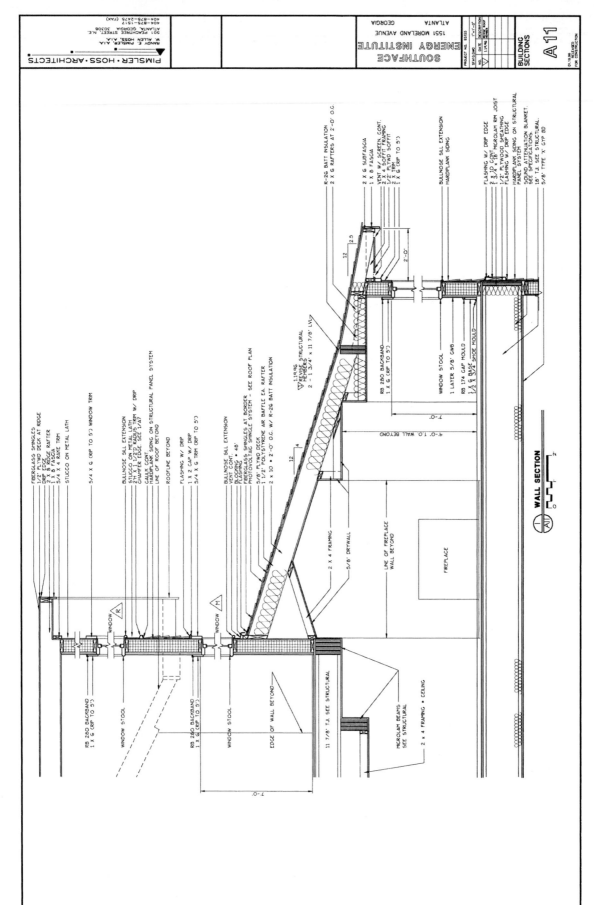

Figure 6–13

WINDOW SCHEDULE

MARK	ORDER #	STYLE	ROUGH OPENG. WIDTH x HEIGHT	FINISH	QUANTITY	REMARKS
ALL WINDOWS				FRAME EXTERIOR/ NATURAL INTERIOR UNLESS NOTED OTHERWISE		HEAD HEIGHT @ 7'-0" A.F.F. UNLESS NOTED OTHERWISE ALL WINDOWS OPERABLE UNLESS NOTED OTHERWISE INSULSHIELD GLASS. NO BRICK MOULD. NO MUNTINS. SINGLE UNIT TYPE. DO NOT GANG.
A	DCWAW3523	AWNING	2'-11 3/4" x 2'-0 7/8"		3	
B	DCWDH3747	DOUBLE HUNG	3'-4 1/2" x 3'-11 1/2"		10	
C	NOT USED					
D	DCWDHVG2967	DOUBLE HUNG	2'-3 1/2" X 3'-7 1/2"		3	
E	DCWDHVG3767	DOUBLE HUNG	3'-4 1/2" X 6'-7 1/2"		6	
F	DCWTRDH2523	FIXED TRANSOM	2'-4 1/2" X 2'-4"		3	
G	DCWDH2563	DOUBLE HUNG	2'-4 1/2" x 3'-3 1/2"		2	
H	SPWCV3048	CORNER VIEW	2'-8 7/8" x 4'-3 3/4"		1	
J	CUSTOM FRAME SIZE 1'-4 1/2" x 3'-10 3/4"	FIXED SIDELITE	1'-2" x 3'-11 1/2"		2	CUSTOM FIT UNSULATED GLASS
K	DCWDH3547	DOUBLE HUNG	2'-9 1/2" x 3'-11 1/2"		4	
L	DCWCM2135	CASEMENT	1'-9 3/4" x 3'-0 7/8"		1	RIGHT HAND
M	DCWCM3541	CASEMENT	2'-11 3/4" x 3'-8 7/8"		12	6 RIGHT HAND, 5 LEFT HAND, 1 FIXED
N	DCWCM3535	CASEMENT	2'-11 3/4" x 3'-0 7/8"		2	1 RIGHT HAND, 1 LEFT HAND
P	DCWDHVG3567	DOUBLE HUNG	2'-9 1/2" x 3'-7 1/2"		2	
R	DCWCM3941	FIXED AWNING	4'-11" x 3'-8 7/8"		1	HEAD HEIGHT @ 15'-4" A.F.F.
S	GLASS BLOCK	6" UNITS 3W x 8H	1'-8" x 4'-2"		1	
T	DCWCM4723	FIXED AWNING	3'-11 3/4" x 2'-0 7/8"		4	WINDOWS AT CUPOLA

NOTES:

1. WINDOWS SPECIFIED ARE PELLA DESIGNER CLASSIC SERIES EXCEPT AS NOTED OTHERWISE. SUBSTITUTES MUST COMPLY WITH SPECIFICATIONS AND SIZE AND BE APPROVED BY ARCHITECT.
2. CONTRACTOR TO VERIFY ALL QUANTITY TAKE OFFS.

DOOR SCHEDULE

DOOR NO.	WIDTH x HEIGHT	THICKNESS	TYPE	HAND	HARDWARE	REMARKS
1	3'-0" X 7'-0"	1-3/4"	METAL CLAD S.C.	RH	DEADBOLT, LOCKSET	THRESHOLD
2	PR. 2'-8" X 7'-0"	1-3/4"	METAL CLAD S.C.		DEADBOLT, LOCKSET	ASTRAGAL, THRESHOLD
3	PR. 3'-0" X 6'-8"	1-3/8"	WOOD S.C. 1/2 LITE	DOUBLE	PASSAGE	
4	3'-0" X 6'-8"	1-3/8"	WOOD S.C.	LH	PASSAGE	
5	3'-0" X 6'-8"	1-3/8"	WOOD S.C.	RH	LOCKSET	
6	PR. 3'-0" X 6'-8"	1-3/8"	FRENCH/ GLASS	DOUBLE	LOCKSET	
7	3'-0" X 6'-8"	1-3/8"	WOOD S.C.	LH	LOCKSET	
8	3'-0" X 6'-8"	1-3/8"	WOOD S.C.	RH	PUSH/ PULL	CLOSER
9	3'-0" X 6'-8"	1-3/8"	WOOD S.C.	RHR	PUSH/ PULL	CLOSER
10	2'-8" ~~3'-0"~~ X 7'-0"	1-3/4"	FRENCH/ GLASS	~~RHR~~ LH	DEADBOLT, LOCKSET	THRESHOLD
11	3'-0" X 6'-8"	1-3/8"		POCKET		
12	3'-0" X 7'-0"	1-3/4"	WOOD S.C. 1/2 LITE	LHR	DEADBOLT, LOCKSET	THRESHOLD
13	3'-0" X 6'-8"	1-3/8"	METAL CLAD	LH	DEADBOLT, LOCKSET	THRESHOLD
14	3'-0" X 6'-8"	1-3/8"	METAL CLAD	~~LH~~ RH	LOCKSET	
15	8'-0" X 7'-0"	1-3/8"	GARAGE DOOR	O.H.	BY MNFG.	
16	8'-0" X 7'-0"	1-3/8"	GARAGE DOOR	O.H.	BY MNFG.	
17	3'-0" X 6'-8"	1-1/8"	WOOD S.C.	RH	PASSAGE	
18	3'-0" X 6'-8"	1-3/8"	WOOD S.C.	LH	PASSAGE	
19	PR. 2'-6" X 6'-8"	1-3/4"	WOOD S.C.	POCKET	PULLS	
20	3'-0" X 6'-8"	1-3/8"	WOOD S.C.	POCKET	PULL	
21	3'-0" X 7'-0"	1-3/4"		LHR	DEADBOLT, LOCKSET	ENTRY DOOR, THRESHOLD
22	3'-0" X 6'-8"	1-3/8"	WOOD S.C.	LH	PASSAGE	
23	2'-6" X 6'-8"	1-3/8"	WOOD S.C.	LHR	CLOSET	
24	2'-6" X 6'-8"	1-3/8"	WOOD S.C.	RHR	CLOSET	
25	3'-0" X 6'-8"	1-3/8"	WOOD S.C.	LH	PASSAGE	
26	3'-0" X 6'-8"	1-3/8"	WOOD S.C.	LHR	LOCKSET	
27	3'-0" X 6'-8"	1-3/8"	WOOD S.C.	RHR	LOCKSET	
28	3'-0" X 6'-8"	1-3/8"	WOOD S.C. 1/2 LITE	RH	PASSAGE	
29	3'-0" X 6'-8"	1-3/8"	WOOD S.C. 1/2 LITE	LH	PASSAGE	
30	3'-0" X 6'-8"	1-3/8"	WOOD S.C. 1/2 LITE	RH	PASSAGE	
31	3'-0" X 6'-8"	1-3/8"	WOOD S.C. 1/2 LITE	LH	PASSAGE	
32	3'-0" X 6'-8"	1-3/8"	WOOD S.C. 1/2 LITE	RH	PASSAGE	
33	2'-8" X 6'-8"	1-3/8"	WOOD S.C. 1/2 LITE	RH	PASSAGE	
34	2'-6" X 6'-8"	1-3/8"	LOUVERED	RH BIFOLD	PULL	
35	3'-0" X 6'-8"	1-3/8"	WOOD S.C. 1/2 LITE	LH	PASSAGE	
36	2'-6" X 6'-8"	1-3/8"	LOUVERED	LH BIFOLD	PULL	
37	3'-0" X 6'-8"	1-3/8"	WOOD S.C.	LHR	LOCKSET	
38	3'-0" X 6'-8"	1-3/8"	WOOD S.C. 1/2 LITE	RH		
39	3'-0" X 7'-0"	1-3/4"	METAL CLAD	LH	DEADBOLT, LOCKSET	2'-0" x 3'-0" LITE, THRESHOLD
40	3'-0" X 6'-8"	1-3/8"	WOOD S.C.	RH		

1 1.19.96 CHANGE SIZE DOOR 10

1 1.19.96 REVERSE DOOR 14

NOTE: ALL DOORS TO HAVE LEVER OPERATING HARDWARE.

DOOR SCHEDULE ABBREVIATIONS

DOOR TYPE:		**SILL/ THRESHOLD**	
HM	HOLLOW METAL	CC/ CR	CONCRETE TO CARPET
H.W.	HOLLOW WOOD	CC/ TL	CONCRETE TO TILE
S.C.W.	SOLID CORE WOOD	CR/ TL	CARPET TO TILE
O.H.	OVERHEAD	TL/ VCT	TILE TO V.C.T.
G.A.	GLASS/ ALUMINUM STOREFRONT	EG	EDGE GUARD
FRAME TYPE:		**HINGE:**	
H.M.	HOLLOW METAL	PIV	PIVOTAL
ALUM	ALUMINUM STOREFRONT	BB	BALL BEARING
S.C.	STEEL CHANNEL	F	FLAT
O.H.	OVERHEAD		
G.A.	GLASS/ ALUMINUM STOREFRONT		
HARDWARE:		**CLOSER**	
L/S	LOCKSET	SF/I	SURFACE MOUNTED, INTERIOR
P/S	PASSAGE SET	SF/E	SURFACE MOUNTED, EXTERIOR
P/P	PUSH/ PULL		
		STOP	
THR	WEATHER STRIPPING	F	FLOOR STOP
PT	PAINTED	W	WALL STOP

PIMSLER • HOSS • ARCHITECTS

RANDY E. PIMSLER, A.I.A.
W. ALLEN HOSS, A.I.A.
501 PEACHTREE STREET, N.E.
ATLANTA, GEORGIA 30308
404-875-1517
404-875-2475 (FAX)

SOUTHFACE RESOURCE CENTER
241 PINE STREET
ATLANTA GEORGIA

PROJECT NO. 95155
DRAWFILE.DWG 1/4"=1'-0"

NO.	DATE	DESCRIPTION
1	1.19.96	REVISE DOOR SCHEDULE

SCHEDULES

A12

01.19.96 RELEASED FOR CONSTRUCTION

Figure 6–14

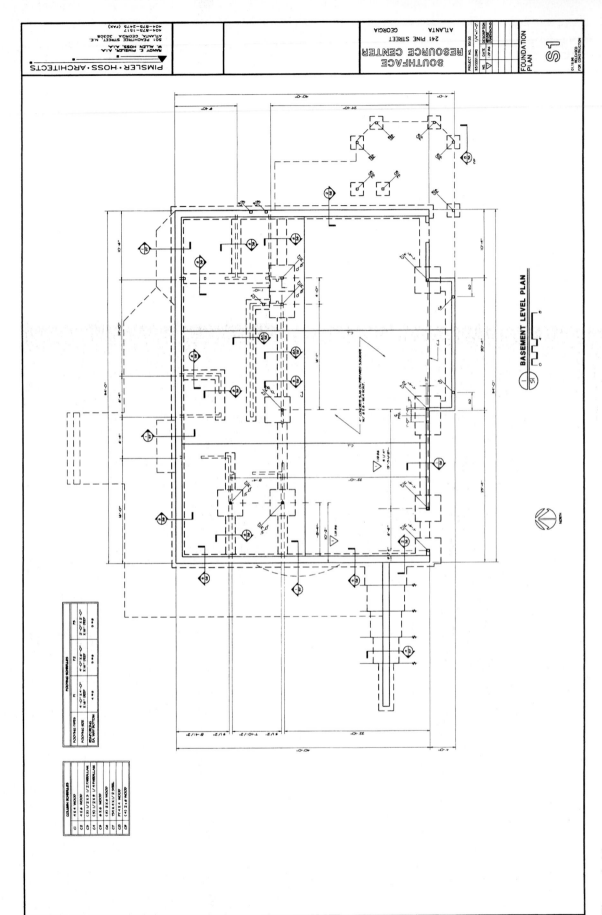

BASEMENT LEVEL PLAN

Figure 6-15

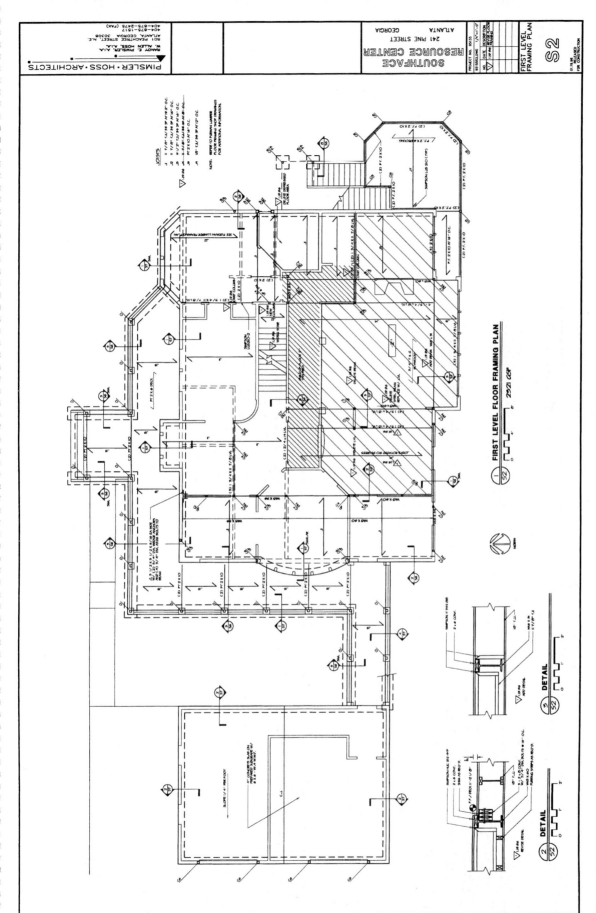

Figure 6-16

313

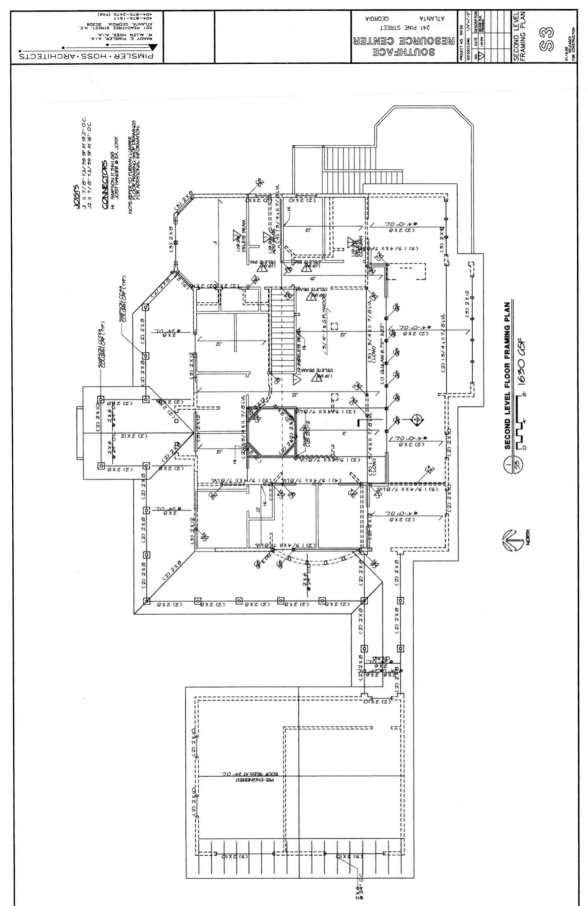

SECOND LEVEL FLOOR FRAMING PLAN

Figure 6–17

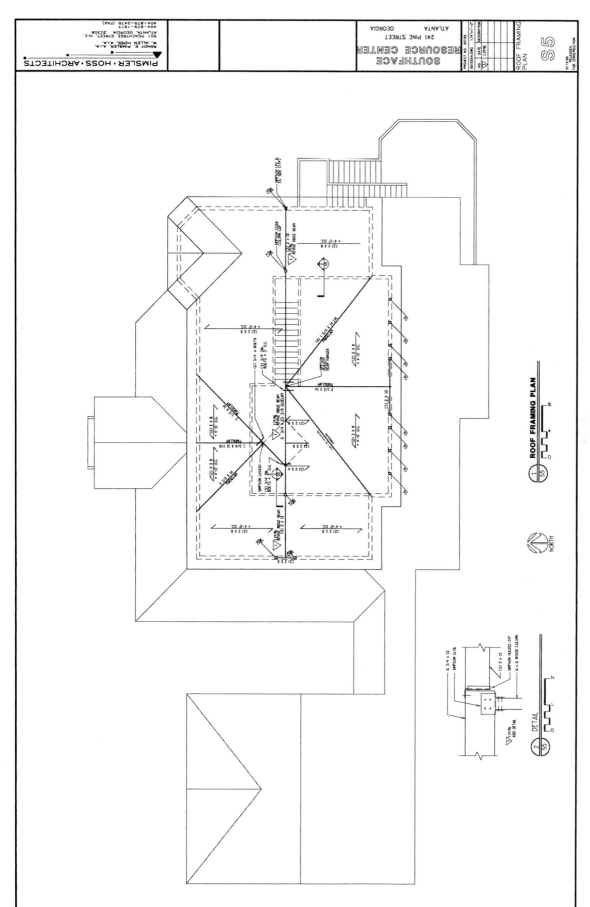

Figure 6–18

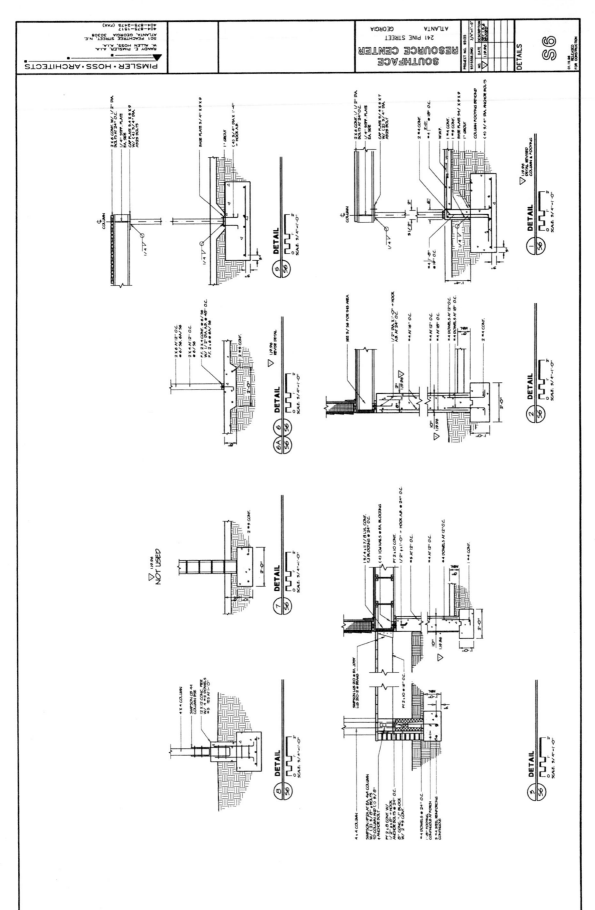

Figure 6-19

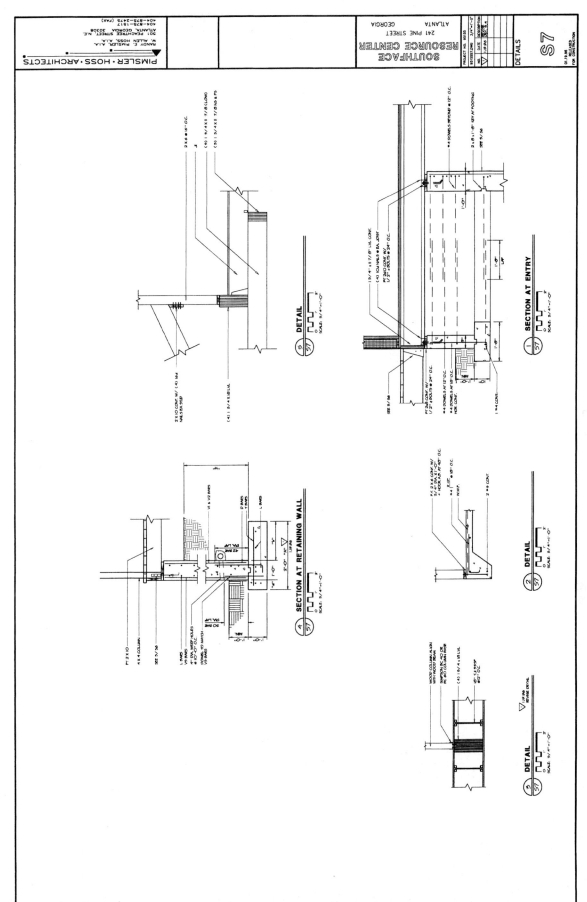

Figure 6-20

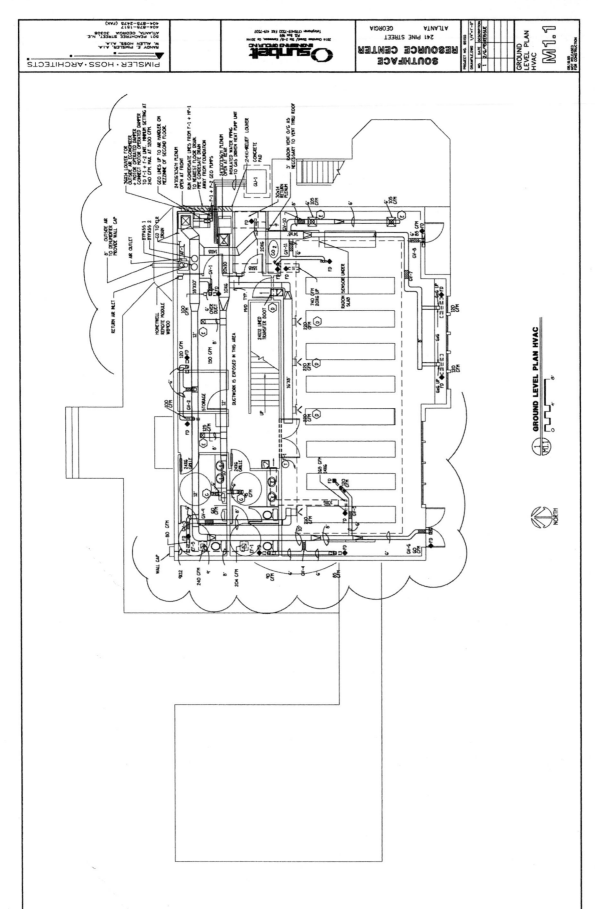

Figure 6-21

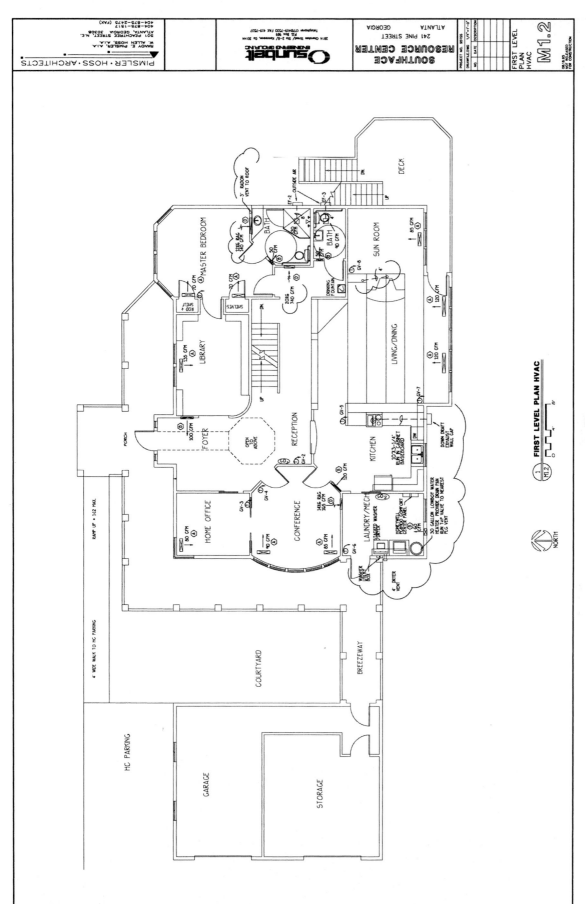

Figure 6–22

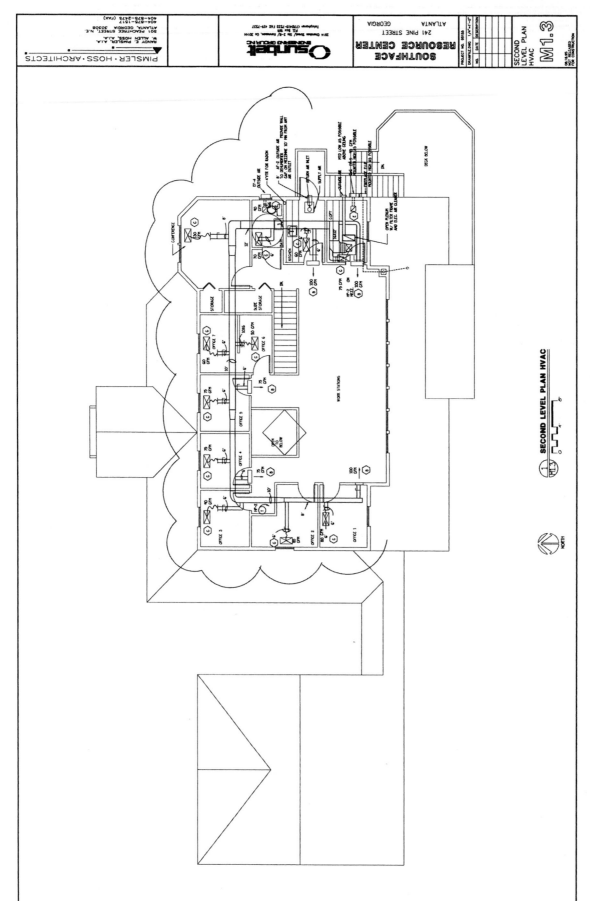

SECOND LEVEL PLAN HVAC

320

Figure 6-23

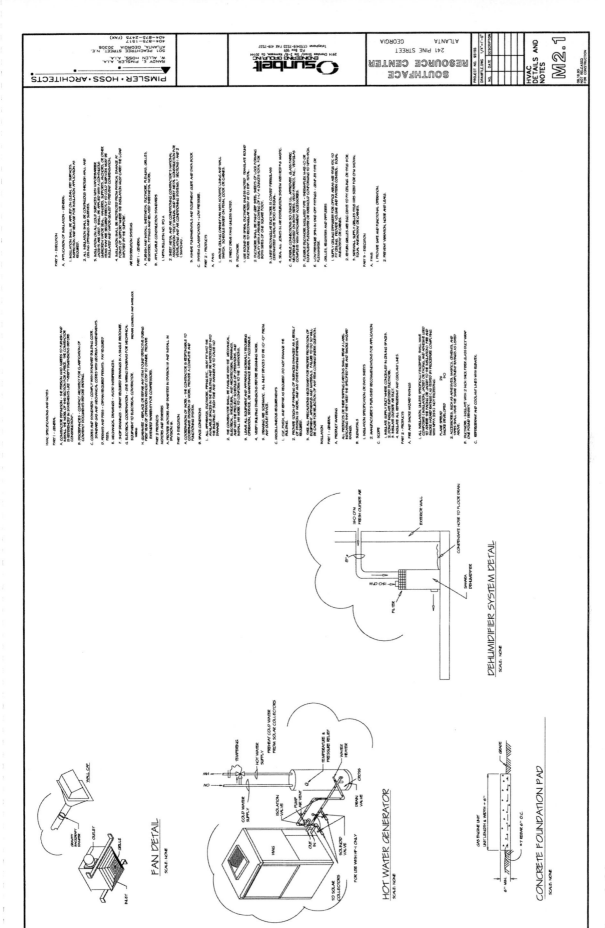

Figure 6-24

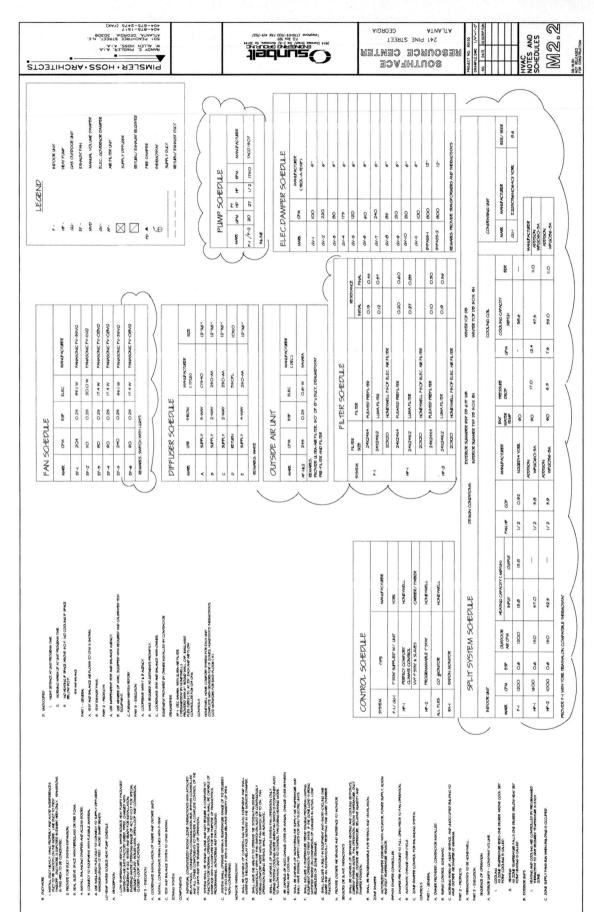

Figure 6-25

322

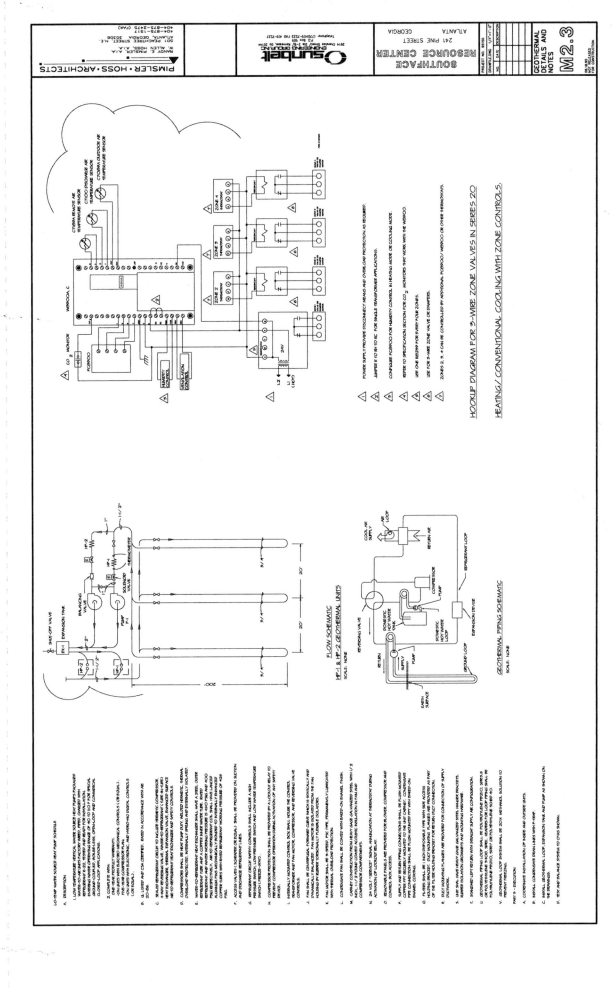

Figure 6-26

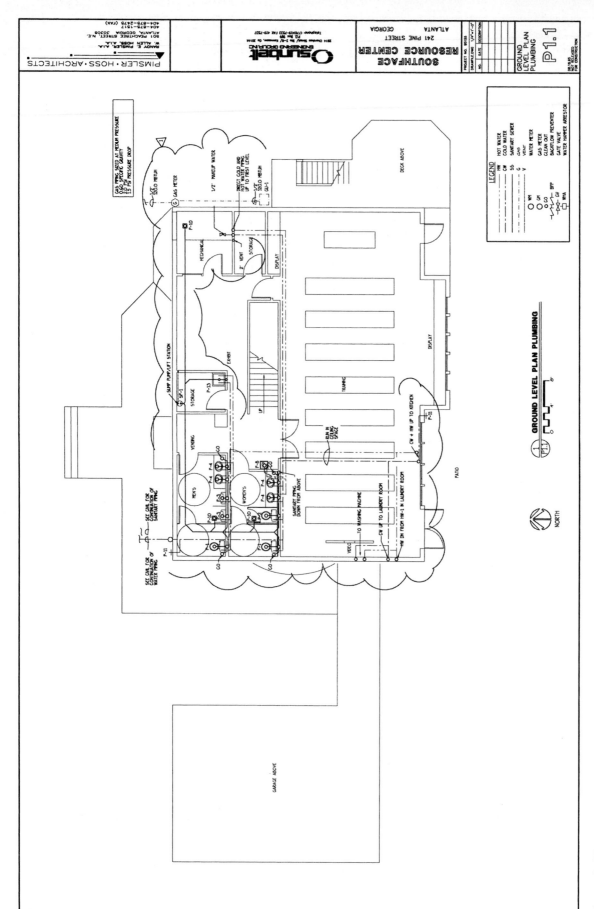

Figure 6-27

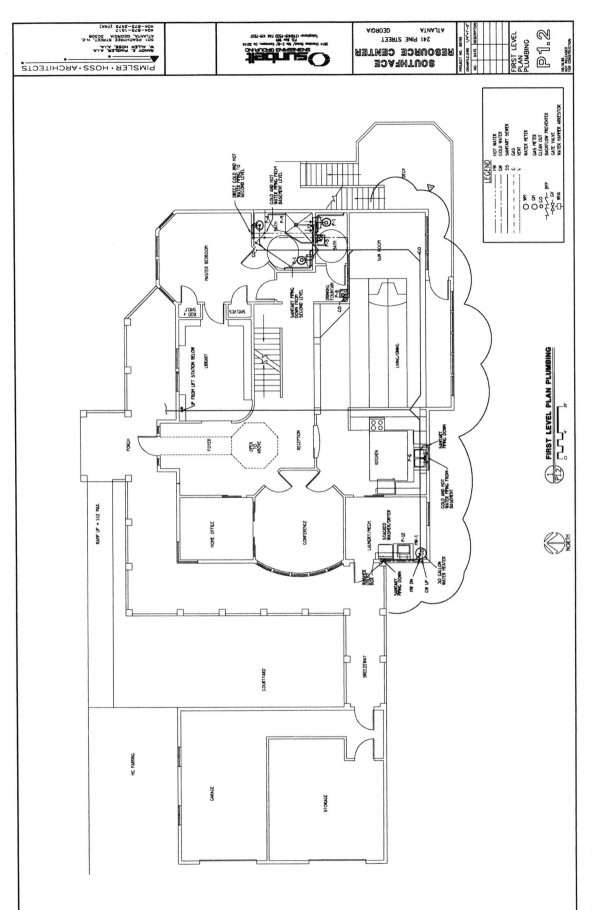

Figure 6-28

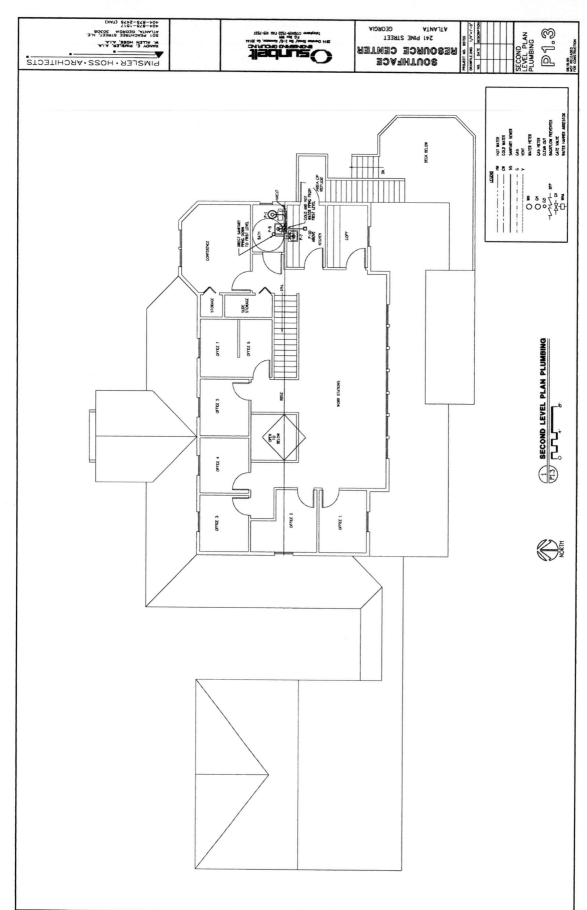

Figure 6–29

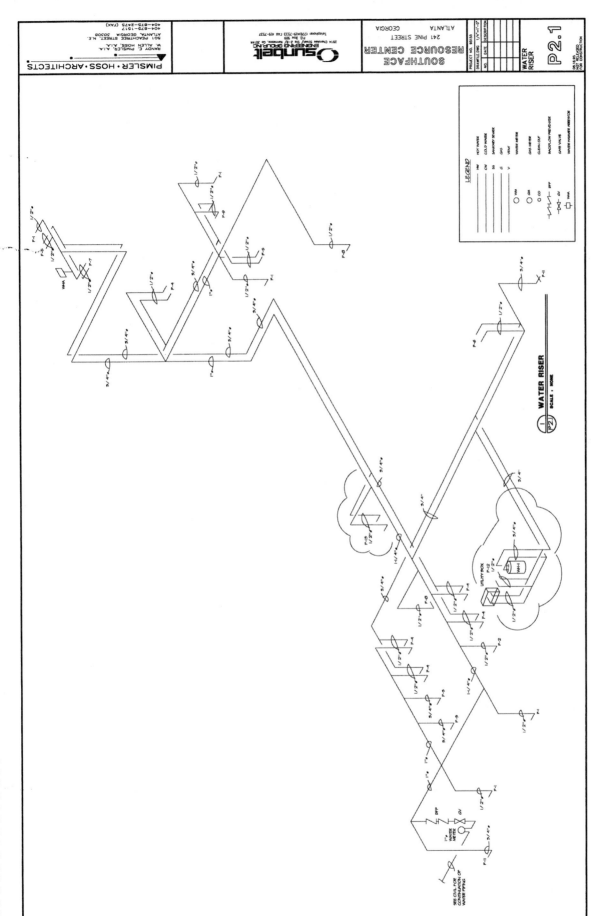

Figure 6-30

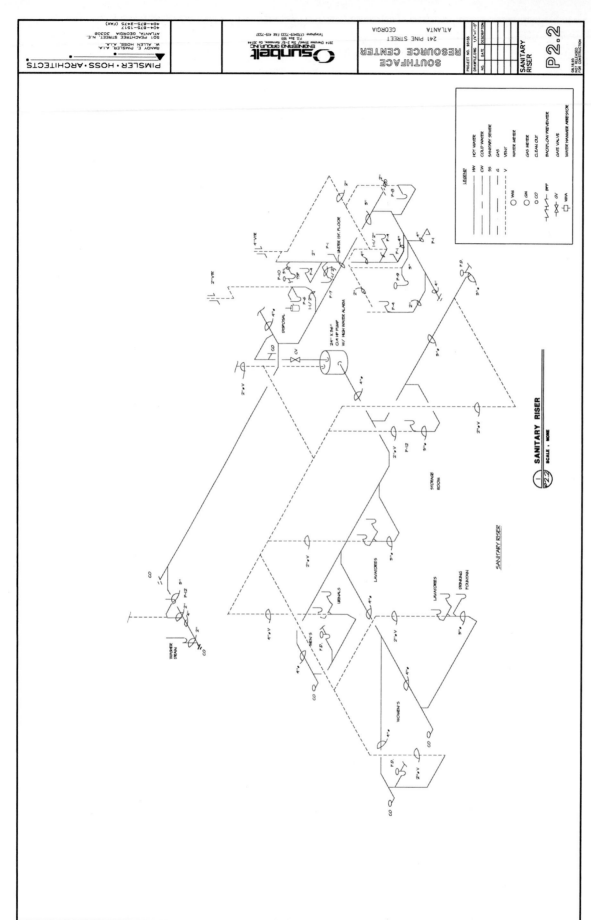

SANITARY RISER

Figure 6-31

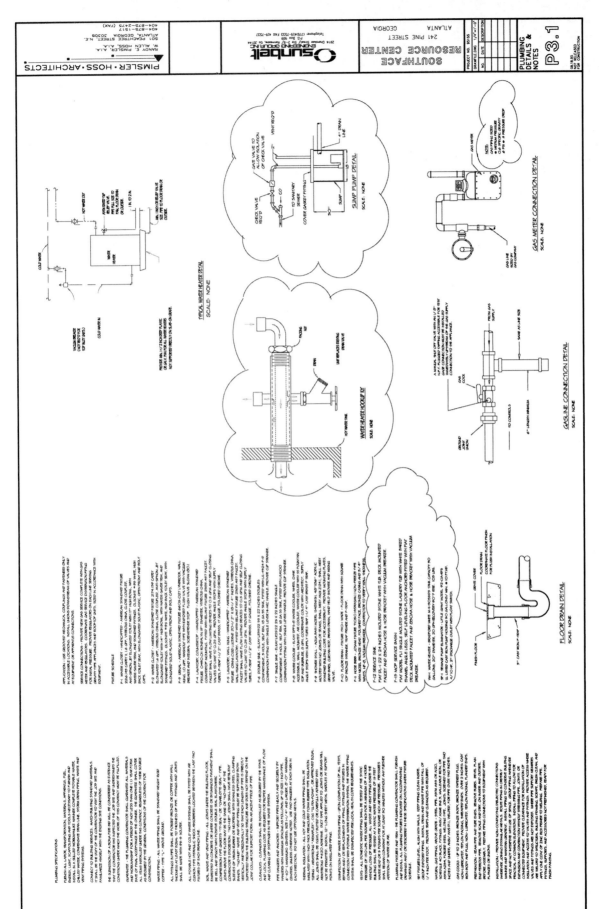

Figure 6-32

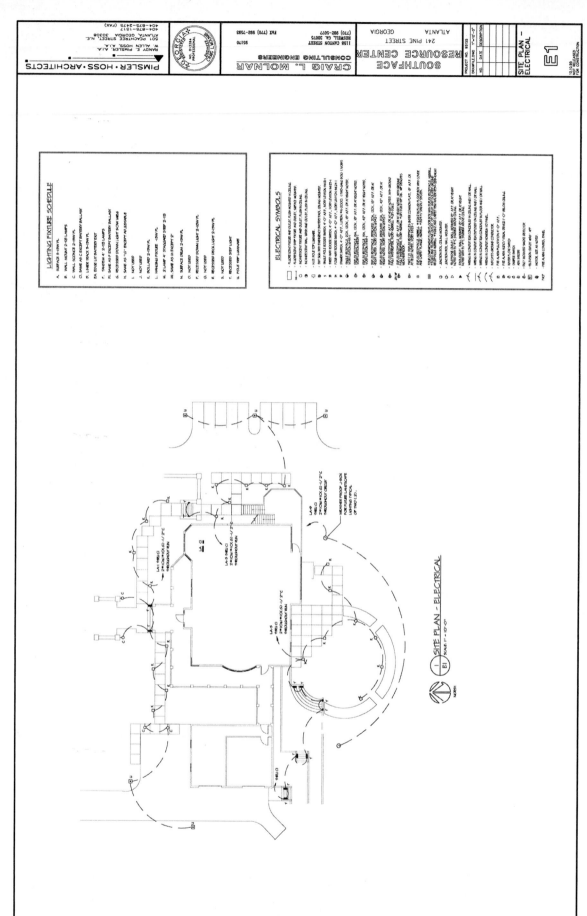

Figure 6-33

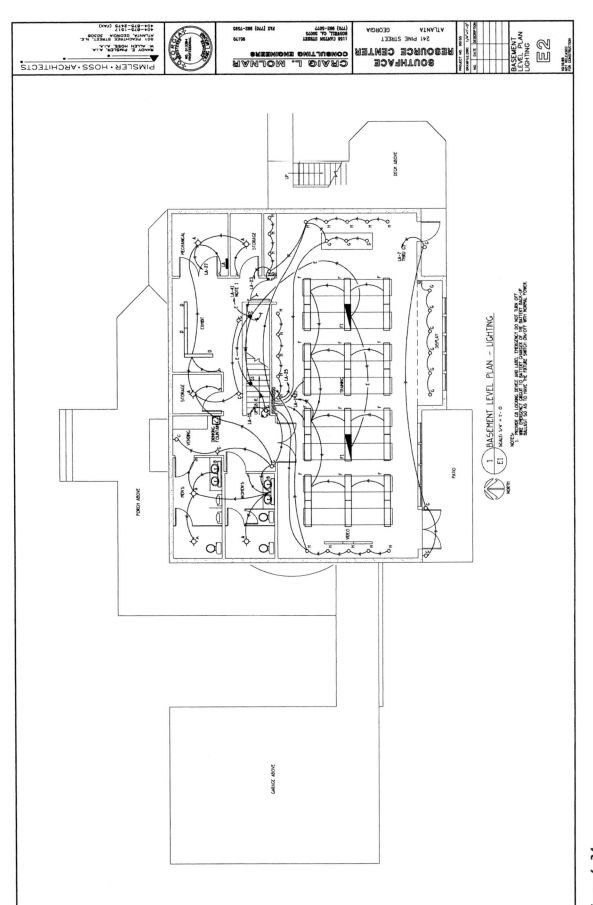

Figure 6-34

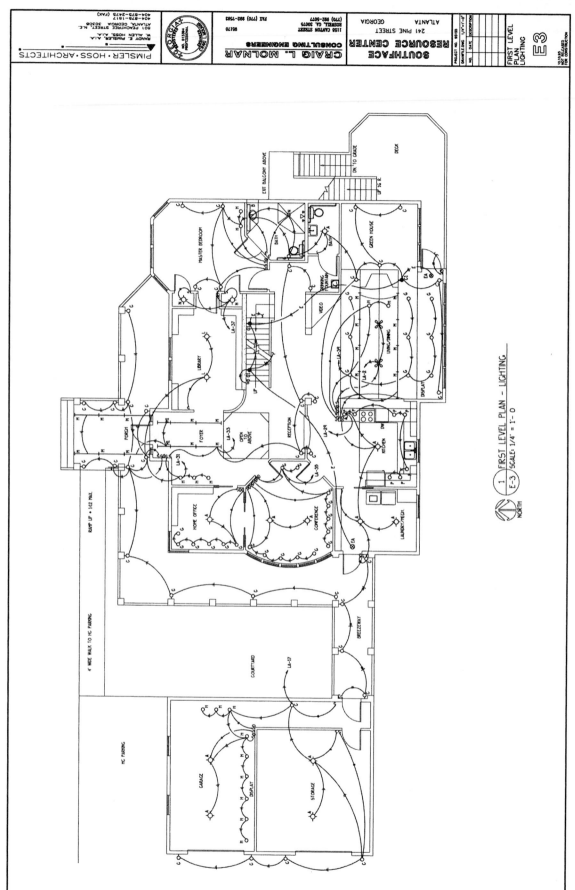

Figure 6-35

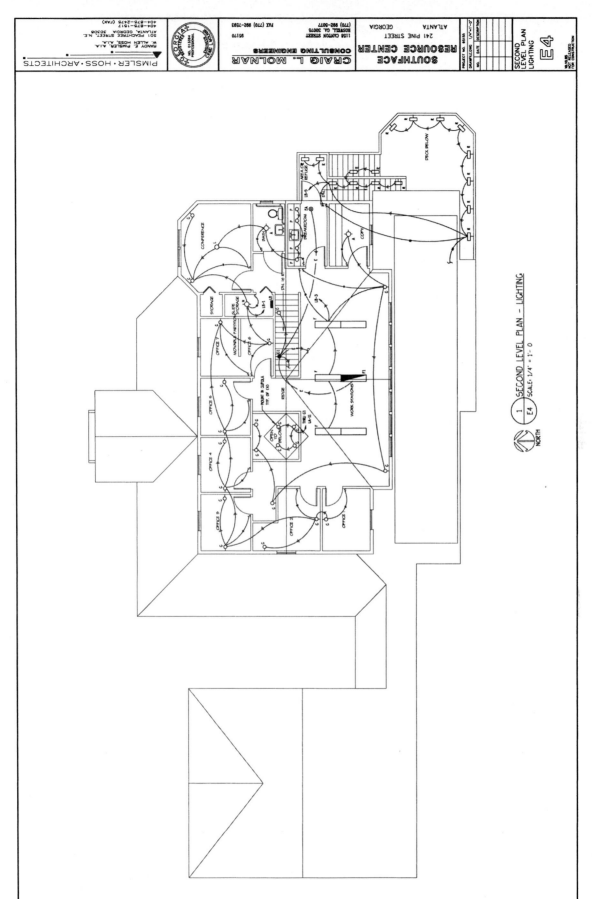

Figure 6-36

333

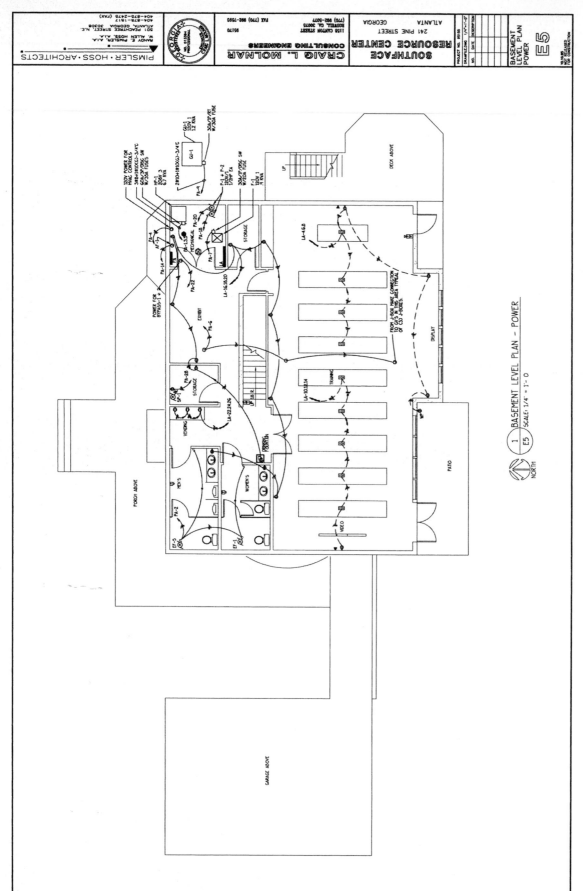

Figure 6-37

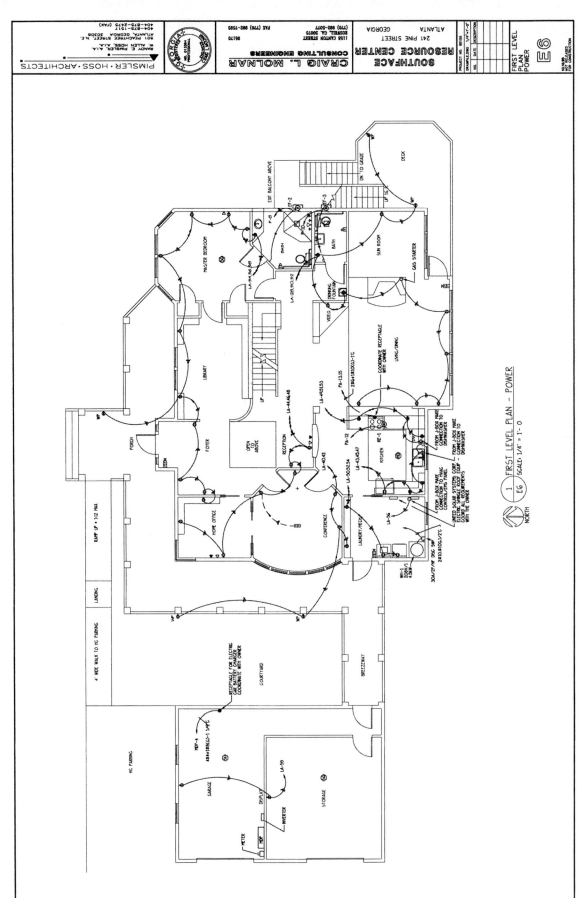

Figure 6-38

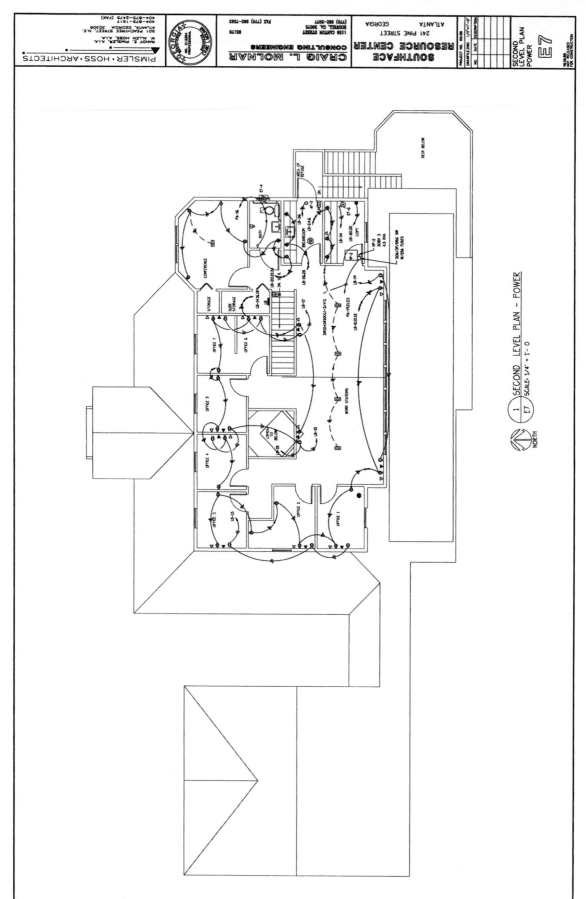

Figure 6-39

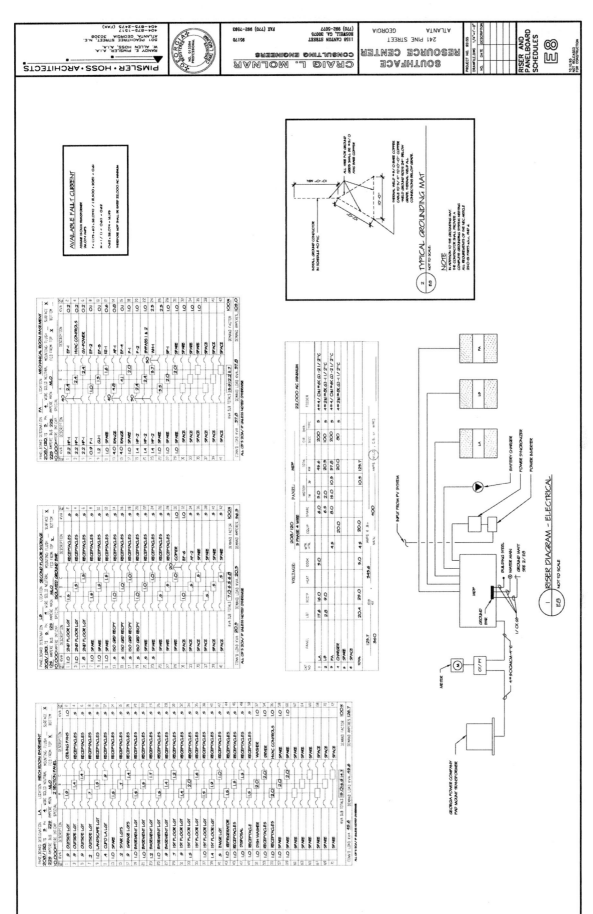

Figure 6-40

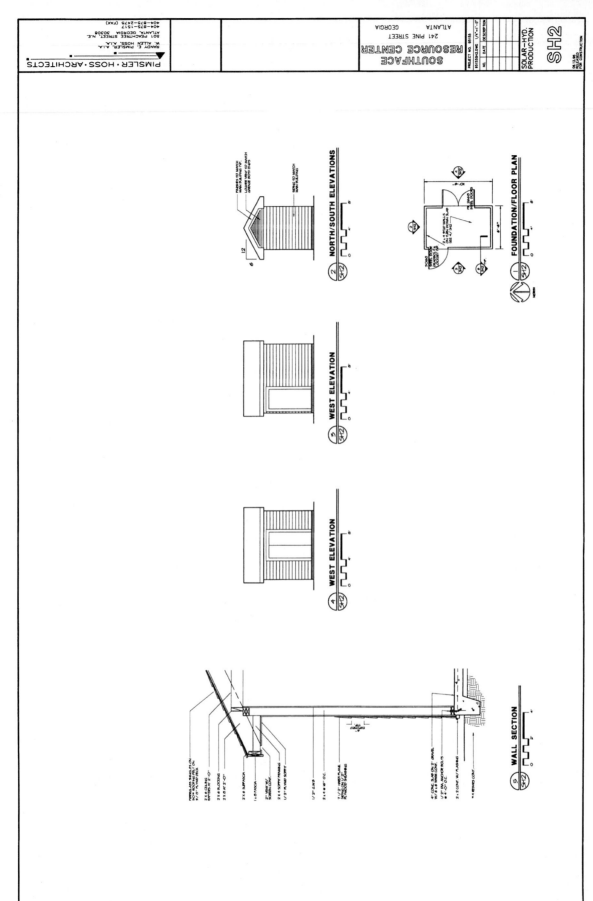

Figure 6-41

EXERCISES

Exercises in planning and drawing commercial buildings are best undertaken under the supervision of your instructor, who can check them occasionally and offer helpful criticism during the development. Start all exercises with sketches.

1. *Wayside rest station.* Design and prepare the working drawings for a small restroom facility to be located on a level, 1-acre lot along a federal highway. Provide for the following facilities:
   (a) Parking for 10 cars, one to be handicapped accessible
   (b) Parking for 3 semitrailer trucks
   (c) Restrooms for men and for women, handicapped accessible
   (d) Trash receptacles
   (e) Water fountains
   (f) Two picnic tables and benches
   Draw the plan, the elevations, the site plan, and the necessary details.

2. *Suburban hardware store.* Design and make the working drawings for a small hardware store on a commercial lot 170' wide and 290' deep. Use C.M.U. bearing wall construction with a concrete slab-on-ground floor and a steel joist roof structure. Provide for the following facilities:
   (a) Floor area of 8000 sq ft
   (b) Display windows across front
   (c) Storage space in rear with unloading doors
   (d) Private office, bookkeeping, and lounge of 1000 sq ft on the second floor above the storage
   (e) Restrooms
   (f) Checkout counter and merchandise counters and racks
   (g) Parking spaces

3. *Small chapel.* Design and draw the working drawings for a small chapel, 6000 sq ft, intended for people of all faiths. Use wood bearing walls and trusses. The lot is 5 acres. Provide for the following facilities:
   (a) Sanctuary to seat 250 people
   (b) Two private offices of 175 sq ft each
   (c) Choir loft to seat 20 people
   (d) Restrooms for men and for women
   (e) Kitchen

   (f) Nursery
   (g) Three classrooms
   (h) Provision for mechanical equipment and janitorial care
   (i) Parking space for 70 cars

4. *Retail sales building.* Design and draw the working drawings for a laundry and retail sales building 65'-0" wide by 70'-0" deep. The lot is 130' wide by 200' deep, and it slopes to the front. Use C.M.U. and brick veneer load-bearing construction with open web roof joists. Provide the following facilities:
   (a) Laundry 1300 sq ft
   (b) Retail sales 2700 sq ft
   (c) Canopy across front of building
   (d) Toilets
   (e) Mechanical equipment room
   (f) Drive-up laundry pickup
   (g) Parking for 23 cars

5. *Library building.* Prepare the working drawings for a suburban library building with two floor levels consisting of a ground floor and a mezzanine. Use C.M.U. and brick veneer walls. The floor is to be poured concrete, and the roof is to be open web joist. The basic width is to be 54'-0", and the length 91'-0". The first-floor-to-floor height is to be 11'-4", and second-floor-to-roof height is to be 12'-8". Put columns on approximate 18'-0" centers; use one elevator, two separate stairwells, toilets, and storage. Reserve space for air-conditioning equipment. Reserve the first-floor level for entry, checkout, conference, receiving, periodicals, reference, and audiovisuals. On the mezzanine level, provide book stacks of various sizes with convenient circulation arrangements around the perimeter of the building.
   Draw the following views, using the scale ¼" = 1'-0":
   (a) Two floor plans, first floor, and second-floor (mezzanine)
   (b) Two elevations
   (c) Site plan (convenient scale)
   (d) Transverse section

"A comfortable house is a great source of happiness. It ranks immediately after health and good conscience."
—SYDNEY SMITH

7

Each of the last three chapters in this manual includes an almost complete set of building plans that is intended for practice in learning to read architectural working drawings. One or two sections of the specifications for each building are also included to help you understand the relationship between the drawings and the specifications. A discussion of the sets of plans is included in the next three chapters as well as relevant tests to help you gain an understanding of architectural working drawings. Presented for study is a one-story bearing-wall and steel-frame building (discussion in Chapter 7 and drawings in Chapter 8), a three-story steel-frame building (discussion in Chapter 7 and drawings in Chapter 9), and a reinforced-concrete building (discussion in Chapter 7 and drawings in Chapter 10). These plans are typical for the three types of buildings and you will find that the drawings increase in complexity from one building to the next.

The actual drawings (which were 24″ × 36″ or 30″ × 42″) have been reduced in size to fit in this manual and some of the original drawings had to be left out. However, many of the details, shown on the omitted drawings, have been added to the drawings presented so that all essential details are included for a thorough understanding of the plans for each building. Because they were added on various drawings, wherever space was available, you will find a discontinuity in the reference system for some of the details that are shown on several of the drawings.

7.1
READING COMMERCIAL BUILDING DRAWINGS

In general, follow the points listed next in orienting yourself to any set of drawings that is unfamiliar to you. Keep in mind that drawings must be interpreted together and that they should not be taken as isolated sheets of information.

7.1.1 Get a General Impression of the Building

First, look over the site plan and the building elevations to create a preliminary mental image of the shape and size of the building. Look for the north arrow on the site plan so that the elevations can be related to the plan view. Some sets of drawings include a perspective view of the building on the cover sheet. When this is the case, relate the elevations to the perspective. Then, try to relate the elevations to the floor plan, and orient yourself to the front entrance where the main traffic will enter. Generally, the floor plan is placed with its front facing the lower edge of the sheet, but this procedure is not always followed (as is the case with the Small Post Office Building). Concern yourself with the exterior features first. Notice the materials used and where they appear. Look for irregular features on the elevations so that you can identify them on the plan and be positive of the orientation. Study the roof plan and notice the direction of the drainage. Of course, remember the purpose of the building and look for those features that you associate with this type of building.

7.1.2 Locate and Identify the "Bones" of the Structure

Study the longitudinal and/or transverse sections through the building. To orient these sections correctly, you may need to examine the plans again, since a building that is almost square in plan makes it questionable as to which is transverse and which is longitudinal. These sections are usually found on the architectural drawings, but the structural sheets will sometimes have full building sections. See if you can determine the structural system being used. If these complete sections are not included, look at the typical wall sections. Turn to the structural sheets to see where columns, girders, beams, etc., are located. You should try to visualize the skeleton that supports the building and its components. The foundation plan will show where columns and walls are placed. Look for grid and reference lines on both the architectural and structural sheets. In most cases, the skeleton members are associated with the reference lines. Try to understand where horizontal members, shown in sections, are supported and how their loads are transferred to columns or bearing walls.

7.1.3 Identify Unusual Drafting Techniques Employed by the Drafter to Show Information

You will find that working drawings done by different offices often vary somewhat in the way in which drawings, notes, and schedules are presented, even though a great deal of standardization exists in the industry. You will find differences on the drawings in the chapters that follow. Observing how these minor variations appear is a part of interpreting the drawings. Notice how leaders relate notes to features, how titles are arranged, and how cutting-plane lines and symbols are used to show the locations of sections. Examine the schedules and observe how they are used and the items that are covered by schedules. Structural, mechanical, and electrical drawings, usually prepared in separate offices, are especially noted for the way minor points are handled differently in comparison with the architectural drawings. Some symbols and abbreviations, too, vary with offices (and with drafters) and are sometimes troublesome for the novice.

7.1.4 Relate Sections and Construction Details to the Larger Views

Notice how sections and details are used to make the information shown on the plans and elevations understandable to the builder and how they identify the various items and materials necessary for construction. After you understand the labeling system employed throughout the drawings, relate the details to their position on the plans or elevations. Reference to various drawings may be necessary before this can be accomplished. Some sections, of course, are labeled as "typical" and have no definite cutting planes, but you should try to identify where, and to what extent, the typical construction applies. Some walls or parts of walls, for example, usually vary from the typical condition, and other specific details may (or may not) be included to explain the variation. It is always helpful to refer back to the longitudinal and transverse sections to relate these specific details to the building as a whole. You may need to examine the plans and elevations again to orient these details correctly and to determine their meaning.

7.1.5 Determine How the Mechanical Equipment, Plumbing, and Electrical Wiring Are Related to the Building

Look for the type of heating and cooling system being employed and how the ductwork fits into the structure. Most often the ducts are concealed above the ceiling, and diffusers are used to conduct the treated air to the spaces of the building. Air-handling units are frequently found on the roof, and the structural drawings then usually show extra supports to carry the weight of these units. Many times the reasons for lower ceiling heights in an area will be found on the mechanical drawings. While plumbing plans will show the domestic water lines and the sanitary sewer lines and vents, they will also frequently show the handling of the rainwater that falls on the roof.

Schedules on these drawings and particularly on the electrical drawings show the kind of equipment and lighting fixtures used in the building. The locations of switches and panel boxes identify places where conduit must be run and sometimes reveal why walls are shaped in an odd way or why structural and other building components are present in some areas.

7.2

READING THE SMALL POST OFFICE BUILDING DRAWINGS

Included in Chapter 8 is a set of working drawings for a one-story building that was designed to be used as a post office. Although not large, it represents a variety of construction features that should be interesting to study. Many energy saving techniques were used in the design of the building, which won an award in the Georgia Energy Design Competition, sponsored by the Georgia Chapter of AIA and the Georgia Power Company. The extensive use of insulation, the *earth-sheltered* effect of the earth berm on the north side of the building (Fig. 7-1), the use of clerestory windows that admit a lot of sunlight (which furnishes some heat and makes the interior bright enough so that interior lights are often unnecessary), and the use of a Trombe wall (Fig. 7-2) to furnish most of the heat during winter months are some of the energy-saving features of this building.

Technically called a *thermal storage wall*, a Trombe wall (see Fig. 7-3) absorbs heat from solar radiation that is transmitted to the wall through insulated glass. Vents in the bottom of the wall allow return air (unheated) to enter the space between the glass and the black-painted

Figure 7–1 Photograph of Small Post Office Building showing entrance and earth-sheltered portion of the structure.

Figure 7–2 Southwest view of the Small Post Office Building showing the windows in front of the Trombe Wall.

surface of the warm wall. When heated, the air rises and is vented into the building at the top of the wall. Distribution of the warm air throughout the building is often accomplished by venting the air into a plenum and moving the heated air with an in-line fan that is placed in the ductwork (as is the case in the Small Post Office Building). Heat is also radiated from the opposite side of the wall into the immediate space adjacent to the wall. To be effective, Trombe walls must have an unobstructed southern exposure, to take advantage of the sun, and must have

some kind of adjustable awning to shade the wall in the summer or when heat is not required.

7.2.1 General Impression of the Building

The site plan shows that the building is rectangular with an irregular shape in the lower-left corner and that north is toward the top of the page. A quick look at the floor plan reveals that the entrance is on the east side

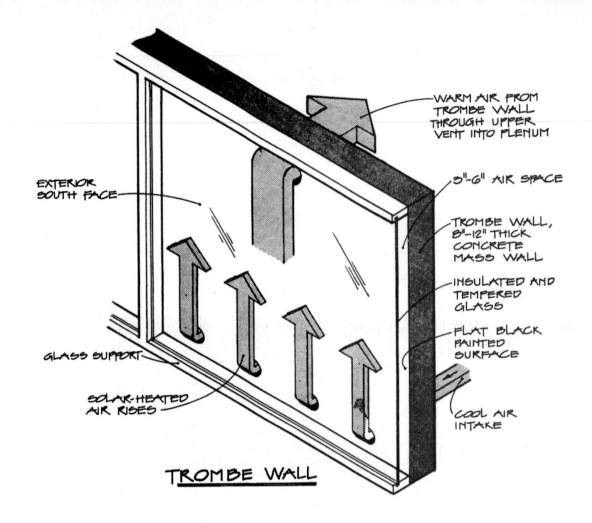

Figure 7–3 Diagrammatic view of a Trombe Wall.

Labels on figure:

WARM AIR FROM TROMBE WALL THROUGH UPPER VENT INTO PLENUM

3"-6" AIR SPACE

TROMBE WALL, 8"-12" THICK CONCRETE MASS WALL

INSULATED AND TEMPERED GLASS

FLAT BLACK PAINTED SURFACE

COOL AIR INTAKE

EXTERIOR SOUTH FACE

GLASS SUPPORT

SOLAR-HEATED AIR RISES

TROMBE WALL

of the building. The elevations indicate that the structure is a one-story building with the north side covered by an earth fill. The south elevation reveals a lot of glass and the Trombe wall, while the east elevation shows the entrance and what appears to be a roof with several levels. The west elevation shows a canopy over a loading dock that is in the southeast corner where the irregular shape in plan was noticed. The roof plan confirms the fact that the roof has four different levels and two clerestory windows that face south and extend across the entire building. It also indicates that all rainwater that falls on the roof will be taken to the ground through roof drains that are carried down into the interior of the building.

A flagpole close to the front of the building and customer parking convenient to the entrance are two of the features that are usually associated with a small post office. Another is the location of post office boxes in the Box Lobby. However, this arrangement of boxes is unlike those in most post offices and appears to offer a considerable advantage to customers in terms of space and light when they come to open their boxes.

A Service Lobby shows a counter and three service stations where stamps, special postage, etc., can be provided to customers.

7.2.2 The "Bones" of the Structure

The full sections on the architectural plans and the structural sheets indicate that a built-up roof on a metal deck is supported by open web joists, which are, in turn, supported by an overhanging steel beam system. The framing of the clerestory windows is unique. The joists of the higher portion of the roof rest on a steel-tube frame that is supported by a line of the overhanging beams, which also carries the load from the joists on the lower portion of the roof. Steel tube columns carry the beam loads to individual concrete footings. Wall footings below the outside of the building support the walls, most of which are reinforced-concrete retaining walls that also act as bearing walls for some of the roof joists. Sections reveal that the roof is cantilevered over the loading dock and that the floor of the entire building is a reinforced-concrete slab-on-grade.

7.2.3 Unusual Drafting Techniques Employed

Section cutting-plane symbols indicate the sheet on which the sections are drawn. The sections are also usually identified by a title, such as "Clerestory Window Section." Details are referenced by portions of circles around the components in question, and the sheet on which the detail is shown is indicated in the detail symbol. The structural plans utilize a special symbol to denote the approximate location of the stepped footings. It is very much like a $ sign, and the top of the footing elevation is given in feet and decimals of a foot alongside the outline of the footings on the foundation plan. Shaded portions on the site plan indicate shrubbery locations. Post office boxes are referred to as "lock boxes" and no details of the individual boxes are given, since the boxes are to be furnished by the Post Office Department.

7.2.4 Sections and Construction Details

The building section looking east shows thick batt insulation above a ceiling that slopes up to the clerestory windows. Other sections reveal that the ceiling heights vary from 8'-6" to 15'-0". A reinforced-concrete vault is shown in the building interior and a tall, reinforced-concrete retaining wall, which also serves as a bearing wall for roof joists, is indicated on the north side of the building. Details of the Trombe wall show the storefront-type windows that admit sunlight to the wall. Vents at the bottom of the wall allow return air to enter the space between the wall and the tempered glass windows. A plenum is indicated at the top of the wall where the duct system will conduct the heated air to other parts of the building. Details show that the parapet walls around the building are carried high enough to shield from view the mechanical equipment on the roof and the clerestory windows that are placed between the different roof levels. All details of the exterior walls show the "exterior wall finish system" (see the specification section shown in Chapter 8, Fig. 8-18) that has varying thicknesses of insulation on the walls, depending on the location.

7.2.5 Mechanical, Plumbing, and Electrical Features

Mechanical plans reveal that the ducts used for the heating and cooling system will be exposed to view below the ceilings and that the air will be released directly into the spaces of the building from diffusers in these ducts. An auxiliary heating unit, called an air-handling unit (heat pump), furnishes cool air or, when necessary, hot air in addition to (or in place of) heat from the Trombe wall. This unit is placed on the roof along with two small air-conditioning units.

The plumbing plans show that water lines will enter the northwest corner of the building and that the sanitary sewer will discharge in the same general area. It also shows that the rainwater carried to the interior of the building from the roof drains will be conducted, under the floor, to the south of the building. The site plan reveals that this rainwater will be discharged into a small retention pond on the south border of the property. A *vee-notched weir* will be used to control the release of the water from this retention pond.

The electrical plans indicate the type and general location of the lighting fixtures with the associated switches and wiring on the lighting plan. The wiring for the mechanical equipment, fan motors, and service outlets is indicated on the power plan. Smoke detector locations, fire alarm pull station locations, and the location of electrical panel boxes and fire control panels are also shown on the power plan.

Figures 8-1 through 8-18 in Chapter 8 are a near-complete set of building plans and a section of the specifications for the Small Post Office Building. Study the plans and specifications thoroughly before using them to take the tests that follow.

READING THE WORKING DRAWINGS FOR A STEEL-FRAME BUILDING

The plans of the Lakeside Centre Building #1 (Fig. 7-4A) are typical of modern office buildings that are built to provide leaseable space for a number of different clients. Because the lease space had not been "sold" at the time the Lakeside Centre drawings were prepared, only the "core" space was developed on the plans, and the design of the leasable space was left for future detailing. As tenants lease space in the building, specific plans are then prepared to fit the requirements of each lessee. This procedure gives the client the advantage of leasing as much (or as little) space as desired and having that space designed to the lessee's specifications. The construction of this type of "speculative office building" has become a popular technique, used by developers, to provide office space for an expanding business community.

Because the construction time required for the completion of the building was most important to the developer, as well as the total cost, the *Instructions to Bidders* and the *Bid Proposal Form* included several unique stipulations. One was the requirement that the contractor selected would accept the prebid contracts for the architectural precast concrete (Fig. 7-4B), the structural steel, and the elevators that had been secured by the developer. This would have the effect of reducing the total time required for construction. Another was that the bidders should submit a proposed time schedule for completing the building, and that this would be one of

Figure 7–4A View of completed Modern Office Building, Lakeside Centre Building #1.

150

Figure 7–4B Erecting the precast concrete panels.

the considerations used when awarding the contract. A further stipulation was that the bidder should submit unit prices for most items that would be required to finish the leasable space. The bidder also was required to agree to complete the work of finishing a portion of the leasable space if directed to do so by the developer. This procedure allowed any space leased during the construction period to be finished, without further bidding, by the same contractor that constructed the building. It also allowed the clients to move into the leased spaces at the earliest possible time.

Although entitled Building #1, this structure is an addition to a group of existing buildings in an office park called Lakeside Centre. Its location in a "campuslike" setting, close to a major transportation artery, makes the Lakeside Centre Building #1 a desirable address for tenants who lease space in the building.

The floor plans and the elevations on the architectural sheets and the framing plans on the structural sheets were drawn at a scale of $^{1}/_{16}" = 1'$-$0"$. This is one-half the usual scale and it makes these plans small, even on the original drawings. Since these plans and elevations are hard to read on the reduced set of drawings in Chapter 9, enlarged views are shown in this chapter.

7.3.1 General Impression on the Building

The site plan shows a building that is semicircular in plan, and the elevations indicate that it is a three-story

building having bands of windows alternating with precast concrete. Several different types of glass are used for the windows, and colored ceramic tile is used to accent the smooth precast concrete that has a sandblast finish (see Fig. 7-5). The floor plan reveals that the main entrance is on the northeast side of the building (facing the bottom of the sheet). A curved glass skylight covers a canopy that is placed over an entrance drive that will give passengers protection from inclement weather as they are discharged from cars at the front entrance. The two indentations on the sides of the building, shown on the site plan, are revealed by the floor plans to be additional first-floor entrances, connected by a long corridor.

The building elevations show that a metal-panel equipment screen covers the elevator penthouse and the HVAC units on the roof. The roof plan reveals that the flat roof slopes down from the edges of a parapet wall toward the interior. Roof drains are placed at the low points to conduct rainwater down roof leaders through the interior of the building. The leaders connect to pipes that run under the first floor slab and discharge the rainwater toward the front of the building. *Scuppers* are placed in the parapet wall to carry off excess rainwater if the drains become clogged.

The floor plans show the large areas of leasable space on each floor surrounding a central core. This core contains a Corridor, an Elevator Lobby with two elevators,

Figure 7–5 Closeup view of the precast concrete panels.

Figure 7–6 View of the skeleton steel frame.

two sets of Stairs, Toilets, and a Telephone/Electrical equipment room. The semicircular nature of the building offers the prospect that each office will have windows with a good view of the surrounding office park area.

7.3.2 The "Bones" of the Structure

The structural plans show the steel beams of the skeleton steel frame (Fig. 7-6) that is to carry the loads of the build-

Figure 7–7 Closeup view of the sprayed fireproofing on the steel beams and columns.

ing. The architectural wall section indicates that the steel frame is to be sprayed with two-hour-rated fire protection for all members except the roof members (Fig. 7-7). The roof consists of an EPDM (ethylene propylene diene monomer) elastic sheet roofing on rigid insulation and metal decking. This is supported by steel joists that rest on a cantilevered beam system that spans from column to column. A ⁵⁄₈″ fire-rated gypsum board suspended ceiling is to be attached below the roof framing. The first floor consists of a concrete slab-on-grade.

The floor framing plans indicate that a beam-and-girder system is employed on the second and third floors. Although the plan of the building is semicircular, the beam framing is rectangular, with beams placed at an angle as the circular wall intersects the rectangular framing. The beams and girders have ¾″ shear-studs welded through the metal decking to their top flanges to act with the poured concrete floors, making the floor system for each floor a *composite slab*. The number of evenly spaced shear-studs is indicated in small squares below each beam and girder.

7.3.3 Unusual Drafting Techniques Employed

Section cutting-plane symbols, as usual, indicate the sheet on which the sections are drawn, but the section and detail numbering system is unusual. Each sheet is divided into a grid with letters across the top and numbers down the side (see Fig. 7-8). The section or detail is numbered according to its placement on the sheet where it is drawn. For example, the **Screen Wall**

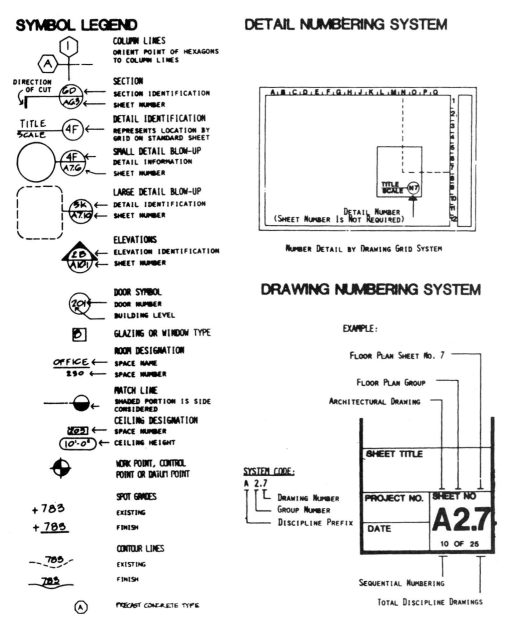

Figure 7–8 Explanation of the reference system used in the working drawings.

Section 10 P (see Fig. 9-4 in Chapter 9) is found opposite grid line 10 and under grid line P. This makes finding the section or detail most convenient. You will find, however, that a few of the sections and details do not conform to this system. The reason, as explained earlier, is that they were taken from drawings that had to be omitted and were placed in blank spaces on drawings that have been included.

The sheet decimal-numbering system is also somewhat different from most working drawings (see Fig. 7-8). Each sheet is given a discipline prefix and a group number within this discipline; then a decimal separates the drawing number within the group of drawings. The abbreviations, materials legend, and symbol legend shown on the cover sheet are a helpful aid to the reader of this set of working drawings.

The grid system used to identify columns and the like on the drawings is unique. The rectangular grid pattern is divided by radii that are numbered in decimals determined by the point where the radius intersects the horizontal grid line. Thus column J-1.3 is a member on grid line J and is located three-tenths of the distance from grid line 1 to grid line 2, where radius line 1.3 intersects the outside of the building. Grid line 0 is not indicated but is located at the top outside edge of the semicircular building.

Figures 7-9 through 7-18 are enlargements of various parts of the working drawings. Revisions on the drawings are clearly shown by the "clouds" (lines forming irregular circles) that surround the material that has been changed or inserted. Small triangles placed within or close to the "clouds" are references to the title block where the date and nature of the revision is shown. This revision section of the title block is important because it indicates whether or not the latest drawings are being used.

Notes on the structural plans identify the methods and symbols used to show tops of footing elevations, tops of structural steel elevations, camber in structural steel members, numbers of steel studs to be used on the beams and girders, and precast concrete connection locations. The column schedule shows the size of the columns used and also indicates the column base-plate sizes, the anchor bolt sizes, the size of footings, and the reinforcing steel required in each footing.

7.3.4 Sections and Construction Details

No transverse or longitudinal sections are shown in the plans, but the wall sections indicate that two distinct types of walls are employed in the building. The precast concrete and window-wall system surrounds most of the building, and a curtain wall covers a portion of the structure. Suspended ceilings of acoustical tile on a common grid system are indicated on the first and second floors, but the ceiling suspended from the roof is required to be constructed as a fire-rated assembly attached to metal studs on the bottom of the roof joists. A note reveals that only the ceiling grid is to be installed in the leasable space and that the acoustical tiles are N.I.C. (not in the contract).

Thick, rigid insulation material is shown between the metal studs that frame the inside of the wall section under the window wall system. Most of the glass in the windows is insulating glass. It is necessary to refer to a section of the specifications (included following the drawings) to determine the meaning of the various types of glass. The sections also show continuous slot diffusers around the edge of the ceiling at the walls. These diffusers are to conduct the heated or cooled air into the spaces of the building.

Details show that the columns are enclosed within metal stud and gypsum board surrounds. They also indicate that the rain leaders are enclosed within the gypsum board surrounds that cover some of the columns. The site plan reveals that the rain leaders empty into catch basins at the front of the building. These catch basins are part of the storm drainage system for the parking lot and are connected by various-sized CMP (corrugated metal pipe). The *invert* (bottom of pipe) elevations are given at each catch basin.

7.3.5 Mechanical, Plumbing, and Electrical Features

Only the first floor mechanical plan is included and it shows the HVAC (heating, ventilating, and air conditioning) system to be one that discharges the conditioned air primarily through the slot diffusers in the ceiling at the edge of the building. Three large HVAC units are shown on the roof plan close to the penthouse, and they are enclosed within the metal-panel mechanical equipment screen. The equipment in the duct system, identified by a notation such as PIU/1-11, refers to the Powered Induction Unit/Electric Duct Heater Schedule, which shows the air-handling capability of the units. Details of these PIU (powered induction units) that supply treated air to the slot diffusers are shown on the drawing along with the schedules. Ducts are located above the ceilings of the leasable spaces and stop at unspecified points. The specific locations for diffusers are not shown. The detailed locations for ducts and diffusers will be determined when tenants lease space on the floor.

The First-Floor Plumbing Plan shows that the cold-water line enters the building at the front through a 2½″ pipe. The water riser diagram is an elevation view rather than the usual isometric type. This is possible in this three-story building because almost all the water pipes are placed along the central core of the building and the toilets are directly over one another. The Sanitary Riser Diagram is also an elevation view, for the same reason, and reveals that there are six vents on the roof. The plan

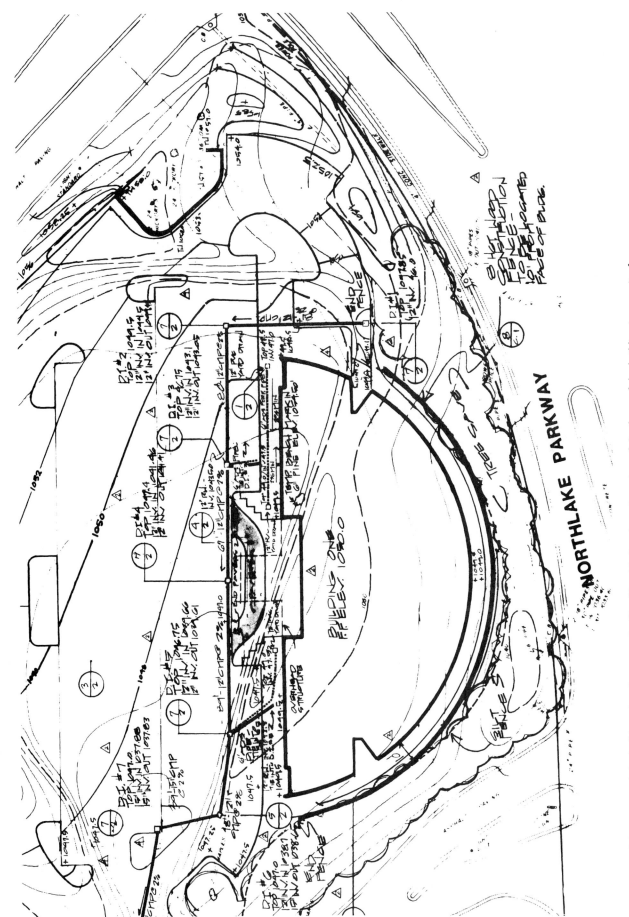

Figure 7–9 Enlargement of the building plan shown on the Site Plan. Notice the orientation of the front of the building is opposite from that shown on the floor plans.

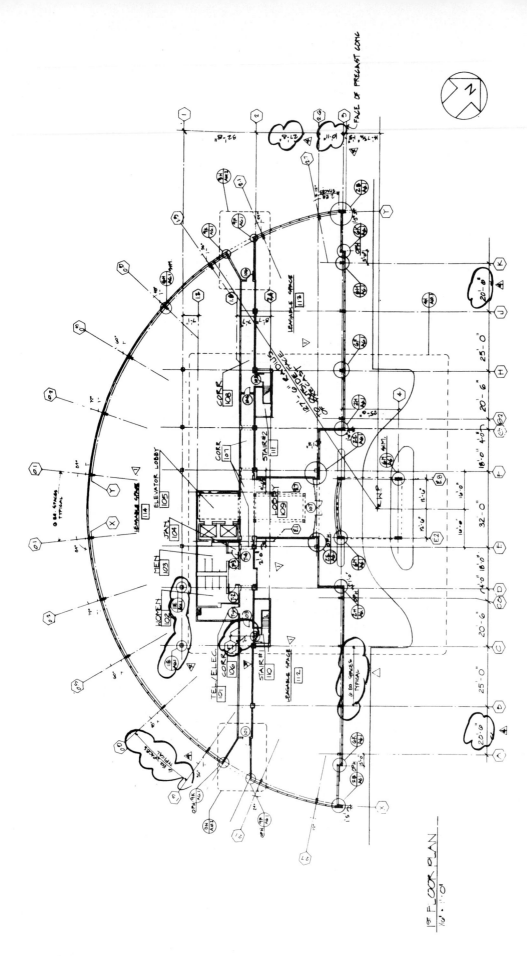

Figure 7–10 Enlargement of the First-Floor Plan.

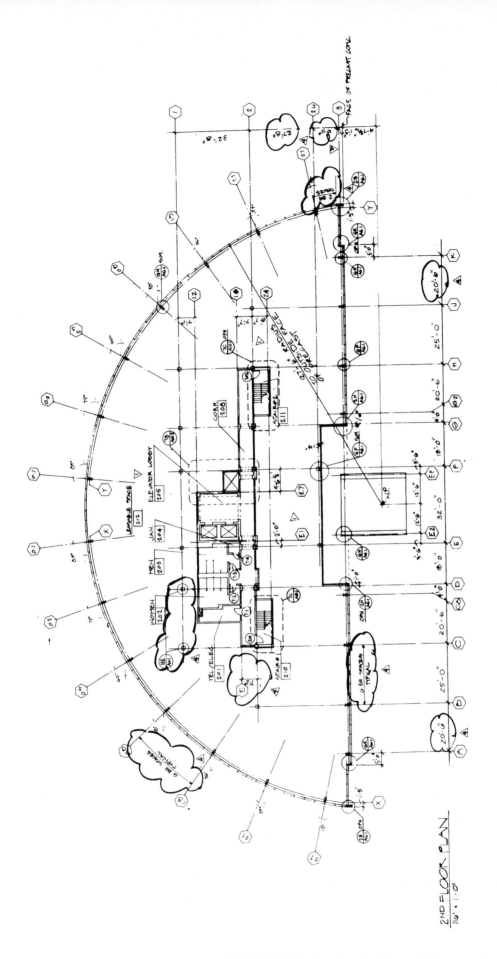

Figure 7–11 Enlargement of the Second-Floor Plan.

SECTION 7.3　Reading the Working Drawings for a Steel-Frame Building　**353**

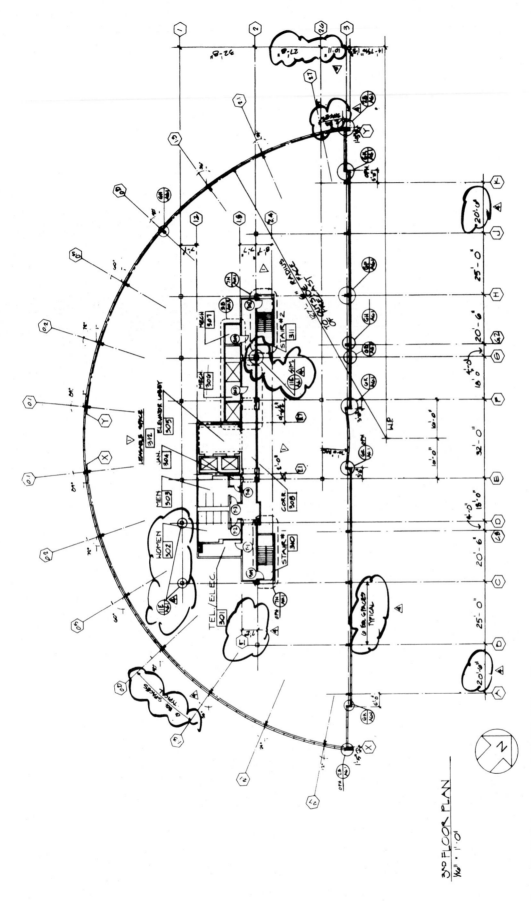

Figure 7–12 Enlargement of the Third-Floor Plan.

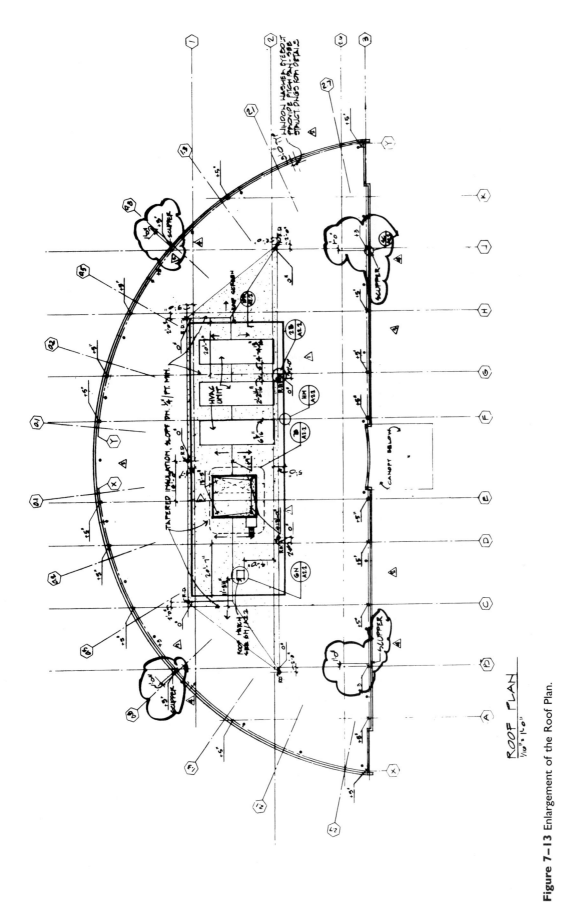

ROOF PLAN
1/16" = 1'-0"

Figure 7–13 Enlargement of the Roof Plan.

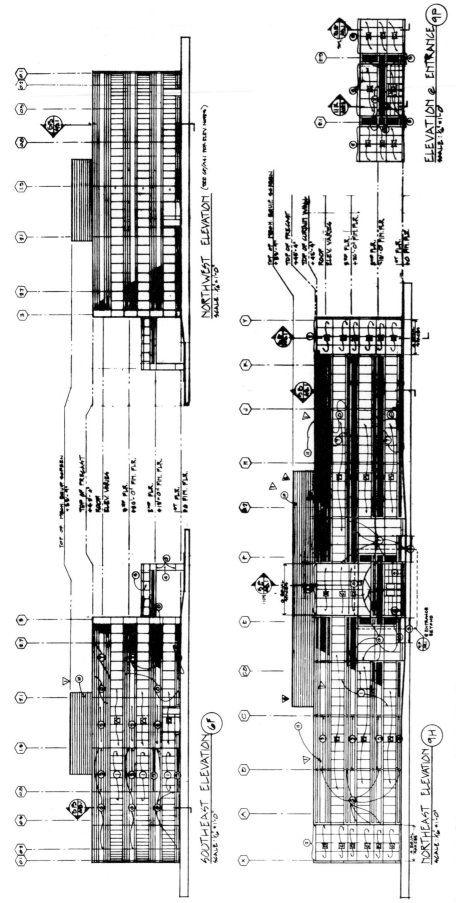

Figure 7–14 Enlargement of the building Elevations.

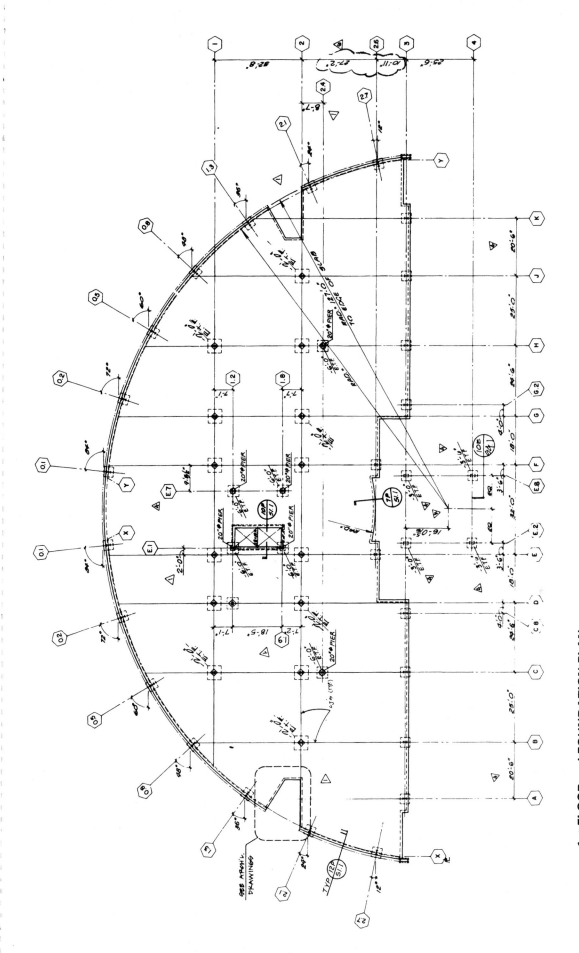

1st FLOOR and FOUNDATION PLAN

Figure 7–15 Enlargement of the structural First-Floor and Foundation Plan.

SECTION 7.3   Reading the Working Drawings for a Steel-Frame Building   **357**

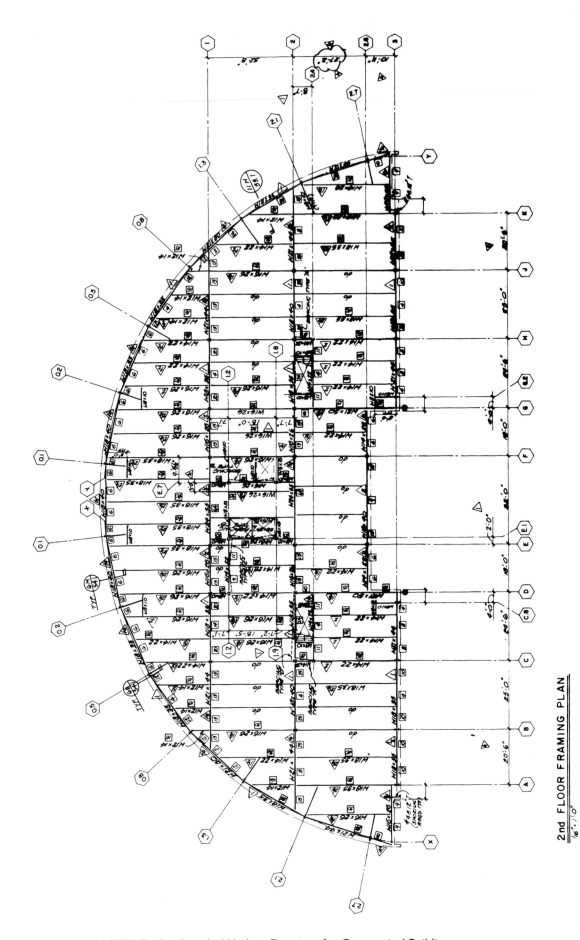

2nd FLOOR FRAMING PLAN
1/16" = 1'-0"

Figure 7–16 Enlargement of the structural Second-Floor Framing Plan.

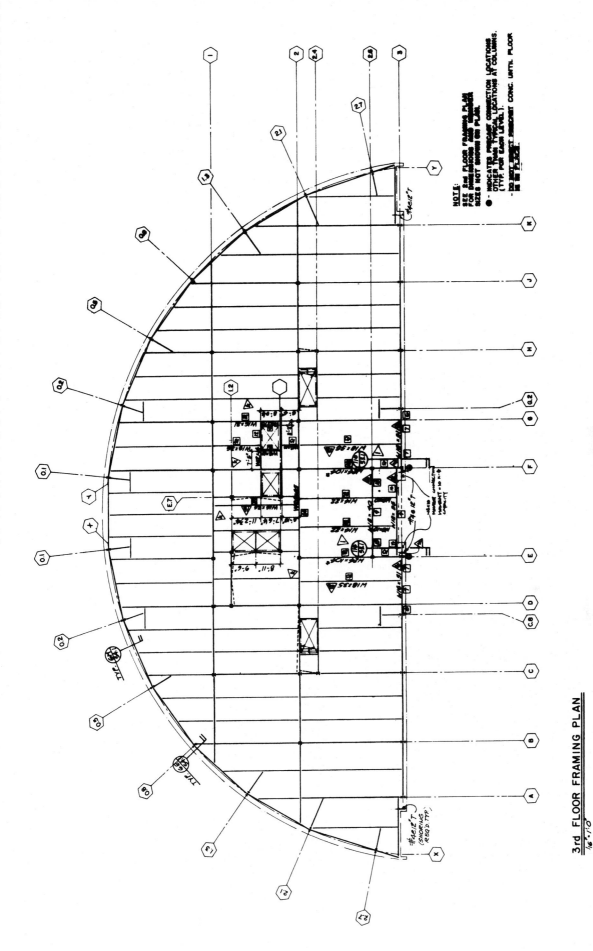

3rd FLOOR FRAMING PLAN
1/16" = 1'-0"

Figure 7–17 Enlargement of the structural Third-Floor Framing Plan.

SECTION 7.3   Reading the Working Drawings for a Steel-Frame Building   **359**

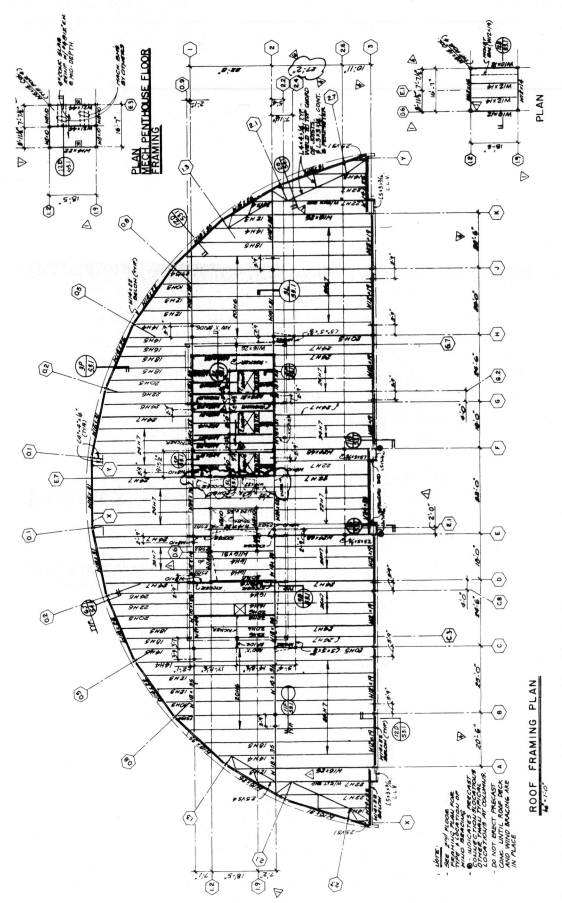

ROOF FRAMING PLAN
¼"=1'-0"

Figure 7–18 Enlargement of the structural Roof Framing Plan.

indicates that the sanitary sewer discharges toward the front of the building.

The First-Floor Electrical Lighting Plan shows that light fixtures are placed only in the central core and indicates that junction boxes are located so that lighting for tenant spaces can be added when those spaces are leased. The Electrical Power Plan shows a more complete treatment since the mechanical units, which are to be supplied with power, are not dependent on leasing tenant spaces. The Mechanical Equipment Schedule shows the electrical requirements of the PIU/EDH equipment. A Fire Alarm Riser Diagram is shown along with the Power Riser Diagram. The Lighting Fixture Schedule shown on sheet **E 4.1** was taken from one of the omitted drawings and refers to the electrical lighting plan.

7.3.6 THE STRUCTURAL STEEL SHOP DRAWINGS

Although not part of the working drawings, the structural steel *shop drawings* form an important link in the construction process. As previously stated, the contract to furnish the structural steel for the Lakeside Centre Building was negotiated prior to the awarding of the general contract. Thus, the work of detailing the steel was well underway before the general contractor had started his work.

Immediately following the set of Lakewood Centre Building #1 working drawings in Chapter 9 are two steel shop drawings for the project. One is a steel fabricator's Third-Floor Framing Plan (see Fig. 9-23), on which the beam sizes and column sizes are noted, and the other is a beam detail sheet (Fig. 9-24). Each identical beam on the framing plan is given a mark (such as **8A**) that identifies the shop drawing (sheet 8) on which the beam is detailed and is unique to the beams on the third floor. You will note that the beam labeled **8A** is on column line **2** and spans from column line **H** to column line **J**. This member is actually a *girder*, since beams frame into it from both sides; but the general term *beam* is used for all horizontal members by the fabricator.

Notice that on the beam detail sheet (Fig. 9-24) the *shop bolt symbol* is used to denote that the connection angles will be attached to the beam in the shop. Gage lines are drawn on the beam detail, 3″ apart, to denote that all bolt holes will be placed somewhere on these lines. The holes on the outstanding legs of the connection angles are offset (1½″) below the beam gage lines. This was done to make the field connection to the column easier. A note on the detail calls for four ¾″ diameter A325 high-strength bolts, 2¼″ long, to connect each end of the beam to the supporting columns.

You will see that all holes in the beam **8A** are dimensioned from the left end of the beam. Both feet and inch dimensions, as well as the total number of inches (given in parentheses), are shown for each set of bolt holes. For example, the distance to the holes on the right end of beam **8A** is shown as **24′-8 ¹³⁄₁₆″** as well as **(296.21)**

(inches). This is done to eliminate any *cumulative measuring error* that could occur by measuring from hole to hole.

The note **Camber 1″** is shown on the detail and is the value indicated on the working drawings as the expected beam deflection (see Fig. 7-17). The notation ***Gr-50*** means that the yield stress of the beam must be 50 ksi to agree with the requirements on the structural drawings. Although you will find only two beams marked **8A** on the fabricator's third-floor framing plan, the note **4-Beams-8A** indicates that the beams for the second floor are included with the third-floor beams since both floors are exactly the same.

The column detail shown on beam detail sheet 8 (Fig. 9-24) was taken from the fabricator's sheet 15 and attached to beam detail sheet 8 to save space in this set of drawings. The base plate **P6** (at the bottom of column **15C**), as well as another column (**15A**), was detailed on the fabricator's sheet 15 and both are shown in Fig. 3-28 in Chapter 3. You may notice that the column schedule on the structural drawings indicates that the W 10 × 49 section would be spliced to a W 8 × 24 section, just above the third floor, extending the column to the roof. The revision symbol and the note (in the Revisions section of title block) **Rev'd cut length of 15C** indicate that the fabricator requested and received approval to extend the W 10 × 49 section all the way from the footing to the roof. This would save the cost of making a connection between the W 10 × 49 section and the W 8 × 24 section. Such a connection would require a butt plate between the column sections because they have different depths (8″ and 10″). Even though the W 10 × 49 shape weighs more per foot of length and therefore costs more than the smaller section, the final cost would be less because of the saving in the cost of labor to make the connection.

Figures 9-1 through 9-22 in Chapter 9 are a near-complete set of building plans and two sections of the specifications for the Modern Office Building. Figures 9-23 and 9-24 are a portion of the structural steel shop drawings for the building. Study the plans, specifications, and shop drawings thoroughly before using them to take the tests that follow.

READING THE WORKING DRAWINGS FOR A REINFORCED-CONCRETE BUILDING

As an example of reinforced-concrete construction, the Outpatient Services Building (Fig. 7-19) was chosen for study in this text because it was designed with a popular type of architectural wall system and a common type of structural floor system. The building was built with a fast-track-type contract and was successfully completed in a minimum time and within budget.

Figure 7–19 View of the completed Outpatient Services Building.

Built as an adjunct to the regular hospital of the Northeast Georgia Medical Center, this building represents a continuing effort on the part of the directors of the center to lower medical costs while providing the best possible care to patients. Although the various treatment facilities are available to area physicians to treat their patients as outpatients and save much of the usual hospital cost, the facilities are also available to patients who must be confined in the hospital. A tunnel and a second-floor bridge connect the two buildings and provide easy access from one building to the other.

The building contract called for only the ground floor and the first two floors to be completely finished and the rest of the four-story building to be left as a shell for completion at a later time when funds were available. The purpose of this procedure was to allow the equipment on the lower floors to be used as soon as possible and to continue to be used while a later contract for finishing the upper floors was being completed. The working drawings and a section of the specifications for the Outpatient Services Building are included in Chapter 10 (Figs. 10-1 through 10-28) along with the preliminary drawings of the building (Figs. 10-29 through 10-31). It is interesting to note how little the exterior of the building was

changed in the final drawings. Some changes were made, however, in the interior location of the various rooms and service areas, and it should be informative for you to look for those changes.

7.4.1 General Impression of the Building

A rectangular building with a drive that circles close to the building is shown on the Site Plan. The Elevations and the Floor Plans reveal that the four-story building has a canopy (Fig. 7-20) built over this drive and that this is the entrance on the ground floor. The perspective on the title sheet indicates the massive nature of this canopy and shows the bands of precast concrete and windows that surround the building. Indentions in the front and back at the first and second stories of the building allow skylights to admit light into the interior of the building. The First Floor Plan reveals that business and patient areas share the portion of the floor that extends into the large canopy, and the Elevations show that the roof of the canopy is at the second-floor level.

The Elevations indicate that other extensions of the building, which overhang the ground floor, are carried all the way to the high roof on the northeast and southwest ends of the building. The Roof Plan indicates that the relatively flat roof has roof drains that carry rainwater down the interior of the building and that window washer anchors are located around the edge of the roof behind a low parapet wall. Two penthouses on the roof provide space for the electrical elevator hoisting equipment and for an opening to the roof area from Stair No. 1.

A small parking lot is revealed on the Site Plan close to the front entrance, and the title sheet perspective shows that a possible future parking facility is planned for the area northeast of the building. A Site Utility Plan indicates that extensive relocation of existing water and sewer lines was necessary before starting construction of the building. It also shows that a new drive, New Gold Street, is to be constructed around the Outpatient Services Building to connect with the existing hospital.

7.4.2 The "Bones" of the Structure

The wall sections and the structural plans reveal that a reinforced-concrete pan-joist floor system is supported by reinforced-concrete beams and columns from the first floor to the roof. A slab-on-grade forms the floor of the ground floor and a reinforced-concrete retaining wall is required on the northwest end of the building. Wall sections indicate that precast concrete panels are supported by spandrel beams around the edge of the structure and that window walls are supported by the precast concrete or by the reinforced-concrete spandrel beams.

Round concrete columns are indicated as supporting the entrance canopy, and square and round columns are located at various points within the structure. Two reinforced-concrete stairs are found in the interior of the building, as well as an elevator shaft that contains two elevators. The penthouses are framed of structural steel and are covered with an exterior insulation and finish system. The bridge connecting the Outpatient Services Building with the hospital is also indicated on the structural plans as being framed of structural steel.

7.4.3 Unusual Drafting Techniques Employed

Because of the complexity of the building, the original drawings required 66 sheets in the set of plans. A number of these sheets that were used to show large-scale

Figure 7–20 Outpatient Services Building showing the massive entrance canopy.

drawings of various areas and to show the unfinished third and fourth floors have been omitted from the set of drawings included in the text. Some of the drawings included in the text have been revised to show many of the details from the omitted sheets. The **Door Schedule,** shown on sheet A-8 (Fig. 10-7), contains only one-half of the total door schedule for the ground floor and the first floor. Floor plans for the second, third, and fourth floors have been omitted. Still, the drawings shown give an accurate impression of the building.

The section and detail reference symbols give the sheet number where the section or detail may be found. While no complete longitudinal or transverse section is presented, the large number of partial sections shown convey sufficient information to gain an understanding of the building.

Several unusual abbreviations are used. **F.O.S.** means "face of stud," where measurements of most spaces are referenced with arrowheads. Measurements to the center line of columns or studs are referenced with small dots. The abbreviation **U.O.N.** means "unless otherwise noted," **I.S.F.** means "inside face," and **O.F.S.** means "outside face."

The pan-joist floor is called a "floor slab" in the schedule shown on the structural drawings. The dimensions of the joists and beams, given on the schedule, are explained in Fig. 6-3. The size notation in the Floor Slab Schedule given as **16MF + 3¾C @ 36 o.c.** means 16″ metal-form joists, plus a 3¾″ concrete slab, spaced at 36″ on center. Double stirrups are used and are indicated as **Dbl.** in the schedule. Closed stirrups are called **hoops** on the structural drawings, the **W stirrups** indicated in the slab schedule are joist stirrups and are detailed on sheet S-10 (Fig. 10-21). Most of the reinforcing that is to be placed in the top of the joists or beams is shown on the Framing Plan by a heavy line, indicating the bar, and by a note, identifying the number and size of the reinforcing bars (see Fig. 7-21). Bar lengths are given as **3 #9 × 31′ + HKs,** which means three #9 bars 31 feet long with standard hooks on each end. Use of the abbreviation **HK** means a hook on one end only.

7.4.4 Sections and Construction Details

The wall sections indicate that the precast concrete panels are *ribbed,* which means that they have a ribbed texture on the face. Two different types are shown: one that supports the window wall at the floor level and one that extends above the floor 2′-8″. This longer panel has a ¼″ × 3½″ *reveal* that forms a horizontal shadow around that part of the building with these precast panels. The panels without the reveal are 5″ thick and the others are from 5⅜″ to 5½″ thick, including the ribbed surface.

The skylight in the Lobby on the ground floor is unusual in that the light that enters the lobby is admitted at the second-floor level. The sloping ceiling and the sloping skylight are shown in the **Lobby Cross Section D-A9** (Fig. 10-8). This section also indicates that Sound Absorption Panels, which have a unique design, are used on the walls of the Lobby. Part of the Lobby extends up through the first-floor level to the second floor.

Suspended ceilings are used in most areas of the building. Sound Attenuation Blankets are placed above the ceilings on each side of the partition walls that divide some rooms from corridors and from other public places. These "sound blankets," which extend a distance of 2′-0″ on each side of the partitions in the ceiling, are also placed in many of the partition walls.

The details indicate that the round columns that are visible in some areas are covered with the vinyl wall covering used on most partition walls. The square columns are covered with ½″ gypsum board in nonrated spaces and with ⅝″ rated gypsum board in one-hour fire-rated areas.

7.4.5 Mechanical, Plumbing, and Electrical Features

The Mechanical Ground Floor Plan shows a heating and cooling system that is placed in the Mechanical Room #29. Ductwork varying from 28″ × 26″ to 6″ × 6″ distributes conditioned air to all spaces on the ground floor. Powered Induction Units **(VAC-PI)** are placed in the distribution system at various points. Most ductwork is placed above the suspended ceilings, and various kinds of ceiling-type diffusers are used to distribute the air. The locations of these diffusers are shown on the Reflected Ceiling Plan of the architectural drawings.

The Ground Floor Plumbing Plan—Soil Waste, Vent, and Rainwater shows that the sewer pipes empty toward the front of the building into an existing sewer manhole. The rainwater pipe, which carries rainwater from the roof (shown as **RW** on the plans), empties into a stormwater drain that is also in the front of the building. The rain leaders from the roof are noted as **DS** (downspouts) on the drawings. The footing drain that is placed around the back of the building is connected into the line that also carries off the rainwater from the roof.

The domestic water, fire, and natural gas lines all enter the building on the north corner. A water meter and a gas meter are placed behind the retaining wall at that location. The pipes are carried up to the floors above through a *pipe chase* that is located in the Mechanical Room.

Since the sheet of the original drawings that contained the electrical symbols was omitted and because the symbols are unusual, the Electrical Symbols chart is shown in Fig. 7-22. The Ground Floor Plan—Lighting shows

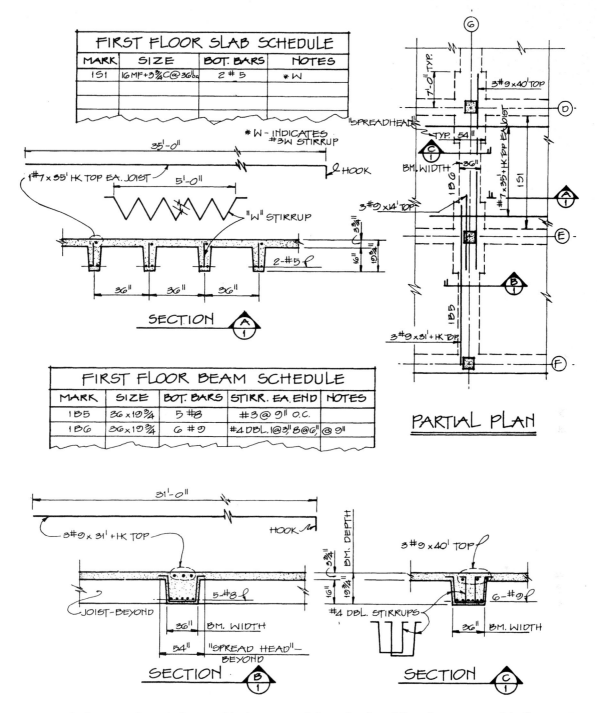

FIRST FLOOR SLAB SCHEDULE

MARK	SIZE	BOT. BARS	NOTES
151	16MF+3¾C@36bₐ	2#5	*W

* W - INDICATES #3W STIRRUP

1#7 x 35' HK TOP EA. JOIST

"W" STIRRUP

ℓ HOOK

2-#5 ℓ

SECTION Ⓐ/1

FIRST FLOOR BEAM SCHEDULE

MARK	SIZE	BOT. BARS	STIRR. EA. END	NOTES
1B5	36 x 19¾	5#8	#3@9" O.C.	
1B6	36 x 19¾	6#9	#4 DBL. 1@3"8@6" @9"	

PARTIAL PLAN

3#9 x 40' TOP

"SPREADHEAD"

TYP. 54"

BM. WIDTH 36"

1#7 x 35' HK TOP EA. JOIST

3#9 x 14' TOP

151

1B6

1B5

3#9 x 31' + HK TOP

SECTION Ⓑ/1

3#9 x 31' + HK TOP

HOOK

JOIST-BEYOND

5#8 ℓ

36" BM. WIDTH

54" "SPREAD HEAD" BEYOND

SECTION Ⓒ/1

BM. DEPTH

3#9 x 40' TOP

#4 DBL. STIRRUPS

6-#9 ℓ

36" BM. WIDTH

Figure 7–21 Explaination of terminology used in the structural sheets for the reinforced concrete pan-joist floor system.

that most fixtures are fluorescent type and are placed in the suspended ceiling. The Ground Floor Plan—Power indicates that the electric power enters the building through the tunnel that connects with the existing hospital. An Auxiliary Power Plan shows the connections to the ceiling speakers and other auxiliary equipment.

Figures 10-1 through 10-31 in Chapter 10 are a near-complete set of building plans, a section of the specifications, and the preliminary drawings for the Outpatient Services Building. Study these plans and specifications thoroughly before using them to take the tests that follow.

- Fluorescent fixture & outlet - Type A unless noted otherwise.
- Incandescent fixture & outlet.
- Incandescent bracket & outlet.
- Exit sign fixture & outlet.
- Duplex receptacle - 16" high - Hubbell #8200 (15A-2P-3W).
- Duplex receptacle - 48" high - Hubbell #8200 (15A-2P-3W).
- Duplex receptacle - 16" high - Hubbell #8300 (20A-2P-3W).
GFI - Duplex receptacle - 48" high - Hubbell #GF8200-I.
WP - Duplex receptacle - 16" high - Hubbell #GF8200/5205WO.
EWC - Duplex receptacle for electric water cooler - 16" high - Hubbell #8200.
- Power receptacle - 50A/208V/1∅-2P+ gnd. Hubbell #9367/9368. Label "X-Ray" - 16" high.
(J) - Junction box.
- Nurse call dome light.
(D) - Automatic door operator motion detector unit.
- Floor box - flush mounted.
- Duplex receptacle flush mounted in floor.
(F) - Fire line flow switch.
(M) - Fire line monitor switch.
(FS) - Firestat - install & connect.
(PE) - Photo-electric control and relay.
(C) - Clock & Clock outlet - 7'-6" high.
(C) - Time elapse clock with reset pushbutton below at 4'-0".
- Emergency call station - 48" high plus pull cord to floor.
- Push button for program bell - 4'-0" high.
- Auto. door push button - 4'-0" high.
- Push button station - push on - push off control - 4'-0" high.
- Electric panelboard.
- Pull box.
(M) - Electric motor connection - HP/volt/∅ as noted.
- Safety disconnect switch - fuse as noted.
- Magnetic starter connection.
(E) - Break-glass station - 4'-0" high.
(E) - Chime - 7'-6" high.
(E) - Audio-visual alarm signal - 7'-6" high.
(T) - Dry type transformer - size as noted.
(SD) - Smoke detector - provide & connect in duct.
(M) - Monitor switch on fire line valve - see plbg.
(L) - Operating light control switch - 4'-0" high.
- Program Bell - 7'-6" high.
(SD) - Smoke detector - ceiling mtd. - provide & connect.
(HD) - Heat detector - ceiling mtd. - provide & connect.
- Nurse call - desk mounted from outlet 16" high.
(N) - Nurse call - wall mounted station 48" high.
(NC) - Nurse call control console (main station).
(NCC) - Nurse call control cabinet - flush mtd. in wall.
S(N) - Nurse call staff station - 48" high.
- Intentional grounding connection per NEC.

S - Single pole switch - Hubbell #1201-I - 4'-0" high.
S₃ - Three-way switch - Hubbell #1201-I - 4'-0" high.
Sₖ - Single pole switch - Hubbell #1201-L-I 4'-0" high.
- Telephone outlet - 16" high.
TEB - Telephone equipment backboard.
- Telephone conduit & pull cord.
- Conduit homerun to T.E.B.
- Nurse call conduit & wiring per mfgr's requirements.
NCC - Conduit homerun to N.C.C.
- Wiring in conduit exposed on ceiling on wall.
- Wiring in conduit concealed in ceiling or wall.
- Wiring in conduit concealed in floor or wall.
- Flexible wiring in flexible conduit.
- Wiring in conduit homerun to panelboard.
- Magnetic door holder - Firemark #FM-997/V to match existing system.
- Flush mounted ceiling speaker, grille, backbox, and baffle.
- Electric door lock connection.
- Surface wall mounted speaker, backbox, and baffle.
(TVC) - Install camera in enclosure with automatic pan drive. Provide flexi-coil video & control, & power connections.
TVC - Fixed camera - ceiling mounted.
TVC - Fixed camera - ceiling enclosure.
WP TVC - Exterior camera.
TVCZL - Roof mounted camera w/zoom lens.
- Belden #8241 in 3/4"C. to T.V. monitor - J.B. mounted under floor under T.V. monitor location and thence up to T.V. monitor through wire way. Locate monitors in security operations room with other monitors.

Figure 7-22 Special electrical symbols used on the Outpatient Services Building.
(Courtesy Chegwidden, Dorsey, and Holmes)

APPENDIX A: ABBREVIATIONS USED IN ARCHITECTURAL DRAWINGS

Above finished floor	AFF
Above finished grade	AFG
Acoustical ceiling tile	ACT
Acoustical tile ceiling	ATC
Adjacent; adjoining; adjustable	ADJ
Administration	ADMIN
Air condition	A/C
Air conditioning unit	A/C UNIT
Air handling unit	AHU
Air vent; acid vent; audio visual	AV
Alternate; altitude	ALT
Alternating current; armored cable; asbestos cement; asphaltic concrete	AC
Aluminum	ALUM
American Architectural Manufacturers Association	AAMA
American Concrete Institute	ACI
American Gas Association	AGA
American Institute of Architects	AIA
American Institute of Steel Construction	AISC
American National Standards Institute	ANSI
American Plywood Association	APA
American Society for Testing and Materials	ASTM
American Society of Heating, Refrigerating, and Air Conditioning Engineers	ASHRAE
American wire gauge	AWG
Americans with Disabilities Act	ADA
Amount	AMT
Ampere	AMP
Anchor bolt	AB

Angle; liter	L
Anodize	ANOD
Apartment; Association for Preservation Technology	APT
Architect	ARCH
Architect/engineer	A/E
Architectural woodwork; acid waste; actual weight	AW
Architectural Woodworking Institute	AWI
Area drain	AD
Asphalt	ASPH
Associated Builders and Contractors; aggregate base course	ABC
Associated General Contractors	AGC
Attention	ATTN
Automatic	AUTO
Avenue	AVE
Average	AVG
Awning window	AWN WDW
Balcony	BALC
Ballast	BLST
Base board radiator	BBR
Base line; building line	BL
Base plate	B PL
Baseboard; bulletin board	BB
Basement	BSMT
Beam; benchmark; bending moment	BM
Beam; wide flange	WF BM
Bearing	BRG
Bedroom	BR
Below ceiling	BLW CLG
Below finish floor	BFF
Benchmark; beam; bending moment	BM
Better	BTR
Between	BTWN
Bevel	BEV
Bituminous	BITUM
Blanket	BLKT

Board; butterfly damper	BD	Celsius; channel	C
Board feet (foot)	BD FT	Cement; cemetery	CEM
Board measure	B/M	Cement finish	CEM FIN
Bookcase; back of curb; between centers; bolt circle; bottom chord; brick color; building code	BC	Cement plaster	CEM PLAS
		Center; contour; cooling tower return	CTR
		Center line; class; close	CL
Borrowed light; built	BLT	Center to center	C TO C
Both faces; bottom face	BF	Centimeter	cm
Both sides	BS	Ceramic	CER
Both ways	BW	Ceramic tile; count; current transformer	CT
Bottom	BOT	Ceramic tile base	CTB
Bottom of steel	BOS	Ceramic tile floor	CTF
Boulevard	BLVD	Ceramic Tile Institute of America	CTI
Breaker	BRKR	Certify	CERT
Brick Institute of America	BIA	Chalkboard	CH BD
Bridging	BRDG	Chilled drinking water	CDW
British thermal unit	Btu	Circle	CIR
Bronze	BRZ	Circuit	CKT
Broom closet	B CL	Cladding	CLDG
Building	BLDG	Class A door	A LABEL
Building line	BL	Class B door	B LABEL
Building Officials and Code Administrators Association International	BOCA	Class C door	C LABEL
		Classroom	CLRM
Building paper	BP	Cleanout; carbon monoxide; cased opening; Certificate of Occupancy; company; cutout	CO
Built-up roofing	BUR		
Cabinet	CAB	Closet	CLO
Cabinet unit heater	CUH	Closet rod; control relay; control room	CR
Cable television	CTV	Clothes dryer	CL D
Calked joint	CLKJ	Coaxial cable	COAX
Canopy	CAN	Coefficient of performance (heating); coping	COP
Cantilever	CANTIL		
Carpet; control power transformer	CPT	Coefficient of utilization; cubic; copper	CU
Carpet and pad	C&P	Column	COL
Carriage bolt; catch basin; cement base; ceramic base; corner bead	CB	Combination; combined	COMB
		Common	COM
Cased opening; carbon monoxide; Certificate of Occupancy; cleanout; company; cutout	CO	Communication	COMM
		Concrete; concentric	CONC
		Concrete floor	CONC FLR
Casement	CSMT	Concrete masonry unit	CMU
Casement window; chemical waste line; clockwise; cold water piping; cool white	CW	Concrete Reinforcing Steel Institute	CRSI
		Condenser, condition	COND
		Conference	CONF
Casework	CSWK	Construction	CONSTR
Casing	CSG	Construction documents; candela; contract documents	CD
Cast concrete	C CONC		
Cast-in-place; cast iron pipe	CIP	Construction joint; control joint	CJ
Cast iron; curb inlet	CI	Construction management; center matched	CM
Cast stone; commercial standard; control switch	CS		
		Construction Specifications Institute	CSI
Catch basin; carriage bolt; cement base; ceramic base; corner bead	CB	Continue; controller	CONT
		Control	CTRL
Cavity	CAV	Control joint; construction joint	CJ
Ceiling	CLG	Control panel; candlepower; concrete pipe	CP
Ceiling diffuser	CLG DIFF		
Ceiling grille	CLG GRL	Coordinate	COORD
Ceiling height	CLG HT	Counter	CNTR

Counter sunk	CSK	Drinking fountain; damage free;	
Counterflashing	CFLG	diesel fuel	DF
Crossbracing	XBRA	Duplex outlet	DX OUT
Cubic feet	CU FT	Duplicate	DUPL
Cubic feet per minute	CFM	Dutch door	DT DR
Cubic feet per second	CFS	Each	EA
Cubic yard	CU YD	Each way	EW
Curb and gutter	C&G	Easement	ESMT
Cut stone	CT STN	East; modulus of elasticity	E
Dampproofing	DMPF	Edge of curb	EC
Decibel	dB	Edge of pavement (paving);	
Demolition; demonstration	DEMO	electrical panel (panelboard)	EP
Demountable partition	DPTN	Edge of slab	EOS
Department	DEPT	Electric	ELEC
Design	DSGN	Electric heater	EH
Detail	DET	Electric water cooler	EWC
Diagonal; diagram	DIAG	Electric water heater	EWH
Diameter	DIA	Elementary; element	ELEM
Difference; differential; diffuser	DIFF	Elevation; each layer;	
Dimension	DIM	easement line	EL
Dining room; door; drain;		Elevator	ELEV
dressing room; drive	DR	Emergency	EMER
Dishwasher; distilled water;		Enamel	ENAM
domestic water	DW	Enclosure	ENCL
Disposal	DSPL	Engineered Wood Association	EWA
Distance; district	DIST	Engineers Joint Contract	
Division; divide	DIV	Documents Committee	EJCDC
Domestic	DOM	Entrance	ENTR
Domestic hot water; double		Environmental Protection Agency	EPA
hung windows	DHW	Equal	EQ
Domestic water heater	DWH	Equipment	EQUIP
Door; dining room; drain;		Equivalent	EQUIV
dressing room; drive	DR	Estimate	EST
Door frame	DR FR	Et cetera; and so forth	ETC
Door stop	DRST	Evacuate	EVAC
Double	DBL	Evaporate	EVAP
Double acting door	DBL ACT DR	Evaporative cooling unit	ECU
Double glaze	DBL GLZ	Example	EX
Double hung (door, window)	DH	Exhaust; exhibit	EXH
Double hung windows; domestic		Existing	EXIST
hot water	DHW	Existing grade	EXST GR
Double joist	DJ	Exit light	EXT LT
Double strength (glass); disconnect		Expansion; expand; exposed	EXP
switch; downspout	DS	Expansion bolt	EXP BT
Douglas fir	DOUG FIR	Expansion joint	EJ
Dovetail	DVTL	Exterior; external; extinguisher	EXT
Downspout; disconnect switch;		Exterior finish; each face	EF
double strength (glass)	DS	Exterior finish system	EFS
Dozen	DOZ	Exterior grade	EXT GR
Drain tile	DT	Fabric	FAB
Drain, waste, and vent	DWV	Face brick	FC BRK
Drawer; domestic water return	DWR	Face of concrete; face of curb	FOC
Drawing	DWG	Face of masonry	FOM
Dressed four sides	D4S	Face of stud; face of slab;	
Dressing area	DR AREA	fuel oil supply	FOS
Dressing room; dining room;		Face of wall	FOW
door; drain; drive	DR	Face to face	F/F

Fahrenheit; female; fire line	F	Glazed concrete masonry unit	GLZ CMU
Fascia; fire alarm station	FAS	Glazed structural unit	GSU
Fascia board	FAS BD	Glazed wall tile	GWT
Federal Housing Administration	FHA	Glazing	GLZ
Feet; fire treated; foot; fully		Glued laminated wood	GLU LAM
tempered (glass)	FT	Grade beam	GR BM
Feet per minute	FPM	Granite	GRAN
Fiberglass	FGL	Ground fault circuit interrupter	GFCI
Figure	FIG	Ground floor	GR FL
File cabinet; footcandle	FC	Grout; grease trap; gross ton	GT
Finish	FIN	Guarantee	GUAR
Finish floor elevation	FF EL	Gutter	GUT
Finish grade	FIN GR	Gymnasium	GYM
Finished opening; field order; fuel oil	FO	Gypsum	GYP
Fire alarm; face area; final		Gypsum Association; gage	GA
assembly; fresh air	FA	Gypsum board	GYP BD
Fire brick	F BRK	Gypsum plaster	GYP PLAS
Fire extinguisher	FE	Gypsum plaster ceiling	GPC
Fire extinguisher cabinet	FEC	Hand dryer; heavy duty	HD
Fireproof; fire protection; flagpole;		Handicap; heating coil; heavy	
freezing point	FP	commercial; hollow core;	
Flashing	FLASH	hose cabinet	HC
Flexible	FLEX	Handicapped	HCP
Float glass	FLT GL	Handrail	HNDRL
Floor; filler	FLR	Hardboard	HDBD
Floor area ratio	FAR	Hardware	HDW
Floor drain	FD	Head joint	HD JT
Floor sink	FLR SK	Header	HDR
Flooring; flange	FLG	Headquarters	HQ
Fluorescent	FLUOR	Heat-strengthened (glass); hand sink;	
Foot; feet; fire treated;		high strength	HS
fully tempered (glass)	FT	Heat absorbing glass	HAGL
Foot board measure	FBM	Heat treated (glass)	HT TRD
Footing	FTG	Heating, ventilating, and	
Foundation	FDTN	air conditioning	HVAC
Freezer	FRZ	Height	HT
Frosted glass	FRST GL	Hemlock	HEM
Full scale; far side; Federal		Hexagon; heat exchanger	HEX
Specification; fire station; full size	FS	Hollow concrete masonry unit	HCMU
Fully tempered (glass); feet;		Hollow core; handicap; heating coil;	
fire treated; foot	FT	heavy commercial; hose cabinet	HC
Furnace; furnish; furniture	FURN	Hollow core wood door	HCWD
Furring	FURG	Hollow metal	HM
Gage; Gypsum Association	GA	Hollow metal door; humidity	HMD
Gallon	GAL	Hollow Metal Manufacturers	
Gallons per minute	GPM	Association	HMMA
Galvanized; galvanic	GALV	Horizontal	HORIZ
Galvanized iron	GI	Horsepower; heat pump; high pressure	HP
Galvanized steel	GALV STL	Hose bibb	HB
Garden	GRDN	Hospital	HOSP
Gas fired water heater	GWH	Hot and cold water	H&CW
Gauge	—	Hot water	HW
General; generator	GEN	House	HSE
General contractor	GC	Hydrant	HYD
Glass; ground level	GL	I beam	IB
Glass block	GL BLK	Identification; inside diameter;	
Glass-fiber-reinforced concrete	GFRC	inside dimension; interior design	ID

Illumination	ILLUM	Louver	LVR
Illumination Engineering Society of North America	IESNA	Louver door	LVDR
		Lumber	LBR
Incandescent	INCAND	Mahogany	MAHOG
Independent; industrial	IND	Mail box; machine bolt; mixing box	MB
Indoor air quality	IAQ	Maintenance	MAINT
Information	INFO	Management	MGT
Insect screen; island	IS	Manhole	MH
Inside diameter; identification; inside dimension; interior design	ID	Manual	MAN
		Manufactured	MFD
Inside face of stud	IFS	Manufacturer; mass flow rate	MFR
Insulation	INSUL	Manufacturing	MFG
Interior	INT	Marble Institute of America	MIA
International Building Code	IBC	Masonry opening; motor operated	MO
Invert	INV	Master bedroom; member	MBR
Invert elevation	INV EL	Material	MATL
Iron pipe	IP	Maximum	MAX
Jalousie	JAL	Mechanical	MECH
Janitor	JAN	Mechanical contractor; manhole cover; medicine cabinet; metal-clad; moisture content; moment connection	MC
Janitor's sink	JS		
Keyway	KWY		
Kickplate	KPL	Mechanical engineer	ME
Kiln dried; knocked down	KD	Mechanical room	MECH RM
Kilowatt	kW	Medical; medium	MED
Kitchen	KIT	Medicine cabinet; manhole cover; mechanical contractor; metal-clad; moisture content; moment connection	MC
Kitchen cabinet	KC		
Knock out panel	KOP		
Laboratory	LAB		
Laminate	LAM	Medium; medical	MED
Laminated glass	LAM GL	Meeting; mounting	MTG
Landing	LDG	Membrane	MEMB
Lath and plaster	L&P	Membrane waterproofing	MWP
Laundry	LAU	Metal	MTL
Lavatory	LAV	Metal flashing	METF
Left hand; latent heat	LH	Metal lath; materials list; monolithic	ML
Left hand reverse; latent heat ratio	LHR	Metal lath and plaster	ML&P
Library	LIB	Metal roof	METR
Light	LT	Meter	m
Light gage	LT GA	Microwave; megawatt	MW
Light switch	LT SW	Middle	MID
Lighting	LTG	Mill finish; mastic floor	MF
Lightweight	LT WT	Millimeter	mm
Lightweight concrete	LWC	Millwork	MLWK
Lightweight concrete masonry unit	LCMU	Minimum; minute	MIN
Limestone	LMST	Miscellaneous	MISC
Limited	LTD	Modified bitumen	MOD BIT
Linear	LIN	Modify; model; module; motor operated damper	MOD
Linear ceiling diffuser	LCD		
Linear diffuser	LD	Moisture resistant	MR
Linear feet (foot)	LF	Molding (moulding)	MLDG
Linen closet	L CL	Mop sink; machine screw; motor starter	MS
Linoleum	LINO		
Living room	LR	Mounted; mean temperature difference	MTD
Load-bearing	LD BRG	Movable	MVBL
Location	LOC	Mullion	MULL
Locker	LKR	Multiple	MULT
Loose fill insulation	LF INS	National Bureau of Standards	NBS

National Electrical Code	NEC	Portland Cement Association	PCA
National Institute of Building Sciences	NIBS	Portland cement plaster	PCP
Natural	NAT	Position; positive	POS
Natural gas; girder; ground	G	Post office; purchase order	PO
Negative	NEG	Post-tensioned concrete	PT CONC
Nickel	NKL	Pounds per cubic foot	PCF
No scale; narrow stile; near side	NS	Pounds per square foot	PSF
Nominal	NOM	Pounds per square inch	PSI
Normal	NORM	Precast concrete; precool coil	PCC
North; newton	N	Precast/Prestressed Concrete Institute	PCI
Not in contract; noise isolation class	NIC	Prefabricate	PREFAB
Not to scale	NTS	Preference	PREF
Number; normally open	NO	Premolded expansion joint	PEJ
Numeral	NUM	Pressure treated; paint; pipe thread; pneumatic tube; post tensioned	PT
Occupational Safety and Health Administration	OSHA	Previous	PREV
Office	OFF	Principal	PRIN
On center	OC	Project	PROJ
Opaque	OPQ	Property	PROP
Opening	OPNG	Property line	PL
Operating room; outside radius	OR	Push/pull; panel point; polypropylene (plastic)	PP
Opposite	OPP		
Optimum; optional	OPT	Quadrant; quadrangle	QUAD
Original	ORIG	Quantity	QTY
Ornamental	ORN	Quarry	QRY
Ounce	OZ	Quarry tile	QT
Out to out	O/O	Radiator; radian; return air duct	RAD
Outside air; overall	OA	Radius; range; riser; thermal resistance	R
Outside face of studs	OFS	Receptacle	RECPT
Overall; outside air	OA	Recessed	REC
Overhang	OH	Rectangle	RECT
Packaged terminal air conditioner	PTAC	Redwood	RWD
Paint; pipe thread; pneumatic tube; post-tensioned; pressure treated	PT	Reference; refrigerator	REF
Pair; pipe rail; pumped return	PR	Reflected ceiling plan; reinforced concrete pipe	RCP
Parallel; parapet	PAR	Refrigerator; reference	REF
Parging	PARG	Regulation; register	REG
Particleboard	PBD	Reinforce	REINF
Partition	PTN	Reinforced brick masonry	RBM
Paved road	PV RD	Reinforced concrete; remote control	RC
Paving	PVG	Reinforcing steel bars	REBAR
Penny (nail); deep; depth	D	Removable	REM
Penthouse; phase	PH	Required	REQD
Perforated; perform	PERF	Resilient	RESIL
Perpendicular	PERP	Restroom	REST
Pharmacy	PHAR	Reveal	RVL
Piece; point of curve; polycarbonate; portland cement	PC	Revision; revolutions	REV
Pilaster	PIL	Revolutions per minute	RPM
Plaster; plastic	PLAS	Right of way	ROW
Plastic; plaster	PLAS	Rigid insulation, solid	RDG INS
Plastic laminate	PLAM	Riser; radius; range; thermal resistance	R
Plate glass	PL GL	Road; refrigerant discharge; roof drain	RD
Plumbing	PLBG	Roof drain; refrigerant discharge; road	RD
Plywood	PLYWD	Roofing	RFG
Portland cement, piece; point of curve; polycarbonate	PC	Room	RM
		Rough opening	RO
		Rough sawn; rapid start	RS

Round	RND	Steel Joist Institute	SJI
Rubber tile floor	RTF	Steel plate	STL PL
Saddle	SDL	Storage	STOR
Sandblast	SDBL	Storeroom	STRM
Sanitary	SAN	Street; single throw; stairs	ST
Sanitary sewer; service sink;		Structural	STRUCT
standing seam (roof); steam		Structural clay tile	SCT
supply; storm sewer	SS	Subfloor	SUB FL
Schedule	SCHED	Substitute	SUB
Schematic	SCHEM	Sump pump	SMP
School	SCH	Surfaced four sides	S4S
Scored joint; slip joint	SJ	Survey	SURV
Sealant	SLNT	Suspended acoustical tile; saturate	SAT
Section	SECT	Suspended acoustical tile ceiling	SATC
Separate	SEP	Tackboard	TK BD
Sewer	SWR	Technical	TECH
Sheathing	SHTHG	Telephone	TEL
Shelving	SHV	Television	TV
Shingles; sensible heat;		Temperature; temporary	TEMP
single hung (window)	SH	Tempered glass	TMPD GL
Shop drawings; smoke detector; soap		Terra cotta	TC
dispenser; storm drain; supply duct	SD	Terrazzo; telephone equipment room	TER
Shower; sensible heat ratio	SHR	Thermostat	TSTAT
Shutter	SHTR	Thousand; kelvin	K
Sidewalk; switch	SW	Thousand board feet	MBF
Siding	SDG	Threshold	THRES
Similar	SIM	Tile Council of America	TCA
Single	SGL	Tongue and groove	T&G
Single hung (window); sensible		Top of beam	TOB
heat; shingles	SH	Top of concrete; table of content;	
Single acting (door); supply air	SA	top of curb	TOC
Sink	—	Top of finish floor	TFF
Skylight	SKLT	Top of floor; top of footing;	
Sliding glass door	SGD	top of frame	TOF
Society of American		Top of joist	TOJ
Registered Architects	SARA	Top of masonry	TOM
Softwood	SFTWD	Top of slab; top of steel	TOS
Solid core; shading coefficient	SC	Topography	TOPO
Solid core wood door	SCWD	Transfer grille	TG
South	S	Transom; transparent	TRANS
Speaker	SPKR	Tread	T
Special	SPCL	True north	TN
Specification	SPEC	Tub/shower	T/S
Splash block	SB	Typical	TYP
Spot elevation	SP EL	Ultimate	ULT
Sprinkler	SPKLR	Undercut door	UCD
Square	SQ	Underwriters Laboratories	UL
Square foot (feet); safety factor;		Unexcavated	UNEX
supply fan	SF	Unfinish	UNFIN
Square yard	SQ YD	Uniform	UNIF
Stained glass	ST GL	Uniform Building Code	UBC
Stainless	STNLS	Universal	UNIV
Stainless steel	SST	Unless noted	UN
Standard	STD	Unless noted otherwise	UNO
Standpipe; solid plastic; sump pit	SP	Vacuum; vacuum line	VAC
Station	STA	Vanity	VAN
Steel joist	STL JST	Vapor retarder; voltage regulator	VR

Variable air volume	VAV	Waterproof membrane	WPM
Velocity	VEL	Waterproofing, water pump;	
Veneer	VNR	weatherproof; working point	WP
Vent stack; voltmeter switch	VS	Weather resistant; water repellent;	
Ventilation; ventilator	VENT	wire rope	WR
Verify in field	VIF	Weep hole; wall hung; wall hydrant;	
Vertical	VERT	water heater	WH
Vestibule	VEST	Weight; water table; watertight	WT
Vinyl base; vacuum breaker;		Welded wire fabric	WWF
valve box	VB	Welded wire mesh	WWM
Vinyl composition tile;		West; waste; watt; wide	W
vitrified clay tile	VCT	Wide flange; wash fountain	WF
Vinyl wall covering	VWC	Window	WDW
Vinyl wall fabric	VWF	Window unit	WU
Vitrified clay tile; vinyl		Wired glass	WGL
composition tile	VCT	With	W/
Volt	V	Without	W/O
Volume	VOL	Wood; wood door	WD
Wainscot	WSCT	Wood blocking	WBL
Wall cabinets	W CAB	Wood door; wood	WD
Wall covering; water closet;		Wood door and frame	WDF
water column	WC	Wood furring strips	WFS
Wall to wall	W/W	Wood panelling	WDP
Water	WTR	Wrought iron	WI
Water closet; wall covering;		Yard; yard drain; yard drainage pipe	YD
water column	WC	Year	YR
Water heater; wall hung; wall			
hydrant; weep hole	WH		

APPENDIX B:
MODULAR VERTICAL BRICK COURSING

Module	Course	Dimension	Module	Course	Dimension
	1C	2⅝"		37C	8'-2⅝"
	2C	5⅜"		38C	8'-5⅜"
1M	3C	8"	13M	39C	8'-8"
	4C	10⅝"		40C	8'-10⅝"
	5C	1'-1⅜"		41C	9'-1⅜"
2M	6C	1'-4"	14M	42C	9'-4"
	7C	1'-6⅝"		43C	9'-6⅝"
	8C	1'-9⅜"		44C	9'-9⅜"
3M	9C	2'-0"	15M	45C	10'-0"
	10C	2'-2⅝"		46C	10'-2⅝"
	11C	2'-5⅜"		47C	10'-5⅜"
4M	12C	2'-8"	16M	48C	10'-8"
	13C	2'-10⅝"		49C	10'-10⅜"
	14C	3'-1⅜"		50C	11'-1⅜"
5M	15C	3'-4"	17M	51C	11'-4"
	16C	3'-6⅝"		52C	11'-6⅝"
	17C	3'-9⅜"		53C	11'-9⅝"
6M	18C	4'-0"	18M	54C	12'-0"
	19C	4'-2⅝"		55C	12'-2⅝"
	20C	4'-5⅜"		56C	12'-5⅜"
7M	21C	4'-8"	19M	57C	12'-8"
	22C	4'-10⅝"		58C	12'-10⅝"
	23C	5'-1⅜"		59C	13'-1⅜"
8M	24C	5'-4"	20M	60C	13'-4"
	25C	5'-6⅝"		61C	13'-6⅝"
	26C	5'-9⅜"		62C	13'-9⅜"
9M	27C	6'-0"	21M	63C	14'-0"
	28C	6'-2⅝"		64C	14'-2⅝"
	29C	6'-5⅜"		65C	14'-5⅜"
10M	30C	6'-8"	22M	66C	14'-8"
	31C	6'-10⅝"		67C	14'-10⅝"
	32C	7'-1⅜"		68C	15'-1⅜"
11M	33C	7'-4"	23M	69C	15'-4"
	34C	7'-6⅝"		70C	15'-6⅝"
	35C	7'-9⅜"		71C	15'-9⅜"
12M	36C	8'-0"	24M	72C	16'-0"

NOTE: A *module* corresponds to 8" concrete block course heights.

APPENDIX C: THE METRIC SYSTEM IN CONSTRUCTION

The following guidelines should help you "see and think metric":[1]

Table C–1 Converting from inch and pound units to metric units.

Measurement	From In./lb Units	To Metric		Multiply by
		Unit	Symbol	
Length	mile	kilometer	km	1.609 344
	yard	meter	m	0.914 4
	foot	meter	m	0.304 8
		millimeter	mm	304.8
	inch	millimeter	mm	25.4
Area	square mile	square kilometer	km²	2.590 00
	acre	square meter	m²	4.046 87
		hectare	ha	0.404 687
	square yard	square meter	m²	0.836 127 36
	square foot	square meter	m²	0.092 903 04
	square inch	square millimeter	mm²	645.16
Volume	cubic yard	cubic meter	m³	0.764 5 55
	cubic foot	cubic meter	m³	0.028 316 8
		liter	L	28.316 85
	cubic inch	milliliter	mL	16.387 064
		cubic millimeter	mm³	16387.064

- 1″ is just a fraction longer ($\frac{1}{64}$″) than 25 mm (1″ = 25.4 mm).
- 4″ is about $\frac{1}{16}$″ longer than 100 mm.
- 1′ is about $\frac{3}{16}$″ longer than 300 mm.
- 4′ is about $\frac{3}{4}$″ longer than 1200 mm.
- 1 millimeter (mm) is slightly less than the thickness of a dime.
- 1 meter (m) is the length of a yardstick plus about 3.3″.
- 1 gram (g) is about the mass (weight) of a large paper clip.
- 10 m equals approximately 11 yd.
- 10 m² equals approximately 12 sq yd.
- 10 m³ equals approximately 13 cu yd.
- The metric equivalent of a typical 2′ × 4′ ceiling grid is 600 × 1200 mm.
- The metric equivalent of a 4′ × 8′ sheet of plywood or drywall is 1200 × 2400 mm.

---

[1] "Seeing Metric," *Metric in Construction* (Sept./Oct. 1992).

Table C–2 Metric/inch-foot length equivalents.

mm	in.	mm	ft	m	ft
1.5	$\frac{1}{16}$	300	1′-0″	1.0	3′-3″
3	$\frac{1}{8}$	400	1′-4″	1.2	4′-0″
6	$\frac{1}{4}$	450	1′-6″	2.0	6′-0″
8	$\frac{3}{8}$	600	2′-0″	2.4	8′-0″
10	$\frac{3}{8}$	750	2′-6″	3.0	10′-0″
12	$\frac{1}{2}$	900	3′-0″	4.8	16′-0″
15	$\frac{5}{8}$	1200	4′-0″	6.0	20′-0″
20	$\frac{3}{4}$	1500	5′-0″	8.0	26′-0″
25	1	1800	6′-0″	12.0	40′-0″
40	$1\frac{1}{2}$	2400	8′-0″		
45	$1\frac{3}{4}$	3000	10′-0″		
50	2				
65	$2\frac{1}{2}$				
75	3				
89	$3\frac{1}{2}$				
95	$3\frac{3}{4}$				
100	4				
125	5				
140	$5\frac{1}{2}$				
150	6				
200	8				
225	9				

Table C–3 Comparison between inch-foot and metric scales.

| In.-Ft. Scales | Ratios | Metric Scales | | Remarks |
		Preferred	Other	
Full Size	1:1	1:1		No change
Half full size	1:2		1:2	No change
4″ = 1′-0″	1:3			
3″ = 1′-0″	1:4			
		1:5		Close to 3″ scale
2″ = 1′-0″	1:6			
1½″ = 1′-0″	1:8			
		1:10		Between 1″ and 1½″ scales
1″ = 1′-0″	1:12			
¾″ = 1′-0″	1:16			
		1:20		Between ½″ and ¾″ scales
½″ = 1′-0″	1:24			
			1:25	Very close to ½″ scale
⅜″ = 1′-0″	1:32			
¼″ = 1′-0″	1:48			
		1:50		Close to ¼″ scale
1″ = 5′-0″	1:60			
³⁄₁₆″ = 1′-0″	1:64			
⅛″ = 1′-0″	1:96			
		1:100		Very close to ⅛″ scale
1″ = 10′-0″	1:120			
³⁄₃₂″ = 1′-0″	1:128			
¹⁄₁₆″ = 1′-0″	1:196			
		1:200		Close to ¹⁄₁₆″ scale
1″ = 20′-0″	1:240		1:250	Close to 1″ = 20′0″
1″ = 30′-0″	1:360			
¹⁄₃₂″ = 1′-0″	1:384			
1″ = 40′-0″	1:480			
		1:500		Close to 1″ = 40′0″ scale
1″ = 50′-0″	1:600			
1″ = 60′-0″	1:720			
1″ = 1 chain	1:792			
1″ = 80′-0″	1:960			
		1:1000		

SOURCE: *Metric Guide for Federal Construction.*

NOTES:

1. Metric drawing scales are expressed in nondimensional ratios.
2. Use only one unit of measure on a drawing; on large-scale site drawings, the unit should be the millimeter (mm).
3. Delete unit symbols, but provide an explanatory note ("All dimensions are shown in millimeters," for example).
4. Whole numbers always indicate millimeters; decimal numbers taken to three places always indicate meters.
5. Where basic modules are used, the recommended basic module is 100 mm, which is similar to the 4″ module (4″ = 101.6 mm).

Table C–4 Metric units used by the construction trades.

Trade	Quantity	Unit	Symbol
Surveying	length	kilometer, meter	km, m
	area	square kilometer hectare (10 000 m^2) square meter	km^2 ha (hm^2) m^2
	plane angle	degree minute second percent	° ′ ″ %
Excavating	length	meter, millimeter	m, mm
	volume	cubic meter	m^3
Paving	length	meter, millimeter	m, mm
	area	square meter	m^2
Concrete	length	meter, millimeter	m, mm
	area	square meter	m^2
	volume	cubic meter	m^3
	temperature	degree Celsius	°C
	water capacity	liter (cubic decimeter)	L (dm^3)
	mass	megagram (metric ton) kilogram	Mg (t) kg
	cross-sectional area	square millimeter	mm^2
Trucking	distance	kilometer	km
	volume	cubic meter	m^3
	mass	megagram (metric ton)	Mg (t)
Masonry	length	meter, millimeter	m, mm
	area	square meter	m^2
	mortar volume	cubic meter	m^3
Steel	length	meter, millimeter	m, mm
	mass	megagram (metric ton) kilogram	Mg (t) kg
	mass per unit length	kilogram per meter	kg/m
Carpentry	length	meter, millimeter	m, mm
Plastering	length	meter, millimeter	m, mm
	area	square meter	m^2
	water capacity	liter (cubic decimeter)	L (dm^3)
Glazing	length	meter, millimeter	m, mm
	area	square meter	m^2

(continued)

Table C–4 *(continued)*

Trade	Quantity	Unit	Symbol
Painting	length	meter, millimeter	m, mm
	area	square meter	m^2
	capacity	liter (cubic decimeter)	$L(dm^3)$
		milliliter (cubic centimeter)	$mL\ (cm^3)$
Roofing	length	meter, millimeter	m, mm
	area	square meter	m^2
	slope	percent	%
		ratio of lengths	mm/mm, m/m
Plumbing	length	meter, millimeter	m, mm
	mass	kilogram, gram	kg, g
	capacity	liter (cubic decimeter)	$L\ (dm^3)$
	pressure	kilopascal	kPa
Drainage	length	meter, millimeter	m, mm
	area	hectare ($10000\ m^2$)	ha
		square meter	m^2
	volume	cubic meter	m^3
	slope	percent	%
		ratio of lengths	mm/mm, m/m
HVAC	length	meter, millimeter	m, mm
	volume (capacity)	cubic meter	m^3
		liter (cubic decimeter)	$L\ (dm^3)$
	air velocity	meter/second	m/s
	volume flow	cubic meter/second	m^3/s
		liter/second (cubic decimeter per second)	$L/s\ (dm^3/s)$
	temperature	degree Celsius	°C
	force	newton, kilonewton	N, kN
	pressure	pascal, kilopascal	Pa, kPa
	energy	kilojoule, megajoule	kJ, MJ
	rate of heat flow	watt, kilowatt	W, kW
Electrical	length	millimeter, meter, kilometer	mm, m, km
	frequency	hertz	Hz
	power	watt, kilowatt	W, kW
	energy	megajoule	MJ
		kilowatt hour	kWh
	electric current	ampere	A
	electric potential	volt, kilovolt	V, kV
	resistance	milliohm, ohm	$m\Omega,\ \Omega$

SOURCE: *Metric in Construction* (March/April 1996)

Table C–5 Metric and U.S. inch softwood lumber sizes.

Metric Size (mm)	U.S. Nominal Size (in.)	U.S. Manufactured Size (in.)
25 × 100	1 × 4	³⁄₄ × 3¹⁄₂
25 × 150	1 × 6	³⁄₄ × 5¹⁄₂
25 × 200	1 × 8	³⁄₄ × 7¹⁄₄
25 × 250	1 × 10	³⁄₄ × 9¹⁄₄
25 × 300	1 × 12	³⁄₄ × 11¹⁄₄
50 × 100	2 × 4	1¹⁄₂ × 3¹⁄₂
50 × 150	2 × 6	1¹⁄₂ × 5¹⁄₂
50 × 200	2 × 8	1¹⁄₂ × 7¹⁄₄
50 × 250	2 × 10	1¹⁄₂ × 9¹⁄₄
50 × 300	2 × 12	1¹⁄₂ × 11¹⁄₄
100 × 100	4 × 4	3¹⁄₂ × 3¹⁄₂
100 × 150	4 × 6	3¹⁄₂ × 5¹⁄₂
100 × 200	4 × 8	3¹⁄₂ × 7¹⁄₄
100 × 250	4 × 10	3¹⁄₂ × 9¹⁄₄
100 × 300	4 × 12	3¹⁄₂ × 11¹⁄₄

Table C–6 Lumber lengths.

m	ft	m	ft
1.8	6	3.9	
2.1	7	4.2	14
2.4	8	4.5	
2.7		4.8	16
3.0	10	5.1	
3.3		5.4	18
3.6	12	5.7	
		6.0	20

Table C–7 Metric steel stud lengths and their U.S. inch equivalents.

Metric (mm)	U.S. (ft and in.)	Metric (mm)	U.S. (ft and in.)
2134	7′-0″	3505	11′-6″
2286	7′-6″	3658	12′-0″
2438	8′-0″	3810	12′-6″
2591	8′-6″	3962	13′-0″
2743	9′-0″	4115	13′-6″
2896	9′-6″	4267	14′-0″
3048	10′-0″	4420	14′-6″
3200	10′-6″	4572	15′-0″
3353	11′-0″		

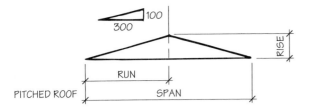

Figure C–1

Table C–8 Roof pitches.

Traditional	Metric
2/12	50/300
4/12	100/300
6/12	150/300
8/12	200/300
10/12	250/300
12/12	300/300

Table C–9 *U* factors for insulating materials.

Insulating Materials	*U* factor[a] (in.-lb)	Metric	Thickness of Material in.	mm
Batt blanket	0.24	1.36	1½	38
Loose wool	0.26	1.48	4	100
Vermiculite	0.24	1.36	1	25
Urethane panel	0.16	0.91	1	25
Polystyrene foam	0.20	1.14	1	25
Foam glass	0.35	1.99	1	25
Insulating board	0.36	2.04	1	25

[a]Inch-pound *U* factor × 5.678 (factor) = metric *U* factor.

Table C–10 Metric dimensions and inch equivalents of roof insulating boards.

Panels and Sheathing		Roof Boards	
Thickness:	11 mm (7/16 in.)	Thickness:	12.5 mm (0.49 in.)
			25.5 mm (0.98 in.)
Width:	1200 mm (47¼ in.)		38 mm (1.50 in.)
			50 mm (1.97 in.)
Length:	2400 mm (7 ft 10½ in.)	Width:	600 mm (23.62 in.)
		Length:	1200 mm (47.24 in.)

Table C–11 Gypsum board: practical metric dimensions.

Thickness	Width	Length
9.5 mm ($3/8$ in.)	400 mm	1200 mm ($47\frac{1}{4}$ in.)
12.7 mm ($\frac{1}{2}$ in.)	600 mm	2400 mm (7 ft $10\frac{1}{2}$ in.)
		2800 mm (9 ft $2\frac{1}{4}$ in.)
		3000 mm (9 ft 10 in.)
15.9 mm ($5/8$ in.)	1200 mm	3600 mm (11 ft $9\frac{3}{4}$ in.)
19.0 mm ($3/4$ in.)		4200 mm (13 ft $9\frac{1}{3}$ in.)
25.4 mm (1 in.)		

Table C–12 Stair riser heights and tread widths[a].

Riser (mm)	Tread (mm)	Two Risers + One Tread (mm)
120	400	640
120	390	640
130	380	640
130	370	630
140	350	630
150	330	630
150	320	620
160	310	630
170	300	640
170	290	630
180	270	630
180	260	620
190	250	630
200	240	640
200	230	630
200	230	630

[a]Metric riser heights and tread widths are in millimeters; 2 risers + 1 tread = 610 to 640 mm.

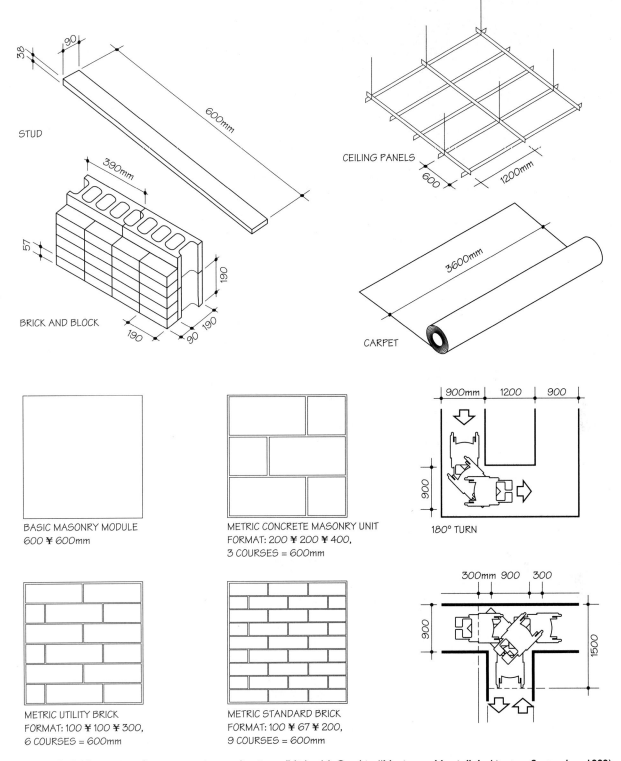

STUD

BRICK AND BLOCK

CEILING PANELS

CARPET

BASIC MASONRY MODULE
600 ¥ 600mm

METRIC CONCRETE MASONRY UNIT
FORMAT: 200 ¥ 200 ¥ 400,
3 COURSES = 600mm

180° TURN

METRIC UTILITY BRICK
FORMAT: 100 ¥ 100 ¥ 300,
6 COURSES = 600mm

METRIC STANDARD BRICK
FORMAT: 100 ¥ 67 ¥ 200,
9 COURSES = 600mm

Figure C–2 Metric sizes for construction applications. (Michael J. Crosbie, "Moving to Metric," *Architecture* September 1992)

Table C-13 Metric minimum and desirable room sizes.

Room	Minimum Size (mm)	m²	Desirable Size (mm)	m²
Kitchen plus dining	4000 × 4000	16		
	2500 × 5500	13.75	3500 × 6000	21
	3000 × 4000	12		
	3000 × 3000	9	3000 × 5000	15
	2500 × 4000	10		
	2500 × 3000	7.5	3000 × 3500	10.5
Kitchen plus family	4000 × 5500	22		
	4000 × 6000	24		
	4000 × 4000	16	4000 × 6000	24
	4000 × 5000	20	4000 × 7000	28
Laundry and utility	2500 × 2500	6.25		
	2000 × 4000	8		
	2500 × 3000	7.5		
	3000 × 3000	9		
	2000 × 3000	6		
Entry, rear	1000 × 1500	1.5		
	1000 × 1200	1.2		
Hall bath	1000 × 1000	1	2000 × 1500	3
	1200 × 1500	4.2		
	900 × 1200	1.08		
Dining room	3000 × 3000	9		
	3000 × 4000	12	3500 × 1500	12.25
	4000 × 4500	18	4000 × 5000	20
	3500 × 4000	14		
Living room	4000 × 5000	20	4000 × 6000	24
	4000 × 6000	24	4500 × 6000	27
Front-entrance foyer	1200 × 1800	2.16		
	2000 × 2400	4.8	2500 × 2400	6
	1600 × 1600	2.56		
Guest coat closet	720 × 1500	1.14		
	610 × 920	0.56		
	700 × 1200	0.84		
	800 × 1200	0.96		
	600 × 1200	0.72		
Den or guest room	3000 × 4000	12	4000 × 4000	16
	4000 × 4000	16	3000 × 4500	13.5

(continued)

Table C–13 *(continued)*

Room	Minimum Size (mm)	m²	Desirable Size (mm)	m²
Master bedroom	3000 × 4000	12	4000 × 4000	16
	4000 × 4000	16	4000 × 5000	20
	4000 × 4500	18		
Closet for master bedroom	2@760 × 1500	2.28	2@730 × 1500	2.19
	2@610 × 1800	2.18	2@910 × 1800	3.27
	2@610 × 1500	1.23	2@910 × 1800	3.27
	2@700 × 1500	2.10	2@680 × 1500	2.04
Bedroom 1	3000 × 4000	12	3500 × 4000	14
	3000 × 3500	10.5	3050 × 3350	10.2
	4000 × 4000	16	4000 × 5000	20
Closet for bedroom 1	750 × 1500	1.12	2@760 × 1500	2.28
	600 × 1800	1.08	910 × 1800	1.65
	600 × 1500	0.9		
	2@750 × 1500	2.24	2@760 × 1500	2.28
Bedroom 2	2400 × 3660	8.78		
	2740 × 3350	9.18		
	3050 × 6100	18.6	3600 × 3660	13.39
	3050 × 3350	10.22	3050 × 3350	10.22
	3660 × 4300	15.74	4260 × 4880	20.78
Closet for bedroom 2	760 × 1500	1.14	2@760 × 1520	2.74
	600 × 1800	1.08	910 × 1830	1.66
	2@700 × 1500	2.10	2@670 × 1520	2.04
	600 × 1500	0.9	2@610 × 1520	1.85
Bath	1500 × 3000	4.5		
	1500 × 2500	3.75		
	2000 × 2500	5.0		
	1500 × 2000	3.0	2400 × 2400	5.76
	2000 × 2000	4.0		
	1800 × 2000	3.6	2000 × 3000	6
Garage, 2-car	7000 × 7000	49		
	5500 × 6000	33	6000 × 7000	42
Garage, 1-car	4500 × 6000	27		
	4000 × 6000	24		
	4000 × 7000	28		

Table C–14 Furniture sizes for the house.

Furniture	Length (mm)	Width (mm)	Height (mm)
Bedroom			
Single bed	2000	950	520
Night table	500	400	650
	550	350	650
King-size bed	2000	1900	520
Double bed	2000	1400–1800	520
Children's bed	1600	750	520
	1700	800	520
Kitchen and Laundry			
Washer, automatic	660–720	650–750	910
Dryer	660–690	760–790	910
Refrigerator	610–850	690–780	1420–1800
Living and Dining Rooms			
Table	1200	800	750
	1500	900	780
Round table	1100		780
Writing table	1300	700	780
	1500	800	780
Grand piano	1600	1500	1100
Sofa	1900	800	430 (seat)
	1750	800	430 (seat)
Chair	450	450	430 (seat)
Armchair	650	600	350 (seat)

C.1

METRIC: WHAT WILL CHANGE AND WHAT WILL STAY THE SAME[2]

C.1.1 Metric Module and Grid

What Will Change

- The basic building module, from 4″ to **100 mm.**
- The planning grid, from 2′ × 2′ to **600 × 600 mm.**

What Will Stay the Same

- A module and grid based on rounded, easy-to-use dimensions.

C.1.2 Drawings

What Will Change

- Units, from feet and inches to millimeters for all building dimensions and to meters for large site plans and civil engineering drawings. Unit notations are unnecessary: If there's not decimal point, it's millimeters; if there's a decimal point carried to one, two, or three places, it's meters. Centimeters are not used in construction.
- Drawing scales, from inch-fractions-to-feet to true ratios. Preferred metric scales are **1:1** (full size); **1:5** (close to 3″ = 1′-0″); **1:10** (between 1″ = 1′-0″ and 1½″ = 1′-0″); **1:20** (between ½″ = 1′-0″ and ¾″ = 1′-0″); **1:50** (close to ¼″ = 1′-0″); **1:100** (close to ⅛″ = 1′-0″); **1:200** (close to ¹⁄₁₆″ = 1′-0″); **1:500** (close to 1″ = 40′-0″); **1:1000** (close to 1″ = 80′-0″).
- Drawing sizes, to the ISO "A" series: **A0 (1189 × 841 mm,** 46.8 × 33.1 in.); **A1 (841 × 594 mm,** 33.1 × 23.4 in.); **A2 (594 × 420 mm,** 23.4 × 16.5 in.); **A3 (420 × 297 mm,** 16.5 × 11.7 in.); **A4 (297 × 210 mm,** 11.7 × 8.3 in.). Of course, metric drawings can be made on any size paper.

What Will Stay the Same

- Drawing contents.

Never use dual units (both inch-pound and metric) on drawings. It increases dimensioning time, doubles the chance for errors, makes drawings more confusing, and delays the learning process.

---

[2] *Metric in Construction* (July/August 1995).

C.I.3 Specifications

What Will Change

- Units of measure, from feet and inches to **millimeters** for linear dimensions, from square feet to **square meters** for area, from cubic yards to **cubic meters** for volume (except use **liters** for fluid volumes), and from other inch-pound units to metric units as appropriate.

What Will Stay the Same

- Everything else in the specification.

Do not use dual units in specifications except when the use of an inch-pound measure serves to clarify an otherwise unfamiliar metric measure. Then place the inch-pound unit in parentheses after the metric, for example, "7.5 kW (10 horsepower)." All unit conversions should be **checked by a professional** to ensure that rounding does not exceed allowable tolerances.

C.I.4 Floor Loads

What Will Change

- Floor load designations, from psf to kilograms per square meter (**kg/m²**) for everyday use and kilonewtons per square meter (**kN/m²**) for structural calculations.

What Will Stay the Same

- Floor load requirements.

Kilograms per square meter often are used to designate floor loads because many live and dead loads (furniture, filing cabinets, construction materials, and so on) are measured in kilograms. However, kilonewtons per square meter or kilopascals, their equivalent, are the proper measure and should be used in structural calculations.

C.I.5 Construction Products

What Will Change

- Modular products: brick, block, drywall, plywood, suspended ceiling components, and raised floors. They will undergo "hard" conversion; that is, their dimensions will change to new rounded "hard" metric numbers to fit the universal **600 × 600 mm** metric planning grid.
- A number of other products, such as concrete reinforcing bars and various kinds of fasteners. They are being converted to hard metric sizes as the result of industry initiatives.

- Products that are custom fabricated for each job (for example, cabinets, stairs, handrails, ductwork, commercial doors and windows, structural steel, and precast concrete) or poured-in-place (concrete). Such products can usually be made to any size, inch-pound or metric, with equal ease, so for metric jobs, they will simply be fabricated or formed in metric.

What Will Stay the Same

- The balance of products, since they are cut to fit at the job site (for example, framing lumber, woodwork, wiring, piping, and roofing) or are not dimensionally sensitive (for example, fasteners, hardware, electrical components, plumbing fixtures, HVAC equipment, and gravel). Such products will be just "soft" converted—that is, relabeled in metric. A 2¾″ × 4½″ wall-switch face plate will be relabeled 70 × 115 mm, and a 30-gal tank, 114 L. Eventually manufacturers may convert many of these products to new rounded "hard" metric sizes, but only when it becomes convenient to do so.

C.I.6 Studs and Other 2 × 3 Framing (Both Wood and Metal)

What Will Change

- Spacing, from 16″ to **400 mm** and from 24″ to **600 mm.**

What Will Stay the Same

- Cross sections.

2 × s are produced in fractional-inch dimensions now, so there is no need to convert them to new rounded "hard" metric dimensions; 2 × 4s may keep their traditional name, or perhaps they'll be relabeled a nominal 50 × 100 mm or a more exact size, such as 38 × 89 mm.

C.I.7 Drywall, Plywood, and Other Sheet Goods

What Will Change

- Widths, from 4′-0″ to **1200 mm.**
- Heights, from 8′-0″ to **2400 mm** and from 10′-0″ to **3000 mm.**

What Will Stay the Same

- Thicknesses, so fire, acoustic, and thermal ratings will not have to be recalculated.

Metric drywall and plywood are readily available, but with a possible cost penalty for small orders. Metric rigid insulation may not be available at this time.

C.1.8 Batt Insulation

What Will Change

- Nominal width labels, from 16" to **16"/400 mm** and from 25" to **24"/600 mm.**

What Will Stay the Same

- Everything else.

Batts will not change in width; they will simply have a tighter "friction fit" when installed among metric-spaced framing members.

C.1.9 Doors

What Will Change

- Height, from 6'-8" to **2050 mm** or **2100 mm** and from 7'-0" to **2100 mm.**
- Width, from 2'-6" to **750 mm**, from 2'-8" to **800 mm**, from 2'-10" to **850 mm**, from 3'-0" to **900 mm** or **950 mm**, and from 3'-4" to **1000 mm.**

What Will Stay the Same

- Door thicknesses.
- Door materials and hardware.

For commercial work, doors can be ordered in any size since they normally are custom fabricated.

C.1.10 Ceiling Systems

What Will Change

- Grids and lay-in ceiling tile, air diffusers, and lighting fixtures—from 2' × 2' to **600 × 600 mm** and 2' × 4' to **600 × 1200 mm.**

What Will Stay the Same

- Grid profiles, tile thicknesses, air diffuser capacities, fluorescent tubes, and means of suspension.

C.1.11 Raised Floor Systems

What Will Change

- Grids and lay-in floor tile, from 2' × 2' to **600 × 600 mm.**

What Will Stay the Same

- Grid profiles, tile thicknesses, and means of support.

C.1.12 HVAC Controls

What Will Change

- Temperature units, from Fahrenheit to Celsius.

What Will Stay the Same

- All other parts of the controls.

Controls are now digital, so temperature conversions can be made with no difficulty.

C.1.13 Brick

What Will Change

- Standard brick to **90 × 57 × 190 mm.**
- Mortar joints, from 3/8" to 1/2" to **10 mm.**
- Brick module, from 2' × 2' to **600 × 600 mm.**

What Will Stay the Same

- Brick and mortar composition.

Of the 100 or so brick sizes currently made, 5 to 10 are within a millimeter of a metric brick, so the brick industry will have no trouble supplying metric brick.

C.1.14 Concrete Block

What Will Change

- Block sizes to **190 × 190 × 390 mm.**
- Mortar joints, from 1/2" to **10 mm.**
- Block module, from 2' × 2' to **600 × 600 mm.**

What Will Stay the Same

- Block and mortar composition.

C.1.15 Sheet Metal

What Will Change

- Designation from "gauge" to millimeters.

What Will Stay the Same

- Thickness, which will be soft converted to tenths of a millimeter.

In specifications, use millimeters only or millimeters with the gauge in parentheses.

C.1.16 Concrete

What Will Change

- Strength designations, from psi to megapascals, rounded to the nearest 5 megapascals per ACI 318M as follows: 2500 psi to **20 MPa**; 3000 psi to **25 MPa**; 3500 psi to **25 MPa**; 4000 psi to **30 MPa**; 4500 psi to **35 MPa**; 5000 psi to **35 MPa**. (*Yes, both 3000 and 3500 psi are rounded to 25 MPa, and 4500 and 5000 psi are rounded to 35 MPa, which indicates the fairly broad allowable tolerances used in concrete strength designations.*)

What Will Stay the Same

- Everything else.

C.1.17 Rebar

What Will Change

- Rebars will change in size per ASTM A615M, A616M, A617M, and A706M. New metric bar sizes are as follows: Nos. 3 and 4 to **10**; No. 5 to **15**; No. 6 to **20**; Nos. 7 and 8 to **25**; Nos. 9 and 10 to **30**; No. 11 to **35**; No. 14 to **45**; and No. 18 to **55**.

What Will Stay the Same

- Concrete.

C.1.18 Glass

What Will Change

- Cut sheet dimensions from feet and inches to millimeters.

What Will Stay the Same

- Sheet thickness, which can be rolled to any dimension and is often rolled in millimeters now. See ASTM C1036.

C.2

METRIC RESOURCES[3]

C.2.1 Design References

- **American Institute of Architects** (AIA Bookstore, 1735 New York Avenue NW, Washington, DC 20006; phone 202–626–7475. All are published by John Wiley & Sons, Professional Reference and Trade Group, 605 Third Avenue, New York, NY 10158; phone 800–225–5945).

---

[3] *Metric in Construction* (July/August 1995).

Architectural Graphic Standards. A metric edition is not due for several years, but current editions include a comprehensive section on metric conversion.

The Architect's Studio Companion: Simplified Technical Guidelines for Preliminary Design, by Edward Allen and Joseph Iano. Includes dual units. 468 pp. $59.95.

Architectural Detailing: Function, Constructability, and Aesthetics, by Edward Allen. Includes dual units. $59.95.

Fundamentals of Building Construction: Materials and Methods, by Edward Allen. Includes dual units. $64.95.

Neufert Architect's Data, by Ernst Neufert. Second International Edition. All units are metric. 433 pp. $55.00.

Wiley Engineer's Desk Reference, by S. I. Heisler. Includes dual units. 566 pp. $79.95.

- **American Society of Civil Engineers** (phone 800–548–2723 for publications).

Metric Units in Engineering—Going SI, by Cornelius Wandmacher and Ivan Johnson. $28.00.

- **Instrument Society of America** (P.O. Box 3561, Durham, NC 27702; phone 919–549–8411).

ISA Guide to Measurement Conversions, by G. Platt. 172 pp. $50.00.

C.2.2 Cost Estimating

- **R. S. Means Company** (P.O. Box 800, Kingston, MA 02364; phone 617–585–7880).

Means Building Construction Cost Data. 1995. Metric edition. $99.95.

- **Frank R. Walker Co.** (P.O. Box 3180, Lisle, IL 60532; phone 708–971–8989).

Building Estimator's Reference Book. 25th Edition. $69.95.

C.2.3 Specifications

- **AIA Master Systems** (phone 703–684–9153).

AIA Masterspec is available in either dual-unit or metric-only versions.

- **Construction Specifications Institute** (601 Madison Street, Alexandria, VA 22314–1791; phone 703–684–0300).

CSRS Spectext contains dual units, as do all other CSI publications.

C.2.4 Building Codes

- **Building Officials and Code Administrators International** (4051 W. Flossmoor Road, Country Club Hills, IL 60477–5795; phone 312–799–2300).

  All *BOCA National Codes* are published in dual units.

- **International Conference of Building Officials** (5360 South Workman Mill Road, Whittier, CA 90601; phone 310–699–0541).

  The *1994 Uniform Codes* are published in dual units.

- **Southern Building Code Congress International, Inc.** (900 Montclair Road, Birmingham, AL 35213–1206; phone 205–591–1853).

  The *1994 Standard Codes* are published in dual units.

- **National Fire Protection Association** (1 Batterymarch Park, P.O. Box 9101, Quincy, MA 02269–9101; phone 800–344–3555).

  NFPA 101, *Life Safety Code*, is published in dual units, as are all NFPA standards.

C.2.5 Metric Standards

- **American Society for Testing and Materials** (1916 Race Street, Philadelphia, PA 19103; phone 215–299–5585). Call ASTM for current prices. All ASTM standards are published in metric or dual units.

  ASTM E621, *Standard Practice for the Use of Metric (SI) Units in Building Design and Construction.*

  ASTM E380, *Standard Practice for Use of the International System of Units (SI).*

  ASTM E713, *Guide for Selection of Scales for Metric Building Drawings.*

  ASTM E577, *Guide for Dimensional Coordination of Rectilinear Building Parts and Systems.*

  ASTM E835, *Guide for Dimensional Coordination of Structural Clay Units, Concrete Masonry Units, and Clay Flue Linings.*

- **American National Standards Institute, Inc.** (11 West 42nd Street, New York, NY 10036; phone 212–642–4900). Call ANSI for current prices. Many ANSI standards are available in metric units.

  ANSI/IEEE 268, *American National Standard Metric Practice.*

  ANSI/AWS A1.1, *Metric Practice Guide for the Welding Industry.*

  ANSI/IEEE 945, *Preferred Metric Units for Use in Electrical and Electronics Science and Technology.*

  ISO 1000, *SI Units and Recommendations for the Use of Their Multiples and Certain Other Units.*

C.2.6 Steel

- **American Institute of Steel Construction** (Metric Publications, 1 East Wacker Drive, Suite 3100, Chicago, IL 60601–2001; phone 800–644–2400 for publications and 312–670–5411 for software).

  Metric Properties of Structural Shapes with Dimensions According to ASTM A6M. Metric version of Part I of the *Manual of Steel Construction.* $20.00.

  Metric Conversion: Load and Resistance Factor Design Specification for Structural Steel Buildings. $20.00.

  Guide to Metric Steel Fabrication. $20.00.

  AISC Database, Version 2.0, Metric Units. An ASCII data file that gives programmers electronic access to the dimensions and properties of all structural shapes—W, M, S, HP, C, MC, WT, MT, ST, L, 2L, TS, P, PX, PXX—in metric units. $60.00.

  AISC for AutoCAD, Version 2.0 (for AutoCAD Releases 12 and 13), a utility that automatically draws plans, side elevations, and end elevations for the above-mentioned structural shapes. The program includes both inch-pound and metric units. $120.

- **Metrosoft** (332 Patterson Avenue, East Rutherford, NJ 07073; phone 201–438–4915). Call for prices.

  ROBOT V6, a metric-based structural analysis program.

- **American Welding Society** (550 N.W. LeJeune Road, P.O. Box 35104, Miami, FL 33135; phone 305–443–9353).

  All AWS standards include dual units.

C.2.7 Concrete

- **American Concrete Institute** (P.O. Box 19150, Detroit MI 48219; phone 313–532–2600).

  ACI 318M/318RM, *Building Code Requirements for Reinforced Concrete and Commentary.* Metric edition of ACI 318/318R. $89.25.

  ACI 318.1M/318.1RM, *Building Code Requirements for Metric Structural Plain Concrete and Commentary.* Metric edition of ACI 318.1/318.1R. $17.75.

- **Portland Cement Institute** (Order Processing, 5420 Old Orchard Road, Skokie, IL 60077; phone 800–868–6733).

  Design and Control of Concrete Mixtures—Canadian Metric Edition. $35.00.

- **Wire Reinforcing Institute** (203 Loudon Street SW, Leesburg, VA 22075; phone 703–779–2339). There is no charge for single copies of the following publications:

Metric Welded Wire Reinforcement. TF-206, a 2-page data sheet.

Metric Welded Wire Reinforcement for Concrete Pipe. TF-311M, a 4-page data sheet.

- **Concrete Reinforcing Steel Institute** (944 N. Plum Grove Road, Schaumburg, IL 60173; phone 708–517–1200).

Contact CRSI for current technical information on the metrication of reinforcing steel.

C.2.8 Wood

- **American Forest and Paper Association**, formerly National Forest Products Association (1250 Connecticut Avenue, NW, Washington, DC 20036; phone 202–463–2700).

Wood Products Metric Planning Package. 1994. 30 pp. $10.00.

- **National Particleboard Association** (18928 Premiere Court, Gaithersburg, MD 20879; phone 301–670–0604).

Metric units have been added to the NPA/ANSI standards for particleboard and medium-density fiberboard. $6.00 each.

- **Hardwood Plywood Manufacturers Association** (P.O. Box 2789, Reston, VA 22090–2789; phone 703–435–2900).

ANSI HPVA 1-1994, *Voluntary Standard for Hardwood and Decorative Plywood.* Includes dual units. 1992. 24 pp. $15.00.

C.2.9 Ceiling Systems

- **USG Interiors** (100 Crocker Road, Westlake, OH 44145–1089; phone 216–871–1000).

Metric Ceiling Systems (SA905ME). No charge.

C.2.10 Metric Scales and Templates

Metric scales are available from graphic arts supply stores. Popular models are **Staedtler-Mars** 987-18-1, **Alvin** 117 PM, and **Charvoz** 30–1261.

Metric plumbing templates are available from **American Standard** (phone 703–841–9585).

C.2.11 Metric Conversion Calculators

Metric conversion calculators include the **Sharp** Model EL-344G Metric Calculator, **Texas Instruments** Model 1895II, and **Radio Shack** Model 65–828.

APPENDIX D:
TABLES FROM THE UNIFORM BUILDING CODE

Table D–1 Asphalt shingle application.

	Asphalt Shingles	
	Not Permitted below 2 Units Vertical in 12 Units Horizontal (16.7% Slope)	
Roof Slope	2 Units Vertical in 12 Units Horizontal (16.7% Slope) to Less Than 4 Units Vertical in 12 Units Horizontal (33.3% Slope)	4 Units Vertical in 12 Units Horizontal (33.3% Slope) and Over
1. Deck requirement	Asphalt shingles shall be fastened to solidly sheathed roofs. Sheathing shall conform to Sections 2322.2 and 2326.12.9.	
2. Underlayment Temperate climate	Asphalt strip shingles may be installed on slopes as low as 2 inches in 12 inches (305 mm), provided the shingles are approved self-sealing or are hand sealed and are installed with an underlayment consisting of two layers of nonperforated Type 15 felt applied shingle fashion. Starting with an 18-inch-wide (457 mm) sheet and a 36-inch-wide (914 mm) sheet over it at the eaves; each subsequent sheet shall be lapped 19 inches (483 mm) horizontally.	One layer nonperforated Type 15 felt lapped 2 inches (51 mm) horizontally and 4 inches (102 mm) vertically to shed water.
Severe climate: In areas subject to wind-driven snow or roof ice buildup.	Same as for temperate climate, and additionally the two layers shall be solid cemented together with approved cementing material between the plies extending from the eave up the roof to a line 24 inches (610 mm) inside the exterior wall line of the building.	Same as for temperate climate, except that one layer No. 40 coated roofing or coated glass base shall be applied from the eaves to a line 12 inches (305 mm) inside the exterior wall line with all laps cemented together.
3. Attachment combined systems, type of fasteners	Corrosion-resistant nails, minimum 12-gage $3/8$-inch (9.5 mm) head, or approved corrosion-resistant staples, minimum 16-gage $15/16$-inch (23.8 mm) crown width. Fasteners shall comply with the requirements of Chapter 23, Division III. Fasteners shall be long enough to penetrate into the sheathing $3/4$ inch (19 mm) or through the thickness of the sheathing, whichever is less.	
No. of fasteners[1]	4 per 36-inch to 40-inch (914 mm to 1016 mm) strip 2 per 9-inch to 18-inch (229 mm to 457 mm) shingle	
Exposure Field of roof Hips and ridges	Per manufacturer's instructions included with packages of shingles. Hip and ridge weather exposures shall not exceed those permitted for the field of the roof.	
Method	Per manufacturer's instructions included with packages of shingles.	
4. Flashing Valleys Other flashing	Per Section 1508.2 Per Section 1509	

[1]Figures shown are for normal application. For special conditions such as mansard application and where roofs are in special wind regions, shingles shall be attached per manufacturer's instructions.
SOURCE: From the Uniform Building Code, © 1994, ICBO.

Table D–2 Wood shingle or shake application.

Roof Slope	Wood Shingles Not Permitted below 3 Units Vertical in 12 Units Horizontal (25% Slope) See Table 15-C	Wood Shakes Not Permitted below 4 Units Vertical in 12 Units Horizontal (33.3% Slope)[1] See Table 15-C
1. Deck requirement	Shingles and shakes shall be applied to roofs with solid or spaced sheathing. When spaced sheathing is used, sheathing boards shall not be less than 1 inch by 4 inches (25 mm by 102 mm) nominal dimensions and shall be spaced on centers equal to the weather exposure to coincide with the placement of fasteners. When 1-inch by 4-inch (25 mm by 102 mm) spaced sheathing is installed at 10 inches (254 mm) on center, additional 1-inch by 4-inch (25 mm by 102 mm) boards must be installed between the sheathing boards. Sheathing shall conform to Sections 2322.2 and 2326.12.9.	
2. Interlayment	No requirements.	One 18-inch-wide (457 mm) interlayment of Type 30 felt shingled between each course in such a manner that no felt is exposed to the weather below the shake butts and in the keyways (between the shakes).
3. Underlayment Temperate climate	No requirements.	No requirements.
Severe climate: In areas subject to wind-driven snow or roof ice buildup.	Two layers of nonperforated Type 15 felt applied shingle fashion shall be installed and solid cemented together with approved cementing material between the plies extending from the eave up the roof to a line 36 inches (914 mm) inside the exterior wall line of the building.	Sheathing shall be solid and, in addition to the interlayment of felt shingled between each course in such a manner that no felt is exposed to the weather below the shake butts, the shakes shall be applied over a layer of nonperforated Type 15 felt applied shingle fashion. Two layers of nonperforated Type 15 felt applied shingle fashion shall be installed and solid cemented together with approved cementing material between the plies extending from the eave up the roof to a line 36 inches (914 mm) inside the exterior wall line of the building.
4. Attachment Type of fasteners	Corrosion-resistant nails, minimum No. 14½-gage $^7/_{32}$-inch (5.6 mm) head, or corrosion-resistant staples, when approved by the building official.	Corrosion-resistant nails, minimum No. 13-gage $^7/_{32}$-inch (5.6 mm) head, or corrosion-resistant staples, when approved by the building official.
	Fasteners shall comply with the requirements of Chapter 23, Division III. Fasteners shall be long enough to penetrate into the sheathing ¾ inch (19 mm) or through the thickness of the sheathing, whichever is less.	
No. of fasteners	2 per shingle	2 per shake
Exposure Field of roof Hips and ridges	Weather exposures shall not exceed those set forth in Table 15-C. Hip and ridge weather exposure shall not exceed those permitted for the field of the roof.	
Method	Shingles shall be laid with a side lap of not less than 1½ inches (38 mm) between joints in adjacent courses, and not in direct alignment in alternate courses. Spacing between shingles shall be approximately ¼ inch (6 mm). Each shingle shall be fastened with two nails only, positioned approximately ¾ inch (19 mm) from each edge and approximately 1 inch (25 mm) above the exposure line. Starter course at the eaves shall be doubled.	Shakes shall be laid with a side lap of not less than 1½ inches (38 mm) between joints in adjacent courses. Spacing between shakes shall not be less than ⅜ inch (9 mm) or more than ⅝ inch (16 mm) except for preservative-treated wood shakes which shall have a spacing not less than ¼ inch (6 mm) or more than ⅜ inch (9 mm). Shakes shall be fastened to the sheathing with two nails only, positioned approximately 1 inch (25 mm) from each edge and approximately 2 inches (51 mm) above the exposure line. The starter course at the eaves shall be doubled. The bottom or first layer may be either shakes or shingles. Fifteen-inch or 18-inch (381 mm or 457 mm) shakes may be used for the starter course at the eaves and final course at the ridge.
5. Flashing Valleys Other flashing	Per Section 1508.5 Per Section 1509	

[1]When approved by the building official, wood shakes may be installed on a slope of not less than 3 units vertical in 12 units horizontal (25% slope) when an underlayment of not less than nonperforated Type 15 felt is installed.

SOURCE: From the Uniform Building Code, © 1994, ICBO.

Table D–3 Maximum weather exposure.

Grade Length	3 Units Vertical To Less Than 4 Units Vertical in 12 Units Horizontal (25% ≤ 33.3% Slope)	4 Units Vertical in 12 Units Horizontal (33.3% Slope)
× 25.4 for mm		
Wood Shingles		
1. No. 1 16-inch	$3\frac{3}{4}$	5
2. No. 2[1] 16-inch	$3\frac{1}{2}$	4
3. No. 3[1] 16-inch	3	$3\frac{1}{2}$
4. No. 1 18-inch	$4\frac{1}{4}$	$5\frac{1}{2}$
5. No. 2[1] 18-inch	4	$4\frac{1}{2}$
6. No. 3[1] 18-inch	$3\frac{1}{2}$	4
7. No. 1 24-inch	$5\frac{3}{4}$	$7\frac{1}{2}$
8. No. 2[1] 24-inch	$5\frac{1}{2}$	$6\frac{1}{2}$
9. No. 3[1] 24-inch	5	$5\frac{1}{2}$
Wood Shakes[2]		
10. No. 1 18-inch	$7\frac{1}{2}$	$7\frac{1}{2}$
11. No. 1 24-inch	10	10
12. No. 2 18-inch tapersawn shakes	—	$5\frac{1}{2}$
13. No. 2 24-inch tapersawn shakes	—	$7\frac{1}{2}$

[1]To be used only when specifically permitted by the building official.
[2]Exposure of 24-inch (610 mm) by ⅜-inch (9.5 mm) resawn handsplit shakes shall not exceed 5 inches (127 mm) regardless of the roof slope.
SOURCE: From the Uniform Building Code, © 1994, ICBO.

Table D–4 Roofing tile application for all tiles.[1]

	Roof Slope 2½ Units Vertical In 12 Units Horizontal (21% Slope) To Less Than 3 Units Vertical In 12 Units Horizontal (25% Slope)	Roof Slope 3 Units Vertical In 12 Units Horizontal (25% Slope) And Over
1. Deck requirements	Solid sheathing per Sections 2322.2 and 2326.12.9	
2. Underlayment In climate areas subject to wind-driven snow, roof ice damming or special wind regions as shown in Figure 16-1 of Chapter 16.	Built-up roofing membrane, three plies minimum, applied per Section 1507.6. Surfacing not required.	Same as for other climate areas, except that extending from the eaves up the roof to a line 24 inches (610 mm) inside the exterior wall line of the building, two layers of underlayment shall be applied shingle fashion and solidly cemented together with an approved cementing material.
Other climate areas		One layer heavy-duty felt or Type 30 felt side lapped 2 inches (51 mm) and end lapped 6 inches (153 mm).
3. Attachment[2] Type of fasteners	Corrosion-resistant nails not less than No. 11 gage, 5/16-inch (7.9 mm) head. Fasteners shall comply with the requirements of Chapter 23, Division III. Fasteners shall be long enough to penetrate into the sheathing 3/4 inch (19 mm) or through the thickness of the sheathing, whichever is less. Attaching wire for clay or concrete tile shall not be smaller than 0.083 inch (2.11 mm) (No. 14 B.W. gage).	
Number of fasteners[2,3]	One fastener per tile. Flat tile without vertical laps, two fasteners per tile.	Two fasteners per tile. Only one fastener on slopes of 7 units vertical in 12 units horizontal (58.3% slope) and less for tiles with installed weight exceeding 7.5 pounds per square foot (36.6 kg/m^2) having a width no greater than 16 inches (406 mm).[4]
4. Tile headlap	3 inches (76.2 mm) minimum.	
5. Flashing	Per Sections 1508.4 and 1509.	

[1] In snow areas a minimum of two fasteners per tile are required.

[2] In areas designated by the building official as being subject to repeated wind velocities to excess of 80 miles per hour (129 km/h) or where the roof height exceeds 40 feet (12 192 mm) above grade, all tiles shall be attached as follows:

2.1 The heads of all tiles shall be nailed.

2.2 The noses of all eave course tiles shall be fastened with approved clips.

2.3 All rake tiles shall be nailed with two nails.

2.4 The noses of all ridge, hip and rake tiles shall be set in a bead of approved roofer's mastic.

[3] In snow areas a minimum of two fasteners per tile are required, or battens and one fastener.

[4] On slopes over 24 units vertical in 12 units horizontal (200% slope), the nose end of all tiles shall be securely fastened.

SOURCE: From the Uniform Building Code, © 1994, ICBO.

Table D–5 Clay or concrete roofing tile application of interlocking tile with projection anchor lugs—minimum roof slope 4 units vertical in 12 units horizontal (33.3% slope).

Roof Slope	4 Units Vertical In 12 Units Horizontal (33.3% Slope) and Over
1. Deck requirements	Spaced structural sheathing boards or solid roof sheathing.
2. Underlayment In climate areas subject to wind-driven snow, roof ice or special wind regions as shown in Figure 16–1.	Solid sheathing one layer of Type 30 felt lapped 2 inches (51 mm) horizontally and 6 inches (153 mm) vertically, except that extending from the eaves up the roof to line 24 inches (610 mm) inside the exterior wall line of the building, two layers of the underlayment shall be applied shingle fashion and solid cemented together with approved cementing material.
Other climates	For spaced sheathing, approved reinforced membrane. For solid sheathing, one layer heavy-duty felt or Type 30 felt lapped 2 inches (51 mm) horizontally and 6 inches (153 mm) vertically.
3. Attachment[1] Type of fasteners	Corrosion-resistant nails not less than No. 11 gage, $\frac{5}{16}$-inch (7.9 mm) head. Fasteners shall comply with the requirements of Chapter 23, Division III. Fasteners shall be long enough to penetrate into the battens[2] or sheathing $\frac{3}{4}$ inch (19 mm) or through the thickness of the sheathing, whichever is less. Attaching wire for clay or concrete tile shall not be smaller than 0.083 inch (2.11 mm) (No. 14 B.W. gage). Horizontal battens are required on solid sheathing for slopes 7 units vertical in 12 units horizontal (58.3% slope) and over.[1] Horizontal battens are required for slopes over 7 units vertical in 12 units horizontal (58.3% slope).[2]
No. of fasteners with: Spaced/solid sheathing with battens, or spaced sheathing[3] Solid sheathing without battens[3]	Below 5 units vertical in 12 units horizontal (41.7% slope), fasteners not required. Five units vertical in 12 units horizontal (41.7% slope) to less than 12 units vertical in 12 units horizontal (100% slope), one fastener per tile every other row. Twelve units vertical in 12 units horizontal (100% slope) to 24 units vertical in 12 units horizontal (200% slope), one fastener every tile.[4] All perimeter tiles require one fastener.[5] Tiles with installed weight less than 9 pounds per square foot (4.4 kg/m^2) require a minimum of one fastener per tile regardless of roof slope. One fastener per tile.
4. Tile headlap	3-inch (76 mm) minimum.
5. Flashing	Per Sections 1508.4 and 1509.

[1]In areas designated by the building official as being subject to repeated wind velocities to excess of 80 miles per hour (129 km/h), or where the roof height exceeds 40 feet (12 192 mm) above grade, all tiles shall be attached as set forth below:
    1.1 The heads of all tiles shall be nailed.
    1.2 The noses of all eave course tiles shall be fastened with a special clip.
    1.3 All rake tiles shall be nailed with two nails.
    1.4 The noses of all ridge, hip and rake tiles shall be set in a bead of approved roofer's mastic.
[2]Battens shall not be less than 1-inch by 2-inch (25.4 mm by 51 mm) nominal. Provisions shall be made for drainage beneath battens by a minimum of $\frac{1}{8}$-inch (3.2 mm) risers at each nail or by 4-foot-long (1219 mm) battens with at least $\frac{1}{2}$-inch (13 mm) separation between battens. Battens shall be fastened with approved fasteners spaced at not more than 24 inches (610 mm) on center.
[3]In snow areas a minimum of two fasteners per tile are required, or battens and one fastener.
[4]Slopes over 24 units vertical in 12 units horizontal (200% slope), nose ends of all tiles must be securely fastened.
[5]Perimeter fastening areas include three tile courses but not less than 36 inches (914 mm) from either side of hips or ridges and edges of eaves and gable rakes.
SOURCE: From the Uniform Building Code, © 1994, ICBO.

Table D-6 Built-up roof-covering application.

	Mechanically Fastened Systems	Adhesively Fastened Systems
1. Deck conditions	Decks shall be firm, broom-clean, smooth and dry. Insulated decks shall have wood insulation stops at all edges of the deck, unless an alternative suitable curbing is provided. Insulated decks with slopes greater than 2 units vertical in 12 units horizontal (16.7% slope) shall have wood insulation stops at not more than 8 feet (2438 mm) face to face. Wood nailers shall be provided where nailing is required for roofing plies.	
	Solid wood sheathing shall conform to Sections 2322.2 and 2326.12.9.	Provide wood nailers where nailing is required for roofing plies (see below).
2. Underlayment	One layer of sheathing paper, Type 15 felt or other approved underlayment nailed sufficiently to hold in place, is required over board decks where openings between boards would allow bitumen to drip through. No underlayment requirements for plywood decks. Underlayment on other decks shall be in accordance with deck manufacturer's recommendations.	Not required.
3. Base ply requirements Over noninsulated decks	Over approved decks, the base ply shall be nailed using not less than one fastener for each 1⅓ square feet (0.124 m²).	Decks shall be primed in accordance with the roofing manufacturer's instructions. The base ply shall be solidly cemented or spot mopped as required by the type of deck material using adhesive application rates shown in Table 15-F.
4. Mechanical fasteners	Fasteners shall be long enough to penetrate ¾ inch (19 mm) into the sheathing or through the thickness of the sheathing, whichever is less. Built-up roofing nails for wood board decks shall be minimum No. 12 gage ⁷/₁₆-inch (11.1 mm) head driven through tin caps or approved nails with integral caps. For plywood, No. 11 gage ring-shank nails driven through tin caps or approved nails with integral caps shall be used. For gypsum, insulating concrete, cementitious wood fiber and other decks, fasteners recommended by the manufacturer shall be used.	When mechanical fasteners are required for attachment of roofing plies to wood nailers or insulation stops (see below), they shall be as required for wood board decks.
5. Vapor retarder Over insulated decks	A vapor retarder shall be installed where the average January temperature is below 45°F. (7°C.), or where excessive moisture conditions are anticipated within the building. It shall be applied as for a base ply.	
6. Insulation	When no vapor retarder is required, roof insulation shall be fastened in an approved manner. When a vapor retarder is required, roof insulation is to be solidly mopped to the vapor retarder using the adhesive application rate specified in Table 15-F. See manufacturer's instructions for the attachment of insulation over steel decks.	When no vapor retarder is required, roof insulation shall be solid mopped to the deck using the adhesive application rate specified in Table 15-F. When a vapor retarder is required, roof insulation is to be solidly mopped to the vapor retarder, using the adhesive application rate specified in Table 15-F. See manufacturer's installation instructions for attachment of insulation over steel decks.
7. Roofing plies	Successive layers shall be solidly cemented together and to the base ply or the insulation using the adhesive rates shown in Table15-F. On slopes greater than 1 unit vertical in 12 units horizontal (8.3% slope) for aggregate-surfaced, or 2 units vertical in 12 units horizontal (16.7% slope) for smooth-surfaced or cap sheet surfaced roofs, mechanical fasteners are required. Roofing plies shall be blind-nailed to the deck, wood nailers or wood insulation stops in accordance with the roofing manufacturer's recommendations. On slopes exceeding 3 units vertical in 12 units horizontal (25% slope), plies shall be laid parallel to the slope of the deck (strapping method).	
8. Cementing materials	See Table 15-G.	
9. Curbs and walls	Suitable cant strips shall be used at all vertical intersections. Adequate attachment shall be provided for both base flashing and counterflashing on all vertical surfaces. Reglets shall be provided in wall or parapets receiving metal counterflashing.	
10. Surfacing	Mineral aggregate surfaced roofs shall comply with the requirements of U.B.C. Standard 15-1 and Table 15-F. Cap sheets shall be cemented to the roofing plies as set forth in Table 15-F.	

SOURCE: From the Uniform Building Code, © 1994, ICBO.

Table D–7 Foundations for stud-bearing walls: minimum requirements.[1,2,3]

Number of Floors Supported by the Foundation[4]	Thickness of Foundation Wall (inches) × 25.4 for mm		Width of Footing (inches)	Thickness of Footing (inches)	Depth Below Undisturbed Ground Surface (inches)
	Concrete	Unit Masonry	× 25.4 for mm		
1	6	6	12	6	12
2	8	8	15	7	18
3	10	10	18	8	24

[1]Where unusual conditions or frost conditions are found, footings and foundations shall be as required in Section 1806.1.

[2]The ground under the floor may be excavated to the elevation of the top of the footing.

[3]Interior stud bearing walls may be supported by isolated footings. The footing width and length shall be twice the width shown in this table and the footings shall be spaced not more than 6 feet (1829 mm) on center.

[4]Foundations may support a roof in addition to the stipulated number of floors. Foundations supporting roofs only shall be as required for supporting one floor.

SOURCE: From the Uniform Building Code © 1994, ICBO.

Table D–8 Wood shingle and shake side-wall exposures.

Shingle or Shake	Maximum Weather Exposures (inches) × 25.4 for mm			
	Single-Coursing		Double-Coursing	
Length and Type	No. 1	No. 2	No. 1	No. 2
1. 16-inch (405 mm) shingles	7½	7½	12	10
2. 18-inch (455 mm) shingles	8½	8½	14	11
3. 24-inch (610 mm) shingles	11½	11½	16	14
4. 18-inch (455 mm) resawn shakes	8½	—	14	—
5. 18-inch (455 mm) straight-split shakes	8½	—	16	—
6. 24-inch (610 mm) resawn shakes	11½	—	20	—

SOURCE: From the Uniform Building Code, © 1994, ICBO.

Table D–9 Exposed plywood panel siding.

Minimum Thickness[1] (inch) × 25.4 for mm	Minimum Number of Plies	Stud Spacing (inches) Plywood Siding Applied Directly To Studs Or Over Sheathing Plywood Siding Applied Directly
³⁄₈	3	16[2]
¹⁄₂	4	24

[1]Thickness of grooved panels is measured at bottom of grooves.
[2]May be 24 inches (610 mm) if plywood siding applied with face grain perpendicular to studs or over one of the following: (1) 1-inch (25 mm) board sheathing, (2) 7/16-inch (11 mm) wood structural panel sheathing or (3) 3/8-inch (9.5 mm) wood structural panel sheathing with strength axis (which is the long direction of the panel unless otherwise marked) of sheathing perpendicular to studs.
SOURCE: From the Uniform Building Code, © 1994, ICBO.

Table D–10 Allowable spans for exposed particleboard panel siding.

Grade	Stud Spacing (inches) × 25.4 for mm	Minimum Thickness (inches) × 25.4 for mm Siding Direct to Studs	Continuous Support	Exterior Ceilings and Soffits Direct to Supports
2-M-W	16	³⁄₈	⁵⁄₁₆	⁵⁄₁₆
	24	¹⁄₂	⁵⁄₁₆	³⁄₈
2-M-1	16	⁵⁄₈	³⁄₈	—
2-M-2				
2-M-3	24	³⁄₄	³⁄₈	—

SOURCE: From the Uniform Building Code, © 1994, ICBO.

Table D–11 Hardboard siding.

Siding	Minimal Nominal Thickness (inch)	Framing (2″ × 4″) Maximum Spacing	Nail Size[1,2]	Nail Spacing	
				General	Bracing Panels[3]
× 25.4 for mm					
I. LAP SIDING					
Direct to studs	3/8	16″ o.c.	8d	16″ o.c.	Not applicable
Over sheathing	3/8	16″ o.c.	10d	16″ o.c.	Not applicable
2. SQUARE EDGE PANEL SIDING					
Direct to studs	3/8	24″ o.c.	6d	6″ o.c. edges; 12″ o.c. at intermed. supports	4″ o.c. edges; 8″ o.c. intermed. supports
Over sheathing	3/8	24″ o.c.	8d	6″ o.c. edges; 12″ o.c. at intermed. supports	4″ o.c. edges; 8″ o.c. intermed. supports
3. SHIPLAP EDGE PANEL SIDING					
Direct to studs	3/8	16″ o.c.	6d	6″ o.c. edges; 12″ o.c. at intermed. supports	4″ o.c. edges; 8″ o.c. intermed. supports
Over sheathing	3/8	16″ o.c.	8d	6″ o.c. edges; 12″ o.c. at intermed. supports	4″ o.c. edges; 8″ o.c. intermed. supports

[1]Nails shall be corrosion resistant in accordance with Division III.
[2]Minimum acceptable nail dimensions (inches).

	Panel Siding (inch)	Lap Siding (inch)
	× 25.4 for mm	
Shank diameter	.092	.099
Head diameter	.225	.240

[3]When used to comply with Section 2326.11.3.
SOURCE: From the Uniform Building Code, © 1994, ICBO.

Table D–12 Allowable spans for lumber floor and roof sheathing.[1,2]

Span (inches)	Minimum Net Thickness (inches) of Lumber Placed			
	Perpendicular to Supports		Diagonally to Supports	
× 25.4 for mm	× 25.4 for mm			
	Surfaced Dry[3]	Surfaced Unseasoned	Surfaced Dry[3]	Surfaced Unseasoned
Floors				
1. 24	3/4	25/32	3/4	25/32
2. 16	5/8	11/16	5/8	11/16
Roofs				
3. 24	5/8	11/16	3/4	25/32

[1]Installation details shall conform to Sections 2326.9.1 and 2326.12.8 for floor and roof sheathing, respectively.
[2]Floor or roof sheathing conforming with this table shall be deemed to meet the design criteria of Section 2322.
[3]Maximum 19 percent moisture content.
SOURCE: From the Uniform Building Code, © 1994, ICBO.

Table D–13 Allowable spans for wood structural panel combination subfloor-underlayment (single-floor) continuous over two or more spans with strength axis perpendicular to supports.[1,2]

Identification	Maximum Spacing of Joists (Inches)				
	× 25.4 for mm				
	16	20	24	32	48
Species Group[3]	Thickness (Inches)				
	× 25.4 for mm				
1	1/2	5/8	3/4	—	—
2,3	5/8	3/4	7/8	—	—
4	3/4	7/8	1	—	—
Span rating[4]	16 o.c.	20 o.c.	24 o.c.	32 o.c.	48 o.c.

[1]Spans limited to value shown because of possible effects of concentrated loads. Allowable uniform loads based on deflection of 1/360 of span is 100 pounds per square foot (psf) (4.79 kN/m²), except allowable total uniform load for 1⅛-inch (29 mm) wood structural panels over joists spaced 48 inches (1219 mm) on center is 65 psf (3.11 kN/m²). Panel edges shall have approved tongue-and-groove joints or shall be supported with blocking, unless ¼-inch (6.4 mm) minimum thickness underlayment or 1½ inches (38 mm) of approved cellular or lightweight concrete is placed over the subfloor, or finish floor is ¾-inch (19 mm) wood strip.
[2]Floor panels conforming with this table shall be deemed to meet the design criteria of Section 2321.
[3]Applicable to all grades of sanded exterior-type plywood. See U.B.C. Standard 23-2 for plywood species groups.
[4]Applicable to underlayment grade and C-C (plugged) plywood, and single floor grade wood structural panels.
SOURCE: From the Uniform Building Code, © 1994, ICBO.

Table D–14 Classification of species.

Group 1	Group 2		Group 3	Group 4
Apitong[a][b]	Cedar, Port Orford	Maple, Black	Alder, Red	Aspen
Beech, American	Cypress	Mengkulang[a]	Birch, Paper	Bigtooth
Birch	Douglas Fir 2[c]	Meranti, Red[a][d]	Cedar, Alaska	Quaking
Sweet	Fir	Mersawa[a]	Fir, Subalpine	Cativo
Yellow	California Red	Pine	Hemlock, Eastern	Cedar
Douglas Fir[c]	Grand	Pond	Maple, Bigleaf	Incense
Kapur[a]	Noble	Red	Pine	Western Red
Keruing[a] [b]	Pacific Silver	Virginia	Jack	Cottonwood
Larch, Western	White	Western White	Lodgepole	Eastern
Maple, Sugar	Hemlock, Western	Spruce	Ponderosa	Black (Western Poplar)
Pine	Lauan	Red	Spruce	Pine
Caribbean	Almon	Sitka	Redwood	Eastern White
Ocote	Bagtikan	Sweetgum	Spruce	Sugar
Pine, Southern	Mayapis	Tamarack	Black	
Loblolly	Red Lauan	Yellow-poplar	Englemann	
Longleaf	Tangile		White	
Shortleaf	White Lauan			
Slash				
Tanoak				

(a) Each of these names represents a trade group of woods consisting of a number of closely related species.

(b) Species from the genus Dipterocarpus are marketed collectively: Apitong if originating in the Philippines; Keruing if originating in Malaysia or Indonesia.

(c) Douglas fir from trees grown in the states of Washington, Oregon, California, Idaho, Montana, Wyoming, and the Canadian Provinces of Alberta and British Columbia shall be classed as Douglas fir No. 1 Douglas fir from trees grown in the states of Nevada, Utah, Colorado, Arizona and New Mexico shall be classed as Douglas fir No. 2.

(d) Red Meranti shall be limited to species having a specific gravity of 0.41 or more based on green volume and oven dry weight.

Source: From the Uniform Building Code, © 1994, ICBO.

Table D–15 Size, height, and spacing of wood studs.

Stud Size (inches)	Bearing Walls				Nonbearing Walls	
	Laterally Stud Stud Height[1] (feet)	Supporting Roof and Unsupported	Supporting One Floor, Roof and Ceiling Only	Supporting Two Floors, Roof and Ceiling	Laterally Ceiling Stud Height[1] (feet)	Unsupported Spacing (inches)
		Spacing (inches)				
× 25.4 for mm	× 304.8 for mm	× 25.4 for mm			× 304.8 for mm	× 25.4 for mm
1. 2 × 3[2]	—	—	—	—	10	16
2. 2 × 4	10	24	16	—	14	24
3. 3 × 4	10	24	24	16	14	24
4. 2 × 5	10	24	24	—	16	24
5. 2 × 6	10	24	24	16	20	24

[1]Listed heights are distances between points of lateral support placed perpendicular to the plane of the wall. Increases in unsupported height are permitted where justified by an analysis.

[2]Shall not be used in exterior walls.

SOURCE: From the Uniform Building Code, © 1994, ICBO.

Table D–16 Allowable spans and loads for wood structural panel sheathing and single-floor grades continuous over two or more spans with strength axis perpendicular to supports.[1,2]

Sheathing Grades		Roof[3]				Floor[4]
		Maximum Span (inches)		Load[5] (pounds per square foot)		Maximum Span (inches)
Panel Span Rating	Panel Thickness (inches)	× 25.4 for mm		× 0.0479 for kN/m²		
Roof/Floor Span	× 25.4 for mm	With Edge Support[6]	Without Edge Support	Total Load	Live Load	× 25.4 for mm
12/0	5/16	12	12	40	30	0
16/0	5/16, 3/8	16	16	40	30	0
20/0	5/16, 3/8	20	20	40	30	0
24/0	3/8, 7/16, 1/2	24	20[7]	40	30	0
24/16	7/16, 1/2	24	24	50	40	16
32/16	15/32, 1/2, 5/8	32	28	40	30	16[8]
40/20	19/32, 5/8, 3/4, 7/8	40	32	40	30	20[8,9]
48/24	23/32, 3/4, 7/8	48	36	45	35	24
54/32	7/8, 1	54	40	45	35	32
60/48	7/8, 1, 1 1/8	60	48	45	35	48

Single-Floor Grades		Roof[3]				Floor[4]
		Maximum Span (inches)		Load[5] (pounds per square foot)		Maximum Span (inches)
Panel Span Rating (inches)	Panel Thickness (inches)	× 25.4 for mm		× 0.0479 for kN/m²		
× 25.4 for mm		With Edge Support[6]	Without Edge Support	Total Load	Live Load	× 25.4 for mm
16 oc	1/2, 19/32, 5/8	24	24	50	40	16[8]
20 oc	19/32, 5/8, 3/4	32	32	40	30	20[8,9]
24 oc	23/32, 3/4	48	36	35	25	24
32 oc	7/8, 1	48	40	50	40	32
48 oc	1 3/32, 1 1/8	60	48	50	50	48

[1]Applies to panels 24 inches (610 mm) or wider.

[2]Floor and roof sheathing conforming with this table shall be deemed to meet the design criteria of Section 2321.

[3]Uniform load deflection limitations 1/180 of span under live load plus dead load. 1/240 under live load only.

[4]Panel edges shall have approved tongue-and-groove joints or shall be supported with blocking unless 1/4-inch (6.4 mm) minimum thickness underlayment or 1 1/2 inches (38 mm) of approved cellular or lightweight concrete is placed over the subfloor, or finish floor is 3/4-inch (19 mm) wood strip. Allowable uniform load based on deflection of 1/360 of span is 100 pounds per square foot (psf) (4.79 kN/m²) except the span rating of 48 inches on center is based on a total load of 65 psf (3.11 kN/m).

[5]Allowable load at maximum span.

[6]Tongue-and-groove edges, panel edge clips [one midway between each support, except two equally spaced between supports 48 inches (1219 mm) on center], lumber blocking, or other. Only lumber blocking shall satisfy blocked diaphragms requirements.

[7]For 1/2-inch (13 mm) panel, maximum span shall be 24 inches (610 mm).

[8]May be 24 inches (610 mm) on center where 3/4-inch (19 mm) wood strip flooring is installed at right angles to joist.

[9]May be 24 inches (610 mm) on center for floors where 1 1/2 inches (38 mm) of cellular or lightweight concrete is applied over the panels.

SOURCE: From the Uniform Building Code, © 1994, ICBO.

Table D-17 Allowable load (lb/sq ft) for wood structural panel roof sheathing continuous over two or more spans and strength axis parallel to supports (plywood structural panels are five-ply, five-layer unless otherwise noted).[1,2]

Panel Grade	Thickness (inch)	Maximum Span (inches)	Load at Maximum Span (psf) × 0.0479 for kN/m²	
	× 25.4 for mm		Live	Total
Structural I	7/16	24	20	30
	15/32	24	35[3]	45[3]
	1/2	24	40[3]	50[3]
	19/32, 5/8	24	70	80
	23/32, 3/4	24	90	100
Other grades covered in U.B.C. Standard 23-2 or 23-3	7/16	16	40	50
	15/32	24	20	25
	1/2	24	25	30
	19/32	24	40[3]	50[3]
	5/8	24	45[3]	55[3]
	23/32, 3/4	24	60[3]	65[3]

[1]Roof sheathing conforming with this table shall be deemed to meet the design criteria of Section 2321.
[2]Uniform load deflection limitations: 1/180 of span under live load plus dead load, 1/240 under live load only. Edges shall be blocked with lumber or other approved type of edge supports.
[3]For composite and four-ply plywood structural panel, load shall be reduced by 15 pounds per square foot (0.72 kN/m2).
SOURCE: From the Uniform Building Code, © 1994, ICBO.

Table D-18 Allowable loads for particleboard roof sheathing.[1,2,3]

Grade	Thickness (inch)	Maximum On-Center Spacing Of Supports (inches)	Live Load (pounds per square foot)	Total Load (pounds per square foot)
		× 25.4 for mm	× 0.0479 for kN/m²	
2-M-W	3/8[4]	16	45	65
	7/16	16	105	105
	7/16[4]	24	30	40
	1/2	16	110	150
	1/2	24	40	55

[1]Panels are continuous over two or more spans.
[2]Uniform load deflection limitation: 1/180 of the span under live load plus dead load and 1/240 of the span under live load only.
[3]Roof sheathing conforming with this table shall be deemed to meet the design criteria of Section 2321.
[4]Edges shall be tongue-and-groove or supported with blocking or edge clips.
SOURCE: From the Uniform Building Code, © 1994, ICBO.

Table D–19 Braced wall panels.[1]

Seismic Zone	Condition	Construction Method[2,3]								Braced Panel Location and Length[4]
		1	2	3	4	5	6	7	8	
0, 1 and 2A	One story, top of two or three story	X	X	X	X	X	X	X	X	Each end and not more than 25 feet (7620 mm) on center
	First story of two story or second story of three story	X	X	X	X	X	X	X	X	
	First story of three story		X	X	X	X[5]	X	X	X	
2B, 3 and 4	One story, top of two or three story		X	X	X	X	X	X	X	Each end and not more than 25 feet (7620 mm) on center
	First story of two story or second of three story		X	X	X	X[5]	X	X	X	Each end and not more than 25 feet (7620 mm) on center but not less than 25% of building length[6]
	First story of three story		X	X	X	X[5]	X	X	X	Each end and not more than 25 feet (7620 mm) on center but not less than 40% of building length[6]

[1]This table specifies minimum requirements for braced panels which form interior or exterior braced wall lines.
[2]See Section 2326.11.3 for full description.
[3]See Section 2326.11.4 for alternate braced panel requirement.
[4]Building length is the dimension parallel to the braced wall length.
[5]Gypsum wallboard applied to supports at 16 inches (406 mm) on center.
[6]The required lengths shall be doubled for gypsum board applied to only one face of a braced wall panel.
SOURCE: From the Uniform Building Code, © 1994, ICBO.

Table D–20 Single-ply gypsum wallboard applied parallel (∥) or perpendicular (⊥) to framing members.

Thickness of Gypsum Wallboard (inch) × 25.4 for mm	Plane of Framing Surface	Maximum Spacing of Framing Member[1] (Center to Center) (inches) × 25.4 for mm	Long Dimension of Gypsum Wallboard Sheets in Relation to Direction of Framing Members ∥	⊥	Maximum Spacing of Fasteners[1] (Center to Center) (inches) × 25.4 for mm Nails[3]	Screws[4]	Nails[2]—to Wood × 25.4 for mm
½	Horizontal	16	P	P	7	12	No. 13 gage, 1⅛″ long, 19/64″ head; 0.098″ diameter, 1¼″ long, annular ringed; 5d, cooler or wallboard[5] nail (0.086″ dia., 1⅝″ long, 15/64″ head).
		24	NP	P			
	Vertical	16	P	P	8	16	
		24	P	P		12	
⅝	Horizontal	16	P	P	7	12	No. 13 gage, 1⅝″ long, 19/64″ head; 0.098″ diameter, 1⅜″ long, annular ringed; 6d, cooler or wallboard[5] nail (0.092″ dia., 1⅞″ long, ¼″ head).
		24	NP	P			
	Vertical	16	P	P	8	16	
		24	P	P		12	

Nail or Screw Fastenings with Adhesives (Maximum Center to Center in Inches)
× 25.4 for mm

(Column headings as above)		End	Edges	Field			
½ or ⅝	Horizontal	16	P	P	16	16	24	As required for ½″ and ⅝″ gypsum wallboard, see above.
		24	NP	P	16	24	24	
	Vertical	24	P	P	16	24	NR	

NOTES: Horizontal refers to applications such as ceilings. Vertical refers to applications such as walls.

∥ denotes parallel.

⊥ denotes perpendicular. P—Permitted. NP—Not permitted. NR—Not required.

[1]A combination of fasteners consisting of nails along the perimeter and screws in the field of the gypsum board may be used with the spacing of the fasteners shown in the table.

For fire-resistive construction, see Tables 7-B and 7-C. For shear-resisting elements, see Table 25-I.

[2]Where the metal framing has a clinching design formed to receive the nails by two edges of metal, the nails shall not be less than ⅝ inch (16 mm) longer than the wallboard thickness, and shall have ringed shanks. Where the metal framing has a nailing groove formed to receive the nails, the nails shall have barbed shanks or be 5d, No. 13½ gage, 1⅝ inches (41 mm) long, 15/64-inch (6.0 mm) head for ½-inch (12.7 mm) gypsum wallboard; 6d, No. 13 gage, 1⅞ (48 mm) inches long, 15/64-inch (6.0 mm) head for ⅝-inch (16 mm) gypsum wallboard.

[3]Two nails spaced 2 inches to 2½ inches (51 mm to 64 mm) apart may be used where the pairs are spaced 12 inches (305 mm) on center except around the perimeter of the sheets.

[4]Screws shall be long enough to penetrate into wood framing not less than ⅝ inch (16 mm) and through metal framing not less than ¼ inch (6.4 mm).

[5]For properties of cooler or wallboard nails, see Chapter 23, Division III, Table 23-III-H.

SOURCE: From the Uniform Building Code, © 1994, ICBO.

Table D–21 Application of two-ply gypsum wallboard.[1]

Thickness of Gypsum Wallboard (Each Ply) (inch) × 25.4 for mm	Plane of Framing Surface	Long Dimension of Gypsum Wallboard Sheets	Maximum Spacing of Framing Members (Center to Center) (inches) × 25.4 for mm	Maximum Spacing of Fasteners (Center to Center) (inches) × 25.4 for mm				
				Base Ply			Face Ply	
				Nails[2]	Screws[3]	Staples[4]	Nails[2]	Screws[3]
Fasteners only								
3/8	Horizontal	Perpendicular only	16				7	
	Vertical	Either direction	16				8	
1/2	Horizontal	Perpendicular only	24	16	24	16	7	12
	Vertical	Either direction	24				8	
5/8	Horizontal	Perpendicular only	24				7	
	Vertical	Either direction	24				8	
Fasteners and Adhesives								
3/8	Horizontal	Perpendicular only	16	7			5	
Base ply	Vertical	Either direction	24	8			7	
1/2	Horizontal	Perpendicular only	24	7	12		5	Temporary nailing or shoring to comply with Section 2511.4
Base ply	Vertical	Either direction	24	8			7	
5/8	Horizontal	Perpendicular only	24	7			5	
Base ply	Vertical	Either direction	24	8			7	

[1]For fire-resistive construction, see Tables 7-B and 7-C. For shear-resisting elements, see Table 25-I.

[2]Nails for wood framing shall be long enough to penetrate into wood members not less than 3/4 inch (19 mm), and the sizes shall conform with the provisions of Table 25-G. For nails not included in Table 25-G, use the appropriate size cooler or wallboard nails as set forth in Section 2340.1.2. Nails for metal framing shall conform with the provisions of Table 25-G.

[3]Screws shall conform with the provisions of Table 25-G.

[4]Staples shall not be less than No. 16 gage by 3/4-inch (19.1 mm) crown width with leg length of 7/8 inch (22.2 mm), 1 1/8 inches (28.6 mm) and 1 3/8 inches (34.9 mm) for gypsum wallboard thicknesses of 3/8 inch (9.5 mm), 1/2 inch (12.7 mm) and 5/8 inch (15.9 mm), respectively.

SOURCE: From the Uniform Building Code, © 1994, ICBO.

APPENDIX E:
SPAN TABLES FOR WOOD STRUCTURAL MEMBERS

FLOOR JOISTS SPAN TABLES

E.1.1 Southern Pine Floor Joists Span Tables

Maximum spans are given in feet and inches.

Table E–1 Southern pine floor joists: 40-psf live load, 10-psf dead load, L/360; all rooms except sleeping rooms and attic floors.

Size inches	Spacing inches on center	Grade										
		Visually Graded				Machine Stress Rated (MSR)				Machine Evaluated Lumber (MEL)		
		Select Structural	No. 1	No. 2	No. 3	2400f-2.0E	2250f-1.9E	2100f-1.8E	1950f-1.7E	M-23	M-19	M-14
2 × 6	12	11-2	10-11	10-9	9-4	11-7	11-4	11-2	10-11	11-2	10-9	10-11
	16	10-2	9-11	9-9	8-1	10-6	10-4	10-2	9-11	10-2	9-9	9-11
	19.2	9-6	9-4	9-2	7-4	9-10	9-8	9-6	9-4	9-6	9-2	9-4
	24	8-10	8-8	8-6	6-7	9-2	9-0	8-10	8-8	8-10	8-6	8-8
2 × 8	12	14-8	14-5	14-2	11-11	15-3	15-0	14-8	14-5	14-8	14-2	14-5
	16	13-4	13-1	12-10	10-3	13-10	13-7	13-4	13-1	13-4	12-10	13-1
	19.2	12-7	12-4	12-1	9-5	13-0	12-10	12-7	12-4	12-7	12-1	12-4
	24	11-8	11-5	11-0	8-5	12-1	11-11	11-8	11-5	11-8	11-3	11-5
2 × 10	12	18-9	18-5	18-0	14-0	19-5	19-1	18-9	18-5	18-9	18-0	18-5
	16	17-0	16-9	16-1	12-2	17-8	17-4	17-0	16-9	17-0	16-5	16-9
	19.2	16-0	15-9	14-8	11-1	16-7	16-4	16-0	15-9	16-0	15-5	15-9
	24	14-11	14-7	13-1	9-11	15-5	15-2	14-11	14-7	14-11	14-4	14-7
2 × 12	12	22-10	22-5	21-9	16-8	23-7	23-3	22-10	22-5	22-10	21-11	22-5
	16	20-9	20-4	18-10	14-6	21-6	21-1	20-9	20-4	20-9	19-11	20-4
	19.2	19-6	19-2	17-2	13-2	20-2	19-10	19-6	19-2	19-6	18-9	19-2
	24	18-1	17-5	15-5	11-10	18-9	18-5	18-1	17-9	18-1	17-5	17-9

SOURCE: Southern Pine Council.

Table E–2 Southern pine floor joists: 30-psf live load, 10-psf dead load, L/360; sleeping rooms and attic floors.

Size inches	Spacing inches on center	Grade										
		Visually Graded				Machine Stress Rated (MSR)				Machine Evaluated Lumber (MEL)		
		Select Structural	No. 1	No. 2	No. 3	2400f-2.0E	2250f-1.9E	2100f-1.8E	1950f-1.7E	M-23	M-19	M-14
2 × 6	12	12-3	12-0	11-10	10-5	12-9	12-6	12-3	12-0	12-3	11-10	12-0
	16	11-2	10-11	10-9	9-0	11-7	11-4	11-2	10-11	11-2	10-9	10-11
	19.2	10-6	10-4	10-1	8-3	10-10	10-8	10-6	10-4	10-6	10-1	10-4
	24	9-9	9-7	9-4	7-4	10-1	9-11	9-9	9-7	9-9	9-4	9-7
2 × 8	12	16-2	15-10	15-7	13-3	16-9	16-6	16-2	15-10	16-2	15-7	15-10
	16	14-8	14-5	14-2	11-6	15-3	15-0	14-8	14-5	14-8	14-2	14-5
	19.2	13-10	13-7	13-4	10-6	14-4	14-1	13-10	13-7	13-10	13-4	13-7
	24	12-10	12-7	12-4	9-5	13-4	13-1	12-10	12-7	12-10	12-4	12-7
2 × 10	12	20-8	20-3	19-10	15-8	21-5	21-0	20-8	20-3	20-8	19-10	20-3
	16	18-9	18-5	18-0	13-7	19-5	19-1	18-9	18-5	18-9	18-0	18-5
	19.2	17-8	17-4	16-5	12-5	18-3	18-0	17-8	17-4	17-8	17-0	17-4
	24	16-5	16-1	14-8	11-1	17-0	16-8	16-5	16-1	16-5	15-9	16-1
2 × 12	12	25-1	24-8	24-2	18-8	26-0	25-7	25-1	24-8	25-1	24-2	24-8
	16	22-10	22-5	21-1	16-2	23-7	23-3	22-10	22-5	22-10	21-11	22-5
	19.2	21-6	21-1	19-3	14-9	22-3	21-10	21-6	21-1	21-6	20-8	21-1
	24	19-11	19-6	17-2	13-2	20-8	20-3	19-11	19-7	19-11	19-2	19-7

These spans are intended for use in enclosed structures or where the moisture content in use does not exceed 19 percent for an extended period of time unless the table is labeled Wet-Service. Applied loads are given in psf (pounds per square foot). Deflection is limited to the span in inches divided by 360, 240, or 180 and is based on live load only. The load duration factor, C_D, is 1.0 unless shown as 1.15 or 1.25. An asterisk (*) indicates the listed span has been limited to 26'-0" based on availability; check sources of supply for lumber longer than 20'. Highlighted sizes/grades are NOT commonly produced.
SOURCE: Southern Pine Council.
NOTE: See notes following Table E–1.

E.1.2 Western Lumber Floor Joists Span Tables

Table E–3 Western lumber floor joists: 40-psf live load, 10-psf dead load, $L/360$. Residential occupancies include private dwelling, private apartment, and hotel guest rooms. Deck is under CABO and Standard Codes.[1]

Species or Group	Grade	2 × 8 12"	16"	19.2"	24"	2 × 10 12"	16"	19.2"	24"	2 × 12 12"	16"	19.2"	24"	2 × 14 12"	16"	19.2"	24"
Douglas Fir-Larch	Sel. Struc.	15-0	13-7	12-10	11-11	19-1	17-4	16-4	15-2	23-3	21-1	19-10	18-5	27-4	24-10	23-5	21-4
	1 & Btr.	14-8	13-4	12-7	11-8	18-9	17-0	16-0	14-9	22-10	20-9	19-1	17-1	26-10	23-4	21-4	19-1
	No. 1	14-5	13-1	12-4	11-0	18-5	16-5	15-0	13-5	22-0	19-1	17-5	15-7	24-7	21-4	19-5	17-5
	No. 2	14-2	12-9	11-8	10-5	18-0	15-7	14-3	12-9	20-11	18-1	16-6	14-9	23-4	20-3	18-5	16-6
	No. 3	11-3	9-9	8-11	8-0	13-9	11-11	10-11	9-9	16-0	13-10	12-7	11-3	17-10	15-5	14-1	12-7
Douglas Fir-South	Sel. Struc.	13-6	12-3	11-7	10-9	17-3	15-8	14-9	13-8	21-0	19-1	17-11	16-8	24-8	22-5	21-1	19-7
	No. 1	13-2	12-0	11-3	10-6	16-10	15-3	14-5	12-11	20-6	18-4	16-9	15-0	23-8	20-6	18-9	16-9
	No. 2	12-10	11-8	11-0	10-2	16-5	14-11	13-10	12-5	19-11	17-7	16-1	14-4	22-8	19-8	17-11	16-1
	No. 3	11-0	9-6	8-8	7-9	13-5	11-8	10-7	9-6	15-7	13-6	12-4	11-0	17-5	15-1	13-9	12-4
Hem-Fir	Sel. Struc.	14-2	12-10	12-1	11-3	18-0	16-5	15-5	14-4	21-11	19-11	18-9	17-5	25-10	23-6	22-1	20-6
	1 & Btr.	13-10	12-7	11-10	11-0	17-8	16-0	15-1	14-0	21-6	19-6	18-3	16-4	25-3	22-4	20-5	18-3
	No. 1	13-10	12-7	11-10	10-10	17-8	16-0	14-10	13-3	21-6	18-10	17-2	15-5	24-4	21-1	19-3	17-2
	No. 2	13-2	12-0	11-3	10-2	16-10	15-2	13-10	12-5	20-4	17-7	16-1	14-4	22-8	19-8	17-11	16-1
	No. 3	11-0	9-6	8-8	7-9	13-5	11-8	10-7	9-6	15-7	13-6	12-4	11-0	17-5	15-1	13-9	12-4
Spruce-Pine-Fir (South)	Sel. Struc.	13-2	12-0	11-3	10-6	16-10	15-3	14-5	13-4	20-6	18-7	17-6	16-3	24-1	21-11	20-7	19-2
	No. 1	12-10	11-8	11-0	10-2	16-5	14-11	14-0	12-7	19-11	17-10	16-3	14-7	23-0	19-11	18-2	16-3
	No. 2	12-6	11-4	10-8	9-8	15-11	14-6	13-3	11-10	19-4	16-10	15-4	13-9	21-8	18-9	17-2	15-4
	No. 3	10-5	9-0	8-3	7-5	12-9	11-0	10-1	9-0	14-9	12-10	11-8	10-5	16-6	14-4	13-1	11-8
Western Woods	Sel. Struc.	12-10	11-8	11-0	10-2	16-5	14-11	14-0	12-9	19-11	18-1	16-6	14-9	23-4	20-3	18-5	16-6
	No. 1	12-6	11-1	10-1	9-0	15-7	13-6	12-4	11-0	18-1	15-8	14-4	12-10	20-3	17-6	16-0	14-4
	No. 2	12-1	11-0	10-1	9-0	15-5	13-6	12-4	11-0	18-1	15-8	14-4	12-10	20-3	17-6	16-0	14-4
	No. 3	9-6	8-3	7-6	6-9	11-8	10-1	9-2	8-3	13-6	11-8	10-8	9-6	15-1	13-1	11-11	10-8

[1]Deck spans are based on normal conditions of use and assume the moisture content of lumber used in decks will not be maintained at a moisture content in excess of 19% for an extended period of time.
SOURCE: Western Wood Products Association.

Table E–4 Western lumber floor joists: 30-psf live load, 10-psf dead load, $L/360$. Residential occupancy sleeping rooms (BOCA and SBCCI only); attics with storage under the Standard Code. Does not apply in UBC areas.

Species or Group	Grade	2 × 6 12"	16"	19.2"	24"	2 × 8 12"	16"	19.2"	24"	2 × 10 12"	16"	19.2"	24"	2 × 12 12"	16"	19.2"	24"
Douglas Fir-Larch	Sel. Struc.	12-6	11-4	10-8	9-11	16-6	15-0	14-1	13-1	21-0	19-1	18-0	16-8	25-7	23-3	21-10	20-3
	1 & Btr.	12-3	11-2	10-6	9-9	16-2	14-8	13-10	12-10	20-8	18-9	17-8	16-5	25-1	22-10	21-4	19-1
	No. 1	12-0	10-11	10-4	9-7	15-10	14-5	13-7	12-4	20-3	18-5	16-9	15-0	24-8	21-4	19-6	17-5
	No. 2	11-10	10-9	10-1	9-3	15-7	14-2	13-0	11-8	19-10	17-5	15-11	14-3	23-4	20-3	18-6	16-6
	No. 3	9-11	8-7	7-10	7-0	12-7	10-11	10-0	8-11	15-5	13-4	12-2	10-11	17-10	15-5	14-1	12-7
Douglas Fir-South	Sel. Struc.	11-3	10-3	9-8	8-11	14-11	13-6	12-9	11-10	19-0	17-3	16-3	15-1	23-1	21-0	19-9	18-4
	No. 1	11-0	10-0	9-5	8-9	14-6	13-2	12-5	11-6	18-6	16-10	15-10	14-5	22-6	20-6	18-9	16-9
	No. 2	10-9	9-9	9-2	8-6	14-2	12-10	12-1	11-3	18-0	16-5	15-5	13-10	21-11	19-8	17-11	16-1
	No. 3	9-8	8-5	7-8	6-10	12-4	10-8	9-9	8-8	15-0	13-0	11-10	10-7	17-5	15-1	13-9	12-4
Hem-Fir	Sel. Struc.	11-10	10-9	10-1	9-4	15-7	14-2	13-4	12-4	19-10	18-0	17-0	15-9	24-2	21-11	20-8	19-2
	1 & Btr.	11-7	10-6	9-10	9-2	15-3	13-10	13-0	12-1	19-5	17-8	16-7	15-5	23-7	21-6	20-2	18-3
	No. 1	11-7	10-6	9-10	9-2	15-3	13-10	13-0	12-1	19-5	17-8	16-7	14-10	23-7	21-1	19-3	17-2
	No. 2	11-0	10-0	9-5	8-9	14-6	13-2	12-5	11-4	18-6	16-10	15-6	13-10	22-6	19-8	17-11	16-1
	No. 3	9-8	8-5	7-8	6-10	12-4	10-8	9-9	8-8	15-0	13-0	11-10	10-7	17-5	15-1	13-9	12-4
Spruce-Pine-Fir (South)	Sel. Struc.	11-0	10-0	9-5	8-9	14-6	13-2	12-5	11-6	18-6	16-10	15-10	14-8	22-6	20-6	19-3	17-11
	No. 1	10-9	9-9	9-2	8-6	14-2	12-10	12-1	11-3	18-0	16-5	15-1	14-1	21-11	19-11	18-3	16-3
	No. 2	10-5	9-6	8-11	8-3	13-9	12-6	11-9	10-10	17-6	15-11	14-9	13-3	21-4	18-9	17-2	15-4
	No. 3	9-3	8-0	7-3	6-6	11-8	10-1	9-3	8-3	14-3	12-4	11-3	10-1	16-6	14-4	13-1	11-8
Western Woods	Sel. Struc.	10-9	9-9	9-2	8-6	14-2	12-10	12-1	11-3	18-0	16-5	15-5	14-3	21-11	19-11	18-6	16-6
	No. 1	10-5	9-6	8-11	8-0	13-9	12-4	11-4	10-1	17-5	15-1	13-10	12-4	20-3	17-6	16-0	14-4
	No. 2	10-1	9-2	8-8	8-0	13-4	12-1	11-4	10-1	17-0	15-1	13-10	12-4	20-3	17-6	16-0	14-4
	No. 3	8-5	7-3	6-8	5-11	10-8	9-3	8-5	7-6	13-0	11-3	10-3	9-2	15-1	13-1	11-11	10-8

[1]Spans for other loads are provided in WWPA's **Western Lumber Span Tables** (572). Spans for other grades and Western Cedars may be calculated with either of WWPA's design aids: **SpanMaster**™ (SM), an electronic hand-held calculator or the WWPA **Span Computer** (SR), which works like a slide rule.
SOURCE: Western Wood Products Association.

CEILING JOISTS SPAN TABLES

E.2.1 Southern Pine Ceiling Joists Span Tables

Maximum spans are given in feet and inches.

Table E–5 Southern pine ceiling joists: 10-psf live load, 5-psf dead load, $L/240$; drywall ceiling, no attic storage.

Size	Spacing	Grade										
inches	inches	Visually Graded				Machine Stress Rated (MSR)				Machine Evaluated Lumber (MEL)		
	on center	Select Structural	No. 1	No. 2	No. 3	2400f-2.0E	2250f-1.9E	2100f-1.8E	1950f-1.7E	M-23	M-19	M-14
2 × 4	12	12-11	12-8	12-5	11-6	13-4	13-2	12-11	12-8	12-11	12-5	12-8
	16	11-9	11-6	11-3	10-0	12-2	11-11	11-9	11-6	11-9	11-3	11-6
	19.2	11-0	10-10	10-7	9-1	11-5	11-3	11-0	10-10	11-0	10-7	10-10
	24	10-3	10-0	9-10	8-2	10-7	10-5	10-3	10-0	10-3	9-10	10-0
2 × 6	12	20-3	19-11	19-6	17-0	21-0	20-8	20-3	19-11	20-3	19-6	19-11
	16	18-5	18-1	17-8	14-9	19-1	18-9	18-5	18-1	18-5	17-8	18-1
	19.2	17-4	17-0	16-8	13-6	17-11	17-8	17-4	17-0	17-4	16-8	17-0
	24	16-1	15-9	15-6	12-0	16-8	16-4	16-1	15-9	16-1	15-6	15-9
2 × 8	12	26-0*	26-0*	25-8	21-8	26-0*	26-0*	26-0*	26-0*	26-0*	25-8	26-0*
	16	24-3	23-10	23-4	18-9	25-2	24-8	24-3	23-10	24-3	23-4	23-10
	19.2	22-10	22-5	21-11	17-2	23-8	23-3	22-10	22-5	22-10	21-11	22-5
	24	21-2	20-10	20-1	15-4	21-11	21-7	21-2	20-10	21-2	20-5	20-10
2 × 10	12	26-0*	26-0*	26-0*	25-7	26-0*	26-0*	26-0*	26-0*	26-0*	26-0*	26-0*
	16	26-0*	26-0*	26-0*	22-2	26-0*	26-0*	26-0*	26-0*	26-0*	26-0*	26-0*
	19.2	26-0*	26-0*	26-0*	20-3	26-0*	26-0*	26-0*	26-0*	26-0*	26-0*	26-0*
	24	26-0*	26-0*	23-11	18-1	26-0*	26-0*	26-0*	26-0*	26-0*	26-0	26-0*

SOURCE: Southern Pine Council.
NOTE: See notes following Table E–6.

Table E–6 Southern pine ceiling joists: 20-psf live load, 10-psf dead load, $L/240$. Drywall ceiling. No future room development, but limited attic storage is available.

Size	Spacing	Grade										
inches	inches	Visually Graded				Machine Stress Rated (MSR)				Machine Evaluated Lumber (MEL)		
	on center	Select Structural	No. 1	No. 2	No. 3	2400f-2.0E	2250f-1.9E	2100f-1.8E	1950f-1.7E	M-23	M-19	M-14
2 × 4	12	10-3	10-0	9-10	8-2	10-7	10-5	10-3	10-0	10-3	9-10	10-0
	16	9-4	9-1	8-11	7-1	9-8	9-6	9-4	9-1	9-4	8-11	9-1
	19.2	8-9	8-7	8-5	6-5	9-1	8-11	8-9	8-7	8-9	8-5	8-7
	24	8-1	8-0	7-8	5-9	8-5	8-3	8-1	8-0	8-1	7-10	8-0
2 × 6	12	16-1	15-9	15-6	12-0	16-8	16-4	16-1	15-9	16-1	15-6	15-9
	16	14-7	14-4	13-6	10-5	15-2	14-11	14-7	14-4	14-7	14-1	14-4
	19.2	13-9	13-6	12-3	9-6	14-3	14-0	13-9	13-6	13-9	13-3	13-6
	24	12-9	12-6	11-0	8-6	13-3	13-0	12-9	12-6	12-9	12-3	12-6
2 × 8	12	21-2	20-10	20-1	15-4	21-11	21-7	21-2	20-10	21-2	20-5	20-10
	16	19-3	18-11	17-5	13-3	19-11	19-7	19-3	18-11	19-3	18-6	18-11
	19.2	18-2	17-9	15-10	12-1	18-9	18-5	18-2	17-9	18-2	17-5	17-9
	24	16-10	15-10	14-2	10-10	17-5	17-2	16-10	16-6	16-10	16-2	16-6
2 × 10	12	26-0*	26-0*	23-11	18-1	26-0*	26-0*	26-0*	26-0*	26-0*	26-0	26-0*
	16	24-7	23-1	20-9	15-8	25-5	25-0	24-7	24-1	24-7	23-8	24-1
	19.2	23-2	21-1	18-11	14-4	23-11	23-7	23-2	22-8	23-2	22-3	22-8
	24	21-6	18-10	16-11	12-10	22-3	21-10	21-6	21-1	21-6	20-8	21-1

These spans are intended for use in enclosed structures or where the moisture content in use does not exceed 19 percent for an extended period of time unless the table is labeled Wet-Service. Applied loads are given in psf (pounds per square foot). Deflection is limited to the span in inches divided by 360, 240, or 180 and is based on live load only. The load duration factor, C_D, is 1.0 unless shown as 1.15 or 1.25. An asterisk (*) indicates the listed span has been limited to 26'-0" based on availability; check sources of supply for lumber longer than 20'. Highlighted sizes/grades are NOT commonly produced.

SOURCE: Southern Pine Council.

E.2.2 Western Lumber Ceiling Joists Span Tables

Table E–7 Western lumber ceiling joists: 10-psf live load, 5-psf dead load, $L/240$. Use these loading conditions for the following: no attic storage, ceilings where the roof slope is not steeper than 3:12, drywall ceilings.

Species or Group	Grade	2 × 6				2 × 8				2 × 10				2 × 12			
		12"	16"	19.2"	24"	12"	16"	19.2"	24"	12"	16"	19.2"	24"	12"	16"	19.2"	24"
Douglas Fir-Larch	Sel. Struc.	20-8	18-9	17-8	16-4	27-2	24-8	23-3	21-7	34-8	31-6	29-8	27-6	42-2	38-4	36-1	33-6
	I & Btr.	20-3	18-5	17-4	16-1	26-9	24-3	22-10	21-2	34-1	31-0	29-2	26-10	41-5	37-8	34-10	31-2
	No. 1	19-11	18-1	17-0	15-9	26-2	23-10	22-5	20-1	33-5	30-0	27-5	24-6	40-3	34-10	31-10	28-5
	No. 2	19-6	17-8	16-8	15-0	25-8	23-4	21-4	19-1	32-9	28-6	26-0	23-3	38-2	33-0	30-2	27-0
	No. 3	16-3	14-1	12-10	11-6	20-7	17-10	16-3	14-7	25-2	21-9	19-10	17-9	29-2	25-3	23-0	20-7
Douglas Fir-South	Sel. Struc.	18-8	16-11	15-11	14-9	24-7	22-4	21-0	19-6	31-4	28-6	26-10	24-10	38-1	34-8	32-7	30-3
	No. 1	18-2	16-6	15-7	14-5	24-0	21-9	20-6	19-0	30-7	27-9	26-2	23-7	37-2	33-6	30-7	27-4
	No. 2	17-8	16-1	15-2	14-1	23-4	21-2	19-11	18-6	29-9	27-1	25-3	22-7	36-2	32-1	29-4	26-3
	No. 3	15-10	13-9	12-6	11-2	20-1	17-5	15-10	14-2	24-6	21-3	19-5	17-4	28-5	24-8	22-6	20-1
Hem-Fir	Sel. Struc.	19-6	17-8	16-8	15-6	25-8	23-4	21-11	20-5	32-9	29-9	28-0	26-0	39-10	36-2	34-1	31-8
	I & Btr.	19-1	17-4	16-4	15-2	25-2	22-10	21-6	19-11	32-1	29-3	27-5	25-5	39-0	35-5	33-4	29-10
	No. 1	19-1	17-4	16-4	15-2	25-2	22-10	21-6	19-10	32-1	29-2	27-1	24-3	39-0	34-5	31-5	28-1
	No. 2	18-2	16-6	15-7	14-5	24-0	21-9	20-6	18-6	30-7	27-8	25-3	22-7	37-1	32-1	29-4	26-3
	No. 3	15-10	13-9	12-6	11-2	20-1	17-5	15-10	14-2	24-6	21-3	19-5	17-4	28-5	24-8	22-6	20-1
Spruce-Pine-Fir (South)	Sel. Struc.	18-2	16-6	15-7	14-5	24-0	21-9	20-6	19-0	30-7	27-9	26-2	24-3	37-2	33-9	31-10	29-6
	No. 1	17-8	16-1	15-2	14-1	23-4	21-2	19-11	18-6	29-9	27-1	25-5	22-11	36-2	32-7	29-9	26-7
	No. 2	17-2	15-7	14-8	13-8	22-8	20-7	19-5	17-8	28-11	26-3	24-2	21-7	35-2	30-8	28-0	25-0
	No. 3	15-0	13-0	11-11	10-8	19-1	16-6	15-1	13-6	23-3	20-2	18-5	16-5	27-0	23-4	21-4	19-1
Western Woods	Sel. Struc.	17-8	16-1	15-2	14-1	23-4	21-2	19-11	18-6	29-9	27-1	25-5	23-3	36-2	32-11	30-2	27-0
	No. 1	17-2	15-7	14-7	13-0	22-8	20-2	18-5	16-6	28-6	24-8	22-6	20-2	33-0	28-7	26-1	23-4
	No. 2	16-8	15-2	14-3	13-0	21-11	19-11	18-5	16-6	28-0	24-8	22-6	20-2	33-0	28-7	26-1	23-4
	No. 3	13-9	11-11	10-10	9-8	17-5	15-1	13-9	12-4	21-3	18-5	16-9	15-0	24-8	21-4	19-6	17-5

SOURCE: Western Wood Products Association.

Table E–8 Western lumber ceiling joists: 20-psf live load, 10-psf dead load, $L/240$. Use these loading conditions for the following: limited attic storage where development of future rooms is not possible; ceilings where the roof slope is steeper than 3:12; where the clear height in the attic is greater than 30"; drywall ceilings.

Species or Group	Grade	2 × 6				2 × 8				2 × 10				2 × 12			
		12"	16"	19.2"	24"	12"	16"	19.2"	24"	12"	16"	19.2"	24"	12"	16"	19.2"	24"
Douglas Fir-Larch	Sel. Struc.	16-4	14-11	14-0	13-0	21-7	19-7	18-5	17-2	27-6	25-0	23-7	21-3	33-6	30-2	27-6	24-8
	I & Btr.	16-1	14-7	13-9	12-3	21-2	19-1	17-5	15-7	26-10	23-3	21-3	19-0	31-2	27-0	24-8	22-0
	No. 1	15-9	13-9	12-6	11-2	20-1	17-5	15-10	14-2	24-6	21-3	19-5	17-4	28-5	24-8	22-6	20-1
	No. 2	15-0	13-0	11-11	10-8	19-1	16-6	15-1	13-6	23-3	20-2	18-5	16-5	27-0	23-4	21-4	19-1
	No. 3	11-6	9-11	9-1	8-1	14-7	12-7	11-6	10-3	17-9	15-5	14-1	12-7	20-7	17-10	16-3	14-7
Douglas Fir-South	Sel. Struc.	14-9	13-5	12-8	11-9	19-6	17-9	16-8	15-6	24-10	22-7	21-3	19-9	30-3	27-6	25-10	23-4
	No. 1	14-5	13-1	12-1	10-9	19-0	16-9	15-3	13-8	23-7	20-5	18-8	16-8	27-4	23-8	21-7	19-4
	No. 2	14-1	12-8	11-7	10-4	18-6	16-0	14-8	13-1	22-7	19-7	17-10	16-0	26-3	22-8	20-9	18-6
	No. 3	11-2	9-8	8-10	7-11	14-2	12-4	11-3	10-0	17-4	15-0	13-8	12-3	20-1	17-5	15-11	14-3
Hem-Fir	Sel. Struc.	15-6	14-1	13-3	12-3	20-5	18-6	17-5	16-2	26-0	23-8	22-3	20-6	31-8	28-9	26-7	23-9
	I & Btr.	15-2	13-9	12-11	11-9	19-11	18-2	16-8	14-11	25-5	22-3	20-4	18-2	29-10	25-10	23-7	21-1
	No. 1	15-2	13-7	12-4	11-1	19-10	17-2	15-8	14-0	24-3	21-0	19-2	17-1	28-1	24-4	22-2	19-10
	No. 2	14-5	12-8	11-7	10-4	18-6	16-0	14-8	13-1	22-7	19-7	17-10	16-0	26-3	22-8	20-9	18-6
	No. 3	11-2	9-8	8-10	7-11	14-2	12-4	11-3	10-0	17-4	15-0	13-8	12-3	20-1	17-5	15-11	14-3
Spruce-Pine-Fir (South)	Sel. Struc.	14-5	13-1	12-4	11-5	19-0	17-3	16-3	15-1	24-3	22-1	20-9	19-3	29-6	26-10	25-3	22-11
	No. 1	14-1	12-9	11-9	10-6	18-6	16-3	14-10	13-3	22-11	19-10	18-2	16-3	26-7	23-0	21-0	18-10
	No. 2	13-8	12-1	11-0	9-10	17-8	15-4	14-0	12-6	21-7	18-8	17-1	15-3	25-0	21-8	19-9	17-8
	No. 3	10-8	9-3	8-5	7-6	13-6	11-8	10-8	9-6	16-5	14-3	13-0	11-8	19-1	16-6	15-1	13-6
Western Woods	Sel. Struc.	14-1	12-9	11-11	10-8	18-6	16-6	15-1	13-6	23-3	20-2	18-5	16-5	27-0	23-4	21-4	19-1
	No. 1	13-0	11-3	10-4	9-3	16-6	14-3	13-0	11-8	20-2	17-5	15-11	14-3	23-4	20-3	18-6	16-6
	No. 2	13-0	11-3	10-4	9-3	16-6	14-3	13-0	11-8	20-2	17-5	15-11	14-3	23-4	20-3	18-6	16-6
	No. 3	9-8	8-5	7-8	6-10	12-4	10-8	9-9	8-8	15-0	13-0	11-10	10-7	17-5	15-1	13-9	12-4

[1]:Refer to footnote at bottom of page 14.
Source: Western Wood Products Association.

RAFTERS SPAN TABLES

E.3.1 Southern Pine Rafters
Span Tables

Maximum spans are given in feet and inches.

Table E–9 Southern pine rafters: 20-psf live load, 10-psf dead load, $L/240$, $C_D = 1.15$. Light roofing, drywall ceiling, snow load.

Size inches	Spacing inches on center	Grade										
		Visually Graded				Machine Stress Rated (MSR)				Machine Evaluated Lumber (MEL)		
		Select Structural	No. 1	No. 2	No. 3	2400f-2.0E	2250f-1.9E	2100f-1.8E	1950f-1.7E	M-23	M-19	M-14
2 × 6	12	16-1	15-9	15-6	12-11	16-8	16-4	16-1	15-9	16-1	15-6	15-9
	16	14-7	14-4	14-1	11-2	15-2	14-11	14-7	14-4	14-7	14-1	14-4
	19.2	13-9	13-6	13-2	10-2	14-3	14-0	13-9	13-6	13-9	13-3	13-6
	24	12-9	12-6	11-9	9-2	13-3	13-0	12-9	12-6	12-9	12-3	12-6
2 × 8	12	21-2	20-10	20-5	16-5	21-11	21-7	21-2	20-10	21-2	20-5	20-10
	16	19-3	18-11	18-6	14-3	19-11	19-7	19-3	18-11	19-3	18-6	18-11
	19.2	18-2	17-9	17-0	13-0	18-9	18-5	18-2	17-9	18-2	17-5	17-9
	24	16-10	16-6	15-3	11-8	17-5	17-2	16-10	16-6	16-10	16-2	16-6
2 × 10	12	26-0*	26-0*	25-8	19-5	26-0*	26-0*	26-0*	26-0*	26-0*	26-0	26-0*
	16	24-7	24-1	22-3	16-10	25-5	25-0	24-7	24-1	24-7	23-8	24-1
	19.2	23-2	22-7	20-4	15-4	23-11	23-7	23-2	22-8	23-2	22-3	22-8
	24	21-6	20-3	18-2	13-9	22-3	21-10	21-6	21-1	21-6	20-8	21-1
2 × 12	12	26-0*	26-0*	26-0*	23-1	26-0*	26-0*	26-0*	26-0*	26-0*	26-0*	26-0*
	16	26-0*	26-0*	26-0*	20-0	26-0*	26-0*	26-0*	26-0*	26-0*	26-0*	26-0*
	19.2	26-0*	26-0*	23-10	18-3	26-0*	26-0*	26-0*	26-0*	26-0*	26-0*	26-0*
	24	26-0*	24-1	21-3	16-4	26-0*	26-0*	26-0*	25-7	26-0*	25-1	25-7

SOURCE: Southern Pine Council.
NOTE: See notes following Table E–10.

Table E–10 Southern pine rafters: 30-psf live load, 10-psf dead load, $L/240$, $C_D = 1.15$. Light roofing, drywall ceiling, snow load.

Size inches	Spacing inches on center	Grade										
		Visually Graded				Machine Stress Rated (MSR)				Machine Evaluated Lumber (MEL)		
		Select Structural	No. 1	No. 2	No. 3	2400f-2.0E	2250f-1.9E	2100f-1.8E	1950f-1.7E	M-23	M-19	M-14
2 × 6	12	14-1	13-9	13-6	11-2	14-7	14-4	14-1	13-9	14-1	13-6	13-9
	16	12-9	12-6	12-3	9-8	13-3	13-0	12-9	12-6	12-9	12-3	12-6
	19.2	12-0	11-9	11-5	8-10	12-5	12-3	12-0	11-9	12-0	11-7	11-9
	24	11-2	10-11	10-2	7-11	11-7	11-4	11-2	10-11	11-2	10-9	10-11
2 × 8	12	18-6	18-2	17-10	14-3	19-2	18-10	18-6	18-2	18-6	17-10	18-2
	16	16-10	16-6	16-2	12-4	17-5	17-2	16-10	16-6	16-10	16-2	16-6
	19.2	15-10	15-6	14-9	11-3	16-5	16-1	15-10	15-6	15-10	15-3	15-6
	24	14-8	14-5	13-2	10-1	15-3	15-0	14-8	14-5	14-8	14-2	14-5
2 × 10	12	23-8	23-2	22-3	16-10	24-6	24-1	23-8	23-2	23-8	22-9	23-2
	16	21-6	21-1	19-3	14-7	22-3	21-10	21-6	21-1	21-6	20-8	21-1
	19.2	20-2	19-7	17-7	13-4	20-11	20-7	20-2	19-10	20-2	19-5	19-10
	24	18-9	17-6	15-9	11-11	19-5	19-1	18-9	18-5	18-9	18-0	18-5
2 × 12	12	26-0*	26-0*	26-0*	20-0	26-0*	26-0*	26-0*	26-0*	26-0*	26-0*	26-0*
	16	26-0*	25-7	22-7	17-4	26-0*	26-0*	26-0*	25-7	26-0*	25-1	25-7
	19.2	24-7	23-4	20-7	15-10	25-5	25-0	24-7	24-1	24-7	23-7	24-1
	24	22-10	20-11	18-5	14-2	23-7	23-3	22-10	22-5	22-10	21-11	22-5

These spans are intended for use in enclosed structures or where the moisture content in use does not exceed 19 percent for an extended period of time unless the table is labeled Wet-Service. Applied loads are given in psf (pounds per square foot). Deflection is limited to the span in inches divided by 360, 240, or 180 and is based on live load only. The load duration factor, C_D, is 1.0 unless shown as 1.15 or 1.25. An asterisk (*) indicates the listed span has been limited to 26'-0" based on availability; check sources of supply for lumber longer than 20'. Highlighted sizes/grades are NOT commonly produced.
*The listed maximum span has been limited to 26'-0" based on material availability.
■ These grades are the most commonly available.
SOURCE: Southern Pine Council.

E.3.2 Western Lumber Rafters
Span Tables

Table E–11 Western lumber roof rafters: 20-psf snow load, 10-psf dead load, $L/240$. Roof slope is 3:12 or less; light roof covering; no ceilings finish.

Species or Group	Grade	2 × 6 12" oc	2 × 6 16" oc	2 × 6 19.2" oc	2 × 6 24" oc	2 × 8 12" oc	2 × 8 16" oc	2 × 8 19.2" oc	2 × 8 24" oc	2 × 10 12" oc	2 × 10 16" oc	2 × 10 19.2" oc	2 × 10 24" oc	2 × 12 12" oc	2 × 12 16" oc	2 × 12 19.2" oc	2 × 12 24" oc
Douglas Fir-Larch	Sel. Struc.	16-4	14-11	14-0	13-0	21-7	19-7	18-5	17-2	27-6	25-0	23-7	21-10	33-6	30-5	28-8	26-5
	No. 1 & Btr.	16-1	14-7	13-9	12-9	21-2	19-3	18-2	16-8	27-1	24-7	22-9	20-4	32-11	28-11	26-5	23-7
	No. 1	15-9	14-4	13-5	12-0	20-10	18-8	17-0	15-3	26-4	22-9	20-9	18-7	30-6	26-5	24-1	21-7
	No. 2	15-6	14-0	12-9	11-5	20-5	17-8	16-2	14-5	24-11	21-7	19-9	17-8	28-11	25-1	22-10	20-5
	No. 3	12-4	10-8	9-9	8-9	15-7	13-6	12-4	11-0	19-1	16-6	15-1	13-6	22-1	19-2	17-6	15-7
Douglas Fir-South	Sel Struc	14-9	13-5	12-8	11-9	19-6	17-9	16-8	15-6	24-10	22-7	21-3	19-9	30-3	27-6	25-10	24-0
	No. 1	14-5	13-1	12-4	11-5	19-0	17-3	16-3	14-8	24-3	21-11	20-0	17-11	29-4	25-5	23-2	20-9
	No. 2	14-1	12-9	12-0	11-1	18-6	16-10	15-8	14-0	23-8	21-0	19-2	17-2	28-1	24-4	22-3	19-11
	No. 3	12-0	10-5	9-6	8-6	15-3	13-2	12-0	10-9	18-7	16-1	14-8	13-2	21-7	18-8	17-1	15-3
Hem-Fir	Sel Struc	15-6	14-1	13-3	12-3	20-5	18-6	17-5	16-2	26-0	23-8	22-3	20-8	31-8	28-9	27-1	25-1
	No. 1 & Btr.	15-2	13-9	12-11	12-0	19-11	18-2	17-1	15-10	25-5	23-1	21-9	19-6	30-11	27-8	25-3	22-7
	No. 1	15-2	13-9	12-11	11-10	19-11	18-2	16-10	15-0	25-5	22-6	20-6	18-4	30-1	26-1	23-10	21-3
	No. 2	14-5	13-1	12-4	11-1	19-0	17-2	15-8	14-0	24-3	21-0	19-2	17-2	28-1	24-4	22-3	19-11
	No. 3	12-0	10-5	9-6	8-6	15-3	13-2	12-0	10-9	18-7	16-1	14-8	13-2	21-7	18-8	17-1	15-3
Spruce-Pine-Fir (South)	Sel. Struc.	14-5	13-1	12-4	11-5	19-0	17-3	16-3	15-1	24-3	22-1	20-9	19-3	29-6	26-10	25-3	23-5
	No. 1	14-1	12-9	12-0	11-2	18-6	16-10	15-10	14-3	23-8	21-4	19-5	17-5	28-6	24-8	22-7	20-2
	No. 2	13-8	12-5	11-8	10-7	18-0	16-4	15-0	13-5	22-11	20-1	18-4	16-4	26-10	23-3	21-3	19-0
	No. 3	11-5	9-10	9-0	8-1	14-5	12-6	11-5	10-3	17-8	15-3	13-11	12-6	20-5	17-9	16-2	14-6
Western Woods	Sel. Struc.	14-1	12-9	12-0	11-2	18-6	16-10	15-10	14-5	23-8	21-6	19-9	17-8	28-9	25-1	22-10	20-5
	No. 1	13-8	12-1	11-0	9-10	17-8	15-4	14-0	12-6	21-7	18-9	17-1	15-3	25-1	21-8	19-10	17-9
	No. 2	13-3	12-0	11-0	9-10	17-5	15-4	14-0	12-6	21-7	18-9	17-1	15-3	25-1	21-8	19-10	17-9
	No. 3	10-5	9-0	8-3	7-4	13-2	11-5	10-5	9-4	16-1	13-11	12-9	11-5	18-8	16-2	14-9	13-2

SOURCE: Western Wood Products Association.

Table E–12 Western lumber roof rafters: 30-psf snow load, 10-psf dead load, $L/240$. Roof slope is 3:12 or less; light roof covering; no ceiling finish.

Species or Group	Grade	2 × 6 12" oc	2 × 6 16" oc	2 × 6 19.2" oc	2 × 6 24" oc	2 × 8 12" oc	2 × 8 16" oc	2 × 8 19.2" oc	2 × 8 24" oc	2 × 10 12" oc	2 × 10 16" oc	2 × 10 19.2" oc	2 × 10 24" oc	2 × 12 12" oc	2 × 12 16" oc	2 × 12 19.2" oc	2 × 12 24" oc
Douglas Fir-Larch	Sel. Struc.	14-4	13-0	12-3	11-4	18-10	17-2	16-1	15-0	24-1	21-10	20-7	19-1	29-3	26-7	25-0	22-10
	No. 1 & Btr.	14-1	12-9	12-0	11-2	18-6	16-10	15-10	14-5	23-8	21-6	19-9	17-8	28-9	25-1	22-10	20-5
	No. 1	13-9	12-6	11-8	10-5	18-2	16-2	14-9	13-2	22-9	19-9	18-0	16-1	26-5	22-10	20-11	18-8
	No. 2	13-6	12-1	11-0	9-10	17-8	15-4	14-0	12-6	21-7	18-9	17-1	15-3	25-1	21-8	19-10	17-9
	No. 3	10-8	9-3	8-5	7-7	13-6	11-8	10-8	9-7	16-6	14-3	13-1	11-8	19-2	16-7	15-2	13-6
Douglas Fir-South	Sel. Struc.	12-11	11-9	11-1	10-3	17-0	15-6	14-7	13-6	21-9	19-9	18-7	17-3	26-5	24-0	22-7	21-0
	No. 1	12-7	11-5	10-9	10-0	16-7	15-1	14-2	12-8	21-2	19-0	17-4	15-6	25-5	22-0	20-1	18-0
	No. 2	12-3	11-2	10-6	9-7	16-2	14-8	13-7	12-2	20-8	18-2	16-7	14-10	24-4	21-1	19-3	17-3
	No. 3	10-5	9-0	8-3	7-4	13-2	11-5	10-5	9-4	16-1	13-11	12-9	11-5	18-8	16-2	14-9	13-2
Hem-Fir	Sel. Struc.	13-6	12-3	11-7	10-9	17-10	16-2	15-3	14-2	22-9	20-8	19-5	18-0	27-8	25-1	23-7	21-11
	No. 1 & Btr.	13-3	12-0	11-4	10-6	17-5	15-10	14-11	13-10	22-3	20-2	18-11	16-11	27-1	24-0	21-11	19-7
	No. 1	13-3	12-0	11-4	10-3	17-5	15-10	14-7	13-0	22-3	19-6	17-9	15-11	26-1	22-7	20-7	18-5
	No. 2	12-7	11-5	10-9	9-7	16-7	14-11	13-7	12-2	21-0	18-2	16-7	14-10	24-4	21-1	19-3	17-3
	No. 3	10-5	9-0	8-3	7-4	13-2	11-5	10-5	9-4	16-1	13-11	12-9	11-5	18-8	16-2	14-9	13-2
Spruce-Pine-Fir (South)	Sel. Struc.	12-7	11-5	10-9	10-0	16-7	15-1	14-2	13-2	21-2	19-3	18-1	16-10	25-9	23-5	22-1	20-6
	No. 1	12-3	11-2	10-6	9-9	16-2	14-8	13-9	12-4	20-8	18-5	16-10	15-1	24-8	21-5	19-6	17-6
	No. 2	11-11	10-10	10-2	9-2	15-9	14-3	13-0	11-7	20-1	17-4	15-10	14-2	23-3	20-2	18-5	16-5
	No. 3	9-10	8-7	7-10	7-0	12-6	10-10	9-11	8-10	15-3	13-3	12-1	10-10	17-9	15-4	14-0	12-6
Western Woods	Sel. Struc.	12-3	11-2	10-6	9-9	16-2	14-8	13-10	12-6	20-8	18-9	17-1	15-3	25-1	21-8	19-10	17-9
	No. 1	11-11	10-6	9-7	8-7	15-4	13-3	12-1	10-10	18-9	16-2	14-10	13-3	21-8	18-9	17-2	15-4
	No. 2	11-7	10-6	9-7	8-7	15-3	13-3	12-1	10-10	18-9	16-2	14-10	13-3	21-8	18-9	17-2	15-4
	No. 3	9-0	7-10	7-2	6-4	11-5	9-11	9-0	8-1	13-11	12-1	11-0	9-10	16-2	14-0	12-9	11-5

SOURCE: Western Wood Products Association.

E.3.3 Representative Roof Truss Spans for Selected Trusses

The following lists apply to Tables E–13 through E–16.

Design Criteria

Top chord live load = 20 psf (958 Pa)

Top chord dead load = 10 psf (479 Pa)

Bottom chord live load = 0 psf (0 Pa)

Bottom chord dead load = 10 psf (479 Pa)

Notes

Given truss spans are examples of truss spans for the given loadings and truss configurations. The tables are not intended to be used for design purposes or specific projects.

Spans have been determined in accordance with the design Specifications for Metal Plate Connected Wood Trusses, TPI-92, of the Truss Plate Institute (TPI) and the 1991 edition of the National Design Specification for Wood Construction (NDS®) of the American Forest and Paper Association (AFPA).

Tables shown are not intended to limit roof trusses to these loads, lumber species, lumber grades, and configurations. See your WTCA member fabricator for actual truss designs and solutions to custom roof profiles. Some representative spans for the configurations shown may vary with each fabricator.

Footnotes

1. Representative spans shown assume that the moisture content of the lumber does not exceed 19% at the time of fabrication and during end use.
2. The representative span for this lumber grade has been limited to the representative truss span that can be achieved by the group of lumber grades provided in these tables.
3. The representative span for this lumber grade has been limited by the representative bottom-chord panel length based on the TPI requirement of applying a 200-lb (890-N) concentrated load to represent a construction worker standing on the bottom chord.

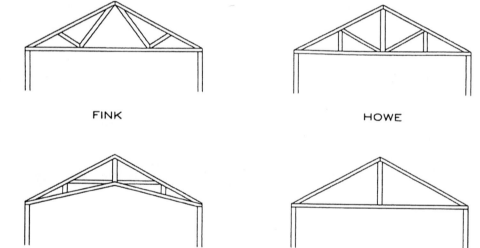

FINK

HOWE

SCISSOR

KING POST

Figure E–I Basic roof truss designs.

Table E–13 Representative roof truss spans for selected Fink trusses: 24″ o.c. spacing; 40-psf total design load; load duration increase of 15% (ft-in.).

			Top Chord		Bottom Chord	
			2 × 4	2 × 6	2 × 4	2 × 6
Southern Pine	3/12	#1 Dense	29-9	42-0[3]	31-11[3]	42-0[3]
		#1	28-11	42-0[3]	30-8[3]	40-9[3]
		#2 Dense	28-7	42-0[3]	28-8	40-7[3]
		#2	27-6	40-6	27-1	38-4
	4/12	#1 Dense	31-11[3]	42-0[3]	31-11[3]	42-0[3]
		#1	31-11[3]	42-0[3]	30-8[3]	40-9[3]
		#2 Dense	31-8	42-0[3]	29-10[3]	40-7[3]
		#2	30-7	42-0[3]	27-10[3]	39-1[3]
	5/12	#1 Dense	31-11[3]	42-0[3]	31-11[3]	42-0[3]
		#1	31-11[3]	42-0[3]	30-8[3]	40-9[3]
		#2 Dense	31-11[3]	42-0[3]	29-10[3]	40-7[3]
		#2	31-10	42-0[3]	27-10[3]	39-1[3]
Douglas Fir-Larch	3/12	Sel. Str.	30-5	43-2[3]	33-2[3]	43-2[3]
		#1 & Better	28-10	42-9	30-6[3]	41-9[3]
		#1	27-10	41-3	28-3[3]	40-3[3]
		#2	26-8	39-5	25-7[3]	37-9
	4/12	Sel. Str.	33-2[3]	43-2[3]	33-2[3]	43-2[3]
		#1 & Better	32-0	43-2[3]	30-6[3]	41-9[3]
		#1	30-11	43-2[3]	28-3[3]	40-3[3]
		#2	29-7	43-2[3]	25-7[3]	38-8[3]
	5/12	Sel. Str.	33-2[3]	43-2[3]	33-2[3]	43-2[3]
		#1 & Better	33-2[3]	43-2[3]	30-6[3]	41-9[3]
		#1	32-3	43-2[3]	28-3[3]	40-3[3]
		#2	30-10	43-2[3]	25-7[3]	38-8[3]
Spruce-Pine-Fir	3/12	Sel. Str.	28-2	38-5[3]	29-4[3]	28-5[3]
		#1	25-9	38-0	23-4	32-7
		#2	25-9	38-0	23-4	32-7
	4/12	Sel. Str.	29-4[3]	38-5[3]	29-4[3]	38-5[3]
		#1	28-9	38-5[3]	25-0[3]	36-5[3]
		#2	28-9	38-5[3]	25-0[3]	36-5[3]
	5/12	Sel. Str.	29-4[3]	38-5[3]	29-4[3]	38-5[3]
		#1	29-4[3]	38-5[3]	25-0[3]	36-5[3]
		#2	29-4[3]	38-5[3]	25-0[3]	36-5[3]
Hem-Fir	3/12	Sel. Str.	29-1	39-9[3]	30-9[3]	39-9[3]
		#1	26-10	39-7	26-10[3]	37-11[3]
		#2	25-8	37-9	24-5[3]	35-2[3]
	4/12	Sel. Str.	30-9[3]	39-9[3]	30-9[3]	39-9[3]
		#1	29-10	39-9[3]	26-10[3]	37-11[3]
		#2	28-6	39-9[3]	24-5[3]	35-2[3]
	5/12	Sel. Str.	30-9[3]	39-9[3]	30-9[3]	39-9[3]
		#1	30-9[3]	39-9[3]	26-10[3]	37-11[3]
		#2	29-8	39-9[3]	24-5[3]	35-2[3]

SOURCE: *Metal Plate Connected Wood Truss Handbook*, Wood Truss Council of America, Madison, WI, 1993. Used by permission of WTCA.

Table E-14 Representative roof truss spans for selected Howe trusses: 24″ o.c. spacing; 40-psf total design load; load duration increase of 15% (ft-in.).

			Top Chord		Bottom Chord	
			2 × 4	2 × 6	2 × 4	2 × 6
Southern Pine	3/12	#1 Dense	29-6	43-9	37-10	43-9[2]
		#1	28-9	42-9	36-3	43-9[2]
		#2 Dense	28-4	41-11	32-3	43-9[2]
		#2	27-4	40-3	30-5	42-10
	4/12	#1 Dense	32-10	48-7	42-5	48-7[2]
		#1	32-0	47-5	40-9[3]	48-7[2]
		#2 Dense	31-6	46-5	37-3	48-7[2]
		#2	30-4	44-7	35-1	48-7[2]
	5/12	#1 Dense	34-3	50-7	42-5[3]	50-7[2]
		#1	33-4	49-5	40-9[3]	50-7[2]
		#2 Dense	32-10	48-4	39-8[3]	50-7[2]
		#2	31-8	46-4	36-11[3]	50-7[2]
Douglas Fir-Larch	3/12	Sel. Str.	30-2	44-9	44-0[3]	44-9[2]
		#1 & Better	28-7	42-6	37-3	44-9[2]
		#1	27-8	40-11	33-8	44-9[2]
		#2	26-6	39-2	30-5	42-8
	4/12	Sel. Str.	33-7	49-8	44-0[3]	49-8[2]
		#1 & Better	31-10	47-1	40-6[3]	49-8[2]
		#1	30-8	45-1	37-5[3]	49-8[2]
		#2	29-5	43-5	33-10[3]	48-11
	5/12	Sel. Str.	35-1	51-9	44-0[3]	51-9[2]
		#1 & Better	33-2	49-1	40-6[3]	51-9[2]
		#1	32-0	47-2	37-5[3]	51-9[2]
		#2	30-8	45-1	33-10[3]	51-4[3]
Spruce-Pine-Fir	3/12	Sel. Str.	27-11	41-4	35-6	41-4[2]
		#1	25-7	37-9	25-9	35-6
		#2	25-7	37-9	25-9	35-6
	4/12	Sel. Str.	31-1	45-11	38-11[3]	45-11[2]
		#1	28-6	42-0	30-2	42-0
		#2	28-6	42-0	30-2	42-0
	5/12	Sel. Str.	32-6	47-11	38-11[3]	47-11[2]
		#1	29-10	43-9	33-2[3]	46-11
		#2	29-10	43-9	33-2[3]	46-11
Hem-Fir	3/12	Sel. Str.	28-10	42-9	40-10[3]	42-9[2]
		#1	26-8	39-4	31-7	42-9[2]
		#2	25-6	37-6	27-11	39-2
	4/12	Sel. Str.	32-2	47-6	40-10[3]	47-6[2]
		#1	29-8	43-8	35-6[3]	47-6[2]
		#2	28-4	41-7	32-3	45-7
	5/12	Sel. Str.	33-8	49-6	40-10[3]	49-6[2]
		#1	30-11	45-5	35-6[3]	49-6[2]
		#2	29-6	43-3	32-5[3]	46-9[3]

SOURCE: *Metal Plate Connected Wood Truss Handbook*, Wood Truss Council of America, Madison, WI, 1993. Used by permission of WTCA.

Table E–15 Representative roof truss spans for selected scissors trusses: 24″ o.c. spacing; 40-psf total design load; load duration increase of 15% (ft-in.).

			Top Chord		Bottom Chord	
			2 × 4	2 × 6	2 × 4	2 × 6
Southern Pine	T.C. 3/12 B.C. 1.5/12	#1 Dense	21-9	32-5	24-6	32-5[2]
		#1	21-2	31-7	23-6	32-5[2]
		#2 Dense	20-11	31-2	20-2	28-6
		#2	20-1	29-11	19-0	26-8
	T.C. 4/12 B.C. 2/12	#1 Dense	24-2	35-11	29-9	35-11[2]
		#1	23-6	35-1	28-5	35-11[2]
		#2 Dense	23-3	34-6	24-9	35-2
		#2	22-5	33-2	23-5	32-10
	T.C. 5/12 B.C. 2.5/12	#1 Dense	25-11	38-7	33-10	38-7[2]
		#1	25-3	37-8	32-5	38-7[2]
		#2 Dense	25-0	37-0	28-6	38-7[2]
		#2	24-1	35-7	26-11	37-11
Douglas Fir-Larch	T.C. 3/12 B.C. 1.5/12	Sel. Str.	22-1	33-1	30-11	33-1[2]
		#1 & Better	21-0	31-5	24-10	33-1[2]
		#1	20-4	30-5	22-0	30-10
		#2	19-6	29-0	19-7	27-1
	T.C. 4/12 B.C. 2/12	Sel. Str.	24-7	36-8	36-6	36-8[2]
		#1 & Better	23-5	34-11	29-9	36-8[2]
		#1	22-8	33-9	26-8	36-8[2]
		#2	21-9	32-3	23-10	33-2
	T.C. 5/12 B.C. 2.5/12	Sel. Str.	26-6	39-5	39-3	39-5[2]
		#1 & Better	25-2	37-6	33-7	39-5[2]
		#1	24-5	36-3	30-2	39-5[2]
		#2	23-5	34-8	27-2	37-11
Spruce-Pine-Fir	T.C. 3/12 B.C. 1.5/12	Sel. Str.	20-4	30-5	22-8	30-5[2]
		#1	18-7	27-7	15-6	21-3
		#2	18-7	27-7	15-6	21-3
	T.C. 4/12 B.C. 2/12	Sel. Str.	22-9	33-10	27-7	33-10[2]
		#1	20-10	30-10	19-4	26-4
		#2	20-10	30-10	19-4	26-4
	T.C. 5/12 B.C. 2.5/12	Sel. Str.	24-6	36-4	31-7	36-4[2]
		#1	22-6	33-3	22-5	30-10
		#2	22-6	33-3	22-5	30-10
Hem-Fir	T.C. 3/12 B.C. 1.5/12	Sel. Str.	21-1	31-5	28-8	31-5[2]
		#1	19-6	29-1	20-3	28-0
		#2	18-8	27-9	17-5	24-2
	T.C. 4/12 B.C. 2/12	Sel. Str.	23-6	34-11	34-1	34-11[2]
		#1	21-10	32-4	24-8	34-5
		#2	20-10	30-10	21-5	29-10
	T.C. 5/12 B.C. 2.5/12	Sel. Str.	25-4	37-6	37-4	37-6[2]
		#1	23-6	34-9	28-2	37-6[2]
		#2	22-5	33-1	24-7	34-6

SOURCE: *Metal Plate Connected Wood Truss Handbook*, Wood Truss Council of America, Madison, WI, 1993. Used by permission of WTCA.

Table E–16 Representative roof truss spans for selected king post trusses: 24″ o.c. spacing; 40-psf total design load; load duration increase of 15% (ft-in.).

			Top Chord		Bottom Chord	
			2 × 4	2 × 6	2 × 4	2 × 6
Southern Pine	3/12	#1 Dense	17-2	25-1	21-6[3]	25-1[2]
		#1	16-9	24-7	20-8[3]	25-1[2]
		#2 Dense	16-4	23-9	20-1[3]	25-1[2]
		#2	15-8	22-7	18-9[3]	25-1[2]
	4/12	#1 Dense	17-10	26-0	21-6[3]	26-0[2]
		#1	17-4	25-5	20-8[3]	26-0[2]
		#2 Dense	16-11	24-6	20-1[3]	26-0[2]
		#2	16-2	23-3	18-9[3]	26-0[2]
	5/12	#1 Dense	18-2	26-7	21-6[3]	26-7[2]
		#1	17-8	25-11	20-8[3]	26-7[2]
		#2 Dense	17-3	25-0	20-1[3]	26-7[2]
		#2	16-6	23-8	18-9[3]	26-3[3]
Douglas Fir-Larch	3/12	Sel. Str.	17-8	25-10	22-4[3]	25-10[2]
		#1 & Better	16-6	24-2	20-7[3]	25-10[2]
		#1	15-9	23-0	19-0[3]	25-10[2]
		#2	15-0	21-10	17-3[3]	25-10[2]
	4/12	Sel. Str.	18-4	26-9	22-4[3]	26-9[2]
		#1 & Better	17-1	24-11	20-7[3]	26-9[2]
		#1	16-3	23-8	19-0[3]	26-9[2]
		#2	15-5	22-5	17-3[3]	26-0[3]
	5/12	Sel. Str.	18-9	27-4	22-4[3]	27-4[2]
		#1 & Better	17-5	25-4	20-7[3]	27-4[2]
		#1	16-7	24-1	19-0[3]	27-0[3]
		#2	15-8	22-10	17-3[3]	26-0[3]
Spruce-Pine-Fir	3/12	Sel. Str.	16-5	24-0	19-9[3]	24-0[2]
		#1	14-9	21-5	16-10[3]	24-0[2]
		#2	14-9	21-5	16-10[3]	24-0[2]
	4/12	Sel. Str.	17-1	24-10	19-9[3]	24-10[2]
		#1	15-3	22-1	16-10[3]	24-6[3]
		#2	15-3	22-1	16-10[3]	24-6[3]
	5/12	Sel. Str.	17-6	25-5	19-9[3]	25-5[2]
		#1	15-6	22-6	16-10[3]	24-6[3]
		#2	15-6	22-6	16-10[3]	24-6[3]
Hem-Fir	3/12	Sel. Str.	17-1	24-11	20-8[3]	24-11[2]
		#1	15-4	22-3	18-1[3]	24-11[2]
		#2	14-7	21-2	16-6[3]	23-8[3]
	4/12	Sel. Str.	17-10	25-11	20-8[3]	25-11[2]
		#1	15-10	22-11	18-1[3]	25-5[3]
		#2	15-1	21-10	16-6[3]	23-8[3]
	5/12	Sel. Str.	18-3	26-6	20-8[3]	26-6[2]
		#1	16-1	23-4	18-1[3]	25-5[3]
		#2	15-4	22-2	16-6[3]	23-8[3]

SOURCE: *Metal Plate Connected Wood Truss Handbook*, Wood Truss Council of America, Madison, WI, 1993. Used by permission of WTCA.

DESIGN DATA FOR BEAMS

Design data for beams are included in Tables E–17 through E–25. Computations for bending are based on the live load indicated plus 10 psf of dead load. Computations for deflection are based on the live load only. All beams in the table were designed to extend over a single span, and the following formulas were used:

For Type A

$$M = \frac{wL^2}{8} \quad \text{and} \quad D = \frac{5wL^4(12)^3}{384EI}$$

To use the tables, first determine the span, the live load to be supported, and the deflection limitation. Then select from the tables the proper size of beam with the corresponding required values for fiber stress in bending (f) and modulus of elasticity (E). The beam used should be of a grade and a species that meet these minimum values. You can determine the maximum span for a beam of specific size, grade, and species by reversing these steps.

Table E–17 Floor and roof beams.

Left half (spans 10'–17'):

Span of beam	Nominal size of beam	6'-0" f	6'-0" E	7'-0" f	7'-0" E	8'-0" f	8'-0" E
10'	2-3x6	1070	780000	1250	910000	1430	1040000
	1-3x8	1235	680000	1440	794000	1645	906000
	2-2x8	1030	570000	1200	665000	1370	760000
	1-4x8	880	485000	1030	566000	1175	646000
	3-2x8	685	380000	800	443000	915	506000
	2-3x8	615	340000	720	397000	820	453000
	2-2x10	630	273000	735	219000	840	364000
11'	2-3x6	1295	1037000	1510	1210000	1730	1382000
	1-3x8	1490	905000	1740	1056000	1990	1206000
	2-2x8	1245	754000	1450	880000	1660	1005000
	1-4x8	1065	647000	1245	755000	1420	862000
	3-2x8	830	503000	970	587000	1105	670000
	2-3x8	745	453000	870	529000	995	604000
	2-2x10	765	363000	890	424000	1020	484000
12'	2-3x6	1545	1346000	1800	1571000	2060	1794000
	1-3x8	1775	1175000	2070	1371000	2370	1566000
	2-2x8	1480	980000	1725	1144000	1970	1306000
	1-4x8	1270	840000	1480	980000	1690	1120000
	3-2x8	985	653000	1150	762000	1315	870000
	2-3x8	890	588000	1035	686000	1185	784000
	1-6x8	755	483000	880	564000	1005	644000
	2-2x10	910	472000	1060	551000	1210	629000
	1-3x10	1090	566000	1275	660000	1455	754000
13'	2-3x6	1815	1711000	2110	1997000	2415	2281000
	1-3x8	2085	1494000	2430	1743000	2780	1991000
	2-2x8	1740	1245000	2025	1453000	2315	1660000
	1-4x8	1490	1067000	1735	1245000	1985	1422000
	3-2x8	1160	830000	1350	969000	1545	1106000
	2-3x8	1045	747000	1215	872000	1390	996000
	1-6x8	885	614000	1040	716000	1185	818000
	2-2x10	1070	600000	1245	700000	1420	800000
	1-3x10	1280	719000	1495	839000	1710	958000
14'	2-2x8	2015	1555000	2350	1815000	2685	2073000
	3-2x8	1340	1037000	1570	1210000	1790	1382000
	2-3x8	1210	933000	1410	1089000	1610	1244000
	1-6x8	1025	766000	1200	894000	1370	1021000
	1-3x10	1485	899000	1730	1049000	1980	1198000
	2-2x10	1235	749000	1445	874000	1650	998000
	1-4x10	1060	642000	1240	749000	1415	856000
	3-2x10	825	499000	965	582000	1100	665000
	2-3x10	740	449000	865	524000	990	598000
15'	3-2x8	1540	1275000	1800	1488000	2055	1699000
	2-3x8	1390	1148000	1620	1340000	1850	1530000
	1-6x8	1180	943000	1375	1100000	1570	1257000
	1-3x10	1705	1105000	1990	1289000	2270	1473000
	2-2x10	1420	921000	1660	1075000	1895	1228000
	1-4x10	1220	789000	1420	921000	1625	1052000
	3-2x10	950	614000	1105	717000	1265	818000
	2-3x10	850	553000	995	645000	1135	737000
	1-6x10	735	464000	855	541000	980	618000
	4-2x10	710	461000	830	538000	945	614000
	2-2x12	960	512000	1120	597000	1280	682000
16'	3-2x8	1755	1548000	2045	1806000	2340	2063000
	2-3x8	1580	1393000	1840	1626000	2105	1857000
	2-2x10	1615	1118000	1890	1305000	2155	1490000
	1-4x10	1385	958000	1615	1118000	1845	1277000
	3-2x10	1075	745000	1260	869000	1435	993000
	2-3x10	970	671000	1130	783000	1290	894000
	1-6x10	835	563000	975	657000	1130	750000
	4-2x10	810	559000	945	652000	1080	745000
	1-8x10	615	413000	715	482000	815	550000
	1-3x12	1310	746000	1530	871000	1750	994000
	2-2x12	1090	621000	1275	725000	1455	828000
17'	2-2x10	1825	1341000	2125	1565000	2430	1787000
	1-4x10	1565	1149000	1825	1341000	2085	1532000
	3-2x10	1215	894000	1420	1043000	1620	1192000

Right half (spans 17'–22'):

Span of beam	Nominal size of beam	6'-0" f	6'-0" E	7'-0" f	7'-0" E	8'-0" f	8'-0" E
17'	2-3x10	1095	804000	1280	938000	1460	1072000
	1-6x10	945	675000	1100	788000	1260	900000
	4-2x10	910	670000	1065	782000	1215	894000
	1-8x10	690	495000	805	578000	910	660000
	1-3x12	1480	894000	1725	1043000	1975	1192000
	2-2x12	1235	745000	1440	869000	1645	993000
	1-4x12	1060	639000	1230	746000	1410	852000
	3-2x12	820	497000	960	580000	1095	663000
18'	2-2x10	2045	1592000	2385	1858000	2725	2123000
	1-4x10	1755	1364000	2045	1592000	2340	1819000
	3-2x10	1365	1061000	1590	1238000	1815	1415000
	2-3x10	1270	955000	1480	1114000	1695	1273000
	1-6x10	1060	801000	1235	935000	1415	1068000
	4-2x10	1020	796000	1195	929000	1365	1062000
	1-8x10	780	588000	910	686000	1040	784000
	1-3x12	1660	1062000	1935	1239000	2210	1416000
	2-2x12	1380	885000	1615	1033000	1845	1180000
	1-4x12	1185	758000	1385	885000	1580	1011000
	3-2x12	920	590000	1075	688000	1230	786000
	2-3x12	830	531000	970	620000	1105	708000
19'	3-2x10	1520	1248000	1775	1456000	2025	1664000
	2-3x10	1365	1123000	1595	1310000	1825	1497000
	1-6x10	1170	943000	1365	1100000	1560	1257000
	4-2x10	1140	936000	1330	1092000	1520	1248000
	2-4x10	975	802000	1140	936000	1300	1070000
	1-8x10	860	691000	1005	806000	1145	921000
	1-3x12	1850	1249000	2155	1457000	2465	1665000
	2-2x12	1540	1041000	1800	1215000	2055	1388000
	1-4x12	1320	892000	1540	1041000	1760	1190000
	3-2x12	1025	694000	1200	810000	1370	926000
	2-3x12	925	624000	1080	728000	1230	832000
	1-6x12	805	531000	940	620000	1070	708000
20'	3-2x10	1685	1456000	1965	1699000	2245	1942000
	2-3x10	1515	1310000	1770	1529000	2020	1747000
	1-6x10	1300	1099000	1515	1282000	1735	1465000
	4-2x10	1260	1092000	1475	1274000	1685	1456000
	2-4x10	1080	936000	1265	1092000	1445	1248000
	1-8x10	960	806000	1120	941000	1280	1075000
	2-2x12	1705	1214000	1990	1417000	2275	1619000
	1-4x12	1465	1040000	1710	1214000	1950	1387000
	3-2x12	1140	809000	1330	944000	1520	1079000
	2-3x12	1025	728000	1195	850000	1365	971000
	1-6x12	970	620000	1130	723000	1295	826000
	2-4x12	730	520000	855	607000	975	694000
21'	3-2x10	1855	1685000	2165	1966000	2475	2247000
	2-3x10	1670	1516000	1950	1827000	2225	2088000
	1-6x10	1430	1273000	1670	1485000	1905	1697000
	4-2x10	1390	1264000	1625	1475000	1855	1686000
	2-4x10	1195	1083000	1390	1264000	1590	1444000
	1-8x10	1050	933000	1225	1089000	1400	1244000
	2-2x12	1880	1405000	2195	1640000	2510	1874000
	1-4x12	1615	1204000	1880	1405000	2150	1606000
	3-2x12	1255	937000	1465	1093000	1670	1249000
	2-3x12	1130	843000	1320	984000	1505	1124000
	1-6x12	970	717000	1130	837000	1295	956000
	2-4x12	805	602000	940	702000	1075	802000
22'	1-6x10	1580	1463000	1845	1707000	2105	1951000
	4-2x10	1525	1453000	1780	1696000	2035	1938000
	2-4x10	1310	1245000	1530	1453000	1745	1660000
	1-8x10	1160	1073000	1355	1252000	1545	1431000
	1-4x12	1770	1384000	2065	1615000	2360	1846000
	3-2x12	1375	1077000	1605	1257000	1835	1436000
	2-3x12	1240	969000	1445	1130000	1655	1291000
	1-6x12	1080	825000	1260	963000	1440	1100000
	2-4x12	885	692000	1035	807000	1180	922000
	4-2x12	1035	808000	1205	943000	1375	1078000
	5-2x12	825	646000	965	754000	1105	862000
	3-3x12	825	639000	965	746000	1105	852000

Required values for fiber stress in bending (f) and modulus of elasticity (E) for the sizes shown to support safely a live load of 20 pounds per square foot within a deflection limitation of l/240.

Table E-18 Floor and roof beams.

SPAN OF BEAM	NOMINAL SIZE OF BEAM	6'-0"		7'-0"		8'-0"	
		f	E	f	E	f	E
10'	2-3x6	1070	975000	1250	1138000	1430	1300000
	1-3x8	1235	850000	1440	992000	1645	1133000
	2-2x8	1030	712000	1200	831000	1370	949000
	1-4x8	880	606000	1030	707000	1175	808000
	3-2x8	685	475000	800	554000	915	633000
	2-3x8	615	425000	720	496000	820	566000
	2-2x10	630	341000	735	398000	840	455000
11'	2-3x6	1295	1296000	1510	1512000	1730	1727000
	1-3x8	1490	1131000	1740	1320000	1990	1508000
	2-2x8	1245	942000	1450	1099000	1660	1256000
	1-4x8	1065	809000	1245	944000	1420	1078000
	3-2x8	830	629000	970	734000	1105	838000
	2-3x8	745	566000	870	660000	995	754000
	2-2x10	765	454000	890	530000	1020	605000
12'	2-3x6	1545	1682000	1800	1963000	2060	2242000
	1-3x8	1775	1469000	2070	1714000	2370	1958000
	2-2x8	1480	1225000	1725	1429000	1970	1633000
	1-4x8	1270	1050000	1480	1225000	1690	1400000
	3-2x8	985	816000	1150	952000	1315	1088000
	2-3x8	890	735000	1035	858000	1185	980000
	1-6x8	755	604000	880	705000	1005	805000
	2-2x10	910	590000	1060	688000	1210	786000
13'	1-3x8	2085	1867000	2430	2179000	2780	2439000
	2-2x8	1740	1556000	2025	1816000	2315	2074000
	1-4x8	1490	1334000	1735	1557000	1985	1778000
	3-2x8	1160	1037000	1350	1210000	1545	1382000
	2-3x8	1045	934000	1215	1090000	1390	1245000
	1-6x8	885	767000	1040	895000	1185	1022000
	2-2x10	1070	750000	1245	875000	1420	1000000
	1-3x10	1280	899000	1495	1049000	1710	1198000
	1-4x10	915	642000	1070	749000	1220	856000
14'	3-2x8	1340	1296000	1570	1512000	1790	1727000
	2-3x8	1210	1166000	1410	1361000	1610	1554000
	1-6x8	1025	957000	1200	1117000	1370	1276000
	1-3x10	1485	1124000	1730	1312000	1980	1498000
	2-2x10	1235	936000	1445	1092000	1650	1248000
	1-4x10	1060	802000	1240	936000	1415	1069000
	3-2x10	825	624000	965	728000	1100	832000
	2-3x10	740	561000	865	655000	990	748000
	1-6x10	640	471000	745	550000	850	628000
	4-2x10	620	468000	720	546000	825	624000
	2-2x12	835	520000	975	607000	1115	693000
15'	3-2x8	1540	1594000	1800	1860000	2055	2125000
	2-3x8	1390	1435000	1620	1675000	1850	1913000
	1-6x8	1180	1179000	1375	1376000	1570	1572000
	1-3x10	1705	1381000	1990	1612000	2270	1841000
	2-2x10	1420	1151000	1660	1343000	1895	1534000
	1-4x10	1220	986000	1420	1151000	1625	1314000
	3-2x10	950	767000	1105	895000	1265	1022000
	2-3x10	850	691000	995	806000	1135	921000
	1-6x10	735	580000	855	677000	980	773000
	4-2x10	710	576000	830	672000	945	768000
	2-2x12	960	640000	1120	747000	1280	853000
	1-4x12	825	549000	960	641000	1100	732000
16'	2-3x8	1580	1741000	1840	2032000	2105	2321000
	2-2x10	1615	1397000	1890	1630000	2155	1862000
	1-4x10	1385	1197000	1615	1397000	1845	1596000
	3-2x10	1075	931000	1260	1086000	1435	1241000
	2-3x10	970	839000	1130	979000	1290	1118000
	1-6x10	835	704000	975	821000	1130	938000
	4-2x10	810	699000	945	816000	1080	932000
	1-8x10	615	516000	715	602000	815	688000
	1-3x12	1310	932000	1530	1087000	1750	1242000
	2-2x12	1090	776000	1275	905000	1455	1034000
	1-4x12	935	666000	1090	777000	1250	888000
	3-2x12	730	518000	850	604000	970	690000

SPAN OF BEAM	NOMINAL SIZE OF BEAM	6'-0"		7'-0"		8'-0"	
		f	E	f	E	f	E
17'	2-2x10	1825	1676000	2130	1956000	2435	2234000
	1-4x10	1565	1437000	1825	1677000	2085	1915000
	3-2x10	1215	1117000	1420	1303000	1625	1489000
	2-3x10	1095	1005000	1280	1173000	1460	1340000
	1-6x10	945	844000	1100	985000	1260	1125000
	4-2x10	910	837000	1065	977000	1215	1116000
	1-8x10	690	619000	805	722000	910	825000
	1-3x12	1480	1117000	1725	1303000	1975	1489000
	2-2x12	1235	931000	1440	1086000	1645	1241000
	1-4x12	1060	799000	1230	932000	1410	1065000
	3-2x12	820	621000	960	725000	1095	828000
	2-3x12	740	559000	865	652000	990	745000
18'	1-4x10	1755	1705000	2045	1990000	2340	2273000
	3-2x10	1365	1326000	1590	1547000	1815	1767000
	2-3x10	1270	1194000	1480	1393000	1695	1592000
	1-6x10	1060	1001000	1235	1168000	1415	1334000
	4-2x10	1020	995000	1195	1161000	1365	1326000
	1-8x10	780	735000	910	858000	1040	980000
	1-3x12	1660	1327000	1935	1549000	2210	1769000
	2-2x12	1380	1106000	1615	1291000	1845	1474000
	1-4x12	1185	947000	1385	1105000	1580	1262000
	3-2x12	920	737000	1075	860000	1230	982000
	2-3x12	830	664000	970	775000	1105	885000
	1-6x12	720	565000	840	659000	960	753000
19'	3-2x10	1520	1560000	1775	1820000	2025	2079000
	2-3x10	1365	1404000	1595	1638000	1825	1871000
	1-6x10	1170	1179000	1365	1376000	1560	1572000
	4-2x10	1140	1170000	1330	1365000	1520	1560000
	2-4x10	975	1002000	1140	1169000	1300	1336000
	1-8x10	860	864000	1005	1008000	1145	1152000
	1-3x12	1850	1561000	2155	1822000	2465	2081000
	2-2x12	1540	1301000	1800	1518000	2055	1734000
	1-4x12	1320	1115000	1540	1301000	1760	1486000
	3-2x12	1025	867000	1200	1012000	1370	1156000
	2-3x12	925	780000	1080	910000	1230	1040000
	1-6x12	805	664000	940	775000	1070	885000
20'	3-2x10	1685	1820000	1965	2124000	2245	2426000
	2-3x10	1515	1637000	1770	1910000	2020	2182000
	1-6x10	1300	1374000	1515	1603000	1735	1831000
	4-2x10	1260	1365000	1475	1593000	1685	1819000
	2-4x10	1080	1170000	1265	1365000	1445	1560000
	1-8x10	960	1007000	1120	1175000	1280	1342000
	2-2x12	1705	1517000	1990	1770000	2275	2022000
	1-4x12	1465	1300000	1710	1517000	1950	1733000
	3-2x12	1140	1011000	1330	1180000	1520	1348000
	2-3x12	1025	910000	1195	1062000	1365	1213000
	1-6x12	970	775000	1130	904000	1295	1003000
	4-2x12	855	759000	995	886000	1135	1012000
21'	2-3x10	1670	1895000	1950	2211000	2225	2526000
	1-6x10	1430	1591000	1670	1857000	1905	2121000
	4-2x10	1390	1580000	1625	1844000	1855	2106000
	2-4x10	1195	1354000	1390	1580000	1590	1805000
	1-8x10	1050	1166000	1225	1361000	1400	1554000
	2-2x12	1880	1756000	2195	2049000	2510	2341000
	1-4x12	1615	1505000	1880	1756000	2150	2006000
	3-2x12	1255	1171000	1465	1366000	1670	1561000
	2-3x12	1130	1054000	1320	1230000	1505	1405000
	1-6x12	970	896000	1130	1046000	1295	1194000
	4-2x12	940	878000	1100	1025000	1255	1170000
	2-4x12	805	752000	940	877000	1075	1002000
22'	4-2x10	1525	1816000	1780	2119000	2035	2421000
	2-4x10	1310	1556000	1530	1816000	1745	2074000
	1-8x10	1160	1341000	1355	1565000	1545	1787000
	1-4x12	1770	1730000	2065	2019000	2360	2306000
	3-2x12	1375	1346000	1605	1571000	1835	1794000
	2-3x12	1240	1211000	1445	1413000	1655	1614000
	1-6x12	1080	1031000	1260	1203000	1440	1374000
	4-2x12	1030	1010000	1205	1179000	1375	1346000
	2-4x12	885	865000	1035	1009000	1180	1153000
	5-2x12	825	807000	965	942000	1105	1076000
	3-3x12	825	799000	965	932000	1105	1065000

Required values for fiber stress in bending (f) and modulus of elasticity (E) for the sizes shown to support safely a live load of 20 pounds per square foot within a deflection limitation of l/300.

SPAN OF BEAM	NOMINAL SIZE OF BEAM	MINIMUM "f" & "E" IN psi FOR BEAMS SPACED:					
		6'-0"		7'-0"		8'-0"	
		f	E	f	E	f	E
10'	2-3x6	1070	1170000	1250	1365000	1430	1560000
	1-3x8	1235	1020000	1440	1192000	1645	1359000
	2-2x8	1030	855000	1200	997000	1370	1140000
	1-4x8	880	727000	1030	847000	1175	969000
	3-2x8	685	570000	800	667000	915	759000
	2-3x8	615	510000	720	600000	820	679000
	1-6x8	525	419000	615	489000	700	558000
11'	2-3x6	1295	1555000	1510	1815000	1730	2073000
	1-3x8	1490	1357000	1740	1584000	1990	1809000
	2-2x8	1245	1131000	1450	1320000	1660	1507000
	1-4x8	1065	970000	1245	1132000	1420	1293000
	3-2x8	830	754000	970	880000	1105	1005000
	2-3x8	745	679000	870	793000	995	906000
	1-6x8	635	558000	740	651000	845	744000
12'	1-3x8	1775	1762000	2070	2056000	2370	2349000
	2-2x8	1480	1470000	1725	1716000	1970	1959000
	1-4x8	1270	1260000	1480	1470000	1690	1680000
	3-2x8	985	979000	1150	1143000	1315	1305000
	2-3x8	890	882000	1035	1029000	1185	1176000
	1-6x8	775	724000	880	846000	1005	966000
	2-2x10	910	708000	1060	826000	1210	943000
	1-3x10	1090	849000	1275	991000	1455	1132000
13'	2-2x8	1740	1867000	2025	2179000	2315	2490000
	1-4x8	1490	1600000	1735	1867000	1985	2133000
	3-2x8	1160	1245000	1350	1453000	1545	1659000
	2-3x8	1045	1120000	1215	1308000	1390	1494000
	1-6x8	885	921000	1040	1074000	1185	1227000
	2-2x10	1070	900000	1245	1050000	1420	1200000
	1-3x10	1280	1078000	1495	1258000	1710	1437000
	1-4x10	915	771000	1070	900000	1220	1028000
14'	3-2x8	1340	1555000	1570	1815000	1790	2073000
	2-3x8	1210	1399000	1410	1633000	1610	1866000
	1-6x8	1025	1149000	1200	1341000	1370	1531000
	1-3x10	1485	1348000	1730	1573000	1980	1797000
	2-2x10	1235	1123000	1445	1311000	1650	1497000
	1-4x10	1060	963000	1240	1123000	1415	1284000
	3-2x10	825	748000	965	873000	1100	997000
	2-3x10	740	673000	865	786000	990	897000
	1-6x10	640	565000	745	660000	850	753000
	4-2x10	620	561000	720	655000	825	749000
	2-2x12	835	624000	975	728000	1115	832000
15'	3-2x8	1540	1912000	1800	2232000	2055	2548000
	2-3x8	1390	1722000	1620	2010000	1850	2295000
	1-6x8	1180	1414000	1375	1650000	1570	1885000
	1-3x10	1705	1657000	1990	1933000	2270	2209000
	2-2x10	1420	1381000	1660	1612000	1895	1842000
	1-4x10	1220	1183000	1420	1381000	1625	1578000
	3-2x10	950	921000	1105	1075000	1265	1227000
	2-3x10	850	829000	995	967000	1135	1105000
	1-6x10	735	696000	855	811000	980	927000
	4-2x10	710	691000	830	807000	945	921000
	2-2x12	960	768000	1120	895000	1280	1023000
	1-4x12	825	659000	960	769000	1100	878000
16'	2-2x10	1615	1677000	1890	1957000	2155	2235000
	1-4x10	1385	1437000	1615	1677000	1845	1915000
	3-2x10	1075	1117000	1260	1303000	1435	1489000
	2-3x10	970	1006000	1130	1174000	1290	1341000
	1-6x10	835	844000	975	985000	1130	1125000
	4-2x10	810	838000	945	978000	1080	1117000
	1-8x10	615	619000	715	723000	815	825000
	1-3x12	1310	1119000	1530	1306000	1750	1491000
	2-2x12	1090	931000	1275	1087000	1455	1242000
	1-4x12	935	799000	1090	932000	1250	1066000
	3-2x12	730	622000	850	725000	970	828000
	2-3x12	655	559000	765	652000	875	745000
17'	2-2x10	1825	2011000	2125	2347000	2430	2680000
	1-4x10	1565	1723000	1825	2011000	2085	2298000
	3-2x10	1215	1341000	1420	1564000	1620	1788000
	2-3x10	1095	1206000	1280	1407000	1460	1608000
	1-6x10	945	1012000	1100	1182000	1260	1350000
	4-2x10	910	1005000	1065	1173000	1215	1341000
	1-8x10	690	742000	805	867000	910	990000
	1-3x12	1480	1341000	1725	1564000	1975	1788000
	2-2x12	1235	1117000	1440	1303000	1645	1489000
	1-4x12	1060	958000	1230	1119000	1410	1278000
	3-2x12	820	745000	960	870000	1095	994000
	2-3x12	740	671000	865	782000	990	894000
18'	3-2x10	1365	1591000	1590	1857000	1815	2122000
	2-3x10	1270	1492000	1480	1671000	1695	1909000
	1-6x10	1060	1201000	1235	1402000	1415	1602000
	4-2x10	1020	1194000	1195	1393000	1365	1593000
	1-8x10	780	882000	910	1029000	1040	1176000
	1-3x12	1660	1593000	1935	1858000	2210	2124000
	2-2x12	1380	1327000	1615	1549000	1845	1770000
	1-4x12	1185	1137000	1385	1327000	1580	1516000
	3-2x12	920	885000	1075	1032000	1230	1179000
	2-3x12	830	796000	970	930000	1105	1062000
	1-6x12	720	678000	840	790000	960	904000
	4-2x12	690	663000	805	774000	920	884000
19'	3-2x10	1520	1872000	1775	2184000	2025	2496000
	2-3x10	1365	1684000	1595	1965000	1825	2245000
	1-6x10	1170	1414000	1365	1650000	1560	1885000
	4-2x10	1140	1404000	1330	1638000	1520	1872000
	2-4x10	975	1203000	1140	1404000	1300	1605000
	1-8x10	860	1036000	1005	1209000	1145	1381000
	2-2x12	1540	1561000	1800	1822000	2055	2082000
	1-4x12	1320	1338000	1540	1561000	1760	1785000
	3-2x12	1025	1041000	1200	1215000	1370	1387000
	2-3x12	925	936000	1080	1092000	1230	1248000
	1-6x12	805	796000	940	930000	1070	1062000
	4-2x12	770	780000	900	910000	1025	1040000
20'	2-3x10	1515	1965000	1770	2293000	2020	2620000
	1-6x10	1300	1648000	1515	1923000	1735	2197000
	4-2x10	1260	1638000	1475	1911000	1685	2184000
	2-4x10	1080	1404000	1265	1638000	1445	1872000
	1-8x10	960	1209000	1120	1411000	1280	1612000
	2-2x12	1705	1821000	1990	2125000	2275	2428000
	1-4x12	1465	1560000	1710	1821000	1950	2080000
	3-2x12	1140	1213000	1330	1416000	1520	1618000
	2-3x12	1025	1092000	1195	1275000	1365	1456000
	1-6x12	970	930000	1130	1085000	1295	1239000
	4-2x12	855	911000	995	1063000	1135	1214000
	2-4x12	730	780000	850	910000	975	1040000
21'	4-2x10	1390	1896000	1625	2212000	1855	2529000
	2-4x10	1195	1624000	1390	1896000	1590	2166000
	1-8x10	1050	1399000	1225	1633000	1400	1866000
	1-4x12	1615	1806000	1880	2107000	2150	2409000
	3-2x12	1255	1405000	1465	1639000	1670	1873000
	2-3x12	1130	1264000	1320	1476000	1505	1686000
	1-6x12	970	1075000	1130	1255000	1295	1434000
	4-2x12	940	1054000	1100	1230000	1255	1404000
	2-4x12	805	903000	940	1053000	1075	1203000
	3-3x12	750	834000	875	973000	1000	1112000
	1-8x12	720	789000	840	921000	960	1052000
	1-10x12	570	623000	665	727000	760	830000
22'	2-4x10	1310	1867000	1530	2179000	1745	2490000
	1-8x10	1160	1609000	1355	1878000	1545	2146000
	3-2x12	1375	1615000	1605	1885000	1835	2154000
	2-3x12	1240	1453000	1445	1695000	1655	1936000
	1-6x12	1080	1237000	1260	1444000	1440	1650000
	4-2x12	1035	1212000	1205	1414000	1375	1617000
	2-4x12	885	1038000	1035	1210000	1180	1383000
	5-2x12	825	969000	965	1131000	1105	1293000
	3-3x12	825	958000	965	1119000	1105	1278000
	1-8x12	790	907000	920	1058000	1055	1209000
	1-10x12	625	716000	730	835000	835	954000

Required values for fiber stress in bending (f) and modulus of elasticity (E) for the sizes shown to support safely a live load of 20 pounds per square foot within a deflection limitation of l/360.

SPAN OF BEAM	NOMINAL SIZE OF BEAM	6'-0" f	6'-0" E	7'-0" f	7'-0" E	8'-0" f	8'-0" E
10'	2-3x6	1430	1170000	1670	1365000	1905	1560000
	1-3x8	1645	1020000	1920	1190000	2195	1360000
	1-4x8	1175	727000	1370	848000	1565	969000
	3-2x8	915	570000	1070	665000	1220	760000
	2-3x8	820	510000	955	595000	1095	680000
	2-4x8	590	364000	690	425000	785	485000
	2-2x10	840	409000	980	477000	1120	545000
11'	2-3x6	1725	1555000	2015	1815000	2300	2073000
	1-3x8	1990	1357000	2320	1584000	2655	1809000
	1-4x8	1420	970000	1660	1132000	1895	1293000
	3-2x8	1105	754000	1290	880000	1475	1005000
	2-3x8	995	679000	1160	792000	1325	905000
	2-4x8	710	485000	830	566000	945	646000
	2-2x10	1020	544000	1190	635000	1360	725000
12'	1-4x8	1690	1260000	1970	1470000	2255	1679000
	3-2x8	1315	979000	1535	1142000	1755	1305000
	2-3x8	1185	882000	1385	1029000	1580	1176000
	2-4x8	845	630000	985	735000	1125	840000
	1-6x8	1005	724000	1175	845000	1340	965000
	2-2x10	1210	708000	1410	826000	1615	944000
	3-2x10	810	472000	945	551000	1080	629000
	2-3x10	725	424000	845	495000	965	565000
13'	1-4x8	1985	1600000	2315	1867000	2645	2133000
	3-2x8	1545	1245000	1805	1453000	2060	1659000
	2-3x8	1390	1120000	1620	1307000	1855	1493000
	2-4x8	990	801000	1155	935000	1320	1068000
	1-6x8	1180	921000	1375	1075000	1575	1228000
	2-x10	1425	900000	1665	1050000	1900	1200000
	3-2x10	950	600000	1110	700000	1265	800000
	2-3x10	855	540000	1000	630000	1140	720000
	1-4x10	1220	923000	1425	1079000	1625	1230000
14'	3-2x8	1790	1555000	2090	1815000	2385	2073000
	2-3x8	1610	1400000	1880	1634000	2145	1866000
	2-4x8	1150	1000000	1340	1167000	1535	1333000
	1-6x8	1370	1149000	1600	1341000	1825	1532000
	2-2x10	1650	1123000	1925	1310000	2200	1497000
	3-2x10	1100	748000	1285	873000	1465	997000
	2-3x10	990	673000	1155	785000	1320	897000
	1-4x10	1415	963000	1650	1124000	1885	1283000
	1-6x10	915	943000	1070	1100000	1220	1257000
	2-4x10	705	481000	825	561000	940	641000
15'	2-4x8	1320	1230000	1540	1435000	1760	1640000
	1-6x8	1570	1414000	1830	1650000	2095	1885000
	2-2x10	1895	1381000	2210	1612000	2525	1841000
	3-2x10	1260	921000	1470	1075000	1680	1228000
	2-3x10	1135	829000	1325	967000	1515	1105000
	1-4x10	1620	1183000	1890	1380000	2160	1577000
	1-6x10	980	696000	1145	812000	1305	928000
	2-4x10	810	592000	945	691000	1080	789000
	4-2x10	945	691000	1105	806000	1260	921000
	1-8x10	720	510000	840	595000	960	680000
	2-2x12	1280	768000	1495	896000	1705	1024000
	1-4x12	1095	658000	1280	768000	1460	877000
16'	2-2x10	2155	1677000	2515	1957000	2875	2235000
	3-2x10	1435	1117000	1675	1303000	1915	1489000
	2-3x10	1290	1006000	1505	1174000	1720	1341000
	1-4x10	1845	1437000	2155	1677000	2460	1915000
	1-6x10	1115	844000	1300	985000	1485	1125000
	2-4x10	925	719000	1080	839000	1235	958000
	4-2x10	1075	838000	1255	978000	1435	1117000
	1-8x10	815	619000	950	722000	1085	825000
	2-2x12	1455	931000	1700	1086000	1940	1241000
	1-4x12	1250	799000	1460	932000	1665	1065000
	3-2x12	970	621000	1130	725000	1295	828000
	2-3x12	875	559000	1020	652000	1165	745000

SPAN OF BEAM	NOMINAL SIZE OF BEAM	6'-0" f	6'-0" E	7'-0" f	7'-0" E	8'-0" f	8'-0" E
17'	3-2x10	1620	1341000	1890	1565000	2160	1787000
	2-3x10	1460	1206000	1705	1407000	1945	1607000
	1-4x10	2085	1723000	2435	2011000	2780	2297000
	1-6x10	1255	1012000	1465	1181000	1675	1349000
	2-4x10	1040	862000	1215	1006000	1385	1149000
	4-2x10	1215	1005000	1420	1173000	1620	1340000
	1-8x10	920	742000	1075	866000	1225	989000
	2-2x12	1645	1117000	1920	1303000	2195	1489000
	1-4x12	1410	958000	1645	1118000	1880	1277000
	3-2x12	1095	745000	1280	869000	1460	993000
	2-3x12	985	671000	1150	783000	1313	894000
	4-2x12	820	559000	955	652000	1095	869000
18'	2-3x10	1695	1432000	1980	1671000	2260	1909000
	1-6x10	1415	1201000	1650	1401000	1885	1601000
	2-4x10	1170	1023000	1365	1194000	1560	1364000
	4-2x10	1360	1194000	1590	1393000	1815	1592000
	1-8x10	1040	882000	1215	1029000	1385	1176000
	2-2x12	1840	1327000	2150	1549000	2455	1769000
	1-4x12	1580	1137000	1845	1327000	2105	1516000
	3-2x12	1230	885000	1435	1033000	1640	1180000
	2-3x12	1105	796000	1290	929000	1475	1061000
	4-2x12	920	663000	1075	774000	1225	884000
	2-4x12	790	569000	920	664000	1055	758000
	5-2x12	735	531000	860	620000	980	708000
19'	2-4x10	1300	1203000	1515	1404000	1735	1604000
	4-2x10	1520	1404000	1775	1638000	2025	1871000
	1-8x10	1145	1036000	1335	1209000	1525	1381000
	1-4x12	1760	1338000	2055	1561000	2345	1783000
	3-2x12	1370	1041000	1600	1215000	1825	1388000
	2-3x12	1230	936000	1435	1092000	1640	1248000
	4-2x12	1025	780000	1195	910000	1365	1040000
	2-4x12	880	669000	1025	781000	1175	892000
	5-2x12	820	624000	955	728000	1095	832000
	1-6x12	1070	796000	1250	929000	1425	1061000
	3-3x12	820	617000	955	720000	1095	822000
	1-8x12	785	584000	915	681000	1045	778000
20'	4-2x12	1680	1638000	1960	1911000	2240	2183000
	1-8x10	1280	1209000	1495	1411000	1705	1611000
	3-2x12	1520	1213000	1775	1415000	2025	1617000
	2-3x12	1365	1092000	1595	1274000	1820	1456000
	4-2x12	1025	910000	1195	1062000	1365	1213000
	2-4x12	975	780000	1140	910000	1300	1040000
	5-2x12	910	728000	1060	849000	1215	970000
	1-6x12	1295	930000	1510	1084000	1725	1239000
	3-3x12	910	720000	1060	840000	1215	960000
	1-8x12	870	682000	1015	795000	1160	909000
	1-10x12	690	538000	805	628000	920	717000
	4-3x12	680	546000	795	637000	905	728000
21'	1-8x10	1400	1399000	1635	1633000	1865	1865000
	3-2x12	1670	1405000	1950	1640000	2225	1873000
	2-3x12	1505	1264000	1755	1475000	2005	1685000
	4-2x12	1255	1054000	1465	1230000	1675	1405000
	2-4x12	1075	903000	1255	1054000	1435	1204000
	5-2x12	1005	843000	1175	984000	1340	1124000
	1-6x12	1295	1075000	1510	1255000	1725	1434000
	3-3x12	1005	833000	1175	972000	1340	1110000
	1-8x12	960	789000	1120	921000	1280	1052000
	1-10x12	760	623000	885	727000	1015	830000
	4-3x12	750	632000	875	737000	1000	842000
	2-3x14	1085	774000	1265	903000	1445	1032000
22'	2-3x12	1655	1453000	1930	1696000	2205	1940000
	4-2x12	1375	1212000	1605	1414000	1835	1615000
	2-4x12	1180	1038000	1380	1211000	1575	1384000
	5-2x12	1100	969000	1285	1131000	1465	1292000
	1-6x12	1440	1237000	1680	1443000	1920	1649000
	3-3x12	1100	958000	1285	1118000	1465	1277000
	1-8x12	1055	907000	1230	1058000	1405	1209000
	1-10x12	830	716000	970	835000	1105	954000
	4-3x12	825	727000	965	848000	1100	969000
	2-3x14	1190	890000	1390	1039000	1585	1186000
	1-6x14	1045	765000	1220	893000	1395	1020000
	3-3x14	795	589000	930	687000	1060	785000
	2-4x14	820	601000	955	701000	1095	801000

Required values for fiber stress in bending (f) and modulus of elasticity (E) for the sizes shown to support safely a live load of 30 pounds per square foot within a deflection limitation of l/240.

Table E-21 Floor and roof beams.

Left section — Spans 10' through 16':

SPAN OF BEAM	NOMINAL SIZE OF BEAM	6'-0" f	6'-0" E	7'-0" f	7'-0" E	8'-0" f	8'-0" E
10'	2-3x6	1430	1462000	1670	1706000	1905	1948000
	1-3x8	1645	1275000	1920	1488000	2195	1699000
	1-4x8	1175	909000	1370	1061000	1565	1212000
	3-2x8	915	712000	1070	831000	1220	949000
	2-3x8	820	637000	955	743000	1095	849000
	2-4x8	590	455000	690	531000	785	606000
	2-2x10	840	511000	980	596000	1120	681000
11'	1-3x8	1990	1696000	2320	1979000	2655	2261000
	1-4x8	1420	1212000	1660	1414000	1895	1615000
	3-2x8	1105	942000	1290	1099000	1475	1255000
	2-3x8	995	849000	1160	991000	1325	1132000
	2-4x8	710	606000	830	707000	945	808000
	2-2x10	1020	680000	1190	793000	1360	906000
	1-3x10	1220	817000	1425	953000	1625	1089000
12'	1-4x8	1690	1575000	1970	1838000	2255	2099000
	3-2x8	1315	1224000	1535	1428000	1755	1631000
	2-3x8	1185	1102000	1385	1286000	1580	1469000
	2-4x8	845	787000	985	918000	1125	1049000
	1-6x8	1005	905000	1175	1056000	1340	1206000
	2-2x10	1210	885000	1410	1033000	1615	1180000
	3-2x10	810	590000	945	688000	1080	786000
	2-3x10	725	530000	845	618000	965	706000
13'	1-4x8	1985	2000000	2315	2334000	2645	2666000
	3-2x8	1545	1556000	1805	1816000	2060	2074000
	2-3x8	1390	1400000	1620	1634000	1855	1866000
	2-4x8	990	1001000	1155	1168000	1320	1334000
	1-6x8	1180	1151000	1375	1343000	1575	1534000
	2-2x10	1425	1125000	1665	1313000	1900	1500000
	3-2x10	950	750000	1110	875000	1265	1000000
	2-3x10	855	675000	1000	788000	1140	900000
	1-4x10	1220	1154000	1425	1347000	1625	1538000
14'	3-2x8	1790	1944000	2090	2268000	2385	2591000
	2-3x8	1610	1750000	1880	2042000	2145	2333000
	2-4x8	1150	1250000	1340	1459000	1535	1666000
	1-6x8	1370	1436000	1600	1676000	1825	1914000
	2-2x10	1650	1404000	1925	1638000	2200	1871000
	3-2x10	1100	935000	1285	1091000	1465	1246000
	2-3x10	990	841000	1155	981000	1320	1121000
	1-4x10	1415	1204000	1650	1405000	1885	1605000
	1-6x10	915	1179000	1070	1376000	1220	1572000
	2-4x10	705	601000	825	701000	940	801000
15'	2-4x8	1320	1537000	1540	1794000	1760	2049000
	1-6x8	1570	1767000	1830	2062000	2095	2355000
	2-2x10	1895	1726000	2210	2014000	2525	2301000
	3-2x10	1260	1151000	1470	1343000	1680	1534000
	2-3x10	1135	1036000	1325	1209000	1515	1381000
	1-4x10	1620	1479000	1890	1726000	2160	1971000
	1-6x10	980	870000	1145	1015000	1305	1160000
	2-4x10	810	740000	945	863000	1080	986000
	4-2x10	945	864000	1105	1008000	1260	1152000
	1-8x10	720	637000	840	743000	960	849000
	2-2x12	1280	960000	1495	1120000	1705	1280000
	1-4x12	1095	822000	1280	959000	1460	1096000
16'	2-2x10	2155	2096000	2515	2446000	2875	2794000
	3-2x10	1435	1396000	1675	1629000	1915	1861000
	2-3x10	1290	1257000	1505	1467000	1720	1675000
	1-4x10	1845	1796000	2155	2096000	2460	2394000
	1-6x10	1115	1055000	1300	1231000	1485	1406000
	2-4x10	925	899000	1080	1049000	1235	1198000
	4-2x10	1075	1047000	1255	1222000	1435	1395000
	1-8x10	815	774000	950	903000	1085	1032000
	2-2x12	1455	1164000	1700	1358000	1940	1552000
	1-4x12	1250	999000	1460	1166000	1665	1332000
	3-2x12	970	776000	1130	905000	1295	1034000
	2-3x12	875	699000	1020	816000	1165	932000

Right section — Spans 17' through 22':

SPAN OF BEAM	NOMINAL SIZE OF BEAM	6'-0" f	6'-0" E	7'-0" f	7'-0" E	8'-0" f	8'-0" E
17'	3-2x10	1620	1676000	1890	1956000	2160	2234000
	2-3x10	1460	1507000	1705	1759000	1945	2009000
	1-6x10	1255	1265000	1465	1476000	1675	1686000
	2-4x10	1040	1077000	1215	1257000	1385	1435000
	4-2x10	1215	1256000	1420	1466000	1620	1674000
	1-8x10	920	927000	1075	1082000	1225	1236000
	2-2x12	1645	1396000	1920	1629000	2195	1861000
	1-4x12	1410	1197000	1645	1397000	1880	1596000
	3-2x12	1095	931000	1280	1086000	1460	1241000
	2-3x12	985	839000	1150	979000	1315	1118000
	4-2x12	820	699000	955	816000	1095	932000
	2-4x12	705	599000	820	699000	940	799000
18'	2-3x10	1695	1790000	1980	2089000	2260	2386000
	1-6x10	1415	1501000	1650	1752000	1885	2000000
	2-4x10	1170	1279000	1365	1492000	1560	1705000
	4-2x10	1360	1492000	1590	1741000	1815	1989000
	1-8x10	1040	1102000	1215	1286000	1385	1469000
	2-2x12	1840	1659000	2150	1936000	2455	2211000
	1-4x12	1580	1421000	1845	1658000	2105	1894000
	3-2x12	1230	1106000	1435	1291000	1640	1474000
	2-3x12	1105	995000	1290	1161000	1475	1326000
	4-2x12	920	829000	1075	967000	1225	1105000
	2-4x12	790	711000	920	830000	1055	948000
	5-2x12	735	664000	860	775000	980	885000
19'	1-6x10	1570	1767000	1830	2062000	2095	2355000
	2-4x10	1300	1504000	1515	1755000	1735	2005000
	4-2x10	1520	1755000	1775	2048000	2025	2339000
	1-8x10	1145	1295000	1335	1511000	1525	1726000
	1-4x12	1760	1672000	2055	1951000	2345	2229000
	3-2x12	1370	1301000	1600	1518000	1825	1734000
	2-3x12	1230	1170000	1435	1365000	1640	1560000
	4-2x12	1025	975000	1195	1138000	1365	1300000
	2-4x12	880	836000	1025	976000	1175	1114000
	5-2x12	820	780000	955	910000	1095	1040000
	1-6x12	1070	995000	1250	1161000	1425	1326000
	3-3x12	820	771000	955	900000	1095	1028000
20'	1-8x10	1280	1511000	1495	1763000	1705	2014000
	3-2x12	1520	1516000	1775	1769000	2025	2021000
	2-3x12	1365	1365000	1595	1593000	1820	1819000
	4-2x12	1025	1137000	1195	1327000	1365	1516000
	2-4x12	975	975000	1140	1138000	1300	1300000
	5-2x12	910	910000	1060	1062000	1215	1213000
	1-6x12	1295	1162000	1510	1356000	1725	1549000
	3-3x12	910	900000	1060	1050000	1215	1200000
	1-8x12	870	852000	1015	994000	1160	1136000
	1-10x12	690	672000	805	784000	920	896000
	4-3x12	680	682000	795	796000	905	909000
	2-3x14	985	836000	1150	976000	1315	1114000
21'	3-2x12	1670	1756000	1950	2049000	2225	2341000
	2-3x12	1505	1580000	1755	1844000	2005	2106000
	4-2x12	1255	1317000	1465	1537000	1675	1755000
	2-4x12	1075	1129000	1255	1317000	1435	1505000
	5-2x12	1005	1054000	1175	1230000	1340	1405000
	1-6x12	1295	1344000	1510	1568000	1725	1791000
	3-3x12	1005	1041000	1175	1215000	1340	1388000
	1-8x12	960	986000	1120	1151000	1280	1314000
	1-10x12	760	779000	885	909000	1015	1038000
	4-3x12	750	790000	875	922000	1000	1053000
	2-3x14	1085	967000	1265	1128000	1445	1289000
	1-6x14	950	832000	1110	971000	1265	1109000
22'	4-2x12	1375	1515000	1605	1768000	1835	2019000
	2-4x12	1180	1297000	1380	1513000	1575	1729000
	5-2x12	1100	1211000	1285	1413000	1465	1614000
	1-6x12	1440	1546000	1680	1804000	1920	2061000
	3-3x12	1100	1197000	1285	1397000	1465	1596000
	1-8x12	1055	1134000	1230	1323000	1405	1511000
	1-10x12	830	895000	970	1044000	1105	1193000
	4-3x12	825	909000	965	1061000	1100	1212000
	2-3x14	1190	1112000	1390	1298000	1585	1482000
	1-6x14	1045	956000	1220	1116000	1395	1274000
	3-3x14	795	736000	930	859000	1060	981000
	2-4x14	820	751000	955	1114000	1095	1001000

Required values for fiber stress in bending (f) and modulus of elasticity (E) for the sizes shown to support safely a live load of 30 pounds per square foot within a deflection limitation of l/300.

Table E–22 Floor and roof beams.

SPAN OF BEAM	NOMINAL SIZE OF BEAM	6'-0" f	6'-0" E	7'-0" f	7'-0" E	8'-0" f	8'-0" E
10'	2-3x6	1430	1754000	1670	2047000	1905	2338000
	1-3x8	1645	1530000	1920	1785000	2195	2039000
	1-4x8	1175	1091000	1370	1273000	1565	1454000
	3-2x8	915	854000	1070	997000	1220	1138000
	2-3x8	820	764000	955	891000	1095	1018000
	2-4x8	590	546000	690	637000	785	728000
	2-2x10	840	613000	980	715000	1120	817000
11'	1-3x8	1990	2035000	2320	2375000	2655	2713000
	1-4x8	1420	1454000	1660	1697000	1895	1938000
	3-2x8	1105	1130000	1290	1319000	1475	1506000
	2-3x8	995	1019000	1160	1189000	1325	1358000
	2-4x8	710	727000	830	848000	945	969000
	2-2x10	1020	816000	1190	952000	1360	1088000
	1-3x10	1220	980000	1425	1144000	1625	1306000
12'	1-4x8	1690	1890000	1970	2206000	2255	2519000
	3-2x8	1315	1469000	1535	1714000	1755	1958000
	2-3x8	1185	1322000	1385	1543000	1580	1762000
	2-4x8	845	944000	985	1102000	1125	1258000
	1-6x8	1005	1086000	1175	1267000	1340	1448000
	2-2x10	1210	1062000	1410	1239000	1615	1416000
	3-2x10	810	708000	945	826000	1080	944000
	2-3x10	725	636000	845	742000	965	848000
	1-4x10	1040	909000	1215	1061000	1385	1212000
13'	3-2x8	1545	1867000	1805	2179000	2060	2489000
	2-3x8	1390	1680000	1620	1960000	1855	2239000
	2-4x8	990	1201000	1155	1401000	1320	1600000
	1-6x8	1180	1381000	1375	1612000	1575	1841000
	2-2x10	1425	1350000	1665	1575000	1900	1799000
	3-2x10	950	900000	1110	1050000	1265	1200000
	2-3x10	855	810000	1000	945000	1140	1080000
	1-4x10	1220	1385000	1425	1616000	1625	1846000
	1-6x10	735	679000	855	792000	980	905000
14'	2-4x8	1150	1500000	1340	1750000	1535	1999000
	1-6x8	1370	1723000	1600	2011000	1825	2297000
	2-2x10	1650	1684000	1925	1965000	2200	2245000
	3-2x10	1100	1122000	1285	1309000	1465	1496000
	2-3x10	990	1009000	1155	1177000	1320	1345000
	1-4x10	1415	1445000	1650	1686000	1885	1926000
	1-6x10	915	1415000	1070	1651000	1220	1886000
	2-4x10	705	721000	825	841000	940	961000
	4-2x10	825	842000	960	983000	1100	1122000
	1-8x10	625	622000	730	726000	835	829000
15'	2-2x10	1895	2071000	2210	2417000	2525	2760000
	3-2x10	1260	1381000	1470	1612000	1680	1841000
	2-3x10	1135	1243000	1325	1450000	1515	1657000
	1-4x10	1620	1775000	1890	2071000	2160	2366000
	1-6x10	980	1044000	1145	1218000	1305	1392000
	2-4x10	810	888000	945	1036000	1080	1184000
	4-2x10	945	1037000	1105	1210000	1260	1382000
	1-8x10	720	764000	840	891000	960	1018000
	2-2x12	1280	1152000	1495	1344000	1705	1536000
	1-4x12	1095	986000	1280	1151000	1460	1314000
	3-2x12	855	768000	1000	896000	1140	1024000
	2-3x12	770	691000	900	806000	1025	921000
16'	3-2x10	1435	1675000	1675	1955000	1915	2233000
	2-3x10	1290	1508000	1505	1760000	1720	2010000
	1-6x10	11.5	1266000	1300	1477000	1485	1687000
	2-4x10	925	1079000	1080	1259000	1235	1438000
	4-2x10	1075	1256000	1255	1466000	1435	1674000
	1-8x10	815	929000	950	1084000	1085	1238000
	2-2x12	1455	1397000	1700	1630000	1940	1862000
	1-4x12	1250	1199000	1460	1399000	1665	1598000
	3-2x12	970	931000	1130	1086000	1295	1241000
	2-3x12	875	839000	1020	979000	1165	1118000
	4-2x12	730	699000	850	816000	975	932000
	2-4x12	625	599000	730	699000	835	798000

SPAN OF BEAM	NOMINAL SIZE OF BEAM	6'-0" f	6'-0" E	7'-0" f	7'-0" E	8'-0" f	8'-0" E
17'	2-3x10	1460	1808000	1705	2110000	1945	2410000
	1-6x10	1255	1518000	1465	1771000	1675	2023000
	2-4x10	1040	1292000	1215	1508000	1385	1722000
	4-2x10	1215	1507000	1420	1758000	1620	2009000
	1-8x10	920	1112000	1075	1298000	1225	1482000
	2-2x12	1645	1675000	1920	1955000	2195	2233000
	1-4x12	1410	1436000	1645	1676000	1880	1914000
	3-2x12	1095	1117000	1280	1303000	1460	1498000
	2-3x12	985	1007000	1150	1175000	1315	1342000
	4-2x12	820	839000	955	979000	1095	1118000
	2-4x12	705	719000	820	839000	940	958000
	5-2x12	655	671000	765	783000	875	894000
18'	2-4x10	1170	1535000	1365	1791000	1560	2046000
	4-2x10	1360	1790000	1590	2089000	1815	2386000
	1-8x10	1040	1322000	1215	1543000	1385	1762000
	2-2x12	1840	1991000	2150	2323000	2455	2654000
	1-4x12	1580	1705000	1845	1990000	2105	2273000
	3-2x12	1230	1327000	1435	1549000	1640	1769000
	2-3x12	1105	1194000	1290	1393000	1475	1591000
	4-2x12	920	995000	1075	1161000	1225	1326000
	2-4x12	790	853000	920	995000	1055	1137000
	5-2x12	735	797000	860	930000	980	1062000
	1-6x12	960	1016000	1120	1186000	1280	1354000
	3-3x12	740	787000	865	918000	985	1049000
19'	2-4x10	1300	1805000	1515	2106000	1735	2406000
	1-8x10	1145	1554000	1335	1813000	1525	2071000
	3-2x12	1370	1561000	1600	1822000	1825	2081000
	2-3x12	1230	1404000	1435	1638000	1640	1871000
	4-2x12	1025	1170000	1195	1365000	1365	1560000
	2-4x12	880	1003000	1025	1170000	1175	1337000
	5-2x12	820	936000	955	1092000	1095	1248000
	1-6x12	1070	1194000	1250	1393000	1425	1592000
	3-3x12	820	925000	955	1079000	1095	1233000
	1-8x12	785	877000	915	1023000	1045	1169000
	1-10x12	620	692000	725	807000	825	922000
	4-3x12	615	702000	715	819000	820	936000
20'	3-2x12	1520	1819000	1775	2123000	2025	2425000
	2-3x12	1365	1638000	1595	1911000	1820	2183000
	4-2x12	1025	1364000	1195	1592000	1365	1818000
	2-4x12	975	1170000	1140	1365000	1300	1560000
	5-2x12	910	1092000	1060	1274000	1215	1456000
	1-6x12	1295	1394000	1510	1627000	1725	1858000
	3-3x12	910	1080000	1060	1260000	1215	1440000
	1-8x12	870	1022000	1015	1193000	1160	1362000
	1-10x12	690	806000	805	941000	920	1074000
	4-3x12	680	818000	795	955000	905	1090000
	2-3x14	985	1003000	1150	1170000	1315	1337000
	1-6x14	860	862000	1005	1006000	1145	1149000
21'	2-3x12	1505	1896000	1755	2213000	2005	2527000
	4-2x12	1255	1580000	1465	1844000	1675	2106000
	2-4x12	1075	1355000	1255	1581000	1435	1806000
	5-2x12	1005	1265000	1175	1476000	1340	1686000
	1-6x12	1295	1613000	1510	1882000	1725	2150000
	3-3x12	1005	1249000	1175	1457000	1340	1665000
	1-8x12	960	1183000	1120	1380000	1280	1577000
	1-10x12	760	935000	885	1091000	1015	1246000
	4-3x12	750	948000	875	1106000	1000	1264000
	2-3x14	1085	1160000	1265	1354000	1445	1546000
	1-6x14	950	998000	1110	1165000	1265	1330000
	3-3x14	725	769000	845	897000	965	1025000
22'	4-2x12	1375	1818000	1605	2122000	1835	2423000
	2-4x12	1180	1556000	1380	1816000	1575	2074000
	5-2x12	1100	1453000	1285	1696000	1465	1937000
	3-3x12	1100	1436000	1285	1676000	1465	1914000
	1-8x12	1055	1361000	1230	1588000	1405	1814000
	1-10x12	830	1074000	970	1253000	1105	1432000
	4-3x12	825	1091000	965	1273000	1100	1454000
	2-3x14	1190	1334000	1390	1557000	1585	1778000
	1-6x14	1045	1147000	1220	1338000	1395	1529000
	3-3x14	795	883000	930	1030000	1060	1177000
	2-4x14	820	901000	955	1051000	1095	1201000
	4-3x14	595	667000	695	778000	795	889000

Required values for fiber stress in bending (f) and modulus of elasticity (E) for the sizes shown to support safely a live load of 30 pounds per square foot within a deflection limitation of l/360.

Table E–23 Floor and roof beams.

SPAN OF BEAM	NOMINAL SIZE OF BEAM	BEAMS SPACED 6'-0" f	E	BEAMS SPACED 7'-0" f	E	BEAMS SPACED 8'-0" f	E
10'	2-3x6	1785	1560000	2085	1820000	2380	2079000
	1-3x8	2055	1360000	2400	1587000	2740	1813000
	2-2x8	1710	1134000	1995	1323000	2280	1512000
	1-4x8	1470	969000	1715	1131000	1960	1291000
	1-6x8	875	558000	1020	651000	1165	744000
	2-2x10	1050	545000	1225	636000	1400	726000
	1-3x10	1260	655000	1470	764000	1680	873000
11'	2-2x8	2070	1509000	2415	1761000	2760	2011000
	1-4x8	1775	1293000	2070	1509000	2365	1723000
	1-6x8	1055	743000	1230	867000	1405	990000
	2-2x10	1275	725000	1490	846000	1700	966000
	1-3x10	1525	872000	1780	1017000	2030	1162000
	1-4x10	1090	623000	1270	727000	1455	830000
	3-2x10	850	484000	990	565000	1135	645000
12'	1-4x8	2110	1680000	2460	1960000	2810	2239000
	1-6x8	1255	965000	1465	1126000	1670	1286000
	3-2x8	1645	1305000	1920	1523000	2190	1739000
	2-2x10	1510	944000	1760	1101000	2010	1258000
	1-3x10	1820	1132000	2125	1321000	2425	1509000
	1-4x10	1300	808000	1515	943000	1735	1077000
	3-2x10	1010	629000	1180	734000	1345	838000
	2-3x10	905	565000	1055	659000	1205	753000
13'	1-6x8	1475	1228000	1720	1433000	1965	1637000
	2-3x8	1735	1493000	2025	1742000	2315	1990000
	2-4x8	1235	1068000	1440	1246000	1645	1423000
	2-2x10	1780	1200000	2075	1400000	2370	1600000
	3-2x10	1185	800000	1380	934000	1580	1066000
	1-3x10	2130	1439000	2485	1679000	2840	1918000
	2-3x10	1070	720000	1250	840000	1425	960000
	1-4x10	1525	1230000	1780	1435000	2035	1640000
	2-4x10	760	514000	890	600000	1015	685000
14'	2-4x8	1435	1333000	1675	1555000	1915	1777000
	3-2x10	1375	997000	1605	1163000	1830	1329000
	2-3x10	1235	897000	1440	1047000	1645	1196000
	1-4x10	1770	1284000	2065	1498000	2360	1711000
	2-4x10	830	641000	1025	748000	1175	854000
	3-3x10	825	599000	960	699000	1100	798000
	1-6x10	1145	1257000	1335	1467000	1525	1675000
	1-8x10	780	553000	910	645000	1040	737000
	4-2x10	1030	749000	1200	874000	1375	998000
	2-2x12	1395	832000	1630	971000	1860	1109000
15'	3-2x10	1575	1228000	1840	1433000	2100	1637000
	2-3x10	1420	1105000	1655	1289000	1890	1473000
	2-4x10	1010	789000	1175	921000	1345	1052000
	3-3x10	945	737000	1100	860000	1260	982000
	1-6x10	1225	928000	1430	1083000	1635	1237000
	1-8x10	900	680000	1050	793000	1200	906000
	4-2x10	1180	921000	1375	1075000	1575	1228000
	2-2x12	1600	1024000	1865	1195000	2130	1365000
	3-2x12	1065	683000	1240	797000	1420	910000
	1-3x12	1920	1229000	2240	1434000	2560	1638000
	4-2x12	800	512000	935	597000	1065	682000
	2-3x12	960	614000	1120	716000	1280	818000
16'	3-2x10	1795	1489000	2095	1738000	2395	1985000
	2-3x10	1610	1341000	1880	1565000	2145	1787000
	2-4x10	1155	959000	1350	1119000	1540	1278000
	3-3x10	1075	894000	1255	1043000	1435	1192000
	1-6x10	1395	1125000	1625	1313000	1860	1500000
	1-8x10	1020	825000	1190	962000	1360	1100000
	4-2x10	1345	1117000	1570	1303000	1790	1489000
	2-2x12	1820	1241000	2120	1448000	2425	1654000
	3-2x12	1210	828000	1410	966000	1610	1104000
	4-2x12	910	621000	1060	724000	1215	828000
	5-2x12	730	497000	850	580000	975	662000
	2-3x12	1095	745000	1280	869000	1460	993000

SPAN OF BEAM	NOMINAL SIZE OF BEAM	BEAMS SPACED 6'-0" f	E	BEAMS SPACED 7'-0" f	E	BEAMS SPACED 8'-0" f	E
17'	2-3x10	1825	1608000	2130	1876000	2430	2143000
	2-4x10	1300	1149000	1520	1341000	1735	1532000
	3-3x10	1215	1073000	1420	1252000	1620	1430000
	1-8x10	1150	989000	1340	1154000	1535	1318000
	3-2x12	1370	993000	1600	1159000	1825	1323000
	4-2x12	1025	745000	1195	869000	1365	993000
	5-2x12	820	596000	955	695000	1095	794000
	2-3x12	1230	895000	1435	1044000	1640	1193000
	3-3x12	820	590000	955	688000	1095	786000
	2-4x12	880	639000	1025	746000	1175	852000
	1-6x12	1070	761000	1250	888000	1425	1014000
	1-8x12	785	558000	915	651000	1045	744000
18'	2-3x10	2120	1909000	2475	2228000	2825	2545000
	2-4x10	1460	1364000	1705	1592000	1945	1818000
	3-3x10	1365	1273000	1595	1485000	1820	1697000
	1-8x10	1300	1176000	1515	1372000	1730	1568000
	3-2x12	1540	1180000	1800	1377000	2050	1573000
	4-2x12	1150	884000	1340	1032000	1530	1178000
	5-2x12	920	708000	1075	826000	1225	944000
	2-3x12	1380	1061000	1610	1238000	1840	1414000
	3-3x12	920	700000	1075	817000	1225	933000
	2-4x12	990	759000	1155	886000	1320	1012000
	1-6x12	1200	903000	1400	1054000	1600	1204000
	1-8x12	880	663000	1025	774000	1175	884000
19'	1-8x10	1430	1381000	1670	1612000	1905	1841000
	3-2x12	1710	1388000	1995	1620000	2280	1850000
	4-2x12	1280	1040000	1495	1214000	1705	1386000
	5-2x12	1025	832000	1195	971000	1365	1109000
	2-3x12	1540	1248000	1795	1456000	2050	1663000
	3-3x12	1025	823000	1195	960000	1365	1097000
	2-4x12	1100	892000	1280	1041000	1465	1189000
	1-6x12	1335	1061000	1560	1238000	1780	1414000
	1-8x12	980	779000	1145	909000	1305	1038000
	3-4x12	735	595000	860	694000	980	793000
	4-3x12	770	624000	900	728000	1025	832000
	2-6x12	670	1063000	780	1240000	895	1417000
20'	3-2x12	1900	1617000	2220	1887000	2530	2155000
	4-2x12	1280	1213000	1495	1415000	1705	1617000
	5-2x12	1135	971000	1325	1133000	1515	1294000
	3-3x12	1135	960000	1325	1120000	1515	1279000
	2-4x12	1220	1040000	1425	1214000	1625	1386000
	1-6x12	1620	1240000	1890	1447000	2160	1653000
	1-8x12	1085	909000	1265	1061000	1445	1212000
	3-4x12	810	693000	945	809000	1080	924000
	4-3x12	850	728000	990	849000	1135	970000
	2-6x12	740	620000	865	723000	985	826000
	1-10x12	860	717000	1005	837000	1145	956000
	2-3x14	1230	891000	1435	1040000	1640	1188000
21'	3-2x12	2090	1873000	2440	2186000	2785	2497000
	4-2x12	1570	1405000	1830	1640000	2095	1873000
	5-2x12	1255	1124000	1465	1312000	1675	1498000
	3-3x12	1255	1111000	1465	1296000	1675	1481000
	2-4x12	1345	1204000	1570	1405000	1795	1605000
	1-8x12	1200	1052000	1400	1228000	1600	1402000
	3-4x12	895	803000	1045	937000	1195	1070000
	4-3x12	935	843000	1090	984000	1245	1124000
	2-6x12	820	717000	955	837000	1095	956000
	1-10x12	950	831000	1110	970000	1265	1108000
	2-3x14	1355	1032000	1580	1204000	1805	1375000
	1-6x14	1190	887000	1390	1035000	1585	1182000
22'	4-2x12	1720	1616000	2005	1886000	2295	2154000
	5-2x12	1375	1292000	1605	1508000	1830	1722000
	3-3x12	1375	1277000	1605	1490000	1830	1702000
	3-4x12	985	923000	1150	1077000	1315	1230000
	4-3x12	1030	969000	1200	1131000	1375	1292000
	2-6x12	900	825000	1050	963000	1200	1100000
	1-10x12	1035	955000	1205	1114000	1380	1273000
	2-3x14	1485	1187000	1730	1385000	1980	1582000
	1-6x14	1305	1020000	1525	1190000	1740	1360000
	2-4x14	1025	801000	1195	935000	1365	1068000
	3-3x14	995	785000	1160	916000	1325	1046000
	3-4x14	680	534000	795	623000	905	712000

Required values for fiber stress in bending (*f*) and modulus of elasticity (*E*) for the sizes shown to support safely a live load of 40 pounds per square foot within a deflection limitation of *l*/240.

Table E-24 Floor and roof beams.

SPAN OF BEAM	NOMINAL SIZE OF BEAM	MINIMUM "f" & "E" IN psi FOR BEAMS SPACED:					
		6'-0"		7'-0"		8'-0"	
		f	E	f	E	f	E
10'	1-3x8	2055	1700000	2400	1984000	2740	2266000
	2-2x8	1710	1417000	1995	1654000	2280	1889000
	1-4x8	1470	1211000	1715	1413000	1960	1614000
	1-6x8	875	697000	1020	813000	1165	929000
	2-2x10	1050	681000	1225	795000	1400	908000
	1-3x10	1260	819000	1470	956000	1680	1092000
	1-4x10	900	585000	1050	683000	1200	780000
11'	2-2x8	2070	1886000	2415	2201000	2760	2514000
	1-4x8	1775	1616000	2070	1886000	2365	2154000
	1-6x8	1055	929000	1230	1084000	1405	1238000
	2-2x10	1275	906000	1490	1057000	1700	1208000
	1-3x10	1525	1090000	1780	1272000	2030	1453000
	1-4x10	1090	779000	1270	909000	1455	1038000
	3-2x10	850	605000	990	706000	1135	806000
12'	1-6x8	1255	1206000	1465	1407000	1670	1607000
	3-2x8	1645	1631000	1920	1903000	2190	2174000
	2-2x10	1510	1180000	1760	1377000	2010	1573000
	1-3x10	1820	1415000	2125	1651000	2425	1886000
	1-4x10	1300	1010000	1515	1179000	1735	1346000
	3-2x10	1010	786000	1180	917000	1345	1048000
	2-3x10	905	706000	1055	824000	1205	941000
	1-6x10	785	594000	915	693000	1045	792000
	2-4x10	650	505000	760	589000	865	673000
13'	1-6x8	1475	1535000	1720	1791000	1965	2046000
	2-3x8	1735	1866000	2025	2178000	2315	2487000
	2-4x8	1235	1335000	1440	1558000	1645	1779000
	3-2x10	1185	1000000	1380	1167000	1580	1333000
	2-2x10	1780	1500000	2075	1750000	2370	2000000
	1-3x10	2130	1799000	2485	2099000	2840	2398000
	2-3x10	1070	900000	1250	1050000	1425	1200000
	1-4x10	1525	1537000	1780	1794000	2035	2049000
	2-4x10	760	642000	890	749000	1015	856000
14'	2-4x8	1435	1666000	1675	1944000	1915	2221000
	3-2x10	1375	1246000	1605	1454000	1830	1661000
	2-3x10	1235	1121000	1440	1308000	1645	1494000
	1-4x10	1770	1605000	2065	1873000	2360	2139000
	2-4x10	880	801000	1025	935000	1175	1068000
	3-3x10	825	749000	960	874000	1100	998000
	1-6x10	1145	1571000	1335	1833000	1525	2094000
	1-8x10	780	691000	910	806000	1040	921000
	4-2x10	1030	936000	1200	1092000	1375	1248000
	2-2x12	1395	1040000	1630	1214000	1860	1386000
15'	3-2x10	1575	1535000	1840	1791000	2100	2046000
	2-3x10	1420	1381000	1655	1612000	1890	1841000
	2-4x10	1010	986000	1175	1151000	1345	1314000
	3-3x10	945	921000	1100	1075000	1260	1228000
	1-6x10	1225	1160000	1430	1354000	1635	1546000
	1-8x10	900	850000	1050	992000	1200	1133000
	4-2x10	1180	1151000	1375	1343000	1575	1534000
	2-2x12	1600	1280000	1865	1494000	2130	1706000
	3-2x12	1065	854000	1240	997000	1420	1138000
	1-3x12	1920	1536000	2240	1792000	2560	2047000
	4-2x12	800	640000	935	747000	1065	853000
	2-3x12	960	767000	1120	895000	1280	1022000
16'	3-2x10	1795	1861000	2095	2172000	2395	2481000
	2-3x10	1610	1676000	1880	1956000	2145	2234000
	2-4x10	1155	1199000	1350	1399000	1540	1598000
	3-3x10	1075	1117000	1255	1303000	1435	1489000
	1-6x10	1395	1406000	1625	1641000	1860	1874000
	1-8x10	1020	1031000	1190	1203000	1360	1374000
	4-2x10	1345	1396000	1570	1629000	1790	1861000
	2-2x12	1820	1551000	2120	1810000	2425	2067000
	3-2x12	1210	1035000	1410	1208000	1610	1380000
	4-2x12	910	776000	1060	905000	1215	1034000
	5-2x12	730	621000	850	725000	975	828000
	2-3x12	1095	931000	1280	1086000	1460	1241000

SPAN OF BEAM	NOMINAL SIZE OF BEAM	MINIMUM "f" & "E" IN psi FOR BEAMS SPACED:					
		6'-0"		7'-0"		8'-0"	
		f	E	f	E	f	E
17'	2-3x10	1825	2010000	2310	2345000	2430	2679000
	2-4x10	1300	1436000	1520	1676000	1735	1914000
	3-3x10	1215	1341000	1420	1565000	1620	1787000
	1-8x10	1150	1236000	1340	1442000	1535	1647000
	3-2x12	1370	1241000	1600	1448000	1825	1654000
	4-2x12	1025	931000	1195	1086000	1365	1241000
	5-2x12	820	745000	955	869000	1095	993000
	2-3x12	1230	1119000	1435	1306000	1640	1492000
	3-3x12	820	737000	955	860000	1095	982000
	2-4x12	880	799000	1025	932000	1175	1065000
	1-6x12	1070	951000	1250	1110000	1425	1268000
	1-8x12	785	697000	915	813000	1045	929000
18'	2-4x10	1460	1705000	1705	1990000	1945	2273000
	3-3x10	1365	1591000	1595	1857000	1820	2121000
	1-8x10	1300	1470000	1515	1715000	1730	1959000
	3-2x12	1540	1475000	1800	1721000	2050	1966000
	4-2x12	1150	1105000	1340	1289000	1530	1473000
	5-2x12	920	885000	1075	1033000	1225	1180000
	2-3x12	1380	1326000	1610	1547000	1840	1767000
	3-3x12	920	875000	1075	1021000	1225	1166000
	2-4x12	990	949000	1155	1107000	1320	1265000
	1-6x12	1200	1129000	1400	1317000	1600	1505000
	1-8x12	880	829000	1025	967000	1175	1105000
	3-4x12	660	632000	770	737000	880	842000
19'	3-3x10	1520	1872000	1775	2184000	2025	2495000
	3-2x12	1710	1735000	1995	2025000	2280	2313000
	4-2x12	1280	1300000	1495	1517000	1705	1733000
	5-2x12	1025	1040000	1195	1214000	1365	1386000
	2-3x12	1540	1560000	1795	1820000	2050	2079000
	3-3x12	1025	1029000	1195	1201000	1365	1372000
	2-4x12	1100	1115000	1280	1301000	1465	1486000
	1-6x12	1335	1326000	1560	1547000	1780	1767000
	1-8x12	980	973000	1145	1135000	1305	1297000
	3-4x12	735	744000	860	868000	980	992000
	4-3x12	770	780000	900	910000	1025	1040000
	2-6x12	670	1329000	780	1551000	895	1771000
20'	3-2x12	1900	2021000	2220	2358000	2530	2694000
	4-2x12	1280	1516000	1495	1769000	1705	2021000
	5-2x12	1135	1214000	1325	1417000	1515	1618000
	3-3x12	1135	1200000	1325	1400000	1515	1600000
	2-4x12	1220	1300000	1425	1517000	1625	1733000
	1-6x12	1620	1550000	1890	1809000	2160	2066000
	1-8x12	1085	1136000	1265	1326000	1445	1514000
	3-4x12	810	866000	945	1011000	1080	1154000
	4-3x12	850	910000	990	1062000	1135	1213000
	2-6x12	740	775000	865	904000	985	1033000
	1-10x12	860	896000	1005	1046000	1145	1194000
	2-3x14	1230	1114000	1435	1300000	1640	1485000
21'	4-2x12	1570	1756000	1830	2049000	2095	2341000
	5-2x12	1255	1405000	1465	1640000	1675	1873000
	3-3x12	1255	1389000	1465	1621000	1675	1851000
	2-4x12	1345	1505000	1570	1756000	1795	2006000
	1-8x12	1200	1315000	1400	1535000	1600	1753000
	3-4x12	895	1004000	1045	1172000	1195	1338000
	4-3x12	935	1054000	1090	1230000	1245	1405000
	2-6x12	820	896000	955	1046000	1095	1194000
	1-10x12	950	1039000	1110	1212000	1265	1385000
	2-3x14	1355	1290000	1580	1505000	1805	1719000
	1-6x14	1190	1109000	1390	1294000	1585	1478000
	2-4x14	930	871000	1085	1016000	1240	1161000
22'	4-2x12	1720	2020000	2005	2357000	2295	2693000
	5-2x12	1375	1615000	1605	1885000	1830	2153000
	3-3x12	1375	1596000	1605	1862000	1830	2127000
	3-4x12	985	1154000	1150	1347000	1315	1538000
	4-3x12	1030	1211000	1200	1413000	1375	1614000
	2-6x12	900	1031000	1050	1203000	1200	1374000
	1-10x12	1035	1194000	1205	1393000	1380	1592000
	2-3x14	1485	1484000	1730	1732000	1980	1978000
	1-6x14	1305	1275000	1525	1488000	1740	1700000
	2-4x14	1025	1001000	1195	1168000	1365	1334000
	3-3x14	995	981000	1160	1145000	1325	1308000
	3-4x14	680	667000	795	778000	905	889000

Required values for fiber stress in bending (f) and modulus of elasticity (E) for the sizes shown to support safely a live load of 40 pounds per square foot within a deflection limitation of l/300.

Table E-25 Floor and roof beams.

SPAN OF BEAM	NOMINAL SIZE OF BEAM	6'-0" f	6'-0" E	7'-0" f	7'-0" E	8'-0" f	8'-0" E
10'	1-3x8	2055	2040000	2400	2381000	2740	2719000
	2-2x8	1710	1701000	1995	1985000	2280	2267000
	1-4x8	1470	1453000	1715	1696000	1960	1937000
	1-6x8	875	837000	1020	977000	1165	1116000
	2-2x10	1050	817000	1225	953000	1400	1089000
	1-3x10	1260	982000	1470	1146000	1680	1309000
	1-4x10	900	702000	1050	819000	1200	936000
11'	1-4x8	1775	1939000	2070	2263000	2365	2585000
	1-6x8	1055	1114000	1230	1300000	1405	1485000
	2-2x10	1275	1087000	1490	1268000	1700	1449000
	1-3x10	1525	1308000	1780	1526000	2030	1743000
	1-4x10	1090	934000	1270	1090000	1455	1245000
	3-2x10	850	726000	990	847000	1135	968000
	2-3x10	765	654000	890	763000	1020	872000
12'	1-6x8	1255	1447000	1465	1689000	1670	1929000
	3-2x8	1645	1957000	1920	2284000	2190	2609000
	2-2x10	1510	1416000	1760	1652000	2010	1887000
	1-3x10	1820	1698000	2125	1981000	2425	2263000
	1-4x10	1300	1212000	1515	1414000	1735	1615000
	2-3x10	905	847000	1055	988000	1205	1129000
	3-2x10	1010	943000	1180	1100000	1345	1257000
	1-6x10	785	713000	915	832000	1045	950000
	2-4x10	650	606000	760	707000	865	808000
13'	2-4x8	1235	1602000	1440	1869000	1645	2135000
	2-2x10	1780	1800000	2075	2100000	2370	2400000
	3-2x10	1185	1200000	1380	1400000	1580	1600000
	2-3x10	1070	1080000	1250	1260000	1425	1440000
	1-4x10	1525	1845000	1780	2153000	2035	2459000
	2-4x10	760	771000	890	900000	1015	1028000
	3-3x10	710	719000	830	839000	945	958000
	1-6x10	920	906000	1075	1057000	1225	1208000
	4-2x10	890	899000	1040	1049000	1185	1198000
14'	2-4x8	1435	1999000	1675	2333000	1915	2665000
	3-2x10	1375	1495000	1605	1745000	1830	1993000
	2-3x10	1235	1345000	1440	1570000	1645	1793000
	2-4x10	880	961000	1025	1121000	1175	1281000
	3-3x10	825	898000	960	1048000	1100	1197000
	1-6x10	1145	1885000	1335	2200000	1525	2513000
	1-8x10	780	829000	910	967000	1040	1105000
	4-2x10	1030	1123000	1200	1310000	1375	1497000
	2-2x12	1395	1248000	1630	1456000	1860	1663000
	3-2x12	930	832000	1085	971000	1240	1109000
15'	3-2x10	1575	1842000	1840	2150000	2100	2455000
	2-3x10	1420	1657000	1655	1934000	1890	2209000
	2-4x10	1010	1183000	1175	1380000	1345	1577000
	3-3x10	945	1105000	1100	1289000	1260	1473000
	1-6x10	1225	1392000	1430	1624000	1635	1855000
	1-8x10	900	1020000	1050	1190000	1200	1360000
	4-2x10	1180	1381000	1375	1612000	1575	1841000
	2-2x12	1600	1536000	1865	1792000	2130	2047000
	3-2x12	1065	1024000	1240	1195000	1420	1365000
	1-3x12	1920	1843000	2240	2151000	2560	2457000
	4-2x12	800	768000	935	896000	1065	1024000
	2-3x12	960	921000	1120	1075000	1280	1228000
16'	2-3x10	1610	2011000	1880	2347000	2145	2681000
	2-4x10	1155	1438000	1350	1678000	1540	1917000
	3-3x10	1075	1341000	1255	1565000	1435	1787000
	1-6x10	1395	1687000	1625	1969000	1860	2249000
	1-8x10	1020	1237000	1190	1443000	1360	1649000
	4-2x10	1345	1675000	1570	1955000	1790	2233000
	2-2x12	1820	1861000	2120	2172000	2425	2481000
	3-2x12	1210	1242000	1410	1449000	1610	1655000
	4-2x12	910	931000	1060	1086000	1215	1241000
	5-2x12	730	745000	850	869000	975	993000
	2-3x12	1095	1117000	1280	1303000	1460	1489000
	3-3x12	730	737000	850	860000	975	982000

SPAN OF BEAM	NOMINAL SIZE OF BEAM	6'-0" f	6'-0" E	7'-0" f	7'-0" E	8'-0" f	8'-0" E
17'	2-4x10	1300	1723000	1520	2011000	1735	2297000
	3-3x10	1215	1609000	1420	1878000	1620	2145000
	1-8x10	1150	1483000	1340	1731000	1535	1977000
	3-2x12	1370	1489000	1600	1738000	1825	1985000
	4-2x12	1025	1117000	1195	1303000	1365	1489000
	5-2x12	820	894000	955	1043000	1095	1192000
	2-3x12	1230	1342000	1435	1566000	1640	1789000
	3-3x12	820	885000	955	1033000	1095	1180000
	2-4x12	880	958000	1025	1118000	1175	1277000
	1-6x12	1070	1141000	1250	1331000	1425	1521000
	1-8x12	785	837000	915	977000	1045	1116000
	3-4x12	585	639000	680	746000	780	852000
18'	3-3x10	1365	1909000	1595	2228000	1820	2545000
	1-8x10	1300	1764000	1515	2058000	1730	2351000
	3-2x12	1540	1770000	1800	2065000	2050	2359000
	4-2x12	1150	1326000	1340	1547000	1530	1767000
	5-2x12	920	1062000	1075	1239000	1225	1416000
	2-3x12	1380	1591000	1610	1857000	1840	2121000
	3-3x12	920	1050000	1075	1225000	1225	1400000
	2-4x12	990	1138000	1155	1328000	1320	1517000
	1-6x12	1200	1354000	1400	1580000	1600	1805000
	1-8x12	880	994000	1025	1160000	1175	1325000
	3-4x12	660	758000	770	884000	880	1010000
	4-3x12	690	796000	805	929000	920	1061000
19'	4-2x12	1280	1560000	1495	1820000	1705	2079000
	5-2x12	1025	1248000	1195	1456000	1365	1663000
	2-3x12	1540	1872000	1795	2185000	2050	2495000
	3-3x12	1025	1234000	1195	1440000	1365	1645000
	2-4x12	1100	1338000	1280	1561000	1465	1783000
	1-6x12	1335	1591000	1560	1857000	1780	2121000
	1-8x12	980	1168000	1145	1363000	1305	1557000
	3-4x12	735	892000	860	1041000	980	1189000
	4-3x12	770	936000	900	1092000	1025	1248000
	2-6x12	670	1594000	780	186000	895	2125000
	1-10x12	775	923000	905	1077000	1035	1230000
	2-3x14	1110	1146000	1295	1337000	1480	1528000
20'	4-2x12	1280	1819000	1495	2123000	1705	2425000
	5-2x12	1135	1456000	1325	1699000	1515	1941000
	3-3x12	1135	1440000	1325	1680000	1515	1919000
	2-4x12	1220	1560000	1425	1820000	1625	2079000
	1-8x12	1085	1363000	1265	1591000	1445	1817000
	3-4x12	810	1039000	945	1212000	1080	1385000
	4-3x12	850	1092000	990	1274000	1135	1456000
	2-6x12	740	930000	865	1085000	985	1240000
	1-10x12	860	1075000	1005	1254000	1145	1433000
	2-3x14	1230	1336000	1435	1559000	1640	1781000
	1-6x14	1075	1149000	1255	1341000	1430	1532000
	2-4x14	845	903000	985	1054000	1125	1204000
21'	5-2x12	1255	1686000	1465	1967000	1675	2247000
	3-3x12	1255	1666000	1465	1944000	1675	2221000
	2-4x12	1345	1806000	1570	2107000	1795	2407000
	1-8x12	1200	1578000	1400	1841000	1600	2103000
	3-4x12	895	1204000	1045	1405000	1195	1605000
	4-3x12	935	1264000	1090	1475000	1245	1685000
	2-6x12	820	1075000	955	1254000	1095	1433000
	1-10x12	950	1246000	1110	1454000	1265	1661000
	2-3x14	1355	1548000	1580	1806000	1805	2063000
	1-6x14	1190	1330000	1390	1552000	1585	1773000
	2-4x14	930	1045000	1085	1219000	1240	1393000
	3-3x14	905	1032000	1055	1204000	1205	1375000
22'	5-2x12	1375	1938000	1605	2262000	1830	2583000
	3-3x12	1375	1915000	1605	2235000	1830	2553000
	3-4x12	985	1384000	1150	1615000	1315	1845000
	4-3x12	1030	1453000	1200	1695000	1375	1937000
	2-6x12	900	1237000	1050	1443000	1200	1649000
	1-10x12	1035	1432000	1205	1671000	1380	1909000
	2-3x14	1485	1780000	1730	2077000	1980	2373000
	1-6x14	1305	1530000	1525	1785000	1740	2039000
	2-4x14	1025	1201000	1195	1401000	1365	1600000
	3-3x14	995	1177000	1160	1373000	1325	1569000
	3-4x14	680	801000	795	935000	905	1068000
	1-8x14	955	1122000	1115	1309000	1275	1495000

Required values for fiber stress in bending (f) and modulus of elasticity (E) for the sizes shown to support safely a live load of 40 pounds per square foot within a deflection limitation of l/360.

APPENDIX F:
HEAT LOSS/GAIN
CALCULATION EXAMPLES[1]

In the following examples of heating and cooling calculations using the *Manual J Worksheet*, there are numerous references to tables contained in *Manual J*. These tables are quite extensive, and it would not be appropriate to include them here. You should obtain a copy of *Manual J* and review the calculation procedures using values from the tables appropriate for their location. The footnote below lists the source for *Manual J*.

F.1

EXAMPLE PROBLEM: HEAT LOSS CALCULATION

Data must be obtained from drawings, or by a field inspection, before load calculations can be made. The data required includes the following:

A. **Measurements to determine areas:**
   1. Overall area of windows and doors
   2. Gross areas of walls exposed to outside conditions
   3. Gross area of partitions
   4. Gross areas of walls below grade
   5. Area of ceilings or floors adjacent to unconditioned space
   6. Floor area for each room

Closets and halls are usually included with adjoining rooms. Large closets or entrance halls should be considered separately. Wall, floor, or ceiling dimensions can be rounded to the nearest foot. Window dimensions are recorded to the nearest inch. Measure the size of the window or door opening. Do not include the frame.

B. **Construction details:**
   1. Window type and construction
   2. Door type and construction
   3. Wall construction
   4. Ceiling construction
   5. Roof construction
   6. Floor construction

C. **Temperature differences:**
   1. Temperature differences across components exposed to outside conditions
   2. Temperature differences across partitions, floors, and ceilings adjacent to unoccupied spaces

---

[1]The heat loss and heat gain calculation examples contained in this appendix were taken from *Manual J*, 7th ed., *Residential Load Calculation*, Air Conditioning Contractors of America (ACCA), 1712 New Hampshire Avenue NW, Washington, DC 20009.

Table 1, located in back of *Manual J*, lists the outside design temperatures for various locations. Room temperatures are determined by the owner or the builder based on recommendations by the heating and cooling contractor, or they are prescribed by applicable codes. ACCA recommends 70°F.

F.1.1 Calculation Procedure

Once areas, construction details, and temperature differences are determined, the tables in the back of *Manual J* and the *Worksheet for Manual J* (Fig. F–3), can be used to calculate heat loss. The total heat loss for a room is the sum of the heat lost through each structural component of the room. To calculate the heat lost through any component, multiply the HTM found in the tables by the area of the component.

HTM values for temperature differences that fall between those listed in the tables can be interpolated as follows: For example, a brick wall above grade, construction number 12-F, is subjected to a design temperature difference of 63°F. Table 2 in *Manual J* indicates an HTM of 4.2 Btu/h per square foot at 60°F and 4.6 Btu/h per square foot at 65°F. Select HTM = 4.4 Btu/h per square foot, which is approximately equal to 4.2 + 3/5 (4.6 − 4.2) Btu/h per square foot.

> **EXAMPLE 1:** Figure F–1 represents a house located in Cedar Rapids, Iowa. Table F–1 lists the construction details. Assume that the inside design temperature is 70°F. From Table 1 in *Manual J*, the outside design temperature is −5°F.

Figure F–2 illustrates the completed worksheet. The following is a line-by-line explanation of the procedure:

Line 1. Identify each area that is heated.

Line 2 and 3. Enter the room dimensions. The dimensions shown were from Fig. F–1.

Line 4. Enter the ceiling height for reference. The direction the room faces is not a concern when you are making the heat loss calculation, but it is used in the heat gain calculations.

Lines 5A through 5D. Enter the gross area for the walls. For rooms with more than one exposure, use one line for each exposure. For rooms with more than one type of wall construction, use one line for each type of construction. Find the construction number in the tables in the back of *Manual J*. Enter this number on the appropriate line.

Example: The gross area of the west living room wall is 168 sq ft. This wall is listed in Table 2 in *Manual J*. The construction number is 12-D.

Lines 6A through 6C. Enter the area and the orientation of windows and glass doors for each room. Determine construction numbers from the tables, and enter them. Determine the temperature difference

Table F–1 Assumed design conditions and construction (heating).

	Const. No.	HTM
A. Determine outside design temperature, 5° db, (Table 1 in *Manual J*)		
B. Select inside design temperature, 70° db		
C. Design temperature difference, 75°		
D. Windows		
Living room and dining room—Clear, fixed glass, double glazed, wood frame (Table 2 in *Manual J*)	3A	41.3
Basement—Clear glass, metal casement windows, with storm (Table 2)	2C	48.8
Others—Double-hung, clear, single glass and storm, wood frame (Table 2)	2A	35.6
E. Doors: Metal, urethane-core, no storm (Table 2)	11E	14.3
F. First-floor walls: Basic frame construction with ½″ asphalt board (R-11) (Table 2)	12d	6.0
Basement wall: 8″ concrete block (Table 2)		
Above-grade height: 3′ (R = 5)	14b	10.8
Below grade height: 5′ (R = 5)	15b	5.5
G. Ceiling: Basic construction under vented attic with insulation (R-19) (Table 2)	16d	4.0
H. Floor: Basement floor, 4″ concrete (Table 2)	21a	1.8
I. All movable windows and doors have certified leakage of 0.5 cfm per running foot of crack (without storm); envelope has plastic vapor barrier; and major cracks and penetrations have been sealed with caulking material. No fireplace all exhausts and vents are dampered; all ducts are taped.		

across the glass, and read the HTM for heating from the tables. Enter these values. Multiply the window area by its HTM to determine the heat loss through that window. Enter the heat loss in the column marked "Btuh Htg."

Example: The living room has 40 sq ft of wood frame, fixed double-glass windows. The construction number of the window is 3A. The temperature difference across the window will be based on winter design conditions. The design temperature difference is 70° − (−5°) = 75°F. The HTM listed for 75°F on line 1–C of the tables is 41.3 Btu/h per square foot. The heat loss through the window is 40 sq ft × 41.3 Btu/h per square foot = 1652.

Example: The workshop has 4 sq ft of metal frame awning glass (plus storm) windows. The construction number is 2C. If the shop temperature is 70°F, the design temperature difference is 70 − (−5) = 75°F. The HTM is 48.8 Btuh/h per square foot. Heat loss through the window is 4 sq ft × 48.8 Btu/h per square foot = 195 Btuh.

Line 7. Not required for the heating calculation.

Line 8. Enter the area, the construction number, and the HTM for wood or metal doors. Multiply the HTM by the door area, and enter the heat loss through the door.

Example: The main entrance (hall A) has a 20-sq-ft, metal, urethane-core door. The construction number of the door is 11-E. The design temperature difference is 70° − (−5) = 75°F. The HTM is 14.3 Btu/h per square foot. The heat loss through the door is 14.3 Btu/h per square foot × 20 sq ft = 286 Btuh.

Lines 9A through 9D. For each room, subtract the window and door areas from the corresponding gross wall, and enter the net wall areas and the corresponding construction number. Determine the temperature difference across each wall, and enter the HTM. Multiply the HTM by the wall area, and enter the heat loss through the wall.

Example: The west wall in the living room has a net area of 128 sq ft (168 sq ft − 40 sq ft). The wall construction number is 12-D. The temperature difference

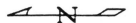

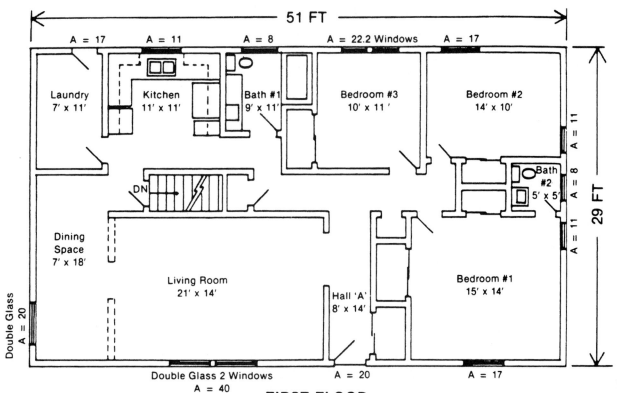

FIRST FLOOR
Ceiling Height 8' 0"
Figure 3-1 First Floor Plan.

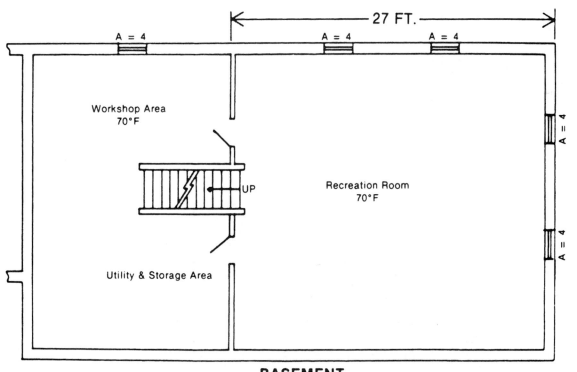

BASEMENT
Ceiling Height Including Joist Space 8' 0"
Wall: Above Grade 3' 0"
Below Grade 5' 0"

Figure F–1 Heat loss example problem: basement and first-floor plans.

FIGURE 3-3 EXAMPLE HEAT LOSS CALCULATION
DO NOT WRITE IN SHADED BLOCKS

			Name of Room	Entire House	1 Living	2 Dining	3 Laundry	4 Kitchen	5 Bath 1
		2	Running Ft. Exposed Wall	160	21	25	18	11	9
		3	Room Dimensions Ft.	51 x 29	21 x 14	7 x 18	7 x 11	11 x 11	9 x 11
		4	Ceiling Ht. Ft Directions Room Faces	8	8 West	8 North	8	8 East	8 East

TYPE OF EXPOSURE	Const No.	HTM Htg	HTM Clg	Area or Length	Btuh Htg	Btuh Clg	Area or Length	Htg	Clg	Area or Length	Htg	Clg	Area or Length	Htg	Clg	Area or Length	Htg	Clg	Area or Length	Htg	Clg
5 Gross	a 12-d			1280			188			200			144			88			72		
Exposed	b 14-b			480																	
Walls &	c 15-b			800																	
Partitions	d																				
6 Windows	a 3-A	41.3		60	2478		40	1652		20	826										
& Glass	b 2-C	48.8		20	978																
Doors Htg.	c 2-A	35.8		105	3738											11	392		8	285	
	d																				
7 Windows	North																				
& Glass	E&W																				
Doors Clg.	South																				
8 Other Doors	11-E	14.3		37	529								17	243							
9 Net	a 12-d	6.0		1078	6468		128	768		180	1080		127	762		77	462		64	384	
Exposed	b 14-b	10.8		460	4968																
Walls &	c 15-b	5.5		800	4400																
Partitions	d																				
10 Ceilings	a 16-d	4.0		1479	5916		294	1176		126	504		77	308		121	484		99	396	
	b																				
11 Floors	a 21-a	1.8		1479	2662																
	b																				
12 Infiltration HTM	70.6			222	15673		40	2824		20	1412		17	1200		11	777		8	565	
13 Sub Total Btuh Loss = 6+8+9+10+11+12					47806			6420			3822			2513			2115			1630	
14 Duct Btuh Loss	0%			—			—			—			—			—				
15 Total Btuh Loss = 13 + 14					47806			6420			3822			2513			2115			1630	
16 People @ 300 & Appliances 1200																					
17 Sensible Btuh Gain = 7+8+9+10+11+12+16																					
18 Duct Btuh Gain	%																				
19 Total Sensible Gain = 17 + 18																					

DO NOT WRITE IN SHADED BLOCKS

	6 Bedroom 3	7 Bedroom 2	8 Bath 2	9 Bedroom 1	10 Hall	11 Rec. Room	12 Shop & Utility	
	10	24	5	29	8	83	77	2
	10 x 11	14 x 10	5 x 5	15 x 14	8 x 14	27 x 29	24 x 29	3
	8 East	8 E & S	8 South	8 S & W	8 West	8 E & S	8 East	4

Area or Length	Htg	Clg	Area or Length	Htg	Clg	Area or Length	Htg	Clg	Area or Length	Htg	Clg	Area or Length	Htg	Clg	Area or Length	Htg	Clg	Area or Length	Htg	Clg	
80			192			40			232			64			249			231				5
															415			385			
															16	781		4	195		6
22	783		28	997		8	285		28	997												
																					7
												20	286								8
58	348		164	984		32	192		204	1224		44	264								9
															233	2516		227	2452		
															415	2283		385	2118		
110	440		140	560		25	100		210	840		112	448								10
															783	1409		696	1253		11
22	1553		28	1977		8	565		28	1977		20	1412		18	1130		4	282		12
	3124			4518			1142			5038			2410			8119			6300		13
	—			—			—			—			—			—			—		14
	3124			4518			1142			5038			2410			8119			6300		15
																					16
																					17
																					18
																					19

Figure F-2 Example heat loss calculation. (Do not write in the shaded blocks.)

is 75°F, and the HTM is 6.0 Btu/h per square foot. The heat loss through the wall is 128 sq ft × 6.0 Btu/h per square foot = 786 Btuh.

Example: The basement wall surrounding the recreation room has a net area of 233 sq ft (above grade), and the construction number is 14-B. The HTM for a 75°F temperature difference is 10.8 Btu/h per square foot. The heat loss above grade is 10.8 × 233 = 2516 Btuh. The net area below grade is 415 sq ft. The construction number is 15-B. The HTM is 5.5 Btu/h per square foot. The heat loss below grade is 415 sq ft × 5.5 Btu/h per square foot = 2283 Btuh.

Lines 10A and 10B. Enter the ceiling area and the construction number for ceilings exposed to a temperature difference. Determine the temperature difference across the ceiling, and enter the HTM. Multiply the HTM by the ceiling area, and enter the heat loss through the ceiling.

Example: An *R*-19 insulated living room ceiling has an area of 294 sq ft. The construction number is 16-D. Since the attic is vented, the temperature difference is 70° − (−5°) = 75°F. The HTM is 4.0 Btu/h per square foot and the heat loss through the ceiling is 294 sq ft × 4.0 Btu/h per square foot = 1176 Btuh.

Example: The recreation room ceiling will have no heat loss since the temperature difference is zero.

Lines 11A and 11B. Enter the floor area and the floor construction number for floors subject to a temperature difference. Determine the HTM, and calculate the heat loss through the floor.

Example: The recreation-room slab floor has an area of 783 sq ft. The construction number is 21. The design temperature difference is 75°F, and the HTM is 1.8 Btu/h per square foot. The heat loss through the floor is 783 sq ft × 1.8 Btu/h per square foot = 1409 Btuh.

Line 12. Use Table 5 and Calculation Procedure A in *Manual J* to calculate the winter infiltration HTM, and enter this value on line 12. For each room, enter the total sq ft of the window and door openings on line 12. Finally, compute the infiltration heat loss due to infiltration for each room by multiplying the winter infiltration HTM value by the appropriate sq ft of window and door openings. Enter these results on line 12. Refer to Fig. F–6 for an example of the infiltration HTM calculation.

Line 13. Calculate the subtotal heat loss for each room and for the entire house. (Add lines 6, 8, 9, 10, 11, and 12.)

Line 14. Calculate and enter the duct heat loss for each room. In this problem, the ducts are in the heated space, so duct losses can be ignored.

Line 15. Add the duct losses to the room losses. This sum is the total heat required for each room and for

the structure. If ventilation air is not introduced through the equipment, you can use the sum for the "Entire House" column to size the heating equipment.

If ventilation air is used, the heat required to temper this air must be added to the total heat required by the structure. This calculation can be made on the front of the *Worksheet for Manual J* form (Fig. F–3) in the panel titled "Heating Summary." In either case, the output capacity of the heating equipment shall not be less than the calculated loss.

Since ventilation was not included in the example problem, the design heating load is calculated as follows:

Line 15 heat loss (Btuh) = 47,808 (Entire house)

Ventilation cfm = 0

Ventilation heat (Btuh) = 0

Design heating load = 47,808 (House) + 0 (Vent)
= 47,808 Btuh

If this problem included 100 cfm of outside air for ventilation, the design heating load would be calculated as follows:

Line 15 heat loss (Btuh) = 47,808 (Entire house)

Ventilation cfm = 100

Design temperature difference = 75°F

Ventilation heat (Btuh) = 1.1 × 100 cfm × 75°F
= 8250 Btuh

Design heating load = 47,808 + 8250
= 56,058 Btuh

F.2

EXAMPLE PROBLEM: HEAT GAIN CALCULATION

The heat gain calculation will be made for the same structure used for the heat loss calculation. In both examples, the measurements and the construction details are the same.

F.2.1 Design Temperature Differences

The design temperature difference is the air temperature difference across a structural component. Table 1 in *Manual J* lists the outside design temperatures for various locations. Assume the inside design temperature to be 75°F, 55% relative humidity. You should estimate unconditioned space temperatures as closely as possible by considering the location and the use of the space in question. Use the design temperature difference to select the appropriate HTM for the structural components.

FORM J—1
Including Calculation Procedures A, B, C, D
Copyright by the
Air Conditioning
Contractors of America
1513 16th Street N.W.
Washington, D.C. 20036
Printed in U.S.A.
1986

Plan No. _____
Date _____
Calculated by _____

WORKSHEET FOR MANUAL J

LOAD CALCULATIONS FOR RESIDENTIAL AIR CONDITIONING

For: Name _Example Problem_____

Address _____

City and State or Province _____

By: Contractor_____

Address _____

City _____

Design Conditions

Winter	Summer

Outside db ____·5____ °F Inside db ____70____ °F   Outside db ____88____ °F Inside db ____75____ °F

Winter Design Temperature Difference ____75____ °F   Summer Design Temperature Difference ____15____ °F

Room RH____55%____ Daily Range____M____

Heating Summary

Total Heat Loss for Entire House (Line 15) = ____47,808____ Btuh

Ventilation CFM = ____none____ Winter Design Temperature Difference = ____°F

Heat Required for Ventilation Air = 1.1 X _____ CFM X _____ °F = ____0____ Btuh

Design Heating Load Requirement = ____47,808____ (house) ____0____ (Vent) = ____47,808____ Btuh

Cooling Summary

Total Sensible Gain ____16,669____ Btuh (Calculation Procedure D) Design Temperature Swings

Total Latent Gain + ____3,835____ Btuh (Calculation Procedure D) Normal 3° (X) 4.5° ( )

Total = Sens. + Lat. = ____20,504____ Btuh   Ventilation CFM = ____none____

Equipment Summary

Make _____ Model _____ Type _____

Heating Input (Btuh)_____ Heating Output (Btuh)_____ Efficiency_____

Sensible Cooling (Btuh _____ Latent Cooling (Btuh) _____ Total (Btuh) _____

COP/EER/SEER/HSPF _____ Cooling CFM _____ Heating CFM _____

Space Thermostat   Heat ( )   Cool ( )   Heat/Cool ( )   Night Setback ( )

Construction Data

Windows _____ Floor _____

_____

_____ Partitions _____

Doors_____

_____ Basement Walls_____

Walls _____

_____

Roof _____ Ground Slab_____

Ceiling _____

Figure F–3 Example load calculation summary.

F.2.2 Calculation Procedure

Once the area, construction details, and temperature differences are determined, you can use the data in the back of *Manual J* and the *Worksheet for Manual J* (Fig. F–3) to determine the heat gain. The total heat gain is the sum of the heat gains through the building envelope (solar gain, transmission, infiltration, and internal loads). The HTMs for various structural components are in Tables 3 and 4. The IITM values for temperature differences that fall between those listed in the table should be interpolated as discussed. Caculate internal gains and infiltration gains by using the procedures outlined in Section V in *Manual J*.

Data must be obtained from drawings or by a field inspection before load calculations can be made. The data required include the following:

A. Measurements to determine areas:
1. Running feet of exposed wall
2. Length and width of rooms and house
3. Ceiling heights
4. Dimensions of windows and doors

B. Area calculations:
1. Gross area of walls exposed to outdoor conditions
2. Gross area of partitions

Table F–2 Assumed design conditions and construction (cooling).

	Const. No.	HTM
A. Outside design temperature: rounded to 90° db, 38 grains (Table 1 in *Manual J*)		
B. Daily temperature range: Medium (Table 1) 88° db		
C. Inside design conditions: 75°F, 55% RH; design temperature difference = (90 − 75 = 15)		
D. Types of shading: Venetian blinds on all first-floor windows, no shading, basement		
E. Windows: All clear, double-glass on first floor (Table 3A in *Manual J*)		
North		14
East or west		44
South		23
All clear, single-glass (plus storm) in basement, Table 3A; use double glass		
East		70
South		36
F. Doors: Metal, urethane-core, no storm, 0.50 cfm/ft	11e	3.5
G. First-floor walls: Basic frame construction with $\frac{1}{2}''$ asphalt board (R-11) (Table 4 in *Manual J*)	12d	1.5
Basement wall: 8″ concrete block, above grade: 3′ (R-5) (Table 4)	14b	1.6
8″ concrete block, below grade: 5′ (R-5) (Table 4)	15b	0
H. Partition: 8″ concrete block furred, with insulation (R-5), ΔT approx. 0°F (Table 4)	13n	0
I. Ceiling: Basic construction under vented attic with insulation (R-19), dark roof (Table 4)	16d	2.1
J. Occupants: 6 (Assumed 2 per bedroom, but distributed 3 in living, 3 in dining)		
K. Appliances: Add 1200 Btuh to kitchen		
L. Ducts: Located in conditioned space (Table 7B in *Manual J*)		
M. Wood and carpet floor over unconditioned basement, ΔT approx. 0°F	19	0
N. The envelope was evaluated as having average tightness. (Refer to the construction details at the bottom of Figure 3–3 in *Manual J*.)		
O. Equipment to be selected from manufacturers' performance data.		

3. Gross area of walls below grade
4. Areas of windows and doors
5. Areas of ceilings under an attic or unconditioned space and/or roof ceiling combinations
6. Areas of floors exposed to the outdoors or floors over an unconditioned space or over a crawl space and/or basement floors
7. Running feet of exposed perimeter for slab-on-grade floors

Closets and halls are usually included with adjoining rooms. Entrance halls should be considered separately. Wall, floor, or ceiling dimensions can be rounded to the nearest foot. Window dimensions are recorded to the nearest inch. Measure the size of window or door openings; do not include the frame.

C. Construction details:
1. Exposed walls and partitions
2. Windows and glass doors
3. Panel doors
4. Ceilings and roof ceilings
5. Floors and ground slabs

D. Temperature differences:
1. Temperature differences across all components exposed to outdoor conditions
2. Temperature differences across partitions and all floors and ceilings that are adjacent to unconditioned spaces

EXAMPLE 2: Figure F–4 represents a house located in Cedar Rapids, Iowa. Table F–2 lists the construction details. Assume that the inside design temperature is 75°F. From Table 1 in *Manual J*, the summer design temperature is 88°db, 75°wb, with 38-grain moisture difference and a medium (M) daily range. Figure F–2 shows the completed worksheet. Note that the outside design temperature is rounded from 88°db to 90°db to expedite the calculations. Rounding the design temperature difference up by 3° or down by 1° will not produce any serious errors in the calculations.

The following is a line-by-line explanation of the procedure:

Line 1. Identify each area.

Lines 2 and 3. Enter the pertinent dimensions from Fig. F–4.

Line 4. For reference, enter the ceiling height and the direction the glass faces.

Lines 5A through 5D. Enter the gross wall area for the various walls. For rooms with more than one exposure, use one line for each exposure. For rooms with more than one type of wall construction, use one line for each type of construction. Find the construction number in the tables in the back of *Manual J*. Enter this number on the appropriate line.

Example: The gross area of the west living room wall is 168 sq ft. This wall is listed in Table 4, number 12, line D, in *Manual J*. The construction number is 12-d.

Line 6. Not required for cooling calculations.

Line 7. Enter the areas of windows and glass doors for the various rooms and exposures. Use the drawings and construction details, or determine by inspection the types of windows used in each room. Also note the shading and the exposure. Refer to the tables in the back of *Manual J*, and select the HTM for each combination of window, shading, and exposure. Enter the HTM values in the column designated "Btuh Clg." Multiply each window area by its corresponding HTM to determine the heat gain through the window. Enter this value in the column "Btuh Clg."

Example: The living room has 40 sq ft of west-facing glass. The window is double pane with drapes or blinds. The design temperature difference is rounded to 15°F. The HTM listed in Table 3A in *Manual J* (double glass, drapes or venetian blinds, design temperature difference of 13°F) is Btu/h per square foot. The heat gain is

44 Btu/h per square foot × 40 sq ft = 1760 Btuh.

Example: The dining area has 20 sq ft of north-facing glass. The HTM listed in Table 3 A (double glass, draperies, 15°F temperature difference) is 14 Btu/h per square foot. The heat gain is

14 Btu/h per square foot × 20 sq ft = 280 Btuh.

Example: The glass in the basement recreation room is single pane with storm. The design temperature difference is rounded to 15°F. The room has 8 sq ft of east-facing glass and 8 sq ft of south-facing glass. From Table 3A (double pane, clear glass, 15°F design temperature difference), the HTMs are 70 Btu/h per square foot for the east and 36 Btu/h per square foot for the south. The heat gain for the east window is

70 Btu/h per square foot × 8 sq ft = 560 Btuh

The heat gain for the south window is

36 Btu/h per square foot × 8 sq ft = 288 Btuh

Line 8. For each room, enter the area of any doors that are not glass. From Table 4 of *Manual J*, No. 11-E, select the HTM, and enter this value on the worksheet. To calculate the heat gain through the door, multiply the HTM by the area of the door. Enter the heat gain in the appropriate column:

Laundry door 17 sq ft × 3.5 Btu/h per square foot = 60 Btuh

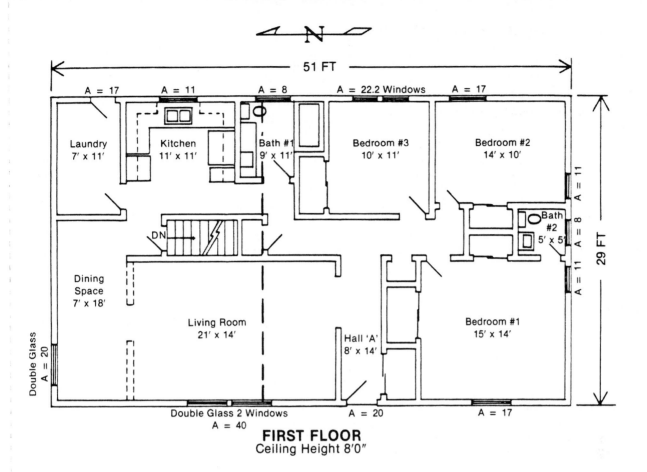

FIRST FLOOR
Ceiling Height 8′0″

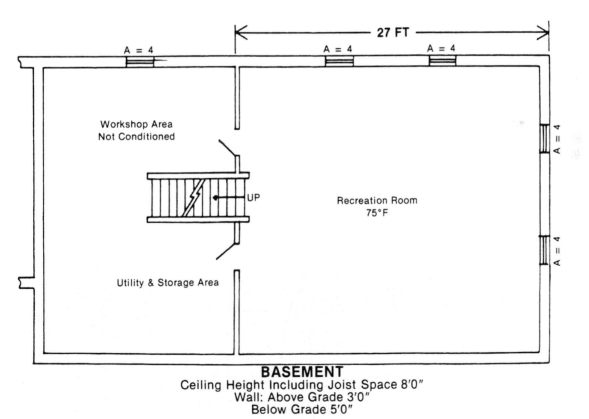

BASEMENT
Ceiling Height Including Joist Space 8′0″
Wall: Above Grade 3′0″
Below Grade 5′0″

Figure F–4 Heat gain example problem: basement and first-floor plans.

EXAMPLE HEAT GAIN CALCULATION
DO NOT WRITE IN SHADED BLOCKS

	TYPE OF EXPOSURE	Const No.	HTM Htg.	HTM Clg.	Entire House Area/Length	Entire House Btuh Htg.	Entire House Btuh Clg.	1 Living Area/Length	Living Btuh Htg.	Living Btuh Clg.	2 Dining Area/Length	Dining Btuh Htg.	Dining Btuh Clg.	3 Laundry Area/Length	Laundry Btuh Htg.	Laundry Btuh Clg.	4 Kitchen Area/Length	Kitchen Btuh Htg.	Kitchen Btuh Clg.	5 Bath-1 Area/Length	Bath-1 Btuh Htg.	Bath-1 Btuh Clg.
1	Name of Room				Entire House			Living			Dining			Laundry			Kitchen			Bath-1		
2	Running Ft. Exposed Wall				160			21			25			18			11			9		
3	Room Dimensions Ft.				51 x 29			21 x 14			7 x 18			7 x 11			11 x 11			9 x 11		
4	Ceiling Ht. Ft / Directions Room Faces				8			8 West			8 North			8			8 East			8 East		
5	Gross a	12-d			1280			168			200			144			88			72		
	Exposed b	14-b			480																	
	Walls & c	15-b			800																	
	Partitions d	13N			232																	
6	Windows a																					
	& Glass b																					
	Doors Htg. c																					
	d																					
7	Windows	North	14		20		280				20		280									
	& Glass	E & W	44		115		5060	40		1760							11		484	8		352
	Doors Clg.	South	23		30		690															
		Basement	70/38		8/8		848															
8	Other Doors	10-e	3.5		37		130							17		60						
9	Net a	12-d	1.5		1078	1617		128	192		180	270		127	191		77	116		64	96	
	Exposed b	14-b	1.6		233	373																
	Walls & c	15-b	0																			
	Partitions d	13-n	0																			
10	Ceilings a	16-d	2.1		1479	3105		294	617		126	265		77	162		121	254		99	208	
	b																					
11	Floors a	21-a	0																			
	b	19-f	0																			
12	Infiltration HTM		7.18		218	1565		40	287		20	144		17	122		11	79		8	57	
13	Sub Total Btuh Loss = 6+8+9+10+11+12																					
14	Duct Btuh Loss %																					
15	Total Btuh Loss = 13 + 14																					
16	People @ 300 & Appliances 1200				3000			3 900			3 900			—			1200			—		
17	Sensible Btuh Gain = 7+8+9+10+11+12+16				16000			3756			1859			535			2133			713		
18	Duct Btuh Gain %				—			—			—			—			—			—		
19	Total Sensible Gain = 17 + 18				16000			3756			1859			535			2133			713		

NOTE: USE CALCULATION PROCEDURE D TO CALCULATE THE EQUIPMENT COOLING LOADS

*Answer for "Entire House" may not equal the sum of the room loads if hall or closet areas are ignored or if heat flows from one room to another room.

DO NOT WRITE IN SHADED BLOCKS

	6 Bedroom 3 Area/Length	Htg	Clg	7 Bedroom 2 Area/Length	Htg	Clg	8 Bath 2 Area/Length	Htg	Clg	9 Bedroom 1 Area/Length	Htg	Clg	10 Hall Area/Length	Htg	Clg	11 Rec. Room Area/Length	Htg	Clg	12 Shop & Utility Area/Length	Htg	Clg	
	Bedroom 3			Bedroom 2			Bath 2			Bedroom 1			Hall			Rec. Room			Shop & Utility			1
	10			24			5			29			8			83			88			2
	10 x 11			14 x 10			5 x 5			15 x 14			8 x 14			27 x 29			24 x 29			3
	8 East			8 E & S			8 South			8 S & W			8 West			8 E & S			8 East			4
	80			192			40			232			64			249			231			5
																415			385			
																232						
																						6
																						7
	22		968	17		748				17		748				8/8		560				
				11		253	8		184	11		253				8/8		288				
													20		70							8
	58		87	164		246	32		48	204		306	44		66							9
																233		373				
	110		231	140		294	25		53	210		441	112		236							10
																						11
	22		158	28		201	8		57	28		201	20		144	16		115				12
																						13
																						14
																						15
			—			—			—			—			—			—			16
			1444			1742			342			1949			516			1336			17
			—			—			—			—			—			—			18
			1444			1742			342			1949			516			1336			19

Figure F–5 Example heat gain calculation.

Lines 9A through 9D. For each room, subtract the window and door areas from the corresponding gross wall area, and enter the net wall areas and corresponding construction numbers. From Table 4, select the HTM for each wall. Multiply the HTM by the appropriate net wall area, and enter the heat gain through the wall.

Example: The west wall in the living room has a net area of 168 sq ft − 40 sq ft = 128 sq ft. The design temperature difference is rounded to 15°F, and the daily range is M. From Table 4, No. 12-D, the HTM is 1.5 Btu/h per square foot. The heat gain through the living room wall is

1.5 Btu/h per square foot × 128 sq ft = 192 Btuh

Example: The basement wall in the recreation room has a net area of 233 sq ft above grade and 410 sq ft below grade. From Table 4, No. 14-B the HTM is 1.6 Btu/h per square foot. The heat gain through the above-grade wall is

1.6 Btu/h per square foot × 233 sq ft = 373 Btuh

(Below-grade walls need not be included in the heat gain calculation.)

Lines 10A and 10B. Enter the ceiling area for the various rooms and the construction number for the corresponding ceiling. Determine the HTM from Table 4, and enter it. Multiply the HTM by the ceiling area, and enter the heat gain.

Table 5

Infiltration Evaluation

Winter air changes per hour

Floor Area	900 or less	900 - 1500	1500 - 2100	over 2100
Best	0.4	0.4	0.3	0.3
Average	1.2	1.0	0.8	0.7 *
Poor	2.2	1.6	1.2	1.0

For each fire place add:		Best	Average	Poor
		0.1	0.2	0.6

Average - Plastic vapor barrier, major cracks and penetrations sealed, tested leakage of windows and doors between 0.25 and 0.50 CFM per running foot of crack, electrical fixtures which penetrate the envelope not taped or gasketed, vents and exhaust fans dampered, combustion air from indoors, intermittent ignition and flue damper, some duct leakage to unconditioned space.

Procedure A - Winter Infiltration HTM Calculation

1. Winter Infiltration CFM
   0.70 AC/HR x 16269 Cu. Ft. x 0.0167   =   190 CFM
                  Volume

2. Winter Infiltration Btuh
   1.1 x 190 CFM x 75 Winter TD   = 15675 Btuh

3. Winter Infiltration HTM
   15675 Btuh ÷ 222 Total Window   =   70.6 HTM
              & Door Area

* Includes Full Basement

Above Grade Volume = 51x29x(8 + 3) = 16269

Figure F-6 Infiltration HTM calculation.

Example: The living room ceiling has an area of 294 sq ft. The (dark roof) construction number is (16-D), the design temperature difference is 15, and the daily range is M. From Table 4, No. 16-D, the HTM is 2.1 Btu/h per square foot. The heat gain through the living room ceiling is

2.1 Btu/h per square foot × 294 sq ft = 617 Btuh

Lines 11A and 11B. For a room that will experience a gain through the floor, enter the floor area and the corresponding construction number. Determine the HTM from Table 4, and enter it. Multiply the HTM by the appropriate area, and enter the heat gain.

Line 12. Use Table 5 and Calculation Procedure B in *Manual J* to calculate the summer infiltration HTM, and enter this value on line 12. For each room, enter the total sq ft of the window and door openings on line 12. Finally, compute the infiltration heat gain due to infiltration for each room by multiplying the summer infiltration HTM value by the appropriate sq ft of window and door openings. Enter these results on line 12. Refer to Figure 6–4 in *Manual J* for an example of this calculation.

Lines 13 through 15. These lines are not used for the cooling calculation.

Line 16. Enter sensible internal loads due to appliances and occupants for the rooms.

Line 17. For each room, add all of the cooling loads (lines 7, 8, 9, 10, 11, 12, and 16), and enter the totals on line 17.

Line 18. If the duct system is installed in an unconditioned space, enter an allowance for the duct gain for each room on line 18. Refer to Table 7-B in *Manual J* for the duct gain multipliers.

Line 19. For the entire house and for each room, add line 17 (structure gain) to line 18 (duct gain), and enter the space-sensible gain on the form.

Note: Line 19 on the form provides information only on the space-sensible loads. Equipment selection requires calculation of the space-latent loads, and if ventilation is used, the sensible- and latent-ventilation loads must also be calculated.

Calculation Procedure C. Use Calculation Procedure C in *Manual J* to calculate the latent infiltration load for the entire house. Refer to Figure 6–5 in *Manual J* for an example of the Procedure C calculation.

Calculation Procedure D. Use Calculation Procedure D in *Manual J* to estimate the sensible- and latent-ventilation loads and to estimate the latent loads that are produced by internal sources. Also use Calculation Procedure D to estimate the total sensible and the total latent loads that must be satisfied by the cooling equipment. Refer to Figure 6–5 for an example of these calculations. For equipment to be selected from manufacturers' performance data, use RSM = 1.0 (refer to Table 6).

Glossary of Construction Terms

A

Abut To join the end of a construction member.

Acre A unit of land measurement having 43,560 sq ft.

Adhesive A natural or synthetic material, usually in liquid form, used to fasten or adhere materials together.

Adobe construction Construction using sun-dried units of adobe soil for walls; usually found in the southwestern United States.

Aggregate Gravel (coarse) or sand (fine) used in concrete mixes.

Air-dried lumber Lumber that has been dried by unheated air to a moisture content of approximately 15%.

Anchors Devices, usually metal, used in building construction to secure one material to another.

Angle A piece of structural steel having an L-shaped cross section and equal or unequal legs.

Apron Inside window trim placed under the stool and against the wall.

Arcade An open passageway usually surrounded by a series of arches.

Arch A curved structure designed to support itself and the weight above.

Areaway Recessed area below grade around the foundation to allow light and ventilation into a basement window.

Arris The sharp edge formed by two surfaces; usually on moldings.

Asbestos board A fire-resistant sheet made from asbestos fiber and portland cement.

Ash pit An enclosed opening below a fireplace to collect ashes.

Asphalt shingles Composition roof shingles made from asphalt-impregnated felt covered with mineral granules.

ASTM American Society for Testing and Materials.

Astragal T-profiled molding usually used between meeting doors or casement windows.

Atrium An open court within a building.

Attic The space between the roof and the ceiling in a gable house.

Awning window An outswinging window hinged at the top of the sash.

Axis A line around which something rotates or is symmetrically arranged.

B

Backfill Earth used to fill in areas around foundation walls.

Backsplash A protective strip attached to the wall at the back edge of a counter top.

Balcony A deck projecting from the wall of a building above ground level.

Balloon frame A type of wood framing in which the studs extend from sill to eaves without interruption.

Balusters Small, vertical supports for the railing of a stairs.

Balustrade A series of balusters supporting the railing of a stairs or balcony.

Bannister A handrail with supporting posts on a stairway.

Bargeboard The finish board covering the projecting portion of a gable roof.

Bar joist A light steel structural member fabricated with a top chord, a bottom chord, and web members.

Baseboard The finish trim board covering the interior wall where the wall and the floor meet.

Batt A type of insulation designed to be installed between framing members.

Batten The narrow strips of wood nailed vertically over the joints of boards to form board-and-batten siding.

Batter boards Horizontal boards at exact elevations nailed to posts just outside the corners of a proposed building. Strings are stretched across the boards to locate the outline of the foundation for workers.

Bays Uniform compartments within a structure, usually within a series of beams, columns, and so on.

Bay windows A group of windows projecting from the wall of a building. The center is parallel to the wall, and the sides are angular. A bow window is circular.

Beam Horizontal structural member, usually heavier than a joist.

Bearing plate A metal plate that provides support for a structural member.

Bearing wall A wall that supports a weight above in addition to its own weight.

Bench mark A mark on some permanent object fixed to the ground from which land measurements and elevations are taken.

Bidet Low plumbing fixture in luxury bathrooms for bathing one's private parts.

Blind nailing Method of nailing to conceal nails.

Blocking Small wood pieces in wood framing to anchor or support other major members.

Board measure The system of lumber measurement. A unit is 1 board ft, which is 1' sq by approximately 1" thick.

Bond beam Continuous, reinforced concrete block course around the top of masonry walls.

Bonds The arrangement of masonry units in a wall.

Brick Small masonry units made from clay and baked in a kiln.

Brick veneer A facing of brick on the outer side of wood frame or masonry.

Bridging Thin wood or metal pieces fastened diagonally at midspan between floor joists to act as both tension and compression members for the purposes of stiffening and spreading concentrated loads.

Buck Frame for a door, usually made of metal.

Building line An imaginary line on a plot beyond which the building may not extend.

Built-up roof A roofing composed of layers of felt impregnated with pitch, coal tar, or asphalt. The top is finished with crushed stone or minerals. It is used on flat or low-pitched roofs.

Bullnose Rounded edge units.

Butt Type of joint having the pieces edge to edge or end to end. Also a type of door hinge allowing the edge of a door to butt into the jamb.

Buttress Vertical masonry or concrete support, usually larger at the base, which projects from and strengthens a wall.

C

Call out A note on a drawing with a leader to the feature.

Cantilever A projecting beam or structural member anchored at only one end.

Cant strip An angular board used to eliminate a sharp, right angle, usually on roof decks.

Cap Covering for a wall or post.

Carport A garage not fully enclosed.

Casement window A window with one or two sashes that hinge on their sides. They may open either in or out.

Casing The trim around a window or door opening.

Caulking A soft, waterproof material used to fill open joints or cracks.

Cavity wall A masonry wall having a 2" air space between brick wythes.

Cement A fine, gray powder made from lime, silica, iron oxide, and alumina that when mixed with water and aggregate produces concrete.

Chamfer The beveled edge formed by removing the sharp corner of a material.

Channel A piece of structural steel having a C-shaped cross section.

Chase A vertical space within a building for ducts, pipes, or wires.

Chord The lower horizontal member of a truss.

Cleanout Accessible fitting on plumbing pipe that can be removed to clean sanitary drainage pipe.

Cleat A small board fastened to another member to serve as a brace or support.

Clerestory A portion of an interior rising above adjacent roof tops and having windows.

Collar beam A horizontal member tying opposing rafters below the ridge in roof framing.

Column A vertical supporting member.

Concrete A building material made from cement, aggregate, and water.

Concrete masonry unit (C.M.U.) A concrete block extruded from cement, aggregate, and water.

Conduit, electrical A metal pipe in which wiring is installed.

Contour A line on a map connecting all points with the same elevation.

Coping A cap or top course of masonry on a wall to prevent moisture penetration.

Corbel A projection of masonry from the face of a wall, or a bracket used for support of weight above.

Core The inner layer of plywood. It may be veneer, solid lumber, or fiberboard.

Corner board A vertical board forming the corner of a building.

Corner brace A diagonal brace at the corner of a wood frame wall to stiffen and prevent cracking.

Cornice The molded projection of the roof overhang at the top of a wall.

Cornice return The short portion of a molded cornice that returns on the gable end of a house.

Counter flashing Flashing used under cap flashing.

Cove A concave molding usually used on horizontal inside corners.

Crawl space The shallow space below the floor of a house built above the ground. Generally, it is surrounded with the foundation wall.

Cricket A device used at roof intersections to divert rain water.

Cripple A structural member that is cut less than full length, such as a studding piece above a window or door opening.

Crown molding A molding used above eye level, usually the cornice molding under the roof overhang.

Cul-de-sac A court or street that has no outlet and that provides a turnaround for vehicles.

Cupola A small, decorative structure that is placed on a roof, usually a garage roof, and that can be used as a ventilator.

Curtain wall An exterior wall that provides no structural support.

D

Dado joint A recessed joint on the face of a board to receive the end of a perpendicular board.

Damper A movable plate that regulates the draft through a flue or duct.

Dampproofing Material used to prevent passage of moisture.

Dead load The weight of the structure itself and the permanent components fastened to it.

Deck Exterior floor, usually extended from the outside wall.

Deflection The deviation of the central axis of a beam from normal when loaded.

Dimension lumber Framing lumber that is 2″ thick and 4″–12″ wide.

Dome A roof in the shape of a hemisphere used on a structure.

Doorjamb Two vertical pieces held together by a head jamb forming the inside lining of a door opening.

Doorstop The strips on the doorjambs against which the door closes.

Dormer A projection on a sloping roof framing a vertical window or vent.

Double glazing Two pieces of glass with air between to provide insulation.

Double-hung A type of window having two sashes that can be operated vertically.

Downspout A pipe for carrying rainwater from the roof to the ground or sewer connection.

Dressed size The actual finish size of lumber after surfacing.

Drip A projecting construction member or groove below the member to throw off rainwater.

Drywall construction Interior wall covering with sheets of gypsum rather than traditional plaster.

Ducts Sheet-metal conductors for air distribution throughout a building.

Duplex outlet Electrical wall outlet having two plug receptacles.

E

Earth berm An area of raised earth.

Easement A right or privilege to a piece of property held by someone other than the owner. Usually the right to run utility lines, underground pipe, or passageways on property.

Eaves The lower portion of the roof that overhangs the wall.

Efflorescence The forming of white stains on masonry walls from moisture within the walls.

Ell An extension or wing of a building at right angles to the main section.

Escutcheon The decorative metal plate used around the keyhole on doors or around a pipe extending through the wall.

Excavation A cavity or pit produced by digging the earth in preparation for construction.

Expansion joint A flexible joint used to prevent cracking or breaking because of expansion and contraction due to temperature changes.

Exterior insulation finish system (E.I.F.S.) An exterior wall finish made from styrofoam, cement, fiberglass, and an acrylic coating.

F

Façade The face or front elevation of a building.

Face brick Brick of better quality used on the face of a wall.

Fascia The outside horizontal member on the edge of a roof or overhang.

Fasteners General term for metal devices, such as nails, bolts, screws, and so on, used to secure structural members within a building.

Fenestration The arrangement of window and door openings in a wall.

Fiberboard Fabricated structural sheets made from wood fiber and adhesive under pressure.

Fill Sand, gravel, or loose earth used to bring a subgrade up to a desired level around a building.

Firecut An angular cut at the end of a floor joist resting on a masonry wall.

Fire rating A fire-resistance classification assigned to a building material or assembly.

Firestop A tight closure of a concealed space with incombustible material to prevent the spreading of fire.

Fire wall A fire-resistant masonry wall between sections of a building for the purpose of containing a fire.

Flagstone Thin, flat stones used for floors, steps, walks, and so on.

Flange The top or bottom pieces that project from a web of a structural steel member.

Flashing Sheet metal or other material used in roof or wall construction to prevent water from seeping into the building.

Flat-plate collector A solar energy collector made from metal piping with glass over.

Flitch beam A built-up beam formed by a metal plate sandwiched between two wood members and bolted together for additional length.

Floor joist Structural member of a floor.

Flue The passage in a chimney through which smoke, gases, and fumes escape to the outer air.

Footing Poured concrete base upon which the foundation wall rests.

Frieze The flat board of cornice trim that is fastened to the wall.

Frost line The deepest level of frost penetration in soil. This depth varies in different climates. Footings must be placed below the frost line to prevent a rupturing of the foundation.

Furring strips Thin strips of wood fastened to walls or ceilings for leveling and for receiving the finish surface material.

G

Gable The triangular end of a gable-roofed house.

Gambrel roof A roof with two pitches, the lower slope steeper than the upper.

Girder A heavy structural member supporting lighter structural members of a floor or a roof.

Glazing Placing of glass in windows and doors.

Grade beam A horizontal member that is between two supporting piers at or below grade and that supports a wall or a structure above.

Gradient The inclination of a road, piping, or the ground, expressed in percent.

Gravel stop A strip of metal with a vertical lip used to retain the gravel around the edge of a build-up roof.

Grounds Wood strips fastened to walls before plastering to serve as screeds and nailing base for trim.

Grout Thin cement mortar used for leveling and filling masonry cavities.

Gusset A plywood or metal plate used to strengthen the joints of a truss.

Gutter A metal or wood trough for carrying water from a roof.

Gyp board Gypsum sheets covered with paper that are fastened to walls and ceilings with nails or screws.

H

Hanger A metal strap used to support piping or the ends of joists.

Header In framing, the joists placed at the ends of a floor opening and attached to the trimmers. In masonry work, the small end of a masonry unit.

Hearth The incombustible floor in front of and within the fireplace.

Heartwood The central portion of wood within the tree, which is stronger and more decay-resistant than the surrounding sapwood.

Hip rafter The diagonal rafter that extends from the plate to the ridge to form the hip.

Hip roof A roof that rises by equally inclined planes from all four sides of a building.

Hose bibb A water faucet made for the threaded attachment of a hose.

House drain Horizontal sewer piping within a building that carries the waste from the soil stacks.

House sewer The watertight soil pipe extending from the exterior of the foundation wall to the public sewer.

Humidifier A device, generally attached to the furnace, that supplies or maintains correct humidity levels in a building.

I

I beam A structural steel shape with a web and flange components, having an I-shaped cross section.

Incandescent lamp A lamp within which a filament gives off light when sufficiently heated by an electric current.

Insulating concrete Concrete with vermiculite added to produce lightweight, insulating concrete for subfloors and roofs.

Interior trim The general term for all of the finish molding, casing, baseboard, and so on, applied within a building by finish carpenters.

J

Jack rafter A rafter shorter than a common rafter; especially used in hip-roof framing.

Jalousie A type of window having a number of small, unframed yet movable pieces of glass.

Jamb The vertical members of a finished door opening.

Joinery A general woodworking term used for all better-class wood-joint construction.

Joist A horizontal structural member supported by bearing walls, beams, or girders in floor or ceiling framing.

Joist hanger A metal strap to carry the ends of floor joists.

K

Keystone The wedged center stone at the crown of an arch.

Kiln-dried lumber Lumber that has been properly dried and cured to produce a higher grade of lumber than that which has been air dried.

King post The center upright strut in a truss.

Kip A unit of 1000-lb load.

Knee wall A low wall resulting from 1½-story construction.

Knocked down Unassembled; refers to construction units requiring assembly after being delivered to the job.

L

Laitance Undesirable surface water that forms on curing concrete.

Lally column A steel column used in light construction.

Laminated beam A beam made of superimposed layers of similar materials by uniting them with glue and pressure.

Landing A platform between flights of stairs or at the termination of stairs.

Lap joint A joint produced by lapping two similar pieces of material.

Lath A metal, wood, or gypsum base for plastering.

Lattice A framework of crossed or interlaced wood or metal strips.

Leader A vertical pipe or downspout that carries rainwater from the gutter to the ground or storm sewer.

Ledger strip A strip of lumber fastened to the lower part of a beam or girder on which notched joists are attached.

Light A single pane of glass in a window or door.

Lineal foot A 1' measurement along a straight line.

Lintel A horizontal support member across the head of a door or window opening.

Live load Loads other than *dead loads* on a building, such as wind, snow, and people.

Load-bearing wall A wall designed to support the weight imposed upon it from above.

Lookout A short wooden framing member used to support an overhanging portion of a roof. It extends from the wall to the underside surfacing of the overhang.

Lot line The line forming the legal boundary of a piece of property.

Louver An opening or slatted grill allowing ventilation while providing protection from rain.

Luminaire An electric lighting fixture used within a room.

M

Mansard roof A hip-type roof having two slopes on each of the four sides.

Masonry A general term for construction of brick, stone, concrete block, or similar materials.

Mastic A flexible adhesive for adhering building materials.

Matte finish A finish free from gloss or highlights.

Membrane A thin layer of material used to prevent moisture penetration.

Metal wall ties Corrugated metal strips used to tie masonry veneer to wood walls.

Millwork A general term that includes all dressed lumber that has been molded, shaped, or preassembled at the mill.

Miter joint A joint made with ends or edges of two pieces of lumber cut at a 45° angle and fitted together.

Modular construction Construction in which the size of all components has been based on a standardized unit of measure.

Moisture barrier A sheet material that retards moisture penetration into walls, floors, ceilings, and so on.

Monolithic Term used for concrete construction poured and cast in one piece without joints.

Mortar A mixture of cement, sand, lime, and water used to bond masonry units.

Mortice A hole, slot, or recess cut into a piece of wood to receive a projecting part (tenon) made to fit.

Mosaic Small, colored tile, glass, stone, or similar material arranged to produce a decorative surface.

Mullion The structural member between a series of windows.

Muntin A small bar separating the glass lights in a window.

N

Newel post The main post supporting a handrail at the bottom or top of a stairs.

Nominal size The size of lumber before dressing, rather than its actual size.

Nonbearing wall A wall supporting no load other than its own weight.

Nonferrous metal A metal containing no iron, such as copper, brass, or aluminum.

Nosing The rounded edge of a stair tread.

O

On-center A method of indicating the spacing between framing members by stating the measurement from the center of one member to the center of the succeeding one.

Open web joist *See* Bar joist.

Outlet Any type of electrical box allowing current to be drawn from the electrical system for lighting or appliances.

Overhang The projecting area of a roof or upper story beyond the wall of the lower part.

P

Pallet A rugged wood skid used to stack and mechanically handle units of masonry.

Panel A flat, rectangular surface framed with a thicker material.

Parapet A low wall or railing, usually around the edge of a roof.

Parge coat A thin coat of cement plaster applied to a masonry wall for refinement of the surface or for dampproofing.

Parquet flooring Flooring, usually of wood, laid in an alternating or inlaid pattern to form various designs.

Parting stop Thin strips set into the vertical jambs of a double-hung window to separate the sash.

Partition A wall that divides areas within a building.

Party wall A wall between two adjoining buildings in which both owners share, such as a common wall between row houses.

Passive solar system An integral energy system using only natural and architectural components to utilize solar energy.

Penny A term used to indicate the size of nails, abbreviated "d." Originally, it specified the price per hundred nails (for example, 6-penny nails cost 6¢ per hundred nails).

Pergola An open, structural framework over an outdoor area, usually covered with climbing shrubs or vines to form an arbor.

Periphery The entire outside edge of an object.

Pier A masonry pillar usually below a building to support the door framing.

Pilaster A rectangular pier attached to a wall for the purpose of strengthening the wall. Also a decorative column attached to a wall.

Pile A long shaft of wood, steel, or concrete driven into the earth to support a building.

Pitch The slope of a roof, usually expressed as a ratio.

Plastic laminate A thin, melamine-surfaced sheet used to cover counter tops.

Plat A graphic description of a surveyed piece of land, indicating the boundaries, location, and dimensions. The plat, recorded in the appropriate county official's office, also contains information as to easements, restrictions, and lot numbers, if any.

Plate The top horizontal member of a row of studs in a frame wall.

Plumb Said of an object when it is in true vertical position as determined by a plumb bob or a vertical level.

Plywood A relatively thin building material made by gluing layers of wood together.

Poché The darkening of areas on a drawing to aid in readability.

Post-and-beam construction A type of building frame in which roof and floor beams rest directly over wall posts.

Precast Concrete units that are cast and finished at the plant rather than at the site of construction.

Prime coat The first coat of paint that serves as a filler and sealer in preparation for finish coats.

Purlins Horizontal roof members laid over trusses to support rafters.

Q

Quarry tile Unglazed, machine-made tile used for floors.

Quarter round Small molding presenting the profile of a quarter circle.

Quarter-sawed oak Oak lumber, usually flooring, that has been sawed so that the medullary rays showing on end-grain are nearly perpendicular to the face of the lumber.

Quoins Large, squared stones set in the corners of a masonry building for appearance's sake.

R

Rabbet (or Rebate) A groove cut along the edge or end of a board to receive another board, producing a rabbet joint.

Radiant heating A method of heating with the use of radiating heat rays.

Rafter A roof structural member running from the wall plate to the ridge. There are jack, hip, valley, and common rafters. The structural members of a flat roof are usually called *roof joists*.

Rake joint A mortar joint that has been recessed by tooling before it sets up.

Rake molding Gable molding attached on the incline of the gable. The molding must be a different profile to match similar molding along the remaining horizontal portions of the roof.

Random rubble Stonework having irregularly shaped units and coursing.

Register Opening in air duct, usually covered with a grill.

Reinforced concrete Concrete containing steel bars or wire mesh to increase its structural qualities.

Retaining wall A heavy wall that supports an earth embankment.

Reveal The side of an opening for a window or door, between the frame and the outer surface of a wall.

Ribbon A wood strip set into studs to support floor joists in balloon framing.

Ridge The top edge of a roof where two slopes meet.

Ridgeboard The highest horizontal member in a gable roof; it is supported by the upper ends of the rafters.

Riprap Irregular stones thrown together loosely to form a wall or soil cover.

Rise The vertical height of a roof or stairs.

Rocklath Paper-covered gypsum sheets used as a plaster base.

Rough hardware All of the concealed fasteners in a building such as nails, bolts, hangers, and so on.

Rough opening As unfinished opening in the framing into which doors, windows, and other units are placed.

Rowlock A special brick coursing placed at the exterior windowsill.

Rubble Irregular, broken stone.

Run The horizontal distance of a flight of stairs, or the horizontal distance from the outer wall to the ridge of a roof.

R-value The unit of thermal resistance in rating insulating materials; higher values indicate better insulators.

S

Saddle A small gable roof placed in back of a chimney on a sloping roof to shed water and debris.

Sanitary sewer Drainage pipe that transports sewage from buildings.

Sash An individual frame into which glass is set.

Scab A short piece of lumber fastened to a butt joint for strength.

Schedule A list of similar items and information about them, such as a window schedule.

Scribing Marking and fitting a piece of lumber to an irregular surface such as masonry.

Scuttle A small opening in a ceiling to provide access to an attic or roof.

Section A unit of land measurement, usually 1 mile square. A section contains approximately 640 acres, and there are 36 sections to a township. Also a drawing showing the cut-open view of an object.

Septic tank A concrete or steel underground tank used to reduce sewage by bacterial action.

Shake A handsplit wood shingle.

Sheathing The rough boarding or covering over the framing of a house.

Shim A thin piece of material used to true up or fill a space between two members.

Shoe mold The small molding covering the joint between the flooring and the baseboard on the inside of a room.

Shoring Planks or posts used to support walls or ceilings during construction.

Siding The outside finish covering on a frame wall.

Sill The horizontal exterior member below a window or door opening. The wood member placed directly onto the foundation wall in wood frame construction.

Skylight A window in a flat roof.

Sleepers Wood strips placed over or in a concrete slab to receive a finish wood floor.

Smoke chamber The enlarged portion of a chimney flue directly above the fireplace.

Soffit The underside of an overhang such as a cornice or stairs.

Soil stack The vertical pipe in a plumbing system that carries the sewage.

Solar collector A device used to collect the sun's heat.

Soleplate The horizontal member of a frame wall resting on the rough floor, to which the studs are nailed.

Span The horizontal distance between supports for joists, beams, or trusses.

Specifications The written instructions that accompany a set of working drawings.

Square A unit of measure—100 sq ft. Commonly used in reference to the amount of roofing material to cover 100 sq ft.

Stile The vertical member on a door or panel.

Stirrup A metal, U-shaped strap used to support the end of a framing member.

Stool The horizontal interior member of trim below a window.

Story A complete horizontal portion of a building having a continuous floor.

Stretcher course A row of masonry in wall with the long side of the units exposed to the exterior.

Stringer The inclined structural member supporting the treads and risers of a stairs; sometimes it is visible next to the profile of the stairs.

Stucco A cement plaster finish applied to exterior walls.

Studs The vertical framing members of a wall.

Subflooring Any material nailed directly to floor joists. The finish floor is attached over the subflooring.

Sunspace A glassed-in area for the collection of solar heat.

Suspended ceiling A finish ceiling hung below the underside of the building structure, either the floor or the roof.

T

Tail joist An relatively shorter joist that joins against a header or trimmer in floor framing.

Tensile strength The greatest longitudinal stress that a structural member can bear without adverse effects (breaking or cracking).

Termite shield Sheet metal placed over masonry to prevent the passage of termites into wood.

Terra-cotta Baked clay and sand formed into masonry units.

Terrazzo flooring Wear-resistant flooring that is made of marble chips or small stones embedded in cement and that has been polished smooth.

Thermal conductor An substance capable of transmitting heat.

Thermostat A automatic device for controlling interior temperatures.

Threshold The beveled metal, stone, or wood member directly under a door.

Title Legal evidence of the ownership of property.

Toe nail Nailing at an angle to the wood fiber.

Tongue The narrower extension on the edge of a board that is received by the groove of an adjacent board.

T post A post built up of studs and blocking to form the intersection of the framing of perpendicular walls.

Transom A hinged window over a door.

Trap A U-shaped pipe below plumbing fixtures to create a water seal and to prevent sewer odors and gases from being released into the habitable areas.

Tread The horizontal surface member of a stairs upon which the foot is placed.

Treated wood Wood that has been chemically treated to prevent decay and insect infestation.

Trim A general term given to the moldings and finish members on a building. Its installation is called *finish carpentry*.

Trimmer The longer floor framing member around a rectangular opening into which a header is joined.

Trombe wall A passive-heating concept consisting of a south-facing masonry wall with glazing in front. Solar radiation is absorbed by the wall, converted to heat, and conducted and radiated into the building.

Truss Structural members arranged and fastened in triangular units to form a rigid framework for support of loads over a long span.

Truss joists A structural framing member fabricated with a thin wood web and wood flanges.

V

Valley rafter The diagonal rafter at the intersection of two intersecting, sloping roofs.

Vapor barrier A watertight material used to prevent the passage of moisture or water vapor into and through walls.

Veneered construction A type of wall construction in which frame or masonry walls are faced with other exterior surfacing materials.

Vent stack A vertical soil pipe connected to the drainage system to allow ventilation and pressure equalization.

Vestibule A small entrance room.

W

Wainscot The surfacing on the lower part of an interior wall that is finished differently from the remainder of the wall.

Wallboard Large sheets of gypsum or fiberboard that are usually nailed to framing to form interior walls.

Wall tie A small metal strip or steel wire used to bind tiers of masonry in cavity-wall construction, or to bind brick veneer to the wood frame wall in veneer construction.

Water closet A toilet.

Water table A horizontal member extending from the surface of an exterior wall so as to throw off rainwater from the wall. Water level below ground.

Weatherstripping A strip of fabric or metal fastened around the edges of windows and doors to prevent air infiltration.

Web The member between the flanges of a steel beam, or the vertical and diagonal members between the top and bottom chords of a truss or bar joist.

Weep hole Small holes in masonry cavity walls to release water accumulation to the exterior.

Wide flange A structural steel beam with a web and top and bottom flanges.

Winder The radiating or wedge-shaped treads at the turns of some stairs.

Wythe Pertaining to a single-width masonry wall.

Index

Numbers in **bold** type indicate figures in chapters 8, 9, and 10.

A

Absolute coordinates, 19
Air flow:
    airtight drywall air barriers (ADAs), 156–158
    moisture, 155
All-Weather Wood Foundation System, 59–60, 61, 62, 63
Allowances in specifications, 276
Alpine Engineered Products, Inc., 195
Alternates in specifications, 276
Aluminum:
    siding, 146
    windows, 208–209
American Institute of Architects (A.I.A.):
    architectural services, 289
    project manuals, 267
American Institute of Steel Construction, 169
American Institute of Timber Construction (AITC), 176–177
American Iron and Steel Institute, 113, 118, 173
American Plywood Association (APA)/Engineered Wood Association, 76
American Society of Heating, Refrigeration, and Air Conditioning Engineers (A.S.H.R.A.E.), 152
Anchor bolts:
    brick cavity walls, 111
    CMU foundation walls, 56
    platform framing, 68
Angular displacement, 19–20
Angular slopes, 205, 206
Appliances, 18–19
Applications packages, 26, 27
ArchiCAD, 14

Architectural Graphic Standards:
    CD-ROM version, 15
    fireplaces, 225
    weights for structural members, 172
Architectural services, 289, 291
Areaways, 57
As-built records, 299
Asphalt shingles, 134–135
AutoCAD, 14, 25
AutoLISP, 25
Automation systems, home, 260
Awning windows, 209, 211

B

Balloon frame construction, 96, 98, 147
Balusters, 227, 232, 233
Barrel-vault roofs, 128, 131
Basements:
    foundations, 45–47, 56
    frost depth, 34
    radon, 40, 41, 42–44
Bathrooms, 66
Beams:
    plank-and-beam construction, 101–107, 189–193
    platform framing, 64–68
    structural members, 68, 70, 109, 173–177
Bearing, 70–72, 73
Bearing-wall construction, 110
Bevel siding, 143–144
Bidding process:
    commercial construction, 297, 298
    conditions, specifying, 345, 347
    contract documents, 267
    online access, 18
Bird's mouth cuts, 89, 90
Block commands, 23–25
Block systems for ICF systems, 121, 122, 123

H

Half-lapped bond, 111
Half-timber style, 147
Handrails, 227, 228, 230, 232
Hardware, computer, 8–14
Header courses, 108, 109
Headers:
    balloon framing, 96
    loads, determining, 181, 186–187
    platform framing, 72–73, 74, 75
Headroom for stairways, 227, 230, 231, 232
Hearths, 221, 224
Heat mirror glass, 209
Heat transfer, 151–154
Hip roofs, 90, 92, 128, 129–130
Hollow-core doors, 213, 214
Home automation systems, 260
Hopper windows, 209, 211
Horizontal sliding windows, 209
Housed stringers, 227
HP-GL/2 language, 12

I

I-joists, 78, 181, 182
I.C.E. Block™, 123, 240–243, 251, 252, 254, 256,
    260–261
Icynene Insealation System™, 258
Information:
    availability of, for innovative systems, 260
    operating instructions for systems and equipment,
        299
    resources for, 15–17, 163–166
Inkjet plotters, 11–12
Inquiry commands, 21
Insulating concrete form (ICF) systems, 121–123,
    240–243, 251, 252, 256, 260–261
Insulating Concrete Forms: A Construction Manual
        (VanderWert and Munsell), 121
Insulating glass, 209
Insulation
    See also R values
    basement foundations, 46–47
    brick cavity walls, 111
    flat roofs, 127, 129
    frame structures, 151–154
    innovative systems, 258
    moisture considerations, 154
    plank and beam construction, 102–103
    post office building, **8–18**, 345
    slabs, 51–52
    steel framing, **9–6**, 118, 119, 350
Integral slabs and footing, 51
Integrated networking, 7

Interior finishes, 149–151

Interior finishes, 149–151
International Residential Code 2000, 172
Internet, 15, 16–17
Isocyanurate foam insulation, 154

J

Jack rafters, 90, 92
Jalousie doors, 216
Jalousie windows, 209, 211
Joists:
    balloon framing, 96, 98
    ceiling, 89, 90, 91
    concrete, 113
    flat roofs, 93, 127, 129
    framing openings, 72–75
    I-joists, 78, 181, 182
    loads, determining, 179–181, 182–184
    platform framing, 66–68, 68–70, 72–73, 74
    second floor framing, 89, 90
    steel, 112–113, 114, 115, 116, 117
    TJI®, 181
    truss joists, 78–79

K

Keyboards, computer, 9, 10
Kitchens, 66

L

Labor, 102, 260, 261
Laminated veneer lumber (LVL), 78, 176–177
Landings for stairways, 227
Layers in CAD drawings, 22
LED (electrophotographic) plotters, 12
Let-in bracing, 85
Light construction, 31–166
Linear displacement, 19
Lintels:
    balloon framing, 96
    foundation walls, 56–57
    platform framing, 89
LISP, 25
Live-load creep, 171
Load bearing walls:
    autoclaved, aerated concrete block, 124, 125
    straw bale construction, 125, 126
Loads:
    basement walls, on soil, 45, 46
    CMU foundation walls, 54, 56
    dead loads, 35, 38, 39, 66
    footings, 35, 37–39